MYSTICS, VISIONARIES, AND PROPHETS

MYSTICS, VISIONARIES, AND PROPHETS

A Historical Anthology of Women's Spiritual Writings

Edited by
Shawn Madigan, C.S.J.

Foreword by
Benedicta Ward, S.L.G.

Fortress Press Minneapolis

MYSTICS, VISIONARIES, AND PROPHETS
A Historical Anthology of Women's Spiritual Writings

Cover design by: Mike Mihelich and Debbie Finch
Original cover art by: Jane Pitz

Library of Congress has cataloged the hard cover edition as follows

Mystics, visionaries, and prophets : a historical anthology of women's spiritual writings / edited by Shawn Madigan ; foreword by Benedicta Ward.

p. cm.
Includes bibliographical references and index.
ISBN 0-8006-3145-5 (alk. paper)
1. Spiritual life – Christianity. 2. Christian women.
I. Madigan, Shawn.
BV4495.M97 1998
248.8'43 – dc21 98-36261

The paper used in this publication meets the minimum requirements of American National Standard for Information Sciences—Permanence of Paper for Printed Library Materials, ANSI Z329.48-1984.

ISBN 0-8006-3420-9

Manufactured in the U.S.A.

CONTENTS

FOREWORD

There are as many texts about the union of holy persons with God as there are texts about the ways in which human beings relate to each other. Among believers and unbelievers alike today, knowledge of oneself and others is a central preoccupation. For believers there is a point of enlightenment. Human relationships are seen to be contingent on—and enlightened by—the mystery of personal relationship to God. The categories we use to order and divide human experience—for example, the gender categories of female and male—take on somewhat new and cohesive meanings in a spiritual realm that perceives all humans as feminine in their relationship to God.

In looking at spiritual writings by women, the intention is not to insist on a special "female spirituality" that somehow excludes men from knowing an intimate God. Rather, the writings of women in this collection are of interest for other reasons. First, they are not known by very many people, so their inclusion here makes them more broadly accessible. Second, the many-sided approach to prayer and communion with Jesus Christ these writings present is of great contemporary interest.

This is not to say that the writings of these women's male contemporaries are of less interest or importance. In a sense, women have more often been the enablers of written texts by men rather than the producers of texts. It is a matter of historical fact that the Roman women who asked Jerome to clarify his explication of the Scriptures inspired him to do so. A group of Anglo-Saxon nuns found the words of the Canticle of Habakkuk obscure, even though they prayed it weekly in the Office of Lauds. They asked Bede to analyze it for them so that they could pray it with understanding. Great women of the eleventh century asked Anselm of Canterbury to provide them with texts that would help them in their main work of prayer.

Such a combination of enabling and producing was not so much a statement about gender potential for union with God as it was about the availability of different kinds of learning. The human categories of male and female had little to do with the essence of communion with God. Bernard of Clairvaux wrote to Hildegard of Bingen, "You are said to be able to search the secrets of heaven and to discern by the light of the Holy Spirit things that are beyond human knowledge" (Letter 390 of Bernard of Clairvaux). Bernard is indicating here that women as well as and men have a potential receptivity to the mysteries of God. The recognition does not, however, imply a difference of function based on gender.

In the present work, Dr. Madigan has brought together translations of spiritual writings from the church of the martyrs to twentieth-century Uganda. In accomplishing this, she has greatly expanded the material that is available for growth into the "art of arts and science of sciences," namely, praying always. That the works are all by women or about women draws attention to the contribution women have made down through the centuries to Christian spirituality. Highlighting this role is especially timely in this age when women's involvement in other areas of life—social, legal, and economic—is increasingly stressed.

–Benedicta Ward, S.L.G.

MYSTICS, VISIONARIES, AND PROPHETS

INTRODUCTION

> "There are different gifts, but the same Spirit. There are different ministries but the same Lord. There are different works, but the same God who accomplishes all of them in everyone. To each person, the manifestation of the Spirit is given for the common good" (1 Cor 12:4–7).

This anthology seeks to gather the religious wisdom, social vision, and personal insight of Christian women over twenty centuries. Their faith stories, personal stance, and visionary writings illustrate how deeply women's intimacy with God has entailed prophetic social witness.

The Christian women who are included in this book are examples of a larger community of women mystics, visionaries, and prophets who used their gifts for the common good. These women differ in personality, vocation, time in history, and cultural-ecclesial settings. They also differ in their initial response to their gifts. They are the same insofar as each knows that the gifts come from the spirit of Christ. Yet some of these women experience self-doubt or fear, particularly if church and society teach that God does not want women to receive the particular gifts that were given. Others are simply happy to have received the gifts and to use them. All do use the gifts for the good of the community to whatever extent it is possible in their milieu.

The women included here are mystics, visionaries, and prophets. Because these titles are used in different ways by different people, I will summarize the meanings of *Christian mystic, visionary,* and *prophet* as the terms are used in this text.

A Christian mystic is one whose experiential awareness of Jesus Christ enables life to be lived with an increasing depth of faith-vision and love-dynamism. Christian mystics have both a conscious desire to grow into the maturity of loving freedom and a willingness to undertake whatever this quest may require. The mystic is willing to be a lifelong discerner of the Spirit's wisdom. Often this means following Christ's directives even if there is little understanding of where the journey is leading. Sometimes it means altering a practice or view that once was "right" but is no longer. At yet other times it may mean being led into the discipleship that cannot give any answers to the question "why."

The Christian mystic is not someone who chooses separation from others out of fear that human love may be an obstacle to loving God. As the women treated here demonstrate, intimacy with Jesus Christ opens the door to the growing inclusiveness of human love. The times of more intimate solitude with Christ open the heart to a greater sense of the presence of Christ that is manifest through other people, places, and events. An authentic Christian mystic relates to others with a gracious hospitality that testifies to the presence of Christ everywhere and in all people.

It may seem odd that the holiest mystics claim to be so unholy and unworthy of the gift of Christ's love. This humility or honesty comes, however, out of the experience of the holiness of Jesus Christ. Once there is a mystical experience of that loving goodness, a new awareness of one's personal lack of holiness occurs. This humility or truthfulness will be evident in different ways in the women represented in this volume. For each the strength of humility or truthfulness is a safeguard against egoism or self-delusion. Humility helps all Christians to acknowledge that everything good comes from God. It liberates Christians to see that, because all are sinners, no human being can judge another with self-righteousness.

At the same time, truthfulness or humility does not mean that mystics are incapable of critical judgments about injustices, sins, and evil. But in the denouncement of the actions, there remains the hope that the doers of the injustices will be enlightened to change their ways. This hope leads many mystics to continue their prayer and work not only for victims of injustice but also for those who are the oppressors.

The heightened consciousness of God's justice and compassion is the result of intimacy with Jesus Christ. This intimacy leads the Christian mystic into a life lived for all and prayer prayed for all. It will be seen that Christian universality of love characterizes these women. Their prayer and life have no boundaries to love as they serve others. Regardless of the century in which the women lived, each will eventually see the integral relationship between prayer prayed and life lived.

Many of the qualities of a Christian mystic are also qualities of a Christian visionary. An additional dimension that characterizes a Christian visionary is—as the word suggests—a "seeing" of Jesus Christ. This seeing experience may be mediated by sensory vision or by intuitive inner vision. It is described by the person as a "seeing," a "showing," or occasionally a "knowing." Christian visionaries are as old as the first postresurrection disciples, who proclaimed, "We have seen the Lord" (Mark 16; Matt 28; Luke 24ff.; John 20ff.).

Because many people can claim to have seen the Lord, some criteria for discerning true from false "seers" have been part of Christian history from its beginnings. For the earliest disciples the test of an authentic seeing of the Lord was the manner of living in imitation of Christ's life. As later ages saw growing numbers of Christians claiming to be "visionaries," the Christian church drew up specific criteria for discernment of true and false visions. Although slight differences occurred from age to age, the general criteria can be summarized in four guidelines.

First, the vision's content must not contradict the Scriptures, an authentic teaching, or an interpretation of that teaching. Second, the visionary's life must bear witness to the liberation of Christ. This liberation may be experienced in some form of inner or outer healing as well as in a life lived with Christ's love. Third, the faith community that knows the visionary must affirm that he or she is a holy person. This assumes a mature faith within the community. Fourth, someone other than the person—usually a spiritual director—will affirm the visionary experience.

Sometimes visions are accompanied by a cure from illness, a cure that authenticates the vision. In medieval times, this experience provided a type of liberation from the need for male clerics to test the visions. In the Middle Ages, the many women visionaries experienced a power through their visions that other women lacked. Visions were a desirable gift that liberated women from restraints of husband or church. The popularity of visions during those ages was one reason that guidelines became necessary for discerning true visions.

It is understandable that those who "see" with bodily eyes or with the inner eye are called visionaries, but it must be recognized that the sense of hearing will be involved as well. Without hearing the word, the meaning of what has been seen can be misinterpreted. Other senses might also be a part of the overall visionary experience. Each of the visionaries in these books will inform the reader about what was heard as well as what was seen. The reader will then know whether the vision was a sensory or an intuitive one.

Some authors have classified visions by their content. The classifications can briefly be summarized as visions of devotion, of doctrine, or of prophecy. Frequently, the same vision may be of two or three kinds, especially if it lasts for a long time. The kinds of vision are not difficult to recognize.

A devotional vision is one in which love is aroused and deepened. The dialogue that accompanies the vision or the mystic's later reflection on its meaning will reveal this love. A doctrinal or intellectual vision clarifies, enhances, or creatively interprets some teaching of the Christian tradition. A prophetic vision can be predictive or revelatory of God's love and hope for the people. A predictive vision clarifies what is happening or indicates what will happen. A revelatory vision affirms the hope and compassion of God for some person, a group, or the world.

Visionaries are enlightened by their seeing and hearing to act as Jesus Christ advises them. Jesus Christ may command the visionary to receive communion more frequently, to perform some ministry, for example, to write, to teach, to preach, to hear confessions, to advise others, or to do a host of other ministries.

If it is a true vision, the women do what they are told in spite of cultural or ecclesial restrictions.

It may seem that there are some congruent strains that ground the meanings of mystics, visionaries, and prophets. This is true, for many prophets were also visionaries and mystics. At the same time, biblically a prophet is someone who proclaims the hope of God for the people of a particular time and place. The prophet teaches the meanings of God's loving word for a particular community. The prophet is usually unpopular because the word that is preached calls for deeper conversion of heart. The teaching of the prophet must be in accord with the evolving living meaning of the Scriptures and the authentic teachings of the believing community. In many cases, the same person is prophet, visionary, and mystic.

Are there any gender differences that can be noted between male and female mystics, visionaries, and prophets? This issue is not directly addressed in this text. The debate of similarity and difference continues to gather ever increasing data that lead to different responses to the question. A brief overview of the women selected for this text does, however, support the following observations.

These women use the ordinary images of life as symbols of revelation. There is a confidence that somehow everything is related to everything else. For all the women, regardless of their time and place, love is the guiding and integrating force of all things. There is an immanence about their experience of Jesus Christ that reveals transcendence. Jesus Christ is not king, warrior, and power-symbol as much as friend, servant, and lover.

The women use female gender images differently than do the males of their period. When the women use female images such as mother, bride, lover, or wife, they do so to indicate an assurance that women are as fully redeemed and loved as men. The use of the feminine image as a full imaging of God differs from male usage of the feminine which needs the masculine to be full imaging of God. At the same time, the masculine imaging of God does not need the feminine for its fullness.

The women in this text do not emphasize the otherness of Jesus Christ to the degree that male mystics of their period do. Most males have used an analytic hierarchical arrangement of stages of prayer, ladders of perfection, degrees of the spiritual life, progressive steps of holiness, and other indications of advancement. The women were more interested in assessing Christian holiness through the quality of loving relationships. Teresa of Ávila was the first woman to engage in a more analytic approach to her visionary experience.

The women treated here also use symbols differently than do the men of their time. Women generally use symbols to say who they are, whereas men use symbols to say who they are not. Women mystics use symbols to unify or integrate; male mystics tend to use the same symbols to separate and order. For example, male mystics tended to separate as dichotomies the realities of male and female, soul and body, earth and heaven, Christ and church. Once the realities were separated, one was placed higher than the other. Women tended to use similar imagery, but they did so in a manner that relativized or integrated all of the images as partial revealers of the mystery of God. One was not higher than the other. Women speak of humanity made in God's image, of this earth as revealing the heavenly, of all prayer—regardless of kind—as a relational experience of God and all people, and of faith as a growing sense of communion with all in Christ.

Whether these differences are grounded in cultural-ecclesial stereotypes or basic physiological-psychological differences of male and female remains an interesting debate. What the texts included in this collection affirm is that the women mystics, visionaries, and prophets were affected by the cultural and ecclesial conditioning of women's perceived inferiority. This conditioning affected men as well. If women were perceived as temptresses, good men would have to engage in a spirituality of renunciation of things sexual. For many male mystics the choice of renunciation symbols such as fasting, poverty, solitary existence, celibacy, and community was viewed as means of gaining control over questionable desires of sexuality, wealth, status, power, and pride.

Women's similar renunciation symbols were interpreted differently. Fasting can serve as an example. Although both men and women fasted to further their hunger for Christ, men saw it as a way to subjugate bodily desires. Women fasted as a means of affirming their body as a source of life for others and of communion with the body of Christ that was life-giving. Their motivation was not so much the control of desires as an integration of giving that finds expression in devotion to the Eucharist.

Particularly in ages when frequent communion was not allowed for laity and women religious, fasting preceded being fed by Christ. It is noteworthy that the fasting from the Eucharist that was imposed by the church was a fast from which Jesus Christ occasionally exempted the women. It is necessary to point out that such differences between the perception and experience of women and men may reside more in cultural-ecclesial limitations of vision than in any gender-related differences.

Finally, it is legitimate to ask why only women were selected for this particular collection. Anyone who has taught in the areas of Christian spirituality or women's studies in religion will already know the reason. Comprehensive histories of Christian spirituality still contain very few women in proportion to the number of men. Texts by or about women's evolving spirituality are increasing, but there is not one work that traces both texts and context through the centuries. There are a number of very good sources that document certain periods of history, complete works by one woman, and biographical works.

Why were these particular women chosen? One pragmatic criterion was the availability and the accessibility of data and texts. A second criterion was the introduction of women and texts from a diversity of cultures, times, Christologies, ecclesial settings, adult vocations, and personalities. It will be evident that a richer ethnic diversity needs to find its way into future anthologies of this type. A final criterion was the potential enlightenment that each woman from the past and present could bring to the enrichment of Christian spirituality today, a time when the Spirit seems to be calling many to again use their gifts for the common good.

In spite of the limitations of this collection, I hope that it will demonstrate two realities, namely, the vast richness in the Christian storehouse that holds things new and old, and the empowering dreams of God for the world that will continue to move faithful hearts to bring them to completion.

To those who have sustained me in this work, I extend my thanks: Professors John Barton, Sarah Coakley, Benedicta Ward, S.L.G., and Sr. Martha Reeves for aiding my senior scholar residency in Oxford, England; Dr. Patrick Henry, Sr. Dolores Shuh, and other resident scholars at the Ecumenical Institute for Religious and Cultural Research during the spring semester; the Abigail Quigley McCarthy Center, the Bush Foundation, and the College of St. Catherine; graduate research assistants Lyn Klug and Lonnie Burkhart; Marshall Johnson and Deborah Finch of Fortress Press; copyeditor Mary Byers; my community of women mystics, visionaries, and prophets—the Sisters of St. Joseph of Carondelet; and last but not least, the earliest community of Christians I remember, Earl, Grace, and John, who insisted that "wings" and not "things" were the best we could give to each other as Christians of love and humor.

– 1 –

PERPETUA

(c. 203)

I Knew the Lord Was with Me

Perpetua lived in the late second and early third century in Carthage, a North African city with a long history of colonization. By the eighth century B.C.E., the Phoenician colonizers had built up Carthage as a primary maritime and commercial center. Economic ties were maintained with the mother city of Tyre. After the Persian invasion and occupation of Tyre in 538 B.C.E., Carthage assumed dominance over Phoenician colonies. Carthage also ruled over a large number of Libyan Berbers who converted to Phoenician culture in the second century B.C.E. Recruits from Libya and Munidia were part of Carthage's army.

Three wars with Rome ended the dominance of Carthage. The last war resulted in the ruthless destruction of Carthage by the Roman army in 146 B.C.E. In 122 B.C.E., six thousand Roman colonists and discharged Roman soldiers were sent to settle there. By the reign of Caligula in 40 C.E., Rome controlled the fertile areas of North Africa. Roman power in Africa reached its peak under the rule of Septimius Severus in the third century C.E.[1]

Unlike the Phoenicians, the Romans imposed their culture on the indigenous population, the Berbers. Latin became the language used for education and for trading. Berbers as well as Phoenicians had to be Latinized if they wished to be integrated into the culture brought by the Romans.

In the Carthage of Perpetua's time the urban elite were Latinized. Three strata composed this elite urban society. The Romans were the top stratum. The Phoenicians constituted the second stratum, retaining a fair amount of power through their involvement in agriculture and commerce. The Berbers made up the third stratum. Having lost whatever power they once held, they worked in the grain fields and olive groves of the Romans or else remained nomadic. The Berbers never accepted the gods of the Romans but chose to retain their own native African traditions.

The pre-Christian primal religions of the North African people centered on the spirits of natural objects, deities from Phoenicia, and the gods of the Roman pantheon. All three of these religious expressions tended toward a monotheism that recognized Saturn (or spirit of the sun) as the supreme God. All three accepted that the worship of the supreme God demanded a total submission to whatever that Supreme Being asked, including death. There was a general belief that a judgment of some kind occurred in the life beyond death. Native religions believed in a literal rising of the bodies of the dead. Religious practices included sacrifice of one's own life as well as that of one's children if that was what Baal-Haamon-Moloch demanded. Exorcisms and use of talismans during this period have also been reported.

Christianity probably arrived during the persecution of Nero in the late first century. Jesus Christ was followed in different ways by the indigenous Africans. Some of the native converts simply added Yahweh and Jesus Christ to their other deities when they became Christians. Others identified the Father of Jesus Christ with the one supreme deity, Saturn. Still others added the externals of Christianity to their existing beliefs. In spite of the plurality of religious interpretations, all agreed that there must be a willingness to suffer and die for one's belief.[2]

Initially there was no formal opposition to the preaching of the Christian God and Jesus Christ. However, as members of the urban elite began to abandon their native gods, the Roman gods, and emperor worship, the Christian gospel became politically dangerous. Christians refused to take part in emperor worship. Their belief that Jesus Christ was coming soon provided a source of joy to them even as they endured torture and martyrdom for their refusal to call Caesar "lord." History's first account of Christianity in North Africa is the martyrdom of seven men and five women who were beheaded at Carthage in 180 C.E.[3]

In 202, the Roman emperor Septimius Severus (193–211), who was born in North Africa, issued an edict that prohibited any further conversions to Christianity. Historians cite two possible reasons for this decree.

First, the emperor wanted no disruption of the peace of Carthage, for the port was a key to Roman prosperity. Trade of all kinds, including slave trade, flowed through the city. Second, there were minor insurrections on the borders of North Africa for which Septimius Severus blamed Christians. Some historians claim the emperor was ill-advised about who caused the insurrections. The Montanists were the more probable offenders since they were politically and militarily anti-Roman. The Christians were not anti-Roman, nor did they wish political gains. They simply refused to worship the emperor and would not engage in military service.[4]

Regardless of the cause, the edict of Septimius Severus required all citizens to take a loyalty test, namely, to sacrifice to the gods of the Roman Empire. It also forbade Christians to teach, to proclaim their faith publicly, and to attempt to convert others to their way of life. Those who boldly disregarded this edict would be punished to deter others from doing the same. In North Africa, the proconsul Scapula applied the decree with great cruelty to women and men alike.

The upper class of Roman descent, the middle class of Phoenician descent, and the lowest class of Berber descent were subject to the same edict and the same punishment for refusing the sacrifice demanded by the emperor. Women as well as men, children as well as the aged, were part of the early church of the martyrs. What did Scapula hope to achieve by the public displays of bloody deaths in the arena?

First, he sought to remove any temporal benefit the Christian religion might bring to its adherents. If they died, their religion could not help them. Second, if the tortures and deaths were disgusting enough to onlookers, they would be dissuaded from joining the cult of Christians. Third, watching the violence in the arena could be a good way for the crowd to be released of any anger they might feel toward Roman rule. Fourth, watching the slow deaths of Christians could enhance the moral strength of emotional control. Finally, the crowd would relearn who held ultimate power in Carthage.

In fact, these desired effects of martyrdom were not so easily attained. When the accused were brought to trial, they generally had an opportunity to defend their position. This allowed them to do precisely what the edict forbade, namely, to teach about Jesus Christ and their convictions of faith. For many who witnessed events in the arena, the strength and joy of the Christians caused onlookers to wonder about the truth of the faith that such martyrs proclaimed.

The entire process of martyrdom became a way to teach others about the meaning of Christian faith. It proclaimed the hope that human beings, like Christ, would rise in glory. In the North Africa of Perpetua's time there was a sense that Christ would come again soon. The joy of this coming reign of God was evident as the martyrs embraced death. This process of martyrdom in the early centuries is quite different from the experience of martyrdom in the twentieth century, which a later chapter will address.[5]

After Constantine's official rescripting of Milan in 313, the persecution of Christians ended. The prefect of North Africa was obliged to return the church properties that had been seized. The practice of branding criminals on the face ceased, and bishops were given civil powers, in 315. Sunday became a state holiday in 321. Pagan religion was declared false worship in 323. By 395, Emperor Theodosius began persecuting pagans in the name of the Christian church.

The martyrdom of Perpetua and her companions belongs to the earlier century of persecutions. The writer who introduces the text of *The Passion of Saints Perpetua and Felicity* tells the reader that Perpetua is from the noble Roman family, Vibii. The willingness of someone in this upper class to die when she had a small child and the means to live well raised questions. The loving friendship of Perpetua and her maidservant, Felicity, and the love among the different classes of people who were their companions, also raised questions. Christianity's discipleship of equals confused a populace living in a stratified society.

The Passion of Saints Perpetua and Felicity is an early Christian account of a protest against the restrictive demands of Roman power. It is a unique account, not only because of its age, but also because it is a woman's personal diary. Unlike later acts of the martyrs, this is a firsthand account. Perpetua herself writes the middle chapters about her experience in prison and her impending martyrdom.[6]

By the latter part of the third century, the stories of martyrs—called *Acta martyrum*—would have distinct forms. In time a web of mythical as well as historical threads would weave together for the sake of edifying the people. The story of Felicity and Perpetua is still relatively unidealized. It was used with other acts of the martyrs by St. Augustine and his community at Hippo in liturgical prayer.

Chapters 3–10 of the diary are written by Perpetua. Felicity, her friend and maidservant, who is pregnant, is a vital part of these chapters. The visions that Perpetua sees help her unfold the meaning of her suffering and the well-being of a brother about whom she must have had some concern. Visions provide the hope to which she would cling as she leaves her infant son and his future to God.

From one perspective, Perpetua could be considered a mother of future visionaries. Her visions support her commitment to Christ, her active leadership of the group about to be martyred, and her sensitivity to the pain of others. Like other visionaries, she will experience a joyful liberation as the meaning of her visions becomes clear. The authentication of visions at this time is often through others having visions that clarify them. This will be seen in the visions of Saturus, a companion of Perpetua's.

It will be clear to the reader that another hand introduces and concludes the reflections of Perpetua. *The Passion of Saints Perpetua and Felicity* was written in Latin. The original text has three styles of Latin, pointing to three different authors of the text as it has come down to us.[7]

The author of the first two chapters states that saints are those people whose lives proclaim the justice and compassion of God in ways appropriate for their time and place in history. In this sense, what it means to be holy will change as the context of Christian life changes. Thus, lives of saints will need to be part of Christian teaching about holiness in every age. As ages change, so will the criteria for sainthood.

Perpetua wrote chapters 3–10, which describe actual events, feelings, and prophetic visions. One of Perpetua's brothers, who died at age seven, is a subject of these visions. The healing power of water in the visions becomes an important symbol of hope. A brother who is still living helps her interpret the meaning of her visions. Perpetua's vision of herself as a male warrior getting ready for battle is a sign to her that she will die as a martyr. She will not receive the clemency that was sometimes shown to pregnant women or mothers of infants. The frequent allusions to the "second baptism" refer to the faith conviction that martyrs were symbolically "baptized in blood." In other words, they would be received into the kingdom of Jesus Christ as soon as they died.

The third hand that concludes the story adds a few details that are worth noting here. The author could be commenting on Perpetua's flair in real life as well as her symbolic actions as death was near. Perpetua does two things that would hold particular meaning for the early hearers of this account. First, she pins up her hair; second, she pulls her robe around herself. These acts would have significance for those who witnessed her death as well.

It was customary for married women to mourn by loosening their hair and letting it hang down. Second, tearing one's clothes was a sign of deep grief. The final commentator points out that Perpetua does just the opposite when thrown into the arena. She carefully pins up her hair and pulls her torn robe over herself to appear untorn. She is joyful about the nearness of God's kingdom.

Perhaps to indicate the power of Perpetua over her own life, the final author makes a point in describing the ineptitude of the young gladiator. He has hit the wrong part of the throat, prolonging both pain and time of death. Perpetua's guidance of his hand testifies to her imitation of Jesus Christ, who chose to give up his spirit. Throughout the account Perpetua encourages others and retains the staunch conviction that death is but a passage to new life.[8]

Perpetua, Felicity, and their male and female companions were part of an early Christian reaction against the oppressive and brutal society of their time. The final author of the text is clear in hoping that their deaths will inspire others to follow Christ. Perpetua, Felicity, and their companions entered eternal life on March 7, 203.[9]

The Passion of Saints Perpetua and Felicity[10]

1

The ancient examples of faith have given testimony to the grace of God and have edified and encouraged believers. The stories have been put into writing both to glorify God and also to strengthen the faith of those in future ages. If this is true for legends of older times, then it is equally true for new stories of our own time. Someday these new stories will be old and useful for posterity, even if contemporary believers hold them in less esteem than older legends, merely because they are of our own time.

But let those who discern the one Spirit that acts in all times and seasons consider the following. Should not the new stories be deemed greater because they are "later than the last"? This seems to flow from the preeminence of God's grace that has been promised to the later ages of the world. For God has said:

> In the last days I will pour forth my Spirit upon all flesh, and their sons and daughters shall prophesy; and on my servants and on my handmaidens I will pour forth my Spirit. Their young shall see visions and their old shall dream dreams.

We recognize and honor not only the prophecies of the old but also the visions of the new, for both were promises of the Spirit. The powers of the Holy Spirit were intended for the building of the church. These gifts of the Spirit are given to the community. Each receives the gifts that the Lord gives. Our desire is to tell of the gifts given and make them known for the greater glory of God. Let no one with weak or despairing faith suppose that the grace of martyrdom and revelation is to be found only among the ancient ones.

Our God continues to be true to the promise so that there is witness given to unbelievers and a blessing given to believers. Thus, "What we have heard and touched, we also declare to you," adult believers and children, "that you also" who were eyewitnesses may remember the glory of the Lord. May you who now learn by hearing "have communion with" the holy martyrs and through them with the Lord Jesus. To him belongs splendor and honor forever and ever. Amen.

2

During the reign of Septimius Severus, certain young catechumens were arrested, including Revocatus and his fellow slave Felicity, Saturninus and Secundulus, and Vibio Perpetua. Perpetua was wellborn, and her parents were still living. She was liberally educated, honorably married, and one of her two brothers was a catechumen like herself. She was twenty-two when she was arrested, and had an infant son that she was still nursing. The following story of her martyrdom has been written by herself. This is just as she left it in her own hand and as composed by herself.

3

She writes: When I was still with my companions, my father tried to dissuade my resolution out of his deep affection for me. Then I finally said, "Father, do you see this vessel lying here, this waterpot or whatever it may be?" "I see it," he said. So I continued, "Can it be called by any other name than what it is?"

He answered, "No." "So neither can I be called by any other name than who I am, a Christian."

My father grew furious at the word *Christian.* He threw himself upon me so violently that I thought he would pluck out my eyes. But he did not, for he wished only to upset me. He was, in fact, simply upset that he and his devil's arguments to me were not heard. I thanked the Lord that I would not have to see my father for a few days. His absence was refreshing for me. During those few days of his absence, we were baptized. The Holy Spirit inspired me to make no other petitions except the one for bodily endurance. It was only a few days after this that we were imprisoned. I was very fearful, for I had never experienced such a darkness before. It was a day of horror.

There was a terrible heat, since there were great crowds of people. The soldiers handled us very roughly. To add to this, I was extremely anxious about the well-being of my baby, who was not with me. Tertius and Pomponius, the deacons who ministered to us in the prison, paid our keepers so that we could get to a better part of the prison for a few hours and refresh ourselves. Then everyone went out of the prison and we were left alone. My baby was brought to me and I nursed him, for he was already weak from not being fed.

I spoke with anxiety to my mother about him. I encouraged my brother to keep faithful, and then I commended my little son to their care. I was terribly saddened because of their deep sadness for me. I suffered doubly from these things for many days. At last I obtained permission for my baby to stay in the prison with me so that I could care for him. This was granted me. As soon as my baby was given to me, I not only recovered my health, but my fears for my baby and my own sadness left. Suddenly, that prison became like a palace to me. I would rather be there than anywhere else.

4

It was then that my brother said to me, "Lady sister, you are now held in great honor. It is so great that you could pray for a vision that would tell you whether your freedom or more suffering lies ahead for you." I knew that the Lord was with me. It was for the Lord's sake that I had already gone through so much. So it was with confidence that I assured my brother, "Tomorrow I will bring you word." I made the request to the Lord to see a vision that would enlighten me about all this.

This is what was shown to me. I saw a brazen ladder of wondrous height reaching up to the heavens. But it was so narrow that only one person could ascend it at a time. All kinds of iron weapons were fastened to the sides of the ladder. There were swords, lances, hooks, and daggers fastened in such a way that if anyone was careless about climbing the ladder or looked upward too soon, they could be mangled and their flesh caught on the weapons. Just beneath the ladder was a reclining dragon of great size. He was lying in wait for those who were going up the ladder, and tried to frighten them from going up.

Saturus was the first who went up the ladder, saying he wished to do this for our sakes because he was the one who first instructed us in the faith. He had not been with us when we were seized and imprisoned. He reached the top of the ladder, turned, and said to me, "Perpetua, I await you. But be careful that the dragon does not bite you." I said, "In the name of Jesus Christ, the dragon will not hurt me!" The dragon at the foot of the ladder put out his head very gently, almost as if he were afraid of me. I stepped on that head as if it were the first step of the ladder.

As I went up the ladder, I soon saw a garden of great proportions. A tall man with white hair, who was dressed as a shepherd, was in the midst of the garden milking sheep. Thousands of others dressed in white were surrounding him. As he raised his head to look at me, he said, "My child, you are welcome." He called to me to come near. Then he gave me some of the milk from his milking, which I held in my cupped hands and drank. All of those who were standing around said, "Amen." I was still eating something sweet as I woke up with the sound of the word *Amen*. I told my brother about this immediately and we both understood that I would have to suffer. From that time on, we had no further hope in this world.

5

After a few days passed, it was rumored that we were to be examined. My father came up the hill from the city to see me, immensely troubled. He tried to make me change my mind. "Have pity on my old age, my daughter. Have pity on me if you believe I am worthy to be called your father. Pity me if I have brought you up to your prime of life with these hands, and if I have preferred you to all your brothers. Do not make me a laughingstock to others. Have some consideration for your brothers, your mother, your aunt, and most especially your little son, who cannot live once you are gone. Lay aside your pride and do not ruin all of us. None of us will ever speak freely again if anything should happen to you."

My father spoke all of this out of his love for me, kissing my hands, casting himself at my feet, and calling me not by the name of daughter, but of lady. I grieved for my dear father, for he—unlike my relatives—could have no joy in my suffering. I tried to comfort him by saying, "What happens will be what God desires. We are in the power of God, not in our own power." He then left with a heavy heart.

6

One day, when we were having the midday meal, we were hurried away to be interrogated. We were brought to a marketplace, where a vast crowd gathered. We went up on a platform. Those before me confessed their faith upon being examined. When it came to my turn to be interrogated, I saw my father holding my little son. He drew me down from the platform saying, "Have pity on your baby." The procurator, whose name was Hilarion, had the power to grant life or death in the wake of the death of the proconsul Minucius Timinianus. Hilarion said to me, "Have pity on your father's age and on your young son. Offer a sacrifice for the safekeeping of the emperors."

"No," I answered. "Are you a Christian?" "I am." My father persisted in trying to make me change my mind. Finally, Hilarion ordered my father to be thrown down, and the judge struck him with his rod. I felt deep grief for my father. It felt like I had been struck instead of him, for I was moved with great compassion for his old age. Then the sentence was passed on all of us. We were condemned to be fed to the beasts in the arena. We went joyfully down into the prison. Because my baby son was used to being nursed by me and also used to being with me in prison, I sent the deacon Pomponius to my father to ask for my baby. My father now refused to give my baby to me. Then, in God's providence, my baby had no further need for breast feeding. Neither did my breasts become inflamed. Thus I was not tortured either by anxiety for my baby's health or by pain in my breasts.

7

A few days later while we were praying, I spoke the name of Dinocrates in the middle of our prayer. It was astonishing that I had not remembered him until then. I was sorrowful over what had happened to him. I saw immediately that I should pray for him. So I did pray for him and make my lamentations. As I did, this was shown to me immediately.

I saw Dinocrates coming forth from a place of darkness. He was very hot and thirsty. His countenance was pale and squalid. The wound from which he died was still very visible on his face. Dinocrates was my seven-year-old brother, who died of gangrene of the face. The death had left all in a loathing. As I prayed, there seemed to be such a great gulf between us that neither could reach the other.

In the place where Dinocrates was, there was a font full of water, but the rim was way above his head. Dinocrates stood on tiptoe to drink. I felt badly because, although the font had water in it, Dinocrates could not drink from it because the rim was too high. I woke up and knew my brother was in trouble.

I trusted that I could relieve the trouble, so I prayed for him every day until we were transferred to the garrison prison. We were sent here because we were to fight the beasts at the garrison games on the caesar Geta's birthday. I prayed for Dinocrates day and night with lamentation and tears so that he might be healed.

8

This vision was shown to me during the daytime while we were in the stocks. I saw the same place I had seen before. Dinocrates was now clean, well clothed, and refreshed. There was a scar where the wound had been. Now the font had its rim as low as the child's waist. Water poured forth from the font unceasingly. A golden bowl full of water was on the rim of the font. Dinocrates came toward it and began to drink from it. The bowl did not run out. After he had drunk enough of the water, he began to play as children do. Then I woke up, knowing that he had been released from any punishment.

9

After a few days the adjutant Pudens, who was in charge of the prison, sensed there was some great power within us and he began to show us great respect. He admitted others to see us so that both we and they could be mutually strengthened by our company. As the day of the games came closer, my father came once again. He was overcome with grief and began to pluck out his beard and cast the hair on the ground. He threw himself down on the ground, cursed his age, and continued to utter unbelievable curses. I deeply pitied his grief in his old age.

10

The day before we were to fight the beasts, I had a vision of Pomponius the deacon knocking loudly at the prison door. I opened the door and went out to see him. He was clad in a white robe without the usual sash around the waist. He wore unusual shoes. He said to me, "Perpetua, we are waiting for you. Come." He then held my hand as we passed through rough and rocky country. Breathing heavily and in pain, we finally arrived at an amphitheater. Pomponius led me into the middle of the arena. Then he said, "Do not be afraid, for I am with you now and suffer with you." He then left, and I saw a large crowd of people looking on with anticipation. I knew that I was condemned to fight the beasts, so I marveled that there were no beasts set free to destroy me. Then an Egyptian, accompanied by his attendants, came forward to fight against me. But good young men also came to be my attendants and supporters.

Then I was stripped and changed into a man. My supporters began to rub me with oil as is done before combat. I saw the Egyptian opposite me rolling in the sand. Then a wondrously tall man who rose higher than the top of the amphitheater came forward. He was dressed in a purple robe with two stripes that ran down the left and right of the middle of the breast. His shoes were made of gold and silver and in a style different from ours. He carried a wand like the trainers use and had a green bough with golden apples. He asked for silence. Then he said, "If this Egyptian conquers Perpetua, he shall kill her with the sword. If she conquers him, she shall receive this bough." Then he departed.

We approached each other and used our fists. My adversary tried to catch hold of my feet, but I kept striking his face with my heels. I was then lifted up into the air and began to strike him in a way that no earthly being could. When I saw that the fight was slowing down, I joined my two hands by linking the fingers of one hand with the fingers of the other. I then caught hold of his head and he fell on his face. I walked on his head and all the people began to shout. My supporters started to sing psalms. Then I came forward to receive the bough from the trainer. He kissed me and said to me, "Peace be with you, my daughter." I began to walk triumphantly to the Gate of Life. I awoke.

Then I understood that I would be fighting not with the beasts but with the devil. I knew the victory was to be mine, however. Such were the things I envisioned and what I did up to the day before the games. Whatever is to happen in the games will have to be written now by another who desires to write of them.

11

The blessed Saturus also has made known this vision of his own, which he wrote himself: I thought we had suffered and died, and were being borne to the east by four angels, who did not seem to touch us. Now we moved not by looking upward as if we were on our backs, but by climbing a gentle slope. When we had been raised above the earth below, we saw a great light. I said to Perpetua, who was at my side, "This is what the Lord promised us. We have received the promise."

While we were carried by those four angels, we were brought to an immense space. It seemed like a garden that had rose trees and all kinds of flowers. The rose trees were as high as the cypress, whose leaves sang without ceasing. There were four angels in the garden who were more glorious than any others. When they saw us, they paid us homage and said in wonder to the other angels, "They have come. They have come."

The four angels who had carried us set us down. We walked over a place that had violets scattered on the ground. Here we found the three who had been burned alive in the same persecution, Jucundus, Saturninus, and Artaxis. Quintus was also here. He had died as a martyr in the prison. We asked them where they were. The other angels said to us, "First, come and enter and greet the Lord."

12

Then we came near to a place that looked as if it had been built of light. Four angels stood before the gate there and clothed us in white robes as we entered. Then we heard the sound of many saying unceasingly with one voice, "Holy, holy, holy!" We saw a Man there with hair as white as snow and face like a young man. We did not see his feet. Four elders were on the right and the left of him. Many other elders were behind them. We entered and stood in wonder before the throne. The four angels lifted us up and we kissed the young Man. He stroked our faces with his hand. The other elders said to us, "Let us stand." We stood and gave the kiss of peace. Then the elders said to us, "Go and play."

I said to Perpetua, "You have your wish." She then said to me, "Thanks be to God. I was happy while I was in my earthly body, but here I am even happier."

13

As we walked forward, we saw Optatus the bishop standing before the right door and Aspasius the priest-teacher standing before the left door. They were at a distance from each other and sorrowful. They said, "Make peace between us, for you have now gone forth from this life and have left us apart like this." We then replied, "Are you not our bishop and you our priest? Why do you fall before our feet?" We were very moved and embraced them.

Perpetua began to speak in Greek with these elders as we drew them into the garden under a rose tree. While we talked with them, the angels said to them, "Refresh yourselves, and if you have any quarrels among yourselves, then forgive one another." The angels made them feel ashamed and said to Optatus, "Reform your people, for they act like they are coming back from a circus and fighting about its factions." It seemed to us that the angels were trying to shut the gates. But we began to recognize many of our brothers and sisters there, and there were martyrs among them. We were all fed with a fragrance beyond description, which fully contented us. It was then that I awoke with joy.

14

These are the famous visions that the blessed martyrs Saturus and Perpetua wrote with their own hands. Secundulus was called by God while he was still in prison so that he might escape the beasts. However, this grace from God does not mean that he did not experience the sword.

15

Felicity was also visited by the grace of God in this way. She was eight months pregnant when she was arrested. As the day of the fighting with the beasts drew near, she was filled with sorrow because she feared her pregnancy would delay her martyrdom. It is against the law to punish any pregnant woman. This is because she could shed her sacred and innocent blood among those who were her enemies. The other martyrs were deeply saddened at the thought of leaving such a good friend and brave companion behind on their mutual journey to the reign of God.

Thus they petitioned the Lord in one flood of common prayer two days before the games were to start. It was soon after this that her labor pains started. The eighth-month labor pains caused her to suffer much in childbirth. One of her guards said to her, "You who suffer so badly now, what will you do when you are fed to the beasts because you refused to sacrifice?" She answered by saying, "Now I suffer what I alone can suffer in childbirth. But Another will suffer for me and in me as I shall suffer for him." She gave birth to a baby girl, who was given to one of her sisters to bring up as her own daughter.

The Holy Spirit has permitted—and so willed—that the story of the games be written, so we shall carry out that wish. We are unworthy to carry out that special request of the most holy Perpetua. At the same time, we wish to give one additional example of her steadfastness and loftiness of soul.

The commanding officer had treated the Christians with unusual cruelty because he was superstitious. Some foolish people had made him fear that the Christians might be carried off from prison by magic spells. Perpetua challenged the man to his face. "Why can you not allow us to refresh ourselves? We are the most noble among the condemned, belonging as we do to Caesar and even fighting on his birthday. Or will it not be to your credit to have us appear in the arena in good shape?" The commanding officer trembled and blushed. He then ordered that the noble persons be treated with more kindness, allowing brothers and other persons to visit so that each could be strengthened by the other. By this time the governor of the prison was already converted to belief.

On the day before the games the Christians celebrated the so-called last supper of "the free festivity." Theirs was not so much a "festivity," but a "love feast" insofar as they could make it that. They were steadfast, flinging words here and there to the crowds and threatening them with the judgment of God as they called for them to witness to the happiness that their coming passion gave them. They laughed at the inquisitiveness of the crowd. Saturus said, "Tomorrow does not satisfy you. That is because what you hate you love to see. Friends today, but foes tomorrow. Yet, remember our faces well, so that when the final day comes, you will recognize us again." All the onlookers left the place amazed, and many of them became believers.

18

The day of their triumph finally dawned. They proceeded from the prison to the amphitheater as if they were on the way to heaven. They had gracious and happy countenances. If they trembled, it was not with fear but with joy. Perpetua followed the group with light steps, as a true bride of Christ. She, the beloved of God, moved all who saw her with that great spirit in her eyes. Felicity was also rejoicing that she was well enough to fight the beasts. She had emerged from bloodshed to bloodshed again, from midwife to gladiator. This second baptism of blood was her childbirth washing of life. They were led within the gate and were forced to put on the dress of the women dedicated to Ceres, while the men had to wear the dress of the priests of Saturn. The noble Perpetua resisted to the last.

She said to them, "We came to this of our own free will, so that our liberty would not be violated. We have pledged our lives to do no such thing as worship another. This was our pact with you." Injustice then acknowledged justice. The commanding officer gave his permission for them to enter the arena in their ordinary dress. Perpetua was already singing a psalm of triumph, as if she were already treading on the head of the Egyptian. Revocatus, Saturninus, and Saturus were threatening the onlookers with retribution. When they came within the sight of Hilarion, they signaled him by their nods and gestures that "you are judging us, but God shall judge you."

The people were infuriated at such pronouncements and demanded that they be scourged before the line of the beast fighters. They were joyful at this, for they had won a deeper share in the sufferings of their Lord.

19

The one who had said, "Ask and you shall receive," granted them the death that they had desired. Whenever they had talked among themselves about their hopes of martyrdom, Saturninus had said he wanted to be thrown before all the beasts. Then he could wear a more glorious crown in the heavens. At the beginning of the games, he was matched with a leopard and later mauled on the platform by a bear. Saturus had a great fear of the bear, but had prayed to be quickly killed by one bite of the leopard.

When he was offered to a wild boar, the fighter of beasts who had bound him to the boar was gored by the same boar. He died only after the days of the games were over. Saturus, however, was dragged by the boar, but not gored. When he was tied up on the bridge before the bear, the bear refused to come out of the den. Saturus was unhurt for the second time.

20

The devil made a mad heifer ready to attack the young women. The animal was selected to match the sex of the accused. The young women were stripped and then enclosed in nets before being brought into the arena. The people were horrified to see the young mothers Felicity and Perpetua. Perpetua was still such a young woman, and Felicity had clearly given birth recently because she had milk dripping from her breasts. Because of the reaction of the crowd, Perpetua and Felicity were recalled and dressed in tunics.

Perpetua was tossed in first, and fell face down. She sat and then pulled her torn tunic from her side to cover her thighs. She seemed more concerned about her nakedness than her suffering. She asked for a hair ornament to fasten her disordered hair. It was not seemly that a martyr should suffer with disheveled hair, for that could make it seem like she was sad at this hour of her glory.

Perpetua then rose and saw that Felicity was bruised. She went to her, extended her hand, and helped her to get up. The two stood side by side. The cruelty of the people was soon appeased, and the young women were called close to the Gate of Life. Perpetua was supported by the catechumen Rusticus, who remained close to her. She had been so completely in ecstasy in the Spirit that she was aroused as if from sleeping.

Those around her were amazed when she began to look around and said, "I cannot tell when we are going to be thrown to that heifer." When they told her what had already taken place, she could not believe it until she observed the injuries and blood on her body and on her dress. Then she summoned her brother and spoke to him and to another catechumen. "Be steadfast in the faith, and love one another. Do not be too disturbed by our sufferings."

21

At another gate, Saturus was encouraging Pudens, a soldier. Saturus said, "What I was hoping for and foretold has happened. Not one beast has touched me. Now that you may trust me with your whole heart, watch how I shall go forth and see that all is over with one bite of the leopard." As the show was ending, the leopard was let loose. With one bite, Saturus was so drenched in blood that the other Christians shouted out, affirming him in this second baptism. "Bless you! Bless you! You are washed well!"

Saturus was blessed, indeed, having been washed in this bath of blood. Then he said to the soldier Pudens, "Farewell! Remember me and my faith. Do not let these things make you anxious but rather confirm you in faith." With that, he asked Pudens for his ring. He took it and plunged it in his wound, before returning it as a legacy, a promise, and a memorial of his blood.

Then, his lifeless body was flung with the rest of the dead to the place set aside for throat cutting. The people asked for the living to be brought into the open so that they could see the sword pierce them. By seeing, they were partners in the murders. Without hesitation, the Christians rose, embraced each other with the rite of peace (the Pax) to complete their martyrdom. Then they made their way to the place the people wished them to come. In silence, they received the sword.

Saturus was the first to climb the ladder, for he was the first to die. Now, as before, he awaited Perpetua. Perpetua, however, was struck on the bone of the throat and cried out in pain. She had to guide the wavering hand of the untried young gladiator to the right spot. Perhaps so great a woman, who was feared by the unclean spirit, could only be killed as she willed it.

O courageous and blessed martyrs! You were truly called and chosen to the glory of Jesus Christ our Lord! Whoever magnifies, honors, and praises the glory of Christ should tell these stories for the good of the church. They are not less important than the stories of older times. They are told because such new instances of virtue testify that one and the same Spirit is working through these times with the Father, God Almighty, and with the Son, Jesus Christ our Lord, to whom belong splendor and infinite power for ever and ever. Amen.

NOTES

1. Harry Gailey, *History of Africa* (New York: Holt, Rinehart and Winston, 1970) 10–48.

2. Mercy Amba Oduyoye, *Hearing and Knowing: A Theological Reflection on Christianity in Africa* (Maryknoll, N.Y.: Orbis, 1986) 15–22.

3. Joanne Turpin, *Women in Church History* (Cincinnati: St. Anthony Messenger Press, 1989) 13–14.

4. John C. Dwyer, *Twenty Centuries of Catholic Christianity* (New York: Paulist Press, 1985) 209.

5. Bruno Chenu, Claude Prudhomme, France Quere, and Jean-Claude Thomas, *The Book of Christian Martyrs* (New York: Crossroad, 1990) 61.

6. Ibid. 1–21.

7. Rosemary Rader, "The *Martyrdom of Perpetua:* A Protest Account of Third-Century Christianity," in *A Lost Tradition: Women Writers of the Early Church*, ed. Patricia Wilson-Kastner (Boston: University Press of America, 1981) 1–32.

8. *Medieval Women's Visionary Literature*, ed. Elizabeth Alvilda Petroff (Oxford: Oxford University Press, 1986) 61.

9. Ibid. 60–63.

10. Unfortunately, the names of Perpetua and Felicity—as well as other women except Mary, Mother of Jesus—are usually omitted in the revised Eucharistic Prayer 1.

11. This translation is from "Passio Sanctarum Perpetuae & Felicitatis," cum sociis earum. Ex. 2. codd. mss. et Editione Holstenii. The text is found in P. Theodorici Ruinart, *Acta martyrum* (Ratisbon: G. Joseph Manz, 1859) 137–46. Additional history about manuscripts, glosses, textual discrepancies, and different days for celebration can be found on 146–68.

BIBLIOGRAPHY

Brown, Peter. *The Cult of the Saints*. Chicago: University of Chicago Press, 1981.

Chenu, Bruno, Claude Prudhomme, France Quere, and Jean-Claude Thomas. *The Book of Christian Martyrs*. New York: Crossroad, 1990.

Dronke, Peter. *Women Writers of the Middle Ages: A Critical Study of Texts from Perpetua to Marguerite Porete*. Cambridge: Cambridge University Press, 1984.

Musurillo, H. R. *The Acts of the Christian Martyrs*. Oxford: Clarendon Press, 1972.

Petroff, Elizabeth Alvilda. *Medieval Women's Visionary Literature*. Oxford: Oxford University Press, 1986.

Rader, Rosemary. "The *Martyrdom of Perpetua:* A Protest Account of Third-Century Christianity." In *A Lost Tradition: Women Writers of the Early Church*. Edited by Patricia Wilson-Kastner. Boston: University Press of America, 1981. 1–32.

Turpin, Joanne. *Women in Church History*. Cincinnati: St. Anthony Messenger Press, 1989.

– 2 –

PELAGIA THE ACTRESS

(FOURTH CENTURY?)

My Choice Is the Riches of Christ

As the preceding chapter indicated, women in the early stages of Christianity were encouraged to follow the call of Christ, even if that meant going against the desires of parents, husbands, brothers, or other family members. The diary of Perpetua points to the difficulty this devotion caused not only to her but also to her father.

The narrative of Pelagia the actress traces another dimension of the freedom of women to follow the call of Christ. As early as the second century, Christian women were refusing to adhere to the social requirement to marry and have children if they felt their vocation was to follow Christ as celibate women. The Christian regard for celibacy for women as well as men was based on the lifestyle of Jesus Christ. Consequently, women and men were considered equals in their identification of this vocation as a legitimate way to imitate the love of Jesus Christ.

This Christian freedom, especially for women, would eventually put Christians on a collision course with Roman law. Caesar Augustus attempted to eliminate all forms of celibacy in the empire. Later Roman emperors promulgated and enforced these laws. Bringing forth many children populated the Roman Empire with good citizens and provided potential soldiers for the Roman legions.[1]

The Christian emphasis on following the Spirit, regardless of social or legal custom, made Christians seem like an indifferent group of citizens. How could true Roman citizens so blatantly disobey laws that were for the good of the people? What disorders would arise as women were liberated from paternal, fraternal, or spousal control? The conflicts between Christian liberation and Roman laws caused problems until Constantine's Edict of Milan (313) finally allowed Christians to follow their religious practices without persecution.[2]

Within the Christian church the development of the order of widows clearly approved of a woman not marrying a second time. Widows were already an institutionalized and official order within the church hierarchy by the late second century. Clement (150–215) and Origen (185?–?254) clearly include the order of widows in their hierarchies.[3]

By the third century the order of widows in Syria required that its official members be at least fifty years old and in need of support from the church. The bishop was now in charge of providing that support for their services in the church.[4] The widows served through prayer and good works. Their care of the sick was linked to both fasting and the imposition of hands. The earlier functions, however, which included direct care of the altar, were by the third century restricted in the East. Widows were forbidden to teach or to baptize, and it was only with the official permission of the bishop that they could perform their limited functions.[5]

The charismatic origin of ministries for women and for widows was virtually forgotten as their roles became hierarchically controlled. By the middle of the third century, there were already claims that the Gospels provided no precedent for women being teachers or baptizers. This inaccurate claim continued to be made in various forms throughout successive centuries. A favorite argument, already picked up in the *Didascalia*, asserts that "if it were lawful to be baptized by a woman, our Lord... would have been baptized by Mary."[6]

The discipleship of equals expressed in the pre-Pauline baptismal formula of Galatians 3:27–28, the ministries of Apphia (Phil 2), Lydia (Acts 16:14), Nympha (Col 4:15), Prisca (1 Cor 16:19; Rom 16:3–5; Acts 18:2ff.), Chloe (1 Cor 1:11), Euodia (Phil 4:2), Junia (Rom 16:7), Deacon Phoebe (Rom 16:1ff.), and a host of other gospel women point to the ministries that women performed in the early charismatic period of the Christian movement.[7] As the movement slowly evolved toward a centralized hierarchical system concerned with social and cultural acceptance, the countercultural boldness of Jesus Christ was tamed by his followers. The prophetic, teaching, and liturgical roles of women in the early church indicated in the Gospels of John and Luke were apparently forgotten or else rejected.[8] The order of widows would have some of its earlier liturgical functions taken over by the order of deaconesses.[9]

By the fourth century the patriarchal ordering of the church in both the East and the West had placed restrictions on the minimal ministries that remained for women. At the same time, it was evident that the charismatic nature of the church of Jesus Christ was not to be suppressed by official ministries. The rise of the monastic movement was not an official idea. The monastic movement in the East and in the West was of charismatic origin.

The early monastic women, like their charismatic predecessors, the widows, prayed for the community and sacrificed for its good as well as for their own good. Monastic women were celibate. In the fourth century, women like Pelagia undertook the rigors of a desert asceticism that would have been denied to women at an earlier time. Although it may be difficult for modern readers to understand why this is a liberating choice for women, the underlying reality is that the choice was one made by a woman following the direction of her life as a personal response to Christ's call. The direction was not chosen for her.

It was not the throwing off of traditional female roles that the monastic movement was concerned with at this time, however. There was a faith reality guiding this choice of life direction. The Roman Empire was disintegrating, and values of power, wealth, and self-indulgence were treated as ends in life rather than as means. The monastic movement served as a protest statement pointing to the value of eternal life rather than passing good.

When the monastic movement to the desert began, it was somewhat similar to contemporary protest movements. A protest movement says in word and deed that something is wrong with the way life is being lived. Protest movements are value statements by those who feel the human community is living a falsehood that oppresses the human spirit.

Those who see things differently are compelled to act out their vision. The men and women who went into the desert to undertake a life of prayer and sacrifice for the world were kicking the dust from their feet. They were marching to a different drummer. Their preaching was a way of life rather than a well-developed verbal sermon. This form of preaching was as open to women as it was to men, in spite of the mandates against women preaching.

Just as Jesus Christ was driven by love to suffer and die for the people, so were the desert solitaries or hermits. Their hope was that their life of prayer and sacrifice would somehow mediate the life of Christ's kingdom on earth as it is in heaven. The early mothers and fathers of the desert were well aware of the need for deep faith that enabled them to trust that their life had meaning. They did not consider themselves holier than those who followed other vocations. Like other holy people, they considered themselves the least holy.

The stories that circulated through the monastic groups of the fourth century and after point to the ongoing need for the conversion of one's own sinfulness before casting stones at others. Those who have an awareness of their own sinfulness and need for continuous repentance in all likelihood will not judge others badly. The collections of stories that circulated throughout the desert communities made this point over and over again.

Stories like that of Pelagia the actress do not emphasize someone's evil. Their intent, rather, is to stress the divine love that gently or boldly pursues human hearts. This is the hopeful love that characterizes the lives of the hermits. In the story of Pelagia, she moves Bishop Nonnus as deeply as he moves her.[10]

In the fourth-century monastic communities, stories of harlots are not to be read with literal eyes and heart. The obvious sinners in such stories are symbols of all the baptized, including the monastics. The women who appear as harlots but then turn to the Lord are honored for their conversion of heart. They are signs of hope for a church that is sinful and yet is loved into ongoing conversion.

We must remember that the hearers are primarily monks who have made a vow of lifelong chastity as part of a vocation of conversion of heart. Two facts make the particular story of Pelagia important for its early hearers.

> The first is the clear recognition of the reality and force of sexual desire in human experience; the second is the equally clear realization that such desire has a true and central role in human life as desire for God, whether it is lived out in the sacrament of marriage or the sacrament of the monastic life. Both are equally an image of the union between Christ and his Church.[11]

The desire for God that was lived out in the desert did not do away with human passions, in spite of the fasting and sacrifices that accompanied the life of prayer. Desert stories and sayings are very realistic about the greatest sin being pride or self-assurance of one's goodness. No one is free from the bondage of human desires. Even human love can be a bondage. For those who discover this, and who fall into the bondage before they realize they are falling, the important thing is not the sin but the repentance that follows.

The tears that seem to flow so freely in desert stories constitute a second baptism, a sign of the desire to return to God with all that one is and is not. Actions will show the sincerity of the tears and their meaning. Bishop Nonnus is led to tears and repentance through Pelagia. Pelagia is moved to repentance through Nonnus.

A reflective reader cannot miss the love each has for the other, though this would not be played up in the early centuries as it would later be in the times of Héloïse and Abelard. There is a disciplined wisdom in the actions both of Nonnus and of Pelagia. Each knows their vocation and each makes the choices that must be made to live lovingly in that vocation.

Assuming there was such a woman, who was the historical Pelagia the actress of Antioch? Historically, actresses were considered to be a second kind of "prostitute" since their costuming and roles meant they publicly pleased (i.e., "seduced") an audience by their use of the body. There are a number of sources for the story of Pelagia and Nonnus, but there has also been a long history of telling and retelling the story.[12]

Pelagia the actress would have been considered a prostitute by fourth-century standards. The word refers not only to those women who were sold into prostitution or who chose it as their only means of staying alive. It also refers to any public use of the body for eliciting pleasure. Both kinds of prostitutes, owing to the social connection of prostitutes with pagan rites and orgies, were forbidden to receive the sacraments.[13] The woman Pelagia is listed in the Roman martyrology on October 8. She is simply identified as a solitary or hermit of Jerusalem.[14]

The Pelagia of the following narrative is one of many other holy women who are remembered only through such a narrative genre. In its context the story of Pelagia points to the strength of a woman's love for Christ that leads her into the rigors of a life of prayer and sacrifice in the desert. It also points to the love that respects and cares for another. The deep spiritual friendship between Pelagia and Nonnus is dependent not on physical presence but on a deeper personal presence in Christ that continues beyond the span of human life.

The Life of St. Pelagia the Harlot[15]

written by the Deacon James
and translated into Latin by Eustochius

Verse Prologue by Eustochius

The words of this writer about holy hidden things
Have I, Eustochius, into Latin rendered;
Good readers, take not of all my labor,
And ask God in your prayers to remember me.

Preface of the Author

We should always have in mind the great mercy of our Lord who does not will the death of sinners but rather that all should be converted by repentance and live (1 Tim 2). So, listen to a wonder that happened in our times. It has seemed good to me, James, to write this to you, holy brothers, so that by hearing or reading it, you may gain the greatest possible aid for your souls. For the merciful God, who wills that no one should perish, has given us these days for the forgiveness of our sins, since in the time to come, he will judge justly and reward everyone according to their works. Now, be silent and listen to me with all the care of which you are capable because what I have to tell you is very rich in compunction for us all.

1

The most holy bishop of Antioch called together all the holy bishops nearby about a certain matter; and so eight bishops came, and among them was Nonnus,[16] the most holy man of God, my bishop, a marvelous man and a most observant monk of the monastery called Tabennisis. Because of his incomparable life and most excellent conduct, he had been snatched away from the monastery and ordained bishop. When we had all assembled in the aforesaid city, the bishop told us the meeting would be in the church of the most blessed martyr Julianus. So we went out and sat there before the door of the church with the other bishops who had come.

2

When we were seated, the bishops asked my lord Nonnus to speak to them, and at once the holy bishop began to speak words for the edification and salvation of all. Now while we were marveling at his holy teaching, lo, suddenly, there came among us the chief actress of Antioch, the first in the chorus of the theater, sitting on a donkey. She was dressed in the height of fantasy, wearing nothing but gold, pearls and precious stones, even her bare feet were covered with gold and pearls. With her went a great throng of boys and girls all dressed in cloth of gold with collars of gold on their necks, going before and following her.

So great was her beauty that all the ages of mankind could never come to the end of it. So they passed through our company, filling all the air with traces of music and the most sweet smell of perfume. When the bishops saw her bareheaded and with all her limbs shamelessly exposed with such lavish display, there was not one who did not hide his face in his veil or his scapular, averting their eyes as if from a very great sin.

3

But the most blessed Nonnus gazed after her intently for a very long space of time. And after she had gone by, he turned around and still gazed after her. Then he turned toward the bishops sitting round him and said, "Were you not delighted by such great beauty?" When they did not reply, he buried his face on his knees over the holy Bible that he held in his hands and all his emotion came out in tears; sighing deeply, he said again to the bishops, "Were you not delighted by her great beauty?" Still they did not answer, so "Indeed," he said, "I was very greatly delighted and her beauty pleased me very much. See, God will place her before his awful and tremendous judgment seat and he will judge her on her gifts, just as he will judge us on our episcopal calling."

And he went on to say to the bishops, "What do you think, beloved brothers, how many hours does this woman spend in her chamber giving all her mind and attention to adorning herself for the play, in order to lack nothing in beauty and adornment of the body? She wants to please all those who see her, lest those who are her lovers today find her ugly and do not come back tomorrow. Now, consider ourselves! We have an almighty Father in heaven offering us heavenly gifts and rewards, our immortal Bridegroom, who promises such good things to us. These things cannot be valued, which 'eye has not seen, nor ear heard, nor has it entered into the heart to know what things God has prepared for those who love' (1 Cor 2:9).

What else can I say? When we have such promises, when we are going to see the great and glorious face of our Bridegroom which has a beauty beyond compare, 'upon which the cherubim do not dare to gaze' (1 Pet 1:12), why do we not adorn ourselves? Why do we not wash the dirt from our unhappy souls? Why do we let ourselves lie so neglected?"

4

When he had said all this, Bishop Nonnus took me, his sinful deacon, with him. We went to the rooms we had been given for our lodging. Going into his bedchamber, the bishop threw himself on the ground with his face to the floor, and beating his breast he wept saying, "Lord Jesus Christ. I know I am a sinner and unworthy, for today the ornaments of a harlot have shown more brightly than the ornaments of my soul. How can I turn my face toward you? What words can justify me in your sight? I will not hide my heart from you, for you know all its secrets. Alas, I am a sinner and unworthy, for I stand before your altar and I do not offer you a soul adorned with the beauty you want to see in me. She promises to please many people. I have promised to please you; and my filthiness makes me a liar. I am naked before earth and heaven, because I do not keep your commandments. I cannot put my hope in anything good that I do, but I place my trust in your mercy which saves." He said this kind of thing and wept for many hours; that day was a great festival of tears for us.

5

The next day was Sunday. After we had completed our night prayers, the holy bishop Nonnus said to me, "I tell you, brother deacon, when I was asleep I was deeply disturbed, and I do not understand it." Then he told me the dream he had had. "At the corner of the altar was a black dove, covered with soot, which flew around me and I could not bare the stench and filth of it. It stood by me until the prayer for the dismissal of the catechumens, 'Depart.' No more was seen of it. After the prayer of the faithful, and the complete oblation had been offered and everyone had been dismissed, I came to the threshold of the house of God.

There I saw the dove again, covered grievously with filth, and again it fluttered around me. Then I held out my hands and drew it to me, and plunged it into the font which was in the antechamber of the holy church and washed off all the dirt with which it was covered and it came out of the water as white as snow. It flew up to the highest heaven and was lost from my sight." When the holy man of God, Bishop Nonnus, had recounted his dream, he took me with him and brought me to the cathedral with the rest of the bishops and there we greeted the bishop of Antioch.

6

He went in and preached to the people who came and sat around his throne and when he had read the canon of the holy Gospel, the same bishop of that city held the Gospel book toward the most blessed Nonnus and asked him to speak to the people. Nonnus then opened his mouth and spoke by the wisdom of God, without any set speech or philosophy and with no indiscretion. Filled with the Holy Spirit, he exhorted and urged the people, speaking very earnestly about the future judgment and the good gifts in store in eternity. All the people were moved with compunction by his words, and the floor of the church was awash with the tears of the hearers.

7

Now by the guiding hand of the mercy of God it happened that there came into the church that very harlot about whom I am speaking. What was even more marvelous was that she who was outside the church and had never before entered the house of God and had never before even considered her sins, was now suddenly pierced by the fear of the Lord when she heard Bishop Nonnus preaching to the people. She was so struck that she despaired of herself and her tears flowed in such a flood that she could not control them. At once she gave orders to two of her servants: "Stay in this place and when holy Nonnus the bishop comes out follow him, find out where he is lodging, and come and tell me."

The servants did as their mistress ordered them, and followed us as far as the Basilica of St. Julianus, which was near the place where we were lodging. They returned home and told their mistress, "He is in the church of the most blessed Julianus." When she heard this, she immediately sent the same servants for the diptychs[17] and on them she wrote: "To the holy disciple of Christ, greetings from a sinner and disciple of the devil. I have heard of your God, how he came down from the heavens to earth not for the righteous but for the salvation of sinners. So greatly did he humble himself that he came near to publicans. He whom the cherubim do not dare to look upon (1 Pet 1:12) spoke with sinners.

"My lord, you are very holy. Just as your lord Jesus showed himself to the harlot in Samaria at the well (John 8:48)[18] will you look upon me, as he did whose follower you are, as I have heard Christians say? If you are a true disciple of Christ, do not reject me, for through you, I may deserve to see his face." The holy bishop Nonnus wrote in reply, "Whoever you are, show yourself to God and you will be saved. But I tell you, I am a man, a sinner, and a servant of God, and you would tempt my humanity. But if you really do desire God, have strength and faith and come to me among the other bishops, for I cannot let you see me alone."

When the harlot read this, filled with joy, she came running to the church of the blessed martyr Julianus, and we were told that she was there. When Nonnus heard this, he called all the bishops around him, and ordered that she should be brought to him. When she came in where the bishops were gathered, she threw herself on the floor and seized the feet of the holy bishop Nonnus. "I beg you, my lord, imitate your master the Lord Jesus Christ and pour out on me your goodness and make me a Christian. My lord, I am an ocean of sin, a deep pit of iniquity and I ask to be baptized."

8

Bishop Nonnus could hardly persuade her to get up. But when she did, he said, "The holy canons say that a harlot may not be baptized unless she has her sponsors who will guarantee that she will not return to her old way of life." When she heard this ruling of the bishops, she threw herself on the floor again and seized the feet of Nonnus. She washed them with her tears and wiped them with the hair of her head (Luke 7:38), saying, "You will give account for my soul. To you I will confess all the sins I have committed. You will wash away by baptism all my great sins and wickedness. You will not now find a place with the saints before God unless you put away from me my evil deeds. Unless you give me my rebirth as a bride of Christ and present me to God, you are no more than an apostate and idolater."

Then all the bishops and clergy who were there, when they saw how greatly this sinner desired God, were amazed and said they had never before seen such faith and such desire for salvation as in this harlot. At once they sent me, the sinful deacon, to the bishop of Antioch to tell him all about it and to ask him to send one of his deaconesses back with me. When he heard about it, he rejoiced with great joy saying, "It is right, Bishop Nonnus, that this great work should have waited for you. I know that you will speak for me in this matter."

At once he sent back with me the lady Romana, the first of the deaconesses. When we got back, we found the harlot still at the feet of the holy bishop Nonnus, who was with difficulty urging her to get up. "Get up, my daughter, so that I may forgive your sins."[19] Then he said to her, "Do you confess all your sins?" To which she replied, "I have looked so closely into my heart that I cannot find there any single good action. I know my sins and they are more than the sand upon the seashore. Water like the sea is little compared to the extent of my sins. But I trust in your God that he will forgive me the whole extent of my sinfulness and look upon me again."

The holy bishop Nonnus said, "Tell me, what is your name?" And she replied, "I was called Pelagia by my parents but the people of Antioch have called me Margaret (a pearl) because of the amount of jewelry with which my sins have adorned me. I am decked out as a slave for the devil." Nonnus said to her, "Your natural name is Pelagia?" To which she replied, "Yes, my lord." Then Nonnus exorcised her and baptized her, placing on her the sign of the cross. He gave her the Body of Christ. With the lady Romana, he was godparent to her. The deaconess received her and took her to the place of the catechumens while we remained where we were. Then the bishop said to me, "I tell you, brother deacon, today we are rejoicing with the angels of God, with the bread and wine of spiritual joy beyond measure, because of Pelagia's salvation."

9

While we were eating some food, a devil cried out like a man suffering violence, saying, "Alas, alas, what am I suffering from this decrepit old man? It was not enough for you to snatch from me three thousand Saracens and baptize them, and obtain them for your God. It was not enough for you that you took over Heliopolis and gave it to your God, when it belonged to me. Those who lived there worshiped me. But now you have taken my greatest hope from me and now more than ever I cannot bear your schemes. Oh, how I suffer because of that accursed man! Cursed be the day on which you were born! I am so weakened that a river of tears flows from me, for my hope is taken away."

The devil said all this outside, crying and lamenting, and everyone heard him. When she returned, he said to the newly baptized woman, "My lady Pelagia, why are you doing this to me? Why have you become my Judas? For was not he also crowned with glory and honor and became an apostate by betraying his lord? This is what you have done to me!" The holy Nonnus said to her, "Make the sign of the cross in the name of Christ." She made the sign of the cross in the name of Christ and she blew it at the demon and at once he disappeared.

10

Two days later, when Pelagia was asleep in the room with the holy Romana, her godmother, the devil appeared to Pelagia in the night. He awakened Pelagia, the servant of God, saying, "I ask you, my lady Margaret, were you not once rich with gold and silver? Did I not adorn you with gold and jewels? Tell me, how have I displeased you? Tell me so that I may make amends, for you have made me a very great cause for mockery among the Christians." Then the handmaid Pelagia made the sign of the cross and blew at the demon, saying, "My God, who snatched me out of your teeth and led me to the heavenly bridal chamber, will resist you for me." At once the devil disappeared.

11

On the third day after the baptism of the holy Pelagia, she called her servant who was in charge of all her goods and said to him, "Go to my rooms and make an inventory of all the gold and silver, the ornaments and the precious clothes, and bring it to me." The servant did as his mistress told him and reported it all to her. At once she sent for holy Nonnus through the holy Romana, her godmother, and she placed all she had in his hands, saying, "Lord, these are the riches with which Satan ensnared me. I place them at your disposal. Do with them whatever you think is right, for my choice is the riches of Christ."

At once the bishop called the senior custodian of the church. In the presence of Pelagia, he gave all her goods to the custodian, saying, "I charge you, by the undivided Trinity, do not let any of this remain with the bishop or with this church. Let it all be expended on the widows and the orphans and the poor, so that whatever evil clings to it may be removed by this good use and the riches of sin become the treasures of righteousness. But if you sit lightly on this promise and either you or anyone else keep any of it, let anathema come upon you and them and their houses. Let them be punished with those who cry, 'Crucify, crucify.' "

Pelagia then called to all her servants, boys and girls, and set them free. She gave each a collar of gold from her own hands. Then she said, "Make haste to free yourselves from this wicked world, so full of sin. Do this so that we who have been together in this world may remain together without grief in that life that is most blessed."

12

On the eighth day when it is the custom for the baptized to take off their white robes,[20] Pelagia rose in the night, though we did not know it. She took off her baptismal dress and put on a tunic and breeches belonging to the holy bishop Nonnus. From that day she was never seen again in the city of Antioch. The holy lady Romana wept bitterly, but the holy bishop Nonnus said to her, "Do not weep, my daughter, but rejoice with great joy, for Pelagia has chosen the better part (Luke 10:42) like Mary whom the Lord preferred to Martha in the gospel." Now Pelagia went to Jerusalem and built herself a cell on the Mount of Olives and there she prayed to the Lord.

13

After a little while, the bishop of Antioch called the bishops together so that they might all go back to their own homes. Three or four years later, I, James the deacon, wanted to go to Jerusalem to worship at the place of the resurrection of Christ. I asked the bishop to let me go. When he gave me his blessing he said to me, "Brother deacon, when you reach the city of Jerusalem, ask the whereabouts of a certain brother Pelagius. He is a monk and a eunuch who has lived there for some years shut up alone. Go and visit him, for truly I think you will be helped by him." I did not at all understand that he was talking about the handmaid of God, Pelagia.

14

So I reached Jerusalem. After I had joined in the adoration of the Resurrection of the Lord Jesus Christ, I made inquiries about the servant of God. I went and found him on the Mount of Olives where he used to pray to the Lord in a small cell which was closed on all sides, with one small window. I knocked on the window. At once she appeared and she recognized me, though I did not recognize her. How could I have known her again, with a face so emaciated by fasting? It seemed to me that her eyes had sunk inward like a great pit.

She said to me, "Where have you come from, brother?" And I replied, "I was sent to you by the order of the holy bishop Nonnus." At once she closed the little window on me, saying, "Tell him to pray for me, for he is a saint of God." At once she began the psalms of the third hour. I prayed beside the cell and then left, much helped by the sight of her angelic face. I returned to Jerusalem and began to visit the monasteries of the brothers there.

15

Throughout these monasteries, great indeed was the fame of the monk Pelagius. So I decided to make another journey to speak with her and receive some saving teaching. When I reached the cell and knocked, calling her name, there was no reply. I waited a second day and also a third, calling the name of Pelagius, but I could not hear anyone. Then I said to myself, "Either there is no one there or he who was a monk has left."

But warned by a nudge from God, I said to myself, "I had better see if, in fact, he has died." So I broke open the little window. I saw that he was dead. So I closed the opening and I was filled with sorrow. I ran all the way to Jerusalem and told whomever I met that the holy monk Pelagius who had wrought so many wonders was now at rest. Then the holy fathers came with the monks from several monasteries and the door of the cell was broken in.[21]

They carried out his sacred little body as if it had been gold and silver they were carrying. When the fathers began to anoint the body with myrrh, they realized that it was a woman.[22] They wanted to keep such a wonder hidden but could not, because of the crowds of people thronging around. The people cried out with a loud voice, "Glory to you, Lord Jesus Christ, for you have hidden away on earth such great treasures, women as well as men."

So it was known to all the people. Monks came in from all the monasteries and also nuns from Jericho and from the Jordan where the Lord was baptized. They were bearing candles and lamps and singing hymns. Then the holy fathers bore her body to its burial.

May the life of this harlot, this account of total conversion, join us to her and bring us all to the mercy of the Lord on the day of judgment, to whom be glory and power and honor to the ages of ages. Amen.

NOTES

1. Jo Ann McNamara, "Wives and Widows in Early Christian Thought," *International Journal of Women's Studies* 2:6 (1979) 584.

2. Rosamund Nugent, *Portrait of the Consecrated Woman in the Greek Christian Literature of the First Four Centuries* (Washington, D.C.: Catholic University of America Press, 1941) 1–5.

3. Abundant citations are found in Mary L. McKenna, *Women of the Church: Role and Renewal* (New York: P. J. Kenedy and Sons, 1967) 51; Roger Gryson, *The Ministry of Women in the Early Church* (Collegeville, Minn.: Liturgical Press, 1976) 25–34.

4. *Didascalia Apostolorum*, ed. R. Hugh Connolly (Oxford: Clarendon Press, 1929) xliii, 131.

5. Ibid. 138, 140.

6. Ibid. 142.

7. Carolyn Osiek, "Relation of Charism to Rights and Duties of the New Testament Church," *Official Ministry in a New Age* (Washington, D.C.: Catholic University of America, 1981) 41–59; Elisabeth Schüssler-Fiorenza, "Word, Spirit and Power: Women in Early Christian Communities," in *Women of Spirit*, ed. Rosemary Radford Ruether and Eleanor McLaughlin (New York: Simon and Schuster, 1979) 29–70; André Lemaire, "From Services to Ministries: 'Diakonia' in the First Two Centuries," *Concilium* 80 (1972) 35–49.

8. Raymond Brown, "Roles of Women in the Fourth Gospel," *Theological Studies* 36 (1975) 688–99; Constance Parvey, "The Theology and Leadership of Women in the New Testament," in *Religion and Sexism*, ed. Rosemary Radford Ruether (New York: Simon and Schuster, 1974) 117–49; Sandra Schneiders, "Apostleship of Women in John's Gospel," *Catholic Charismatic* 1 (1977) 16–20.

9. Bonnie Bowman Thurston, *The Widows: A Women's Ministry in the Early Church*

(Minneapolis: Fortress, 1989), is a well-documented study of the evolution and decline of the order of widows.

10. Benedicta Ward, S.L.G., *Harlots of the Desert* (London/Oxford: Mobray, 1987) 104–10; this scholarly and readable collection of five stories of women insightfully contextualizes their historical meanings and relevance as models of repentance.

11. Ibid. 102.

12. *Pélagia la pénitente: Metamorphose d'une légende*, vol. 1, Les Textes et leur histoire (Paris, 1981). This is cited by Ward, *Harlots of the Desert* 65.

13. This is described more fully as inclusive of juggling and playing music in Ward, *Harlots of the Desert* 104–10.

14. The Vita Sanctae Pelagiae, Metricis is found in Migne, *Patrologia Latina* (*PL*) 73:663–72; n. 1, col. 671, says that Pelagia is listed in the Roman martyrology, where she is identified as a holy woman penitent of Jerusalem.

15. The translation is taken from Ward, "Pelagia: Beauty Riding By," in *Harlots of the Desert* 67–75.

16. *PL* 73, n. 4, col. 671, states that Nonnus is listed in the Roman martyrology as Bishop of Edessa who converted Pelagia. His feast is December 2.

17. These are tablets that can be used for notes as well as for other things.

18. The citation for this should be John 4:7, which is the citation in the Latin text, *PL* 73:667.

19. This refers to a ritual for casting out evil or the devil called an "exorcism."

20. The "eighth day" is the symbolic day of a new creation ushered in by the resurrection. Sunday was the "eighth day" as measured against Jewish sabbath. The octagonal shape of early baptismal fonts derives from this symbolism.

21. By medieval times a well-developed liturgical ritual, using many of the readings and responses from the burial mass for the dead, accompanied the literal enclosing of a cell, hermitage, or anchorage. Reopening it was no easy task. Whether such a seal is reflected here is difficult to tell. One small window opening was customary.

22. Early liturgical practices of anointing of the body for burial were more extensive than the diminished physical versions today. Respect for the whole body as temple of the Spirit was testified to in this way.

BIBLIOGRAPHY

Bowman Thurston, Bonnie. *The Widows: A Women's Ministry in the Early Church.* Minneapolis: Fortress, 1989.

Connolly, R. Hugh, ed. *The Didascalia Apostolorum.* Oxford: Clarendon Press, 1929.

Gryson, Roger. *The Ministry of Women in the Early Church.* Collegeville, Minn.: Liturgical Press, 1976.

Lemaire, André. "From Services to Ministries: 'Diakonia' in the First Two Centuries." *Concilium* 80 (1972) 35–49.

McKenna, Mary L. *Women of the Church: Role and Renewal.* New York: P. J. Kenedy and Sons, 1967.

McNamara, Jo Ann. "Wives and Widows in Early Christian Thought." *International Journal of Women's Studies* 2:6 (1979) 488–584.

Nugent, Rosamund. *Portrait of the Consecrated Woman in the Greek Christian Literature of the First Four Centuries*. Washington, D.C.: Catholic University of America Press, 1941.

Osiek, Carolyn. "Relation of Charism to Rights and Duties of the New Testament Church." *Official Ministry in a New Age*. Washington, D.C.: Catholic University of America, 1981. 41–59.

Ruether, Rosemary Radford. "Mothers of the Church: Ascetic Women in the Late Patristic Age." In *Women of Spirit*. Edited by Rosemary Radford Ruether and Eleanor McLaughlin. New York: Simon and Schuster, 1979. 71–98.

Schüssler-Fiorenza, Elisabeth. "Word, Spirit and Power: Women in Early Christian Communities." In *Women of Spirit*. Edited by Rosemary Radford Ruether and Eleanor McLaughlin. New York: Simon and Schuster, 1979. 29–70.

Ward, Benedicta, S.L.G. *Harlots of the Desert*. London/Oxford: Mobray, 1987.

–3–

BRIGIT OF IRELAND

(c. 453–518)

She Never Said No to the Poor

Brigit's actual history, by Western standards, is shrouded in narrative. The fact that her story is told through Irish narrative makes the question of the "real Brigit" an even greater puzzle. The oral tradition of the Irish people must be understood to appreciate the value of the Brigit narratives and the strength of the woman beneath the story.

Caesar was correct in assessing the early preference of the Celtic people for oral tradition. Imagination, creative memory, and passing on the tradition from person to person were much preferred to writing things down:

> We have it on Caesar's authority that the druids of Gaul considered it improper to commit their learning to writing, and on this point he is substantially borne out by Irish evidence.[1]

Unlike the rest of western Europe in the fifth century, Ireland possessed its own living culture that was expressed in oral literature. The social and legal form of organization was that of the extended family headed by a king. Certain rights and responsibilities were clearly set forth. With the coming of Christianity, which was a "religion of the book," a new written form of Irish literature and cultural memory would come into being.

Pope Celestine I (423–32) sent Bishop Palladius to the Irish Christians in 431. Since bishops were not sent anywhere unless Christians already lived in that place, Christianity was already present in Ireland before the coming of the British priest, Patrick (390–465), in 432. Patrick came to Ireland from a country that had been under Roman rule for two centuries. Thus, the Christian tradition that had shaped Patrick and that he tried to impose on the Irish was a thoroughly Romanized Christianity. The language, customs, laws, art, governmental and authority structures, as well as the educational criteria with its written language, were part of the Roman Christian culture in which Patrick was raised. This Roman culture and Romanized Christianity had not yet touched Ireland.[2]

The Irish had their own system of order based on the extended family headed by a king for large families or a "subking" for small families. Each tribe had its particular groupings within the royal family. There were the nobles, artisans, and bards or poets who wove the tales of family glories. There were also *brehons*, who were the keepers and tellers of the law, the rituals, and the customs of the family. The brehons could be female or male, a factor that may account for a greater gender equity of laws in early Ireland than in other cultures at that time. These laws included statutes regarding rape.[3] At the same time, the Irish practiced polygamy for centuries after Patrick's Christianity arrived.

Unlike the relationship of king and subjects in other lands, the Irish "king" was a familial ruler with emotional bonds to his extended clan. The social network was more horizontal than vertical. The personal welfare of each member of the social network was important to the king. This is one reason that the image of Jesus Christ as king was one the Irish associated with familial affection rather than with dominance.

Patrick was not very sympathetic to the Irish culture that he discovered upon his arrival. He preferred the ways of his own Romanized Britain. Its language, educational system, written forms of records, hierarchical structures for law and order, clearly defined worldview, and "civilized" behaviors were quite different from the practices of the Irish. Patrick felt that he was bringing "civilization" as well as Christianity to Ireland. At the time of his coming, there were still several Celtic gods and goddesses worshiped by the Irish. Dagda, Maeve, Lugnascal and Brigit were powerful figures in the religious devotion of the people. There was a cult of the sun, a cult of the dead, belief in an underworld, and various fertility cults.[4]

In time, some Christian festivals would grow from the pagan ritual festivals. February 1, the celebration of the goddess Brigit, who was invoked for new life of spring, would be taken over by the Christian saint Brigit. The festival of Samain on November 1 would be taken over by All Saints. The joyous festival of Beltaine or May Day and the harvest festival of Lugnascal would also be Christianized.[5] The Irish belief in the spirit world and demonic possessions was part of most native Irish religions in the fifth century. This belief and fear of demonic possession was countered by the exorcisms preceding Christian baptism.[6] This made Christian baptism a very desirable ritual.

Patrick seems to have "fostered" some of the sons of the kings or subkings. Fostering was a custom whereby a son of a king or noble would be temporarily raised and guided by another king or noble with certain responsibilities attached. Whoever fostered the son of another had the right to protection from the king or noble whose son was fostered. This practice was a symbol of the bonds between the nobles or kings and their respective clans. Because Patrick and other missionaries did not belong to clans, their lives would not be protected by anyone. Thus, fostering was useful for any stranger to practice.

The laws of the clans were retributive as well as protective. If someone in the clan was injured or killed by a member of another clan, specific actions were considered to be just in response. Irish clan laws required that clan kings repay damages a clan member inflicted on another clan. This included payment not only for personal injury but also for loss of livelihood as well as any hardship caused to dependent family members.

The fifth-century Irish people were able to accept many of the Christian teachings, in spite of their Graeco-Romanized clothing. Patrick was successful in baptizing and confirming many Irish people. He was also successful in encouraging many converts to become monks, nuns, or celibates who would continue to live in their clan. His Romanized Christian understandings about the material creation, the body, personal and corporate sin, and the spirit world were not those of the Irish. The Irish who accepted Christian baptism did so with their specifically Irish religious ears.

As long as the bardic institution survived in Ireland—which it did up to the seventeenth century—the old pagan roots would resist the new Romanized Christianity. The Christian religion could only succeed in the long run if it became as universal in Ireland as it had been in early Rome. There is a strength that universality lends to any religion. For Christians, the belief that Jesus Christ is universal gives Christianity the ability to embody the best of cultures. In this context, the incorporation of the Irish culture would be essential to the long-term health of Christianity in Ireland.[7]

Some attempts to Romanize Irish Christians did not fully succeed. An authoritative hierarchical diocesan structure could work in a Romanized society. It did not work well in early Irish society because the social strata of the Irish people were more horizontal than vertical. The Irish Christian monasteries retained a close link to extended families. The abbots and abbesses of monasteries were frequently the sons and daughters of kings who afforded them protection as well as gifts. Abbots and abbesses were not only monastic leaders but were administrators of monastic holdings. When Rome tried imposing a central episcopal authority and the Roman diocesan structure, the monastic tradition posed other difficulties.

Monk-bishops had jurisdictional or administrative power. The diocesan bishops had sacramental power and administrative power over some laity and clergy, but they lacked comparable jurisdiction over the monasteries. In the Irish monastic system laymen could be abbots and laywomen could be abbesses. Sons and daughters of nobility could inherit leadership in monasteries even if they did not intend to make lifelong vowed commitment.[8]

Monasteries could continue growing as they prospered. The Roman diocesan structure could not grow beyond preset regions. The only growth possible would come from joining dioceses under an overlord bishop. Whereas Irish kings or abbots could group clans or monasteries, autonomy was still maintained with a king or abbot acting more as a coordinator for the common good than as an overlord. If the diocesan system was going to be credible, the bishop would have to be like an Irish king whose relationship to the clan was one of personal interest and the preservation of common good.

By the year 630 there was a system of chief bishops and chief abbots or abbesses. Kildare, associated with St. Brigit, and Armagh (Ulster), associated with Patrick, became major centers of rival ecclesiastical power. The Patrick and Brigit stories that have come into Irish lore are often about the historical rivals for power, the bishops of Kildare and Armagh. In 630 Kildare still held prominence. The bishop of Kildare was "the chief bishop of the Irish bishops," and the abbess was "the abbess whom all the abbesses of the Irish venerate."[9] The veneration is based on the bonds of care reflective of Irish horizontal authority rather than upon the Romanized hierarchical ordering.

Irish Christianity was at odds with Romanized Christianity in more ways than the ordering of authority. There was a greater equality between women and men in Irish society than there was in the sixth-century Roman church. Irish male missionaries had female helpers, similar to the apostle Paul's coworkers. A sixth-century letter written by bishops in Gaul to Irish missionaries tried to stop this practice. The men were strongly urged to cease letting the women assist them at the Eucharist. They were also urged not to stay with their women coworkers in the same house. The exception to this could be a grandmother, mother, sister, or niece.[10]

The dichotomies that Patrick brought between soul and body, human and divine, male and female, earthly and heavenly, sinfulness and graciousness, Jesus Christ the human and Jesus Christ the divine, the living and the dead, and so on, could not be interiorized by Irish Christians. Irish spirituality had foundational beliefs that made it quite different from Romanized Christianity.

The Irish felt a permanent nearness and interchange between the spirit world and the human world. God, Jesus Christ, the saints, and the angels surrounded all of life. This conviction influenced the religious imagination of the people to experience sacredness everywhere. The pervasiveness of God's presence through the beauty and joy of the world made the earth an icon for the heavenly beauty that was yet to come.

To the Irish, the natural world and the spiritual world were utterly intertwined. Although God's graciousness and good spirits were everywhere, there were also the mischievous spirits and evil demons who could inhabit sacred spaces. It was believed that certain evil spirits staked their claims in particular holy spaces of the earth: the womb (women), the sanctuary (druids), the place where dramatic meetings of nature occur (like the fiery forge of blacksmiths). For this reason there was need for protection prayers, such as that on St. Patrick's breastplate.[11]

> Christ in the heart of all who know me,
> Christ on the tongue of all who meet me,
> Christ in the eye of all who see me,
> Christ in the ear of all who hear me.[12]

The perceived mutuality of relationships of the material and spiritual world encompassed human relationships. The extended clan saw itself related to other groups through bonds of justice and care. This relationship included the perception that believing Christians are bonded to the larger community of Christianity, the communion of saints, the Trinity, the angels, and everyone. Worship and solitary prayer were forms of participation in this eternal and universal communion of those who praise. The prayers of Irish Christians reflect this abiding sense of the presence and hospitality that mediate the holiness of God.[13]

Journeying to other lands for Christ was one expression of the restlessness of Irish spirituality. Such wanderings denoted an inner sacred space that would be filled only in the process of the journeying. Clearly, such journeying was not limited to the Irish missionaries. Many groups throughout history traveled to new lands. The difference here was that the Celtic or Irish peoples did not go to new lands to conquer, destroy, and dominate. They went to assimilate the culture that was present while at the same time introducing elements that might enrich that culture.[14]

The Christ of Celtic history was not so much a Christ who redeemed humans from a sinful and fallen world as he was a liberator leading humans toward true freedom. Christ was the heroic one whose light reveals how humans throw shadows on God's hope for the world. To be a disciple of Christ meant to suffer and wage war against all that might blot out the light and freedom of the spirit. Asceticism was one means of light and freedom.

For Christian Celts all creation was ordered toward liberation and resurrection in Christ. Loving creation was a way of praising God. All that existed was ordered toward light and love, not toward darkness and sin. This outlook influenced the perspectives of some Irish theologians on matters like original sin and redemption. Their views were quite different from the more highly popularized views of Augustine.[15]

Irish spirituality emphasized the role of the community. At the same time, there was also a love of solitude. Being alone in the midst of natural beauty was conducive to sensing sacredness everywhere. There were not two distinct worlds of spiritual and natural in Irish perspective. Each was part of the other. Celtic spirituality is sensitive to the omnipresence of God, a presence that is within and without, ahead as well as behind, and present.

The narratives of a relational saint like Brigit can thrive in the incarnational context of Irish spirituality. The stories about Brigit, Patrick, Brendan, and other saints need to be read with an appreciation for the intent of such narratives. Like many biblical accounts, they are meant to reveal more about the power of God than the power of any historical figure. The purpose of Irish saint stories was to edify believers and encourage them to undertake the spiritual journey that "sainthood" demands.

Consequently, to construct any historical "life of Brigit" is difficult because Celtic "lives of saints" are not constructed as chronological scientific history. In addition to the difficulties of sorting out historical truth from narratives not intended to present historical truth, there is an another difficulty in the stories of Brigit: there were many legends about the Mother Goddess, Brigit of Ireland, that were seemingly "transformed" into the Christian saint stories of Abbess Brigit of Kildare. Some of the stories that indicate a clash between Brigit of Kildare and some bishop of Armagh are really stories about the two rival churches and rival bishops of those cities.

It is no wonder that more than a few historians have thrown up their hands in despair. Others insist, however, that, in spite of the obvious patterning of the Abbess Brigit stories, there was an influential actual Abbess Brigit who existed and held great influence in the Irish church. The Brigit stories do reflect the Irish devotional assurance that the lives of the holy ones, like Brigit, are continuations of the Jesus stories of the Gospels.

The summaries of selective Brigit tales that follow will illustrate these elements. The full stories can be found in the variety of works that are cited. Brigit tales are retold in this chapter simply to show that Christian stories of holiness have as many forms as there are cultures and peoples. In spite of the endless variety of forms, there remains a unity in function. They reveal that the gospel continues to be written in the lives of Christ's followers of every age and place.

One tale claims that Brigit was born at sunrise on the first day of spring. Angels baptized her and gave the name that means Fiery Arrow.[16] The flame appeared again as Brigit received the veil at her profession as a sister.[17] After her death, a flame was kept burning at her monastery at Kildare by her sisters. The similarities to the sun goddess Brigit are in evidence here. The flaming sun that symbolized goddess Brigit was also a symbol for St. Brigit. As a flame at Kildare was kept burning for the goddess Brigit, a flame at Kildare was kept burning after the death of Abbess Brigit.

In pre-Christian times, the vestal virgins at Kildare performed the customary religious rituals of the people, preserved the traditions, learned about secret healing remedies, learned of the science and laws of the time, and were expected to teach such things to their successors.[18] The woman who headed the college for women at Kildare was considered to be an incarnation of the goddess Brigit, and consequently was held in great love and esteem by the people. Because Kildare and the area around it belonged to the goddess Brigit, its lush green meadows could not be plowed, for these were symbols of a fertility associated with Brigit. The oak tree, especially the giant oak in Kildare, could not be cut down because it was Brigit's sacred tree. Brigit also had a sacred cow whose milk was life. Goddess Brigit, like other female deities, was symbolized by a wisdom serpent. The legend of Patrick driving "snakes" from Ireland grew out of this particular association.

Another story tells of the goddess Brigit lighting the way for Jesus, Mary, and Joseph. The three are journeying in severe winds to the temple at Jerusalem for the ritual of purification. The goddess Brigit holds candles that do not go out. For such heroism and wonder working, Mary grants to Brigit the festival day of February 1, the day preceding the church celebration of the purification or Candlemas (February 2). Another version of the tale has St. Brigit helping Mary by making the crowds who followed her and Jesus stop following them. Brigit holds a flaming harrow above her head, and the crowds go away in fear. As a favor, Mary tells St. Brigit that she will have her festival celebrated on February 1, the day before the ritual of purification in the temple. The pre-Christian Irish celebrated a spring fertility festival of goddess Brigit on February 1. St. Brigit's day also replaces this festival in Christianized Ireland.[19]

To conclude that there never was an Irish saint named Brigit of Kildare misses the intent of oral Celtic tradition. The stories need to be heard in an ancient milieu that was less concerned with chronological history than it was with the meaning and interrelationship of human world and spirit world. Abbess Brigit was loved by the people of Kildare for her graciousness to the poor just as the goddess Brigit of Kildare was loved for her concern for the poor. The numerous Kildare stories point to the lack of concern for chronological time in stories of more spirit-filled content that were told by the bards and felons and *brehons*.[20]

The tradition of Christian legend in Irish history requires that the eyes must see beneath the story to the power and presence of God. Some Brigit stories showing her in conflict with Brendan are tales not about Brigit and Brendan but rather about the dynamic of conflict between the bishops of Kildare and of Armagh. Other tales about Brigit and Brendan reflect disagreement about the role of women in the Irish church, a role that early Celtic Christians represented by Brigit saw differently from the Roman tradition represented by Patrick and—in some stories—by Brendan as well. The following is an example of such a story.

The heroic St. Brendan was on one of his many voyages to other lands. Ferocious sea animals attacked the ship. The crew was frightened and asked God to save them through their leader, St. Brendan. Nothing changed. Then the crew decided to petition God to save them through the glorious St. Patrick. Nothing changed. In great trepidation they decided to beseech God to help them through St. Brigit. Within moments the attacking sea beasts fled.

As soon as the ship landed, Brendan decided he would go to meet this powerful Brigit and reprimand her for using power that was greater than his. He inquired about Brigit and finally located her at the monastery of Kildare. He demanded to see her at once. She came and asked him what he wanted. Brendan, assuming Brigit had some access to evil power, commanded her to make a full confession of her sins to him. Brigit responded that he was the one who should be confessing sins, since he had accused her unjustly. He did confess to her, and she in turn confessed to him.[21]

A later version of the same story shifted the dominance. In it, Brendan still confesses first. This time, however, it is because Brigit acknowledges that Brendan is holier than she. Thus, he "rightly" should go first.[22]

There are a variety of early tales of Abbess Brigit that are altered in later retellings. The alterations reflect the later periods of Romanized patriarchal Christianity. The earlier non-Romanized Christianity retained the narratives of equality among saintly women and men of early Christian tradition in Ireland.

The establishment of a double monastery at Kildare under the guidance of an abbess does have a historical ring. The stories that are told of this monastery retain some elements of earlier sacred stories of Kildare as the city of goddess Brigit. The Kildare tradition in Christianity was a strong one. One part of this tradition even has the saintly abbess Brigit celebrating an early Irish Eucharist.[23] This tradition may be related to the story of Brigit receiving the degrees of bishop when she received the veil from Bishop Mell. "Then the degrees were conferred upon Brigit and it was the degrees of a bishop that Bishop Mell conferred upon her."[24] The pastoral role of Brigit as abbess of Kildare is attested to in the myriad tales about her care for the poor. The debate about what "degrees of bishop" meant as early abbesses received them is too complex to discuss here. Successive chapters will point out that the ecclesial importance of abbesses declined as time went on, particularly after Charlemagne.

At the same time, the abbesses of Kildare who succeeded Brigit did retain concern for the poor. Irish tradition testifies to this concern as it does to the fact that the Kildare abbesses also retained a Christian power of reconciliation that was able to prevent war.[25]

Because Brigit was important in the lineage of the Irish people, an old Irish poem traces her origin to King Bresal Brec, who once ruled Ireland. The same poem names Brigit as abbess of Kildare, an affirmation that is more historically reliable from the perspective of Western "history."[26]

As abbess of the double monastery of Kildare, Brigit put her many gifts to good use. Legends reveal a powerful love for the poor and the afflicted. The legends about Brigit's care for her sheep are actually stories that focus on her love for God's people, whom she perceives as all people. This love testifies to her holiness. In addition to her great love for the poor, ancient lives speak of Brigit's extraordinary intellectual and spiritual gifts. Her graciousness has inspired generations of Irish Christians. One of her biographers summarizes her importance in this way: "St. Brigit received from her people a worship that history accords to no other saint. The people beheld in her the noblest and best type of womanhood.... She is the child of prophecy, the Queen of the South, the Mary of Erin."[27]

The following tales come from a variety of sources. The first nine summarized tales can be found among those recorded by Brigit's nephew, Cogitosus, and a man named Joannes Capgravius.[28] They are samples of the symbolic forms of tales that show Brigit living the gospel in her own way and also in a manner that retains some hints of the tales of goddess Brigit.

Some Tales of St. Bridget

Brigit was born to Brochesa, a handmaiden of a nobleman named Dubtacus of Leinster. Brochesa been sold by Dubtacus to a druid magician. His wife was afraid that Brochesa's child would be more beautiful and powerful than her own children. When Brigit was born, those who were present saw the cloth that covered her head appear as a flame of fire.

The druid magician tried to feed Brochesa and Brigit with meat he had already offered to the pagan gods. Brigit could not eat it, so the magician got her a white cow that could give her milk to drink for the rest of her life. The druid saw that Brigit was growing wiser, more beautiful, and more deeply loving every year that she lived. She became increasingly sensitive to the poor, a fact that made the druid love her more.

Although he loved her as his own daughter and put her in charge of all the cows, the druid became angry with Brigit on occasion. This was especially true when she gave to the poor people of the area all the butter and milk produced by the cows. Such a small amount was left for the druid that Brigit understood his anger with her. She prayed to God, who immediately filled the vessels of the druid with butter and milk. This miracle so moved the holy druid that he believed in Jesus Christ and set both Brochesa and Brigit free.

Meanwhile, Dubtacus also kept in touch with Brigit and loved her well. He too admired her love for the poor, until she gave too many of his things away. One day she gave away his prized sword that he had received as a gift from the king. When the king heard of this, he too was angry and asked Brigit why she did that. She said that she had given it to Christ, for the poor were Christ. The king was moved by her sincerity and piety and gave another sword to her father.

When Brigit was a young woman, her beauty was greater than that of her beautiful mother, Brochesa. So many men wanted to marry her that her family told her to pick one and get married. Because she had already dedicated herself to Jesus Christ, however, she asked God to disfigure her so that she could follow his call. One of her eyes became temporarily damaged, and men stopped proposing to her. At last she was free to request permission to make her profession as a nun. Brigit and three other women went to one of the disciples of St. Patrick, the holy bishop Macaille. They requested him to affirm the vocation of Brigit by giving her the veil. As he contemplated this request, the holy bishop saw a pillar of fire appear over the head of Brigit. Bishop Mel, who was also there, saw the flame. Both laid hands upon her. Bishop Mel also gave her the degrees of bishop. Her beauty was now restored.

One Easter, Brigit made beer from one measure of malt and sent part of that beer to eighteen churches. In spite of the small amount, there was an abundance of beer for everyone who wished to drink it throughout the entire octave of Easter. During this same octave Brigit blessed water to make it holy. One day a leper came to her and asked for help. She sprinkled the leper with holy water and the man was immediately cured of his leprosy. Two sick virgins also drank that blessed water, and they were immediately cured of their sickness.

One day three Britons by birth approached Kildare and asked for Brigit. Two of the Britons were blind and one was leprous. They met Brigit at the door of the church and asked her to cure them. She invited them in to eat and said she would pray for them. They told her that it was because they were Britons and not Irish that she refused to cure them. She was moved by their reproach and took holy water to bless them. Immediately, the blind men could see and the leper was cleansed.

One day a woman with a reputation for being good came with apples to give to Brigit. Although there were lepers begging for food as the woman brought her apples toward the church, the woman did not give them any, but gave her apples to Brigit, who immediately gave them to the hungry lepers. The woman was extremely angry with Brigit for giving the food away. Brigit became angry with the woman, whose reputation for being good was something in which the woman took pride. Brigit told the woman that she was not as good as she thought, for she would not help those in need. Then Brigit told the woman that from that time on, her trees would no longer bear fruit.

One cold and frosty night the holy Brigit decided to walk to a deep pool and stay there to pray throughout the night. She prayed and wept during the night as she reflected on God's love. Since the others of the monastery were sound asleep, they did not know that Brigit spent the night in this fashion. She decided that she would continue this custom instead of sleeping. However, by an act of the Savior, the pool dried up before Brigit came back to pray. She decided to return to bed. In the morning the pool was full of water once again. Brigit decided to go to pray by it in the night hours. But it was dried up at night. Finally Brigit understood that the Lord would lead her in prayer and she should not lead herself. She forgets that her fervor and desire to pray must always be in response to Christ's inspiration, not merely her own. This tale points to the mystery that prayer is a gift and that human beings ought not to force the shape it will take.

What can be the point of those tales of Brigit? As mentioned earlier, the appearance of the flame of fire over her head at birth and when receiving the veil are remnants of the goddess Brigit stories. Goddess Brigit was a sun goddess whose fiery flames were well known and tended by the vestal virgins of Kildare before Christianity included St. Brigit in its ranks. As the goddess Brigit had a cow that was an endless milk producer, Brigit's cow is also one that gives her milk for the rest of her life. Brigit's ability to multiply the foodstuffs, milk, beer, cheese is not unlike the multiplying of food that characterizes some of the prophets like Elijah and Jesus Christ.

Brigit's ability to bless water and have it become a source of healing occurs in many Brigit tales. Whether lepers or other afflicted people seek her out, the holy water becomes a means of Christ's power being revealed. The baptismal imagery is at work in many Brigit stories. The tales of the woman with the apples and of Brigit herself going to the water to pray can be read on many levels. The woman with the apples has a good reputation that resembles the good reputation of the Pharisees in the Gospels. Yet the woman will not share her gifts with those who are most in need of them, namely, the poor lepers who gather around Brigit's church at Kildare. Brigit is rebuffed by the woman for sharing the gifts just as Christ was criticized by the Pharisees.

Many tales of Brigit have her doing wonders similar to those Christ did. Brigit was able to cast out devils from men and women. Sometimes the devils fled when she came on the scene. Sometimes she had conversations with a devil. One such occasion was a friendly visit to another abbess at Armagh. Brigit sat down at the table and saw a devil was also sitting there. Brigit asked the abbess if she saw the devil at her table. The abbess could not see it. Brigit blessed the eyes of the other abbess, who then said that she could see the devil. Brigit asked the devil why he was sitting there at the table. The devil replied that he sat near the abbess because of her sloth. St. Brigit commanded the devil to depart, and the abbess of Armagh was cured of her slothfulness.[29]

Brigit's charity, wisdom, and ecclesiastical importance are found in many tales that involve bishops. The tales do not show Brigit and the bishops competing for power. They reflect the Irish tradition of Brigit and the bishops being brothers and sisters in the Lord who work together for God's glory. Mutual respect is evident in the three examples of these tales that follow.

The fame of Brigit and her convent spread up and down the Irish countryside. Several bishops invited Brigit to visit them and consider the possibility of beginning a monastery. One of these bishops was her friend, Bishop Mel of Armagh. He was a holy man, and Brigit enjoyed conversing with him about spiritual matters. During one visit with Bishop Mel, the prince of Longford gave a banquet and requested the presence of Bishop Mel and Brigit. During the supper one of the servants accidentally dropped a precious vase that shattered into a thousand pieces. The prince was so enraged that he ordered the servant to be cast immediately into prison and executed as soon as possible. Bishop Mel tried to plead for the poor servant with the prince, but to no avail. Then Bishop Mel remembered that Brigit had miraculous powers. She should be the one to remedy this situation. The bishop ordered the servants to bring the fragments to Brigit. St. Brigit prayed to the Lord for the life of the poor servant. As she did, the many fragments of the vase were slowly placed together and then returned to the prince as whole. The prince was pleased. He freed the servant and many conversions to the Lord occurred here.

On one occasion when Brigit accompanied Bishop Mel to a meeting of bishops, St. Patrick presided over the gathering. The purpose of this particular meeting was to discern whether Bronus, one of Patrick's disciples, had fathered a child. Bishop Bronus denied the charge that the child's mother made, but she insisted it was Bronus who was the father of the infant in her arms. Patrick asked Brigit if she would take the woman aside and see if the woman was telling the truth. Brigit did as Patrick asked. The woman insisted it was Bronus who was the true father. Brigit then made the sign of the cross on the lips of the woman; immediately the woman's face began to swell and she became afraid. Brigit then made the sign of the cross on the mouth of the child. The child amazed all, for he began to speak out with a clarity beyond his years. He said that Bishop Bronus was not his father. Then he pointed to another man who was an observer of the meeting and said that that man was his father. The woman who had accused Bishop Bronus admitted that she had been lying and asked pardon. The swelling in her face immediately went down when she acknowledged her guilt. From that time on, Patrick asked a holy chaplain to always accompany Brigit on her journeys.

Brigit spent some time in the eastern parts of Ulster. On one journey with Bishop Ere, Brigit was greeted with great joy by the bishop and priests of Munster. Requested to set up new convents there, she worked zealously to establish some new foundations, and was asked to attend the bishops' synod at Magh Femyn, between Cashel and Clonmel. At the synod the bishops paid tribute to Brigit's zeal and humility. While the synod was going on, there was an outbreak of an infectious disease that made many of the inhabitants of the city very ill. People collected around Brigit and begged her to come to visit their sick relatives and friends, and pray for them. Many of the ill were cured by her prayers and the epidemic was soon over.[30]

Many of the stories about the miraculous power and faith of Brigit clearly are enhancements of the variety of parables, sayings, or acts of Jesus Christ that are narrated in the Gospels. For an oral culture, which is what existed when the earliest tales of Brigit appeared, the stories are intended to invoke the hearers to imitate Jesus Christ. Any of the miracles of Brigit, like the gospel miracles of Jesus Christ, are revelations of the power of God that invite the observers to praise God. Like Jesus Christ of the Gospels, Brigit is moved by love to help anyone who sincerely needs what she can give. Always, it is clear that Brigit invokes Jesus Christ and is aware that Christ's power is at work in and through her.

A final set of Brigit tales demonstrates that the power of Christ continues to visit those who believe. Brigit is clearly one of these believers whose faith and love accomplish all things in Christ. This power extends over the birds of the air as well as over the beasts in the field. It is a power that turns human hearts toward the Lord as well as a power that is manifest in great love for the poor. Brigit never said no to the poor, any more than Jesus Christ has ever said no to those who acknowledge their need for him. These final tales illustrate facets of Brigit's holiness that are rooted in the power of Christ.

More Tales of St. Briget

On one of her travels Brigit was received with great hospitality by a very poor woman. The woman insisted that Brigit stay for the night and was delighted when Brigit agreed. It was a cold night, however, and the woman had used up the last of her wood some nights before. The woman was so grateful to God for sending Brigit to stay with her that she took down part of a wooden frame for her house and used it for kindling. She wanted to prepare a lovely meal for the holy Brigit but lacked food. So she decided to kill the only calf of her one cow.

After a lovely supper and conversation both women slept peacefully through the night. Although it seemed like Brigit had not known how much the poor woman gave when she invited her to spend the night, Brigit had hardly left when the woman discovered her cow had another calf and the house had a new frame.

Once there were many men who were moving a tree to the place where Brigit had instructed them. The tree was harder to move than they anticipated, however. Together the multitude of men, the strength of the oxen, and the variety of engines could not pull the tree. The men were almost ready to give up, but Brigit prayed with faith. The Savior had promised that even if faith were as small as a mustard seed, great things could be done. When Brigit was through praying, the men had no trouble bringing the tree to the place where Brigit wished it to be carried.

Many animals were drawn to Brigit's gentleness and kindness. One day she saw some ducks flying while others were swimming near her in the water. She called to them gently but with a certain command in her voice. They came to her as promptly as if she had called them by name. She gently touched them and they freely flew away. Once a wild boar broke into Brigit's herd of pigs. Hearing the noise, Brigit went out to the boar, blessed it, and it became tame. The pigs, who had been so afraid, were no longer afraid of the boar for it remained tame and stayed with them. It was clear that even the birds of the air and the beasts of the field obeyed the will and pleasure of this great saint.

Once a very wealthy queen visited Brigit's monastery. She brought many expensive presents, including a lovely silver chain. Some of Brigit's sisters took the silver chain and hid it before Brigit saw it. They were afraid that Brigit, who gave away everything to those in need, would give it to the first poor person who came to the door. One day a poor man came to the door. Having nothing of value to give him, Brigit saw the silver chain and gave it to him to obtain whatever he needed. When her sisters saw the poor man going away with the chain, they were angry. They complained to Brigit that she gave everything away, and they were going to be poor themselves one day because of it. Brigit thought for a moment and then told them to look for the silver chain in her place of prayer in the church. To the surprise of her sisters, they found there a silver chain of great value. They kept the chain as a reminder of St. Brigit's holiness and virtue.

Once a holy virgin was at sea, and the ship in which she was traveling was wrecked. With great fear, she prayed to St. Brigit to save her. As she prayed, she began to feel herself lifted on top of the waves. The virgin walked on the water until she was safely ashore.

On another day some of the sisters of Brigit were on their way back to the monastery. Some good-hearted people had given them a large portion of meal to carry with them. This was not difficult when they could travel on land. However, a great body of water separated them from their monastery. Upon arriving at the water, they found they could not carry the meal on their backs, for they were not strong enough. There was no boat or anyone around who could help them to the other side. They decided to invoke their holy superior Brigit for help. In a short time they found that they had been transported to the other side with all their meal.

Brigit never said no to the needs of the poor. Once she even gave away the precious vestments that Bishop Conleath used to wear on the major feasts of the church. No one knew of this except Brigit. She did not think of it until a major festival was coming up, and Bishop Conleath announced he would come to celebrate the sacred Eucharist with them. Brigit knew that Conleath liked to wear special vestments to celebrate the major festivals. Yet she felt justified in having given these vestments to the poor Christ who so often appeared to her in the poor people at her door. While thinking on these things, two horses stopped at the door of the church. They were pulling a wagon, but there was no one to guide the horses. Brigit went out to the wagon and found in it vestments identical to the ones she had given away.

One day Brigit was in the fields feeding her flocks when the same poor person went to her seven times and asked for help. Brigit could never say no to anyone in need, so seven times she gave the person alms and some of her flock. She had such tenderness of heart that she could not tell the poor person to go away. The size of the flock was diminished. Yet at nightfall, when Brigit counted the flock in the field, she discovered that it was the same number as when the day began.

One harvest time Brigit sent for many workers and reapers to come and cut down her grain. She agreed with them on their payment and hired them for a particular day. It happened that on the agreed upon day rain fell on the land in great abundance. Brigit's fields were dry for the harvesting, however. None of the workers hired by others could work on that day; but Brigit's workers worked and were paid in full. They took in the harvest, to the admiration of all who heard of that day.

Brigit's day of death had already been foretold to one of her sisters. When the appointed time came, Brigit simply gave up her spirit to her heavenly spouse.

It was the year 518. In spite of her love for all that was simple, Brigit's sisters placed her body on a monument of gold and silver, adorned with jewels and stones and interred her in her own monastery at Kildare. Bishop Conleath also was buried there.

Later the body of Brigit was transferred to the city of Dune in Ulster. At Ulster it was placed close to the bodies of Patrick and Columba, the other two glorious patrons of Ireland. Yet many miracles were worked at Kildare through the intercession of Brigit. The merits of this great saint have caused many miracles to be worked at many times and places, for she is truly one of the holy ones of God.[31]

NOTES

1. P. MacCana, *Celtic Mythology* (London: Hamlyn, 1970) 16.

2. R. P. C. Hanson, "The Mission of St. Patrick," in *An Introduction to Celtic Christianity*, ed. James P. Mackey (Edinburgh: T. and T. Clark, 1989) 22–44.

3. J. N. Hillgarth, *Christianity and Paganism: 350–750* (Philadelphia: University of Pennsylvania Press, 1986) 120–22; Mary Condren, *The Serpent and the Goddess* (New York: Harper and Row, 1989) 62–63.

4. Hanson, "The Mission" 22–44.

5. Kathleen Hughes, *Church and Society in Ireland: A.D. 400–1200*, ed. David Dumville (London: Variorum Reprints, 1987) 12–13.

6. *Monumenta Germaniae Historica, Scriptores Rerum Merovingicarum*, vol. 3, ed. B. Krusch (Hanover, 1896), "Vitae patrum Iurensium . . . Eugendi," II (Gaul, sixth century); this is cited and translated by Hillgarth, "The Church Frees Men from Devils" 14–15.

7. James P. Mackey, "Introduction: Is There a Celtic Christianity?" in Mackey, *An Introduction* 1–21.

8. Kathleen Hughes, *The Church in Early Irish Society* (London: Methuen, 1966) 81–87.

9. Migne, *Patrologia Latina* 72, col. 778.

10. The letter is cited by Edward Sellner, *Wisdom of the Celtic Saints* (Notre Dame: Ave Maria Press, 1933) 20.

11. This eighth-century prayer is one of many ancient wayfarer prayers and reflects the omnipresence of Christ within and without; see Neil D. O'Donaghue, "St. Patrick's Breastplate," in Mackey, *An Introduction* 45–63.

12. O'Donaghue, "St. Patrick's Breastplate" 62.

13. Diarmuid O'Laoghaire, "Prayers and Hymns in the Vernacular," ibid. 268–304.

14. James P. Mackey does acknowledge two exceptions to this, namely, the sacking of Rome in 390 B.C. and Delphi in 297 B.C.; see ibid. 18–19.

15. The cultural and political overlays of the theological controversies between Pelagius and Augustine are well documented in B. R. Rees, *Pelagius: A Reluctant Heretic* (Woodbridge, Suffolk: Boydell Press, 1988) 21–79, 140–42.

16. Lady Gregory, A *Book of Saints and Wonders* (London: John Murray, 1907) 1.

17. D. P. Conyngham, *Lives of the Irish Saints and Martyrs* (New York: Sadlier, 1870) 150–51.

18. Jan de Vries, *Keltische Religion* (Stuttgart: Kohlhammer, 1961) 217.

19. Ethel Rolt-Wheeler, *Women of the Cell and Cloister* (Milwaukee: Young Churchmen's Association, n.d.) 51.

20. Celtic war gods are reflected in the battles of Columb Cille while Kieran, Kevin, Brigit, Patrick, and many others function like the gods or goddesses of the Celtic peoples; see de Vries, *Keltische Religion* 217, and Condren, *The Serpent* 270–77.

21. *Lives of Saints from the Book of Lismore*, Anecdota Oxoniensia Medieval and Modern Series, no. 5 (Oxford: Clarendon Press 1890) 199, 333–34; Bethada Naem Erenn, *Lives of Irish Saints*, ed. and trans. Charles Plummer, vol. 2 (London: Oxford University Press, 1922) 83–84.

22. Condren, *The Serpent* 75.

23. *Lives of Saints* 193.

24. Conyngham, *Lives of the Irish Saints* 151.

25. Condren, *The Serpent* 77.

26. The lineage is traced in the eulogy "Hail Brigit, an Old Irish Poem on the Hill of Alenn," ed. and trans. Kuno Meyer, in Hillgarth, *Christianity and Paganism* 123–25.

27. Rev. J. A. Knowles, *St. Brigid, Patroness of Ireland* (New York: Benziger, 1907) 7.

28. The life and many tales of Brigit are contained in English Recusant Literature Series: 1558–1640, vol. 210, ed. D. M. Rogers (London: Scolar Press, 1974); these tales are found on 107–20.

29. The Martyrology of Aengus, an ancient source of Irish saints, states that Bishop Mel conferred the degrees of bishop on Brigit and on her successors, the abbesses of Kildare. This is cited in the above source as well as in Conyngham, *Lives of the Irish Saints* 151.

30. Ibid. 153.

31. Ibid. 153–55.

32. Rogers, *English Recusant* 121–40.

BIBLIOGRAPHY

Chadwick, Nora. *The Age of the Saints in the Early Irish Church*. London: Oxford University Press, 1961.

Cogitosus and Capgravius. *Famous Acts and Miracles of Brigit*. English Recusant Literature Series: 1558–1640. Vol. 210. Edited by D. M. Rogers. London: Scolar Press, 1974.

Condren, Mary. *The Serpent and the Goddess: Women, Religion and Power in Celtic Ireland*. San Francisco: Harper and Row, 1989.

Conyngham, D. P. *Lives of the Irish Saints and Martyrs*. New York: Sadlier, 1870.

Erenn, Bethada Naem. *Lives of Irish Saints*. 2 vols. Edited and translated by Charles Plummer. London: Oxford University Press, 1922.

Gregory, Lady. *A Book of Saints and Wonders*. London: John Murray, 1907.

Hillgarth, J. N. *Christianity and Paganism: 350–750*. Philadelphia: University of Pennsylvania Press, 1986.

Hughes, Kathleen. *Church and Society in Ireland:* A.D. *400–1200.* Edited by David Dumville. London: Variorum Reprints, 1987.

Hughes, Kathleen. *The Church in Early Irish Society.* London: Methuen, 1966.

Knowles, Rev. J. A. *St. Brigid, Patroness of Ireland.* New York: Benziger, 1907.

Lives of Saints from the Book of Lismore. Anecdota Oxoniensia Medieval and Modern Series, no. 5. Oxford: Clarendon Press, 1890.

Mackey, J. P., ed. *An Introduction to Celtic Christianity.* Edinburgh: T. and T. Clark, 1989.

Sellner, Edward. *Wisdom of the Celtic Saints.* Notre Dame: Ave Maria Press, 1993.

–4–

BALTHILD, QUEEN OF NEUSTRIA

(died c. 680)

Sold at a Cheap Price

A brief history of the times immediately before Balthild can help to situate her life in a warring world. In the late fifth century, Clovis I began a line of Merovingian kings whose realm rose to great power after the decline of the Roman Empire. Clovis successfully led the German tribe of the Franks in the conquest of Roman Gaul. The Franks and Merovingian kings would gradually take over all of Gaul in the sixth century.

Meanwhile, the population of Roman Gaul, survivors of a vanished empire, and the Roman Catholic bishops struggled to assert some remnant of the civil authority that had been theirs in the later years of the Roman Empire. Clovis and his line of Merovingian rulers did their share of pillaging church properties, but they also learned that they had to work with the bishops who still held favor with the Christian people.

Clovis married Clotilda, a young princess of a royal family of Gaul, whose uncle held a high position in that region. This uncle had murdered Clotilda's parents and brother to secure power in the disintegrating kingdom. Clotilda was a devout Christian, who in time converted Clovis to Christianity. Given the times and his personality, his conversion did not prevent him from continuing to wage war. Like other kings, he murdered members of his own family in order to strengthen his sons' position. They would eventually rule Austrasia because of the power Clovis ensured for them.

Clovis encouraged Clotilda's activities for the poor, made reparation for his sins before he died, encouraged his people to become Christians, and was generous to the bishops and monasteries in his land. Clovis died in 511. His four sons established centers of the kingdom in Metz, Soissons, Paris, and Orleans. Eventually, these were fused into two major centers, Neustria and Austrasia.

Austrasia, also known as German France, occupied the northeastern part of the former Gaul. It had a shifting population as new hordes of invaders arrived from Germany, Frisia, Westphalia, and Saxony. Neustria, sometimes called Roman France, extended from the borders of the northeast province to the Atlantic Ocean and south to the River Loire. Clothar II and his son who succeeded him, Dagobert I, made Neustria the province that received their personal concern. Dagobert I laid the foundation for a system of laws for Neustria. After his death in 639, the power of the Merovingian Empire began its decline.

Two sons of Dagobert I's ruled after his death: Sigebert II in Austrasia, and Clovis II in Neustria and Burgundy.[1] Clovis II named Erchinoald to be his mayor of the palace, a powerful position usually held by one of the most influential landowners who represented other landowners before the king. The position could involve keeping peace in the kingdom by ensuring the landowners' loyalty to the king, or it could be used for personal gain and insurrection. It was Erchinoald who purchased the young Anglo-Saxon woman Balthild.[2]

Erchinoald was an able political mentor for Balthild, who aided him in his palace duties. Erchinoald brought Balthild to the attention of Clovis II. The king was impressed with the young woman and married her when he came of age in 648. History generally portrays Clovis II as an able king and a relatively good husband. "Relatively good" means he is also depicted as a womanizer, glutton, and drunkard.[3]

Their first son, Clothar III, was born in 649. Two other sons, Theuderic III and Childeric II, followed. While Clovis II was alive, Balthild held a strong position in the kingdom. She astutely secured ecclesiastical support by using her power to help loyal men in the court to be named bishops. She endeared herself to many bishops by giving them large sums of money for the poor and for building up their churches. Like others of the Merovingian world, she supported shrines of the saints as well as monasteries. In turn, the bishops and monasteries entreated heaven on behalf of Balthild and her family.

In spite of the fact that Balthild lived in the Dark Ages, a period from which few documents of any kind have been preserved, accounts of her life as a Frankish queen have been preserved. These stories of lives of the saints (hagiography) were a flourishing literary genre of the time.

It is difficult to assess the degree to which the historical Balthild has been clothed in the expectations of holiness that held in Merovingian times. That the personal lives of powerful women were recorded at all testifies to their leadership and influence. They were important in their own right as well as meeting in some way the expectations of holiness.

What were the assumptions about holy women during the Merovingian period? In that violent society, women were expected to foster peace and to suffer for harmony, even to the point of martyrdom. It seemed inevitable that those who tried to make peace and oppose war would suffer.

Christian saintly women were expected to help the poor in many ways. Plundering and warring among the powerful left the poor victimized. In contrast to their warrior husbands, the royal women who held power were expected to use that power for those who had none.

Merovingian husbands used their wealth as a means of gaining power and rewarding loyalty, which in turn enabled them to maintain their power. Early barbarian kings were accustomed to an economy grounded in looting and gift giving. After defeating their rivals in war, the kings would spread out the booty they had confiscated, or that had been given to them in the act of surrender. The wealth taken in war was used to accumulate greater power.

Holy women, in contrast, used personal wealth to alleviate suffering, to support monasteries and convents, and to meet the various needs of favored bishops and their people. Using wealth in this way brought the women a certain loyalty from the recipients. Many women gave their inheritance to the safekeeping and general use of monasteries, for this meant no other family member could have access to it.

The Germanic tradition favored the woman saint who used family wealth for others. It did not emphasize leaving property behind. Voluntary poverty would be part of a later paradigm of holiness. This may be a major reason why the women's lives that have been preserved as "saintly" in the Merovingian period are those of royal women who gave their wealth to the church and to the poor.

Although women could not hold ecclesiastical office, they could strongly suggest to their husbands who ought to be appointed bishop. Queen Balthild, who temporarily ruled for her son, actually appointed bishops. This use of power could be saintly. (This was not always the case, however.)

Because Germanic law upheld women's rights to share in the estates of husbands and fathers, women were free to use their wealth as they chose. Later in history, husbands or sons would have control of money that came to women. In the Dark Ages, however, women started monasteries, became abbesses, and were on equal footing with abbots and bishops. None of this was contrary to saintliness. It was a sign of holiness.

The self-assurance of royal women, some of whom became abbesses, came from a blend of personality and aristocratic training. A royal abbess was most capable of administering the estate of the monastery. She was also capable of enhancing its resources. As heads of monasteries, abbesses could recruit and train new members and discipline those members who required it. The royal abbesses of Merovingia were models of hospitality. The monasteries cared for all people, without regard for class, occupation, or circumstance. In a period when wars were constantly fought against those of differing backgrounds, saintly women embodied the universality of the love of Christ.

In the early Dark Ages an abbess could use her monastery's resources as she chose. An abbess was free to select her rule of life from many existing rules or to modify and interpret any one rule to fit her monastery. Networking with other abbots and abbesses to exchange wisdom about the spiritual journey was an aid in discerning what Christ was asking of them.

During the Dark Ages those who joined monasteries may have had a calling to that particular way of life, or they could have been there for other reasons. Some women came to the monastery for education and a kind of career advancement that was only possible here. Others came with children to escape the abuse of a husband or simply for a place to stay. Still other women were forced into monasteries by their families to do penance for some sin, or to get rid of them so there would be more power for those outside. Such a variety of people meant that the abbess had to show great prudence and wisdom in meting out discipline practices that would foster growth in the Christian life.[4]

This growth included guidance given by the abbess, often more by example than by words. Daily the abbess heard confessions from her nuns about their faults and gave them necessary penances to help change their weakness into strength.[5]

In the Dark Ages, saints were not expected to perform extraordinary acts or miracles as signs of God's power working through them. Their lives were the signs of God's power. If something "miraculous" did occur, there were strict codes for assessing whether it was really a miracle or simply a natural phenomenon. On rare occasions, there might have been a miracle of healing, but this was not significant. Women were supposed to know how to use medicinal herbs and basic medical skill to foster healing.

At the beginning of the Dark Ages royal or noble women were considered equal, or in some cases superior, to bishops in terms of power. The saintly women of this period could be powerful allies or formidable enemies. The practice of Frankish queens and kings appointing bishops ceased by the ninth century, when the Frankish aristocracy became integrated into the church hierarchy.

Saint stories of the Dark Ages were clearly told in order to inspire imitation. Those who were remembered had to have respect for the clergy in their lifetime (since the clergy controlled the historical tradition). Paradigms of holiness were used as vehicles for telling the story and perhaps limited much of the personality from coming through the story. At the same time, in spite of all of these facts, some elements of prophecy, illumination, strength, and holiness can still reach out across the centuries.

Women whose use of power alleviates rather than inflicts suffering will always have a place among the holy ones. Balthild's story portrays the challenge and the need for such holy women in every age. The uniqueness of the personality may have been lost in the telling. But the strength of the woman who makes such a journey for the good of others still shines through.

The rough and brutal age in which women like Balthild lived presumed that women as well as men could endure hardship. At the same time, it was assumed that the suffering of others would stir holy women to act in their behalf. In an age when death was all around, it was expected that holy women would not fear dying. The manner of dealing with death was a final test of holiness. A true Christian leader died in a way that provided illumination for her sisters and brothers. The true saint was more concerned for others as she was dying than she was for herself. Balthild exemplified this manner of Christian death in imitation of the God-man whose concerns were for others, even when dying.

The life of Balthild focuses more on her final years in the convent of Chelles than it does on her early life. Typical of slaves of the period, it is not known when Balthild was born. She was English and was sold as a slave to Erchinoald, the mayor of the palace of Clovis II. After she married Clovis, she ably ran the domestic kingdom while he was off to war.

When Clovis died, Balthild ruled for her youngest son. When Erchinoald died, a year after Clovis, she appointed Ebroïn as mayor of the palace. Ebroïn had the son of a Burgundian mayor killed. Then he had the bishops of Lyons and Autun murdered, for they were enemies of the court of Balthild.

Ebroïn and Balthild appointed two new bishops to take the places of the murdered men. Genesius, a supporter of Balthild and a member of her court, was sent to be bishop of Lyons. Another friend, Leodegar, was made bishop of Autun.

Some historians claim that Ebroïn not only engineered the killing of the bishops of Lyons and Autun but also forced Balthild into a monastery when she objected to the violence. Other historians say Balthild chose to enter a monastery as a sign of opposition to Ebroïn's growing power and the violence that accompanied it. Such a move would give her the means of opposing Ebroïn through alliances with other abbots, bishops, and abbesses, on whose support the ruler depended.

After Balthild was in the monastery of Chelles, Ebroïn was part of a conspiracy that murdered her son Childeric II. Theuderic III, Balthild's youngest son, was easily used by Ebroïn to do whatever Ebroïn thought expedient. Another of Balthild's sons, Chlotar III, died in 673. This allowed Ebroïn to rule Neustria and Burgundy through Theuderic III without any problems. Meanwhile, Balthild was already assuming the duties of a nun and taking on whatever service was needed in her convent.

The nun of Chelles who tells the story of Balthild introduces some pieces of biographical knowledge that suggests they were friends. The nun tells of the virtues of Balthild, virtues characteristic of royal saints of the day. The love and humility that characterize those who serve Christ are found in the universality of hospitality that Balthild demonstrates to all who come to the monastery.

In the midst of a violent society where claims to power caused many deaths, the royal queen and nun Balthild used her power to effect greater love. Even her manner of dying reveals a thoughtfulness toward her abbess and her sister friends, for she does not reveal the extent of her illness. Some are surprised at her death. This royal woman of achievement maintained a domestic power that helped maintain a temporal kingdom. As the following selection indicates, Balthild died quietly in Christ's loving power, her source of an everlasting kingdom.[6]

Here Begins the Prologue to the Life of Lady Balthild the Queen[7]

1. Most beloved, I have been commanded by the prelate Christ to accomplish a simple and pious work.[8] My lack of skill and experience prevents me from setting forth an exquisite narrative in learned language. But the power of heartfelt love more strongly commands us not to be puffed up with vainglory and simply bring the truth to light. We know that the Lord Jesus Christ asked for fruit from the fig tree, not leaves. Likewise we have determined that the fruit of truth shall not be hidden, but shine forth upon a candlestick for the advancement and edification of many.

Although less skilled in scholarship, we are all the more eager to cultivate a plain and open style so as to edify the many people who—like prudent bees seeking sweet nectar from the flowers—seek from simple words the burgeoning truth that edifies but does not flatter and puff up the one who hears it. Thus may the compendium of piety be thrown open to those who desire to imitate her. Therefore in what follows, we have shown forth the truth as best we can, not for detractors but for the faithful.

Here Begins the Life of the Blessed Queen Balthild

2. The blessed Lord who "wills that all be saved and come to the knowledge of the truth" works in all people both "to will and to do" (1 Tim 2:4; 1 Cor 12:6; Phil 2:33). By the same token, by the merits and virtues of the saints, praise should first be sung to the Lord who has made the humble great and has raised the poor from dust and seated them among the princes of the people. Such a one is the woman now present to our minds, the great and venerable lady, Balthild the Queen. Divine providence called her from across the seas. She, who came here as God's most precious and lofty pearl, was sold at a cheap price.

Erchinoald, a Frankish magnate and most illustrious man, acquired her and in his service the girl behaved most honorably.

Her pious and admirable manners pleased the prince and all his servants. For she was kindhearted, sober, and prudent in all her ways, careful, and wishing evil to no one. Her speech was not frivolous, nor were her words presumptuous. In every way, she behaved with utmost propriety. Since she was of the Saxon race, she was graceful in form with refined features, a beautiful woman with a smiling face and serious gait. She so showed herself as she ought in all things that she pleased her master and found favor in his eyes.

Thus, he decided that she should set out the drinking cup for him in his chamber. This meant that she was honored above all others as his housekeeper—standing at his side, always ready to serve him. She did not allow this dignity to make her proud, but rather kept her humility. She was always obedient to her companions and amiable in her ministering to her elders. She would remove their shoes and then wash and dry their feet. She brought them water to wash themselves, and prepared their clothing expeditiously. She performed all these services with good spirits and no grumbling.[9]

3. This noble conduct led her companions to praise and love her. She gained such a reputation that when the wife of Erchinoald died, he wished to marry Balthild, that faultless virgin. When she heard of this, she fled from his sight. When he called her into his chamber, she hid herself in a corner and covered herself with bundles of rags so no one might find her. Because she was humble, she attempted to flee from the honor that was to be hers. She had hoped not to get married but to have Jesus alone for her spouse.

Divine providence intervened, and Erchinoald found a different wife. Thus it happened that Balthild, with God's approval, escaped marriage with this prince, but eventually came to be espoused to Clovis, son of the former king Dagobert. By virtue of her humility, she was thus raised to a higher rank. She was wed to the king by divine dispensation, and honored in this station. She brought forth royal children. These events are known to all, for now her royal progeny rule the realm.

4. She, upon whom God conferred the grace of prudence, obeyed the king with vigilant care as her lord. She acted as a mother to princes, as a daughter to priests, as a most pious nurse to children and to adolescents. She was amiable to all, loving priests as fathers, monks as brothers, and serving as nurse to the poor. She distributed generous alms to everyone. She guarded the prince's honor by keeping their intimate counsels secret. She always exhorted the young to strive for religious achievement. She humbly and assiduously suggested things to the king for the benefit of the church and of the poor. Desiring to serve Christ in the secular way of life, she frequented daily prayers, commending herself with tears to Christ, the king of heaven.

Impressed by her faith and devotion, the pious king delegated his faithful servant, the abbot Genesius, to help her.[10] Through his hands, she ministered to priests and poor alike, feeding the needy, clothing the naked, overseeing the burial of the dead, funneling large amounts of gold and silver through him to convents of men and virgins. In time, Genesius was ordained as bishop of Lyons in Gaul.[11] Genesius was busy in the palace of the Franks. By the order of King Clovis II, as we have said, Lady Balthild followed his advice in providing alms through him to every poor person in many places.

5. In accordance with God's will, King Clovis II migrated from his body (c. 657), leaving behind his three sons and Balthild.[12] Clothar III succeeded his father as King of the Franks, maintaining peace in the realm with the aid of the excellent princes Chrodebert, Bishop of Paris, Lord Quen, Ebroïn, mayor of the palace, other elders and many other people. To promote peace, the elders advised Lady Balthild to name Childeric the king of Austrasia, which the people accepted. This move united the Burgundians with the Franks. We believe that these three realms remained at peace with each other due to Lady Balthild's great faith and God's will.

6. God's will continued to work through Lady Balthild. She followed the advice of good priests, prohibiting the evil of simony. This evil, the naming of bishops according to who could pay for the sacred office, was a depraved custom that stained the church of God. God acted through Balthild in her abolishment of another evil custom of the people. This was the custom of killing their children rather than nurturing them, so that they might avoid the public burdens that were heaped upon them by custom, a practice which caused great damage to their affairs.[13] In her mercy Balthild forbade anyone to carry on any of the practices. For this, her reward in God's realm must be great.

7. Who can count how many and how great her services were to religious communities? She showered great estates and whole forests upon them for the construction of their cells and monasteries. At Chelles, in the region of Paris, she built a great community of virgins as her own special house of God. She named the maiden Bertilla, a servant of God, as the superior of the group. In time the venerable Lady Balthild would decide to go there to live under the rule of religion and to rest in peace. In truth, she followed her desire with willing devotion.[14]

Whatever wonders God works through the saints and the chosen ones should not be easily passed over, for all contribute their praise to God. As the scripture says, "God does wonders in the saints" (Ps 37:38). The Holy Spirit, the Paraclete, dwells within and cooperates with the benevolent heart as it is written, "All things work together for good for those who love God" (Rom 8:25). This was spoken truly of this holy woman. As we have said, neither our tongue nor that of any other can voice all the good that Lady Balthild did.

How much consolation and help she lavished on the houses of God and on the poor for the love of Christ! How many advantages and comforts did she confer on them! The monastery of Corbie in the parish of Amiens was built at her own expense. There the venerable Lord Theofredus, now a bishop but then an abbot, ruled a great flock of brothers whom Lady Balthild had requested from the most saintly Lord Waldebert. Waldebert was abbot of the monastery of Luxeuil, and sent the brothers to Corbie, which all agree to praise even in this day.[15]

8. What else did this saintly lady do? She gave the very holy man Philibert a large woods where his community has now settled. Other pastures and land were given for the building of this same monastery. How many great farms and coins of gold and silver she gave to Lord Lagobert at Corbie! She took off the precious waist belt from her royal clothing and gave it to the brothers to use for alms. She gave all these things away with a kind and joyous soul, for as the Scripture says, "the Lord loves a cheerful giver" (2 Cor 9:7).

She gave many precious gifts to the convents of Fontanelle and Logium. Who can number the many whole farms and innumerable gifts of money that were given to Luxeuil and the monasteries in Burgundy? What did she do for Jouarre, the convent from which she gathered Lady Bertilla, abbess of Chelles, and other sacred virgins? Many gifts of wealth and land were given to them! Similarly, she often directed gifts to holy Fara's monastery.[16] She granted many great estates to the basilicas of the saints and the monasteries of the city of Paris, enriching them with many gifts. What more? As we have said, we cannot recount all of the things this great lady did, not even half of them. To give an account of all the blessings she bestowed is utterly beyond our powers!

9. We should not pass over, however, what she did in her zealous love of God for the older basilicas of the saints, Lord Denis and Lord Germanus, Lord Medard, Saint Peter, Lord Anianus, Saint Martin, or anything else that came to her notice. She would send orders and letters warning bishops and abbots that the monks dwelling in those places ought to live according to their holy rule and order. That they might agree more freely, she ordered their privileges confirmed and granted them immunities that they might beseech Christ, the highest king, to show mercy to the king and to give peace to the land.

Let it be remembered, since this increases the magnitude of her own reward, that she prohibited the sale of captive Christian folk to outsiders, and gave orders through all the lands that no one was to sell captive Christians within the borders of the Frankish realm![17] In addition, she ordered that many captives should be ransomed, paying for many of them herself. She established many of the captives she released in monasteries as well as many others of her own people. She could thus care for them. Those that she could persuade joined already established communities and prayed for her. She even gave gifts to Rome, particularly to the basilica of Saints Peter and Paul. She also directed many large gifts to go to the poor people of Rome.[18]

10. As we have said before, it was the intention of Balthild to join the monastery at Chelles, which she had built and endowed. The Franks did not want this to happen, for they loved her dearly and wished her to remain their good queen. However, the wretched Bishop Sigobrand caused a great commotion among the Franks; his pride among the Franks caused him mortal ruin.[19] A plan was formed to kill this bishop against the will of Lady Balthild. They were afraid that the lady would punish them severely and avenge the death, so they permitted her to enter the monastery. There can be no doubt that the princes' motives were far from pure![20]

But the lady, considering the will of God rather than their counsel, thought it a dispensation from God that, in spite of the circumstances, she might have the chance to fulfill her holy plan under Christ's rule. Conducted by several elders, she came to the monastery of Chelles. There she was received into the holy congregation by the holy maidens, as was fitting, honorably and with love. At first, she experienced anger at those who betrayed her, for she had been very good to them. They were suspicious of her motives for joining the congregation, though they were the ones who had been evil to her when she had acted for their good. She spoke with the priests about all of this and begged them to forgive the commotion that was in her heart. In time, by the grace of God, peace was fully restored among them all.

11. She loved her sisters with the most pious affection as her own daughters, and she obeyed the holy abbess as a mother. Lady Balthild had previously shown herself a servant, the lowliest bondwoman to them from holy devotion, even while she still ruled over the public palace and was only a visitor to the community. One example of her great humility was the way she would valiantly take care of the dirtiest cleaning jobs for the sisters in the kitchen, personally cleaning up the dung from the latrine.[21] She did all this gladly and in perfect joy of spirit, doing such humble service for Christ's sake.

Who would believe that one so sublime in power would take care of things so vile? Only if she were driven by the purest love of Christ could such actions be expected! She prayed constantly, persistently, devoutly, tearfully. She frequently attended divine reading and gave constant comfort to the sick through holy exhortation and frequent visits. Her sincere charity enabled her to grieve with the sorrowful and rejoice with the joyful. With humility she often made suggestions to the lady abbess that could lighten the burdens or bring comfort. The lady abbess listened to these humble suggestions for improvement and amiably granted the petitions. Truly with them, as with the apostles, there was but one heart and one soul, for they loved each other tenderly in Christ.

12. When the Lady Balthild became ill, suffering greatly from pain caused

by an infection in the bowel, she would have died without the efforts of doctors. Yet her confidence was placed more heavily in heavenly medicine than in earthly cures. With a holy and just conscience, she thanked God for the chastisement. She gave wise advice when asked. She provided a pattern of piety in her service to her sisters in great humility. She often consulted with the abbess regarding the gifts they might bring the king and the queen and their nobles. This was customary so that the house of God would not lose the good reputation with which it began.

It would thus remain in close affection with all its friends and also grow ever stronger in the name of God. "It is fitting to have loving bonds with those who are without" (1 Tim 3:7). Lady Balthild particularly urged the sisters to always care for the poor and for guests with the utmost zeal, out of love and mercy. The abbess heard the admonitions of Balthild in the love of Christ and did all with a gladness of heart. Lady Balthild never ceased to carry out such works and thus increased the holiness of her community.

13. As her glorious death approached, a clear vision was shown to them. Before the altar of holy Mary, a ladder stood upright whose height reached to the heavens. Angels of God were going up and down the ladder, and the Lady Balthild was making her ascent. Through this revelation she understood that her merit, patience, and humility would take her to the heights of the eternal king, who would swiftly reward her with an exalted crown. The lady knew, from this clear vision, that it would not be long before she would die and come to the place where she had already laid up her true treasure.

She ordered that this vision be concealed from the other sisters so that they would not grieve unnecessarily before her passing. She now devoted herself with greater piety and good spirits to holy prayer, commending herself even more zealously, more humbly, and with greater contrition to the celestial king, the Lord Jesus Christ. As much as she could, she concealed the weight of her pain and consoled Lady Bertilla and the rest of the sisters, saying that her illness was not serious, that she was getting better, dissimulating what was to come so that afterward they might take comfort in believing that the blow of death came suddenly to her and she went unexpectedly from this life to the next.

14. When the lady felt her end to be truly near, she raised her holy mind to heaven. Having been made certain that she would receive the great prize, she vehemently forbade her attendants to say how sick she was to the other sisters or to the abbess who was ill herself. She did not want the abbess distracted by a multitude of even heavier sorrows. At the time that Lady Balthild was dying, there was a child who was her goddaughter whom she wished to take with her. This child died suddenly and preceded Balthild to the tomb.[22] Full of faith, she made the sign of the cross. Raising pious eyes and holy hands to heaven, the saint's spirit was released from the chains of the body. Immediately, the chamber

glittered brightly with the light of divine splendor. No doubt with the light, a chorus of angels and her faithful old friend Bishop Genesius came to receive that most holy woman as her great merits deserved.

15. For a little while, the sisters attending her stifled their sorrow. They said nothing of her death as she had ordered. They remained silent with the exception of telling the priests who commended Balthild to the Lord. When the abbess and the rest of the community learned what had happened, they asked how this jewel could have been so quickly snatched away from them without knowing that the hour of death was near. Shocked, they all prostrated themselves on the ground in grief and with profuse tears and sobs gave thanks to the pious Lord and praised him.

Then they commended her soul to Christ, the pious king, that he might escort her to holy Mary in the chorus and company of the saints. They buried her with great honor and much reverence as was proper. Lady Bertilla, the holy abbess, earnestly commended her to the holy priests in several churches so that the holy name of Lady Balthild would be carefully commemorated in the sacred prayers of the Mass. She is still celebrated in many places for her holiness.

16. She left an example of holiness to her followers. Her humility, patience, mildness, and overflowing zeal for love, infinite mercy, astute and prudent vigilance, and pure confessions were an example to many. She showed that everything should be done as a result of consultation and that nothing should be done without consent, but that all actions should be temperate and rational. She left this rule of piety as a model to her companions and now for her holy virtues and many other merits, she has received the prize of the crown that the Lord set aside for her long ago. So she is happy among the angels in the Lord's sight. She rejoices forever among the white-robed flock of virgins enjoying the immense and everlasting joy she had always desired.

In order to make known her sublime merits to the faithful, God in goodness allowed many miracles to be worked at her tomb. Whoever came there seized by fever, vexed with demons, or even sick with toothaches, was cured through divine power and through the intercession of Balthild if they had faith. Whatever plague or illness they experienced, they could leave the sight safe and sound as they left in the name of the Lord. This was manifest most recently in the case of a certain boy.

17. The venerable Bishop Leudegund came from Provence. He was a faithful friend to the monastery of Chelles. A demon possessed his son. The demon was so violent that the son's companions could only control him if his hands and feet were bound. Otherwise, he tore apart all that he could reach. When the friends brought him to the place of the holy sepulcher and laid him half alive on the pavement, the ferocious demon grew terrified with the fear of God and grew silent and stiff. Divine power made the demon flee from the boy immediately.

The boy rose up confidently, made the sign of the cross, gave thanks to God, and returned to his family and friends unharmed and in his right mind.

18. Now let us remember that there have been other noble queens of the Franks who worshiped God. Clothild, King Clovis's queen of old, niece of King Gundobad. Her husband was a strong pagan, but she drew him and many other Frankish leaders to Christianity and the Catholic faith by holy exhortation. She led them to construct a church in honor of St. Peter at Paris. She built the original community of virgins for St. George at Chelles. In honor of the saints, and to store up her future reward, she founded many other communities which she endowed with much wealth.

Likewise, we are told of Queen Ultragotha and of the most Christian king Childebert. Ultragotha was a comforter of the poor and a helper of the monks who served God. There was also the faithful handmaid named Radegund. She was a wife of King Clothar, a queen of older times. The grace of the Holy Spirit was given to her to relinquish her husband during her life and consecrate herself to the Lord Christ as a nun. We can read in her acts all the good she did in her life for Christ, her true spouse.

19. But it is right for us to meditate here on Queen Balthild, whose many good deeds have been done in our time and whose acts are well known to us. We have commemorated a few of these acts and cannot believe that her merits are any less than the good performed by others before her. We know she surpassed them in zealous striving for what is holy. After performing many good deeds to the point of evangelical perfection, she surrendered herself freely to holy obedience and happily ended her life as a religious, a true nun. Her sacred feast is celebrated on January 30.[23]

She lies entombed in her monastery of Chelles, while she reigns gloriously with Christ in heaven in perpetual joy. We trust she will never forget her faithful friends. As well as we could, we have followed your orders, dear lady. Forgive our lack of skill. We pray that, in your love for us, you ask the good Lord to exonerate us from our sins of negligence. May the peace of the Lord be with you and to the Lord be glory from everlasting to everlasting. Amen.

NOTES

1. A Secular Priest, *Lives of Sainted Queens* (London: Burns and Oates, n.d.) Clotildis 1–20; Radegund 1–11; Balthildis 1–7. Each section of this work beings its pagination with 1. A map of Merovingian rulers and descendants is found in Suzanne Wemple, *Women in Frankish Society* (Philadelphia: University of Pennsylvania Press, 1981) viii–x.

2. Janet L. Nelson, "Queens as Jezebels: The Careers of Brunhild and Balthild in Merovingian History," in *Medieval Women*, ed. Derek Baker (Oxford: Basil Blackwell, 1978) 46–48.

3. *Liber historiae Francorum*, ed. and trans. Bernard Bachrach (Lawrence, Kans.: Coronado Press, 1973) 43–44.

4. *Sainted Women of the Dark Ages*, ed. and trans. Jo Ann McNamara, John E. Halborg, and E. Gordon Whatley (Durham: Duke University Press, 1992) 1–15.

5. Rule of Donatus of Besançon, c. 23; the entire rule can be found in Migne, *Patrologia Latina* 87:273–98, Donatus episcopi Vesontionensis, *Regula ad virgines;* this is cited in McNamara, *Sainted Women* 10 n. 28.

6. McNamara, *Sainted Women* 264–68.

7. Ibid. 268–78.

8. The writer of this text is usually identified as a nun of Chelles, a popular training center for Anglo-Saxon nuns. She will use the authoritarian "we"—meaning the Holy Spirit and herself.

9. The virtues and actions described here were those to be found in rules for nuns at this time.

10. "Pious king" indicates the writer may be unaware of the reputation of Clovis II as a glutton, liar, and womanizer. This suggests the writer may be from a later generation.

11. The murder of Aunemund is discreetly omitted.

12. In time each of the three sons, Clothar III, Childeric, and Theuderic, would all succeed to the throne.

13. The precise meaning of these reasons for infanticide at this time is obscure. Infanticide in the early Middle Ages was a common practice.

14. Lady Balthild was forced into the convent at Chelles, though the emphasis that it was her own choice could be consistent with the pious character of Balthild.

15. Waldebert was schooled in the monastic discipline of St. Columbanus, instructed his monks in that rule, and authored a rule for women that was very popular in the Frankish communities.

16. This was a convent of Anglo-Saxon nuns, loosely connected to Chelles in Balthild's time. They had some connection to the Irish monks at Luxeuil, headed by Waldebert.

17. This effectively blocked the slave trade of the day. Queen Balthild had herself been a slave.

18. The use of her royal authority for good is a constant theme of holiness in the story of Balthild.

19. Bishop Sigobrand succeeded Chrodebert as bishop of Paris. He attempted to restore wealth to his own diocese, not the realm. This caused the Franks to plot his death, although they knew Balthild would never allow this. Ebroïn helped plan the killing.

20. Ebroïn, who owed his position to the queen, forced her into the cloister between 664 and 667. He would eventually be exiled to Luxeuil from 673 to 675.

21. This task was associated with the preparation of food, since the fowl, fish, or other animals required slaughter, dissection, preparation, and so forth.

22. A seven-year-old girl named Radegund was buried in the same tomb with Queen Balthild. The name of this goddaughter was the name of a former holy queen whom Balthild took as her model of piety.

23. The text uses the dating of the third calends of February 680. This is January 30 in the present calendar.

BIBLIOGRAPHY

Brown, Peter. *The Cult of the Saints: Its Rise and Function in Latin Christianity*. Chicago: University of Chicago Press, 1981.

Brown, Peter. *Society and the Holy*. London: Faber and Faber, 1982.

Eckenstein, Lina. *Women Under Monasticism, 500–1500*. Cambridge: Cambridge University Press, 1896.

Geary, Patrick J. *Before France and Germany: The Creation and Transformation of the Merovingian World*. Oxford: Oxford University Press, 1988.

Hillgarth, J. N. *Christianity and Paganism*. Philadelphia: University of Pennsylvania Press, 1986. 350–750.

McNamara, Jo Ann. "A Legacy of Miracles: Hagiography and Nunneries in Merovingian Gaul." In *Women of the Medieval World: Essays in Honor of John Mundy*. Edited by Julius Kirschner and Suzanne Wemple. New York: Basil Blackwell, 1985. 36–52.

McNamara, Jo Ann. "The Ordeal of Community: Hagiography and Discipline in Merovingian Convents." *Vox Benedictina* 3 and 4 (1986) 293–326.

McNamara, Jo Ann, John Halborg, and E. Gordon Whatley, eds. and trans. *Sainted Women of the Dark Ages*. Durham: Duke University Press, 1992.

– 5 –

DHUODA OF SEPTIMANIA

(NINTH CENTURY)

My Son, Search Eagerly for God

Charlemagne became king of the Franks in 768. He was a gifted ruler and warrior, and established the Franks as a kingdom with new lands and wealth. Charlemagne's dream was to create a common European culture through unifying the political and ecclesial powers of his time. He saw that an alliance with Rome was for the mutual good of church and state. His title, Holy Roman Emperor, if not accurate, was as least a famous one by which later centuries would remember him.

Charlemagne brought great scholars to his court in 777. His plan was that they would teach others, so that his whole realm would be educated. In 782, he enticed the well-known scholar Alcuin to head the court schools and direct monastic learning. Courts and monasteries were influential as means of cultural transmission, and the Frankish empire soon became a center for learning. The royal court and the monasteries were the vehicles for Latin culture which was both translated and taught.[1] Successful as the education was, the political and ecclesiastical unity of Europe was not accomplished in Charlemagne's lifetime.

Charlemagne upheld the teachings of church councils in his realm and enforced Roman laws that reversed the earlier equality of men and women. In addition to the restrictions of church councils, he forbade abbesses to bless male members of their double monasteries. Abbesses also had to cease blessing their nuns with priestly benedictions. Nuns could no longer approach the altar, touch sacred vessels, or distribute the body and blood of Christ. When altar linens needed to be washed, it had to be the priest who removed them from the altar. Then he gave them to women at the altar rail for washing. Similarly, offerings brought to the altar by women now had to be received by the priests outside the sacred space, that is, by the altar rail. These issues would be more formally decreed in 829, but their origin is traced to the time of Charlemagne.[2]

Four of Charlemagne's five wives and all six of his palace concubines provided him with many daughters and sons. The son destined to be the next ruler was Louis the Pious, son of Charlemagne and Hildegarde.[3] Louis the Pious (778–840) received the promise of inheritance at his baptism. In 781, Pope Hadrian I (722–95) blessed him in Rome and invested him with the royal crown, although he was only three years old at the time. Charlemagne named Louis king of Aquitaine in 781.

In 794, Louis married Iminigard, daughter of the powerful Count Ingramnus. Louis and Iminigard had three sons, Lothair, Pepin, and Louis the German. Louis the Pious, personally trained by Charlemagne from childhood, was well beloved by warriors and people. He was not only a just and pious king, but an able leader who extended the empire of Charlemagne to great proportions even before his official crowning.

Charlemagne did not officially crown Louis the Pious as his successor until September 13, 813, when Charlemagne knew death was near. He died within five months on January 20, 814. The new emperor, Louis, called an assembly to affirm and sanction his overseeing of the empire. He gave each of his brothers, sisters, half-brothers, and half-sisters an inheritance. This included placing some of his sisters and half-sisters in convents so that they would not be threats to his rule. Louis and his eldest son, Lothair, served as co-rulers of the empire, though Louis retained the title of emperor.

In 819, Louis wed Judith of Bavaria, a powerful Saxon woman who was half his age. Beautiful, cultivated, and politically astute, Judith made both friends and enemies at the court as she exerted her influence on Louis. Louis and Judith had two daughters and one son, Charles the Bald, born in 823.[4]

Louis named Bernard, a count from Septimania, as his trusted counselor. Bernard was responsible for governing a fair amount of land and people in his region. As a result of his military victories for Louis, Bernard later was named to the powerful position of the chamberlain of the palace.

Because chronicles of the time were more concerned with the courtly class involved in political struggles and wars, more is known of Bernard of Septimania than of his wife Dhuoda of Septimania. They were married in the palace chapel at Aix-la-Chapelle on June 29, 824. So little was known about Dhuoda that she was a victim of mistaken identity for a period in the eighteenth century when some historians thought she was a daughter of Charlemagne.[5]

The little that is known of Dhuoda comes primarily from her manual of instruction for her son.[6] Dhuoda could have been a countess of noble origin, a probability that is validated by her education in the classics and in theology. These sources are abundant and are accurately cited in her manual. Charlemagne's educational programs did bear fruit in many women like Dhuoda. Although many of the manuscripts written by women in the eighth and ninth centuries have not been preserved, those that remain point to a similarly sound education. This included the use of Latin, for the church of this period was already proclaiming Latin, Greek, and Hebrew as the "sacred languages."

The citations that are made throughout Dhuoda's manual show a disciplined logic. She has the ability to verbalize reasons for her alternative positions about the increasingly limited perspectives of women's roles. At the same time, she carries out the socially expected role of managing the large estate while her husband is off to war or at court. Dhuoda is not only running the estate in Bernard's absence, she is also trying to pay off his excessive debts from his overindulgence in the royal way of life. This causes her difficulties of conscience as well as social ones. She has to borrow money from Jews to pay off some of Bernard's outstanding debts.[7]

Like other aristocratic women whose husbands were away at war, Dhuoda carried the administrative burdens. Charlemagne had tried to ease the burden for women in this situation by issuing an edict allowing a noble who was called off to war to leave four men behind. These men were to help protect the wife and family and also to help with administration of and work on the estate. This small amount of help was not enough for someone like Dhuoda, who was running a large estate, caring for a great number of workers, and trying to repay the staggering debts her husband left behind.

Although Bernard's courtly career kept him at Louis's palace most of the time, he and Dhuoda did have two sons. The first, William, was born on November 29, 826, and it was for him that Dhuoda composed her manual. Less than a year after the birth of William, Bernard had led successful battles for Louis's army. His brilliant victory at the March d'Espagne in 827 secured him in favor.[8] Within two years Bernard was given the second highest position in the realm, chamberlain of the palace at Aix-La-Chapelle. Although unpopular with some at court, he was an important figure in the life of Judith, Louis's young wife.

In 830, some nobles from the court of Pepin, son of Louis and his first wife, informed Louis that Judith and Bernard were lovers. The nobles urged Pepin to punish Bernard and Judith and then to remove Louis from the throne. Louis heard of Pepin's plan and sent Judith to a monastery. Bernard fled to Barcelona to hide from the nobles. Pepin's troops tried to force Louis into a monastery so that Pepin could rule, but Louis's loyal armies rallied to defeat Pepin.

Louis declared Judith an adulteress but did not have her killed. This was due to the decrees of the four reform councils of the church held in 829, which urged reconciliation in cases of adultery. Because Louis had publicly punished men who had killed their adulterous wives, he felt compelled to set an example of a more Christian approach.[9] He forgave Judith and was reconciled to Bernard in 831. Bernard and Pepin were brought before Louis to swear an oath of fealty in 832. When Bernard fought for Louis in Burgundy in 833, he was restored to the office of chamberlain of the palace. In 837, Louis named Bernard the ruler of Septimania, despite the complaints of the aristocracy of Septimania.

Between his various court duties and wars, Bernard visited Dhuoda in 839 or 840. A second son, Bernard, was born on March 22, 841.[10] The infant Bernard was only a few weeks old when Bernard of Septimania summoned the infant to live at the court. A bishop friend took little Bernard to his father. Young Bernard, as well as his older brother, William, would eventually be used to help secure the political ambitions of his father.[11]

These ambitions continued in various directions after Louis's death in 840. The two sons, Pepin and Charles the Bald, were uneasy co-rulers. Bernard had thrown in his lot with Pepin, and served as a counselor to him even as Louis was finishing his last years. Louis discovered the shift in loyalty and stripped Bernard of the titles he had given him. Bernard did well at Pepin's court at Aquitaine, however. When Bernard sent for his infant son to be raised at Aquitaine, it was a tribute to Pepin that secured Bernard in his favor.

Meanwhile Judith, who had been "repenting" for her life at a convent in Poitiers, was released from her religious vows by Pope Gregory IX. Given the situation that led her to the convent, the pope declared her vows null and void. Judith decided to go to Aquitaine with Pepin rather than to the court of Charles the Bald. Once in Pepin's court, she urged Bernard to use his influence with Pepin to force a battle between Charles the Bald and Lothar, who sided with Pepin.

In time the brothers would fight for supremacy. At the Battle of Fontenoy in 841 Pepin and Lothar fought Charles the Bald. Bernard's troops watched the battle from a distance before Bernard decided to enter. Typically, Bernard wanted to wait to see whose troops were going to be victorious before he took sides. When it looked as if Charles would win, Bernard sent his son William to pay homage to Charles and request benefices if his army aided Charles.[12] Charles defeated Pepin and Lothar. He honored Bernard's request but never trusted Bernard after this time.

How much Dhuoda knew about her husband's courtly intrigues cannot be discovered from her manual for William. She does encourage William to be very careful about whom he chooses to be his counselors. This might indicate her awareness that the changing power struggles could be devastating for a young man who formed the wrong alliances. William is close to sixteen at the time Dhuoda completes her manual. She is naturally concerned about the sons that she has not seen in two years.

Through references in her manual we can determine that Dhuoda is writing this book between November 30, 841, and February 2, 843. She says she is beginning the manual on the feast of St. Andrew (November 30) in the second year after the death of Louis the Pious. The manual is written to commemorate William's sixteenth birthday.

Throughout her manual Dhuoda refers to Bernard as "my lord." This title of respect flowed from the perspective that the husband ruled the house "in God's name" just as the king or emperor ruled the nation "in God's name." Augustine, one of Dhuoda's favorite authors, was one source for this perception. Augustine stressed that all humans were made in God's image. A woman, however, was made in God's image in her rational mind but not in her inferior body with its inferior sexual characteristics. Thus, women were subordinate to men "by nature" and could only grow in God's image through the tutelage of their husbands.[13] Dhuoda's references to Bernard as "my lord" do not reveal antipathy toward him for the debts he has forced on her. She is a respectful wife.

Dhuoda's manual reflects a hope and a strong conviction that nothing happens in vain. God has some purpose that will come through all that humans do not quite understand or accept. Although Dhuoda honestly names her disappointments and sorrows, especially in the epitaph, she does not despair of God's love. She urges William to follow her example.

Dhuoda's humility will be noticed in two different ways. First, her claims of inadequacy are typical of women in this period. Second, she acknowledges truthfully that she has certain competencies. Citing 2 Corinthians 11:23, she justifies her ability to teach her son just as Paul justifies his ability to teach. The *Statuta ecclesiae antiqua*, compiled c. 475 by Gennadius of Marseilles, forbade women to teach men and to baptize.[14] Dhuoda asserts boldly that life lived in God's presence can be a source of holy wisdom. The uniqueness of a mother's love provides an additional source of wisdom for guiding one's son, regardless of what church fathers have said to the contrary.[15]

The manual is written for William, but Dhuoda hopes that her loving wisdom will be helpful to many, including her younger son, Bernard. She urges William to guide Bernard and also to share the book as he sees fit. Dhuoda is confident that her teaching is sound and will lead to virtue. She claims an inner authority that is given by God, but does not claim to be a woman who is holy, who is a great mystic, or who is a visionary. Her claims are to the contrary.

She is one who—with her son—is on the journey toward God, with all the searching this implies. Her hope is that William will continue the journey, and help his brother to do the same. She reminds him of his duty to take over any bills that may still be owed after Dhuoda dies. This settling of debts was considered part of the obligations of Christians who hoped for heaven.

Careful reflection on the text will reveal a humble and strong woman struggling against the abandonment of sons and husband. She does not anticipate that she will see her sons in the near future, nor does she know when she will see her husband again. Her hope for the reunion at the end of their common journey carries her through the difficulties of daily responsibilities.

What Dhuoda could not know as she was writing the manual was the tragic end of her husband and of William. In 844, Bernard was beheaded for treason against Charles the Bald. In 848, Pepin of Aquitaine and William, the son for whom the manual is written, were taken as prisoners during the Battle of Spain and then beheaded. Bernard, the remaining son, would eventually be executed as well.

Although Dhuoda's epitaph is written prior to any of these tragedies, it conveys a realism about life's sufferings as well as an underlying hope that this all must have meaning. Courage is needed to accept what cannot be changed, as well as to change what can be changed. Regardless of what happens in life, Dhuoda assures both her son and all who pass by that God's love remains.

Her manual itself is a fruit of her prayer as well as a hope that all who read it may become more aware of God's love. Like many saints, Dhuoda asks all who pass by to remember her in prayer, for she lived her life as best she could in trying circumstances.[16]

Manual for My Son[17]

Prologue

Here begins the manual of Dhuoda. In the name of the Holy Trinity, this book is written for her son, William.

[*In the original manuscript, an acrostic appears here introducing the work and also spelling* DHUODA DILECTFIL JOU VILHELM SALUTE M'LEGE.]

Many things that are clear to many other people are hidden from my understanding. Like myself, others have intelligence that lacks understanding. Yet the wisdom of the One who opens the mouth of the mute and enables the tongues of children to speak is present with me.

Even if I am not as intelligent as many, and even if I am unworthy among women, I am Dhuoda, your mother, and you, William, are my son. It is to you that I send my reflections in this manual. For the moment, chess remains the most habitual and appropriate recreation for young people. Some women are accustomed to habitually looking in the mirror to remove blemishes, refresh their beauty, and thus keep their husbands happy as they are meant to do. In the same habitual way I wish you to read this little book addressed to you so that you will remember me. I am aware of the profusion of worldly activities in which you must engage. But I wish you to read this just as frequently as young people play chess or women look in mirrors.

May you often read this small volume I am sending you, though your own collection of books will increase by many volumes. I pray that you, with the help of the omnipotent God, will grow in deep understanding of this book, since it is for your own good. Whatever you choose to know, you will find in this manual in a short form. In this manual you also have a mirror in which to examine your soul in order to discover not only how to satisfy the world in all things but also how to satisfy the One who has formed you out of clay. William, my son, it is imperative that you be equally competent in matters that lead in both directions; you must be competent in your worldly affairs and also capable of pleasing God in all things.

My son, I have been most careful in composing this word of salvation to you. It has been an ardent and vigilant concern of mine to compose a written account of your birth by God's grace in this manual. Therefore I shall continue as I have previously planned.

In the eleventh year of the reign of Louis, by God's graciousness, I was married to my lord and your father, Bernard. This took place in the palace at Aix-la-Chapelle, the year of five concurrent days on the third calends of July.[18] Two years later, on the third calends of December, you were born through the grace of God.[19] You were my most yearned for, my firstborn son.

The calamities of this unhappy time continued to occur and reached their crest in many fluctuations and battles of fortune in the kingdom. Louis followed the path common to all. During the twenty-eighth year of his reign, before he reached old age, his life ended as a debt to the world.[20] In the year after his death God mercifully enabled your brother, Bernard, to be born in the city of Uzes on the eleventh calends of April.[21] Before he was baptized, thus when he was still an infant, Bernard, my lord and your father, had you both brought to him at Aquitaine.[22] You were accompanied by Bishop Elephantus of Uzes and others of his faithful people.

I remained in that city a long time, separated from both you and your brother by the command of my lord and your father. He was already rejoicing at his public combat. I decided to lessen my grief due to my separation from you by writing this small book which I now send to you. It is written with the understanding that is now mine.

1:1. On the Love of God

Not only the choirs of heaven but also every creature who walks on the earth and moves toward heaven ought to praise God. I challenge, you my son, along with all who are worthy and capable of loving God, to search eagerly for God with all your strength, and to scale the summit. May you be strong like them in attaining the kingdom that will never end.

I speak to you now as if I were with you and in the presence of those who may read this book because you offer it to them. From the height of your nobility and youthfulness, do not condemn or reproach me for daring to address written words about God to you. I have not undertaken this casually, knowing it demands sharpness of mind. I know better than anyone else how human and frail I am. I am but dust and ashes and reproach myself unceasingly. I am aware that patriarchs, prophets, and all the other saints from the creation until now could not fully understand the pattern of holy things. Insignificant and of low birth as I am, how can I hope to understand these things? What am I capable of saying about the mystery of God when the Scriptures say that even the heavens cannot contain the greatness of God?

Genesis says that Moses wanted to see the Lord face to face, after having an intimate conversation with God. "If I have found favor in your sight," Moses said, "show yourself to me that I might see you." But God said, "You cannot see my face, because no one can see me and continue to live." If it is like this for Moses on the heights, what can you expect from someone like me upon the earth? My soul grows very feeble thinking on this, for I have no such vision. Yet feeling burns in my mind.

1:2. On the Search for God

My son, we must both search for God since we live in the will of God. It is in God that we live and move and have our being. I seek the Lord in order to be strong, for of myself I am as unworthy and inconsequential as a shadow. It is absolutely necessary for me to ask the Lord's help unceasingly so that I might know and understand. Even a problematic puppy, who sits under the master's table with the others, can often succeed in catching and eating the crumbs that fall from the master's table. The One who could make the mouth of dumb animals speak with understanding is indeed most powerful.

This Lord who prepares a table in the desert for faithful followers and gives them a measure of wheat to fulfill their needs, can also satisfy my desires as a handmaid of the Lord from that goodness. Within the holy church I am at least under the table, able to watch the small dogs there (that is, the ministers of the holy altars) even if it is at a distance. But I can still collect crumbs of spiritual understanding from under that table. Such crumbs of beautiful, valuable, and clear insights are appropriate both for you and for me. I am sure of this, for our God does not abandon the poor in spirit.

The Lord, here and everywhere, remains the same now as in times past and in the future. All that is good and profitable originates and is completed in our God. For the Lord says, "I am the alpha and omega," as well as, "I am who am." "The One who is sent me," says Scripture. There are many more examples.

1:3. The Greatness of God

My son William, our God is great above all. The holy One knows the high and mighty, the proud who are from afar, and looks with favor on the lowly. God withdraws from the mighty and raises up the weak. With compassion the Lord lowers himself to descend to the humble, to those in need. Therefore, frequently acknowledge your own need for God so that you may always be raised up by the Lord. The Lord alone knows our weaknesses and evils. For Scripture says, "The eyes of the Lord look down upon the children of the earth to see if there is one who is wise enough to seek the mystery." Yes, our God knows all our actions from the rising of the sun until its setting.

This means not only each day, but our lifetime, from the moment of our birth until the last moment of our death. "From the first light of morning until the evening" also means that the Lord watches over all people who have ever lived, from the moment of the first formed Adam until the last moment when the last person will die at the end of the world. God knows everything that humans in their weakness think, say, and do. The holy One recognizes the chosen ones among the multitudes and gathers them from the lowest and highest places to give them the kingdom. The Lord rewards all of those who fight for riches that last. Each is awarded according to the individual merits.

1:4. The Unfathomable Mystery of God

The apostle Paul says that no mortal being has ever yet been able to comprehend fully the sublimity and greatness of God. "Oh, the height of the riches and wisdom and knowledge of God. How incomprehensible are the judgments and how unsearchable are the ways of the Lord" (Rom 11:33). "For who has known the mind of the Lord, or who can be God's counselor" (Rom 11:34; 1 Cor 2:16)? "Who in the heavens is like the Lord or who can be equal to God" (Ps 138:7)? The answer is clearly no one. Why? Because God alone knows the hearts of human children and is the most high over all the earth.

I may be as fragile as a shadow, yet I shall lead you now into whatever depth of understanding you may attain, my son. I am not capable of offering you a perfectly logical lecture even if it were appropriate for me to do so. Instead, I will compose a work that imitates a learned lecture by assembling the most useful ideas for you.

1:5. Only God Remains

I exhort you to constantly meditate upon the words of the holy Gospels and the writings of the fathers concerning wisdom, daily actions, and bodily senses.

If you think, speak, and act rightly, you shall believe the triune nature of the everlasting God, who remains one in trinity and triune in unity. No one can measure the mystery of God. Scripture affirms that God is the One whom the morning stars and all the children of the earth joyfully praise with one voice. God alone measured and laid the foundations of the earth, enclosed the sea, and covered it with clouds (Job 38:4–5, 8–9).

This God who rules over all things with power can bring you to the height of perfection, forever nourishing and increasing you in the divine image and likeness. After reflecting upon the great mystery of God, who and what God is, you shall finally acknowledge that you cannot fully understand the Lord or find another equal to God. Then by this very unknowing you shall begin to know that this is God. As a poet said, God is the one "who commanded and they were created, who spoke and everything was fashioned, heaven and earth, underwater depths, and the orbit of the sun and the moon" (Ps 104).

In this world we speak and think about all things in relation to our power and purposes. This is not the true reality of things. For example, after struggling hard, someone in the world may confidently assert, "the kingdom is mine" or refer to "my whole kingdom." This person has not yet stopped to consider the reality that the kingdom and all else that is passing belongs to the Lord. The unbelieving and wicked Nabuchodonosor, when he was defeated and left prostrate, finally gained true understanding. For at last he observed, "God alone is the King who governs and rules over all. God alone has the power to raise up whomsoever the holy One chooses and to bring down those who walk in pride. The kingdom belongs to this God, who alone can give it to whomsoever is chosen by the Lord" (Deut 3:22–24; 4:31).

Another person may claim, "The earth is mine." This person does not consider carefully the words of the psalmist: "The earth is the Lord's. The birds of the air and the fish of the sea belong to him. God gives the birds the air and the food in the forest and the fish are given the pathways of the sea. The ends of the earth are in the hands of the Lord, who rules and directs all that dwell therein" (Ps 8:9). Quite contrary to this, we on earth may claim, "This is mine, all of it." This is partially true, of course, because it is and it isn't. Some things will pass away and some will remain. Earthly things belong to someone for a little while but not forever. In due time such things shall pass away.

There are many stories that I have heard and known about my ancestors and yours, my son. Some of them behaved as if they were all-powerful in the world, but they were not. Perhaps because of their good works they are with God. However, they are no longer held as important by the world. For them as well as for others, I say the prayer for the dead upon my knees. Although I may be thought of as the least important in my family, I have the wisdom to know that which is to come to us all through loss and in death.

Only God, the all-powerful and forever undiminished Lord, is the one to be feared, loved, and believed in as the immortal One. The Lord alone rules and does whatever is desired. Indeed, all things are established in the will and power of the Lord. There is no one who can resist the will of the Lord by complaining, "Why have you done this?" To the God of the universe belong power and reign and glory. Daniel spoke with assurance of that power. "The power of God is an eternal power which may not be taken away. The kingdom of the Lord will not be destroyed" (Dan 7:14). There are many similar affirmations.

1:6. Integrity or Goodness

Fragile vessel of the earth that I am, what more can I add? I am already on the way to death, a companion to all those who have already gone before me. The greatness, the height, the depth, and the width of the sublime and all-powerful God can never be fathomed by all of humankind taken together. Even if the heavens and the earth were like a giant leaf of parchment unrolled into the air and all the curved bridges on the world were sharpened as pens and dipped into different inks, and even if all the people born into all the different cultures of the world were to be made into the most brilliant of writers, which is clearly impossible, they would still be unable to capture the mystery of God.

They could not tell of the richness, knowledge, piety, and infinite mercy of the Lord. Because our Lord is so great that no one can grasp the mystery, I urge you to fear and love this Lord with your whole soul, your whole intellect, and in all that you do and say. I, Dhuoda, your mother, urge you to say repeatedly, "My God, you are good and your mercy remains forever."

Believe that God is above you, below you, within, and outside of you, for our God is everywhere, within and without. God is the reality above because the Lord presides over us and rules us all. God is on high, as the psalmist says, because the glory of the Lord is above the heavens (Ps 8:2). God is the foundation of all because the Lord bears us all. In God alone we live and move. In God, we have our being and make our stand. God is the interior reality because we are filled with the good things of the Lord. As the Scriptures say, we are filled to satisfaction. "The earth is filled with the fruit of your works" (Ps 103:13).

The Scripture also proclaims, "and every creature is filled with your blessing" (Ps 104:27).The Lord is the reality around us because the impregnable wall of God surrounds us all. We are secure, protected, and defended by our God. It has been written that the love of the Lord protects us as a wall and a shield. This describes my faith. Blessed be God forever. I, your mother, have faith that far exceeds the limits and poverty of my understanding.

My beautiful and lovable son William, I encourage you not to be reluctant to acquire many books by the most holy doctors and by your teachers. These should help you discern and understand more about God and instill deeper ideas about God our creator than what I have written. Beg for this learning, choose it, and love it. If you do this, it will be many things for you. Learning shall be a guardian, a leader, your companion and your homeland, the way, the truth, and the life. Learning will bring you great prosperity in the world and help your enemies to be converted to peace.

In addition, you must gird your loins like a man, as Job has written. You should be humble in heart, chaste in body, and upright in your grandeur. Adorn yourself with splendor. Always know that I, Dhuoda, your orator, shall always be here for you, my son. When I leave you in death, as will certainly happen, you will have this manual as a memorial.

By reading this manual and by praying to God, you will be able to behold my body and mind, as in a mirror. You will find the duties you owe me upon death detailed in this book. You will have many teachers, my son. They will offer you instructions that are longer and more useful. But no other teacher will give you instructions like mine in character, nor with such a burning heart as I, your mother, lovingly give you, my firstborn son.

Read these words that I send you, understand them, and put them into practice. When your little brother has received the grace of Christ in baptism, I ask you to not be reluctant to instruct, support, and love him. Challenge him always to go from the good to the better. When he is of an age to speak well and to read, show him this bound copy of the manual that I have put together and in which I have written your name. I, your mother, urge you both to do this as if you were near and already able to respond.

At least from time to time, lift up your hearts from among the burdens and cares of this life. Keep your eyes on God who reigns in heaven. Unworthy as I am to speak of God so often, may this Lord make you happy and joyous at this present moment, along with your father, my master and lord, Bernard. May everything you do prosper. And after the journey of this life is finished, may you enter rejoicing into the heaven of the holy ones. Amen.

2:1. Faith, Hope, and Charity

My son, there are three virtues that will order your life, though love is the most precious of these three. Love survives the changing times and seasons that come and go. However, hope is necessary for us now. Faith requires this hope. This is because our lives are lived within the realms of the visible and the invisible.

What the apostle says is true. Although there are these three, faith, hope, and charity, the greatest of these is charity (1 Cor 13). While you are on earth, my son, work to acquire the virtue of heaven. To know joy in this world, we must pray to live now as if the future were already here. As the psalmist says,

"My eyes are turned to you, O God, in you I take refuge. Do not strip me from life" (Ps 141:8).

Lead a life of prayer even in the midst of your troubles. If you believe that God will be your help, God indeed will guide you and be good to you. Hope in God and all will come out well in the end. Return to God as often as you can and ask for help. Our God is ever near. As the psalmist says, "Put your trust in the Lord and do good.... Be still before the Lord and wait patiently for him.... Take delight in the Lord who will give you your heart's desire" (Ps 37:3, 7, 4).

Take delight in the Lord, and make your petitions with a sincere heart. If you do this, my son, and reflect upon the greatness and goodness of God, you will know joy. Pray this prayer often, "Your love, O God, reaches to the heavens.... Continue your loving kindness to those who know you and your favor to those who are true of heart" (Ps 36:5, 10).

I pray that you will believe so that you can know the mystery of the most sublime Trinity. Live your faith, grow through hope, and live in the love that is God.

10:4. The Sweetness of My Love and Self-Forgetfulness

I have put my interests aside because of the greatness of my love for you and my desire to see your beauty, my son. But now, I will enter again within myself, "closing the doors." Even if I am not worthy to be counted among the saints, nevertheless I ask that you include me in that number through affection. I ask you to pray unceasingly for the healing of my soul.

You probably know that my continual infirmities and certain other circumstances have led me to bear many hardships. These sufferings are in accord with the sentiments of the one who said, "I am in danger from my own nation, and in danger from Gentiles." I have had to bear similar things, though being both weak in body and lacking the merit I need. Through the power of your father, Bernard, and with God's help, I have confidently escaped many dangers.

However, there were times when I was overcome by things beyond my control. I was negligent in divine praise, and what I ought to have done during the seven liturgical hours, I did quite haphazardly seven times seventy times. With all my strength I beg you to pray joyfully, and with sincere petitions, that God will have mercy on all my offenses and negligences. Pray that the Lord will deign to raise my broken and saddened spirit to the heights.

With a vigilant heart be zealous in your vigils and prayers as well as in giving alms to the poor while you know that I am still alive. This you should do so that I can be freed bodily from the chain of my sins, and deserve to be received by the merciful judge without reservation and with great kindness.

Your frequent prayer and the frequent prayer of others for me are necessary now. The prayers will be even more necessary after what is soon to take place. My spirit is upset with great fear and sadness about what might happen to me in the future. I am uncertain about how I may be freed at the end. Why? Because I know I have sinned in thought and word. Useless speech itself leads to sinful action. Yet, though all this may be true, I will never despair of God's mercy. I don't despair now and I never will despair. I know that at some future time I will eventually regain God's mercy because I have a son like you. No one will struggle on my behalf as you will, noble son, and as your noble descendants will also.

My lord and master, Bernard, has left me weighed down with heavy debts. I took on these debts so that I might not fail in my feudal obligation to him. As he led the march and went to many other places, I took over his debts so that he would not separate himself from me and from you as so many other men have done. I have frequently borrowed a great deal of money from the hands of both Jews and Christians because I was in such need. I have paid back as much as I can, and I will continue to do so. However, if something is still owed after my death, I now beg you to search out my debtors diligently. When you have found them, pay them back for absolutely everything. With God's help pay them not only from my estate if anything remains, but also from what you have or may justly acquire.

Is there more? Yes, there is. Although I have urged you to look after your little brother before, now I ask you again. If he grows to maturity, may he also deign to pray for me. I feel as if I have already exhorted both of you together to have the frequent pouring out of sacrifices and offering of the Mass for me.

When the Redeemer summons me from this world, may he have a place of refreshment prepared for me. May God, the all-holy One, have me pass over with the saints to the eternal kingdom. May this come to be through your prayers as well as the worthy prayers of others.

May this be the word of God. This work is finished here. Amen. Thanks be to God.

10:5. The Names of Relatives

Here are the names of certain deceased persons omitted from those named above. They are: William, Cunegunda, Gerberg, Withburg, Thierry, Guacelm, Warner, Rothlind.

There are some from your genealogy who are still alive with God's grace. It is the business of him who created them as he wished to call them when he desires. For them, my son, we can only say with the psalmist, "We who are living, we bless the Lord, now and forever."

When someone related to you dies, it happens only with the power of God and when the Lord orders it. This is the case with your uncle, Lord Heribert. If you survive him, order that his name be written into the list transcribed above so that he might be prayed for.

10:6. The Epitaph for My Tomb

Please have my name written on the list of the dead when I die. On the stone covering the tomb that marks my burial place, I beseech you with all my strength to order the following verses be deeply inscribed. I deeply wish this so that all who see this epitaph will pour out worthy prayers to God for me, for I am so unworthy.

Also, if someone reads this manual that you now read, let all meditate on the words that follow. In so doing may they commend me to God, that I might be released. Even as I write this, I already feel as if I were enclosed within a tomb.

Reader, read here the verses of my epitaph:

> Thrown here in this mound of earth, is
> the earthly body of Dhuoda, formed from the earth.
> Receive her, infinite King,
> as the earth has received her fragile clay
> into its depths.
> Pardon her, gracious King.
>
> She is bathed from her wounds; only the tomb remains
> with its absolute darkness.
> O King, absolve her sins.
>
> All of you of every age and sex, who pass by here,
> I ask you to pray this prayer.
> O Great and Holy One, remove her chains.
>
> She ended life with a piercing, deep, and serious wound.
> She was entombed in bitterness.
> O King, forgive her sins.
>
> Let not the evil serpent seize her soul.
> Praying will you please say this:
> Merciful God, come to her aid.
>
> Let no one pass by until this is read.
> I conjure all of you to pray, saying:
> Loving God, give her rest.
>
> O most compassionate God, order perpetual light
> to wash her so that she is with the saints at the end.
> May she receive the "Amen" after the funeral rites.

NOTES

1. Edward James, *The Origins of France* (New York: St. Martin's Press, 1982) 49–92, 157–70.

2. 789, *Admonitio generalis* 76. *Monumenta Germaniae historica*. Legum sectio 2: Capitularia Regum Francorum. 1, 60 829, *Conc. Parisiense* 45. Legum Sectio III: Concilia 2, 639.

3. A detailed list of wives, concubines, and children can be found in *Son of Charlemagne*, trans. Allen Cabaniss (Syracuse: Syracuse University Press, 1961) 135, n. 5.

4. *Son of Charlemagne* provides a clear and detailed picture of the life and times of Louis the Pious.

5. An eighth-century *L'histoire littéraire de la France* (Paris: 1740), vol. 5, 17, made this claim, which was first contested by Migne, *Patrologia Latina* 106:109–18. The error was then corrected in a later edition of the history in vol. 2, 274, col. 2, n. 2.

6. The *Manual de Dhuoda* can be found in *Acta sanctorum* (1877), saec. 4, pars 1, 750–57; Migne, *Patrologia Latina* 106:109–18; also in Pierre Riche, Bernard de Vregille, and Claude Mondesert, eds., *Manuel pour mon fils*, Sources chrétiennes, no. 225 (Paris: Éditions du Cerf, 1975) 84–359.

7. Dhuoda, *Manuel pour mon fils / Dhuoda; introduction, texte critique, notes*. Sources chrétiennes, no. 225, 350–52.

8. James, *The Origins of France* 160–70.

9. Suzanne Wemple, *Women in Frankish Society* (Philadelphia: University of Pennsylvania Press, 1981). This well-documented work uses primary sources to detail social and ecclesial laws as well as conflicts of this period; see esp. 76–88.

10. Prologue, Sources chrétiennes, no. 225, 45–49.

11. Wemple, *Women in Frankish Society* 89–97.

12. Allen Cabaniss, "The Woes of Dhuoda, or France's First Woman of Letters," *Mississippi Quarterly* 11:1 (Winter 1958) 38–49.

13. *Ancient Christian Writers*, trans. John Hammond Taylor (New York: Newman, 1982) vol. 41, 99, 175.

14. The Apostolic Constitutions had also claimed this in the late fourth century; see *Constitutiones Apostolorum* 3.6, 3.9 in Migne, *Patrologia Graeca* 1:782, 798; also *Statuta ecclesiae antiqua* 37, 41, 100 in Corpus Christianorum, Series Latina, vol. 148, 172, 173, 184.

15. Wemple, *Women in Frankish Society* 127–48.

16. Edouard Bondurand traces the history, translations, and authenticity of three manuscripts of Dhuoda's manual in *Le Manuel de Dhuoda*, trans. Edouard Bondurand (Paris: Picard, 1887).

17. *Manuel pour mon fils*, Sources chrétiennes, no. 225, 45–49; 84–87; 96–117; 122–25; 349–59. A more literal translation from portions of the Latin text can be found in Marie Anne Mayeski, *Women: Models of Liberation* (New York: Sheed and Ward, 1988) 41–53; also James Marchand, *Medieval Women Writers*, ed. Katharina Wilson (Athens: University of Georgia Press, 1984) 12–26.

18. June 29, 824.

19. November 29, 826.

20. June 20, 840.

21. March 22, 841.

22. This occurred in 841.

BIBLIOGRAPHY

Cabaniss, Allen, trans. *Son of Charlemagne.* Syracuse: Syracuse University Press, 1961.

Cabaniss, Allen. "The Woes of Dhuoda, or France's First Woman of Letters." *Mississippi Quarterly* 11:1 (Winter 1958) 38–49.

James, Edward. *The Origins of France: From Clovis to the Capetians, 500–1000.* New York: St. Martin's Press, 1982.

McNamara, Jo Ann, and Suzanne Wemple. "Marriage and Divorce in the Frankish Kingdom." In *Women in Medieval Society.* Edited by Susan Mosher Stuard. Philadelphia: University of Pennsylvania Press, 1976. 95–124.

McNamara, Jo Ann, and Suzanne Wemple. "Sanctity and Power: The Dual Pursuit of Medieval Women." In *Becoming Visible: Women in European History.* Edited by Renate Bridenthal and Claudia Koonz. Boston: Houghton-Mifflin, 1977. 90–118.

Marchand, James. "The Frankish Mother: Dhuoda." In *Medieval Women Writers.* Edited by Katharina M. Wilson. Athens: University of Georgia Press, 1984. 1–29.

Mayeski, Marie Anne. *Women: Models of Liberation.* New York: Sheed and Ward, 1988. 31–56.

Riché, Pierre, Bernard de Vregille, and Claude Mondesert. *Manuel pour mon fils,* Sources chrétiennes, no. 225. Paris: Éditions du Cerf, 1975.

Wemple, Suzanne. *Women in Frankish Society.* Philadelphia: University of Pennsylvania Press, 1981.

– 6 –

HILDEGARD OF BINGEN

(1098–1179)

Love Overflows into All Things

Hildegard of Bingen was born near the end of the eleventh century. Two particular currents of that century would continue to affect her life and times.

First, efforts to reform and renew the church and its clergy would continue, although there was a renewed fervor and stability of the people. Second, power clashes between church and civil rulers would continue, although some partial resolutions were achieved during this century.

The efforts at church reform fostered by Pope Gregory VII (in 1073–85) achieved certain positive results. This Benedictine pope could effect reforms in the church because Emperor Otto I allowed monasteries, churches, and cathedrals to be independent of civil rulers. Gregory VII had tried to restore some order to chaotic situations both within the church and within the larger society. His plans for the church included clerical and monastic reforms.

He forbade the clergy to marry and punished both clergy and nobility for selling or buying church offices. Gregory's monastic reforms included liturgical renewal and closer observance of the rule of life. He also desired to integrate the laity into the church's worship life, a goal that was not appreciated by most people. Although this desire led to some liturgical reforms, the language of liturgy was no longer understood by the majority of laity. Consequently, a more privatized devotional spirituality continued to grow.

The long history of power struggles between Roman pontiffs and civil or national rulers could not be resolved during the pontificate of Gregory VII and would continue well into the twelfth century.[1] Gregory VII tried to impose the theological reasoning that emanated from the Pseudo-Dionysian construct of reality. The attempts were not fully successful, although future church hierarchies and theologians would interiorize this perception as foundational to their reflections. An overview of the construct might assist the reader in understanding the worldview that continued its influential hold for centuries.

The Pseudo-Dionysian construct used the heavenly order (the celestial hierarchy) as an ideal model for the earthly order (the ecclesiastical hierarchy). The construct assumed that people were not socially equal. Because God caused people to be born into particular classes, the social inequality of clergy, nobility, or commons was perceived as God's will.[2] To imitate heavenly peace, the earthly society had to order these inequalities so that all might know their place in the social order. Staying in one's place was "holy," since this ensured peace in society.

The higher estates of clergy and nobility were closest to God's light and love. These higher groups mediated love, wisdom, and light to the lower groups. The lower groups owed obedience and love to successively higher groups. The higher groups owed the lower groups love but not obedience, since the former, being closer to the top, were wiser. Jesus Christ was at the top of the heavenly order, whereas the pope was at the top of the ecclesiastical order. In diagram form, the construct looked like the following.[3]

Celestial Hierarchy	**Ecclesiastical Hierarchy**
JESUS CHRIST	ROMAN POPE
First Choir of Angels	*The Sacraments*
Seraphim	Eucharist/Body of Christ
Cherubim	Unction
Thrones	Baptism
Second Choir of Angels	*The Clergy*
Dominations	Bishop—perfecting order
Virtues	Priest—illuminating order
Powers	Deacon—purifying order
Third Choir of Angels	*The Laity*
Principalities	Monks—perfected order
Archangels	Contemplatives—illumined order
Guardian Angels	Catechumens/Penitents—in need of purification

Since many clergy of this time were nobility, the order of the clergy and the order of nobility were seen as equal in the eyes of the nobility. The clergy did not look at it in that fashion. Clergy, including Pope Gregory VII, put clergy at the top and nobility beneath them. This caused dissension for two basic reasons.

First, there was a history of kings and queens effecting reforms in the church as well as in society during the ages when rulers looked on themselves as God's representatives on earth. The royalty had also known a history of appointing bishops and lesser clergy to their tasks in the kingdom. The church was a vehicle of the empire, not vice versa, in their eyes.

As Gregory VII assumed a plenitude of power over the ecclesiastical hierarchy and was perceived as "Christ's vicar on earth," he was fostering an image that rulers opposed. Christian kings and queens felt they were Christ's vicars on earth.

Gregory VII had theologians who could argue for the supremacy of pope over emperor or king. The argument was based on the notion of jurisdiction or ordering of society. The pope, not the king, had jurisdiction over the church universal, the monasteries and convents of the world, the bishops and the other clergy, and the laity. Although jurisdiction was a spiritual power, Gregory reasoned that temporal power was necessarily a manifestation of spiritual power. This was the general interpretation after 1216. By 1250, jurisdiction was considered to be a power residing in the office of bishop, but as given or delegated through the universal jurisdiction of the Bishop of Rome.[4]

Gregory VII believed the unification of the world in Christ would only be accomplished if the universal pope were the ultimate authority. Nationalistic emperors, kings, or queens were too occupied with their own nation's well-being to be considered universal rulers. The theory of papal supremacy over royal supremacy seemed to have validity in a period that had seen multiple wars between groups and nations vying for power. However, tensions continued over this matter well into the twelfth century, the century in which Hildegard of Bingen lived her adult life.

Hildegard was born in 1098, into a noble family at Bermersheim. Very little is known of her childhood. Her parents brought her to the anchoress Jutta of Spanheim for instruction when Hildegard was about seven years old. Jutta's cell or living space was attached to the Benedictine monastery of Disibodenberg. Liturgical services could be prayed in the cell or living space. These prayers could be prayed with the monastic community, for their prayer was able to be heard. Spiritual direction would be made available through the monks as well. Some fasting, some disciplined instruction about prayer, appropriate manual labor, and reflection on the Scriptures were part of Hildegard's daily routine as Jutta directed.[5]

Hildegard acknowledges that her visions began in childhood, although she did not speak of them when she was a child. Later she recounts that her visions came while she was mentally awake.[6] At fifteen she decided to follow the Benedictine way of life. Other women came to join Jutta and Hildegard, and so the monastery of Disibodenberg became a double monastery. Jutta died in 1136, and Hildegard was chosen to be her successor as overseer of the nuns. It was not till five years after the death of Jutta that Jesus Christ told Hildegard she was to write and preach about her visions.[7]

The thought of this filled her with fear. She was finally convinced by her monk friend, Vollmar, to write down the visions. When she did this, the illnesses connected with the visions ceased. Hildegard's visions filled her with a gamut of emotions—from wonder to terror, from exultation to a fear of mortality, and from glory to a sense of useless pride. She was taught theology through her visions rather than from a disciplined study, for women were not allowed to study theology in universities. Her anthropology, typical of the time, saw humans at the center of the universal web of life. She claimed an authority as Christ instructed her to claim it. Her prophetic voice, her preaching activities, and her teachings were eventually verified by church leaders in spite of the prohibitions against women teaching men.[8]

Hildegard's first visionary work, *Know the Ways* (the *Scivias*), was in still in process during the Synod of Trier in 1147. The *Scivias* would not be completed until 1152, but her friends, Archbishop Henry of Mainz and Bernard of Clairvaux, asked Pope Eugenius III to review the work. Eugenius read a portion of it to the bishops at the Synod of Trier, and it was quickly acclaimed.

Hildegard's recognition as a prophet grew rapidly after this. More women came to join her community at Disibodenberg, making it necessary to move to a new place. There was some opposition to this by the abbot of Disibodenberg. However, Hildegard had a vision that predicted evil days would fall on the monastery if the women weren't allowed to leave. Her letters to the abbot make this quite clear.[9] The nuns moved to Rupertsberg near Bingen in 1150 with Hildegard as their abbess.

Hildegard's role as abbess of Bingen brought her into ever widening circles of relationships. She corresponded with at least four popes, Eugenius III (1145–53), Anastasius IV (1153–54), Adrian IV (1154–59), and Alexander III (1159–81).[10] She also exchanged correspondence with the German emperor Frederick I (Barbarossa or red beard), Bernard of Clairvaux, and Elisabeth of Schönau.[11] The volume of letters to so many people indicates her breadth of influence as a prophetic visionary and discerner of hearts.

But Hildegard's prayerful life, her preaching tours, and her letters to popes and prelates did not reform the church. She saw a dozen popes and ten antipopes during her lifetime. She also witnessed continual tensions between Frederick and Adrian IV over the power to invest bishops with ring and crozier.[12] In 1178–79, Hildegard had a confrontation with the clergy of Mainz, the diocese within which Bingen was located.

The clergy of Mainz claimed that an excommunicant had been buried on the monastery property and that the body should be removed from the sacred ground. Hildegard said the man had been reconciled to the church before died. The clergy said that there was still a ban of excommunication, so the body had to be exhumed and buried elsewhere. Hildegard decided to conceal the grave. The bishop then put the convent under interdict, which meant that the nuns could not sing the divine office or receive communion or any other sacrament. Hildegard's letter to the clerics and bishop of Mainz asks that the interdict be lifted, for she had a vision of evil overtaking the convent if the body of the dead man were taken away.[13]

When the clerics did not change their position, Hildegard called in her friend, the powerful Archbishop Philip of Cologne, to go to Mainz and plead her case. The archbishop took a knight with him who claimed to have been absolved at the same time as the dead man. Archbishop Philip lifted the interdict, as did the archbishop of Mainz. Hildegard's friends were very true to her, a fact that made many of her time say she was someone that one would like as a friend, but definitely not as an enemy.

Hildegard's intense mystical and visionary life did not keep her secluded in her convent. She undertook four preaching tours of Germany in the years 1159, 1160, 1163, and 1170. The volume and range of works attributed to her reflect an intelligence that extended through many disciplines of that time. In addition to the *Scivias*, she completed two further books of visions, the *Book of Life's Merits* and the *Book of Divine Works*.[14]

Hildegard's visionary theology and cosmology reflect the anthropology of her age. Her perspective asserts that all creation is somehow contained in humanity, and humanity in turn leaves its outlines on all of creation. There is a pastoral concern about the human orientation toward the love of God. Love is the base of all that is, for creation itself takes place through the love of God. The Christocentric perspective of creation through the Word is summed up in the cosmic Christ in whom all remain. Creation is brilliant with divine life and reveals the God who cannot be seen.

There is a "greenness" or life power that appears frequently in the works of Hildegard. This greenness is a spark of God's life and love manifest in all creation. Greenness is like the earthly expression of the heavenly in an integrity that overcomes dualisms. Jesus Christ is the "green" wood that caused all greening power to flood the earth and human life.[15]

Hildegard's love of music and skill at musical composition are evident in many of her liturgical antiphons and hymns. Her songs and morality play, *The Play of the Virtues*, are a tribute to her musical skills.[16] Her medical and scientific works are available under a number of different titles, the two most common being included in *The Subtleties of the Divine Nature of Created Things*.[17] She claims to be an unlearned woman, yet her *Vita* tells of varieties of medical advice she gave and various cures from exorcisms that she herself enacted.[18]

Her friendship with Richardis, a sister who recorded many of Hildegard's visions, shows her warm human nature. Shortly after the move to Rupertsberg, Richardis, as was her niece Adelheid, was elected abbess of another Benedictine convent. Richardis was to go to the Benedictine convent of Bassum in the diocese of Bremen, where her brother was the archbishop. Adelheid was to be abbess of Gandersheim and later of Quedlinburg. Hildegard tried to dissuade

Richardis from leaving. She even appealed to the mother of Richardis, to the archbishop of Mainz, and to Eugenius III to block the appointment. When these failed, she appealed to Archbishop Hartwig, Richardis's brother, to beg her to return to Rupertsberg. Richardis died suddenly, and her brother wrote to say that she had intended to return. He also confessed to Hildegard, whom he knew to be a good friend to Richardis, that it was his fault she had left Bingen in the first place. Hildegard's response is a letter that expresses her love and forgiveness and also justifies her position by saying the Lord had given her a vision about Richardis.[19]

Although Hildegard is in many ways a woman of her own time, she represents a creativity in her interpretation of theology. On the one hand, she felt that her monastery should not allow novices who were from a different class than nobility because it could put them in an inferior position. On the other hand, in her reflections on the equality of men and women, she insists that "woman may be made from man, but no man can be made without woman."[20]

Hildegard referred to her time as an "effeminate age." She felt that because so many men had become fearful or "womanish," God would make women strong or "virile." In a letter to a negligent bishop, Hildegard described a vision of pure knowledge as a female figure dressed in the bishop's pallium. This could have been a representation of Hildegard herself in her role as prophet to those who ought to have been prophetic.

When Hildegard of Bingen died on September 17, 1179, her sisters claimed that two streams of light appeared in the skies and crossed over the room in which she was dying. During her life she was marked by her visions of light. In her dying, it seemed she was marked by the same eternal light. When a commission was set up to seek witnesses for her canonization, other sisters said there was often the illumination of the Holy Spirit as she walked through the cloisters chanting one of her favorite liturgical compositions.[21]

Regardless of the scientific truth of that witness, the works of Hildegard testify to a holy leader in an age of turmoil. Her works and music continue to be appreciated today. The brief selections that follow are from her visionary works, which she composed in three major parts.

Part One focuses on God the creator and contains six visions in which is depicted the relationship of various aspects of creation to God. Vision 4 of this first part depicts humanity and life. The last three parts of the vision (4.27, 4.28, and 4.29) are included here because they give the reader a brief glimpse of the theological anthropology of Hildegard.

Part Two of the visions depicts the mystery of Jesus Christ, fully God and fully human, who brought saving love to the world. There are seven major visions of this second part, each with subdivisions. Vision 2 describes the coming and meaning of the Word. Since Jesus Christ, the "sapphire man," is often artistically depicted in illustrations of Hildegard's works, visions 2:2, 2:3, and 2:4 have been chosen because they set forth part of Hildegard's theology of the incarnation as an expression of love.

Part Three continues with the centrality of the human mystery and the love of Christ, concluding with a heavenly setting that represents the final liberation in Christ Jesus. The thirteen visions, the sum of the visions of Parts One and Two, point to the happy resolution of the world in Christ. Part Three focuses on the Holy Spirit, who empowers the world toward the final fulfillment in Christ. Vision 13 is also the earliest liturgical morality play in existence, *Ordo virtutum* or *The Play of the Virtues.* It was composed between 1141 and 1151. Hildegard set this play to music and it is still available to us. Visions 13:10, 13:11, 13:12, 13:14, and 13:16 provide a hint of Hildegard's musical sensitivity as well as insight into the joy of the heavenly celebration of the holy ones.

Scivias by Hildegard of Bingen[22]

The Beginning of the Book[23]

Here Begins the Book: May you know of upright humanity.

Here begins the First Part of the Book: May you know proof of the truthfulness of the visions flowing from God.

Behold, in the forty-third year of my passing journey, when I clung to a heavenly vision with fear and trembling, I saw a very great light from which a heavenly voice spoke and said to me:

> O weak person, both ashes of ashes and decaying of the decaying, speak and write what you see and hear. Because you are timid about speaking and simple about explaining and unskilled about writing those things, speak and write those things not according to the mouth of a person nor according to the perception of human inventiveness nor according to the wishes of human arrangement. But speak and write according to the extent that you see and hear those things in the heavens above in the marvelousness of God, bring to light those things by way of explanation, just as even a listener, understanding the words of a teacher, explains those things according to the course of the teacher's speech—willingly, plainly, and instructively. So therefore even you, O person, speak those things which you see and hear; and write those things not according to yourself nor according to another person, but according to the will of the one knowing, see and arrange all things in the secrets of the divinity's own mysteries.

A second time I heard a heavenly voice speak and say to me:

> Speak therefore these marvelous things and write and speak those things taught in this manner.

In the year 1141 of the incarnation of Jesus Christ the Word of God, when I was forty-two years and seven months old, a burning light coming from heaven poured into my mind. Like a flame which does not burn but rather enkindles, it inflamed my heart and my breast, just as the sun warms something with its rays. And I was able to understand books suddenly, the psaltery clearly, the evangelists and the volumes of the Old and New Testament, but I did not have the interpretations of the words of their texts nor the division of their syllables nor the knowledge of their grammar. Previously, though, I had felt within myself the gift of secret mysteries and wondrous visions from the time I was a little girl, certainly from the time I was five years old right up to the present time.

I revealed my gift to no one except to a select few and some religious who were living in my area, and I concealed my gift continuously in quiet silence until God wished it to be manifest by God's own grace. I truly saw those visions; I did not perceive them in dreams, nor while sleeping, nor in a frenzy, nor with the human eyes nor with the external ears of a person, nor in remote places; but I received those visions according to the will of God while I was awake and alert with a clear mind, with innermost eyes and ears of a person, and in open places. There may be a reason why I received those visions in this manner, but it is difficult for a human person to understand why. But after I had passed through the turning point of young womanhood, when I had arrived at the beginning of the age of perfect fortitude, I again heard a heavenly voice speaking to me:

> I, the living light and the obscured illumination, appointed the person whom I wished, wondrously according to what pleased me, with great wonders across the boundaries of ancient people, who have seen many secrets in me; indeed, I struck people down on earth so that they might not lift themselves up in any exaltation of their own minds. The world also had no joy in it nor playfulness nor practice in those things which belong to the world, because I restrained it from stubborn daring, having fear and quaking in its own labors. People indeed suffered pain in their hearts and in the veins of their flesh, having bound together soul and senses, and sustaining the many passions of the body, so that diverse peace of mind was not concealed in them, but they judged themselves blameworthy in all their motives.... Whence they searched through my love in their own souls, where they came upon the one who hastened the way of salvation. And the one came upon those people and loved them, acknowledging that they had been faithful and similar to the one in some part of that

labor which they had done for me. And holding themselves together with that one, they strained in all these things with heavenly zeal, so that my hidden miracles might be revealed. And the same people did not place themselves above that one with an ascent of humility and with the intention of goodwill, the one bent over them with warm protection. You therefore, O person, who receive these things, not in the turmoil of deceit but in the purity of simplicity, who receive these things straight for the manifestation of the things concealed, write what you see and hear.

Although I saw and heard these things, I nevertheless refused to write them because of doubt and evil opinion, and because of the diversity of other people's words, not so much out of stubbornness, but out of humility, until I became sick, pressed down by the scourge of God. I was sick for a long time with many different illnesses. Eventually, with the testimony of a nobleman and a young woman of good wishes, I started to write what I had searched out and come upon secretly. As soon as I did that, I became healthy with a received strength, and knowing—as I said—the profoundness of the narration of books, I was able to bring my work to completion with difficulty, taking ten years.

These visions were written in the days of Henry Moguntin, archbishop, and Conrad, king of the Romans, and Cunon, abbot of the mountain, and blessed Disibod, high priest, under Pope Eugenius. I spoke and wrote these things, not according to the invention of my or any person's heart, but as I saw, heard, and perceived them in the heavens through the hidden mysteries of God. And again I heard a heavenly voice speaking to me, "Proclaim and write this!"

Part One

Vision 4:27

You, O person, reflect on these things which you see. I saw many storms approach the earth. These storms tried to bend the burning sphere that was in the body of the person. This signifies that as long as a person lives in soul and body, many invisible trials will disturb the soul. Through the pleasures of the body, these trials will bend the soul many times toward the sins of earthly concupiscence. But that sphere worked vigorously to renew the person. That inner burning sphere resisted these storms strongly. This signifies that a faithful person who has been disturbed by sin is often urged on by a gift from God. The person hurls away the deceits of the devil and seeks the creator faithfully.

Vision 4:28

Why do you see these many storms rushing into another sphere, wishing to hurl it down even though they are not strong enough to do so? Because the many snares of the devil try to entice the soul to sinning with many evil deeds, but these snares are not strong enough with their deceitfulness. The soul, resisting strongly, does not give in to these raging storms. Guarding itself with heavenly inspiration, the soul drives the darts of false deceptions away from itself, and it rushes back to its savior. This was shown earlier in the words of the complaint of the soul, just as it was prophesied.

Vision 4:29

Then truly you see another sphere, drawing itself together out of the lines of its form and loosening its knots. This signifies the soul forsaking the members of its fleshly dwelling place. It leaves behind its relationship to the body when the time of the dissolution of the body has come. The soul extracts itself from the body with a groan. Grieving, it shatters its seat. By removing itself from the body with distress, it allows the place of its dwelling to fall away with much trembling. It will then know the merits of its works by the just judgment of God. This was shown earlier in the complaint of the soul. When the soul unties itself in this way, various spirits of both light and darkness come. These spirits are companions of the conversation that takes place in the dwelling place of the soul.

At the time of the resolution of the conversation—when the soul of the person leaves its dwelling—the angelic spirits of both good and evil are present according to the just and true plan of God. They are like inspectors for the work of the person, checking to see what was performed with the body while the soul was in the body. They expect the resolution, and after the soul has untied itself from the body, they will lead the soul away with themselves. They pay attention to the knowledge of the just judge concerning the soul as it is separated from its body. The heavenly judge will judge according to the merits of the works of that person. This was also faithfully prophesied to you.

Whence, whoever has knowledge in the Holy Spirit and wings in faith, let that person not pass over my warning, but let that person lay hold of it by embracing it in enjoyment of the soul.

Second Part[24]

Vision 2:2

Next I saw a very bright light. Inside it was a person who was the color of a sapphire. The bright light signifies God, who is without any blemish of illusion, defect, and falsehood. The person signifies the Word who is without blemish of any halfheartedness, ill will, and unfairness. The Word was begotten before time according to the divinity of God, but the Word was made flesh afterward in time according to the humanity of the world. This person was completely surrounded by a very pleasant fire of reddish color. This fire signifies the Holy Spirit, who is without any blemish of dryness, death, and darkness.

The only begotten one of God was conceived in flesh from the Holy Spirit and was born within time from the Virgin—the light of true brightness poured out into the world. The very bright light completely surrounded this light of reddish color, and at the same time this fire completely surrounded the light. Both the fire and the light surrounded the person, existing as one light with one force of potentiality. This signifies that God, the Word, and the Holy Spirit are inseparable in the majesty of their divinity. God is the most just justice, but is not without the Word and the Holy Spirit. The Word is the fullness of fruitfulness, but is not without God and the Holy Spirit. The Holy Spirit is the attendant of faithful hearts, but is not without God and the Word. For God is not without the Word nor the Word without God, and neither God nor the Word is without the Holy Spirit. And the Holy Spirit is not without God and the Word.

All of these three persons exist as one in the whole divinity of majesty. The unity of the divinity flourishes in God—neither God nor the Word without the Holy Spirit—nor the Holy Spirit without them. These three persons exist as one in the whole divinity of majesty, and the unity of divinity flourishes in these three inseparable persons because divinity is not able to be split since it exists without any change. God is shown through the Word, the Word through the birth of creatures, and the Holy Spirit through the Word being made flesh. What does this mean? God is the one who begot the Word before time. The Word is the one through whom all things from God have been done in creatures, and the Holy Spirit is the one who appeared in the form of a dove at the baptism of the Word who existed in time for a certain amount of time.

Vision 2:3

People must never forget to call upon myself alone, God in these three persons. I showed these three persons to people so that they would burn more vividly in my love when I sent the Word into the world because of my love. John, my chosen one, speaks about this.

Vision 2:4

The love of God appeared in us in this way, because God sent the only begotten one into the world so that we may have life through the only begotten one Love is in this, not that we chose God but because God chose us first and sent the only begotten one as propitiation for our sins (1 John 4:9–10). What does this mean? Because God chose us in this way, another salvation sprang up rather than the first one that we had when we were the heirs of innocence and holiness. Because God showed love for us in our perils, when we were subject to earning punishment, God sent the Word through birth to be the one among people who was full of holiness through the various virtues. God sent the word into the darkness where the Word performed all kinds of good things and led those who had fallen into the uncleanness of sin back to life. They were not strong enough to get back into a state of holiness by themselves. What does this mean?

The beloved of the love of God came through the fountain of life to nourish us back to life and to help us in our dangerous state. The Word is the deepest and sweetest love preparing us for repentance. How did this happen?

Mercifully, God remembered the Creator's own great work and most precious pearl, namely, human beings whom God formed from the slime of the earth and breathed into life. So God provided life again through repentance since the sly serpent had deceived humanity with proud advice. God hurled humanity into the humility of repentance, which the devil did not do nor know about because the devil did not know how to stand up to the right way.

Therefore the salvation of love did not originate with us. We did not know how to—nor were we strong enough to—choose God in salvation. Since the creator and Lord of all things loved people so much, God sent the Word—leader and savior of the faithful—for our salvation. The Word washed and dried off our wounds. The Word sweat [blood], from which all the good things of salvation flowed. You, O person, understand that no changeableness ever touches God. For God is God, the Word is the Word, and the Holy Spirit is the Holy Spirit. These three persons clearly flourish indivisibly in the unity of their divinity.

Part Three[25]

Vision 13:10[26]

Praises ought to be given to the heavenly creator with the unceasing voice of heart and mouth. For the creator gives grace not only to those standing and erect but also to those sliding and falling out of their very high seats.

Thereupon, you see, O people, the sky got very bright. This stands for the joy of the heavenly city. And I heard all the previously mentioned virtues sing in a wondrous manner to the various types of music. They persisted strongly in the way of truth as they sang the praises of the city of celestial joy. They persisted strongly as they called those with complaints back to praising with joy. This signifies that you hear a pleasant and sweet musical performance sounding forth from the chosen ones with wondrous joy as they sing about all the wonderful things of God which have been prophesied to you. This is just like the air containing and sustaining all those things which are under heaven.

This musical performance exists in the heavenly city and perseveres in God with pleasant devotion. It also exists in the complaints of those whom the old serpent has tried to destroy, but whom divine virtue nevertheless has led through to the company of blessed joy. The blessed joy contains those mysteries which the human mind cannot know while on earth. The virtues persisted in exhorting and encouraging themselves so that they might fight back the snares of the devil and help people gain salvation. But these virtues do overcome the snares of the devil, so that the faithful may pass over at last from sin through to celestial reward through repentance.

This means that the virtues resist in the minds of the faithful the various faults by which they have been wearied by the devil. And with these having been overcome with the strongest strength, the people who had fallen into sin are then turned back to divine nourishment. This happens when they march through and bewail their earlier deeds and then contemplate and provide for their later deeds.

Vision 13:11

And the sound was that of the voice of a multitude singing a musical performance with a harmony in praise of the celestial orders. This is because the musical performance recalls the glory and honor of the heavenly city. And it bears glory and honor upward again since it brings forth the word of God publicly.

Vision 13:12

The words of the musical performance stand for the body, and the musical performance itself stands for the spirit. The celestial harmony announces the divinity, and the words truly uncover the humanity of the Word of God.

Vision 13:14[27]

A musical performance also softens hard hearts, leads in the humor of reconciliation, and summons the Holy Spirit. These voices were the voice of a multitude. This refers to the praises of jubilation which are found in the simplicity of agreement and to the love shown to the faithful. These praises lead through to that agreement—where there is not any disagreement—when they make the people who have been placed on earth sigh with their heart and with their mouth for their heavenly reward.

The sound of these voices passed through me, and I did not have any slowness or difficulty understanding them. This is because wherever divine grace will have worked, it casts forth all the shadows of darkness—making those things pure and light which had been concealed by the fleshly senses in the weakness of the flesh.

Vision 13:16

Praise God with the sound of the trumpet; praise God with lyre and harp. Praise God with timbrel and dance; praise God with strings and organ. Praise God with cymbals sounding forth well; praise God with the cymbals of jubilation. Let every spirit praise the Word (Ps 150:3–6). This has the following meaning.

You who know, adore, and love God with a simple intention and pure devotion, praise God with the sound of a trumpet—that is, with a sense of reason. Do this because when the destroyed angels and followers fell into destruction, the armies of the blessed spirits stood firm and reasonable in truth. And they clung to God with faithful devotion.

And praise God with the lyre of profound devotion and with the harp of a soft flowing sound. Just as the trumpet is played before the lyre, and the lyre is played before the harp, likewise also the prophets first rose up in the wondrous voices of the blessed angels who persevered in the love of truth. And then the prophets spoke through created people, to be followed by the apostles who spoke with the sweetest words.

And praise God with the timbrel of mortification and the dance of exultation. For after the harp, the timbrel exults; after the timbrel, the dance follows. Similarly, after the apostles prophesied the words of salvation, the martyrs suffered various bodily punishments in honor of God. And from the martyrs, the truthful teachers of the priestly office rose up.

Praise God with the strings of human redemption and with the organ of divine protection. When strings are played, the voice of both the strings and the organ are heard. Similarly, the virgins went out as true teachers when they showed the truth in the office of their blessedness. And the virgins loved the Word of God as a true human—the strings—and they adored the Word as true God—the organ. For they believed the Word to be true human and true God. What does this mean? When the Word of God took on flesh for the salvation of the human race, the Word did not set aside the glory of the Word's divinity. So the blessed virgins have chosen the Word as their bridegroom. They have seized the Word with faithful devotion as a true man in marriage and as true God in chastity.

But also praise God with cymbals sounding forth well, that is, with the protections which sound forth with true joy. This takes place when people, lying in the lowest of sins, bear themselves upward from the lowest places to the celestial heights by the means of divine inspiration.

And praise God with the cymbals of jubilation, clearly with divine praise. For in divine praise, the virtuous virtues are strongly victorious as they oppress the faults within people and lead those who persevere in doing good deeds by having a strong desire to do so, to the blessedness of true reward.

Again I heard the voice speak from the very bright sky and say: "O most high, praise be to you who do these things in simple and untaught people." Still again, the voice from heaven cried aloud with the greatest crying (Josh 6:5) and said:

Hear and pay attention, all you who long for your celestial reward and blessedness. You who have a believing heart and expect your celestial reward, receive these sermons and place them in your inner hearts (Luke 9:44). Do not refuse to listen to this warning. For I am the living and true witness of truth and the speaking and not-being-silent God. I say and again I say: Who will be able to be stronger (2 Chron 2:6) than I am? Whoever will try this, I will cast that one down (2 Kings 19:7). A person cannot seize a mountain and wish to move it; a person can only make a stand in the valley of humility.

Who can spring across ways without going across waters? Clearly only the kind of person who fans himself or herself into confusion, and who cuts up a piece of fruit without eating it. And how can my tent be there? But my tent is there—any place where the Holy Spirit pours out water. What does this mean? I am in the middle (Luke 22:27). In what way? Whoever seizes me worthily, this one will decline neither in height nor in depth nor in breadth. What does this mean?

For I am that love which neither blazing pride casts down nor the deepest falls tear to pieces, nor the breath of evil rubs away. What was I able to build on the height of the sun? Brave people, who show their strength in valleys, despise me. Dull people hurl me down with the sound of trumpets. Wise people reject my food. And whoever prepares a tower for themselves according to their will also despises me. But I will confuse all of these with a very little and tiny one, just as I cast Goliath down with a boy, and as I conquered Holofernes with Judith.

Whoever will have rejected the mystical works of this book, I will stretch my bow above that person and I will pierce that person with the arrows of my quiver. I will cast the crown from their head, and I will make them like those who fell at Horeb (Sinai), when they murmured against me. And whoever will bring forth evil sayings against this prophet, that curse which Isaac brought forth will come upon them. Let people be satisfied with the heavenly rose when they embrace it and when they hold it in their heart and when they lead it forth into the level ways (Isa 40:4 and Luke 3:5).

And whoever has tasted the mystical works of this book and has placed them in their memory, let this person be like a mountain of myrrh and frankincense, and all other aromas. Let this person ascend by means of many blessings from blessing to blessing, just as Abraham did. Let the new wedded bride of the lamb join that column to herself in the sight of God. And let the shadow of the hand of the Word protect this person.

But if any person will conceal these words of the finger of God fearfully and will lessen them through their own madness, or will have led them forth into a strange place by reason of some other human sense, let this person be condemned. The finger of God will rub this one away.

Praise, praise God, therefore, you blessed flesh in all those wondrous things which God has established in your tender form of outward appearance. God foresaw all of you in the first sight of the rib of the first person whom God created.

Whoever has keen ears for understanding clearly, let this person pant for my words with a burning love of my image. Let this person write these words down in the consciousness of their soul.

NOTES

1. Yves Congar, "The Sacralization of Western Society in the Middle Ages," *Concilium* 47 (1969) 60–65. Sabina Flanagan, *Hildegard of Bingen (1098–1170): A Visionary Life* (London: Routledge, 1989) 3–18.

2. Ruth Mohl, *The Three Estates in Medieval and Renaissance Literature* (New York: Columbia University Press, 1933) 15–44.

3. René Rogues, *L'Univers dionysien* (Aubier: Montaigne, 1954) 319–29. *Dionysius, the Pseudo-Areopagite: The Ecclesiastical Hierarchy*, trans. Thomas L. Campbell (Washington, D.C.: University Press of America, 1981) 12–15, 70–78.

4. For descriptions of the history and controversies over the meaning of justification, see Walter Ullman, *Medieval Papalism: The Political Theories of the Medieval Canonists* (London: Methuen, 1948) 90–93; Donald Heintschel, *The Medieval Concept of an Ecclesiastical Office* (Washington, D.C.: Catholic University of America, 1956) 1–15.

5. *Hildegard of Bingen: An Anthology*, ed. Fiona Bowie and Oliver Davies (London: SPCK, 1990) 34–50; Flanagan, *Hildegard of Bingen* 9–40.

6. This is stated in her preface to the *Scivias*, *S. Hildegardis abbatissae opera omnia*, Migne, *Patrologia Latina* 197:383A.

7. Bowie and Davies, *Hildegard of Bingen: An Anthology* 34–50.

8. Benedicta Ward, "Saints and Sybils: Hildegard of Bingen to Teresa of Avila," in *After Eve: Women, Theology and the Christian Tradition*, ed. Janet Martin Soskice (London: Marshall Pickering, 1990) 102–8.

9. *Epistolae* 38, 39, in Migne, *Patrologia Latina* 197:203, 204–5.

10. *Epistolae* 1, 2, 3, 4, in Migne, *Patrologia Latina* 197:145–50, 150–53, 153–54, 154–56.

11. *Epistolae* 27, 29, 45, in Migne, *Patrologia Latina* 197:186–87, 189–90, 214.

12. The compromise reached at the Concordat of Worms, 1122, between the German emperor Henry V and Pope Callistus II, was ignored by Frederick I. This compromise allowed the emperor to attend the ceremony but not to bestow symbols of office, a basic restatement of the Gregorian reforms; see Karl E. Morrison, "The Gregorian Reforms," in *Christian Spirituality: Origins to the Twelfth Century*, ed. Bernard McGinn, John Meyendorff, and Jean LeClerq (New York: Crossroad, 1985) 177–93.

13. Acta, *Epistolae* 8, 9, in Migne, *Patrologia Latina* 197:63–65, 158–61.

14. *Liber vitae meritorum*, in *Sanctae Hildegardis opera*, ed. J. B. Pitra (Monte Cassino, 1882); *Liber divinorum operum*, in Migne, *Patrologia Latina* 197:739–1052.

15. *The Book of Divine Works*, ch. 1, 2, 4, 9, and 10, uses the image frequently. A translation of this work can be found in *Hildegard of Bingen's Book of Divine Works, with Letters and Songs*, ed. Matthew Fox (Santa Fe: Bear, 1987).

16. *Hildegarde von Bingen: Lieder*, ed. P. Barth, M. I. Ritscher, and J. Schmidt-Gorg (Salzburg, 1969); some of these songs are translated in Fox, *Hildegard of Bingen's Book of Divine Works.*

17. This is a translation from the abbreviated Latin title, *Liber subtilitatum*; this includes both her *Natural History* (*Physica*) and *Causes and Cures* (*Causa et curae*). A readable but well-annotated source tracing both the development and content of these works can be found in Flanagan, *Hildegard of Bingen* 80–105.

18. "Vita sanctae Hildegardis," esp. bk. 3, ch. 2, in Migne, *Patrologia Latina* 197:122–27.

19. The story is documented in Bowie and Davies, *Hildegard of Bingen: An Anthology* 23–33.

20. *Scivias* I, vision 2, ch. 12.

21. B. Newman, "Hildegard of Bingen: Visions and Validations," *Church History* 54 (1985) 163–75.

22. *Scivias by Hildegard of Bingen*, trans. Bruce Hozeski (Santa Fe: Bear, 1986).

23. Ibid. 56–57.

24. Ibid. 87–90.

25. Part Three has thirteen visions, the sum of the visions in Parts One and Two. Vision 13 is the conclusion of the story, a new creation. These excerpts are from vision 13, ibid. 389–95.

26. Hildegard's morality play, *The Play of the Virtues*, is the earliest morality play known in the church. It is found within vision 13. She composed this play and set it to music between 1141 and 1151.

27. Throughout these sections Hildegard's love for music will be apparent.

BIBLIOGRAPHY

Bowie, Fiona, and Oliver Davies. *Hildegard of Bingen: An Anthology*. London: SPCK, 1990.

Flanagan, Sabina. *Hildegard of Bingen (1098–1170): A Visionary Life*. London: Routledge, 1989.

Fox, Matthew, ed. *Hildegard of Bingen's Book of Divine Works, with Letters and Songs*. Santa Fe: Bear, 1987.

Hildegard of Bingen: Scivias. Edited by Mother Columba Hart and Jane Bishop. Classics of Western Spirituality. New York: Paulist Press, 1990.

Hozeski, Bruce, trans. *Scivias by Hildegard of Bingen*. Santa Fe: Bear, 1986.

Lachman, Barbara. *The Journal of Hildegard of Bingen*. New York: Bell Tower, 1993.

Newman, B., ed. *Saint Hildegard of Bingen Symphonia: A Critical Edition of the "Symphonia armoniae celestium revelationum" ("Symphony of the Harmony of Celestial Revelations")*. London and Ithaca: Cornell University Press, 1988.

Silvas, Anna, trans. *Vita Sanctae Hildegardis*. Published in four parts in the Arcadia, Australia, periodical *Tjurunga* 29 (1985), 30 (1986), 31 (September 1986), and 32 (May 1987).

Strehlow, W., and G. Hertzka. *Hildegard of Bingen's Medicine*. Santa Fe: Bear, 1988.

RECORDINGS OF HILDEGARD'S MUSIC

"A Feather on the Breath of God." Sequences and hymns by Abbess Hildegard of Bingen. Gothic voices, directed by Christopher Page, with Emma Kirby, Margaret Philpot, Emily Van Evera. Hyperion A 66039. Recorded in London, 1981.

Hildegarde von Bingen: "Ordo virtutum." Sequentia, directed by Klaus Neumann. Harmonia Mundi 20395/96. Recorded in France, June 1982.

– 7 –

HÉLOÏSE

(c. 1098–1164)

Unite Us Forever in the World to Come

The twelfth century was a profoundly religious century. A new sense of nature and humanity, legal developments that gave rise to canon law in a codified form, the rise of universities and scholastic theology, the crusades as one expression of lay piety, the so-called military orders, renewed visionary literature, the development of purgatory as a doctrine, and collections of miracle accounts and legends all contributed to the spirituality of the period.[1] There was a more speculative approach to theology than that of prior centuries. At the same time, affective understandings of faith continued. Bernard of Clairvaux and the Cistercians and Anselm of Canterbury had a marked influence on this age and on subsequent ages.[2]

Women did not fare well in this century. The romantic and devotional literature of the twelfth century could suggest that women were placed on a pedestal and lived a life of relative comfort and adulation. The opposite was true. Whereas devotional literature emphasized the angelic status of virginity, living women were looked upon as temptresses. Marriage as a vocation of holiness did not fare well, either. The highest state was the virginal state. Men who studied sacred sciences like philosophy and theology took a vow of celibacy as an aid to their higher speculative calling.

The renewed religious fervor drew many to monastic life. Abbot Hugh of Cluny drew so many married men to his foundation that he felt some compassion for their wives. He did succeed in getting some land for a monastery for women. New orders of the century drew thousands of women. Some orders, like the Premonstratensians, initially admitted women as well as men and reinstituted the double monastery tradition. As was typical of the times, however, a male religious would head the double monastery. A male prior would take care of the women's donations and decisions about community finances. Although many noblewomen brought impressive holdings with them to the monastery, they had nothing to say about their use. In time, the antifeminism of the age resulted in decisions to simply close some of the women's monasteries and send them out on their own. Innocent II (1138), Celestine II (1143), Eugenius III (1147), and Adrian IV (1154) tried to enforce the care that male orders ought to have for their sisters in the Lord.[3] But the suppression of women's monasteries continued. One of the abbots of the community bluntly states why this must be:

> We and our whole community of canons, recognizing that the wickedness of women is greater than all the other wickedness of the world, and that there is no anger like that of women, and that the poison of asps and dragons is more curable and less dangerous to men than the familiarity of women, have unanimously decreed for the safety of our souls . . . that we will avoid them like poisonous animals.[4]

Héloïse was born at the turn of the century, probably around 1098. The exact date of her birth is not known, nor are the names of her parents. It is known that Héloïse was schooled at the convent of Notre Dame at Argenteuil, six miles from Paris. This convent had a great reputation for learning. In the ninth century Charlemagne's daughter was abbess there and built it into a center of learning for women. Although the school was destroyed during Norman invasions, it had been rebuilt into a reputable school by 1100. Héloïse lived here, where she was well educated, till she was sixteen.

When Héloïse finished her education at this convent, she was not ready to marry. Since women were usually married by age thirteen or fourteen, and also since Héloïse would have no support, an uncle named Fulbert shared his home with her and saw to it that her education continued. Fulbert was a canon of Notre Dame in Paris.[5] He knew many influential scholars of the time, including the brilliant young master of Notre Dame, Peter Abelard. Abelard was made master of Notre Dame when he was only thirty-four. His brilliance and arrogance had already made for him enemies among older scholars of his time.[6] Students, fascinated by his learning, followed him everywhere. Women were taken with his manners and demeanor as well.

Peter Abelard agreed to tutor Héloïse in exchange for room and board at Fulbert's house. Héloïse had a mind that Abelard admired. In time, he began to be taken with her other attractive qualities as well. It did not take long before his pupils noticed a change in him. He wrote love songs that became very popular and well known. Some named Héloïse as his love. The gossip grew, but Fulbert did not believe it, primarily because his niece was trustworthy and had good sense.

Passion prevailed over good sense. The love between Héloïse and Abelard eventually led to Héloïse becoming pregnant. Abelard was afraid of what Fulbert might do to Héloïse when he found this out, so he asked his sister Lucilla to help them by giving them a safe place to stay. The two escaped to Lucilla's house in the darkness of night. Peter Abelard wished to marry Héloïse, but she knew that a public marriage would ruin his career as a philosopher. Like other philosophers and theologians of the twelfth century, he had taken a vow of celibacy as a sign of his dedication to scholarly commitment of the divine sciences.

Héloïse finally convinced Abelard that his career should be respected and his future influence considered. The two were secretly married by a cleric friend who agreed not to tell anyone. The child that was eventually born was named Peter, and he was raised by his aunt Lucilla. Abelard convinced Héloïse to enter the convent of the Argenteuil. He took her there and watched her receive the veil. Whether his motivation was one of jealousy or one of concern can only be speculated from his letters.

Meanwhile, Fulbert wished to have revenge on Abelard for disgracing his niece, though there may have been other reasons as well. Fulbert hired some men to find Abelard and castrate him. This event awakened Abelard to the suffering brought upon Héloïse as well as that now brought on himself. He decided to enter the Benedictine monastery of St. Denis in 1119. This monastery was only a short distance from the Argenteuil, the community that had received Héloïse.[7]

From this point on, Abelard's troubles increased. The monks at his monastery were crude, vicious, hypocritical, and warlike. His letter to console a friend details his sufferings in this monastery; the jealousies that led to a condemnation of his book *The Majesty of the Trinity* by the Council of Soissons in 1121; the reasons for his expulsion from the Monastery of St. Denis by Abbot Suger; his time in a cloister in Troyes; his life as a solitary in the diocese of Troyes, where he built a house dedicated to the Trinity and eventually a chapel dedicated to the Paraclete; and finally his residence at St. Giles, where the duke of Brittany assigned him for his own safety. The monks at this abbey elected him superior but eventually tried to poison him.[8]

Héloïse's life at Argenteuil was not as calamity stricken. Her early letters indicate that she did not feel a vocation to the religious life, which would not have made her an exception at this time. Yet she was elected prioress, a position that placed her in charge of the education of children, novices, and women who came to the monastery. The position would also suggest that her spirituality was capable of guiding others along the way.

The Abbey of St. Denis, which was originally responsible for the nuns at Argenteuil, was not always careful about the responsibility. Héloïse appealed to Abelard, the abbot of St. Giles, to petition the bishop of Troyes to release her from this convent to another. Abelard appealed to the bishop, requesting that Héloïse come to the House and Chapel of the Paraclete, which he had built and which had been occupied by monks. The buildings had not been kept up, but Héloïse and some others moved there to follow their rule of life. Peter Abelard wrote a rule for the community, some letters of direction, and some hymns for prayer.[9]

Pope Innocent II confirmed this new community. Héloïse was elected the first abbess of the Paraclete, and in time many women were attracted to the monastery. At least six new foundations were formed from this house while Héloïse was abbess. It is thought that she wrote a later rule for the daughter houses that altered some of Abelard's points. The later rule allows for a woman to be head of double monasteries, and for the sisters to go out for necessary things.[10]

Abbess Héloïse did not fear honesty about the competence of women. Her leadership of the Monastery of the Paraclete and her holiness were well known in her time, although she would never claim the latter. Her attempt to integrate the love of Abelard into a deepening love of God would occupy much of her life. In the letters that are exchanged between Abelard and herself, she makes her points with clarity. The citations of Scripture, the fathers of the church, and the classics point to a mind that comprehends the relationship of disciplines. Some of her communications with popes of the period and their responses have been preserved.[11] The rest of her works have not been found.

Peter Abelard died in good standing as a monk of Cluny in 1142.[12] Abbot Peter the Venerable, a friend of both Abelard and Héloïse, honored her request to have Abelard buried in the cemetery of the Monastery of the Paraclete.[13] When Héloïse died twenty-two years later, she was buried next to Abelard in the small abbey church. This was in 1164. Both bodies were moved at different times in the history of the monastery and as a result of the French Revolution. Today the graves can be located at the cemetery of Père Lachaise near Paris; they are marked by a Gothic-style structure surrounded by iron railings.

The publication history of the letters between Abelard and Héloïse, the summaries of letters that passed for the actual letters, and the colorful history of additional letters composed by imaginative writers testify to the importance of Héloïse and Abelard's story.[14] They wrote to each other in Latin. The Latin collection of Abelard's works was printed in Paris in 1616. The first French translation from the Latin was published in 1693 at The Hague. A 1736 English translation claims use of a French dictionary as an additional source for the translation.[15]

The majority of the first and second letters are printed in the pages that follow. These letters from Héloïse are from the Latin text. The response of Abelard to the first letter will be summarized to provide some context for understanding. In the second letter of Héloïse to Abelard, the theology of the twelfth century about women as well as the literal interpretation of Scripture will be evident. Finally, a letter from Peter the Venerable will be included, which is his response to the request Abbess Héloïse made for assurance of the status of

Peter Abelard upon his death. The letter reveals his affection and admiration for Abbess Héloïse, an admiration that she does not indicate for herself.

First Letter of Héloïse to Abelard[16]

To Abelard, her master, her father, her spouse, her brother
from Héloïse, his servant, his daughter, his wife, his sister.

My beloved, by accident it seems, someone recently brought me a letter that you sent a friend to help him. As soon as I saw the greeting, I knew that you wrote it. I read it with the same affection which I would have embraced the writer. Through the words of the letter, I tried to recreate the image of the writer in his absence from me. The letter was full of so much suffering, retelling as it did the tragic story of our lives, our conversion, and the crosses which you alone continue to carry.

You truly did what you promised to do in the beginning of your letter. You made him see that his troubles were small when compared to your own. The persecutions you suffered at the hands of your teachers, the injury done to your body, the terrible envy and even dangerous pens of Alberic of Rheims and Lotulf of Lombardy, fellow students, were all explained. Through their instigation, what was done to your glorious theological work was also included. You were given something like a prison sentence as well.

The plotting and evils your abbot heaped upon you, as well as the attack of your brother monks and the serious attacks on your reputation that were stirred up against you by those two false apostles, the rivals previously mentioned, was followed by the scandal that occurred, naming your oratory for the Paraclete. [This was a scandal because Abelard had already been condemned for his works that "separated" the persons in the Trinity. Separating out the Paraclete looked like he was unrepentant.] You ended the awful story by describing the ongoing persecutions of yourself by your brother monks.

I do not think anyone could read or hear what you say and have dry eyes. The many details narrated in the letter have greatly increased my sorrow in proportion to the dangers that increase even until now. All of us here, as a consequence, have been driven to despair of your life. Our hearts pound fearfully as, awaiting rumors, we daily expect to hear final words about your death. Although Christ still protects you in some way, we who are his handmaids and yours, plead with you to write us. Let us share in your sorrows and joys, for sorrows which are shared usually bring relief; whenever many carry a burden, it is lighter and may even be set aside. Even if this storm has lessened, the more quickly the letters come, the more joy they will be bring in the receiving. Whatever you may write about, it will demonstrate that you still remember us, and thus it will be a means of healing.

Seneca teaches us by his own example how welcome the letters of absent friends are. He writes these words to Lucilius, his friend:

> Thank you for your frequent letters. They are the one way your presence is with me. Whenever I receive your letter, it seems that we are immediately one. If pictures of absent friends are welcome, even though they revive our memories, and make us long for those who are gone, giving a false and empty comfort, so much more welcome are the letters sent to us by absent friends in their own handwriting.

Thank God your presence can be restored to us at least in this way, a way which neither malice nor difficulty can obstruct. Do not let negligence slow down this process. I implore you to heal us whom you have hurt even though your hands are full as you cure someone else. As both a friend and a companion, you have done what is right. You have given your friend the benefit of your friendship and of your companionship.

At the same time, do you not owe us as much friendship, since we are not only friends but very good friends and also your daughters—or whatever name is holier and endearing? If you have any doubt about your obligations to us, there are many arguments and witnesses that I could suggest. But even if these factors remain silent, the reality shouts forth of itself. After God, you alone are the founder of this place. You alone built the chapel. You alone designed the rule of this congregation.[17] You did not build on anyone else's foundation. Everything here is your creation. In this forsaken place of wild animals and robbers, you built a divine tabernacle and dedicated the chapel to the Paraclete. You did not bring any riches from princes or kings, even though you did have influence with the wealthiest and most powerful people. Thus anything built here is all your doing.

This is in spite of the fact that the clerics and scholars who met here to be taught by you also ministered to your needs. Even those who knew how to receive but not how to give, because they were supported by the church, insisted that you accept their generous offers to help. The young plant, this monastery whose members are dedicated to a holy way of life, can be credited to you and only to you. Until now, you have planted young shoots in great number, but watering is necessary if they are to live and grow. Even if our house was not new, it would still remain weak because it is composed entirely of the frail feminine sex.

Therefore, frequent and diligent cultivation is needed just as the apostle himself said, "I planted, Apollos watered, and God, however, gave the increase." The apostle planted the Corinthians to whom he was writing, and founded them in faith by the preaching of doctrine. Afterward, Apollos, the disciple of that apostle, watered them by sacred exhortations and thus divine grace was showered on them, bringing an increase in virtue.

Yet you cultivate the vines of another's vineyard which you have not planted, and these vines are bitter in their turning against you. Your admonitions to them are fruitless and your sacred words have no effect. You teach and admonish rebellious men who do not profit from your exhortations. In vain you scatter the pearls of divine wisdom before swine. You spend yourself tirelessly on the stubborn; in contrast, what do you owe to the obedient? Do you have no responsibility for your daughters when you can give so much care to your enemies? Although I omit the rest, think of how obligated you are to me. The debt that you owe to these women as a community you owe more abundantly to one who is yours alone.

Given your superiority, you know better than our humble selves how many impressive treatises the fathers wrote for the teaching, exhortation, and even comfort of women. You also know the care that went into such teachings. This makes your initial neglect of this young abbey even more astonishing to me. Although you knew our conversion of heart was still in its fragile beginnings, the fact that reverence for our God, for our love, or even the example of the holy fathers, did not move you to offer me some words of comfort astonishes me. If you could not do this face-to-face, at least a letter could have been sent in your absence. Meanwhile, I was wavering in my choice and almost succumbed to prolonged grief over everything.

As you know, I am the one to whom you were bound by the great obligation of love, an obligation that became even greater when it was reinforced by the lasting bonds of the sacrament of marriage. You know that you have been made subject to me by the great love with which I have always surrounded you, a love which has been publicly exposed as excessive. My beloved, you and everyone else knows that I lost much in losing you.

Truly, the greater the cause of any sorrow, the greater must be the means to remedy or console it. Since you alone are the cause of my sorrow, the consolation must come only from you. Only you can bestow the grace of consolation. Insofar as you alone are the one who brings me sadness, you alone can bring me joy. You alone owe me the most, for I have done everything you ordered. I did this so completely that I found strength in your command to enter this abbey, since I was unable to oppose you in anything you desired. It was at your command that I instantly changed my dress along with my mind to prove to you that my heart, my body, and soul were your possession.

God knows that I asked nothing of you except yourself. My love for you was not motivated by any desire for your possessions. I did not expect you to marry me, nor did I expect you to give me any marriage portion. I can truly say that I never tried to satisfy my own pleasure and wishes, but only yours. You yourself surely know this. Even if the name of wife sounds holier and truer to others, the word mistress will always remain sweeter to me. If you do not get angry at this, even the name of concubine or prostitute is sweet to me. I choose these so as to win fuller gratitude from you as well as to do less damage to the glory of your reputation.

You have not forgotten all this if the letter sent to console your friend can be used as an example. In that letter you explained that I did not wish us to enter into a public marriage. However, you did not give the main reasons for my claim that I preferred love over marriage, or liberty over chains. God is my witness to the depth of my love. Even if Augustus, ruler of the entire world, thought me worthy of the honor of marriage and gave me the whole world for my possession, I would consider it more valuable and more of an honor to be called your whore than to be called his empress.

Someone is not made better because they are rich or have power. These things depend on luck, but goodness and love are matters of virtue. A woman should be considered no more than a slave who is for sale if she marries a rich man more willingly than a poor one, or if she desires man's possessions in marriage more than the man himself. Any woman who marries for these reasons should be given wages, not gratitude. This is what the philosopher Aspasia has in mind in the logical argument she put forth to Xenophon and his wife. (This is according to Aschines Socratius.) When Aspasia proposed a way of reconciling them, this is how she ended her argument:

> Unless you decide once and for all that the one you have is the best one for your needs and that you each have the best woman and the best man, you will continue to question in your mind whether there is a better man or woman on earth who may be chosen.

Her thought is more than a simple philosophy. It is a holy thought that ought to be called wisdom. Perfect love thinks this way, even though it could be a holy error and a blessed fallacy in those who are married. This enables marriage bonds to be kept through a loving modesty of spirit rather than through bodily continence alone. Sometimes error brings people to that point. It is simply a clear truth that brought me there. What others believed about their husbands, I believed about you. The whole world also believed it and knew it to be true of you. Thus my love was all the more true to the degree that it was free of error.

Who was there among kings or philosophers that could equal your fame? Was there any region, city, or village that did not wish eagerly to see you? Was there anyone who did not rush to see you when you were in public places? Didn't everyone stretch the neck or strain the eyes to follow your departure? What wife or virgin did not secretly covet you in your absence or glow with excitement in your presence? What queen or powerful woman did not envy me because of my joys or because we shared our bed?

You had two special gifts, in addition to many others, with which you could immediately draw women to you. Your gifts of speaking and of singing are talents that have rarely been given to philosophers. Although these gifts were more for refreshment and relaxation from the demanding work of philosophic exercises, you wrote many love songs and poems composed in meter and rhythm. The lyrics and the melodies had such sweetness in them that everyone knew your name, and even illiterate people could not forget your songs. These melodies and lyrics made all women sigh for love of you. Because most of these songs sang of our special love, I became famous everywhere in a short time. Many women burned with envy of Héloïse. What gift of body or mind did not adorn your young manhood?

Does not my present misfortune compel those women who once envied me to pity me now in the loss of such delights? Does not the compassion that is due to me now soften the hearts of every previous enemy, man or woman? Although I am considered most guilty, you know that I am most innocent. It is not only the thing done, but, more importantly, the intention of the doer that makes the crime. Therefore justice ought to weigh not on the actions alone but on what was in the heart. You alone can judge what I have had in my heart toward you, for you have put it to the test. I give everything to your examination and in all things yield to your testimony.

Can you give me one reason why you so neglected me after this conversion to a life in religion, a life which you alone insisted upon for me? Why have I been so forgotten that you have neither spoken to me to revive my strength nor sent me a letter to console me? Tell me if you can. If you cannot, I will at least tell you what I feel and what everyone suspects. My desire joined me to you more powerfully than friendship, and the fires of my lust united me to you more powerfully than ever. Therefore, when what you desired ceased to be possible, your display of affection vanished with it. Beloved, this is not my conjecture alone. Everyone believes this. My opinion is not one opinion among many but expresses the universal view. This view is not only held in private but is expressed in public. If this were my personal opinion only, and others could find excuses for your love, that would lessen my sorrow. If I could fabricate excuses for you that would cover up your cheap behavior toward me, I would.

I beg you to pay attention to what I am about to ask, for it is a small and easy thing for you to do. Since I am deprived of your physical presence, at least send me a letter, a sweet image of yourself in words. You have enough of those. If I have to put up with your stinginess in words, I surely wait in vain for generous deeds. Yet I still believe that you will do much for me because I have done everything for you. I am obedient to you even now. It was your command, not religious devotion, that forced me to embrace the monastic way of life while I was still a young woman. You can judge my situation for yourself. If you do nothing for me, are not my efforts in vain?

I cannot expect God to reward me for anything I have done up to now. Love for God has not been my motivation. I only followed you when you were hastening after God. I took the religious habit before you did. As if moved by the memory of Lot's wife who turned back, you gave only God the title to me by monastic investiture and profession. This was before you yourself made that commitment. I suffered violently because of this. I was ashamed that you had so little confidence in my love in this situation. God knows that I would not have hesitated either to precede you or to follow you if you commanded it.

My soul belonged to you more than to me. In fact, it is more yours now, for if it is not with you, it does not exist. Without you, there is no purpose for my existence. I beg you to treat my soul well so that it may remain with you. If it experiences your kindness, if you repay gracious acts with my gracious act, a small grace in return for my great deed, mere words in return for my love, my soul will flourish in your possession. I beg you to remember what I have done and consider how much you owe me. When I enjoyed carnal pleasure with you, many were uncertain whether I acted through love or lust. The end of the affair now shows its origin. I have given up all pleasure in order to serve you. Weigh your injustice with care. I beg you to send your presence to me the only way you can. Write some comforting message to me, or at least agree to do so. Then my obedience will be revived and I will again be at peace for God.

Farewell, my only love.

Response of Abelard to Héloïse[18]

This is written from the Monastery of St. Giles after Abelard has made real efforts at repentance, has suffered much for his theology, and has made sincere efforts to live as a monk. By the time this letter is written, Abelard seems to feel a need to affirm some of his faith beliefs to Héloïse, for he has been attacked by Bernard of Clairvaux for questionable positions. He does not want Héloïse to worry about this. He affirms his early love for her and his desire that he wished to keep her only for himself because he loved her without measure. He feels that early love has now been transformed in him and that he loves her in the Lord.

After asking for her prayers, he claims that his salvation is really in her hands because she is the one who loves purely. She must battle for both of them since he does not face the same battles over their passion that she does. He composes a prayer for both of them:

God, at the creation of the human race, you fashioned woman from a rib of man and sanctified the great mystery of the nuptial union. You bestowed the highest honor on marriage by being born in wedlock and by performing your first miracle at the wedding feast at Cana. You also wished to grant me this refuge for my frail and passionate nature. Now do not be angry with the prayer of your humble servant. I pour out my petitions before the face of your majesty because of my own excesses and those of my beloved. You who are most merciful, pardon our many offenses, great as they are. Let the immensity of your boundless mercy be greater than the multitude of our faults. I beseech you to punish us in this life so that we may be spared in the next life. Punish us in time so that you can save us in eternity. Raise your rod of correction against us, your servants, rather than the sword of your wrath. Afflict our flesh if that will save our souls.

Come as a redeemer, not as an avenger. Come as the God of mercy, not as a God of justice. Come as a compassionate father, not as a stern lord. Lord, prove us and try us, in the manner in which the prophet asked you to deal with him: "Test me, Lord, put me to the proof; consider my secret desires and thoughts"—that is, consider first my strength and then measure my burden of temptations accordingly. This is the promise St. Paul made to the faithful when he said: "God will be faithful to you; the Lord will not allow you to be tempted beyond your powers. God will decide which temptations you endure, and will enable you to overcome them."

Lord, you have brought us together. You have also separated us at the time and in the manner that you desired. Now complete this work that you began in your mercy with an abundance of mercy. You who have separated us in this world, unite us forever in the world to come. For you alone are our hope, our heritage, our expectation and our consolation, Lord blest forever and ever. Amen.

The Second Letter from Héloïse to Abelard[19]

To him who is her only beloved after Christ
from her who is his alone in Christ.

My only beloved, you surprised me in the greeting of your letter by acting contrary to custom. The greeting that headed your letter placed me first, contrary to the natural order, for you placed my name before your own, woman before man, wife before husband, servant before master, nun before monk and priest, and abbess (deaconess) before abbot. Surely you know the accepted order. Those who write to superiors or equals should put the name of these before their own. In writing to inferiors, those taking precedence in rank take precedence in the order of address.

We were also greatly surprised that your letter increased our desolation rather than bestowing the balm of comfort to us. You caused tears to flow when you should have wiped them away. Who among us could hear the words you wrote at the end of your letter with dry eyes? You said: "But if the Lord shall deliver me into the hands of my enemies so that they prevail over me and slay me," and so on. What makes you think such a thought? How could you bear to put it into words? May God never forget us who serve so as to let us outlive you. May God never grant us a life without you, for that would be more grievous to bear than any kind of death. You should perform the last rites over us and commend our souls to God. You should thus send us whom you have gathered into the Lord's service ahead of you so that you may no longer be anxious on our account. May you be happier dying after us, because then you are free of any solicitude for our salvation.

I beg you, master, to spare us words of this kind. Such words only make those who are already unhappy more unhappy. Before death, do not take away from us the source of our existence. "Sufficient unto the day is the evil thereof." That day of death, when all death finds here, will be wrapped about with every kind of bitterness, and with enough distress. For "To what purpose is it," Seneca says, "to summon evil in advance and to destroy life before death has come?"

My beloved, you have asked that your body be brought to our burial place here should you die far from this place. This was so that our thoughts could be continually set on you and you could reap a richer harvest in our prayers. How could you imagine your memory could ever fade from among us? Besides, when excess of grief allows us no tranquillity, do you think that is really a fruitful time for prayer? When the soul will have lost the power of reason, the tongue the use of speech, the mind distraught instead of at rest, that will be a time—if I may so speak—for rage against God, for provoking God with complaints rather than being appeased through supplications. In such sorrow, we shall not be able to pray but only to lament. We will be hastening to follow you through death rather than to bury you. We shall be more desirous of being laid in the grave ourselves than to lay you in yours. In losing you, we shall have lost our own life. We shall not be able to live if you leave us. May we never survive to see that day! If the mere mention of your death is already a death to us, what will be the reality if it finds us living....

A heart overwhelmed with grief cannot be at peace. A mind disturbed with deep anxiety cannot devote itself sincerely to God. I pray that you do not place obstacles to our service of God to which you have especially committed us. If bitter grief must come, let it come suddenly. That should be our prayer so that grief may not torment us with vain dread long before it actually comes. This grief cannot be relieved by any foresight. The poet says as much when he prays to God:

> Whatever thou hast in store, may it be sudden.
> Let our minds be blind to what the future holds.
> Permit our fears to hope.

But what have I to hope for if you are gone? For what reason would I prolong this pilgrimage on which I have no support except yours, a support based upon the knowledge that you live? I am denied all pleasure in you even now, separated from that presence which could restore me to myself at least from time to time.

I am the unhappiest woman among unhappy women. Among the unfortunate, I am the most unfortunate. I was lifted to such a height when I was chosen by you. Correspondingly, when I was flung down, my fall brought the greater suffering to you and most of all to myself. For the higher one is raised, the heavier is the fall. Was there a great or noble woman that Fortune ever set above myself or raised to the same degree? Whom else has Fortune so cast down and crushed with grief? What glory Fortune bestowed on me through you! But now, what ruin she has brought me in you! She has been violent to the extreme, not showing moderation in either good or evil. She first made me happier than any woman so that she could make me the most wretched of any woman. Now as I remember the great joy that once was mine, my intense grief matches it through the ill fortune that overtook me. My regret for what I have lost is no less than had been the joy of possession. Ecstasy has found its counterpoint in despair.

In our case, what heightens my indignation at the outrage you suffered is the overturning of the laws of justice. God's anger spared us while we enjoyed the pleasures of unbridled love, surrendering ourselves to fornication. Pardon this shameful word but it is precise. Yet, when we had corrected what was unlawful by what was lawful, when we at last covered the shame of fornication by an honorable marriage, then the wrath of the Lord's hand fell upon us. The God who had long allowed our unchaste union would not allow our chaste one. The punishment that you suffered was one that would be fitting for men taken in flagrant adultery. But what others merit through adultery, you incurred through a marriage, when you were confident you had now made amends for all your wrongdoing.

What adulterous women have brought upon their lovers, your own wife brought upon you! This was not when we were given over to our pleasures as formerly. Rather it was when we were temporarily apart. You were directing the schools in Paris. I was living among the nuns at Argenteuil as you commanded. We were separated that we might devote ourselves to our work; you the more zealously to the schools and I more freely to prayer and Scripture study. Then, when we were living a chaste and holy life, you alone paid the penalty in your body for what we both committed. You alone were punished, although we were both at fault. You, who were less to blame, bore all. You had made more than due reparation in humbling yourself for my sake and in lifting me up and with me all my family. You were less deserving of punishment, both in God's sight and in the sight of those traitors.

How unhappy I am to have caused such wickedness through being born into the world! Must women always be the ruin of great men? Proverbs does say to be careful of women. "Listen to me, O children, and attend to the ways of my mouth. Let not your heart give in to her ways; do not go astray in her paths. For she hast cast down and wounded many. Many strong men have been slain by her. Her house is the way to hell, a pathway to the chambers of death." Ecclesiastes says, "I applied my heart to know her. But I found the woman whose heart is snares and nets more bitter than death. Her hands are like strong bands. Whoever wishes to please God shall escape from her wiles. But the sinner shall be overcome by her."

At the beginning of the world it was a woman who caused the man to be banished from Paradise. She who had been created by the Lord as a helpmate for man was the instrument of his downfall. Samson the Nazirite, that powerful man of God whose conception was announced by an angel, was overcome by Delilah. She was the one who betrayed him to his enemies. She deprived him of his sight, and drove him to such despair he brought ruin upon himself as he was bringing ruin upon his enemies. Solomon, the wisest of all men, was so infatuated by a woman whom he had taken to himself that he was driven into madness. He whom the Lord had chosen to build his temple (in preference to David his father, who was a righteous man) was pushed into idolatry till the end of his life by this woman. Thus Solomon left the service of God which he had proclaimed and taught in his words and writings. Job, a most holy man, fought his last and hardest battle against his wife, who was urging him to curse God. From repeated experience the clever tempter knew well that the ruin of men is accomplished most easily through their wives. This tempter directed his usual malice against us in the same way. By means of marriage he overthrew one whom he could not overthrow through fornication. He was not permitted to effect evil by evil, so he effected evil through what is good.

I thank God for at least this much. I did not consent to do evil through the persuasion of the tempter as the women did about whom I have spoken. However, he did turn my love into a cause of evil. Yet, though I did not consent to the guilt of this crime, and though my heart be purged through innocence, so many sins went before this that I am not wholly without blame. I merit what I now suffer for yielding to the delights of carnal pleasure in the past. The sequel is a fitting punishment for my previous sins, for evil beginnings lead to an evil end. Above all, it is for this offense that I ask strength to do fitting penance. In some measure I especially wish to make amends by long contrition for the pain of the wound inflicted on you. I rightly wish to suffer in contrition of heart all the passing hours of my life for what you have suffered in the body. Thus I hope to make reparation at least to you, if not to God.

I admit to the weakness of my unhappy soul, for I know of no penance by which to appease God. I accuse God of the worst cruelty because of the outrage committed against you. My indignation and rebellion against this ordinance of God are such that my repentance cannot please the Lord. Regardless of the degree of mortification of the body, what kind of repentance is it when the mind still wants to sin and burns with its old desires? It is easy to accuse oneself, to confess sins, or even to impose penances upon the body from without. But it is far more difficult to tear the longing for supreme pleasures from the heart. It is with reason that the saintly Job can say the following, "I will make a complaint against myself," that is, "I will let loose my tongue and open my mouth in confession to accuse myself of my sins," and then immediately add, "I will speak in the bitterness of my soul."

St. Gregory comments on this, saying, "There are some who confess their faults aloud, yet in that confession, they do not know how to be sorry. They speak cheerfully of what should be lamented." Thus, "whoever despises their sins and declares them, must declare them in bitterness of heart. It is this bitterness of heart that punishes for the deeds the mind has prompted the tongue to tell." The sorrow that belongs to true repentance is rare, as St. Ambrose remarks. "I have found those who have preserved their innocence more frequently than I have found those who have truly repented." Indeed, the delights that we enjoyed together as lovers were so sweet that I can neither hate them nor forget them except with the greatest difficulty. There are present to me and so is my longing for them wherever I turn. I am not even spared their illusions when I sleep. Their unclean visions take such complete possession of my unhappy soul even during the solemn moments of the Mass when prayer should be the most fervent. Yet even then, my thoughts are fixed on vileness rather than on prayer. When I ought to be deeply sorrowful for what I have done, I am lamenting for what I have lost.

It is not only what we actually did that afflicts me. I live the past over and over again in my mind, the very places and moments we shared together. I have no relief from this even when I sleep. An unguarded word or a movement of my body betrays my thoughts. I am a most unhappy woman. I can truly utter the complaint of the afflicted Paul. "O wretched that I am! Who shall deliver me from the body of this death?" I wish I could add with truth what follows: "I thank God through Jesus Christ our Lord." You, my beloved, have that grace that came to you though you did not seek it. A single wound to your body has healed you from these torments and also healed any wounds in your soul. God has proved to be kind to you, in spite of the apparent cruelty. The Lord is a good physician who causes pain to heal. For me it is not that easy. I am young and passionate. Because I have known the most intense pleasures of love, the attacks directed against me are most fierce, for my nature is frail.

People who say I am so chaste do not see the hypocrite in me. They have turned the purity of the body into a virtue, when it is a virtue not of the body but of the spirit. I am praised by others, but I know I merit none of this in the eyes of God, who tries the heart and knows the hidden places of our deepest selves. I am praised as being religious in this age in which there is little true religion. This too is tainted with hypocrisy, for whoever does not offend against human judgment receives the highest praise. Yet perhaps there is merit acceptable to God in some degree if a person, whatever the intention, avoids giving scandal outwardly to the church, if the name of the Lord is not blasphemed among the infidels, and if the order to which one belongs is not dishonored among the worldly-minded. To do good and to avoid evil is an inspiration of grace from God. Yet avoiding evil is useless if doing good does not follow from it. It is written: "Depart from evil and do good." Both are in vain if they are not done for the love of God.

Yet God knows that I have feared to offend you rather than God and sought to please you rather than the Lord at every stage of my life up to the present time. It was not love of God but your command that made me put on the habit of religion. If I must endure all this in vain, with no thought of reward in the future, reflect on what an unhappy life I must lead, a life that is miserable beyond all others. My pretense deceived you for a long time, just as it did many others, so that you mistook hypocrisy for devotion. Thus, when you commend yourself to my prayers, you are asking of me what I look for from you.

I implore you not to hold me in such high esteem because I fear you will cease to help me with your prayers. Do not withdraw the grace of your healing because you think that all is well with me. Do not delay in aiding me in my adversity because you think that I am not in need. Do not believe that strength is mine, in case I fall because you are not upholding me. False praise has injured many and taken needed support from them. The Lord cries through Isaiah, "O my people, your leaders cause you to err and they destroy the way you should walk." God says through Ezekiel, "Woe to the women that sew pillows to all armholes and make kerchiefs upon the head of every statue to hunt souls." Solomon says, "The words of the wise are as goads and as nails fastened by the masters of assemblies." That is, the words of the wise do not know how to ease the wounds but to pierce them.

Thus, stop using words to praise me or you too will be found guilty of flattery and falsehood. If you suspect there is good in me, the breath of my vanity may carry away the quality you have praised. No one who knows medicine uses outward appearance to diagnose an internal sickness. What is common to both the outcast and the elect wins no favor in the sight of God. Outward actions which are performed more zealously by hypocrites than by saints are like this. "The heart is deceitful above all things and desperately wicked. Who can know it?" "There is a way which seems right to a man, but the end of it is the way of death." It is rash to pass judgment on that which is reserved for the scrutiny of God. This is why it is written, "Judge none blessed before death." That means do not praise anyone when by praising that person, you can make them no longer praiseworthy.

To me your praise is the more dangerous because I find pleasure in it. The more anxious I am to please you, the more your praise delights me and fools me. I implore you to be solicitous and fearful on my behalf. You must be just as afraid for me because I do not have you as a refuge from my passionate nature. Do not exhort me to virtue or rouse me to the fight saying, "For my strength is made perfect in weakness," and: "Yet is he not crowned, except he strive lawfully." I do not seek a crown of victory. For me, it is enough to avoid danger. It is safer to avoid danger than to engage in war.

In whatever corner of heaven God shall place me, the Lord shall do enough for me. Here, none will envy another since what each one will have will suffice. Let me add the weight of authority to what I say. Let us listen to St. Jerome: "I confess my weakness. I do not wish to fight in the hope of victory, because I may, in this fight, lose the victory." What need is there to abandon what is sure and to engage in that which is unsure?

Peter the Venerable: Letter to Héloïse[20]

To our venerable and dearest sister in Christ, the handmaid of God,
Héloïse, guide and mistress of the handmaids of God,
From your brother Peter, humble abbot of Cluny,
the fullness of God's salvation and of our love in Christ.

I was very happy to read the letter from your sanctity, where I learned that my visit to you was no transitory call, and which made me realize that I have not only been with you, but in spirit have never really left you. My stay, I see, was not that of one to be remembered as a passing guest for a single night, nor was I treated as "a stranger and a foreigner among you" (Gn 23:4), but as a "fellow citizen of God's people and member of God's household" (Eph 2:19).

Everything I said or did on that fleeting or flying visit of mine has remained so firmly in your holy mind and made such an impression on your gracious spirit that, to say nothing of my carefully chosen phrases on that occasion, not even a chance, unconsidered word of mine fell to the ground unheeded. You noted all. You committed all to your retentive memory in the warmth of your unbounded sincerity, as if all were the mighty, the heavenly, the sacrosanct words or deeds of Jesus Christ himself. You may have been prompted to remember them in this way by the injunctions on receiving guests in our common rule, which belongs to us both. "Let Christ be worshiped in them who is received in their persons."[21] Perhaps you were also reminded of the Lord's words concerning those given authority, though I have no authority over you. "Whoever listens to you listens to me" (Luke 10:16).

May I ever be granted this grace from you; that you will think me worthy to be remembered and will pray for the mercy of the Almighty upon me, along with the holy community of the flock entrusted to your care. I am repaying you now as far as I can. Long before I saw you, and particularly as I have come to know you, I have kept for you in the innermost depths of my heart a special place of real and true affection. I am therefore sending you, now that I have left you, a ratification of the gift of a trental I made you in person, in writing and under seal as you wished. I am also sending the absolution for Master Peter you asked for, similarly written on parchment and sealed. As soon as I have an opportunity, I will gladly do my best to obtain a prebend in one of the great churches for your Astralabe, who is also ours for your sake. It will not be easy, for the bishops, as I have often found, are apt to show themselves extremely difficult when occasions have arisen for them to give prebends in their churches. But for your sake I will do what I can as soon as I can.[22]

The Absolution for Peter Abelard[23]

I, Peter, abbot of Cluny, who received Peter Abelard as a monk of Cluny and gave his body, removed in secret, to the Abbess Héloïse and the nuns of the Paraclete, by the authority of Almighty God and of all the saints, in virtue of my office, absolve him from all his sins.

NOTES

1. R. W. Southern, *Western Society and the Church in the Middle Ages* (New York: Penguin, 1976) 100–132, 240–99.

2. Benedicta Ward, "Anselm of Canterbury and His Influence," and Basil Pennington, "The Cistercians," provide both concise and well-documented accounts in *Christian Spirituality: Origins to the Twelfth Century*, ed. Bernard McGinn, John Meyendorff, and Jean LeClerq (New York: Crossroad, 1985) 196–205, 205–17.

3. Southern, *Western Society* 304–18.

4. E. L. Hugo, *Annales Praemonstratensis*, vol. 2, 147; this is footnoted by Southern, *Western Society* 314, n. 14.

5. At this time canon referred to a layman or a cleric who lived a life of common prayer and of study and cared for the cathedral church, the church of the bishop, and ministered to the people. In turn, the canon was supported by the bishop and people.

6. Abelard's method of teaching was the disputation and not the more orthodox lecture and lectio of Anselm, William of Champeaux, and other scholars who taught him; see *The Letters of Héloïse and Abelard*, trans. Betty Radice (New York: Penguin, 1974) 10–17.

7. *Letters of Abelard and Héloïse: To which has been attached a particular account of their Lives, Amours, and Misfortunes*, trans. John Hughes, 6th corrected ed. (London: J. Watts, 1736). The preface cited here has no page numbers.

8. "Historia Calamitatum" is a letter to a friend. "Ad Amicum Scripta," in Migne, *Patrologia Latina* 178:3–41.

9. "Seu Regula Sanctimonialum," in Migne, *Patrologia Latina* 178:130–97; "Regula," ibid. 178:198–213; 313–36, 378–80.

10. Radice, *Letters* 30–31.

11. Migne, *Patrologia Latina* 178, Innocent II (1136) 347, 351–52; Celestine II (1143) 355; Eugenius III (1147) 351–52; Adrian IV (1157) 353.

12. The official censoring of Peter Abelard, "Censura Doctorem Parisiensium," is found in Migne, *Patrologia Latina* 178; 6 pages but no numbering prior to the table of contents. *Epistola* 25 of Peter the Venerable testifies to Abelard's repentance; Migne, *Patrologia Latina* 178:345.

13. Migne, *Patrologia Latina* 178, *Epistola* 23, *Epistola* 24, *Epistola* 25. 337–42, 343, 344–45. Absolution of Peter Abelard, 345.

14. This history is well traced in Radice, *Letters* 45–55.

15. Hughes, *Letters of Abelard and Héloïse*; the dictionary of M. Bayle is named as an additional source. This English translation has not received good critical reviews, although the collector claims the letters in it are authentic.

16. *Epistola* 2, "Quae Est Heloissae ad Petrum Deprecatoria," Migne, *Patrologia Latina* 178:42–50.

17. *Epistola* 8, followed by the rule, Migne, *Patrologia Latina* 178:130–97, 198–213.

18. *Epistola* 3, ibid. 48–54.

19. *Epistola* 4, ibid. 54–71.

20. *Epistola* 25, ibid. 344–45.

21. *Regula*, ch. 53.

22. There is a death day of October 29/30 given in the Paraclete necrology for Peter Astralabe, teacher of our son, Peter, but no year is given. Whether the canon of the Cathedral of Nantes in 1150 or the abbot of a Cistercian abbey in the Swiss canon of Fribourg—both named Astralabe—refers to this person is uncertain.

23. Migne, *Patrologia Latina* 178:345.

BIBLIOGRAPHY

Constable, Giles. *The Letters of Peter the Venerable*. 2 vols. Cambridge, Mass.: Harvard University Press, 1967.

Hughes, John, trans. *Letters of Abelard and Héloïse: To which has been attached a particular account of their Lives, Amours, and Misfortunes.* 6th corrected ed. London: J. Watts, 1736.

McGinn, Bernard, John Meyendorff, and Jean LeClerq, eds. *Christian Spirituality: Origins to the Twelfth Century.* New York: Crossroad, 1985.

McLeod, Enid. *Heloise.* 2nd ed. London: Chatto and Windus, 1971.

Migne, J. P., ed. *Patrologia Latina* 178. Paris, 1616.

Moncrieff, C. K. Scott. *The Letters of Abelard and Heloise.* London: Guy Chapman, 1925.

Radice, Betty, trans. *The Letters of Abelard and Heloise.* New York: Penguin, 1974.

Southern, R. W. "The Letters of Abelard and Heloise." In *Medieval Humanism and Other Studies.* Oxford: Blackwell, 1970.

Southern, R. W. *Western Christianity and the Church of the Middle Ages.* New York: Penguin, 1976.

–8–

MECHTHILD OF MAGDEBURG

(c. 1207–1297)

Lead Me in the Dance

The little we know about Mechthild of Magdeburg is primarily found in the prologue to her work and in her own writing.[1] Mechthild was born in Magdeburg, Thuringia, in Lower Saxony. Her date of birth is estimated as about 1207.[2] Mechthild's family seems to be of the nobility, for her familiarity with court life, the courtly love lyrics of the time (*Minnesang*), the images reflecting a cultural refinement, and her ability to use liturgical Latin in the midst of her writing in Low German point to this conclusion.[3]

In the main autobiographical section of her work, book 4, Mechthild says that she received her first deep experience of the Holy Spirit when she was twelve. After this experience the Spirit visited her daily for approximately thirty years. She did not tell anyone about this until she was about forty-three years old. From her reflections on being a favorite in her family, Mechthild indicates that she was a well-loved and happy child. When she was twenty-three, she left her home to be guided by a holy Beguine in Magdeburg.

The Beguines were one of the many organized groups of laywomen who desired to lead a life of prayer and service to the needy. Single, married, and widowed women were equally welcome to join the community if called to its form of prayer and service. The movement drew many women who did not feel a call to enter a monastery or take permanent vows. The Beguines were not cloistered, nor did they wear an official habit. They wore a simple blue dress of the time and took no permanent vows but promised to live celibately while they were Beguines. The women could retain any property or other wealth they may have accumulated from family, from their own industries, from trades, or from any other source.

Beguines were free to gather in communities of various sizes and numbers, to live as solitaries, to live within their own homes, and they could also join third orders of established religious communities. The houses, schools, hospitals, and churches that grouped together as a beguinage had a grand mistress who coordinated and oversaw religious observance. Spiritual guidance was given to younger Beguines by older members. There also were Beguines who sought spiritual direction from clergy, from men or women in religious orders, or from any other holy person. The Beguine way of life could be temporary or permanent, which meant that the women could leave the community if another vocation grew out of this one.

Many social factors of the twelfth and thirteenth centuries contributed to the rapid growth of the Beguines. The religious enthusiasm of the age for an apostolic life caused men and women to seek a more fervent expression of Christian life than what was available to laity. There was an inordinate attachment to wealth and power in the church and in civil society, which led the more fervent people to desire voluntary poverty. There was such a growing inequity between the rich and the poor that more sensitive Christians wished to meet the needs of the people who were basically ignored by civil leaders. Groups like the Beguines, and their male counterparts, the Beghards, provided a life of prayer and ministry to the poor that was attractive to the fervent.

An added social factor that contributed to the numbers of women joining other women in a life of prayer and service was the lack of men as potential marriage partners. Local feuds and wars, the crusades, the expectation of celibacy for philosophers and theologians as well as clergy, and the increasing number of male monastics who had been married and left their wives each led to more women without suitable partners.

Moreover, many male religious groups did not wish to be responsible for female groups, to which was added the fear that women could be a source of temptation for the men who were assigned as chaplains. Double monasteries were becoming uncommon by the twelfth century. Although many women visionaries were living as solitaries scattered around the cities and doing apostolic work, it was not until the twelfth century that there emerged a recorded organization of women's groups for the purposes of prayer and service.

Tracing its roots to Lambert Le Begue (d. 1177), a revivalist preacher of Liège who encouraged the group and contributed to its founding, the Beguine movement spread rapidly throughout Europe after influential women like Marie d'Oignies became members.

Marie d'Oignies (1177–1213) was a married woman who, with her husband, took a vow of celibacy in their efforts to live deeper lives of prayer and service. Jacques de Vitry, a bishop-supporter of the movement, recognized that an official approval by the pope would help the popular movement to continue flourishing without excessive opposition. He obtained official approval of this way of life from Pope Honorius III (1216–27) in 1216.[4] Unfortunately, this approval was only made verbally.

Gregory IX (1227–41) did give an official written approval in his bull *Gloriam virginalem* in 1233, but he also placed the women under stricter clerical control. The Beguines were unpopular with some of the clerics and male religious of the period because they had female superiors and did not turn over their financial resources to the church or a bishop or a cleric. Their resources were directly used for service of the needy, for education, or for community needs.

In 1274, the Franciscan Gilbert of Tourni prepared a tract against the Beguines, "A Collection of Church Scandals." This criticized the Beguines for not observing a cloister, for not wearing a habit, for not heeding their parish clergy, for not being under male authority, for reading publicly from the Bible, for using vernacular translations of the Bible, for presuming to teach the laity publicly, and for claiming that the Spirit was the source of their liberation from male dominance.[5] The Second Council of Lyons affirmed the tract and condemned the Beguines.

Harassment, suspicion, and persecution of the Beguines were intermittent during Mechthild's life. Like some of the other Beguines, she was critical of the abuses of some of the clergy in the church. She drew wrath upon herself from clergy and laity whom she strongly criticized for their lack of fervor. She frequently speaks of a "corrupt Christianity," a "poor church," and a "maiden whose skin is filthy" (5.4).[6] She wrote that God calls the clergy of the cathedral "goats because their flesh stinks of impurity with regard to eternal truth, before the Eternal Trinity" (6.3).

When there was a movement among some of the clerics to burn her writings, God told her, "No one may burn the truth. Those who take this book out of my hands must be stronger than I" (2.26). She was criticized for being an uneducated laywoman when she claimed that John the Baptist said Mass for her in a vision. Her critics said that John could not say Mass, for he was not an ordained priest (2.4; 6.36). Mechthild responded by calling her critics Pharisees. "Never could pope or bishop or priest speak the word of God as well as did John the Baptist.... Was this a layman? Teach me, you blind. Your lies and your hatred will not be forgiven without suffering" (6.36).

The early works of Mechthild circulated during her lifetime. Her confessor, the Dominican Heinrich of Halle, translated her works and organized them into "books." He encouraged the Forest Sisters (groups of Beguines) to reflect on them.[7]

Mechthild lived for forty years as a Beguine. She was in contact with many circles of society and of the church during that period. While ministering to the poor and the sick, she also undertook a life of ascetical practices and contemplation. She tells of periods of illness in her writings. "For twenty years, I was weary, ill, and weak, first from repentance and sorrow, then from holy desire and spiritual striving. Much bodily illness followed" (4.2).

Mechthild left behind some delightful works that show the creativity of the medieval imagination. She describes the beauty of the heavens and a courtly young Christ in the manner of the courtly romance literature of the period. Symbolic birds, colors, and flowers enhance the mystical visions. Jesus Christ, like the lord of the manor, is the personification of the gracious and perfect lover. The description of Mechthild's heavenly dance with Love depicts the splendor of medieval heaven and its holy garden of repose. Love pursues her just as surely as she has pursued Love.[8] Love is a wisdom figure who enlightens Mechthild.

In the passages that follow, Love gently assures Mechthild that she need not fear. "Madam, in this dance of praise, you have done well" (1.44). This dance can be done only if the handsome youth leads. Mechthild informs the youth of this. "I cannot dance, O Lord, unless you lead me" (1.40 ff). Mechthild celebrates the mystery of their love in the dance, in the light of knowledge and wisdom, in a garden of delight, and in the heart of her lover. Her mystical communion is affirmed in her acclamations, "His heart in my heart, His soul in my soul, Enclosed and at peace" (2.4).

Mechthild is capable of lovely poetic imagery as well as clear corrective admonitions. When she corrects some of her sister Beguines (3.15), the corrections are not motivated by malice or ill humor. She wishes for those she admonishes to realize how much they are loved by the heart of Christ. She is among the first of the mystics to perceive the heart of Christ as a fire of love whose sparks can set human hearts on fire (6.13).

Mechthild uses a variety of literary forms in her works. Dialogue, prayer forms, prose narrative, and medieval symbols are woven throughout her seven books. Allegorical sections and metaphorical allusions abound.[9] The title chosen by Mechthild, *The Flowing Light of the Godhead*, expresses the dominant image used in her writing. The image refers not only to light, but to all that flows—water, blood, wine, honey. All these are symbols of the motion and transference of love from God to humans. The translator and writer of Mechthild's works, Heinrich of Halle, is quick to assure readers that he has not changed anything that Mechthild wrote:[10]

> What is written in this book flowed out of the living Godhead into the heart of Sister Mechthild. It is here faithfully recorded as God gave it from his heart and as she wrote it with her own hand. Deo Gratias. (6.3)

Mechthild has a sense that her work may be of lasting value to some of the people who read the book. "Any honest woman or good man who would have liked to speak with me, and after my death cannot do so, should read this little book" (6.1). The value was felt by Heinrich of Nördlingen, a Dominican, who sent the work to two friends of his. He said he was led to do this because the "living radiant love of Christ" was found in it, and "is the most moving love poem I have ever read in our tongue."[11]

At age sixty-three, Mechthild sought refuge at the Cistercian convent of Helfta. The nuns of the monastery were pleased to accept the holy Mechthild because they admired her courage and vision. They may have been aware of her works, since parts of her book were already circulating before her death. Mechthild was at Helfta for a short time before a severe illness left her blind. She wondered what she might do to repay these good women for all that they did to care for her. She was told to dictate the seventh book to them as a gift. This she did before she died in 1297 at the age of ninety.

The works of Mechthild were relatively well known in the fourteenth century. For a variety of reasons they then remained virtually unknown for the next three hundred years. It was not until 1860 that Dr. Carl Greith, later to be bishop of St. Gallen, located the text as he was writing a history of German mysticism. At Einsiedeln he located the book of Mechthild, then known as manuscript 277. The popularity of Mechthild slowly rose again, as translations made the text more accessible. The selections of *The Flowing Light of the Godhead* that follow introduce the warmth and richness of Mechthild's experience of Jesus Christ. The courtly language, style, and medieval imagination have been compared to that of Dante's *Divine Comedy*.[12] The theme of the medieval dance will become a key image. The final prayer and dialogue reveal the older Mechthild, whose life is coming to a close. Her sense of the all-embracing presence of Christ through those around her is clear. So is the gratefulness her body and soul feel for each other. With peace, she awaits the final revelation of her heavenly lover from whom she has never really parted.

The Flowing Light of the Godhead[13]

Of the Revelations to a Loving Soul[14]

In the year of our Lord 1250 and for fifteen years after this, this book was revealed to a sister who was holy in both body and spirit. It was revealed in German by God to Mechthild, a sister who served the Lord with devotion, simplicity, humility, abject poverty, and heavenly contemplation. She suffered oppression from many and scorn as well for almost forty years. Yet, she followed the light and the teaching of the Dominican tradition with earnest and sincere conviction. She increased daily in the path of perfection.

This book was both copied and put together by a Dominican brother of Mechthild. There is wisdom in this book, as can be readily seen from its table of contents.

This Is the First Part of the Book[15]

This book is to be joyfully welcomed for God speaks in it.

This book is now sent forth by myself as a messenger to all spiritual people, both good and evil. The building of the church cannot stand, particularly if its clergy and hierarchy fall into lukewarmness. My book proclaims the holiness of God, to whose praise my own holiness resounds. All who wish to understand this book should read it nine times.

This Book Is Called The Flowing Light of the Godhead

Lord God, who has written this book? I, Mechthild, have written it in my weakness. Why? Because I dare not hide the gift that is in it! Lord, what shall this book be called, for your glory? It shall be called The Flowing Light of the Godhead. It is called this because your flowing light and love flood all hearts that dwell in your mystery without falseness.

1. How Love and the Soul, Who Sits Enthroned as Queen, Speak to Each Other

SOUL: God be with you, Lady! Your name is known to me, for it is Love.

LOVE: God reward you, O Queen!

SOUL: Love, how happy I am to meet you!

LOVE: And I am very honored by your greeting to me.

SOUL: Love, you have spent so many years trying to understand the mystery of the Holy Trinity that the overflow has fallen once and for all into the humble lap of Mary!

LOVE: But my Queen, all these things were done for your delight!

SOUL: Love, you have taken from me all that I won on the earth!

LOVE: Did you not know this was a blessed exchange, O Queen?

SOUL: It is blessed to deprive me of childhood?

LOVE: If it is in exchange for heavenly freedom, yes!

SOUL: Love, you have stolen my youth!

LOVE: But it has been in exchange for strength, for virtues.

SOUL: You have taken my friends and relations!

LOVE: You know that is quite false, Queen!

SOUL: You have also taken all my honor and my possessions!

LOVE: You may look at it like that, Queen. But in one hour, the Holy Spirit shall give you so much more than you have lost.

SOUL: Love, you have tested me so greatly through suffering, that now my body can hardly bear its own weight!

LOVE: It seems you have gained great understanding through that loss.

SOUL: Love, do you realize you have consumed both my flesh and my blood, my life?

LOVE: Yes, but through it you have been enlightened and raised to God!

SOUL: You are a robber, Love. I expect you will make up for all you have stolen from me!

LOVE: You must trust me, O Queen. Please, just take me as I am.

SOUL: I see now, Love, that even here on earth, you have paid me back a hundred times for anything I have given!

LOVE: My Queen, now God and all the realm of heaven are yours.

2. Of Three Persons and Three Gifts

The true greeting of God out of the spring of the flowing Trinity has such power that it takes all strength from the body and bares the spirit. The soul sees itself as one of the blessed in heaven and can acknowledge itself in this glory. The soul seems separated from the body with its power and longing for love. The smallest part of life that remains to the body is a "sweet sleep." The soul sees God as One and Undivided in Three Persons. The Three Persons are seen as One Undivided God.

God greets the soul in the language of the court of heaven, which is not understood by us on the earth. The soul is clothed with such heavenly garments and surrounded with such strength that it may ask whatever it wishes and be sure that the wishes shall be granted.

If anything that is asked for is not granted, then the soul knows it is because it must be taken to a secret place by God. In this place, the soul must not ask or pray for anything or anyone. God alone will play with the soul in a game about which no one knows. This game is such that no one can really penetrate it. It is like a game in which the peasant cannot know a plow nor a knight really know a tournament. In fact, not even Mary the Mother can do anything here. God and the soul soar to a bliss that cannot be described! It is so great that I cannot begin to speak of it, for I remain a sinful creature!

In fact, as the Infinite God brings my unmoored soul into the heights of contemplation, I have lost touch with the earth. I am so awed that I forget I was ever on this earth! When the flight is at its highest, unfortunately, the soul must depart.

Then the all-glorious God speaks. "Maiden, now you must humble yourself and go back to the earth!"

She is frightened and says, "Lord, you have drawn me to the heights where I am out of myself and cannot praise you with any order of my body. I suffer grievously and I work to order my body!"

God speaks again. "My dove, your voice is music to my ears. Your words are pleasant to my mouth. Your longings for me are the gentlest of all gifts!"

She replies, "Dear Lord, All must be as you, the Master, wishes!"

She sighs so deeply that her body is awakened as it asks, "Lady! Where have you been? You now come back with love, beautiful and strong, free and full of spirit! But your wanderings have taken from me all my exuberance, my peace, my health, and my power."

To this the soul replies, "Silence! You are a destroyer and a complainer! I shall guard myself against you! If my enemy is wounded, that shall not trouble me. In fact, I am glad if it happens!"

This encounter surges from the Flowing Godhead into the arid soul. It floods in through many channels and brings forth ever fresh revelations and wisdom.

O Loving God, fire within and radiance without! You have given these gifts to me so that I hunger for the life that your holy ones enjoy. Undeserving as I am of your gifts, I shall gladly suffer here. No soul can receive your gifts or greeting until it has suffered enough to conquer itself. So, in this greeting, I wish that to happen so that I, while living, may still die.

3. Of the Handmaid of the Soul and of the Blow of Love

SOUL: My dearest Love, how long have you waited in vain for me? What can I do, for I am hunted, captured, bound, and terribly wounded. From this, I can never be healed. You have dealt cunning blows. Shall I ever recover from them? Would it not have been better that I should have never known you?

LOVE: I hunted you for my pleasure and caught you for my desire. I bound you for my joy and your wounds have made us one. Yes, my wise blows have made us one. It was I that drove the Almighty One from the heavens and it was I who took his human life and gave it back to him again. This was for the honor of the Father! How could you hope to save yourself from me, you who are so poor?

SOUL: But Queen, listen to my fear! What if I escape you through use of one small gift of God or through food or drink?

LOVE: One gives prisoners bread and water so that they do not die. God has given you more than this as respite for these times. But when death shall come to you, that is, when Easter is yours, I shall be with you, around you, through you. I shall take your body away and give you to your heart's Love.

SOUL: Love, you know I have been your scribe! Seal these words with your sign.

LOVE: Whoever loves God more than oneself knows where to find the seal. The seal lies between you and me. May your Easter come and may God give you the glorious resting place as your eternal home!

4. *The Soul Whom God Knows Appears at the Court*

When the poor soul comes to Court, she is both discreet and modest. With joyful eyes, she looks at her God. How lovingly she is received! Although she longs above all to praise this God, she is silent. But the Lord, with great love, shows her the Divine Heart. This heart glows like red gold in a great fire. God lays the soul bare in his glowing heart.

The great God, and the humble maiden, embrace and are as much one as water is in wine, The maiden is then overcome and out of time, for she is beside herself in weakness. Yet, God is overpowered with love for her as has always been the case. The Lord neither gives nor takes. Then the soul at last says, "Lord! You alone are my beloved! You alone are my desire, the flowing stream, the Light! And I am but your reflection!"

This is how the loving soul comes to the court of God, she who cannot live without the Lord!

5. *Of the Torrent of Love and of the Incessant Longing of Hell*

Although my body is tormented, my soul is in great delight because I have seen and embraced my Beloved! It is because of him that I suffer torment! As he draws me to himself, I give myself to him. I am powerless to hold back, and so he takes me to himself.

I would gladly speak, but I do not dare. I am engulfed in the deep union with the glorious Trinity. I am given a brief period of repose so that I may long with deep longing for him. I wish to sing the praises of this Lord, but I cannot. If this Lord would be loved above all things, I would even be willing to be sent to hell!

But I am able to do little except to look at him and say, "Lord, give me your blessing!" He looks at me, and draws me to himself with a loving greeting that cannot be explained. I mean by this that my body is incapable of expressing it.

Yet my body says to my spirit, "Where have you been? I cannot endure this any longer!"

And my soul replies, "Silence you fool! I will be with my Love even if you cannot begin to understand! For I am his joy and he is my torment."

This is the moment from which I shall never recover. But must I endure it forever and never escape from it?

6. Of the Nine Choirs and How They Sing

Now listen, my love. Hear with spiritual ears what the nine choirs sing.

We praise You, O Lord.
For you have sought us in your humility,
Saved us by your compassion,
Honored us by your humanity,
Led us by your gentleness,
Ordered us by your wisdom,
Protected us by your power,
Sanctified us by your holiness,
Illumined us by your intimacy,
Raised us by your love.

15. How God Comes to the Soul

I come to my love as dew on the flowers.

21. Of Knowledge and Freedom[16]

Love without knowledge is only darkness to the wise soul. Knowledge without revelation is as painful as the pains of hell. Revelation of Love cannot be endured without death.

22. Of the Mission of the Virgin Mary and How the Human Soul Was Made in the Honor of the Trinity

The sweet dew of the uncreated Trinity is distilled from the spring of the eternal Godhead in the flower of the chosen maid. And the fruit of this flower is the immortal God and a mortal man, Jesus. This man is a living comfort of everlasting love. Jesus is our Redeemer who is at the same time our Bridegroom!

The sight of the bride is intoxicated by the sight of the glorious countenance. In her greatest strength, my soul is overcome; in my blindness, I see most clearly. In my greatest clearness, I am still both dead and yet alive. The richer I become, the poorer I am. The more I protest in storm, the more loving God becomes to me. The higher I soar, the brighter I shine from the reflection of the Godhead and the nearer I am to him.

The more I labor, the more sweetly I am able to rest. The more I understand, the less do I speak. The louder I call to the Lord, the greater the wonder that is worked through me, with the power of the Lord. The more deeply God loves me, the more glorious is the course of love. Then, I am nearer to the resting place and I am closer to the embrace of God.

The closer I am to the embrace of God, the sweeter is the kiss of God. The more lovingly we both embrace, the more difficult it is for me to depart. The more God gives me, the more I can give and still have more. The more quickly I leave the Lord, the sooner I must return. The more the fire burns, the more my own light increases. The more that I am consumed by love, the brighter I shall shine! The greater my praise of God, greater my desire is to love the Lord.

How does our Bridegroom share in the jubilation of the Holy Trinity? God willed to no longer remain in himself alone. This is why the Lord created the soul and gave himself in great love to her. Of what are you made, O soul, that you are blessed to soar so high above all creatures of the earth? Yet, while you remain yourself, how are you somehow mingled with the most holy Trinity?

SOUL: You have spoken of my beginning. I was created in love and therefore nothing can express or liberate my nobility except Love alone. Blessed Mary, you are the Mother of this wonder. When did this all happen to you?

THE VIRGIN MARY: The Father's joy was darkened by Adam's fall and he was angry. The everlasting wisdom of God was provoked. It was then that the Father chose me as a bride so that he might have someone to love. This was because his noble bride, the soul, was dead. So the Son chose me as mother and the Holy Spirit accepted me as friend.

Thus, I alone was the bride of the Holy Trinity. I was the mother of orphans that I presented before the sight of God, so that they might not be lost as others before them.

I became the mother of so many noble children! I was full of the milk of compassion that nurtured the wise as well as the prophets who came before the birth of the Son of God. After that, I nurtured Jesus in my youth. As the Bride of God, I nurtured the holy church at the foot of the cross. Then, I became as a dry desert, full of pain and sorrow as the human agony of my son, Jesus, spiritually pierced my soul....

But my soul was reborn through his life-giving wounds and would live again, young and childlike in a new way! If another soul were to fully recover, the mother of God would also be its mother and its nurse as well. Ah, my God, how just and how true! You, my God, are my true Father and my soul is your rightful bride! I resemble you in all my sorrows over the son.

Blessed Mary! In your old age, you nourished the holy apostles with your maternal wisdom and your powerful prayer. This was so that God's honor and will should be fulfilled in their lives. You did also nurture then, as you do now, the hearts of the martyrs with strong faith. You nurture the confessors with the protection of their ears. You nurture the maidens with purity and the widows with constancy.

You nurture the perfect with a gentle spirit and sinners with your assured intercession. My Lady, you must still nurture us . . . until the last day! Then you shall see how God's children and your children are weaned and grown up in that love that brings everlasting Life. Then you shall see and know the fullness of the milk with which you nursed the Lord Jesus from your breasts that he kissed.

26. In This Way, the Soul Leads the Senses and Is Free from Grief

The faithful soul walks in a wondrous and lofty way! The soul leads the senses as someone with sight might lead a blind person. In this way, the soul is free and travels without any grief in the heart. Now the soul sees that it wishes nothing other than what the Lord wills, for the Lord wills only what is best for the soul.

27. How You Are to Become Worthy in the Way, Walk in It, and Be Perfected by the Lord

Three things make the soul worthy of this way so that it recognizes it and walks in it. First, it must will to come to God, renouncing all self-will, joyfully welcoming God's grace, and willingly accepting all its demands against human desires. Second, all things shall be welcome on the way except those that are sinful. Third, the creature shall be made perfect when all that it does is for the glory of God. Then, even the least desire will be as highly praised by God as if it were the highest state of human contemplation that is possible.

If I sin, I am no longer in this way.

35. The Desert Has Twelve Things[17]

You shall love nothing and flee your self. You shall stand alone. You shall seek help from no one so that your being may be quiet. You shall be free from the bondage of all things and shall loose those who are bound. Exhort the free and care for the sick while you—at the same time—dwell alone. You shall drink the waters of sorrow and kindle the fire of love. You shall dwell in the desert with the vessel of virtue.

36. Of Malice, Goodness, and Wonders

You shall be adorned by the malice of your enemies. You shall be honored with the virtues of your heart. Your crown shall be your good works. You shall be raised up with our mutual love. You shall be sanctified with my glorious wonders!

37. The Soul Answers That She Is Not Worthy of Such Graces

My beloved, undeserved contempt delights me! I desire the virtues of the heart. I have little of good works. I have tarnished the beauty of our twofold love. I am most unworthy of your glorious wonders!

38. God Rejoices That the Soul Has Overcome Four Sins

Our Lord delights in heaven because of the loving soul he has on earth. He says, "Look how she who once wounded me has risen! She has cast out the worldliness of her life. She has overcome the bear of impurity and trodden the lion of pride under her feet. She has torn the wolf of desire from his revenge and now comes racing as a hunted deer to the spring which is myself. Yes, she comes soaring like an eagle, swinging herself from the depths to the heights!"

39. God Asks the Soul What It Brings

God: What do you bring me, my Queen, as you sorely hunt for my love?

40. The Soul Responds

Soul: Lord, I bring you my treasure! It is greater than the mountains and higher than the world. It is deeper than the sea, and higher than the clouds! It is more glorious than the sun and more abundant than the stars! In fact, it outweighs the whole earth!

41. God Speaks

God: You are the image of my own heart. You are made noble by my humanity and adorned by my Holy Spirit. What do you call your treasure?

42. The Soul Responds

Soul: Lord, I call it my heart's desire! I have withdrawn it from the world, and denied it even to myself as well as to all other creatures. Now I can bear this no longer. Where shall I lay this treasure, O my God?

43. God Answers

God: You shall lay your heart's desire nowhere except in my Divine Heart and on my human breast. There alone shall you find comfort and be embraced by the Holy Spirit.

44. Of the Way Love Is Found in Seven Things, Three Bridal Robes, and a Dance

God: My loving soul, do you wish to know the way?

Soul: Yes, Holy Spirit, show it to me!

Holy Spirit: You must overcome the need for remorse, the pain of penitence, the labor of confession, the love of the world, the temptation of the devil, the pride of the body, and the annihilation of self-will that drags so many people backward that they never really come to true love. When you have conquered most of these enemies, you shall be weary and cry out, "Beautiful youth! Where can I find you?"

YOUTH: I hear a voice which speaks of love. Many days I have wooed her but I never heard her voice! Now I am moved and I must go to meet her. It is she who bears both grief and love. She bears this in the morning, in the dew of intimate rapture which first penetrates her soul.

THE WAITING MAIDS OF THE FIVE SENSES: Lady, you must adorn yourself!

SOUL: Love, where shall I go?

SENSES: We have heard a whisper that the Prince is coming to greet you in the morning dew and the song of the birds! Do not delay, my Lady!

The soul then dressed in a garment of humility so that none was more humble. Over this was placed a white robe of chastity that was so pure it could not endure any words or desires that might stain it. Next, the soul wrapped herself with the mantle of holy desire, which was woven with all the virtues. It was clothed in this way that she went into the company of the holy people. In their company the sweetest nightingales sing day and night.

She hears as well the song of the birds of holy wisdom. Yet the youth does not come! He sends his messengers to her to invite her to dance. He then sends the faith of Abraham to her, the longings of the prophets, the chaste modesty of our lady, St. Mary, and the sacred perfection of our Lord Jesus Christ and the whole company of the elect. A noble Dance of Praise is prepared. Then at last the Youth comes and speaks to her.

YOUTH: Maiden, you shall merrily dance just as my elect do!

SOUL: I cannot dance, O Lord, unless you lead me. If you wish me to leap joyfully, you must first dance and sing yourself! Then I will leap for love. Then will I dance from love to knowledge, from knowledge to fruition, from fruition to the mystery beyond all human sense. There will I remain and circle forever!

YOUTH: Your Dance of Praise is well done. Now you shall have whatever you wish of the Virgin's son.... But you are weary! Come at midday to the shade by the brook, to the resting place of love. There you can cool yourself.

SOUL: My Lord! It is too much of a gift that you should accompany my love. When the heart has no love of itself, it will be forever aroused to love by you alone!

Then, wearied of the dance, the soul said to the senses, "Leave me alone, for I must cool myself!" The senses responded, "Lady, will you be refreshed by the tears of Mary Magdalene? Will that be sufficient?"

SOUL: Be quiet, for you do not know what I mean! Do not stop me, for I wish to drink of the unmingled wine!

SENSES: Lady, in virginal chastity, the Love of God is ready for you!

SOUL: This may be so, but for me it is not the highest love.

SENSES: You may cool yourself in the blood of the martyrs.

SOUL: I have already been martyred so many times that I cannot go that way.

SENSES: There are many holy souls who live according to the advice of their confessors.

SOUL: I do obey their counsels, but I cannot go that way either!

SENSES: Then surely you will find refuge in the wisdom of the Apostles!

SOUL: I already have their wisdom in my heart. It tells me to choose the better part.

SENSES: Lady, the angels are clear, bright, and fully loving. Ascend to them if you wish to refresh yourself.

SOUL: The angels' joy is only woe unless I see my Lord and my Love!

SENSES: Cool yourself, then, with the holy austerity that God gave to John the Baptist.

SOUL: Pain and suffering cannot refresh unless Love rules over all.

SENSES: Lady, if you wished to be refreshed, kneel down at the Virgin's knee to the tiny babe; then taste and see how the angels drink of eternity from the milk of this joyful maid!

SOUL: It is a childish joy to nourish and rock a babe! I am a full-grown bride and I wish to be at my lover's side!

SENSES: But Lady, if you wish to go there, we shall be blinded for the fiery glory of the Godhead. As you well know, all the flame and glowing in heaven and on the earth which ever burns and shines flows from God alone. From the divine breath of the Lord through his divine lips, and from the counsel of the Holy Spirit, who can abide in this even for one hour?

SOUL: Fish cannot drown in water nor can birds sink in the air. Gold will not perish in the refiner's fire. God has given all creatures the power to nourish and to seek the end for which they were made. How then can I not seek my end? I must return to God who is my Creator through nature, my Brother through humanity, my Bridegroom through love. I belong to him forever! Do you think that fire has only destructive results for my soul? No; love can fiercely scorch but it can also be tender and consoling. Therefore, do not be troubled! You can still teach me. When I return, I shall need your teaching, for the earth is full of snares.

Then the beloved soul goes into the Lover, into that secret hiding place of the sinless Godhead.... There, the soul was fashioned into the very nature of God so that no further hindrance could come between it and God. It was then that the Lord said, "Now stand up, O soul."

SOUL: What do you wish, Lord?

LORD: You must go now.

SOUL: But Lord, what will happen to me if I leave you?

LORD: You are by nature already mine! Nothing can come between us! There is no angel so sublime who, even for an hour, has been granted that which has been given to you forever. Therefore, put all fear and shame and outward faults away forever. It is only those things that keep you sensitive to me by nature that you shall wish to keep for eternity. Those things are your noble longing, and your endless desire for me. In my infinite mercy, I shall fill those forever!

SOUL: Lord, now I have been stripped of all things while you remain a God most glorious! Our mutual communion is Love eternal, which shall never die. Then came a blessed stillness that both welcomed. He gave himself to her and she fully gave herself to him. The soul knows what shall now happen to her and she is comforted by it. Where two lovers come together in secret, they must often part but yet the parting is without parting.

Dear Reader and Friend of God!

I have written down my way of love for you. May God give it to you in your heart. Amen!

The Seventh Part of the Book

43. Of the Simplicity of Love[18]

Those who would know much, but love little
Remain forever at the beginning of a good life.
Therefore, we should always carry wonder in our hearts
If we hope to please God in an inner way.

A simple love, even with a little knowledge
Can work great things within us.

Holy simplicity is the way to all wisdom.
Holy wisdom shows the wise that they are but fools.

When simplicity of heart
Lives in the wisdom of the senses
Great holiness comes to the human soul.

64. *How God Serves Us*[19]

I speak as a beggar woman as I pray this to God:

My Lord,

I thank you that you have taken all earthly riches from me, for since then, you have clothed and fed me through the goodness of others. Because of this, I no longer can clothe my heart in the pride of possessing such things.

My Lord,

I thank you for taking away the sight from my eyes, for that has meant that you serve me through the eyes of others.

My Lord,

I thank you for taking away the power of my hands . . . and the power of my heart, for now you serve me with other hands and hearts.

My Lord,

I pray to you for all of these who so serve me in you. Reward them here on earth with your divine love. May this love enable them to faithfully serve you and please you with all virtues, until they come to a happy end.

I pray too for all those of pure heart who gave up everything for the Love of God. We are all arch-beggars who shall be judged on the last day by Jesus, our Redeemer and Lord. Change in me all that I lament in your presence and all that I lament in all sinners.

All that I ask, I pray you to grant to me and to all imperfect spiritual people for your own glory. Your praise, O Lord, shall never be silent in my heart, no matter what I do or suffer or leave undone. Amen.

65. *How God Adorns the Soul with Suffering*

. . . The suffering body speaks to the downcast Soul:

When will you soar on the wings of your longing to the blissful heights, to Jesus your everlasting Love?
O Soul, thank him there for me, and pray that he may be mine, poor and unworthy as I am in his memory.
For he came to this poor earth and took our human nature upon himself.

Pray that he keep me from sin in his glorious favor, until he gives me a holy end,
When you, most dear soul, will have to part from me.

SOUL: My beloved Body, prison in which I have been bound, I thank you now for all in which you have followed me. Although I have often been troubled by you, yet you have so often come to my aid!

All your needs will be taken account of at the last day.
Therefore, let us lament no more, but be filled with gladness.
Now let us stand firm in joyful hope for all that God has done to us both!

. . . The more the soul loves,
The less the body thinks of itself,
The humbler its work before God,
And before all those of goodwill.

THE END OF THIS BOOK.

NOTES

1. Mechthild of Magdeburg, *Offenbarum der Schwester Mechthild von Magdeburg oder das flissende Licht der Gottheit* (Regensburg: Joseph Mainz, 1869). This is MS. 277 from the monastic library of Einsiedeln. Heinrich of Nördlingen and others translated Mechthild's original text, MS. 277, into High German in 1344. The Latin translation by Heinrich of Halle is still in existence. The original text has not been found.

2. Mechthild says she is forty-three as she writes her visions in book 4 of *The Flowing Light of the Godhead.* According to the prologue, book 4 was composed between 1250 and 1255.

3. John Howard, "The German Mystic, Mechthild of Magdeburg," in *Medieval Women Writers*, ed. Katharina Wilson (Athens: University of Georgia Press, 1984) 153.

4. *Women and Power in the Middle Ages*, ed. M. Erler and M. Kowaleski (Athens: University of Georgia Press, 1988) 1–17; Ernest McDonnell, *The Beguines and Beghards in Medieval Culture* (New Brunswick, N.J.: Rutgers University Press, 1954) 30–46.

5. Malcolm Lambert, *Popular Heresy: Movements from Bogomil to Hus* (New York: Holmes and Meier, 1977) 176; Marygrace Peters, "The Beguines: Feminine Piety Derailed," *Spirituality Today* 43:1 (Spring 1991) 36–52.

6. The numbers in parentheses refer to the book and chapter number in *The Flowing Light of the Godhead.*

7. Howard, "The German Mystic" 153–85.

8. Alice Kemp-Welch, *Of Six Medieval Women* (Williamstown, Mass.: Corner House, 1972) 57–82.

9. Such images include birds in general; blackbirds, doves, eagles, larks, and nightingales image, respectively, demons, Holy Spirit, Christ, communal prayers, and the lovers of God. Green, gold, red, and yellow symbolize human love of Christ, divinity, patience or love, and hope. Particular flowers are also symbols; see Mary Jeremy Finnegan, *Women of Helfta* (Athens: University of Georgia Press, 1991) 47.

10. Examples of the forms of writing in Mechthild as well as an introduction to her work can be found in Finnegan, *Women of Helfta* 15–23.

11. This is cited in ibid. 22.

12. Edmund Gardner, *Dante and the Mystics* (New York: Octagon Books, 1968) 342–48.

13. *Offenbarum der Schwester Mechthild. The Revelations of Mechthild of Magdeburg (1210–1297): or, the Flowing Light of the Godhead*, trans. Lucy Menzies (London/New York/Ontario: Longmans, Green, 1955), based on MS. 277. Page numbers will indicate the German text (G) and the English translation (E). Some wording in the Menzies translation has been altered for the sake of clarity. These minor changes do not alter the meaning or intent of the German text.

14. Pre-Prologue. G 1; E 1.

15. Prologue, 1.1–1.6, 1.15. G 1–8; E 3–10.

16. 1.21–1.27. G 11–14; E 12–15.

17. 1.35–1.44. G 18–22; E 17–20.

18. 7.43. G 241; E 243.

19. 7.64–7.65. G 257–58; E 261–63.

BIBLIOGRAPHY

Bynum, Carolyn Walker. "Mechthild of Magdeburg: Images of God." In *Jesus as Mother: Studies in the Spirituality of the High Middle Ages*. Berkeley: University of California Press, 1982. 229–47.

Clark, Susan L. " 'Ze Glicher Wis': Mechthild von Magdeburg and the Concept of Likeness." In *The Worlds of Medieval Women: Creativity, Influence and Imagination*. Edited by Constance Berman, Charles Connell, and Judith Rice Rothschild. Morgantown, W. Va.: West Virginia University Press, 1985. 41–50.

Colledge, Eric. "Mechthild of Magdeburg." *Month* 211 (June 1961) 325–36.

Finnegan, Mary Jeremy. *The Women of Helfta: Scholars and Mystics*. Athens: University of Georgia Press, 1991.

Howard, John. "The German Mystic, Mechthild of Magdeburg." In *Medieval Women Writers*. Edited by Katharina Wilson. Athens: University of Georgia Press, 1984. 153–85.

Kemp-Welch, Alice. *Of Six Medieval Women*. Williamstown, Mass.: Corner House, 1972.

Koch, Regina. "Mechthild von Magdeburg, Woman of Two Worlds." *14th Century English Mystics Newsletter* 3 (1981) 111–31.

McDonnell, Ernest. *The Beguines and Beghards in Medieval Culture*. New Brunswick, N.J.: Rutgers University Press, 1954.

Menzies, Lucy. *The Revelations of Mechthild of Magdeburg (1210–1297): or, The Flowing Light of the Godhead*. London/New York/Ontario: Longmans, Green, 1953.

Peters, Marygrace. "The Beguines: Feminine Piety Derailed." *Spirituality Today* 43:1 (Spring 1991) 36–52.

– 9 –

GERTRUDE THE GREAT

(c. 1256–1302)

Engrave Thy Wounds upon My Heart

By the time Gertrude the Great was brought to Helfta, the monastery was already renowned for its learning. Elizabeth of Schwartzburg and her husband, Count Burchard of Mansfield, founded the monastery in 1229, locating it near their castle at Mansfield. Seven Cistercian nuns and Cunegund of Halberstadt were its first inhabitants. Because of baronic wars, the monastery moved to Rodarsdorf in Upper Saxony. Gertrude of Hackeborn, who is not the Gertrude named "the Great" (although the accolade could surely have been given to her), was elected abbess of this monastery when she was only nineteen. When a water shortage placed the monastery in jeopardy, Baron Lords Albert and Louis Hackeborn gave an ancestral castle at Helfta to Gertrude and her sister, Mechthild. The nuns moved to this castle, which became the monastery of Helfta.

In spite of the difficult period of anarchy and turmoil after the death of Frederick II in 1250, Abbess Gertrude von Hackeborn brought the monastery of Helfta to the highest level of feminine culture known to the Middle Ages. At Helfta women studied the works of Albert the Great, Thomas Aquinas, and other fathers and doctors of the Church, the Scriptures, and some of the classics. There was a strong grounding in music, choral office, hymnody, and psalmody. Grammar, rhetoric, theology, arithmetic, geometry, astronomy, Latin, and copying of manuscripts were also part of the curriculum. In the monastery, intellectual learning was complemented by a desire for holiness

Helfta in the thirteenth century was a haven of visionary women. These visionaries were confident that the authority given to them by Jesus Christ in their visions ought to be used for the service of others. The women of Helfta show few effects of the negative female stereotyping suffered by other women during this time. At Helfta the intellectual and spiritual equality of women and men was assumed. This is particularly noticeable in women like Gertrude the Great, who was brought to Helfta as a child and was not exposed to the social and ecclesial attitudes of feminine inferiority and sinfulness.[1]

The holiness of the nuns of Helfta was as well known as their scholarship. In the thirteenth century increasing clericalization tended to look on a priest as another Christ. Much of this was due to the focus on the consecration of bread and wine in the liturgy. The moment that the consecratory words were uttered became magnified to such a degree that it was thought the priest at that time was temporarily divinized. The elaboration of canon law, the definition of sacraments, the penitential system, the restriction of theological training in universities to males only, and the theory of the divine character of priesthood all served to place priests in inordinate positions of divine power.

Within this context the Helfta visionaries provide a glimpse of an alternative mediation of Jesus Christ. Priests had a power of office, but the visionaries had the power of mystical union. The clergy could teach because they were ordained by a bishop. Women mystics and visionaries taught because they too were ordained to do so by Jesus Christ. Since the fifth century, some sacraments formerly mediated by laity had become the sole prerogative of ordained priests. Visions of the Helfta mystics affirmed their role as sacramental mediators. A special "moment of consecration" did not temporarily divinize them, but a total union with Jesus Christ did. The mysticism of the Helfta women did not directly challenge the institution of the priesthood. That would not occur to women of this century. Their mysticism complemented the form of institutional priesthood, however, and provided alternative expressions of its meaning.[2]

Devotion to the Eucharist was widespread in the thirteenth century; however, daily communion was not encouraged. Monthly communion was considered normative for women. Abbess Gertrude von Hackeborn did not accept the normative for her sisters at Helfta. She insisted on more frequent communion, urging them to receive communion at least every Sunday and feast day. She is rewarded by Jesus Christ for this brave decision and bold move.[3]

Gertrude von Hackeborn was still abbess at Helfta when the young Gertrude was brought to the monastery for education. It is difficult to know why a child of four or five would be brought to a monastery to spend her childhood. Whether this was a fulfillment of some parental vow to give a child to the Lord, whether Gertrude was an unwanted child from a second marriage, or whether Gertrude was part of a large family whose children could not be cared for remains a matter of speculation. Gertrude only tells the reader that she has happy memories of her childhood.[4]

The sister of Abbess Gertrude, Mechthild of Hackeborn, was placed as guide and caregiver for young Gertrude. The child's acute perception and intelligence were quickly noticed by Mechthild and Abbess Gertrude. Young Gertrude was a precocious child who quickly absorbed the lessons given at Helfta. In time she decided to join the monastery that had been her home. She was twenty-five when she experienced her first vision of Jesus Christ on January 27, 1281.

Subsequent visions would follow for the rest of her life, usually occurring while she was at community office or at the celebration of the Eucharist.

The Christ images of Gertrude are varied. Some images, like lover, bridegroom, and friend, were popular ones in the twelfth century. Other images, like judge, ruler, and powerful authority, are less common in the century, but common to Gertrude.[5] The heart and wounds of Jesus Christ were recurrent symbols in Gertrude's visions. These symbols pointed to the gracious and endless love of Jesus Christ for all people. Gertrude had a number of visions of herself drinking from the heart of Christ through the wound in his side. These visions are a symbolic way of stating that she was in communion with Jesus Christ. The context for Gertrude's devotion to the Sacred Heart, the symbol of the humanity-divinity of Jesus Christ, was not private prayer but community worship.

Gertrude's visions most frequently occurred at liturgical prayer, the prayer of the community. The Christ of her visions emphasized the centrality of community worship. The mystical union of Gertrude with Christ was not so much a source for seclusion as it was oriented toward service of others. This service of others was not seen as detrimental to the mystical life of Helfta, but rather it was an integral part of that life. For the women of Helfta, the hospitality of Christ, who serves all, was manifest through their own service and love of all.

The entire community of Helfta is the object of some visions that affirm the result of their prayers for others. Sometimes the visions of one Helfta visionary affirmed the authenticity of another sister's visions. The content of the visions included some experiences that transcended the normative practices of the church of the period. Gertrude herself receives some sacraments directly from Jesus Christ when she is unable to receive them through priestly mediation.[6]

In some visions Gertrude acts as the priestly channel of mediation to her sisters, binding and loosing as Jesus Christ commands her.[7] Although Gertrude is well aware of the prohibitions of her time against women baptizing, preaching, teaching, hearing confessions, and receiving communion frequently, she acts in accord with the authority grounded in her visions of Jesus Christ. When she has honest questions about doing what he says, he assures her that he is Lord of the church, and her obedience is to him. She eventually can live with some serenity in the claim to this authority. Gertrude is strong in her sense of obedience to the church, but is also convinced that a monastic vocation is one of service for others to the extent Jesus Christ directs it that way. This emphasis is quite different from the emphasis of other women monastics of the twelfth century.

The church as the mystical body of Christ is imaged as male in Gertrude's works, since she did conceive of the fullness of humanity within the erroneous physiology of her time. This may also have contributed to her freedom for envisioning herself in a priestly role as well as the virgin Mary. The Christ of her visions is always one of strong and loving kindness. In her writings, *pietas* is difficult to adequately translate into English. It is like the strong and compassionate affection of a mother or father for a child. It also signifies the loving concern that God has for all people who are forever bonded to God.

Those who lived with Gertrude were aware that God had chosen her to be a herald of this divine love. Her service was to make known the mystery of the divine kindness so that all might live with greater trust and hope in that unique love. Gertrude's own trust in this mercy was so strong that she did not fear even a sudden death or death without the last rites. She knew that Jesus Christ would be with her. His affection was borne as an imprint upon her heart, a union that grew deeper as her life progressed.[8]

Gertrude died in 1302. Her body was laid to rest at Helfta beside the bodies of Abbess Gertrude and her sister, Mechthild. Unfortunately, the frequency of wars forced the Helfta nuns to move to Eisleben. The sisters of Helfta had hoped they would be able to return to Helfta after peace returned. This never happened, and the graves of three of the most significant Helfta women were lost to history.

Innocent XI (1676–89) placed Gertrude's name into the Roman martyrology in 1677. This canonization process also proclaimed that her feast would be celebrated on November 17, the date believed to be her death day. Later ages changed the date to November 15.

The selections that follow are from *The Herald of Divine Love.* This work has five books or major sections. Gertrude herself wrote book 2. The remaining books are compilations of works by Gertrude that the nuns of Helfta put together after her death.[9]

The sections that follow are a brief introduction to Gertrude's visions and the liturgical grounding for her visions. The excerpts from her work are necessarily brief, but they do introduce the reader to some of the affection and warmth of the relationship of Gertrude and Jesus Christ.

The Herald of Divine Love[10]

Book 1[11]

Chapter 14. Gertrude Receives Gifts from God

2. Many people often asked Gertrude what she thought about certain points that they questioned. In particular, many wondered whether they should cease receiving communion, for some reason or other. Gertrude advised those who asked, and who seemed reasonably fervent, that they should approach the Lord's table with confidence, for God was gracious and merciful. Sometimes she almost had to use force to get them to receive communion. However, on one occasion

she became worried. Was she relying on herself more than she ought, for she was an honest and sincere woman. As she had done so often, she took her wondering to her Lord in his great kindness. She confided her fear to him. She felt reassured by his warmth revealed in the answer to her question.

"Do not be afraid, but be comforted. Be strong and confident, for I, the Lord your God and your lover, give you a definite answer. My freely given love has created you and chosen you to be my delight. You can give a sure answer to those who ask me the question through you. You can be sure that I will be true to what I say now. I promise that I will never allow an unworthy person to ask you the question about receiving the life-giving sacrament of my body and blood. Declare to those whom I send to you that it is safe to approach me, for they are weary and oppressed. They can approach my heart because of your grace and your love. I shall open fatherly arms to embrace them and give them the affectionate kiss of peace."

4. Some days later she remembered the promise the Lord made to her. Aware of her own unworthiness, she asked the Lord how he could possibly perform such wonderful things through her, worthless as she was. The Lord answered her.

"Does not the Church's faith rest universally on the promise that I made to Peter when I said, 'Whatever you bind on earth shall be bound in heaven'? Does not the church today believe that this promise is fulfilled through all the ministers of the church? Therefore, why do you not believe with equal faith that I can do whatever I choose to do in love? Believe what my divine mouth has promised you!" Then he touched her tongue and said, "See, I have put my words in your mouth (Jer 1:9). I confirm every word you speak in my name to anyone at the prompting of the Spirit. If you promise anyone on earth my goodness, it will be held in heaven as a valid promise."

Gertrude answered, "Lord, what if I told someone that a guilty act could not remain unpunished and thought I did so under the guidance of the Spirit. I could not rejoice if anyone suffered condemnation as a result." The Lord replied, "Whenever you are moved by justice or by compassion to say such a thing, I will surround the person with my lovingkindness. That will move her to repentance so that she will no longer deserve my punishment."

5. ..."Do not be afraid, my daughter. Have faith in me and the privilege I am conferring upon you. When anyone asks your advice in humility and faith, you will discern that case in the light of my divine truth. Regardless of the matter, you will come to the same conclusion as I would.... Why is it such a great thing for me to grant you discernment when I have allowed you again and again to experience the secrets of my friendship?... I, God dwelling within you, with the boundless lovingkindness of my affection, long to bring many people blessings through you. The joy your heart feels at this is drawn from the joy of the brimming well of my own heart."

6. This receives strong support from the evidence of Dame Mechthild of blessed memory. While she was praying for Gertrude, she was shown the heart of Gertrude in the likeness of a strong bridge. The bridge seemed fortified on one side by Christ's human nature and on the other by his divine nature. Mechthild understood what the vision meant. The Lord was saying that anyone who walked with Gertrude would not be able to fall or wander. Whoever received her words and humbly obeyed her advice would not stray from the true path to the Lord.

Book 2[12]

Chapter 1. The Visitation of the Lord to Gertrude

1. Let the unfathomable depth of uncreated Wisdom cry out to the depths of omnipotent Power. Let all creation praise and exult in your amazing love! O most sweet God of my life and the only love of my soul, your overabundance of mercy has led me through the many obstacles I have placed in the way of your love. I have been led through a desert, through dry lands that had no pathway, for my own doing brought me into a deep valley of my miseries.

I was twenty-five when my conversion began. It was the Monday before the Feast of the Purification of Mary, your most chaste Mother. It was evening, during the joyful hour after compline. You, who are the true light that is clearer than any light and deeper than any depth, chose to enlighten my darkness. How sweetly and gently you began my conversion! You settled the anxiety and restlessness that had plagued me for more than a month....

2. At this time I was in the middle of our dormitory, bowing reverently to an older religious as our rule requires. When I raised my head, I saw you, my gracious love and redeemer. You were the most handsome and amiable young man of sixteen years.[13] How you surpassed all others in beauty! You attracted my heart and eyes by the infinite light of your glory, which you kindly revealed only in proportion to the weakness of my nature. You stood before me, and with wonderful tenderness and love you said, "Your salvation is at hand! Why are you so consumed with grief? Do you have no one to console you that you are so overcome by sadness?"

I knew that I was physically standing in my place in choir as you spoke. This was the place where I offered my tepid prayers. Yet as I heard these words, "I will save and deliver you. Do not be afraid," I saw you put your right hand in mine, as if to ratify your promise. You spoke again. "You have been afflicted in ways similar to my enemies. Though you have sucked honey, it has been amid thorns. Now come back to me. I will receive you and inebriate you with an overflow of my heavenly delights."

My soul melted within me as you spoke these words. When I tried to come to you, I beheld a great distance between you and myself. Between your outstretched right hand and my left hand, there was such a long hedge that I could see neither an end nor a beginning to it! The top of it appeared so full of thorns that I could find no way to come to you who are the only consolation of my soul. I then wept over my faults and crimes. The hedge that divided us stood for these crimes. You knew the sincere fervor with which I desired you, and my weakness as well. Most loving Father of the poor, "whose mercies are greater than all your works," you then took my hand and placed me instantly beside you without any difficulty! In looking at the precious hand you extended to me as a pledge of your promises, I recognized your radiant wounds through which you took away our transgressions (Col 2:14).

You enlightened and opened my mind by such illuminations. These revelations gave me the power to be inwardly detached from an inordinate love of literature and from all my vanities. Soon I counted as nothing those things that had formerly pleased me. Everything that was not you, O God of my heart, appeared vile to me. You alone gave pleasure to my soul....

Chapter 2. Gertrude's Heart Is Enlightened

1. Hail, my light and my salvation! May all in heaven, on earth, and in the depths give thanks to you. You have given me the extraordinary grace to know and consider what passes within my heart. Before this gift I did not care any more about the movements of my heart than I did about what passes through my hands and feet (if I may speak this way). Only after the infusion of your most sweet light did I see so many things in my head that offended your goodness. I even saw that there was such chaos, disorder, and confusion within me that you could not abide there.

Nevertheless, my most loving Jesus, all these defects and all my unworthiness did not prevent you from honoring me with your visible presence. I experienced it nearly every day that I received the life-giving nourishment of your Body and Blood. However, I only saw you indistinctly, as one might see the coming dawn. By this presence, you were slowly and sweetly attracting my soul, so that I might be entirely united to you, by knowing you better and enjoying you more fully.

2. I worked to obtain your favors on your mother's Feast of the Annunciation, celebrating your union with our nature in her virginal womb. You who said, "Here I am before I called you," anticipated this festal day. Unworthy as I am, you poured forth on me the sweetness of your blessing on the vigil of the feast. The sweet benediction was bestowed upon me while I was at the chapter following matins [morning prayer]....

From that time on you gave me a clearer knowledge of yourself. This knowledge awakened such love in me that now I wished to correct all my faults not for fear of your just anger but because of love alone. I do not remember any time in my life when I experienced such deep happiness as these days about which I speak. You invited me to taste the immense delights of your royal table. I am not certain whether it is your wise providence which has now deprived me of them, or whether the pain of their absence is due to my own negligence.

Chapter 3. God's Dwelling in Her Heart

1. You continued to act lovingly toward me and to continually draw my soul from vanity and to yourself. One day between the festival of the Resurrection and the Ascension, I went into our courtyard before prime and seated myself near the fountain. I began to consider the beauty of this place. It charmed me with its clear and flowing stream, the verdure of the trees which surrounded it, and the flight of the birds—especially the doves. Above all, I loved the sweet calm of this place that is apart from everything. I asked myself what would make this place even better for me. I thought that the friendship of a wise and intimate companion, who would sweeten my solitude or render it useful to others, would do that.

It was then that you, my Lord and my God, who are a torrent of inestimable pleasure, not only inspired me with the first impulse of this desire, but also willed to be the fulfillment of it. You inspired me with the thought that if I return your graces to you in continual gratitude, as a stream returns to its source; if I increase in the love of virtue, and put forth the flowers of good works like the trees; if I despise the things of earth and fly upward as freely as the birds, I can free my senses from the distraction of exterior things. Then my spirit would be empty of obstacles and my heart would be an agreeable dwelling for you.

2. I was occupied with the recollection of these things during the same day when I was kneeling for evening prayer after vespers. Before retiring to rest, this passage of the gospel came suddenly to my mind: "If any one love Me, My word will be kept, and my Father will love them and we will make Our abode with them" (John 14:23). At these words my worthless heart perceived your presence in my heart, my most sweet God and my delight. How I wished that all the waters of the sea were changed into blood so that I could be washed with them to remove the evils of my heart, which you have chosen for your dwelling. I wished that my heart might be torn from my body and cast into a furnace. Then it might be purified from its dross and made less unworthy of your presence.

My God, since that hour you have sometimes treated me with sweetness and sometimes with severity, as I have either amended my life or been negligent. However, I speak truthfully when I say this. Even the most perfect amendment which I could ever attain even for a moment or even for a whole lifetime could not merit the most trifling of condescending graces that I have received from you. This is how great my crimes and sins are.

Your overwhelming compassion helps me to believe that the sight of my faults makes you fear you will see me perish. Thus, my faults do not incur your anger. Your patience is supporting my defects even now, and with much kindness. This goodness is even greater than the sweetness with which you patiently bore the weak and untrustworthy nature of Judas during your mortal life.

3. My mind still takes pleasure in wandering and in distracting itself with perishable things. Even so, when I finally return into my heart after some hours, days, or even entire weeks, I still find you there. I cannot complain that you have left me even for a moment from that first time until this year. This is the ninth year since I received this grace.

Well, there is one exception. Once I felt that you left me for the eleven days before the Feast of John the Baptist. I believe this happened on account of a worldly conversation I had on the Thursday before this. Your absence lasted until the Vigil of St. John when the Mass "Ne timeas, Zacharia" is said. ["Fear not, Zachary, thy prayer is heard" is the Introit for the Vigil of John the Baptist.] Then your sweetest humanity and unbounded love moved you to seek me in my disturbed state. I had reached such a place that I thought no more of the greatness of the treasure I had lost. I do not even remember feeling grief at the time that I lost it, nor did I have any real desire of recovering the loss!

Chapter 4. Of the Symbolic Wound of Love Imprinted in her Heart

1. During the winter of the first or second year when I began to receive these favors, I found the following prayer in a book of devotions.

O Lord Jesus Christ, Son of the living God, help me to always be drawn to you with my whole heart. May I seek only your sweetness and delights with a great desire and with a thirsting spirit. May my mind and everything within me long only for you, our true Blessing. O most compassionate Lord, imprint your wounds with your most precious blood upon my heart. For I desire to know both your grief and your love through these wounds and wish the memory of them to remain in my heart forever. May this gift enlighten my compassion for your sufferings and increase your love in me. May you also grant me the grace to despise all creatures so that my heart may delight only in you. Amen.

2. I repeated this prayer frequently, for I quickly learned it with great satisfaction. You heard my petitions, for you hear the prayers of the humble. It was not long after I began saying the prayer, during that same winter, that I was in the dining room after vespers for something to eat. I was sitting near someone to whom I had told my secret.

I am writing this only for the benefit of those who may read what I write, because I have often perceived that the fervor of my devotion is increased by this communication with another. Lord, my God, I do not know whether it was thy Spirit, or perhaps human affection that made me reveal this. I have heard from those more experienced in such matters that it is always better to reveal these secrets. The revelations are not to be told to just anyone, but to those whom we reverence as well as with whom we share friendship.

Yet I am still doubtful, as I have said, about my motives. I commit all to your faithful providence, whose spirit is sweeter than honey. If this fervor arose from any human affection, I am even more bound to have a profound gratitude for it. This is because you have united the depth of my evil to the precious gold of your love so that the jewels of your grace might be encased in me.

I was thinking attentively about these things as I sat in the dining room. Unworthy as I am, I then perceived that what I had asked for in the prayer was granted to me. I knew in spirit that you had imprinted the adorable marks of your sacred wounds in the depth of my heart, even as they are on your body. My restless soul had been cured by the imprinting of these wounds on my heart. You gave me the precious drink of your love to satisfy my thirst.

The depth of your mercy was not exhausted by my unworthiness, for I received a most remarkable gift from your overflowing generosity. Each time during the day when I reflected upon those adorable wounds, saying five verses of the psalm "Benedic, anima mea, Domino" (Ps 103), I never failed to receive some new favor.

At the first verse "Bless the Lord O my soul," I deposited all the rust of my sins and my voluptuousness at the wounds of thy blessed feet. At the second verse "Bless the Lord, and never forget all that he has done for you," I washed away all the stains of carnal and perishable pleasures in the sweet bath of blood and water which you poured forth for me.

At the third verse "Who forgives all your iniquities," I reposed my spirit in the wound of your left hand, even as the dove makes its nest in the crevice of the rock. At the fourth verse "Who redeems your life from destruction," I approached your right hand and took from it all that I needed for my perfection in virtue. Being so magnificently adorned, I passed to the fifth verse "Who satisfies your desire with good things." I asked to be purified from all the defilement of sin and have the indigence of my wants supplied. This was so that I might become worthy of your presence and merit the joy of your embrace, though I know I am utterly unworthy of this.

I declare also that you freely granted my other petition—namely, that I might experience your grief and your love together. Sadly, this did not continue long, although I cannot accuse you of having withdrawn it from me. I lost this due to my own negligence, so I cannot complain against anyone except myself. Your excessive goodness and infinite mercy has procured for me the greatest of your gifts. You have hidden my unworthiness from yourself and impressed your wounds upon my heart without any merit on my part. May all praise, honor, glory, dominion, and thanksgiving be yours forever and ever!

Chapter 5. The Way to Care for the Wound of Divine Love

1. Source of all good, it was your will this event happened seven years later, right before Advent. I asked someone to say the following prayer before a crucifix. "Most loving Lord, pierce the heart of Gertrude with the arrow of thy love through the merit of your own pierced heart. Let nothing that will hinder your presence remain in her heart, so that it may be totally filled with the strength of your divinity."

On the third Sunday of Advent, when we sang "Gaudete in Domino" [Introit for the third Sunday of Advent, formerly called Gaudete Sunday] I believe I was moved by that person's prayers. Through your infinite goodness and excessive mercy, you infused a deep love in me as I approached your adorable body and blood. I could not help myself as I broke forth with these words: "Lord, I am not worthy to receive the least of your gifts. Yet by the merits and prayers of all here present I beg you to pierce my heart with the arrow of your love." I sensed that my words had reached your Divine Heart, for there was a sudden interior abundance of grace. It was accompanied by a vision in which you showed me the image of your crucifixion.

2. I received the sacrament of life and returned to the place where I pray. Then it seemed to me that I saw a ray of light like an arrow coming forth from the wound of the right side of the crucifix. The crucifix was in an elevated place, and the light continued to go back and forth for some time, sweetly warming my cold affections. My desire was not entirely satisfied with these things until the following Wednesday.[14]

After Mass, the faithful meditated on your adorable Incarnation and Annunciation. However imperfect my prayers were, I joined them in this. Suddenly you appeared before me, and it was then that you imprinted a wound in my heart. "May the full tide of your affection flow here," you said. "May all your pleasure, your hope, your joy, your grief, your fear, and every other feeling be sustained by my love!" I recall what I thought at the time. I had heard a wound should be bathed, anointed, and bandaged. You did not teach me how I should do this. Now I know that this was because you wanted me to find this out through another person. She had learned to listen far more insightfully and sensitively than myself to the sweet whisperings of your love.

3. She advised me to meditate upon the love of your heart that was manifest as you hung upon the cross. She said I should drink the waters of true devotion from this fountain. This would wash away all my sins and thus bathe the wound. She advised me as well to take the oil of gratitude from the unction of your mercy, for this would care for the wound. The sweetness of your immeasurable love has produced this as a remedy for all evils. This most effective and powerful love would serve as the binding force of justification which would wrap the

wound. Thus the union of all my thoughts, words, and works with your heart would occur in a powerful and indissoluble way.

4. May your love that abides in me in such fullness make up for all the deprivations of love that my own evil and wickedness have caused. The fullness of love abides in the Lord, seated at the right hand of the Father. He has truly become "bone of my bones, and flesh of my flesh!" Through him, through the power of the Holy Spirit, you have placed the noble virtues of compassion, humility, and reverence in me so that I can speak to you, my God. In, with, and through Jesus, I now complain to you about the sufferings I endure.

They are so many! They have caused me to offend your divine goodness by my thoughts, words, and deeds in so many ways. The worst of my offenses is the bad use I have made of your many graces through my unfaithfulness, negligence, and irreverence. Unworthy as I am, even if you had given me a thread of flax as a remembrance of you, you know that I would have respected it more than I have respected all these favors.

5. My God, from whom nothing is hidden, you know well that I did not wish to write down all these things. Yet, you know my reason for writing these things. It is because I have profited so little from your goodness that I cannot believe your revelations were made known to me for myself alone. Your eternal wisdom cannot be deceived. I pray to you, O Giver of Gifts, for all those who may ever read these things. You have so freely and generously bestowed gifts upon me.

May you enable those who read these things to be touched with tenderness and compassion for you. May they praise, adore, and glorify your mercy, for your great love for all and your desire for their salvation is the reason you have left such royal gems in my defiled heart. With their hearts may these readers supply for my own deficiency as they pray, "Praise, honor, glory, and benediction be to you, O God the Father, from whom all good things come!"

Chapter 6. The Infant Jesus Is Intimately United with Gertrude

2. . . . This happened on that most sacred night in which the sweet dew of divine grace gently showered over the world. It was the night when the heavens had already dropped celestial rain as I meditated in the court of the monastery. My spirit was waiting like a mystic fleece as I prepared to assist at this divine birth. This was the night in which a virgin—like a star that produces its bright light—brought forth a son, truly God and truly man.

In this night I suddenly saw a delicate child before me. The child had just been born, but already it could be seen that he possessed the greatest gifts of perfection. I imagined that I received this precious child within my bosom with the tenderest affection. While I possessed him to me, it seemed that I was suddenly changed into the color of this divine infant. I say that knowing I am calling something color which cannot be compared to anything visible.

3. At last I understood the meaning of those sweet, mysterious words: "God will be all in all" (1 Cor 15:28). My spirit was magnified by the presence of my spouse. By the rapture that I felt, I knew I had received my bridegroom. I heard the following with a desire that made them appear like a delicious beverage that satisfied the source of my thirst.

"As I am the image and presence of the divine substance of God, my father, so you shall be the image of my substance in my humanity. Your glorified soul shall receive the indwelling of my divinity as the air receives the light of the sun's rays. You will be transformed by this so that you can attain the closest union with me."

Most noble balm of the divinity! Like an ocean of love, you empty yourself in eternal light and in eternal budding of life. You transform as you diffuse yourself until the end of time. O invincible strength of the hand of the most high God! You enable a weak vessel to receive such a precious liquor within itself when that vessel is only fit to be cast away in contempt. You did not abandon me when I wandered in the devious ways of sin, but kept joining me to yourself as far as my own misery would allow. O most divine goodness, what greater testimony can there be to the depth of your care!

Chapter 7. The Divinity Is Imprinted as a Seal on Wax

1. On the feast of the most holy Purification, I was in bed, having had a serious illness. As morning was dawning, I was quite sad for missing the worship that so often brought me the divine visitation. But on that day it was the mediatrix, the Mother of God, who consoled me in the name of the only Mediator. "You know that you have never suffered more severe corporal sufferings than those caused by your illness. At the same time, remember this. You have never received greater gifts from my son than those which will be given to you now. It is these gifts for which your sufferings have prepared you."

This was a wonderful consolation. After the procession, as I received the living bread, I thought only of God and myself. I beheld my soul like wax softened by the fire, impressed like a seal upon the bosom of the Lord. Then I saw it being both surrounded and partly drawn into the treasure house, the dwelling of the ever-peaceful Trinity in the plenitude of the divinity. My soul was radiant with its glorious impression.

2. O burning fire of my God. You contain, produce, and imprint those living flames that attract the humid waters of my soul and dry up the torrents of earthly delights. O fire that softens my self-centeredness so hardened by time! O consuming fire that gives sweetness and peace to be found in you alone! Only in you can we receive this grace of being reformed to the image and likeness in which we were created. O burning furnace, we enjoy the true vision of peace only in you. You judge and purify the gold of the elect and lead the soul to eagerly search for you in your eternal truth, our highest good.

Chapter 8. Union of her Soul with God

1. On the next Sunday when we sang "Esto Mihi" [Introit for Quinquagesima Sunday], you inflamed my spirit and increased my desires to receive the most noble gifts you intended to bestow. Two antiphons moved my soul deeply at nocturne [night prayer]. These were the versicle of the first response, "With blessings I will bless you," and the versicle of the ninth response, "I will give all these lands to you and to your posterity" (Gen 26). It was then that you showed me the lands which your boundless goodness had promised.

2. O blessed country where blessings flow upon blessings! O field of delights! Your least grain can satisfy the hungers of faithful human hearts for everything that is considered desirable, delightful, amiable, sweet, and joyful....

4. (I will try to express as far as I can that which is utterly inexpressible.) I saw the part of his blessed heart where the Lord received my soul on the Feast of the Purification under the form of wax softened by the fire. His heart seemed to be sweating through that wax with a violence. It seemed like the substance of the wax was melted by the excessive heat burning in the hidden depth of his heart. This sacred reservoir attracted these drops of sweat to itself with surprising force, powerfully, inexpressibly, and even inconceivably. As I saw this, it was evident that love, which could not be hindered from communicating itself, had an absolute power in this place. Great, hidden, and impenetrable secrets could be discovered here.

5. O eternal light! O secure mansion containing all that is desirable! O paradise of unchanging delights! Continual fountain of immeasurable pleasures! In you there is eternal springtime which soothes the soul by its sweet song, or rather by its delicious and intellectual melodies. The soul rejoices in the odor of this springtime's vivifying perfumes and is inebriated by the soothing sweetness of its mystic liquors. It is transformed by those secret caresses.

Chapter 9. The Communion of God with Her Soul

1. During Lent, which was soon after this, I was confined to bed for the second time by a severe sickness. I was left alone one morning since the other sisters were busy elsewhere. But the Lord never abandons those who are deprived of human consolation. He came to me to verify the words of the psalmist: "I am with you in tribulation" (Ps 90). Then he turned his right side toward me. A pure and solid stream, which was like crystal, came forth from his blessed and inmost heart. A most precious ornament that resembled a necklace was on his chest. The ornament seemed to alternate its color between gold and rose.

Then our Lord spoke to me. "This sickness which you suffer will sanctify your soul. Each time you go forth from me with the intention of doing good to your neighbor in thought, word, or deed, it will be like the stream I have shown you.

The purity of the crystal stream, your going forth with a purity of intention, makes the color of the gold more brilliant. The precious gold of my divinity, and the rose of the perfect patience of my humanity, will make your going forth pleasing to me."

Chapter 10. The Indwelling of Divinity

1. My conscience would not consent for me to publish these writings because I considered it so unsuitable. For this reason, I put it off until the feast of the Exaltation of the Holy Cross [September 14]. Before Mass I had decided that I would occupy myself with other things that day. The Lord conquered the repugnance I had to publishing this by saying, "Be assured that you will not be released from the prison of the flesh until you have paid this debt which still binds you." I then reflected that I had already employed the gifts of God for the advancement of my neighbor.

Perhaps my spoken words were enough to satisfy the debt. But the Lord made me remember the words from the preceding matins. "If the Lord had wished to teach his doctrine only to those that were present, he would have taught only by spoken word and not by writing. However, now his words are written for the salvation of many." Then he added, "I desire that your writings bear testimony to my divine goodness in these latter times, for I shall continue to do good to many."

2. These words depressed me as I began to reflect upon the difficulty and impossibility of my thoughts and words to begin to explain my revelations. How could this be made known to the human intellect without scandal resulting? Again the Lord delivered me from my inner battles. The Lord poured an abundance of rain like a waterfall which weighed me down like a young and tender plant.

Being the obstinate creature that I am, I could find no profit in his deluge. A more gentle watering might have made me increase in perfection. His few weighty words made some sense of it all, but I was not really able to penetrate the full meaning of them. So I found myself even more depressed. I asked myself "What would be the advantage of these writings?"

Your goodness, my God, brought me consolation with your wonderful sweetness. You refreshed my spirit by your reply. "Since this deluge appears useless to you, behold how I will now hold you near my divine heart. This will make your words gentle and encouraging, according to the capabilities of your mind."

3. You faithfully fulfilled your promise, my Lord and my God. For four days, at a convenient hour each morning, you suggested clearly and sweetly what I composed. For this reason I have been able to write it without difficulty and without reflection. It was as if I had learned all this by heart. Before this it was not possible for me to write a sufficient quantity, although I applied my whole

mind to it. I could not find even a single word to express the things which I could write freely on the following day. I was thus instructed and learned to discipline my impetuosity.

Scripture teaches, "Let no one so apply themselves to action as to omit contemplation." You are jealous for my welfare, my Lord. While you give me leisure to enjoy the embraces of Rachel, you still do not allow me to be deprived of the glorious fruitfulness of Leah. May your wise love always accomplish both of these things in me.

Epilogue

Chapter 24. Conclusion of This Book

1. Behold, O loving Lord, I offer you the talent that your condescending intimacy has revealed to me, unworthy as I am. I have used it to obtain the love of your love through what I have written or may yet write. With your grace I can boldly declare my only motive in saying or writing these things has been to obey your will, to promote your glory, and to show concern for the salvation of all. I desire that everyone should praise you and give you thanks that my unworthiness has not caused you to withdraw your mercy from me. I desire also that you should be praised for those who, reading these things, are charmed with the sweetness of your charity and are drawn to desire that love.

I desire as well that you be praised by any who study these works. Just as a new learner begins study by learning an alphabet but then attains to philosophy, may those who study this work be led to higher things. As they peruse these things, with imagination and reflection, may they continue to search for the hidden manna. This is the manna that increases the hunger of those who partake of it. It is a manna so profound that it cannot be found in corporeal substances.

2. You alone are the almighty dispenser of all good things. Pasture us during our exile until, "Beholding the glory of the Lord with unveiled countenance, we are transformed into his image, from glory to glory by the power of the Spirit" (2 Cor 3:18). In accord with your faithful promises and the humble desire of my heart, I beg you to give the peace of your love to all who read these writings with humility.

May they also have compassion for my miseries and a salutary compunction for their growth in perfection. By elevating their hearts toward you with burning love, may they be like so many golden censers, whose sweet smells and colors shall abundantly supply for all my negligence and ingratitude. Amen.

NOTES

1. Mary Jeremy Finnegan, *The Women of Helfta: Scholars and Mystics* (Athens: University of Georgia Press, 1991) 1–10.

2. Carolyn Walker Bynum, *Jesus as Mother: Studies of Spirituality in the High Middle Ages* (Berkeley: University of California Press, 1982) 16–21, 247–63.

3. Finnegan, *The Women of Helfta* 117 (citation is from Gertrude von Hackeborn, *Livre* 5.2); see also Jean Bainvel, "Devotions to the Heart of Jesus," in *Catholic Encyclopedia* (New York: Appleton, 1910) 7:165.

4. *Gertrude the Great: The Herald of God's Loving Kindness*, bk. 2, 18.1; cited by Alexandra Barratt, *Gertrude the Great* (Kalamazoo, Mich.: Cistercian Publications, 1991) 10.

5. *Oeuvres spirituelles* 3, trans. Pierre Doyere, Sources chrétiennes, no. 143 (Paris: Cerf, 1968) *L'Heraut*, bk. 3, ch. 15, 65–66; ch. 20–23, 110–19; ch. 63, 250–52. *Oeuvres spirituelles* 4, trans. Jean-Marie Clément and Bernard de Vregille, Sources chrétiennes, no. 255 (Paris: Cerf, 1978), *L'Heraut*, bk. 4, ch. 5, 82–89; ch. 9, 108–12; ch. 16, 174–83.

6. *Oeuvres spirituelles* 3, *L'Heraut*, bk. 3, ch. 10, 42–43; ch. 44, 198–202; ch. 60, 244–47; ch. 68, 274–75.

7. *Oeuvres spirituelles* 2, *L'Heraut*, bk. 1, ch. 14, 196–203; *Oeuvres spirituelles* 4, *L'Heraut*, bk. 4, ch. 32, 278–81.

8. Barratt, *Gertrude the Great* 20–25.

9. The original work was in German. In 1536, Lanspergius of Cologne, a Carthusian monk, translated *The Herald of Divine Love* into Latin. By the middle of the sixteenth century a number of editions had been published in various languages.

10. The five books of *The Herald of Divine Love* have been published in the following volumes of Sources chrétiennes (SC). Books 1 and 2, Gertrude d'Helfta, *Oeuvres spirituelles* 2, SC 139; bk. 3, *Oeuvres spirituelles* 3, SC 143, trans. Pierre Doyere (1968); bk. 4, *Oeuvres spirituelles* 4, SC 255 (1978); bk. 5, *Oeuvres spirituelles* 5, SC 331, trans. Jean-Marie Clement and Bernard de Vregille (1986).

11. *Oeuvres spirituelles* 2, *L'Heraut*, bk. 1, ch. 14, 196–203.

12. *Oeuvres spirituelles* 2, *L'Heraut*, bk. 2, 256–77; 350–53.

13. This was considered to be the perfect age of manhood.

14. At this time the feast of the Annunciation was celebrated on the third Wednesday of Advent.

BIBLIOGRAPHY

Barrett, Alexandra. *The Herald of God's Loving Kindness*. Kalamazoo, Mich.: Cistercian Publications, 1991.

Bynum, Carolyn Walker. *Jesus as Mother: Studies in the Spirituality of the High Middle Ages*. Berkeley: University of California Press, 1982.

Bynum, Carolyn Walker. *Holy Feast and Holy Fast*. Berkeley: University of California Press, 1987.

Dolan, Gilbert. *St. Gertrude the Great*. St. Louis: Herder, 1916.

Finnegan, Mary Jeremy. "Idiom of Christ in Women Mystics." *Mystics Quarterly* 13 (June 1987) 65–72.

Finnegan, Mary Jeremy. *Women of Helfta: Scholars and Mystics*. Athens: University of Georgia Press, 1991.

Gertrude the Great. *Gertrude the Great of Helfta: Spiritual Exercises*. Translated by G. Jaron and J. Lewis. Kalamazoo, Mich.: Cistercian Publications, 1989.

Gertrude the Great. *Gertrude of Helfta: The Herald of Divine Love*. Translated by Margaret Winkworth. Classics of Western Spirituality. New York: Paulist Press, 1993.

Jedin, H., ed. *From the High Middle Ages to the Eve of the Reformation*. Vol. 4 of *History of the Church*. New York: Seabury, 1980.

McLaughlin, Eleanor Como. "Equality of Souls, Inequality of Sexes: Women in Medieval Theology." In *Religion and Sexism: Images of Woman in the Jewish and Christian Traditions*. Edited by Rosemary Radford Ruether. New York: Simon and Schuster, 1974. 213–66.

– 10 –

HADEWIJCH

(THIRTEENTH CENTURY)

I Am All Love's and Love Is All Mine

Hadewijch probably lived in the thirteenth century, a century of many diverse movements. On the one hand, the papacy had reached a height of political power. On the other hand, the papal office had lost its influence as a spiritual and moral force. There was an increased desire for authentic religious experience among many of the clergy and laity. At the same time, there was an abundance of heretical groups as well. Scholastic theology with its Aristotelian reflections on faith dominated the university scene. A more experiential affective theology and spirituality flourished among other groups. A few sentences about each of these diverse strands may further the understanding of the age in which Hadewijch likely lived and wrote.[1]

The last pope of the twelfth century, Innocent III (1198–1216), brought the papal office to the summit of political power even as that office began its decline as a spiritual and moral force. The Decretals of Gratian had provided legal and juridical arguments for the superiority of the power and prerogatives of the papacy. From this point on, the reforms begun by successive popes would mean reform of political and ecclesial institutions, but not reform of the papal power and its papal court, the Curia.

Like campaigns earlier, which started with the intent of winning the world for Christ, the crusades of the thirteenth century continued with the same fervor. In retrospect, in "winning the world for Jesus Christ," the crusades brought about the death of many thousands of people and caused irreparable destruction of cities, cultures, and the bonds between Eastern and Western Christianity.[2] The Children's Crusade of 1212 resulted in the death or enslavement of thousands of French and German children. Two later crusades in the century succeeded in doing nothing more than costing lives on both sides.

The monastic and cathedral schools that developed through the twelfth century began to serve the needs of growing cities by the end of that century. In the thirteenth century, groups of these schools came together to form the universities in major cities such as Paris and Bologna. The best of Greek thought, particularly that of Aristotle, influenced the mode of thinking about faith. The monumental work of Dominicans like Thomas Aquinas (1225–74) furthered a systematic and reasonable approach to Christian faith.

At the same time, there was more of a renewal than simply thinking about faith. New apostolic orders, for example, the Dominicans and Franciscans, grew as people felt called to a more apostolic way of life, a way of life manifested in the sharing of goods, the renunciation of wealth, and in care for the poor, orphans, the sick, and the aged (Matt 5:3–12; Luke 10:1–10). Voluntary poverty was undertaken by many laity and clergy as a criticism of the abuses of wealth and power by some of the church hierarchy, including the popes and the Curia. Various thirteenth-century popes called for reform of the church as an institution. They and their papal court were skilled, however, at resisting the pressure to reform. By the end of the century, the papacy would be simply a well-organized bureaucracy that secured a steady flow of money into its coffers to keep the Curia running well.[3]

The perceived value of women in the thirteenth century was extremely low, and they were treated as a surplus commodity. Canon law allowed wife beating if a woman did not obey her husband. The twelfth-century theologian Peter Lombard had tried to alter this perception of a wife as her husband's property:

> God did not make woman from Adam's head, for she was not intended to be his ruler; nor from his feet, for she was not intended to be his slave; but from his side, for she was intended to be his companion and friend.[4]

In spite of Lombard's efforts, women were still considered to be essentially inferior to men. Society and the church believed that men needed to channel the religious energies of women to curtail excessive enthusiasm, heresy, or other abuses to which women were judged to be susceptible. At the same time, the religious enthusiasm of the time, which affected men as well as women, left women without an organized way to live out their apostolic call. Men could be clerics, monks, canons, or join any number of male communities. Women had the option of joining a cloistered community, and these were linked to male religious orders, many of whom refused to supervise or add on more dependent convents of women. The only other options for women were to be solitaries and live under some form of pious rule in their own homes, or to become recluses attached to a monastery or church.

Another popular option was to become a Beguine. In the thirteenth century, the Beguines posed a challenge to both social and ecclesial perceptions of women's place. The Beguines were more of a movement than an official order. Their day-to-day lives were shaped by their piety and their response to a more intense Christian life. Each particular group of Beguines could develop its own rule of life and order of the day. Aspiring Beguines lived under the direction of a more experienced Beguine. The daily order of their life included attendance at Mass when possible, the divine office, prayers in honor of Mary and the passion of Christ, meditative reading and contemplation, communal penance, and monthly confession. Vigils and major feasts were days for recollection.

Groups of Beguines who lived in community also had houses for widows or other women who were not members of the group but needed a place of refuge that would be free from the plundering and abuse that often came to single women. The activities of the Beguines included education of poor as well as economically stable boys and girls, care for the sick and elderly, aid to the outcasts of society, training of housewives to run their estates, arts and crafts, and contemplative prayer.[5]

The reaction toward the Beguines ranged from sincere admiration for their holiness to great disgust and fear. Some churchmen like Lambert Le Begue and Jacques de Vitry, the bishop of Liège who helped organize the movement, felt the Beguines were the new mothers of the church. The saintly Marie d'Oignies (1177–1213), was an enthusiastic patron and promoter of the Beguines.[6] This woman's holiness was acknowledged by many. On the other hand, the Second Council of Lyons and the Council of Vienne judged the group as a whole quite harshly.

In spite of the mixed reviews the Beguines were getting in the thirteenth century, Hadewijch joined the movement. Little is actually known about her. If a life of Hadewijch was written, it has not survived. It is known that she lived in the thirteenth century and that her works were familiar to the Canons Regular of Windesheim and the Carthusians of Diest by the fourteenth century.

Her familiarity with the language and customs of chivalry and courtly love suggests that she was born into a higher class. Wherever she acquired her education, she had amassed a broad range of knowledge. Her works indicate an ability to use metaphors that were part of the academic curriculum. She is familiar with the Latin language, rules of rhetoric, numerology, Ptolemaic astronomy, music theory, the church fathers, and most canonical twelfth-century writers.

She may have founded a Beguine group or else she became a leader of such a group. Her letters provide a clear indication that she is a spiritual director for younger Beguines. A theme that runs throughout her works is apparent in her letters directed to them. Love ought to be the dominant quality of their life:

> The greatest radiance anyone can have on earth is truth in works of justice performed in imitation of the Son, and to practice the truth with regard to all that exists, for the glory of the noble love that God is. (1 John 4:16)[7]

Her theological perspectives on self-knowledge differ from those of Bernard of Clairvaux, whose works influenced her. Bernard stressed that self-knowledge would lead to the awareness that humans are in fact poor images of God because of their sinfulness. Hadewijch stresses that self-knowledge should not stop with the awareness of personal poverty, but go on to recognize that God's power is greater than human weakness:

> Anyone who is truly faithful will know that the goodness of the Beloved is greater than human failure ... live for God in such a way, this I implore you, that you be not wanting in the great works to which God has called you.[8]

The extant works of Hadewijch include thirty-one letters, forty-five poems in stanzas, fourteen visions, and sixteen poems in couplets. Letter 6 is a manifesto about the Beguine way of life, detailing what it means to live love in the world of her time and in a community of apostolic women. Letter 11 is an autobiographical one that describes her own journey into the meaning of love. The frequent reference to love as the core of Christian spirituality and its thematic reappearance places Hadewijch in the school of "love mysticism."

This mysticism, reflected in Bernard of Clairvaux and others, shifts the scholastic focus from intellectual knowledge of God to experiential love of God. There are different shades of meaning for *love* as Hadewijch uses the term. In some cases it is an experience and in others it is the beloved, a person.

The romantic tradition and the Middle Dutch tradition of love songs have affected the poetic reflections of Hadewijch. The images of courtly love, of a lover who is never quite attainable, of the submissive service to love, and the complaints against the power of love and its paradox are part of this courtly love tradition. The tension between "having" love and "losing" love runs throughout her works. She is probably writing in the period when the courtly poetry of the Netherlands was at its height. At the same time, it is not copied by Hadewijch, for her own experiences and expressions that illumine divine and human love relationships are uniquely her own.[9]

Whatever role Hadewijch had in the Beguine community, there seems to have been opposition to her as time went on. It has been mentioned earlier that various groups in the church did not look upon women like the Beguines with favor. Their independence from ecclesiastical control made them a source of dissension. Their public teaching and reading from the Scriptures in the vernacular caused concern. Although Hadewijch seems to have been more of a recluse than a wandering Beguine teacher, her life was not one of simple repose. Scholars generally believe that the Beguine community evicted her. This could be the reason for her pain of separation from her sister Beguines, namely, Sara, Margriet, and Emma:

> But I, unhappy as I am, ask this with love from all of you—who should offer me comfort in my pains, solace in my sad exile, and peace and

> sweetness. I wander alone and must remain far from him to whom I belong. . . . Why does he hold me so far from him and from those who are his?[10]

Hadewijch had been so consistent in her urgings of the Beguines to care for the sick that she may have spent her own last days offering her services to a leprosarium or to the sick poor. In such settings, she could not only nurse the sick but also have ready access to the chapel or church that was always attached to these kinds of establishments. Unfortunately, no more is known of her last years than is known of her early years. When and where she died has been lost to history.

In the excerpts from her love songs that follow, it will be seen that love is a paradox for Hadewijch. Yet she seems to enjoy the challenge of the paradoxical presence and absence of her beloved. The demands of love are like food that satisfies but simultaneously leaves even deeper hungers. One engaged in the love chase may have ever-deepening love, but then "the more crushing her burden" (2). Love consoles, gives peace, and empowers noble hearts to hold firmly to the challenge (2, 3, 5, 7, 8), even though there are conflicts that can make one weary. There can be no true love without sacrifice that enables setbacks to be overcome (6, 9, 10).

Hadewijch dares to enter the wilderness of the ambiguous journey and encourages others to "risk the adventure" (6). She is assured that what seems like loss is actually gain (2); no action is lost, in spite of appearances. In the end, more is given than taken (4). Love is always faithful, although it can seem like love has abandoned the lover. Limited comprehension of the mystery of divine love is the cause of not understanding the love that humans receive. At the same time, the pain involved in the desire for greater love can open the heart to ever-increasing proportions for experiencing the mystery of eternal love.

Excerpts from Love Songs

31. Melody and Song[11]

1

I wish to devote all my time
To noble thoughts about great Love.
For she, with her infinite strength,
So enlarges my heart
That I have given myself over to her completely,
To obtain within me the birth of her high being.

But if I wish to take free delights,
She casts me into her prison!

2

I fancied I would suffer without harm,
Being thus fettered in love,
If she willed to make me understand
All the narrowest paths of her requirements.
But if I think of reposing in her grace,
She storms at me with new commands.
She deals her blows in a wonderful way;
the greater her love, the more crushing her burden!

3

This is a marvel difficult to understand—
Love's robberies and her gifts;
If she gives me any consolation to taste,
It becomes fear and trembling.
I pray and invite Love
That she may incite noble hearts
To sing in tune the true melody of Love
In humble anxiety and high hope.

4

Consolation and ill treatment both at once,
This is the essence of the taste of love.[12]
Wise Solomon, were he still living,
Could not interpret such an enigma.
We are not fully enlightened on the subject in any sermon.
The song surpasses every melody!
That springtime of eternity I continually long for
Keeps in store for me the reward.

5

Learning, delaying, and long awaiting
This springtime, which is Love itself,
Makes us despise associations with aliens
And shows losses and great gains.
The pride of Love counsels me to hold

So firmly to her that I may encompass
Union above comprehension:
The melody surpasses every song!

6

When I speak of the melody which surpasses every song,
What I mean is Love in her might.
I say a little yet it serves not to enlighten
The alien hearts that are cold
And have met small suffering for the sake of Love:
They do not know that Love reveals
Her glory to the noble-minded, who are bold
And are cherished in Love.

7

Love's invincible might
Is unheard-of by our understanding:
It is nearly when we are lost, and far away when we grasp it;
It is a peace that disturbs all peace:
A peace that is conquered in love,
By which he who sets his whole mind on Love
Is cherished by her consolation,
And thus she loves him with love in love.

8

He who wishes thus to progress in love
Must not fear expense or harm,
Or pain; but faithfully confront
The strictest commands of Love,
And be submissive with faultless service
In all her comings and in all her goings;
Anyone who behaved thus, relying on Love's fidelity,
Would stand to the end, having become all love in Love.

32. Nobility in Love

1

Soon the flowers will open for us,
And other plants in great numbers.

But at the same time, men will condemn the noble hearts
Who live under the dominion of Love.
In Love, I place my salvation,
And my power in her hands;
I demand no other consolation from her
Than to remain wholly in her chains.

2

With anyone who now bears the chains of veritable Love,
As man's debt to Love requires,
The cruel aliens before long
Will quite openly interfere.
They find many ways to intimidate
Those who trust high Love's protection;
But any harm they cause them,
Thanks be to God amounts to very little.

3

He who is to serve high Love
Must fear no pain;
He shall give himself all for all,
To content high Love;
But if it happens that he delays somewhat,
He will indeed learn this truth:
That he will positively never become
Master of veritable Love.

4

Love is master of contraries;
She is ready to give bitter and sweet;
Since I first experienced the taste of her,
I lie at her feet continually;
I pray her it may be her pleasure
That I endure, for her honor's sake,
Suffering, to the death, without recovery,
And I will not complain of it to aliens.

5

If anyone made known to aliens
What we suffer for the honor of Love,

It would truly break her heart
And deeply wound her being;
For aliens understand nothing at all
Of what we must suffer for veritable Love—
What adventures and changes of destiny—
Before she will rejoice in our love.

6

When souls truly wish to please Love,
I counsel them that they spare nothing,
And that they accord with her
So as to persevere in the storms with longing
In spite of their faultfinders,
Who are so bent on harming them.
No matter how such foes may oppress them,
These souls are privileged to be ever free.

7

A free man's nobility we can recognize
In jousts and noble deeds;
With the pride of noble minds, he wades through
Where the storm of Love withstands him.
For in jousts a knight receives praise
Of which he appears worthy because of love.
Love is so strong a buttress:
It is right that men suffer for her sake.

8

People afraid of any pains in love
Certainly cannot understand
What can be won by souls
Who are always submissive to Love,
Who receive from her hand heavy blows
Of which they remain wholly unhealed,
And who mount on high and are knocked down again
Before they please Love.

9

From slothful hearts and ignoble minds
Remains hidden the great good

Which those well understand
Who live in the madness of love;
For they make many a gallant stand
In storm and adventure;
It is right that they should have success
In the high nature of Love.

10

God grant success to those who strive
To please the will of Love,
Who for her sake gladly receive
Great burdens with heavy weights,
And who always endure on her account many sufferings,
Of which they judge Love worthy,
I truly wish they should yet behold
The wonders of Love's wisdom.

33. Hunger for Love

1

The season is renewed with the year;
The days, dark a short time ago, grow lighter.
When souls desire Love but possess her not,
It is a wonder they do not go to wrack and ruin.

2

The new year already begins
For anyone who has resolved
To spare neither much nor little
For Love; pain becomes pure profit.

3

But they who spare any pain for Love,
Thus betraying their baseness,
And expect profit from joys unrelated to love,
Inevitably find the service burdensome.

4

But lovers who are trueborn
And chosen to bear Love's likeness
Spare no pain in her service
And live continually in holy affliction.

5

They whom high Love's nature touches
Always suffer gladly,
As in their deeds clearly appears;
They ever think them imperfect.

6

For the perfect ones, it would be a pity
If, by the counsel of baseborn aliens,
They ceased performing those noble deeds,
Which create hunger in new satisfaction.

7

Inseparable satiety and hunger
Are the appendages of lavish Love,
As is ever well known by those
Whom Love has touched by herself.

8

Satiety: for Love comes and they cannot bear her;
Hunger: for she withdraws and they complain.
Her fairest enlightenments are heavy burdens;
Her sharpest assaults, renewed pleasures.

9

How does Love's coming satiate?
Filled with wonder, we taste what she is;
She grants possession of her sublime throne;
She imparts the great treasure of her riches.

10

How does Love's refusal create hunger?
Because we cannot come at which we wish to know

Or enjoy what we desire:
That increases our hunger over and over.

11

How does Love's enlightenment overwhelm us?
Because we cannot receive her great gifts,
And we can elaborate nothing so beautiful as she:
So we do not know where to seek rest.

12

How does noble Love make assault and blow
Always welcome, night and day?
Because we can fall back on nothing else
But confidence with reliance on Love.

13

To holy Love I now recommend
All of you who wish to know Love,
And who therefore spare nothing
So as to dwell in Love with new ardor.

14

May new light give you new ardor;
New works, new delights to the full;
New assaults of Love, new hunger so vast
That new Love may devour new eternity!

34. Becoming Love with Love

1

In all seasons new and old,
If one is submissive to Love,
In the hot summer, the cold winter,
Love will be received from Love.
We shall satisfy with full service
   In encountering high Love;
So it especially becomes love with Love;
   That is bound to happen.

2

Bitter and dark and desolate
Are Love's ways in the beginning of love;
Before anyone is perfect in Love's service,
We often become desperate:
Yet where we imagine losing, it is all gain.
   How can one experience this?
By sparing neither much nor little,
   By giving oneself totally in love.

3

Many are in doubt about Love;
Love's labor seems to them too hard,
And at first they receive nothing in it.
They think, "Should you wander there?"
If their eyes clearly saw the reward
   That Love gives at the end,
I dare indeed say openly:
   They would wander in Love's exile.

4

In love no action is lost
That was ever performed for Love's sake;
Love always repays, late or soon;
Love is always the reward of love.
Love knows with love the courtly manners of Love;
Her receiving is always giving;
Not least she gives by her adroitness
   Many a death in life.

5

It is very sweet to wander lost in love
Along the desolate ways Love makes us travel.
This remains well hidden from aliens;
But they who serve Love with truth
Shall in love walk with Love.
All round that kingdom where Love is Lady,
And united with her receive all that splendor
And taste to the full her noble fidelity.

6

As for the tastes that fidelity gives in Love—
Whoever calls anything else happiness
Has always lived without happiness,
To my way of thinking.
For it is heavenly joy, free,
To the full devoid of nothing:
"You are all mine, Beloved, and I am all yours."[13]
There is no other way of saying it.

7

I can well keep silent about how it is
With those who have thus become one in love:
Neither to see nor to speak is my part;
For I do not know this in myself,
How the Beloved and the loved soul embrace each other
And have fruition in giving themselves to each other.
What wonder is it that grief strikes me
Because this has not yet fallen to my share?

8

That I was ever short of love
Causes me sadness; that is no wonder.
Rightly do I suffer pain for it,
That I ever descended so low.
For Love promises me all good,
If I would conceive the high plan
Of working in the realm she assigned me,
In her highest possible service.

9

That realm to which Love urges me on,
And the service she commands us to perform,
Is to exercise love and nothing else,
With all the service this entails.
He who truly understands this,
How to work in every respect with fidelity,
Is the one whom Love completely fetters
And completely unites to herself in love.

10

To this I summon all the perfect,
Who wish to content Love with love,
Thus to be in Love's service
In all her comings and in all her goings.
If she lifts them up, if she knocks them down,
May it all be equally sweet to them;
So will they speedily become love with Love:
In this way may God help us!

35. Unloved by Love

1

The season is dark and cold:
On this account, bird and beast grow sad.
But suffering of a different kind envelops hearts
Who know Love's proud nature
And that she will remain out of their reach.
Whoever ascends, I stay in the valley,
Robbed of rich consolation,
Continually burdened with heavy loads.

2

The load is all too heavy for me,
And is never laid down, though need be great.
How could a heart keep on
When it must endure as many deaths
As one experiences who knows that he
Is ever unloved by Love,
And that everyone she receives is refused
Help and consolation and confidence?

3

If Love will not admit me to favor as her loved one,
Why was I ever born?
If I am thus ill-starred before Love,
I am lost and no mistake;
So I can complain bitterly,
All my time from now on.

I hope for no prosperity,
Since Love will thus be out of my reach.

4

I showed Love my pains;
I prayed her to have pity on them;
By her behavior she gave me to understand
That she had neither inclination nor time.
What becomes of me is all the same to her.
How she ever showed herself favorable to me,
Her strange fickleness has put out of my head.
Therefore I must live in night by day.

5

Whereabouts is Love? I find her nowhere.[14]
Love has denied me all I love.
Had it ever happened to me by Love
That I lived for a moment
In her affection, supposing I did,
I would have sought amnesty in her fidelity.
Now I must keep silence, suffer, and face
Sharp judgments ever anew.

6

I am brought to ruin by these decrees
That Love must thus remain out of my reach.
Even if I wished to secure her affection,
I have no good fortune or success in the attempt.
Disheartenment has so set itself against me,
I cannot receive any comfort
That may ward off from my heart
This unheard of adversity.

7

Love, you were present at the council
Where God called me to become a human being.
You willed me to exist in disquiet;
All that happens to me, I impute to you!
I fancied I was loved by Love;

I am disowned; that is clear to me.
My confidence, my high false assurance,
Is all concluded in grief.

8

Sweet as Love's nature is,
Where can she come by the strange hatred
With which she continually pursues me
And transpierces the depths of my heart with storm?
I wander in darkness without clarity,
Without liberating consolation, and in strange fear.
Give love to noble spirits, O Love,
And perfect all you have begun in me!

9

It is plain that Love has dealt with me deceitfully.
From whom shall I now seek remedy?
I shall seek it from fidelity, if she will receive me
And, for the sake of her high achievement,
Lead me before Love, that I may give myself up
Fully to her, in the hope she will show some concern.
I do not pray for her consolation or any remedy,
But only that she may acknowledge me as hers.

10

Alas, Love, do all your pleasure!
Your law is my best consolation;
I will wholly conform myself to it,
Whether I am a prisoner or liberated.
I will abide above all by your dearest will,
In torment, in death, in disaster.
Grant, Love, that I may acknowledge you as Love:
That is richness above all gain.

36. Daring the Wilderness

1

Whatever season of the year it is,
O you who are lovers!

So control your ardor
That nothing too much depress or too much gladden you,
But everything be in the just middle—
Whatever Love does with you or omits to do,
Whether it be misfortune or benefit.
For these are attitudes
Through which Love blesses
Your abiding
In Love.

2

Let they whom Love has ever blessed
Be—according to the season of the year—
Sad or joyful,
And always on Love's side,
And let them be continually available
Where each knows the will of Love
In ease, in harshness,
In pleasure, in pain:
That wilderness
Each dares
In Love.

3

Who wills to dare the wilderness of Love
Shall understand Love:
Her coming, her going,
How Love shall receive love with love,
Perfectly.
So Love has kept nothing hidden from them,
But she shows them her wilderness and her highest palace
—Know well, everyone—
Because each has kept on to the end
With suffering
In Love.

4

Those who wish that Love heal their suffering
Shall behave toward Love

According to her pleasure,
With confidence that disregards all that befalls them,
According to true love:
They suffer all grief indeed, without pain
In order to content high Love.
They let it appear
That they shall read
All judgments passed on them
In love.

5

Judgment of Love
Pierces deep within
Through the inward senses;
This cannot be known by the ignoble heart
That spares anything for Love;
But they who fare high-mindedly
Through all Love's nature—
Where the loving soul with love gazes upon Love—
Because they have conquered
Remain enlightened
In love.

6

O soul, creature
And noble image,
Risk the adventure!
Consider your law and your nature—
Which must always love—
And love the best good of Love.
To have fruition of her, defend yourself boldly;
Thus you will have success.
And spare no hour,
But ever keep on to the end
In love.

7

They who, according to love,
Understand Love's counsel

And who dare through Love
Many a great exertion for Love's sake,
All perseveringly,
Find that to be less than love is great pain;
On this subject, Love shows them her rich teaching
Ever new.
Irrevocably
They remain high-minded
In love.

8

But you who reject Love's counsel
In which fidelity lies,
And on whom pain weighs heavy,
I take it that you will be grieved again,
And without avail.
For you never did what Love urged
While Love promised you love with love,
And this you fled;
So you remain cast out
Of what Love provides
In love.

9

Let them whom Love provides with any favor
Live, from then on, free,
And in this liberty say:
"I am all Love's and Love is all mine!"[15]
High-minded and bold,
Each summons all the love of Love as owed,
For this she gives diverse riches;
She is kind to them in all things.
They alone
Have full power
In love.

10

Of herself, Love is good.
What she does to anyone

Makes them wise;
How Love causes the high-minded to love
She so teaches them
That they can nevermore forget it.
So Love has taken possession of them with love.
What happens to them then?
By the fury of Love
Each is all devoured
In love.

11

Alas! Where then is Love,
When someone cannot find her—
Someone, that is,
Who employs all that is had
And nevertheless does not find Love—
Someone to whom Love sends love
So that Love keeps them revolving in woe,
And yet they cannot experience her?
But another to whom she gives favor
Has quickly become perfect
In love.

12

Love is indeed there,
Beyond, I know not where,
Free, without fear.
That for me Love is inaccessible
Causes me anguish,
And still more woe to anyone who clings fast
To Love in her oppressive power.
But this did not last long;
Love gave unmistakably
Her embraces
In love.

13

Now may God help those
Who would gladly do all things

According to Love's wishes,
And who will gladly traverse the deep wilderness
To the land of love,
Where they are often placed in afflictions
And are subject to Love in all things
In heavy chains:
Thus Love holds them heavy laden
In the continual fire
Of love.

Here is Love's guarantee:
When Love with love finds fidelity in anyone
Who for Love's sake undergoes all pains,
Sweet and harmless,
Full satisfactions shall be known to him
In love.

37. Love's Great Power

1

The season approaches us rapidly
When summer will set up for us
A banner with all sorts of flowers;
Many noble lovers will rejoice at this.

2

For the days become long for us,
And the birds raise their song;
They for whom Love sweetens all distress
Can give her grateful thanks.

3

I also would thank you, Love, had you deserved it
To the full—just like one of your poor friends.
But since you first bowed me under your yoke,
You have always spoiled my happiness.

4

You do good to those whom you favor;
I think you can never bear anyone's success.
At this my heart is sad; at this my mouth complains,[16]
At this my strength is truly broken.

5

O Love, if you were love, as you actually are,
Where would you have come by the strange hatred
With which you transpierce those
Who give you a kiss at all times?

6

Yes, you are all, Love; you are so wise;
Your name is Love, and it is of high renown;
All you do ever gives delight,
No matter what remains under oppression.

7

Your name adds grace, your presence breathes joy;
Your refusal annihilates, but your gift crowns.
However sorely you have distressed us,
With one kiss, you give us full reward.

8

Thus, Love's work surpasses all,
And all things are beleaguered by her powers;
Her burden has outweighed all burdens;
There is no escaping her; we must go out to meet her!

9

God bless Love!
If anyone so will, let Love make them free in a different way.
As for her wonders and her cunning tricks,
I cannot avow many in my favor.

10

Since you, O Love, can do all with love,
Give me, for the sake of love, the fruition
That delights the loving soul through your highest goodness!
But you have consumed all my youth.

11

Love wills that the loving soul lovingly demand total love.
She has set up her highest banner.
From this we learn what kind of works she requires,
With clear truth and without doubt.

12

O noble souls! Apply yourself to the exercise of love,
And adorn yourselves with the light of truth,
So that no darkness may assail you,
But you may consort with your Beloved according to the law of love.

13

Love wills all love from noble spirits,
And that they bring their works into conformity with it,
And that they rejoice with memory
And delight in Love with joy.

Praise and honor be to Love,
To her great power, to her rich teaching;
And by her consolation may she heal the pain
Of all who gladly brave Love's vicissitudes.

NOTES

1. R. W. Southern, *Western Society and the Church of the Middle Ages* (New York: Pelican, 1976) 100–132, 272–309.

2. The fourth crusade, which destroyed the city of Constantinople in 1204, resulted in a tragic separation of Eastern and Western branches of Catholic Christianity, a separation that still exists.

3. John C. Dwyer, *Church History: Twenty Centuries of Catholic Christianity* (New York: Paulist Press, 1985) 172–91.

4. Peter Lombard, *Opera omnia*, tomus primus. 191–92 liber secundus. "De rerum corporalium et spiritualium creatione et formatione, aliisque pluribus eo pertinentibus."

Distinctio 18. "De formatione mulieris." 3 (Aug. lib. 9 de Gen. ad litteram, cap. 13). C 688, in Migne, *Patrologia Latina* 191–92.

5. Fiona Bowie, ed., *Beguine Spirituality: An Anthology* (London: SPCK, 1989); Ernest McDonnell, *The Beguines and Beghards in Medieval Culture* (New Brunswick, N.J.: Rutgers University Press, 1954) 1–49.

6. Brenda Bolton, "Vitae Matrum: A Further Aspect of the Frauenfrage," in *Medieval Women*, ed. Derek Baker (Oxford: Blackwell, 1978) 253–73.

7. Hadewijch, Letter 1, "In God's Radiance," in *Hadewijch: The Complete Works*, trans. Mother Columba Hart (New York: Paulist Press, 1980) 1:18, 47.

8. Letter 2, "Serve Nobly," ibid. 2:3, 2:39, 48–49.

9. Ria Vanderauwera, "The Brabant Mystic, Hadewijch," in *Medieval Women Writers*, ed. Katharina Wilson (Athens: University of Georgia Press, 1984) 186–93.

10. Letter 26, "Coping with Separation," Hart, *Hadewijch* 26:24, 26:31, 106–7.

11. The excerpts are from Hart, *Hadewijch*, 217–37.

12. See Job 30:31.

13. See Song of Songs 2:16.

14. See Job 21:8–9.

15. See Song of Songs 2:16.

16. Job 23:4.

BIBLIOGRAPHY

Bolton, Brenda. "Vitae Matrum: A Further Aspect of the Frauenfrage." In *Medieval Women*. Edited by Derek Baker. Oxford: Blackwell, 1978. 253–73.

Bowie, Fiona, ed. *Beguine Spirituality: An Anthology*. London: SPCK, 1989.

Dwyer, John C. *Church History: Twenty Centuries of Catholic Christianity*. New York: Paulist Press, 1985.

Hart, Mother Columba, trans. *Hadewijch: The Complete Works*. New York: Paulist Press, 1980.

Southern, R. W. *Western Society and the Church of the Middle Ages*. New York: Pelican, 1976.

Vanderauwera, Ria. "The Brabant Mystic, Hadewijch." In *Medieval Women Writers*. Edited by Katharina Wilson. Athens: University of Georgia Press, 1984.

– 11 –

JULIAN OF NORWICH

(1342–1420?)

In Our Mother Christ We Profit and Mature

The first extant book by a woman in the English language was written by Julian of Norwich. Very little else is known about her, however, except the few pieces of information included here and some annotations in the archives at Norwich, England. Her mother is mentioned in one of her revelations or "showings," but nothing more is known about her family. Her name may have been taken from the Church of St. Julian at Norwich to which her cell was attached.

What is known about Julian is that she received her showings when she was thirty years old. These came successively for one day and one night after she had almost died from a severe chest infection. These showings would later be referred to as the "short showings." Dame Julian reflected on their meaning for at least twenty years. The reflections would eventually be referred to as the "long showings."[1]

Julian's reflections on her showings would provide a ray of hope in the darker side of fourteenth-century England. The Hundred Years War, bubonic plague, and fears of death and brutal punishments were all a part of the fourteenth century. Cutting off a hand or foot, blinding, and other forms of mutilation were not uncommon punishments for theft, disloyalty, and other offenses. Human life was cheap, and fear of punishment by God ran high. A certain degree of pessimism, fear, and anxiety characterized the darker side of English life.

The joyful hope that weaves through Julian's presentation of God was needed in this century. Julian's showings emphasize a God whose power is expressed in love, not in punishment.[2] To an age of anxiety about sudden death and the possibility of hell, Julian could write with assurance, "God loves us and delights in us . . . all shall be well."[3]

Julian's showings are not naive. She was as challenged in hope as those around her. Like others throughout human history, she raised clear concerns: Why do humans sin? Why is there evil when God could simply not allow evil? What is the purpose of suffering? After reflecting on her revelations for some time, Julian answered her own questions. The only answer is to place the questions in the mystery of God's love, which is not understood by humans:

> It is in this knowledge (of God's love) that we are most blind, for some of us believe that God is almighty and may do everything, and that God is all wisdom and can do everything, and that God is all love and will do everything. There we fail! It is this ignorance that most hinders God's lovers, as I see it.[4]

The God of Julian's revelations calms human fears and anxieties. The motherly and gracious God of the *Showings* lovingly creates, compassionately restores, and gently sustains (ch. 5). The courteous Lord is a loving servant who raises all humanity to the heavens (ch. 23). The compassionate God does not wish any harm to come to the children, but desires only to forgive all the wrong the children do (ch. 53). Even if an individual becomes honestly discouraged about personal evil, the community of the church stands ever near to mediate the Spirit (ch. 61). God desires communion with all humans that is as intimate as Julian's. Julian is led into the side of Christ, a symbol of their intimate union (ch. 24).[5]

Julian's *Showings* are a unique contribution to mystical literature. She is aware of the biblical tradition of maternal God imaging.[6] She can read Latin and knows sources, which may have included the patristic sources that imaged God as mother.[7] Her education by the Benedictines of Carrow probably provided some introduction to the lyric poetry of her age, some of which (for example, the popular "feeding imagery") used maternal images of Jesus. Among women, the nursing, nourishing, birthing Christ imagery was as popular as the bridegroom image.[8] The Ancren Riwle, a rule of life followed by an anchoress like Julian, also made use of some feminine imagery for God.[9]

Julian of Norwich was not the first writer to employ maternal imagery for Jesus Christ; it was already used by patristic writers and earlier medieval writers. The imagery is found among male religious as well as female religious writers. The imagery of Jesus as mother was particularly popular among men in the Cistercian tradition, who also used maternal imagery for the role of abbots.[10]

Contemporaries of Julian's are familiar with the imagery of mother Jesus, especially the feeding imagery. Margery Kempe relates an account in which the Lord Jesus tells her to stop eating meat and feed on him instead. Margery then visits a holy male anchorite who tells her to thank God and continue to suck on the breasts of Jesus Christ.[11] Catherine of Siena incorporates feeding imagery as well. A popular literary work of fourteenth-century England made abundant use of the maternal Christ imagery.[12]

This being said, it is also necessary to say that Julian's use of maternal imaging is distinct for at least three reasons. First, Julian relies on metaphors and not similes in the maternal imagery of God. This is done at least eighty-three times.[13] Second, Julian's abundance of feminine metaphors for God does not include a single reference to Matthew's "God as mother hen" (Matt 23:37), a favorite image for male writers. Third, Julian demonstrates an integrity and creativity with her development of maternal God imagery. This latter trait makes her work unique.

This third aspect of Julian's distinctiveness deserves elaboration to indicate the various ways in which her maternal imaging is truly unique among mystical writers. She develops the image of God's motherhood in a way that affirms its equivalence to God's fatherhood. She uses maternal imagery for each person of the Trinity. Julian's maternal image of God does not stand over and against the value of women. Rather, she develops the maternal metaphor as that which surrounds and guides humans throughout the life cycle. Each of these aspects is intertwined with the other throughout the longer showings.

Unlike others before her, Julian has no difficulty in naming God "mother" in a sense that is equivocal to "father" (ch. 52, 58). Others before her had difficulty imagining a creator as anything other than father. This was connected to the physiology of the period, which believed that the male seed contained the full potential for human life.[14] The female simply received it and nourished it. Thus, God could only be like a father and not like a mother, for God was the source of life.[15] Thus, to call God a mother in a manner equivalent to father was to upset the system of male superiority based on males perceived as "fully in God's image" and females as not fully in God's image. If God is mother as surely as God is father, then women are also "fully in God's image."[16]

A second dimension of uniqueness is the integrity of Julian's use of maternal imaging for God and her perspectives on the dignity of real women. In the medieval period the imaging of Jesus Christ as maternal did not further the position of women's dignity or equality. Whereas men like Bernard of Clairvaux could be tender in describing Jesus as mother and abbot as mother, flesh-and-blood mothers were still looked on as a potential source of temptation.[17] As earlier chapters have stated, it is one thing to have ideal women and mothers—like the virgin Mary—on romanticized pedestals, but quite another thing to see how women are treated in society and in the church. Julian's theology does not suffer from that dichotomous approach.

Julian uses physical motherhood as a powerful metaphor of likeness to God's expressions of self-giving. She is unique not only in her treatment of each person of the Trinity with maternal imagery, but also in her maternal imaging of the Trinity as Unity. There is an integral use of the maternal symbol of womb throughout her development of the human life cycle in its journey toward God.

Life begins in the womb of God, where it is nourished in love. The birth pangs of love cause suffering and the cross, but the journey that is always sustained by the motherly God will come to eternal life in the womb of heavenly eternal beginnings. Images of enclosure, birth, growth, feeding, nourishing, giving and guiding life to its fruition abound in Julian (ch. 6, 43, 52–55, 57, 60, 61, 63–64, 80).

Like a mother who loves her children, Jesus Christ continues to teach, to bathe all who desire it, to forgive and to welcome back the children with open loving arms (ch. 12, 35, 40, 57–63, 74, 77). It may be necessary to apply discipline or to give medicine for healing, even if neither is desired or understood by the child (ch. 48, 60, 61, 63, 77–78, 82). At the same time, God's motherly touch encourages the child to go forth, for there is always the welcome embrace upon return (ch. 34, 36, 40, 48, 52–53, 55, 74, 77, 82–83, 86).

The full cycle of life is completed as death becomes the gateway to the fullness of life. This is symbolized by the gracious return to the womb of eternal beginnings (ch. 53, 57, 63–64). Through the entire cycle Julian sees only gentleness and love in the compassionate mother God. "I saw no manner of wrath in God" (ch. 49). Courtesy, tenderness, sweetness, humility, and compassion mark the God of Julian's visions.[18]

Although Julian strikes the expected female pose of self-disparagement in the short *Showings,* she asserts her confidence in speaking about God's love even if she is a woman (ch. 6, 13). It is worth noting that the long text, written some twenty years later, omits the disparaging references.[19] The earlier references to the soul, to humanity, and to God as "he" are deliberately changed to "she," "we," and "us" in later chapters (ch. 29, 34, 65, 74).

Julian's imaging of the maternal God is a bold assertion. If mother Jesus feeds with his body and blood to sustain the life of the children, then women are more uniquely fitted to act *in persona Christi* than men. If the maternal God encloses all creation in the womb of life and gently brings humans to the womb of eternal beginnings, then women as well as men are made in the full image of God. These were both bold assertions for a fourteenth-century woman to make.

Julian's perceptions of creation, redemption, afterlife, and imaging of God by women as well as men represent a narrow path between orthodoxy and heresy in her day. Her literary and theological skill in the use of biblical and literary images and contrasts makes her entire work an integral presentation of the bonding of all creation in the maternal and paternal God. The brief excerpts from her longer showings that follow are but a brief introduction to the work of this gentle and hopeful English woman. In England the feast of Dame Julian of Norwich is celebrated on May 8.

Showings

51[20]

Then our courteous Lord answered very mysteriously, by revealing a wonderful example of a lord who has a servant, and gave me the sight for the understanding of them both. The vision was shown doubly with respect to the lord, and the vision was shown doubly with respect to the servant. One part was shown spiritually, in a bodily likeness. The other part was shown more spiritually, without bodily likeness. So, for the first, I saw two persons in bodily likeness, that is to say, a lord and a servant; and with that, God gave me spiritual understanding. The lord sits in state in rest and in peace. The servant stands before his lord, respectfully, ready to do his lord's will.

The lord looks on his servant very lovingly and sweetly and mildly. He sends him to a certain place to do his will. Not only does the servant go, but he dashes off and runs at great speed, loving to do his lord's will. And soon he falls into a dell and is greatly injured; and then he groans and moans and tosses about and writhes, but he cannot rise or help himself in any way. And of all this, the greatest pain which I saw him in was lack of consolation, for he could not turn his face to look on his loving lord, who was very close to him, in whom is all consolation; but like a man who was for the time extremely feeble and foolish, he paid heed to his feelings and his continuing distress, in which distress he suffered seven great pains.

The first was the severe bruising which he took in his fall, which gave him great pain. The second was the clumsiness of his body. The third was the weakness which followed these two. The fourth was that he was blinded in his reason and perplexed in his mind, so much so that he had almost forgotten his own love. The fifth was that he could not rise. The sixth was the pain most astonishing to me, and that was that he lay alone. I looked all around and searched, and far and near, high and low, I saw no help for him. The seventh was that the place in which he lay was narrow and comfortless and distressful.

I was amazed that this servant could so meekly suffer all this woe; and I looked carefully to see if I could detect any fault in him, or if the lord would impute to him any kind of blame, and truly none was seen, for the only cause of his falling was his goodwill and his great desire. And in spirit he was as prompt and as good as he was when he stood before his lord, ready to do his will.

And all this time his loving lord looks on him most tenderly, and now with a double aspect, one outward, very meek and mild, with great compassion and pity, and this belonged to the first part; the other was inward, more spiritual, and this was shown with a direction of my understanding toward the lord, and I was brought again to see how greatly he rejoiced over the honorable rest and nobility which by his plentiful grace he wishes for his servant and will bring him to.[21] And this belonged to the second part of the vision. And now my understanding was brought back to the first, keeping both in mind.

Then this courteous lord said this: "See my beloved servant, what harm and injuries he has had and accepted in my service for love, yes, and for his goodwill. Is it not reasonable that I should reward him for his fright and his fear, his hurt and his injuries and all his woe? And furthermore, is it not proper for me to give him a gift, better for him and more honorable than his own health could have been? Otherwise, it seems to me that I should be ungracious."

For twenty years after the time of this revelation, except for three months, I received an inward instruction and it was this: "You ought to take heed to all the attributes, divine and human, that were revealed in the example, though this may seem to you mysterious and ambiguous." I willingly agreed with a great desire, seeking inwardly with great care all the details and the characteristics which were at that time revealed, so far as my intelligence and understanding will serve, beginning with when I looked at the lord and the servant, at how the lord was sitting and the place where he sat, and the color of his clothing and how it was made, and his outward appearance and his inward nobility and goodness; and the demeanor of the servant as he stood, and the place where and how, and his fashion of clothing, the color and shape, his outward behavior and his inward goodness and willingness.

I understood that the lord who sat in state in rest and peace is God. I understood that the servant who stood before him was Adam; that is to say, one man was shown at that time and his fall, so as to make it understood how God regards all humans and their falling. For in the sight of God all humans are one man, and one man is all humanity. This man was injured in his powers and made most feeble, and in his understanding he was amazed, because he was diverted from looking on his lord, but his will was preserved in God's sight. I saw the lord (God the Father) commend and approve him for his will, but he himself was blinded and hindered from knowing this will. And this is a great sorrow and a cruel suffering to him, for he neither sees clearly his loving lord, who is so meek and mild to him, nor does he truly see what he himself is in the sight of his loving lord. And I know well that when these two things are wisely and truly seen, we shall gain rest and peace, here in part and the fullness in the bliss of heaven, by God's plentiful grace.

The place where the lord sat was unadorned, on the ground, barren and waste, alone in the wilderness. His clothing was wide and ample and very handsome, as befits a lord. The color of the clothing was azure blue, most dignified and beautiful. His demeanor was merciful, his face was a lovely pale brown with a seemly countenance, his eyes were black, most beautiful and seemly, revealing all his loving pity, and within him there was a secure place of refuge, long and broad, all full of endless heavenliness. And the loving regard which he kept constantly on his servant, and especially when he fell, it seemed to me that it could melt our hearts for love and break them in two for joy. This lovely regard had in it a beautiful mingling which was lovely to see. Part was compassion and pity, as far as heaven is above earth. The pity was earthly and the bliss was heavenly.

The blueness of his clothing signifies his steadfastness; the brownness of his fair face with the blackness of the eyes was most suitable to indicate his holy solemnity; the amplitude, billowing (shining) splendidly all about him, signifies that he has enclosed within himself all heavens and all endless joy and bliss; and this was shown in a brief moment, when I perceived that my understanding was directed to the lord. In this I saw him greatly rejoice over the honorable restoration to which he wants to bring and will bring his servant by his great and plentiful grace. And still I was amazed, contemplating the lord and the servant as I have said.

I saw the lord sitting in state and the servant standing respectfully before his lord, and in this servant there is a double significance, one outward, the other inward. Outwardly, he was simply dressed like a laborer, prepared to work, and he stood very close to the lord, not immediately in front of him but a little to one side, and that on the left; his clothing was a white tunic, scanty, old and all worn, dyed with the sweat of his body, tight fitting and short, as if it were a hand's breadth below his knee, looking threadbare as if it would soon be worn out, ready to go to rags and to tear.

And in this I was much amazed, thinking, "This is not fitting clothing for a servant so greatly loved to stand in before so honorable a lord." And, inwardly, there was shown in him a foundation of love, the love which he had for the lord, which was equal to the love which the lord had for him. The wisdom of the servant saw inwardly that there was one thing to do which would pay honor to the lord; and the servant, for love, having no regard for himself or for anything which might happen to him, went off in great haste and ran when his lord sent him, to do the thing which was his will and to his honor; for it seemed by his outer garment as if he had been a constant laborer and a hard traveler for a long time. And by the inward perception which I had of both the lord and the servant, it seemed that he was newly appointed, that is to say, just beginning to labor, and that this servant had never been sent out before.

In the servant is included the second person of the Trinity, and in the servant is included Adam, that is to say, all humanity. And therefore when I say "the Son," that means the divinity which is equal to the Father, and when I say "the servant," that means Christ's humanity, which is the true Adam. By the closeness of the servant is understood the Son, and by his standing to the left is understood humanity, Adam. The lord is God the Father, the servant is the Son, Jesus Christ, the Holy Spirit is the equal love which is in them both.

When Adam fell, God's Son fell; because of the true union which was made in heaven, God's Son could not be separated from Adam, for by Adam, I mean all humanity. Adam fell from life to death, into the valley of this wretched world, and after that into hell. God's Son fell with Adam, into the valley of the womb of the maiden who was the fairest daughter of humanity, and that was to excuse Adam from blame in heaven and on earth; and powerfully, the Son brought humanity out of hell. By the wisdom and the goodness which were in the servant is understood God's Son; by the poor laborer's clothing and the standing close by on the left is understood Adam's humanity with all the human weakness which follows. For in this our good Lord showed his own Son and Adam as only one humanity. The strength and the goodness that we have are from Jesus Christ; the weakness and blindness that we have are from Adam, which two were shown in the servant.

And so has our good Lord Jesus taken upon him all our blame; and therefore our Father does not wish to assign more blame to us than to his own beloved Son, Jesus Christ. So the Son was the servant before he came on earth, standing ready in purpose before the Father until the time when the Father would send the Son to do the glorious deed by which humankind was brought back to heaven. That is to say, even though he is God, equal with the Father as regards his divinity, but with his prescient purpose that he would become human to save humankind in fulfillment of the will of his Father, so he stood before his Father as a servant, willingly taking upon himself all our responsibilities. And then he rushed very readily at the Father's bidding, and soon he fell very low into the maiden's womb, having no regard for himself or for his cruel pains.

The white tunic is his flesh; the scantiness signifies that there was nothing at all separating the divinity from the humanity. The tight fit is poverty; the age is Adam's wearing;[22] the wornness is the sweat of Adam's labor; the shortness shows the servant-laborer.

The hurt that he took was our flesh, in which at once he experienced mortal pains. That he stood fearfully before the lord and not immediately in front symbolizes that his clothing was not seemly enough for him to stand immediately in from of the lord, nor could nor should that be his office while he was a laborer; nor further might he sit with the lord in rest and peace until he had duly won his peace with his hard labor; and that he stood to the left symbolizes that the Father by his will permitted his own Son in human nature to suffer all humanity's pain without sparing him. By his tunic being ready to go to rags and to tear is understood the rods and the scourges, the thorns and the nails, the pulling and the dragging and the tearing of his tender flesh, of which I had seen a part. The flesh was torn from the skull, falling in pieces until when the bleeding stopped; and then it began to dry again, adhering to the bone. And by the tossing about and writhing, the groaning and the moaning, is understood that he could never with almighty power rise from the time he fell into the maiden's womb until his body was slain and dead, and he had yielded his soul into the Father's hand, with all humanity for whom he had been sent.

Now the Son does not stand before the Father on the left like a laborer, but he sits at the Father's right hand in endless rest and peace. But this does not mean that the Son sits on the right hand side as one man sits beside another in this life, for there is no such sitting, as I see it, in the Trinity; but he sits at his Father's right hand, that is to say, right in the highest nobility of the Father's joy.

52[23]

And so I saw that God rejoices that he is our Father, and God rejoices that he is our Mother, and God rejoices that he is our true spouse, and that our soul is his beloved wife. And Christ rejoices that he is our brother, and Jesus rejoices that he is our Savior. These are five great joys, as I understand, in which he wants us to rejoice, praising him, thanking him, loving him, endlessly blessing him, all who will be saved.

During our lifetime here we have in us a marvelous mixture of both well-being and woe. We have in us our risen Lord Jesus Christ, and we have in us the wretchedness and the harm of Adam's falling. Dying, we are constantly protected by Christ, and by the touching of his grace we are raised to true trust in salvation. And we are so afflicted in our feelings by Adam's falling in various ways, by sin and by different pains, and in this we are made dark and so blind that we can scarcely accept any comfort. But in our intention we wait for God, and trust faithfully to have mercy and grace; and this is his own working in us, and in his goodness he opens the eye of our understanding, by which we have sight, sometimes more and sometimes less, according to the ability God gives us to receive.

And now we are raised to the one, and now we are permitted to fall to the other. And so that mixture is so marvelous in us that we scarcely know, about ourselves or about our Christian friends, what condition we are in. For these conflicting feelings are so extraordinary, except for each holy act of assent to God, which we make when we feel him, truly willing with all our hearts to be with him, and with all our soul and with all our might. And then we hate and despise our evil inclinations, and everything which could be an occasion of spiritual and bodily sin. And even so, when this sweetness is hidden, we fall again into blindedness, and so in various ways into woe and tribulation.

But then this is our comfort, that we know in our faith that by the power of Christ who is our protector we never assent to that. But we complain about it, and endure in pain and woe, praying about it until the time that he shows himself again to us. And so we remain in this mixture all the days of our life. But he wants us to trust that he is constantly with us in three ways.

He is with us in heaven, true man in his own person, drawing us up; and that was revealed in the spiritual thirst. And he is with us in earth, leading us; and that was revealed in the third revelation where I saw God in a moment of time. And he is with us in our soul, endlessly dwelling, ruling and guarding.

If we, through our blindness and our wretchedness, at any time fall, then let us quickly rise, knowing the sweet touching of grace, and willingly amend ourselves according to the teaching of Holy Church, as may fit the grievousness of the sin, and go on our way with God in love, and neither on the one side fall too low, inclining to despair, nor on the other side be too reckless, as though we did not care; but let us meekly recognize our weakness, knowing that we cannot stand for the twinkling of an eye except with the protection of grace, and let us reverently cling to and trust only God.

For God sees one way and humans see another way. For it is for humans to accuse themselves, and it is for our Lord God's own goodness courteously to excuse us.

54[24]

My understanding accepted that our substance is in God, that is to say, that God is God, and our substance is a creature in God. For the almighty Truth of the Trinity is our Father, for God made us and keeps us. And the deep Wisdom of the Trinity is our Mother, in whom we are enclosed. And the high Goodness of the Trinity is our Lord, and in him we are enclosed and he in us. We are enclosed in the Father and we are enclosed in the Son and we are enclosed in the Holy Spirit. And the Father is enclosed in us and the Son is enclosed in us and the Holy Spirit is enclosed in us.

56[25]

I saw most surely that it is quicker and easier for us to come to the knowledge of God than it is for us to know our own soul. For our soul is so deeply grounded in God and so endlessly treasured that we cannot come to knowledge of it until we first have knowledge of God, who is the creator and to whom it is united. God is closer to us than our own soul, for God is the foundation on which the soul stands. Our soul sits in God in true rest, and our soul stands in God in sure strength, and our soul is naturally rooted in God in endless love. Therefore, if we want to have knowledge of our soul, and communion and discourse with it, we must seek in our Lord God in whom it is enclosed.

The honorable city in which our Lord Jesus sits is our sensuality in which he is enclosed. Our natural substance is enclosed in Jesus, with the blessed soul of Christ sitting in rest with the divinity. I saw very certainly that we must necessarily be in longing and in penance until the time when we are so deeply led into God that we verily and truly know our own soul. I saw certainly that our good Lord himself leads us into this high depth in the same love with which we were created and in the same love with which he redeemed us through the power of his blessed passion.

All this notwithstanding, we can never come to the full knowledge of God until we know clearly our own soul. For until the time that it is in its full powers, we cannot be all holy. In nature we have our life and our being, and in mercy and grace we have our increase and fulfillment. God wants us to understand, desiring with all our heart and all our strength to have knowledge of these things, always more and more until the time when we are fulfilled. To know them fully and to see them clearly is nothing else than the endless joy and bliss which we shall have in heaven, which God wants us to begin here in knowledge of divine love.

58[26]

God the blessed Trinity, who is everlasting being, eternal without beginning, in eternal purpose created human nature, which fair nature was first prepared for the Son, the second person. And by full agreement of the whole Trinity, God created us all. And in our creating, God joined and united us to himself. In this union we are kept as pure and as noble as we were created. By the power of that same precious union, we love and delight in our Creator. In God, we delight, praise, give thanks, and endlessly rejoice.

And so in our making, God almighty is our loving Father, and God all wisdom is our loving Mother, with the love and goodness of the Holy Spirit, which is all one God, one Lord. And in the joining and the union the Lord is our very true spouse and we his beloved wife and his fair maiden, with which wife he was never displeased. For he says, "I love you and you love me, and our love will never divide in two."

I contemplated the work of all the blessed Trinity, in which contemplation I saw and understood these three properties: the property of the fatherhood, and the property of the motherhood, and the property of the lordship in one God. In our almighty Father we have our protection and our bliss, as regards our natural substance, which is ours by our creation from without beginning; in the second person, in knowledge and wisdom we have our perfection, as regards our sensuality, our restoration, and our salvation, for he is our Mother, brother, and savior; and in our good Lord the Holy Spirit we have our reward and our gift for our living and our labor, endlessly surpassing all that we desire in marvelous courtesy, out of great plentiful grace. All our life consists of three: In the first we have our being, and in the second we have our increasing, and in the third we have our fulfillment. The first is nature; the second is mercy; the third is grace.

As to the first, I saw and understood that the high might of the Trinity is our Father, and the deep wisdom of the Trinity is our Mother, and the great love of the Trinity is our Lord; and all these we have in nature and in our substantial creation. And furthermore I saw that the second person, who is our Mother, substantially the same beloved person, has now become our mother sensually, because we are double by God's creating, that is to say, substantial and sensual. Our substance is the higher part, which we have in our Father, God Almighty; and the second person of the Trinity is our Mother in nature of our substantial creation, in whom we are founded and rooted, and he is our Mother of mercy in taking our sensuality.

And so our Mother is working on us in various ways, in whom our parts are kept undivided; for in our Mother Christ we profit and increase, and in mercy he reforms and restores us, and by the power of his passion, his death, and his resurrection he unites us to his substance. So our Mother works in mercy on all his beloved children who are docile and obedient to him, and grace works with mercy, and especially in two properties, as it was shown, which working belongs to the third person, the Holy Spirit. He works, rewarding and giving. Rewarding is a gift for our confidence which the Lord makes to those who have labored; and giving is a courteous act which he does freely, by grace, fulfilling and surpassing all that creatures deserve.

Thus in our Father, God Almighty, we have our being and in our Mother of mercy we have our reforming and our restoring, in whom our parts are united and we are made perfect, and through the rewards and the gift of grace of the Holy Spirit we are fulfilled. And our substance is in our Father, God Almighty, and our substance is in our Mother, God all wisdom, and our substance is in our Lord God, the Holy Spirit, all goodness, for our substance is whole in each person of the Trinity, who is one God.

And our sensuality is only in the second person, Christ Jesus, in whom is the Father and Holy Spirit; and in him and by him we are powerfully taken out of hell and out of the wretchedness on earth, and gloriously brought up into heaven, and blessedly united to our substance, increased in riches and nobility by all the power of Christ and by the grace and operation of the Holy Spirit.

59[27]

And we have all this bliss by mercy and grace, and this kind of bliss we never could have had and known, unless that property of goodness which is in God had been opposed, through which we have this bliss. For wickedness has been allowed to rise in opposition to that goodness; and the goodness of mercy and grace opposed that wickedness, and turned everything to goodness and honor for all who will be saved. For this is that property in God which opposes good to evil. So Jesus Christ, who opposes good to evil, is our true Mother. We have our being from him, where the foundation of motherhood begins, with all the sweet protection of love which endlessly follows.

As truly as God is our Father, so truly is God our Mother. This is revealed in everything, and especially in those sweet words where God says, "I am Lord." That is to say, I am God, the power and goodness of fatherhood; I am God, the wisdom and lovingness of motherhood; I am God, the light and the grace which is all blessed love; I am God, the Trinity; I am God, the unity; I am God, the great supreme goodness of every kind of thing; I am God, who makes you to love; I am God, who makes you to long; I am God, the endless fulfilling of all true desires. For where the soul is highest, noblest, most honorable, still it is lowest, meekest, and mildest.

And from this foundation in substance, we have all the powers of our sensuality by the gift of nature, and by the help and furthering of mercy and grace, without which we cannot profit. Our great Father, almighty God, who is being, knows us and loved us before time began. Out of this knowledge, in most wonderful deep love, by the prescient eternal council of all the blessed Trinity, God wanted the second person to become our Mother, our brother, and our savior. From this it follows that as truly as God is our Father, so truly is God our Mother. Our Father wills, our Mother works, our good Lord the Holy Spirit confirms. And therefore it is our part to love our God in whom we have our being, reverently thanking and praising this God for our creation, mightily praying to our Mother for mercy, and pity, and to our Lord the Holy Spirit for help and grace. For in these three is all our life: nature, mercy and grace, of which we have mildness, patience, and pity, and hatred of sin and wickedness. For the virtues of themselves must hate sin and wickedness.

And so Jesus is our true Mother in nature by our first creation. And he is our true Mother in grace by taking our created nature. All the lovely works and all the sweet loving offices of beloved motherhood are appropriated to the second person, for in him we have this godlike will, whole and safe forever, both in nature and in grace, from his own goodness proper to him.

I understand three ways of contemplating motherhood in God. The first is the foundation of our nature's creation; the second is God taking our nature, where the motherhood of grace begins; the third is the motherhood at work. And in that, by the same grace, everything is penetrated, in length and in breadth, in height and in depth without end; and it is all one love.

60[28]

But now I should say a little more about this penetration, as I understood our Lord to mean: how we are brought back by the motherhood of mercy and grace into our natural place, in which we were created by the motherhood of love, a mother's love which never leaves us.

Our Mother in nature, our Mother in grace, because he wanted altogether to become our Mother in all things, made the foundation of divine work most humbly and most mildly in the maiden's womb. And God revealed that in the first revelation, when he brought that meek maiden before the eye of my understanding in the simple stature which she had when she conceived. That is to say, that our great God, the supreme wisdom of all things, arrayed and prepared himself in this humble place, already in our poor flesh, himself to do the service and the office of motherhood in everything.

The mother's service is nearest, readiest, and surest. It is nearest because it is most natural; readiest because it is most loving; and surest because it is truest. No one ever might or could perform this office fully, except only him. We know that all our mothers bear us for pain and for death. Oh, what is that? But our true Mother Jesus, he alone bears us for joy and for endless life; blessed may he be. So he carries us within him in love and travail, until the full time when he wanted to suffer the sharpest thorns and cruel pains that ever were or will be, and at the last he died.

And when he had finished, and had borne us so for bliss, still all this could not satisfy his wonderful love. And he revealed this in these great surpassing words of love: "If I could suffer more, I would suffer more." He could not die anymore, but he did not want to cease working. Therefore, he must needs nourish us, for the precious love of motherhood has made him our debtor.

The mother can give her child to feed on her milk, but our precious Mother Jesus can feed us with himself, and does, courteously and most tenderly, with the blessed sacrament, which is the precious food of true life. With all the sweet sacraments he sustains us most mercifully and graciously. This he meant in those blessed words where he said, "I am he whom the church preaches and teaches to you." That is to say: All the health and the life of the sacraments, all the power and the grace of my word, all the goodness which is ordained in holy church for you, I am he.

The mother can lay her child tenderly to her breast, but our tender Mother Jesus can lead us easily into his blessed breast through his sweet open side, and show us there a part of the godhead and the joys of heaven, with inner certainty of endless bliss. And that he revealed in the tenth revelation, giving us the same understanding in these sweet words spoken as one looks into his blessed side rejoicing: See how I love you.

The fair, lovely word "Mother" is so sweet and so kind in itself that it cannot truly be said of anyone or to anyone except of him and to him who is our true Mother of life and of all things. To the property of motherhood belong nature, love, wisdom, and knowledge, and this is God. For though it may be so that our bodily bringing to birth is only little, humble, and simple in comparison with our spiritual bringing to birth, still it is he who does it in the creatures by whom it is done.

The kind, loving mother who knows and sees the need of her child guards it very tenderly, as the nature and condition of motherhood will have. And always as the child grows in age and in stature, she acts differently, but she does not change her love. And when it is even older, she allows it to be chastised to destroy its faults, so as to make the child receive virtues and grace. This work, with everything which is lovely and good, our Lord performs in those by whom it is done. So he is our Mother in nature by the operation of grace in the lower part, for love of the higher part. And he wants us to know it, for he wants us to have all our love attached to him.

In this I saw that every debt which we owe by God's command to fatherhood and motherhood is fulfilled in truly loving God, which blessed love Christ works in us. This was revealed in everything, and especially in the great bounteous words when he says, "I am he whom you love."

63[29]

Here we may see that it truly belongs to our nature to hate sin, and truly it belongs to us by grace to hate sin. Nature is all good and fair in itself. Grace was sent out to save nature and destroy sin and bring it back again to the blessed place from which it came, which is God, with more nobility and honor by the powerful operation of grace. For it will be seen before God by all his saints in joy without end that nature has been tried in the fire of tribulation, and that no lack or defect is found in it.

So are nature and grace of one accord. For grace is God as uncreated nature is God. He is two in his manner of operation, and one in love, and neither of these works without the other, for they are not separated. And when by the mercy of God and with his help, we reconcile ourselves to nature and to grace, we shall see truly that sin is incomparably worse, more vile and painful than hell. For sin is in opposition to our fair nature. For as truly as sin is unclean, so truly is sin unnatural. All this is a horrible thing to see, for the loving soul would wish to be all fair and shining in the sight of God, as nature and grace teach. But do not let us be afraid of this, except insofar as fear may be profitable.

Let us meekly lament to our beloved Mother, and he will sprinkle us all with his precious blood, and make our soul most pliable and most mild, and heal us most gently in the course of time, just as it is most glory to him and joy to us without end. And from this sweet and gentle operation he will never cease, until all his beloved children are born and brought to birth. He revealed that when he gave understanding of the spiritual thirst which is the longing in love that will last till the day of judgment.

So in our true Mother Jesus our life is founded in his own prescient wisdom from without beginning, with the great power of the Father and the supreme goodness of the Holy Spirit. And in accepting our nature he gave us life. In his blessed dying on the cross he bore us to endless life. And since that time, now and ever until the day of judgment, he feeds us and fosters us, just as the great supreme lovingness of motherhood wishes, and as the natural need of childhood asks. Fair and sweet is our heavenly Mother in the sight of our soul. Precious and lovely are the children of grace in the sight of our heavenly Mother, with gentleness and meekness and all the lovely virtues which belong to children by nature. For the child does not naturally despair of the mother's love. The child does not naturally rely upon itself. Naturally the child loves the mother, and each of them the other.

These and all others that resemble them, are such fair virtues, with which our heavenly Mother is served and pleased. I understood no greater stature in this life than childhood, with its feebleness and lack of power and intelligence, until the time that our gracious Mother has brought us up into our Father's bliss. And there it will be truly made known to us what God means in the sweet words when God says, "All will be well. You will see it yourself, that every kind of thing will be well."

85[30]

I marveled greatly at this vision. For despite our foolish living and our blindness here, still our courteous Lord endlessly regards us, rejoicing in this work. And we can please God best of all by wisely and truly believing it, and rejoicing with and in God. As truly as we shall be in the bliss of God without end, praising and thanking him, so truly have we been in God's love and knowledge in endless purpose from without beginning.

In this love without beginning, God created us. In the same love, God protects us and does not allow us to be hurt in a way that might decrease our bliss. Therefore, when the judgment is given and we are all brought up above, we shall clearly see in God the mysteries which are now hidden from us.

Then shall none of us be moved to say in any manner, "Lord, if it had been so, it would have been well." But we shall all say with one voice, "Lord, blessed may you be, because it is so, it is well. Now we truly see that everything is done as it was ordained by you before anything was made."

NOTES

1. Brant Pelphrey, *Julian of Norwich* (Wilmington, Del.: Michael Glazier, 1989) 17–22.

2. Anna Marie Reynolds, "Woman of Hope," in *Julian, Woman of Our Day*, ed. Robert Llewelyn (London: Darton, Longman, and Todd, 1985) 11–26.

3. *Julian of Norwich, Showings*, ed. and trans. Edmund Colledge and James Walsh (New York: Paulist Press, 1978) ch. 68, p. 315.

4. Ibid. ch. 73, p. 323.

5. Mary Paul, S.L.G., "Julian of Norwich and the Bible," in *Julian of Norwich*, ed. A. M. Allchin (Fair Acres, Oxford: SLG Press, 1980) 11–23.

6. Pss 28:9; 34:9; 78:24, 25; 80:11; 84:4; Wis 7; Isa 46:3–4; 49:15; 63:9; 66:13; Hosea 11:3–4; 13:13–14; Matt 23:37; Luke 13:34; James 1:18; 1 Peter 1:3; 2:2–3; John 6; John 21:5–6; 1 Cor 10:3–4, etc.

7. Clement of Alexandria, "Exhortation to the Greeks," "The Rich Man's Salvation," in *Clement of Alexandria*, trans. G. W. Butterworth (Cambridge, Mass.: Harvard University Press, 1953) 201, 319, 347; Clement of Alexandria, *Christ the Educator*, trans. Simon Wood in The Fathers of the Church, vol. 23 (New York: Fathers of the Church, 1954) 39–40; Sr. Ritamary Bradley names other sources in "The Motherhood Theme in Julian of Norwich," *Fourteenth Century English Mystics Newsletter* 2:4 (1976) 25–30.

8. J. Edgar Bruns, *God as Woman, Woman as God* (New York: Paulist Press, 1973) 84–85; *Richard Rolle of Hampole and His Followers*, ed. C. Horstman, Yorkshire Writers Series, vol. 1 (New York: Macmillan, 1895) 368; *Political, Religious and Love Poems*, ed. Frederick James Furnival, Early English Text Society, Original Source no. 15 (London: EETS, 1866) republished (London: Oxford University Press, 1965) 187.

9. *The English Text of the Ancren Riwle*, ed. E. J. Dobson, Early English Text Society, Original Source no. 267 (London: Oxford University Press, 1972) 172.

10. This is well documented in Caroline Walker Bynum's *Jesus as Mother* (Berkeley: University of California, 1982) esp. 110–66; Eleanor McLaughlin, "'Christ, My Mother': Feminine Naming and Metaphor in Medieval Spirituality," *Nashotah Review* (Fall 1975) 228–48; Benedicta Ward, "Faith Seeking Understanding: Anselm of Canterbury and Julian of Norwich," in Allchin, *Julian of Norwich* 25–31.

11. *The Book of Margery Kempe*, trans. Barry Windeatt (London: Penguin, 1985) ch. 5, pp. 51–52.

12. *The Monk of Farne*, ed. Hugh Farmer (Baltimore: Helicon, 1961) esp. 41, 64, 69, 72.

13. Similes appear twice, i.e., ch. 61 and 74. However, the simile is used more to describe the role of the child than the role of God.

14. Thomas Aquinas, *Summa theologica*, ed. English Dominican Province, 3 vols. (New York: Benziger, 1947–48) 1, 92, 1 ad 1; 1, 91, 3; 1, 92, 2 and 3.

15. Guerric of Igny, Second Sermon for Lent, ch. 2, *Liturgical Sermons*, 2 vols., Cistercian Fathers Series 8 and 32 (Spencer, Mass.: Cistercian Publications, 1970–71) vol. 1, 142; 2:30. Additional sources naming Jesus "mother" can be found in Bynum, *Jesus as Mother* 118–25.

16. Men used the maternal image for Jesus Christ but not for God the Creator, for God the Father was considered to be the origin of life. This perception was based upon the physiology of the times. The male seed was thought to contain all life; thus, males

were the whole image of God and women were undeveloped males. See the abundant references in Bynum, *Jesus as Mother;* Thomas Aquinas, *Summa theologica* 1, 92, 1.

17. Letter 322 in S. *Bernardi, Opera omnia,* Migne, *Patrologia Latina* 182:533.

18. Jennifer Heimmel documents this well in *"God Is Our Mother": Julian of Norwich and the Medieval Image of Christian Feminine Divinity,* Salzburg Studies in English Literature, vol. 92:5 (Salzburg: University of Salzburg, 1982) 46–102.

19. This is with the exception of a remark in ch. 2 that is negated in ch. 19.

20. The excerpt is from Colledge and Walsh, *Julian of Norwich: Showings* 267–78.

21. This may refer to Revelation 9, ch. 22, where Julian describes how her understanding was lifted up to the heavens.

22. The phrase refers to the long period of waiting for the light of Christ.

23. Colledge and Walsh, *Julian of Norwich: Showings* 279–82.

24. Ibid. 285–86.

25. Ibid. 288–90.

26. Ibid. 293–95.

27. Ibid., 295–97

28. Ibid. 297–99.

29. Ibid. 303–5.

30. Ibid. 341.

BIBLIOGRAPHY

Alchin, A. M., ed. *Julian of Norwich.* Fair Acres, Oxford: SLG Press, 1980.

Colledge, Edmund, and James Walsh, eds. and trans. *Julian of Norwich: Showings.* Western Classics of Spirituality. New York: Paulist Press, 1978. Short and long texts.

Cressy, Dom Serenius, ed. *Revelations of Divine Love,* 1670. A modern edition of this text has been done by Dom Roger Hudleston. London: Burns, Oates, Washbourne, 1927.

Gillespie, Vincent, and Maggie Ross, "The Apophatic Image: The Poetics of Effacement in Julian of Norwich." In Marion Glasscoe, ed., *The Medieval Mystical Tradition in England.* Cambridge: D. F. Brewer, 1992. 53–77.

Glasscoe, Marion, ed. *Julian of Norwich. A Revelation of Love.* Exeter: University of Exeter Press, 1976. Middle English text only.

Heimmel, Jennifer. *"God Is Our Mother": Julian of Norwich and the Medieval Image of Christian Feminine Divinity.* Salzburg Studies in English Literature, vol. 92:5. Salzburg: University of Salzburg, 1982. 46–102.

Julian of Norwich. *Enfolded in Love and in Love Enclosed.* Trans. by members of the Julian shrine. 2 vols. London: Darton, Longman and Todd, 1980, 1985.

Llewelyn, Robert, ed. *Julian, Woman of Our Day.* London: Darton, Longman and Todd, 1985.

Pelphrey, Brant. *Julian of Norwich.* Wilmington, Del.: Michael Glazier, 1989.

Reynolds, Anna Marie, ed. and trans. *A Showing of God's Love.* London: Sheed and Ward, 1974. Short text only.

Wolters, Clifton, ed. and trans. *Julian of Norwich: Revelations of Divine Love.* Harmondsworth: Penguin Classics, 1966. Long text only.

– 12 –

CATHERINE OF SIENA

(1347–1380)

I Ask Mercy for the World

Caterina Benincasa, Catherine of Siena, was born on March 25, 1347, the twenty-fourth child of Lapa Piacenti and Giaciomo Benincasa. A twin sister, Giovanna, died, but Catherine flourished. Her lively chatter, disarming directness, quick intelligence, and stubborn independence gave her a favored status with both parents. Her biographer, friend, and spiritual director, the Dominican Raymond of Capua, states that Catherine dedicated her virginity to God when she was only seven.[1]

Catherine decided to join the Third Order of St. Dominic when she was fifteen, the age when young women usually married. Catherine's parents wanted her to be married like their other daughters. Catherine refused, and her parents in turn refused to allow her to join the Third Order. Catherine decided she would cut her hair to make herself unattractive to potential suitors. Then she undertook an even stricter regime of prayer and fasting. Finally, her parents allowed her to follow her desires.

Catherine received the Dominican habit in 1365. Returning to her parents' home to pray, fast, and eventually to engage in a number of outreach works for the poor of the city, she was well known for the variety of deeds she performed. At the same time, she grew in contemplative prayer and continued a severe fast for the good of the church. In 1368, while at prayer in her room, she experienced the mystical communion with Jesus Christ that would grow throughout her life.

Catherine's intensely busy life remained deeply prayerful. In time, her life was interwoven with the difficulties of the church. Catherine's visions and dialogues with Jesus Christ provided her with the courage to speak out against the abuses of power that were still plaguing the church of the fourteenth century. Her life was lived in the midst of the struggles between French and Italian churchmen over papal candidates. In one vision Jesus Christ tells Catherine that he does not want the ministers of his church to be "bloated with pride in their hankering after high office."[2]

The French and Italian power struggles had a long history. Between 1250 and 1300 four of the thirteen popes were French, a factor that added tension to the relationships of French and Italian nations as well as to the tensions among powerful French and Italian churchmen. At the beginning of the fourteenth century, King Philip IV of France forbade the French bishops to contribute money to Rome until power lines were straightened out. Pope Boniface VIII (1294–1303) excommunicated Philip for his boldness. Philip responded by sending his representatives to harass the pope.

Boniface VIII died a few months later. His successor, Benedict XI, died within a year of taking office. A Frenchman, Bertrand de Got, was elected Pope Clement V (1305–14). This pope decided he would remain at Avignon, since he felt his life would be safer there than in the midst of the warring border factions around Rome. Clement V sent his delegates to rule Italy, a move that turned Italians against him.

The period of the Avignon papacy lasted almost seventy years, 1308–77. Strong national rulers influenced their bishops to vote for the papal candidate who would favor particular interests.[3] As long as the pope was in France, cities of Italy vied for control of the Italian states. Florence and Siena were the strongest contenders for this power. They simultaneously tried to gain independence from the French papacy.[4] An antipapal league formed with an aim to cut off relations with the Avignon papacy and to regain some privileges that had been lost, such as rulers' power to appoint bishops.

Catherine went to Pisa in 1375 to dissuade leaders of Pisa and Lucca from joining an antipapal league, the Tuscan League. While in Pisa, she learned that Gregory XI (1370–78) was blocking grain supplies to Florence. This move added fuel to the antipapal fire for the formation of the Tuscan League. In 1376, Gregory placed Florence under interdict. He excommunicated any person or group that supported Florence. Other Italian states withdrew their support for the city.

Catherine directly interceded with Gregory XI to stop the destructive clash of wills that was ruining the unity of the church. She urged him to return to Rome and start acting with a compassion fitting the papal office:

> In the name of Christ crucified, I am telling you.... Be a courageous man for me, not a coward. Respond to God who is calling you to come and take possession of the place of the glorious shepherd, St. Peter, whose representative you still are.[5]

In 1376 Catherine met with Gregory. She implored him to deal gently with the Florentines and to return to Rome. Gregory returned to Rome on January 13, 1377. In 1378 he asked Catherine to mediate with the Florentines for him. However, since he had not yet lifted the interdict against the Florentines, some of them mobbed Catherine and she narrowly escaped with her life. Gregory XI died on March 27, 1378, still at odds with the Florentines.

An authoritarian Italian pope, Urban VI (1378–89), was elected to succeed Gregory XI. French cardinals contested the election, claiming that fear of the Italian mobs had forced the election, thereby rendering it invalid. On September 20, 1378, dissident French cardinals with some sympathetic friends elected a ruthless cardinal, Count Robert of Geneva, as Clement VII. Clement VII decided to reside at Avignon. Urban VI, needing support, negotiated peace with the Florentines. In 1379, this pope requested Catherine to come to Rome to serve as both a mediator and a counselor.

Although the relationships with popes and national leaders took up much of Catherine's life, her energies were not solely concerned with this ministry. Her abundance of personal correspondence in close to four hundred preserved letters and her *Dialogue* point to other areas of her personal life that were part of her ministry for the church. Like other women of the fourteenth century, she experienced some resentment and obstacles in following the path to which Jesus Christ had called her:

> My very sex, as I need not tell you, puts many obstacles in the way. The world has no use for women in work such as that, and propriety forbids a woman to mix so freely in the company of men.[6]

At the same time, the Christ of her visions made it clear that he was the giver of gifts, regardless of the thoughts of political or ecclesial rulers of the time. When gifts were given, they were to be used as Christ directed. If those representing his church had difficulty with that, then Catherine would have to ignore such restrictions and do as he commanded.

> Does it not depend on my own will where I shall pour out my grace? With me, there is no longer male and female, nor lower and upper class. All stand equal in my sight.[7]

Catherine's suffering was as much a ministry for the body of Christ as her prayerful solitude and her more public activities. Her suffering bore fruit, a reality affirmed by a number of her miracles, which are food miracles.[8] In the *Miracolo* the Virgin Mary assures Catherine that souls are being freed from purgatory because of her suffering. Her mother and father are among those who benefit from it.[9]

Accounts of Catherine's life accentuate her severe fasting, a contrast to the excessive feasting of the age. Yet in her letters, Catherine is sensible, gentle, and clear in letting circumstances affect how one interprets fasting:[10]

> If the body is weak, fallen into sickness . . . not only ought fasting to be put aside, but meat should be eaten; if once a day isn't enough, let it be eaten

four times a day. If one cannot stand up, stay in bed. If one can't kneel, sit down or lie down.... This is what discretion wants. For this reason, discretion proposes that penance be done as a means and not as a principal desire.[11]

Catherine attracted many people by her human warmth and joyful vitality. "She had nothing out of the ordinary in the way of good looks," says Raymond of Capua.[12] Her gentleness and love drew others to her as disciples and spiritual directees. Raymond was one of Catherine's friends and admirers, as well as her confessor. He admits, in spite of his love for Catherine, that he sometimes fell asleep as she waxed eloquently about heaven or the things of God. Catherine would be so absorbed in her topic that she would only eventually notice that Raymond was dozing. With exasperation she would say, "I might as well be talking to the wall as to you about the things of God."[13]

Catherine's advice to her correspondents is always clothed with a humility that is truth. She strongly urges those who have care of others not to be too harsh in their judgments and corrections. To one such woman, Blessed Daniella, she urges this respect for the unique working of God within the heart of each person. There is a gentle way to point out faults: "The vice that you might have seemed to recognize in others, ascribe to them and to you together, always using true humility."[14]

This humility is a form of self-knowledge that all are in need of God's help to become better. Catherine links self-knowledge to humility, patience, and a nonjudgmental attitude:

> I pray you then, you and me and every other servant of God, that we devote ourselves to understanding ourselves perfectly, in order that we may more perfectly recognize the goodwill of God, so that enlightened, we may abandon judging our neighbor, and acquire true compassion.[15]

This perspective of compassion, nonjudgment, and humility may seem to be contradicted by Catherine's identification of greed and power abuses by some of the clergy. Her letters reveal, however, that the basis for her sadness is that those who have great gifts and abuse them grieve the heart of God. In one vision Christ says to her, "I have dignified my ministers and thus grieve more over their wickedness."[16]

In the fourteenth century, priesthood was looked on as an elevated state of life. The priest was almost transfigured when he said the words of consecration and then lifted up the bread and wine during the Mass. The elevation of the host was accompanied by ringing bells and sweet incense smells. Many of the clergy and people believed Jesus Christ "arrived" at this moment. Seeing the body and blood was important, for "seeing" was "receiving." Laity did not receive the blood of Christ at this time. There was a fear that some drops of the precious blood might fall to the floor. Soon after the death of Catherine, the Council of Constance would condemn any priest who gave the laity communion under both forms.[17]

In late medieval Italy, devotion to the precious blood was very popular. At this time the Lamb of God taking away sin was a more important image than the Lamb of God sensed as food. The sacred wounds of Jesus Christ (the stigmata) also symbolized love that took away sin. The sacred blood was perceived as more important than sacred bread, for blood was necessary to give life to the body. This devotional perspective was particularly strong in Tuscany, which may help explain the strong devotion of Catherine of Siena to the precious blood.[18]

The precious blood was not the only object of devotion. The humanity of Jesus Christ was also the focal point of devotional theology. Catherine's intimate dialogues with the human Christ reveal his blood that was given for all. When Christ was lifted up on the cross, he drew all to himself. This desire for communion of all people was one of Catherine's strong desires. Her own life was given for this unity. Her life of fasting was for the good of the church and the world.

Given Catherine's strong concern for unity, it is not surprising that communion or receiving the body of Christ was central to her spirituality. Catherine strongly urged the frequency of communion, not only to her own followers but to others as well.[19] She is explicit in her disapproval of priests who believe they control the Eucharist and thus deny it to those who crave it. Catherine tells of two times when Christ fed her directly because the clergy would not.[20]

Her intense devotion to Jesus Christ and the body of Christ, the church, is the source for her own sadness at the disruptions in that church. Like Jesus Christ, Catherine gave her life and her body for the good of the world. Her final letter to her friend, Raymond of Capua, informs him of the living martyrdom her life had been for the unity of the church.[21]

Soon after Catherine wrote the letter, on January 1, 1380, she was afflicted with a paralyzing attack. From February 26 of that year, Catherine was unable to eat or drink. In the final days of her life, the period after Sexagesima Sunday, she felt like a personal failure for all that remained undone. The sorrow was deepened by the sensation of demons attacking her as death neared. She was finally released from her suffering on April 29, 1380.

Although Catherine's holiness was well established in her lifetime, the fifteenth-century theologian John Gerson strongly opposed her teachings. Like that of others, his literal reading of 1 Timothy 2:12 led him to restrictive conclusions:

> All women's teaching, particularly formal teaching by word and by writing, is to be held suspect unless it has been diligently examined, and indeed

much more fully than men's. The reason is clear: ... the law from on high forbids it. And why? Because women are more easily seduced and determined seducers; and because it is not proved that they are witnesses to divine grace.[22]

Raymond of Capua, reminded his readers that God sent unschooled apostles to teach the multitudes. If this was true, why couldn't God send holy women filled with the power and wisdom of God to church leaders? If leaders humbly listened, welcoming the women God sends, divine mercy will be poured out on the church.[23]

Pope Paul VI declared Catherine of Siena a doctor of the church in 1970.[24] Her festival is celebrated on April 29.

The excerpts that follow are from *The Dialogue*. Catherine began this work in 1377 and completed it in October 1378. During this period she was convincing the pope to return from Avignon to Rome. Many of her letters preceded this work.[25]

These selections point to the universality of Christ's love that Catherine lived intensely as she gave her life for the unity of the church. The Christ of Catherine's dialogue is a loving and personal Christ who cares for all his people. For Catherine, there is no one best way to follow this Christ, but only the way that Christ inspires in each one of his followers.

The Dialogue

24.[26] The Vines That Are Tended by the Divine Gardener

You then are my workers. You have come from me, the supreme eternal gardener, and I have engrafted you onto the vine by making myself one with you.

Keep in mind that each of you has your own vineyard. But everyone is joined to the neighbors' vineyards without any dividing lines. They are so joined together, in fact, that you cannot do good or evil for yourself without doing the same for your neighbors.

All of you together make up one common vineyard, the whole Christian assembly, and you are all united in the vineyard of the mystic body of holy church from which you draw your life. In this vineyard is planted the vine, which is my only begotten Son, into whom you must be engrafted. Unless you are engrafted into him you are rebels against holy church, like members that are cut off from the body and rot.

It is charity that binds you to true humility—the humility that is found in knowing yourself and me. See, then, that it is as workers that I have sent you all. Now I am calling you again, because the world is failing fast. The thorns have so multiplied and have choked the seed so badly that it will produce no fruit of grace at all.

I want you, therefore to be true workers. With deep concern, help to till the souls in the mystic body of holy church. I am calling you to this because I want to be merciful to the world as you have so earnestly begged me.

26.[27] *The Bridge*

On the cross, my Son drew everything to himself, for he proved his unspeakable love, and the human heart is always drawn by love. He could not have shown you greater love than by giving his life for you. You can hardly resist being drawn by love, then, unless you foolishly refuse to be drawn.

I said that, having been raised up, he would draw everything to himself. This is true in two ways. First, the human heart is drawn by love, as I said, and with all its powers: memory, understanding, and will. If these three powers are harmoniously united in my name, everything else you do, in fact or in intention, will be drawn to union with me in peace through the movement of love. All will be lifted up in the pursuit of crucified love. So my Truth indeed spoke truly when he said, "If I am lifted up high, I will draw everything to myself." For everything you do will be drawn to him when he draws your heart and its powers.

What he said is true also in the sense that everything was created for your use, to serve your needs. But you who have the gift of reason were made not for yourselves but for me, to serve me with all your heart and all your love. So when you are drawn to me, everything is drawn with you, because everything was made for you.

41.[28] *Love Experienced in Heaven*

The just who die in loving charity and are bound by love can no longer grow in virtue once time has passed. But they can forever love with that same affection with which they came to me, and by that same measure will it be measured out to them. They desire me forever and forever they possess me, so their desire is not in vain. They are hungry and satisfied, satisfied yet hungry—but they are far from bored with satiety or pained in their hunger.

Although they are all joined in the bond of charity, they know a special bond of sharing with those whom they loved most closely with a special love in the world. Through this love, they grew in grace and virtue. They helped each other proclaim the glory and praise of my name in themselves and in their neighbors. Now, in everlasting life, they have not lost that love. No, it is shared by all their just companions, my beloved people, and by all the angels. When someone reaches eternal life, everyone shares in her good and she shares in the good of everyone.

Everyone is full with delight and can grow no more. Each finds joy in me and in all the blessed ones, tasting in them the sweetness of my love. Their desires are a continual cry to me for the salvation of others. They finished their lives loving their neighbors. They did not leave that love behind but brought it with them when they passed through that gate which is my only begotten Son. So you see that whatever bond of love exists as they finish their lives, that bond is theirs forever and lasts eternally.

What these blessed ones want is to see me honored in you who are still on the way, pilgrims running ever nearer your end in death. Because these blessed ones seek my honor, they desire your salvation. So they are constantly praying to me for you. I do my part to fulfill their desire, provided only that you do not foolishly resist my mercy.

I have told you of the good of the glorified body in the glorified humanity of my Son. This is the guarantee of your own resurrection. You will all be made like him in joy and gladness, eye for eye, hand for hand, your whole bodies made like the body of the Word, my Son. You will live in him as you live in me, for he is one with me. But your bodily eyes will delight in the glorified humanity of the Word, my only begotten Son. Why? Because those who finish their lives delighting in my love will keep that delight forever. Not that they can do any further good now, but they rejoice in the good that they have brought with them. In other words, they cannot do anything more deserving of merit, for it is only in this life, by the choice of free will, that one can either merit or sin.

The face of my Son will appear to them neither terrifying nor hateful, for they have finished their lives in love. They delighted in me and were filled with goodwill toward their neighbors. To them the Lord will appear with mercy and love.

55.[29] *Christ Is the Safe Bridge to the Father*

When you are gathered together in my name, you are thirsty for living water. So you move forward and cross over the bridge, following the teaching of my Truth who is that bridge, Jesus. You run after his voice that calls out after you, "Let whoever is thirsty come to me and drink, for I am the fountain of living water."

I have told you that this is the way to climb onto the bridge. In this climbing, you are all gathered together and united, loving each other, carrying your hearts and wills like vessels.

This is the way you must keep, no matter what your situation in life. Every person gifted with reason has this obligation. No one can draw back and say, "My position or my children or other earthly obstacles keep me from following this way." Nor can the difficulties you encounter along the way excuse you. You are not to talk that way, because I have already told you that every state of life is pleasing and acceptable to me if it is held to with a good and holy will.

All things are good and perfect, since they were made by me. I am supreme goodness. I made them all and give them to you to use them, not to embrace death, but to have life through them.

It is an easy matter, for nothing is so easy and delightful as love. What I ask of you is nothing other than love and affection for me and for your neighbors. This can be done any time, any place, and in any state of life by loving and keeping all things for the praise and glory of my name.

64.[30] *Love Your Neighbor as I Love You*

I would have you know that every good, whether perfect or imperfect, is acquired and made manifest in me. It is acquired and made manifest by means of your neighbor. Even simple people know this, for they often love others with a spiritual love. If you have received any love sincerely, without self-interest, you will drink your neighbor's love sincerely. This love is like a vessel you fill at the fountain. If you hold your vessel in the fountain while you drink, it will not get empty. Indeed, it will always be full. So the love of your neighbor, whether spiritual or temporal, is meant to be drunk in me, without any self-interest.

I ask you to love me with the same love with which I love you. Without me, you cannot do this, for I loved you without being loved. Whatever love you have for me, you owe me. So you love me, not gratuitously, but out of duty, while I love you, not out of duty, but gratuitously. You cannot give me the kind of love I ask of you. This is why I have put you among your neighbors: so that you can do for them what you cannot do for me—that is, love them without concern for thanks and without looking for any profit for yourself. And whenever you do this, I will consider it done for me.

66.[31] *Dialogue on Prayer and Good Works*

Perfect prayer is achieved, not with many words, but with loving desire when the soul rises up to me with knowledge of herself, each movement seasoned by the other. In this way, she will have vocal and mental prayer at the same time, for the two stand together like the active life and the contemplative life. Still, vocal and mental prayer are understood in many different ways. This is why I told you that holy desire, that is, having a good and holy will, is continual prayer. This will and desire rises at the appointed time and place to add actual prayer to the continual prayer of holy desire. As long as the soul remains firm in holy desire and will, she will make it at the appointed time. But sometimes beyond the appointed times, she makes this continual prayer, as charity asks of her for her neighbor's good and according to the need she sees and the situation in which I have placed her.

The principle of holy will means that each of you must work for the salvation of souls according to your own situation. Whatever you do in word or deed for the good of your neighbor is a real prayer. (I am assuming that you actually pray as such at the appointed time.) Apart from your prayers of obligation, however, everything you do can be a prayer, whether in itself or in the form of charity to your neighbors, because of the way you use the situation at hand.

85.[32] *The Enlightenment of God's Love*

The light given by grace, given to whoever wants to receive this light beyond natural light, shows us the Truth. Every light that comes from Holy Scripture has come and still comes from that light. This is why foolish, proud, and learned people go blind even though it is light, because their pride and the cloud of selfish love have covered and blotted out this light. So they read Scripture literally rather than with understanding. They taste only its letter in their chasing after a multiplicity of books, never tasting the marrow of Scripture because they have let go of the light by which Scripture was formed and proclaimed. Such as these, then, wander and fall to whining when they see so many uncultured and unschooled in biblical knowledge, yet as enlightened in knowledge of the truth as if they had studied for a long time. But this is no wonder at all, for they possess the chief source of light from which learning comes. But because proud people have lost that light, they neither see nor know my goodness or the light of grace that is poured out in my servants.

I tell you, therefore, that it is better to walk by the spiritual counsel of a humble and unschooled person with a holy and upright conscience than by that of a well-read but proud scholar with great knowledge. For one cannot share what one does not have inside oneself. Because some persons live a life in the darkness, they often share the light of the Holy Scripture in darkness. You will find the opposite in my servants, for they share the light within them in hunger and longing for others' salvation.

I have told you this, my dearest daughter, to let you know the perfection of this unitive state in which souls are carried off by the fire of my charity. In that charity, they receive supernatural light and in that light they love me. Love follows upon understanding. The more they know, the more they love. The more they love, the more they know. Each nourishes the other. By this light, they reach that eternal vision of me in which they see and taste me in truth when soul is separated from body.

This is that superb state in which the soul, even while mortal, shares the enjoyment of the immortal. In fact, she often attains such union that she hardly knows whether she is in the body or out. She tastes the pledge of eternal life through her union with me as well because her own will is dead. It is by that death that she realizes her union with me, and in no other way could she perfectly accomplish that.

These souls have then a taste of eternal life. They have let go of the hell of self-will. But those who live by self-willed sensuality have in that a pledge of hell, as I have told you.

110.[33] *The Mystery of Divine Presence in the Sacred Species*

The sun never leaves its orbit, never divides. It gives light to all the world, to everyone who wants to be warmed by it. This sun is not defiled by any uncleanness. Its light is one. So is the Word, my Son, one with me and I with him. His most gracious blood is a sun, wholly God and wholly human.

This sun, this light, has in it the color of your humanity, the one united with the other. So the light of my Godhead became lightsome with the color of your humanity. That color became lightsome, fully divinized by the resurrection. The person of the Incarnate Word was penetrated and kneaded from one dough with the light of my Godhead, the divine nature, and with the heat and fire of the Holy Spirit. By this means, you have come to receive the light. To whom have I entrusted this light? To my ministers in the mystic body of holy church, so that you might have life when they give you his body as food and his blood as drink.

I have said that this body of his is a sun. Therefore, you could not be given the body without being given the blood as well. You could not be given either the body or the blood without the soul of this Word, nor the soul of the body without the divinity of me, God eternal. For the one cannot be separated from the other.... It is the whole divine being that you receive in that most gracious sacrament under the whiteness of bread.

Just as the sin cannot be divided, so neither can my wholeness as God and as human be divided. Even if the host is divided, I would be there, wholly God and wholly human. Nor is the sacrament itself diminished by being divided any more than fire. If you had a burning lamp, and all the world came to you for light, the light of your lamp would not be diminished by the sharing. Yet each person who shared it would have the whole light. True, each one's light would be more or less intense depending on what sort of material each one brought to receive the fire.

Imagine that many people brought candles. Each candle, the smallest as well as the largest, would have the whole light. Yet the person who carried a one-ounce candle would have less than the person whose candle weighed a pound. This is how it is with those who receive the sacrament. Each one of you brings your own candle, that is, the holy desire with which you receive the sacrament. Your candle is unlit and is lighted when you receive the sacrament. It is I who have given you the candle with which you can receive the light and nourish it within you. Your candle is love, because it is for love that I created you. Without love, you cannot have life.

Your being was given to you for love. In Holy Baptism, which you received by the power of the blood of this Word, you were made ready to share this light.

There is no other way you could come to share it. Indeed, you would be like a candle that has no wick and therefore can neither burn nor receive the light. So if you would bear this light, you must receive the wick that is faith. To this grace that you received in baptism, you must join your own soul's love. For I created your soul with a capacity for loving—so much so that you cannot live without love. Indeed, love is your food.

It is with this love that you come to receive my gracious glorious light, the light I have given you as food to be administered to you by my ministers. But even though all of you receive the light, each of you receives it in proportion to the love and burning desire you bring with you.

So you see that in no way can the heat and color and brightness that are fused in this light be divided—not by the scant desire the soul brings to this sacrament, nor by any fault in the soul who receives it or in the one who administers it. It is like the sun, which is not contaminated by the filth it shines upon. Nothing can contaminate or divide the light in this sacrament. Its brightness is never diminished and it never strays from its orbit, though the whole world shares in the light and heat of this Sun.

So this Word, this Sun, my only begotten Son, never strays from me, the eternal Sun and Father. In the mystic body of holy church, he is administered to everyone who will receive him. He remains wholly with me and wholly you have him, God and man. Even if all the world would ask for his light, all would have it whole and whole it would remain.

113.[34] *The Dignity of the Ministers of Christ*

O dearest daughter, I have told you this so that you may better know how I have dignified my ministers, and thus grieve the more over their wickedness. It is impossible to have a greater dignity than theirs in this life.

They are my anointed ones. I call them other Christs because I have appointed them to be my ministers to you and have sent them like fragrant flowers into the mystic body of holy church. No angel has this dignity, but I have given it to those I chose to be my ministers. I have sent them like angels, and they ought to be earthly angels in this life.

Just as these ministers want the chalice in which they offer the sacrifice to be clean, so I shall demand that they themselves be clean in heart and soul and mind. I want them to keep their bodies as instruments of the soul in perfect purity. I do not want them feeding and wallowing in the mire of impurity, nor bloated with pride in their hankering after high office, nor cruel to themselves and their neighbors—for they cannot abuse themselves without abusing their neighbors. If they abuse themselves by sinning, they are abusing the souls of their neighbors, for they are not giving them an example of good living.

114.[35] The Desire That the Ministers Serve Well

I want them to be generous and not avariciously selling the grace of my Holy Spirit to feed their own greed. They ought not to do so. Rather, as they have received charity freely and generously from my own goodness, so ought they to give to everyone who humbly asks, lovingly, freely, and with a generous heart, moved by love for my honor and for the salvation of souls.

Nor ought they to take anything in payment for what they themselves have not bought, but have received gratuitously so they might administer it to you. But they may accept alms. So also should those who receive from the ministers give alms if they are able. My ministers ought to be provided for with material help in their needs. You ought to be provided for and nourished by them with spiritual gifts, the holy sacraments I have established in holy church to be administered for your salvation.

134.[36] Catherine's Prayer for the Church

Immeasurable Love! By revealing this, you have given me a bittersweet medicine so that I might rise up once and for all from the sickness of foolish indifference and run to you with concern and eager longing. You would have me know myself and your goodness, and the sins committed against you by every class of people and especially by your ministers, so that I might draw tears from the knowledge of your infinite goodness and let them flow as a river over my wretched self and over those wretched living dead.

Therefore, it is my will, ineffable Fire, joyous Love, eternal Father, that my desire should never weary of longing for your honor and the salvation of souls. I beg you, let my eyes never rest, but in your grace make of them two rivers for the water that flows from you, the sea of peace. Thank you for granting to me what I ask of you and for what I did not ask because I did not know how. You have given me both the invitation and the reason to weep and to offer tender, loving, tormented longings in your presence with constant humble prayer.

Now, I beg you, be merciful to the world and to holy church. I am asking you to grant what you are making me ask. Do not delay any longer in granting your mercy to the world. Bow down and fulfill the longing of your servants! It is you who make them cry out, so now listen to their voices.

Your Truth said that we should call out and we would be answered, that we should knock and the door would be opened to us, that we should ask and it would be given to us. O eternal Father, your servants are calling to you for mercy. Answer them then. I know well that mercy is proper to you, so you cannot resist giving it to anyone who cries out for it. Your servants are knocking at the door of your Truth. They are knocking because in your Truth, your only begotten Son, they have come to know your unspeakable love for humankind.

Therefore, your burning love neither can nor should hold back from opening to those who knock with perseverance.

Open, then, and unlock and shatter the hardened hearts of your creatures. If you will not do it for their failure to knock, do it because of your infinite goodness and for love of your servants who are knocking at the door for them. Grant it, eternal Father, because you see how they stand at the door of your Truth and ask. For what are they asking? For the blood of this door, your Truth. In this blood you have washed away iniquity and drained the pus of Adam's sin. His blood is ours because you have made it a bath for us. You neither can nor will refuse it to those who ask it of you in truth.

Give, then, the fruit of your blood to these creatures of yours. Put onto the scales the price of your Son's blood so that the demons may not carry off your sheep. You are a good shepherd to have given us your only begotten Son to be our true shepherd. In obedience, he laid down his life for the sheep, and made his blood a bath for us. It is this blood that your servants, hungry as they are, are asking at this door. They are asking for you, through this blood, to be merciful to the world, and make holy church blossom again with the flowers of good holy shepherds whose perfume will dispel the stench of the putrid evil flowers.

Your servants seek the honor and salvation of many souls. Give them the bread of life, the fruit of the blood of your only begotten Son, which they are begging of you for the glory and praise of your name and the salvation of souls. It would seem that you receive more glory and praise by saving many people rather than let them persist in their hardness of heart. To you, eternal Father, everything is possible. Though you created us without help, it is not your will to save us without our help.

So I beg you to force the wills of those who refuse you to want what they think they do not want. I ask this of your infinite mercy. You created us out of nothing. So now that we exist, be merciful and remake the vessels you created and formed in your image and likeness. Reform them to grace in the mercy and blood of your Son.

148.[37] *Humans Are Created for Union with Each Other*

Enlarge your heart, daughter, and open your mind's eye to the light of faith. See with what great love and providence I have created and ordained humankind to rejoice in my supreme eternal reward.

In this mortal life, so long as you are pilgrims, I have bound you with the chain of charity. Whether you want it or not, you are so bound. If you should break loose by not wanting to live in charity for your neighbors, you will still be bound by it by force. Thus, that you may practice charity in action and in will, I in my providence did not give to any one person or to each individually the knowledge for doing everything necessary for human life.

No, I gave something to one, something else to another, so that each one's need would be a reason to have recourse to the other. So, though you may lose your will for charity because of your wickedness, you will at least be forced by your own need to practice it in action. Thus, you see the artisan turn to the worker and the worker to the artisan. Each has need of the other because neither knows how to do what the other does. So also the cleric and the religious have need of the layperson and the layperson of the religious. Neither can get along without the other. So with everything else.

Could I not have given everyone everything? Of course. But in my providence, I wanted to make each of you dependent on the others, so that you would be forced to exercise charity in action and will at once. I have shown you my generosity, goodness, and providence toward people.

I have so ordered the charity of those in heaven that no one simply enjoys his or her own reward in this blessed life without its being shared by the others. This is not how I have willed it to be. Rather, their charity is so well ordered and perfect that the great find joy in the reward of the small, and the small find joy in the reward of the great. I mean small in the sense of capacity, not that the small are any less full than the great.

Thus, all of them in this joyous charity rejoice in each other's reward and exult in me with jubilation and mirth without any sadness, sweet without any bitterness. This is because while they lived and died they enjoyed me in loving charity through charity for their neighbors.

167.[38] *Catherine's Thanks to God*

Thanks be to you, eternal Father, that you have not despised me, your handiwork, nor turned your face from me, nor made light of these desires of mine. You, Light, have disregarded my darkness. You, Life, have not considered that I am death, nor have you considered these grave weaknesses of mine. You, eternal Purity, have disregarded my wretched filthiness. You who are infinite have overlooked the fact that I am finite, and you, Wisdom, the fact that I am foolishness.

For all these, and so many other endless evils and sins of mine, your wisdom, your kindness, your mercy, your infinite goodness have not despised me. No, in your light you have given me light. In your wisdom, I have come to know the truth. In your mercy, I have found your charity and affection for my neighbors.

Let this same love compel you to enlighten the eye of my understanding with the light of faith, so that I may know your truth, which you have revealed to me. Let my memory be great enough to hold your favors, and set my will ablaze in your charity's fire. Let that fire burst the seed of my body and bring forth blood; then with that blood, given for love of your blood, and with the key of obedience, let me unlock heaven's gate.

I heartily ask the same of you for every reasoning creature, all and each of them, and for the mystic body of holy church. I acknowledge and do not deny that you loved me before I existed, and that you love me unspeakably much, as one gone mad over your creature.

O eternal Trinity! O Godhead! That Godhead, your divine nature, gave the price of your Son's blood its value. You, eternal Trinity, are a deep sea. The more I enter you, the more I discover. The more I discover, the more I seek you. You are insatiable, you in whose depth the soul is sated yet remains always hungry and thirsty for you, eternal Trinity, longing to see you with the light of your light.

Just as the deer longs for the fountain of living water, so does my soul long to escape from the prison of my darksome body and see you in truth. Oh, how long will you hide your face from my eyes?

O abyss! O eternal Godhead! O deep sea! What more can you have given me than the gift of your very self?

You are a fire always burning but never consuming. You are a fire consuming in your heat all the soul's selfish love. You are a fire lifting all chill and giving light. In your light, you have made me know your truth. You are that light beyond all light who gives the mind's eye supernatural light in such fullness and perfection that you bring clarity even to the light of faith. In that faith I see that my soul has life, and in that light receives you who are Light.

Who could reach to your height to thank you for so immeasurable a gift, for such generous favors, for the teaching of truth that you have given me? A special grace this, beyond the common grace you give to other creatures. You willed to bend down to my need and that of others who might see themselves mirrored here.

You responded, Lord. You yourself have given and you yourself answered and satisfied me by flooding me with a gracious light, so that with that light, I may return thanks to you. Clothe me with yourself, eternal Truth, so that I may run the course of this mortal life in true obedience and in the light of most holy faith. With that light, I sense my soul once again becoming drunk. Thanks be to God! Amen.

Here ends the book composed by the blessed virgin, the faithful spouse and servant of Jesus Christ, Catherine of Siena, dictated in ecstasy. She was clothed in the habit of St. Dominic. Amen.

NOTES

1. Raymond of Capua, *Legenda major,* 1:3, in *The Life of Catherine of Siena,* trans. Conleth Kearns (Wilmington, Del.: Michael Glazier, 1980) 28; hereafter this source will be cited as *Leg.* and page numbers will refer to the translation by Kearns.

2. Catherine of Siena, *The Dialogue*, trans. Suzanne Noffke (New York: Paulist Press, 1980) *Dial.* 113, 213; references to the *Dialogue* are from this translation.

3. Martin Gillet, *The Mission of Catherine of Siena* (St. Louis: Herder, 1955) 1–78.

4. *Leg.* 2:10, 264.

5. *Selected Letters of Catherine Benincasa: St. Catherine of Siena as Seen in Her Letters*, trans. and ed. Vita Dutton Scudder (New York: E. P. Dutton, 1927) 201.

6. *Leg.* 2:1, 217.

7. Ibid.

8. *Leg.* 2:3, 140–41; 2:16, 298–99.

9. *Leg.* 2:8, 212–18; 2:9, 220–23; 3:7, 417; 2:11, 241–44.

10. *Leg.* 2:4, 155, 162, 163; 3:7, 412, 414.

11. Letter to Sister Daniella of Orvieto, in *Medieval Women's Visionary Literature*, ed. Elizabeth Alvilda Petroff (New York: Oxford University Press, 1986) 268.

12. *Leg.* 1:7, 66.

13. *Leg.* 1:6, 58.

14. Petroff, *Medieval Women's Visionary Literature* 264.

15. Ibid. 265.

16. *Dial.* 113, p. 212.

17. "Condemnatio communionis sub utraque." Session 13, June 15, 1415. Concilium Constantiense, 1414–18. In *Decrees of the Ecumenical Councils*, ed. Norman Tanner (London: Sheed and Ward, and Washington, D.C.: Georgetown University, 1990) 418–19.

18. Caroline Walker Bynum, *Holy Feast and Holy Fast* (Berkeley: University of California Press, 1987) esp. 150–88.

19. Letters 184, vol. 3, 146; 358, vol. 5, 284; these are footnoted in Bynum, *Holy Feast and Holy Fast*, 375, n. 127.

20. *Dial.* 142, pp. 294–95.

21. Letter T 373 to Raymond of Capua, in Catherine, *Selected Letters* 348–49.

22. John Gerson, *De examinatione doctrinum*, pt. 1, considerations 2a, 3a, in *Joannis Gersonii . . . Omnia opera*, ed. Louis Ellies-Dupin, 5 vols. (Antwerp, 1706) 1:14–26; this is quoted in Caroline Walker Bynum, *Jesus as Mother* (Berkeley: University of California Press, 1982) 136, n. 85.

23. *Leg.* 2:1, 217.

24. Mary Ann Fatula, *Catherine of Siena's Way* (Wilmington, Del.: Michael Glazier, 1987); this well-documented work has abundant citations and an excellent bibliography of primary sources.

25. The letters of Catherine of Siena are published in a six-volume work, *La Lettere di S. Caterina da Siena*, ed. Niccolò Tommaseo (Florence: Barbiera, 1970); excerpts of these letters are found in the *Selected Letters* cited previously. A translation project of all the letters is in process, *The Letters of Catherine of Siena*, vol. 1, trans. Suzanne Noffke (Binghamton, N.Y.: Medieval and Renaissance Texts and Studies, 1988–). Subsequent volumes will follow.

26. *Dial.* 24, pp. 62–63.

27. *Dial.* 26, pp. 65–66.

28. *Dial.* 41, pp. 82–85.

29. *Dial.* 55, pp. 109–10.

30. *Dial.* 64, pp. 120–21.

31. *Dial.* 66, pp. 126–27.
32. *Dial.* 85, pp. 157–58.
33. *Dial.* 110, pp. 206–9.
34. *Dial.* 113, pp. 212–13.
35. *Dial.* 114, p. 213.
36. *Dial.* 134, pp. 274–76.
37. *Dial.* 148, pp. 311–13.
38. *Dial.* 167, pp. 364–66.

BIBLIOGRAPHY

Bynum, Caroline Walker. *Holy Feast and Holy Fast.* Berkeley: University of California Press, 1987.

Catherine of Siena. *Catherine of Siena: The Dialogue.* Translated by Suzanne Noffke. New York: Paulist Press, 1980.

Catherine of Siena. *I, Catherine: Selected Writings of Catherine of Siena.* Translated and edited by Kenelm Foster and Mary John Ronayne. London: Collins, 1980.

Catherine of Siena. *Selected Letters of Catherine Benincasa: Saint Catherine of Siena as Seen in Her Letters.* Translated and edited by Vita Dutton Scudder. New York: E. P. Dutton and Co., 1927.

Catherine of Sienna. *The Letters of Catherine of Siena.* Vol. 1. Translated by Suzanne Noffke. Binghamton, N.Y.: Medieval and Renaissance Texts and Studies, 1988–. More volumes will follow.

Fatula, Mary Ann. *Catherine of Siena's Way.* Wilmington, Del.: Michael Glazier, 1987.

Gillet, Martin. *The Mission of Catherine of Siena.* St. Louis: Herder, 1955.

Kearns, Conleth. *The Life of Catherine of Siena.* Wilmington, Del.: Michael Glazier, 1980.

Perrin, J. M. *Catherine of Siena.* Westminster, Md.: Newman, 1965.

– 13 –

MARGERY KEMPE

(c. 1373–1440)

I Ask God's Mercy for Everyone

In the late fourteenth century, English spirituality was characterized by strong emotion, exactly weighed sin, explicit doctrines, physical penance for sins, and contrition for personal evil. Most believers favored a literal interpretation of life and religion. Scripture was also literally interpreted by many of the faithful. The people sensed a closeness between earth and heaven. The heavenly world of saints or the hellish world of demons could affect the daily events of people's lives. Authentic devotion was not far removed from superstition.

Devotional people experienced a closeness to the humanity of Jesus Christ. The passion and sufferings of Jesus Christ were the focal points of piety. Obtaining merit to assure the forgiveness of sins and the attainment of heaven were major concerns. Pious practices like prayer and pilgrimages were important ways to show devotion and to obtain the merit that was needed on the journey to heaven.

If someone was inspired by God, it was expected that there would be tangible evidence of that inspiration. There were various heresies that caused suspicion of people like Margery Kempe, whose visions and tears were well known among the people. Because visions or miracles could be caused by either devils or Jesus Christ, fourteenth-century visionaries were a source of both fear and respect.

One of the developments of English piety in the fourteenth century was the growing awareness of the laity that they, the laity, were called to holiness. Formerly holiness was expected more of the clergy and the religious estate than of laity. In the fourteenth century, devotional literature was translated and made available to the laity, and this encouraged a more contemplative life. The popularity of such literature continued throughout the later Middle Ages. By the fifteenth century the popularity of works like those of Margery Kempe and Julian of Norwich pointed to the devotion of the people and their love for the human Christ. The appeal of Margery Kempe's experiences of Jesus Christ is obvious from the fact that selections of her meditations were published by Wynken de Worde in 1501 and then republished in 1521.[1]

Margery's colorful and holy life still shows through her book, even though she did not write it.[2] Her honesty and independence are clear in her relations with people of all states. Although she could neither read nor write, her acute memory enabled her to cite sources that she had heard about from others. She was able to think well on her feet and to respond clearly and directly to monks, archbishops, clerics, friends, husband, and anyone else who questioned her authenticity. That she was a laywoman, married, and had little formal education endeared her to laity who were desirous of a living a holy life in the midst of their vocation.

Like other women of her time, Margery would be suspected of Lollardism for being so public in her teaching and so enthusiastic about her spirit-filled mission.[3] Unlike the Lollards, she still went on pilgrimages, sought out spiritual counseling, and received the Eucharist. One of the women with whom she consulted was the anchoress Julian of Norwich. Margery tells us that Julian gave her sound advice:

> Said she, "The Holy Ghost never moves contrary to charity, for this would be contrary to the self that is all charity...when God visits a creature with tears of contrition, devotion, and compassion, the creature may and ought to believe that the Holy Ghost is in the soul...I pray God grant you perseverance."[4]

What else is known of Margery Kempe? She was the daughter of John Brunham, mayor of Lynne, and was born in King's Lynne, Norfolk, around 1373. John Brunham loved being important, which he was in the city of Lynne. He was not only the mayor but also a member of Parliament, a coroner, and a justice of the peace. Margery was happy to be the daughter of such an important man, since she was made to feel important herself.

When Margery married John Kempe, she felt she had married beneath her dignity. After her ale consistently spoiled, she decided this could be a punishment for her pride in feeling of a higher estate than her husband. John was quite handsome and very much in love with Margery, whose independent spirit was attractive to him. Margery decided she ought to be a more loving wife to her husband, who loved her so well.[5]

After the birth of their first child, the first of fourteen children, Margery became seriously ill. She was about twenty at the time, and the process of childbirth had been difficult. Since she seemed to be near death, a priest was summoned to hear her confession of sins. When he came, she tried to confess a sin that had been bothering her for a long time. Before she could state it, the priest started his reproof of her. Her fear for not confessing this sin, as well as her own illness, sent her into a tormented period of madness. Not until Jesus Christ sat on her bed, consoled her, and assured her that her sins were forgiven did she come back to her senses.[6]

Margery's visionary intimacy began with this experience and continued throughout the rest of her life. In some cases, the descriptions Margery gives of her intimacy with Jesus Christ may seem too physical for readers.[7] In the context of the times, however, this personal intimacy affirmed the reality of their friendship. Loving Jesus Christ meant experiencing a deeply personal friendship. The reflections of Margery Kempe are clearly not the abstractions of an earlier theology. Her work is a distinctive step away from that of most of the prior English mystics. It provides an inkling of the future effects of humanism on mystical experience, resembling Continental mystics.[8]

From the beginning of the sensory visions that she has of Jesus Christ, Margery can describe Jesus clearly with typical medieval symbolism. He wears a purple silk garment, a medieval English symbol of divinity. Thus, whatever he tells her to do, she must. Jesus tells Margery to take off her hair shirt. She needs to learn that it is the hair shirt of the heart that is more important than external penance.[9] When Margery's husband wants her to eat with him on Fridays instead of fasting, Jesus tells her to give up her Friday practice.[10] What is fitting for one stage of the spiritual journey may no longer be fitting for a future stage.

Margery is also told to lessen her verbal devotional prayers and meditate as the Lord will teach her. After the pilgrimage to Jerusalem when Margery receives the gift of tears, she will be told to cease her practice of abstaining from meat, for she needs the energy her tears drain away.[11] When her husband needs her to care for him in his old age, Jesus tells Margery to give up the time she spends in contemplation and care for her husband. He informs her that her loving deeds for her husband are just as important to him as her hours of contemplation.[12] This was a new way for Margery to look at the potential holiness of all of life.[13]

The one devotional expression of Margery Kempe that made her well known in her time and in her travels was her gift of tears. The excessive outbursts had one of two effects on those who witnessed the weeping. Either the witnesses thought she was possessed by demons and mad, or they thought the weeping was an affirmation of her holy and tender love of Jesus Christ. When Margery had her visions, she often participated in the sorrow if the vision was sorrowful. Margery wept for the sufferings of the Lord, shared in the feelings of Mary, Mary Magdalene, Peter, and other saints who were part of the scenes. Sometimes she even consoled those who were sorrowing.[14]

Upon first reading her book, a modern reader may simply dismiss Margery as a hysterical woman of little account in the mystical tradition, the way many interpreters of the spiritual life considered her for 430 years. She was judged by many as an "apprentice mystic," a religious "enthusiast," a deluded woman, an embarrassment to the "real" English mystics, and so on.[15]

Two basic things need to be remembered in defense of Margery. First, she was surrounded by people who believed that God acted through sensory phenomena. Whereas Margery's public displays of emotion irritated some people, they clearly inspired others because these tears demonstrated her compassion and love for Jesus Christ. This form of public display, along with her public refutation of sinful monks and clergy, was all she had to verify her authenticity. If she were a cleric or a religious, she would have had an organized group or an "institutionalized" form of sanctity to contextualize her holiness and to affirm the visionary life that flowed from the expectations of holiness.

Second, the gift of tears was not as familiar or as strong a tradition of piety in fourteenth- and fifteenth-century England as it was in Eastern Christianity. The long spiritual tradition of holy tears in Russia, Syria, and Byzantium was apparently unfamiliar to Margery Kempe, for she never uses this tradition as a reason for defending her experience.[16] She does not seem aware that there were contemporaries of hers on the Continent who experienced holy tears and were also considered mystical women, namely, Dorothea of Prussia and Bridget of Sweden. Fortunately, some of her counselors are aware of this reality.

Margery tried to contain her tears and asked Jesus Christ to relieve her of this burden because her weeping made her an object of ridicule. Jesus instructed her that his gifts were given as he wished. Neither she nor anyone else could dictate to him those on whom he bestowed particular gifts.[17] Neither ecclesial nor social boundaries and expectations about who could receive which gifts actually controlled the giving of gifts. While Margery did not appreciate the particular gift she had that disturbed others, she also learned that gifts must be used to draw others to God, whether the receiver liked the gift or not.

Margery claimed that Jesus Christ wished her to teach the Gospel even if the official church forbade women to preach.[18] She continued to teach the Gospel as long as Jesus Christ commanded her to do so. The official teachers in the church were suspicious of—and nervous about—this illiterate woman preaching, for there were many heretical groups. Margery was able to give signs of her authenticity. She could name the sins of those who believed she was not inspired by Christ. This assured the doubters that she was in conversation with God.

Like many medieval pilgrims, Margery felt she must go to Jerusalem. She was a robust traveler, going to many places of pilgrimage. Sometimes her husband accompanied her, and sometimes he did not. Margery was often put out of a group for her weeping. Some pilgrims are rude to her, ridicule her, or act in many unkind ways. In each case, Christ assures her that she is loved by him and that she must be charitable in her responses.

Margery's role models on her journey include popular women saints of her day. Catherine of Alexandria, Catherine of Siena, Mary of Egypt, Mary Magdalene, and Bridget of Sweden were some of her favorites.[19] Her life unfolded through a variety of dialogues with Jesus Christ, who tenderly reminded her of his love. She in turn shared his mercy for all people. In a vision recounted near the end of Book One, Jesus thanked her for the mercy her prayers showed for all people.[20] Like that of other authentic Christian visionaries, her intimacy with the Lord encouraged universality in her love, her prayer, and her life.

A manuscript was sent for repair to the Victoria and Albert Museum in 1934. It was identified by Hope Emily Allen as a copy of *The Book of Margery Kempe*.[21] This was translated into more modern English and published for the Early English Text Society in 1940.[22] *The Book of Margery Kempe* was dictated, perhaps to one of her sons. The illegible text was finally rewritten and tidied up by a priest whom Margery convinced to rewrite it. Then the last ten chapters were added. In spite of the rewriting, the book still reflects the vigor of Margery Kempe, "a medieval English woman of unforgettable character, undeniable courage, and unparalleled experience."[23]

Although the following selections do not reveal the color of this woman that a reading of the entire text reveals, they do provide a snapshot of her character. The intuitive learning that Margery experienced through her visions of Jesus Christ, and the enlargement of her own horizons about the compassion of Christ for all, can be glimpsed through the excerpts.

The change in Margery from a self-important woman to one who humbly and strongly believes in God's mercy is less evident in the excerpts than it is in her book as a whole. What can come through in the following selections, however, is the model that Margery can be for anyone who believes that Jesus Christ freely gives gifts, surprises us on the journey, and guides each of us to discover the uniqueness of Christian holiness to which we are called.

The Book of Margery Kempe[24]

Chapter 1[25]

When this creature was twenty years of age or somewhat more, she was married to an important burgess of Lynne and was with child within a short time as nature would. After she had conceived, she was belabored with great illness until after the child was born. Then, because of the great difficulties in childbirth, and the illness before, she despaired of her life, thinking she might not live. Then she sent for a priest, for she had something on her conscience which she had never revealed before in her life.

She was always prevented by the devil, who kept telling her that as long as she was in good health, she needed no confession, but should do penance by herself alone and all should be forgiven, for God is merciful enough. Therefore and oftentimes this creature did great penance in fasting on bread and water and other deeds of alms with devout prayers. But she would not reveal her sin in confession.

When she was at any time sick or diseased, the devil said in her mind that she would be damned because she was not forgiven for that fault. Thus, after her child was born, she—fearing for her life—sent for her confessor as was said above. She willed to be forgiven for all the sins of her lifetime as much as she could remember them. When she came to the point of saying the thing which she had so long concealed, her confessor was a little too hasty and began sharply to reprove her before she had fully said her intent, and so she would say no more, regardless of anything he might do. With the dread she had of damnation on the one side, and his sharp reproving her on the other, this creature went out of her mind and was vexed and tormented with spirits for half a year, eight weeks, and odd days.

In this time, she thought she saw devils opening their mouths all inflamed with burning waves of fire, as if they would swallow her. Sometimes they were trying to grab her, sometimes threatening her, pulling her and dragging her night and day during the aforesaid time. The devils cried out with great threats and demanded that she forsake Christianity, her faith, and deny her God, his Mother, all the saints in heaven, her good works and all good virtues, her father, her mother, and all her friends. So she did. She slandered her husband, her friends, and her own self. She said many a wicked and cruel word, knew no virtue nor goodness, desired all wickedness, and said and did what the spirits tempted her to do. She would have destroyed herself many a time at their stirrings and have been damned with them in hell, and in witness thereof, she bit her own hand so violently that the mark was seen for the rest of her life.

She spitefully tore the skin over her heart with her nails, for she had no other instruments. She would have done worse, but she was bound and kept still with restraints day and night so that she might not have her will. When she had labored with these and many other temptations so that people thought she would never escape or live, she lay alone and her keepers were far from her. On that day, our merciful Lord Jesus Christ, ever to be trusted, worshiped be his name, never forsaking his servant in time of need, appeared to his creature who had forsaken him in the likeness of a man, most handsome, most beauteous, and most amiable that ever might be seen with human eyes. He was clad in a mantle of purple silk, sitting upon her bedside, looking upon her with so blessed a face that she was strengthened in all her spirit. He said to her these words. "Daughter, why have you forsaken me when I never forsook thee?"

As he said these words, she really saw how the sky opened as bright as any lightening, and he rose up into the air, not right hastily and quickly, but fair and easily, so that she might well behold him in the air until the sky closed again.

And this creature became calmed in her wits and reason, as well as ever she was before. She begged her husband, as soon as he came to her, to give her the keys of the buttery to take her meat and drink as she had done before. Her maidens and her keepers told him not to give her the keys. They said she would give away the goods that were there, for she knew not what she said.

Nevertheless, her husband, ever having tenderness and compassion for her, commanded that they should deliver the keys to her. She took her meat and drink as her bodily strength would permit and knew her friends and her household and all others that came to see how our Lord Jesus Christ had wrought his grace in her, so blessed may he be who is ever near in tribulation. When people think he is far from them, he is ever near....

Chapter 5[26]

On a Friday before Christmas Day, as this creature was kneeling in a chapel of St. John, within the Church of St. Margaret, weeping and asking mercy and forgiveness for her sins and trespasses, our merciful Lord Christ Jesus, blessed may he be, ravished her spirit and said unto her, "Daughter, why are you weeping so severely? I am coming to thee, Jesus Christ who died on the cross, suffering bitter pains and passions for thee. I, the same God, forgive thy sins to the uttermost point, and thou shalt never come into hell or purgatory, but when thou shalt pass out of this world, within a twinkling of an eye, thou shalt have the bliss of heaven. I am the same God that hath brought thy sins to thy mind and forgiven thee. I grant thee contrition to thy life's end. Therefore, I bid thee and command thee, boldly call me 'Jesus Christ thy love,' for I am thy love, and shall be thy love without end. Daughter, thou hast a hair shirt on thy back. I will that thou take it off and I shall give thee a hair shirt in thy heart that shall please me much more than all the hair shirts in the world. Also, my dearest daughter, thou must forsake that which thou lovest best in this world, the eating of meat. Instead of meat, thou shalt eat my flesh and my blood that is the very body of Christ in the sacrament of the altar. This is my will, daughter, that thou receive my body every Sunday and I shall flow so much grace into thee that all the world shall marvel....

"I shall give thee grace enough to answer every cleric in the love of God. I swear to thee by my majesty that I will never forsake thee.... Daughter, I will thee to give up saying so many beads and rather thou think such thoughts as I will put into thy mind. I shall give thee leave to pray till six o'clock, saying what thou wilt. Then shalt thou be still and speak to me in thought, and I shall give to thee high meditation and true contemplation. I bid thee go to the anchorite at the Preaching Friars and tell him my secrets and my counsels that I show to thee... my spirit shall speak in him to thee."

Then this creature went forth to the anchorite . . . who thanked God. "Daughter . . . I charge thee to receive such thoughts as God gives as meekly and devoutly as ye can, and to come to me and tell me what they are, and I shall, with the grace of our Lord Jesus Christ, tell you whether they are of the Holy Spirit or of your enemy the devil."

Chapter 11[27]

It happened on a Friday on Midsummer's Eve, in very hot weather as this creature was coming from York carrying a bottle of beer in her hand and her husband carrying a cake, that he asked his wife this question:

"Margery, if there came a man with a sword, who would cut off my head unless I made love with you as I have done before, tell me on your conscience—for ye say ye will not lie—whether ye would allow my head to be cut off, or whether ye would allow me to make love with ye again as I did at one time?"

"Alas, sir," said she. "Why raise this matter, when we have been chaste these eight weeks?"

"Because I want to know the truth of your heart."

Then she said with great sorrow, "In truth I would rather see ye being killed than that we should turn again to our uncleanness."

He replied, "Ye are not a good wife."

Then she asked her husband why he had not made love to her for the last eight weeks, since she lay with him in his bed every night. He said he was made so afraid when he would have touched her that he dare do no more.

"Now, good sir, change your ways and ask God's mercy, for I told ye nearly three years ago that your lust would be lessened and now is the third year, and so I hope I shall have my desire. Good sir, I pray ye grant me what I ask, and I will pray for ye that ye shall be saved through the mercy of our Lord Jesus Christ, and ye shall have more reward in heaven than if ye wore a hair shirt or a coat of mail as a penance. I pray ye allow me to make a vow of chastity . . . before whatever bishop's hand God chooses."

"No," he said. "That I will not grant you, for now I may be intimate with you without mortal sin and then I may not do so." Then she replied, "If it be the will of the Holy Spirit to fulfill what I have said, I pray God that ye may consent. If it be not the will of the Holy Spirit, I pray God that ye never consent."

Then they went on toward Bridlington. . . . As they came to a cross, her husband sat down under the cross calling his wife to him and saying these words unto her: "Margery, grant me my desire, and I will grant ye your desire. My first desire is that we shall lie together in one bed as we have done before; the second, that ye shall pay my debts before ye go to Jerusalem; and the third, that ye shall eat and drink with me on the Friday as ye used to do."

"No, sir," she said. "I will never break my Friday fast as long as I live."

"Well," he said, "then I shall have sex with you again." She begged him to let her say her prayers and he kindly agreed. Then she knelt down beside a cross in the field and prayed in this way with a great abundance of tears.

"Lord God, thou knowest all things. Thou knowest what sorrow I have had to be chaste in my body these three years, and now I might have my will, and dare not for love of thee. For, if I should break that custom of fasting that thou commandest me to keep on the Friday, I should now have my desire. But, Blessed Lord, thou knowest that I will not go against thy will.... Now, Blessed Jesus, make thy will known to me that I may follow it thereafter and fulfill it with all my might."

Then our Lord Jesus Christ, with great sweetness, spoke to her, commanding her to go again to her husband and to pray him to grant her what she desired. "And he shall have what he desireth. For, my beloved daughter, this was the reason that I asked thee to fast, so that you should the sooner obtain your desire ... I no longer wish you to fast. Therefore I command you in the name of Jesus, eat and drink as your husband does."

Then this creature thanked our Lord Jesus Christ for his grace and his goodness, and rose up and went to her husband, saying to him:

"Sir, if it please ye, ye shall grant me my desire, and ye shall have your desire. Grant me that ye will not come into my bed, and I will pay your debts before I go to Jerusalem. Make my body free for God ... asking no debt of matrimony. After this day, as long as you live, I shall eat and drink on the Friday at your bidding."

Then said her husband, "As free may thy body be for God as it hath been to me."

This creature thanked God, greatly rejoicing that she had her desire. She asked her husband to pray with her three Our Fathers in worship of the Trinity for the great grace God had given them. And so they did, kneeling under a cross, and afterward they ate and drank together in great gladness of spirit. They then went to Bridlington and many other places, speaking with God's servants ... to find out if any deceit were in her feelings.

Chapter 12[28]

This creature was sent by our Lord to diverse places of religion and among them, she came to a place of monks where she was made most welcome for our Lord's love, except for the monk with great office in that place who despised her.... Nevertheless, she sat with the abbot.... She uttered many great words as God put them in her mind and the same monk who had so despised her slowly inclined his affection toward her and he began to savor her words. And so, afterward, this monk came to her and said, "I hear it said that God speaketh unto thee. I pray thee tell me whether I shall be saved or not, and in what sins I have most displeased God, for I will not believe unless thou can tell me my sin."

The creature said to the monk, "Go to your Mass, and if I may weep for you, I hope to have grace for you." He followed her counsel and went to his Mass. She wept amazingly for his sins. When Mass was ended, the creature said to our Lord Jesus Christ, "Good Lord, shall he be saved?"

"My beloved daughter, say in the name of Jesus, that he has sinned in lechery, in despair, and in keeping worldly goods.... He will be saved if he will give up his sin, and follow thy counsel. Tell him to give up his sin, to confess and be forgiven of it, and to give up the office that he has outside."

Then came the monk again. "Margery, tell me my sins."

She said, "Sir, I understand that ye have sinned in lechery, in despair, and in keeping worldly goods."

Then the monk stood still, somewhat ashamed, and afterward said, "Say whether I have sinned with wives or single women."

"Sir, with wives."

Then he said, "Shall I be saved?"

"Yea, sir, if you follow my advice... I shall help you to feel sorrow. Confess and be forgiven your sin and give it up. Leave the office you hold outside, and God shall give you grace for love of me."

The monk took her by the hand... gave her a great dinner, and afterward gave gold to pray for him, and she left. When she returned sometime later, the monk had done all that was asked, was now subprior of the place... and highly blessed God that he ever saw her.

Chapter 28[29]

The company of pilgrims had excluded Margery from their meals (because of her weeping, her abstinence from meat, and her holy speech) and arranged a ship for themselves to sail in. They bought containers for their wine, and obtained bedding for themselves, but nothing for her.[30] She, seeing their unkindness, went to the man they had been to and bought herself bedding... and showed them what she had done, intending to sail with them in that ship.

Afterward, as this creature was in contemplation, our Lord warned her in her mind that she should not sail in that ship, and he assigned her to another ship, a galley, that she should sail in. Then she told this to some of the company.... They sold away the vessels they had got for their wines and were quick to come to the galley where she was, and so, though it was against her will, she went forth with them in their company, for they were afraid to do otherwise.

When it was time to make up their beds, they locked up her bedclothes, and a priest, who was in the company, took away a sheet from the aforesaid creature, and said it was his. She swore to God that it was her sheet. Then the priest swore a great oath, by the book in his hand, that she was as false as she could be, and despised her and strongly rebuked her.

So she had much tribulation till she came to Jerusalem.[31] Before she arrived there, she said to them that she supposed they were annoyed with her. "I pray you, be in charity with me for I am in charity with you and forgive me that I have annoyed you along the way. If any of you have in any way trespassed against me, God forgive you for it and I do."

So they went forth into the Holy Land till they could see Jerusalem. When this creature saw Jerusalem . . . praying for God's mercy, she asked that just as God brought her to see the earthly city of Jerusalem, God would grant her grace to see the blissful Jerusalem above, the city of Heaven. Our Lord Jesus Christ, answering her thought, granted her desire.

Then for the joy she had and the sweetness she felt in her conversation with our Lord, she was on the point of falling off the donkey, for she could not bear the sweetness and grace God worked in her soul. Then two German pilgrims went to her and kept her from falling. The one was a priest and he put spices in her mouth to comfort her. . . . They went to the temple in Jerusalem (the Church of the Holy Sepulcher).

They were let in at evensong time on one day and remained until evensong of the next day.[32] Then the friars lifted up a cross and led the pilgrims to the places where our Lord suffered his passion, every man and woman bearing a wax candle in one hand. And the friars always, as they went about, told them what our Lord suffered in every place. The aforesaid creature wept and sobbed as plenteously as if she had seen our Lord with her bodily eyes suffering his passion at that time. And when she came up on to the Mount of Calvary, she fell down because she could not stand or kneel . . . and cried with a loud voice as though her heart would have burst apart. For in the city of her soul, she saw truly and vividly how our Lord was crucified. Before her face, she saw and heard the mourning of our Lady, of St. John and Mary Magdalene and of many others that loved our Lord.

She had such deep compassion and such great pain, at seeing our Lord's pain, that she could not keep herself from crying and roaring, even if she should have died for it. This was the first crying that she ever cried in any contemplation.[33] This manner of crying endured for many years, no matter what anyone did, and she suffered much from it, enduring reproof. The crying was so loud and so strange that it astonished people unless they had heard it before or knew its cause. She had these cries so often that it made her physically weak, especially if she heard of our Lord's passion. . . .

First when she had her cryings in Jerusalem, she had them often, and in Rome as well. When she first came home to England, she cried less often, once a month or so, then once a week, and afterward daily. Once she had fourteen in a day, and another day she had seven, and so on as God desired. Sometimes, this crying would occur in church, sometimes in the street, sometimes in her room, and sometimes in the fields, wherever God would send them.

As soon as she knew she was going to cry, she would hold it in as much as she could so that people would not be too annoyed with her. For some said she was troubled by a wicked spirit; some said it was a sickness; some said she had drunk too much wine; some banned her; some wished she were drowned in the harbor; some wished she were put to sea in a bottomless boat.... Some spiritual men loved her and honored her more. Some great clerics said our Lady never cried that way, nor any saint in heaven. But these clerics knew little of what she felt, nor would they believe that she could not stop crying as she wished.

Therefore, when she knew she was going to cry, she held it in as long as she could... until she grew blue as lead.... When it was granted this creature to see our Lord's precious, tender body, all torn and rent with scourges, more full of wounds than a dove house is full of holes, hanging on the cross with the crown of thorns on his head, his blissful hands, his tender feet nailed to the hard tree, the rivers of blood flowing out of every limb, the grisly and grievous wound in his precious side shedding blood and water for her love and her salvation... she could not keep herself from crying... for the fire of love that burned so deeply in her soul with pure pity and compassion.

Chapter 52[34]

There was a monk preaching in York who heard much slander and evil spoken about Margery... he repeated these things in his sermons... which caused her friends to be afraid with grief.[35] Margery responded, "I have reason to be merry and glad in my soul if I suffer anything for our Lord, for he suffered much more for me."

She was brought into the archbishop's chapel at York, and there many of the archbishop's household, despising her, calling her "Lollard" and "heretic," were swearing many a horrible oath that she should be burned.

She, through the strength of Jesus, replied, "Sirs, I fear you shall be burned in hell without end unless you stop swearing of oaths, for you are not keeping the commandments of God. I would not swear as you do for all the money in this world." They went away as if they had been shamed.

She prayed inwardly, asking to behave that day in a manner pleasing to God.... Our Lord, answering her, said all would be well. At last, the archbishop came into the chapel with his clerics and said sharply to her, "Why do you dress in white? Are you a virgin?"

Kneeling before him, she said, "No, sir, I am no virgin. I am a wife."[36] He commanded his men to put her in fetters, for she was a heretic.

Then she said, "I am no heretic, nor shall you prove me one."

The archbishop went away and left her standing alone. Then she made her prayers to our Lord God Almighty to help her and save her from her enemies, spiritual and physical. She trembled and shook so much that she hid her hands in her sleeves so no one could notice. After a time, the archbishop came back to the chapel with many clerics, among whom was the same doctor who had examined her before and the monk who had preached against her in York. Some people asked if she were a Christian woman or a Jew. Some said she was a good woman and some said she was not.

Then the archbishop took his seat and his clerics did so too, each according to his degree, since many people were present. The whole time that the people were gathering together and the archbishop was taking his seat, the said creature was standing at the back praying for help against her enemies. She prayed so devoutly for so long that she melted into tears.

She began to cry so loudly that the archbishop and his clerics and many people were astonished, for they had never heard such crying before. When her crying had passed, she came before the archbishop and fell down on her knees. The archbishop said sharply to her, "Why do you weep this way, woman?"

She replied, "Sir, someday you will wish you had wept as bitterly as I."

Then, the archbishop questioned her on the Articles of Faith, which God gave her the grace to answer well and truly and readily without any hesitation so that the archbishop could not find fault with her. Then he said to the clerics, "She knows the Articles of Faith well enough. What shall I do with her?"

The clerics said, "She knows the Articles of Faith, but we shall not let her live among us. The people have faith in what she says, and she might lead some of them astray."[37]

. . . Finally the archbishop said to her, "Lay your hand on the book before me and swear you will go out of my diocese as soon as you can."

"No, sir," she said. "Not until you give me permission to go back to York and to say good-bye to my friends." He gave her permission to stay for one or two days. . . .

Then he said, "You must swear that you will not teach nor challenge the people in my diocese!"

"No, sir, I will not swear," she said. "For I will speak of God, and rebuke those who swear great oaths wheresoever I go until the pope and holy church have ordained that no one shall be so bold as to speak about God. For God Almighty does not forbid any of us to speak about God. Also the Gospel mentions that when the woman heard our Lord preach, she came before him and said with a loud voice: 'Blessed be the womb that bore thee and the breasts that nursed thee.' Then our Lord replied, 'Truly, they are blessed who hear the word of God and keep it' [Luke 11:27–28]. Therefore, sir, I think that the Gospel gives me permission to speak of God."

"Sir," said the clerics, "now we know she has a devil inside her, for she speaks of the Gospel!"

Quickly, an important cleric brought out a book and quoted St. Paul, saying that women should not preach (1 Cor 14:34–35). Answering that, she said, "I do not preach, sir, for I do not use a pulpit. I rely on good words and good deeds only, and that I will continue to do as long as I live."[38]

Then the doctor who had examined her previously said, "Sir, she told me the worst tales about priests that I have ever heard!" The archbishop commanded her to tell the tale.... He praised it, saying it was a good story.

The cleric who had examined her earlier without the archbishop said, "Sir, this story pierces me to the heart."

The aforesaid creature said to the cleric, "There is an honorable cleric, sir, where I generally live, who is a good preacher. He has said many times, 'If anyone is not pleased by my preaching, notice who it is, for that person feels guilty.' Sir," she said to the cleric, "is this why you have responded to me in this way? May God forgive you."

The cleric did not know what he could say to her then. Afterward, he came to her and begged forgiveness for having been against her. Also, he asked her to pray especially for him.

Then the archbishop said, "Where can I find someone who will lead this woman away from here?" Quickly, many young men jumped up, but the archbishop answered, "You are too young." A good earnest man from the archbishop's household said he would guide her. The archbishop gave him money and said, "Lead her out of here immediately." Asking her to pray for him, he blessed her and let her go. Then she returned to York and was well received by many people, and many worthy clerics. These rejoiced in our Lord, who had given an unlettered woman the wit and wisdom to answer so many learned men without a mistake or fault.

Chapter 76[39]

This happened when the husband of the creature was past sixty. He was coming from his bedroom with bare feet and bare legs. He slipped and fell down the steps to the ground. His head was twisted beneath him, badly broken and bruised. He had five linen plugs in his head (to drain the wound) for many days....

Then the said creature, his wife, was sent for and so she came to him. Then he was lifted up and his head sewn up, and he was sick a long time after, so that people thought he would die. The people said, if he died, his wife deserved to be hanged for his death. They did not live together, nor did they sleep together, because they both freely vowed to each other to live chaste. But in order to live chastely, they dwelt in different places so no suspicion could be had about their incontinence. For at first they dwelt together after they had made their vow, and then people slandered them, and said they satisfied their lust and pleasure just as they did before making their vow.

To avoid this gossip, they agreed to live in different places. She also would have more time for contemplation.... After John had his accident, Margery prayed to our Lord that her husband might live a year and that she might be rescued from slander, if it was God's will. Our Lord said, "Daughter, thou shalt have thy wish, for he shall live. I have done a great miracle for you that he has not died. I bid thee to take him home and take care of him for my love."

She said, "No, good Lord, for I shall not then attend to thee as I do now."

"Yes, daughter," said our Lord. "Thou shalt have as much reward looking after him in his need at home as if thou were in church saying your prayers. Thou have said many times that thou would like to serve me. I ask thee now to serve him for the love of me, for he hath fulfilled both thy will and my will. He hath made thy body free to me, so that thou shouldst serve me, and live chaste and clean. Therefore I wish that thou be free to help him in his need in my name."

"Ah, Lord," said she. "For thy mercy, grant me grace to obey and fulfill thy will, and never let my spiritual enemies have any power to keep me from fulfilling your will."

Then she took her husband home with her and looked after him for as many years as he lived and had much hard labor with him; for in his last days, he turned very childish again and lost touch with everything. So he could not—or would not—control his bowels or go to a stool to relieve himself. Like a child, he discharged his excrement in his linen clothes, where he sat by the fire or at the table, whichever it was. He would spare no place.

Therefore her labor was all the greater in washing and wringing out his clothes and in keeping the fire going so the clothes could dry. This hindered her from her contemplation, so that many times she would have loathed her labor, except she remembered the delectable thoughts, fleshly lusts, and inordinate love she had for his body in her youth.

Chapter 81[40]

When our Lord was buried, our Lady lay still on her bed as if she were dead, and St. John took her up in his arms and Mary Magdalene went on the other side to support and comfort our Lady, as much as they could or might... this creature heard St. Peter knocking at the door, and St. John asked who was there.

Peter answered, "It is I, sinful Peter, who hath forsaken my Lord Jesus Christ."

Saint John would have made him come in, but Peter would not, till our Lady bade him come in. Then Peter said, "Lady, I am not worthy to come in to you," and he stayed outside the door. . . .

And the creature beheld St. Peter come before our Lady and fall down on his knees, with great weeping and sobbing, and say, "Lady, I beg your mercy, for I have forsaken your dear son and my sweet master, who hath loved me so well, and therefore Lady, I am never worthy to look upon him or upon thee either. . . . "

"Ah, Peter," said our Lady. "Do not fear, for though thou hast forsaken my son, he has not forsaken thee. He shall come again and comfort us all, for he promised me, Peter, that he would come again on the third day. . . . "

Then Mary Magdalene and our Lady's sisters left to go and buy ointment to anoint our Lord's body. This creature felt like it was a thousand years until the third day came. . . . That day she was with our Lady in a chapel where our Lord Jesus Christ appeared and said, "Hail, holy parent . . . I am your son, Jesus."[41] Then he took his mother and kissed her very sweetly.

Then this creature thought that she saw our Lady feeling and searching all over our Lord's body to see if there was any soreness or pain. She heard our Lord say, "Dear mother, my pain is all gone. Now I shall live forever. Mother, thy pain and sorrow shall also be turned into great joy. Mother, ask what ye will. . . . "

When he had allowed his mother to ask what she wished and had answered all her questions, he said, "Mother, now excuse me, for I must go and speak with Mary Magdalene." Our Lady said, "That is well done, Son, for she has very great sorrow over your absence."

Once, this creature was present with Mary Magdalene, mourning and seeking our Lord at the grave. She heard and saw our Lord Christ appear to Mary in the likeness of a gardener, saying, "Woman, why dost thou weep?"

Mary, not knowing who he was, all inflamed with the fire of love, answered, "Sir, if you have taken my Lord away, tell me and I will take him back again."

Then our merciful Lord, having pity and compassion on her, said, "Mary." With that word, she recognized our Lord and fell down at his feet and tried to kiss them, saying, "Master."

Our Lord said to her, "Touch me not."

Then this creature thought that Mary Magdalene said to our Lord, "Ah, Lord, I see you do not want me to be as much at home with thee as I was before." She now looked very sad.

"Mary," said our Lord, "I shall never forsake thee, but I shall always be with thee without end." Then our Lord said to Mary Magdalene, "Go tell my brothers and Peter that I have risen."

Then the creature thought that Mary went forth with great joy. This was a marvel, for if our Lord had spoken to this creature as he did to Mary Magdalene (Do not touch me), she could never have been merry. . . . Whenever she heard these words in a sermon, as she often did, she wept, she sorrowed, and she cried, as though she would have died of the love and desire she felt to be with our Lord.

Chapter 84[42]

Daughter, I promise thee that thou shalt have the same reward in heaven for good acts toward others as if thou had done them to me. I know all the thoughts of thy heart, and thy love for all people. I thank thee for the charity thou hast for everyone, desiring that I should deliver all from sin. I also thank thee for the charity that you have in your prayer for all Jews, Saracens, and all nonbelievers, that they should come to faith. Your holy tears and weeping, your praying and desiring that I should hear thy prayer, are heard.

Furthermore, daughter, I thank thee for the general charity that thou hast toward all people now living in this world, and all those that are to come until the end of the world.... Daughter, for all these good desires, thou shalt have a most high reward in heaven. Believe it well and never doubt. Every good thought and desire is the speech of God in your soul. So great is my love for thee that I shall not never withdraw it....

I wish the grace I have shown to thee to be manifest on the earth. I have been so gracious and merciful to thee that no one in the world will ever despair of sin. They shall have mercy and grace if they wish it.

Book Two, Chapter 10[43]

Good Lord Jesus, I ask for thy mercy on all who are in our church, the order of priesthood, of religious men and women, for those too busy to save and defend the faith of holy church. For all that are in grace at this time, God send them perseverance until the end of their lives, and make me worthy to partake of their prayers as they do of mine, each of the others.

I cry your mercy for the king of England, the lords and ladies, that they use authority well. I ask your mercy for the rich and powerful that thou give them thy grace to use these for your pleasure. I ask mercy for the Jews and Saracens, for unbelievers, for thou hast spread mercy to all on this earth. If there is anyone who is not drawn to thee, I ask thee to draw them to you now, for thou hast drawn me and I did not deserve it.

I ask mercy for all misbelievers, false tithe-payers, thieves, adulterers, common women, those who are tempted, the wicked... I ask mercy for all my spiritual and bodily children, for all people in this world, for my friends and my enemies, for the sick, lepers, bedridden, prisoners, and all who have spoken well or ill of me until the world ends. Be as gracious to all of these as thou hast been to me.

May the peace and rest that thou hast bequeathed to your blessed friends in heaven be mine and be to all who ask thee for mercy. I thank thee for the sins thou hast prevented me from doing. I thank thee for all those who shall have faith and trust in my prayers until the world's end, for I pray to you to grant them all the abundance of your mercy. Amen.

NOTES

1. Margaret Deanesly, "Vernacular Books in England in the Fourteenth and Fifteenth Centuries," *Modern Language Review* 15 (1920) 349–58. The title of Worde's publication was *A shorte treatyse of contemplacyon taught by our lorde ihesu cryste.*

2. *The Book of Margery Kempe*, ed. Sanford Brown Meech and Hope Emily Allen (Oxford: Oxford University Press, 1940). Original Series, vol. 212 of the Early English Text Society.

3. The Lollards, judged heretical by the Roman Church, believed the fullness of the Spirit could be given to women as well as men. Thus, priests and bishops had no more spiritual authority than any devout man or woman. Diverse further interpretations by sects of Lollards included denial of the need for images, pilgrimages, sacraments, and ordained priests. Women could preach, teach, and lead prayers in the Spirit. See Claire Cross, "Great Reasoners in Scripture: The Activities of Women Lollards, 1380–1530," in *Medieval Women*, ed. Derek Baker (Oxford: Blackwell, 1978) 359–80.

4. "Dame Julian of Norwich and Margery Kempe," in *Women and Religion*, ed. Elizabeth Clark and Herbert Richardson (New York: Harper and Row, 1977) 112.

5. Meech and Allen, *The Book of Margery Kempe*, 9–11, 16.

6. *The Book of Margery Kempe*, trans. Barry Windeatt (London: Penguin, 1985) ch. 1, 41; all future references to *The Book of Margery Kempe* will be from this source unless otherwise indicated.

7. Chapter 14 has Jesus Christ name Margery, by analogy, "wife," 65–67; ch. 35 mentions Margery being wedded to the Godhead, 122–25.

8. Pseudo-Dionysius was one of the most popular "saints" of the Middle Ages, confused with the person identified in Acts 17. His theological works had tremendous influence on medieval religious imagination; see Jean Ritzke-Rutherford, "Anglo-Saxon Antecedents of the Middle English Mystics," in *The Medieval Mystical Tradition in England*, ed. Marion Glasscoe (Exeter: University of Exeter Press, 1980) 216–23.

9. Ch. 5, 51.

10. Ch. 11, 60.

11. Ch. 5, 52; ch. 36, 126–27; ch. 66, 200.

12. Ch. 76, 219–21.

13. Anthony Goodman, "The Piety of John Brunham's Daughter, of Lynne," in Baker, *Medieval Women*, 347–58.

14. Stephen Medcalf, "Medieval Psychology and Medieval Mystics," in Glasscoe, *The Medieval Mystical Tradition* 120–55.

15. Maureen Fries critiques those who negate the value of Margery Kempe as a "real" mystic. See Fries, "Margery Kempe," in *An Introduction to the Medieval Mystics of England*, ed. Paul E. Szarnach (Albany: State University of New York Press, 1984) 217–35.

16. The spiritual homilies of Isaac the Syrian are one of many works illustrating the Eastern tradition. A readable modern approach to holy tears can be found in Maggie Ross, *The Fountain and the Furnace* (New York: Paulist Press, 1987) esp. 159–286.

17. Ch. 57, 179–81.

18. Ch. 52, 161–67.

19. See Ch. 17, 20, 21; 73–76, 83–86.

20. Ch. 84, 244–47.

21. Meech and Allen, *The Book of Margery Kempe* xxxii–xlvi.

22. Meech and Allen, *The Book of Margery Kempe*. The manuscript was acquired by the British Library in 1980; it is now B. L. Add. MS 61923. Windeatt, *The Book of Margery Kempe*, 298 n. 1.

23. Windeatt, *The Book of Margery Kempe* 10.

24. These excerpts are taken from *The Book of Margery Kempe: Fourteen Hundred and Thirty Six*, a modern version by W. Butler-Bowdon (New York: Devin-Adair, 1944). The meanings of occasional words or phrases that are no longer part of English usage have been retained, although the precise words are not used.

25. Butler-Bowdon, *The Book of Margery Kempe* 1–3.

26. Ibid. 10.

27. Ibid. 16–18. Since Margery and John Kempe had fourteen children, John is surprised at the suggestion of a vow of chastity.

28. Ibid. 18–20.

29. The full text can be found on 102–7.

30. William Wey, *Itineraries to Jerusalem, 1458* (Roxburghe Club, 1857), indicates that pilgrims should bring specific bedding, a chest with a good lock, utensils, medicines, laxatives, and food and drink. This is cited in Windeatt, *The Book of Margery Kempe* 312 n. 1.

31. Part of this tribulation could have been caused by the conditions in which debarking pilgrims lived until they could be processed at the port of Jaffa. See ibid. 312 n. 3.

32. Muslim officials guarded the door, controlled admission, charged pilgrims entrance fees, and locked them in the church for their vigil; see ibid. 312 n. 5.

33. Margery distinguishes between this form of tears or crying, which would be her experience for the next ten years, and the weeping that occurred prior to the visit to Jerusalem; see ibid. 313 n. 8.

34. Butler-Bowdon, *The Book of Margery Kempe* 110–15. Margery's trial at York occurred in 1417.

35. Parliament passed an act that allowed for the burning of heretics in 1401. Louise Collis, *The Apprentice Saint* (London: Michael Joseph, 1964) 19.

36. The bishop forbade Margery to wear the symbolic white clothing of a virgin. She was also forbidden to wear the widow's symbolic dress and ring. Obedience to the church was considered one sign of orthodoxy at this time.

37. The fear of women teaching was one of the reasons for the condemnation of the Beguines by the Council of Vienne, 1311–13. The council believed that God did not wish women to teach sacred things.

38. This could refer to the authenticity test for true Christian teachers, that is, "By their fruits you will know them" (Matt 12:33–37).

39. Butler-Bowdon, *The Book of Margery Kempe* 164–66. Margery's husband, John, died about 1431.

40. This excerpt is taken from meditations on the passion and resurrection of Jesus Christ, ch. 81, ibid. 178–81. Chapters 79–81 are meditations on the passion and resurrection.

41. Medieval tradition held that the risen Christ appeared to his mother before he appeared to anyone else, even though the Gospels do not state this.

42. Butler-Bowdon, *The Book of Margery Kempe*, 186–88.

43. This is a portion of the prayer found in book 2, ch. 10; the excerpts are from Butler-Bowdon, 228–30.

BIBLIOGRAPHY

Atkinson, Clarissa W. *Mystic and Pilgrim: The Book and World of Margery Kempe*. Ithaca, N.Y.: Cornell University Press, 1983.

Baker, Derek, ed. *Medieval Women*. Oxford: Blackwell, 1978.

Collis, Louise. *Memoirs of a Medieval Woman: The Life and Times of Margery Kempe*. New York: Thos. Y. Crowell, 1964.

Glasscoe, Marion, ed. *The Medieval Mystical Tradition in England*. Exeter: University of Exeter Press, 1980.

Glasscoe, Marion, ed. *The Medieval Mystical Tradition in England*. Cambridge: Cambridge University Press, 1984.

Riehle, Wolfgang. *The Middle English Mystics*. London, Boston, Henley: Routledge and Kegan Paul, 1981.

Stuard, Susan Masher, ed. *Women in Medieval Society*. Philadelphia: University of Pennsylvania Press, 1976.

Windeatt, Barry, trans. *The Book of Margery Kempe*. London: Penguin, 1985.

– 14 –

TERESA OF ÁVILA

(1515–1582)

Study Diligently How to Walk in Truth

Sixteenth-century Spain witnessed a religious intensity marked by mystical quests and a desire for holiness. The renewal councils of Florence, Basel, and Constance were beginning to renew the fervor of the church as a whole. Tribunals of the Inquisition were set up in Spain on November 1, 1478, during the reign of Ferdinand and Isabella. In 1492 the Moors of Granada were overcome, leading many to be more firmly convinced that God was "on their side." Ferdinand and Isabella had the Jews deported so that they could create one Catholic state. Even if the Jews were converted Christians, they had to leave the country. In 1512 the Illuminati (or Adunbradoes) were attacked as heretics in spite of their great similarity to the Rhineland mystics.

Theories of prayer and spirituality were of interest to many .of the people as the apostolic spirituality of Ignatius of Loyola (1491–1556) took hold. At the same time, the desire for a more traditional "contemplative" life was also drawing many to monasteries. Abandonment of earthly power or titles and an asceticism that disciplined the body to free the spirit were undertaken by the poor and the powerful alike. There was an increase in varieties of devotionalism that bordered on the superstitious. Patriotism became mixed with spiritism and the misguided zeal that justified forcing inhabitants of the Spanish-dominated "New World" to become Christians or die. Slavery was not considered evil, but simply part of the result of conquest.

The cultural and religious climate influenced the intensity of the Spanish predilection for "stamping out heresy" at all costs. The fact that Spain controlled half of Europe, the Low Countries, and much of Italy lent a certain euphoria to the age. Spain had the finest army and navy in the world. The Spanish ruler, Philip II, devoted himself to austere practices and a strict monastic prayer life.

Clergy were now given moral and doctrinal training in a structured way. Imaginative mystical extravagance, however, fed many at the cost of biblical and theological orthodoxy. By the middle of the sixteenth century, the Inquisition had succeeded in stamping out the majority of heresies and heretics in Spain. There was a great interest in and desire for mystical visions, with the usual excesses that accompany such enthusiastic religious desires.

The Jesuits, founded by Ignatius of Loyola, were a strong force for supporting the Catholic Church in Spain against the reformers of northern Europe. The *Spiritual Exercises* of Ignatius were responsible for nurturing an impressive number of contemplative people, including Teresa of Ávila. Contemplation that supported an intensely active life was one of the gifts of the Ignatian tradition to Teresa.[1]

Teresa was born in Castile in 1515, into a loving and wealthy family (her mother died giving birth to her). She was a charming and headstrong child, and after being educated by Augustinian nuns, she entered the convent of Carmel in 1535. Her initial fervor affected her health, and she endured a mysterious illness that left her paralyzed for a year. Her father insisted that she be allowed to come home where he could oversee her care. Upon her recovery, Teresa insisted on returning to Carmel.

It was during this time that visions and revelations started coming to her. She was told to reform the life of the Carmelite community of nuns, which was not as fervent as it once had been. With the blessing of superiors, she founded a reformed house, or discalced house, of Carmelites in 1562. She continued to found more reformed houses in spite of some strong opposition to this effort. She insisted that mystical union with Jesus Christ is something to which all Christians are called.[2]

Teresa's raptures, ecstasy, and visions were not understood by her confessors and spiritual directors. She had a hard time trying to get them to grasp what she was talking about, since most had not had her deep experiences of prayer. John of the Cross (1542–91) did understand. He and Teresa became great friends and co-reformers of Carmel. John was also a fitting spiritual director for her.

There were differences and similarities in background, personality, and prayer experiences between Teresa and John. John of the Cross was born in poverty, whereas Teresa was born into wealth. Teresa's mother died in childbirth; John's widowed mother raised him. Teresa had no formal theological education; John was educated by the Jesuits. Teresa experienced the ecstasies about which she wrote; John's prayer experiences were not consistently ecstatic.

These two saints resemble each other insofar as both agree on the unity of the human person and the interdependence of the body and spirit. Both give less guidance on prayer as such than on the spiritual life in general. Both insist upon three prerequisites for Christian life: love for God and for one another, emotional detachment from people and created things, and true humility. The quality of prayer and the quality of life are mutually influential. The cross will be some part of the journey toward God, but its form will be decided by God and not by humans. Teresa is convinced that heaven will mean enjoying God, but it will also mean a continuation of human friendships and love. John is not as clear on that point.[3]

Both undertook the reform of their Carmelite communities for a five-year period. Both disapproved of ostentatious asceticism and self-annihilation for its own sake. Both downplayed any connection between visions as certification of holiness.[4] Both were realistic about the lifelong process of growth into Christian maturity that involved a blending of self-discipline for love's sake and cooperation with God's graciousness.[5] Both saints described the observable path into communion with God, yet there is no expectation that people would conform to the described stages. Teresa and John were wise counselors who realized that God leads each person differently. In every case, God provides all that is necessary for the journey.

Teresa's works show a human personality with a warmth and humor about herself and life. True to the Carmelite tradition, she shows a preference for the bridegroom image of Jesus Christ. For Teresa the progress anyone makes in the spiritual journey is actually God's progress within the person. God calls and sustains all who are willing to undertake the path of holiness that is communion with God. The few works that Teresa left were written under obedience to her superiors.

The Book of Her Life, Spiritual Testimonies, The Way of Perfection, Meditations on the Song of Songs, and *The Interior Castle* constitute her written works.[6] It is the latter from which the excerpts in this chapter are taken. Teresa began writing *The Interior Castle* in June 1577 and completed it that November. She considered this her best work.

The term *interior castle* refers to the inward journey toward loving communion with God. The castle has a number of rooms or concentric circles that lead from outer to inner. Each circle is a mansion or resting place for enjoying God. There is no need to hurry or worry on the journey to the center because God will lead each person in whatever way is appropriate. It is simply the liberty to follow that is at issue. The journeying person should not be distressed if the journey is long and diverse. Many variations are possible as one becomes more enlightened about the ways of God's love.[7]

The first three rooms describe the obstacles on the journey from self-concern to prayerful God concern. The fourth room describes the growing process of recollection in God. The fifth mansion presents the various forms that deeper union with God may take and the need for discernment. The sixth presents some differences between true and false locutions, ecstasies, and raptures. The seventh mansion clarifies some differences between betrothal and spiritual marriage as symbols of the mystic's communion with God. Throughout the work Teresa affirms that holiness is demonstrated by active love and not by ecstatic gifts.

Throughout her works Teresa shows a basic trust in God and in the goodness of people. She has a strong sense of being loved for no reason other than God's graciousness. She has a wholesome personality that is open to the newness and the challenge of life. With gentleness and firmness, she urges her sisters to follow wherever the Lord leads. They are told to be content with whatever path is theirs, and not to measure themselves against anyone else. They should not link the experiencing of visions with holiness. The chapters from *The Interior Castle* that follow give Teresa's advice about this.

Teresa delivered her new book, *The Interior Castle,* to a friend, Father Gratian, in 1577. He took the work to Seville for safekeeping in 1580. The Inquisition was still examining *The Book of Her Life* for possible heretical opinions. Teresa died in 1582 after a long life spent as reformer, superior, theologian, visionary, and spiritual director. She was canonized in 1622. Her feast is celebrated on October 15. She was declared a doctor of the church in 1970 by Pope Paul VI.

In the selections that follow, the common sense of Teresa will be evident. Chapters nine through eleven are the final chapters in the Sixth Dwelling Place. These will be followed by chapters one through four of the Seventh Dwelling Place, the heart of the journey.

The Interior Castle[8]

Chapter Nine[9]

Treats of how the Lord communicates with the soul through an imaginative vision; gives careful warning against desiring to walk by this path and the reasons for such a warning. The chapter is very beneficial.

1. Now let us come to imaginative visions, for they say the devil meddles more in these than in the ones mentioned, and it must be so.[10] But when these imaginative visions are from our Lord, they in some way seem to me more beneficial because they are in greater conformity with our nature. I'm excluding from that comparison the visions the Lord shows in the last dwelling place. No other visions are comparable to these.

2. Well, now, let us consider what I have told you in the preceding chapter about how this Lord is present. It is as though we had in a gold vessel a precious stone having the highest value and curative powers.[11] We know very certainly that it is there, although we have never seen it. But the powers of the stone do not cease to benefit us provided that we carry it with us. Although we have never seen this stone, we do not cease on that account to prize it. Through experience we have seen that it has cured us of some illnesses for which it is

suited. But we do not dare to look at it or open the reliquary, nor can we. This is because the manner of opening the reliquary is known solely by the one to whom the jewel belongs. Even though the Lord loaned us the jewel for our own benefit, he has kept the key to the reliquary. He will open it, as something belonging to him, when he desires to show us the contents, and he will take the jewel back when he wants to, as he does.

3. Well, let us say that sometimes he wants to open the reliquary suddenly in order to do good to the person to whom he has loaned it. Clearly, a person will be much happier afterward as the admirable splendor of the stone is remembered, and hence, it will remain more deeply engrained in memory. So it happens here. When our Lord is pleased to give more delight to this soul, he shows it clearly his most sacred humanity in the way he desires. This will be either as he was when he went about in the world or as he is after his resurrection. Even though the vision happens so quickly that we could compare it to a streak of lightning, this most glorious image remains so engraved upon the imagination that I think it would be impossible to erase it until it is seen by the soul in that place where it will be enjoyed without end.

4. Although I say "image," let it be understood that, in the opinion of the one who sees it, it is not a painting but truly alive, and sometimes the Lord is speaking to the soul and even revealing great secrets. But you must understand that even though the soul is detained by this vision for some while, it can no more fix its gaze on the vision than it can on the sun. Hence this vision always passes very quickly, but not because its brilliance is painful, like the sun's, to the inner eye. It is the inner eye that sees all of this. I wouldn't know how to say anything about a vision that comes through the exterior gift of sight. This is because the person I mention[12] about whom I speak so particularly had not undergone such a vision, and one cannot be sure about what one has not experienced. The brilliance of this inner vision is like an infused light coming from a sun covered by something as sparkling as a properly cut diamond. The garment seems made of a fine Dutch linen. Almost every time God grants this favor, the soul is in rapture, for in its lowliness it cannot suffer so frightening a sight.

5. I say "frightening" for this reason. The Lord's presence is the most beautiful and delightful a person could imagine even if that person lived and labored for a thousand years thinking about it (for it far surpasses the limitations of our imagination or intellect). Yet, this presence bears such extraordinary majesty that it causes the soul extreme fright. Certainly it is not necessary here to ask how the soul knows, without having been told who the Lord is, for it is clearly revealed that he is the Lord of heaven and earth. This is not true of earthly kings, for in themselves they would be held of little account were it not for their retinue, or unless they tell who they are.

6. O Lord, how we Christians fail to know you! What will that day be when

you come to judge, for even when you come here with so much friendliness to speak with your bride, she experiences such fear when she looks at you? O daughters, what will it be like when he says in so severe a voice, "Depart you who are cursed by my Father"?

7. As a result of this favor granted by God, let us keep in mind the above thought, for it will be no small blessing. Even St. Jerome, though he was a saint, kept it in mind. Thus, all that we suffer here in the strict observance of the religious life will seem to us as nothing. For however long it lasts, it lasts but a moment in comparison with eternity. I tell you truthfully that as wretched as I am I have never had fear of the torments of hell. These torments would be nothing compared to what I recall the condemned will experience on seeing the anger in these eyes of the Lord, so beautiful, meek, and kind. It doesn't seem my heart could suffer such a sight. I've felt this way all my life. How much more will the person fear this sight to whom the Lord has represented himself, since the experience is so powerful that it carries that person out of his senses. The reason the soul is suspended must be that the Lord helps its weakness, which is joined to his greatness in this sublime communication.

8. When the soul can remain a long while gazing on this Lord, I don't believe it will be experiencing a vision but some intense reflection in which some likeness is fashioned in the imagination. Compared with a vision, this likeness is similar to something dead.

9. It happens to some persons that their imagination is so weak, or their intellect so effective, or I don't know what the cause is, that they become absorbed in their imagination to the extent that everything they think about seems to be clearly seen. (I know this is true, for these people have spoken with me—not just three or four but many.) Yet if they were to see a real vision, they would know without any doubt whatsoever their mistake, for they themselves are composing what they see with their imagination. This imagining doesn't have any effect afterward, but they are left cold—much more so than if they were to see a devotional image. It's very wise not to pay any attention to this kind of imagining, for what was seen is then forgotten more easily than a dream.

10. That is not so in the vision about which I spoke above. The soul is far from thinking that anything will be seen, or even having the thought pass through its mind. Suddenly, the vision is represented to it all at once and stirs all the faculties and senses with a great fear and tumult so as to place them afterward in that happy peace. Just as there was a tempest and tumult that came from heaven when St. Paul was hurled to the ground,[13] here in this interior world there is a great stirring. In a moment, as I have said, all remains calm. This soul is left so well instructed about so many great truths that it has no need of any other master. Without any effort on the soul's part, true Wisdom has taken away the mind's dullness and leaves a certitude, which lasts for some

time, that this favor is from God. However much the soul is told the contrary, others cannot then cause it fear that there could be any deception. Afterward, if the confessor puts fear in it, God allows it to waver and think that—because of its sins—it could possibly be deceived. But it does not believe this. Rather, as I have said concerning those other things, the devil can stir up doubts, as he does with temptations against matters of faith, that do not allow the soul to be firm in its certitude. But the more the devil fights against that certitude, the more certain the soul is that the devil could not have left it with so many blessings, as they really are. For the devil cannot do so much in the interior of the soul. The devil can present a vision, but not with this truth and majesty and these results.

11. Since the confessors cannot witness this vision—nor, perhaps, can it be explained by the one to whom God grants this favor—they fear and rightly so. Thus, it's necessary to proceed with caution, wait for the time when these apparitions will bear fruit, and move along little by little looking for the humility they leave in the soul and the fortitude in virtue. If the vision is from the devil, he will soon show a sign, and will be caught in a thousand lies. If the confessor has undergone these experiences, he needs little time for discernment. Immediately in the account given, he will see whether the vision is from God or the imagination or the devil. This is especially true if His Majesty (God) has given the confessor the gift of discernment of spirits. If the confessor has discernment of spirits as well as learning, even though he may have no personal experience, he will recognize the true vision very well.

12. What is necessary, sisters, is that you proceed very openly and truthfully with your confessor. I don't mean in regard to telling your sins, for that is obvious. I mean truth in giving an account of your prayer. If you do not give such an account, I am not sure you are proceeding very well, nor that it is God who is teaching you. God is very fond of our speaking as truthfully and clearly to the one who stands in his place as we would to him, and of our desiring that the confessor understand all our thoughts and even more our deeds, however small they may be. If you do this, you don't have to go about disturbed or worried. Even if the vision is not from God, it will do you no harm if you have humility and a good conscience. His Majesty knows how to draw good from evil, and the road along which the devil wanted you to go astray will be to your greater gain.

Thinking that God grants you such wonderful favors, you will force yourselves to please God more and be even more constantly aware of His Majesty's image. As a very learned man once said, the devil is a great painter. If the devil were to show this man I mentioned a living image of the Lord, the man wouldn't be grieved but would allow the image to awaken his devotion. Thus, he would wage war on the devil by using the wickedness of the evil one. Even though a painter may be a very poor one, a person should not on that account fail to reverence the image that is made if it is a painting of our good God.

13. That same learned man was strongly opposed to the advice some gave about making the fig when seeing a vision. He said, instead, that whenever we see a painting of our king we must reverence it. I see that he is right. Even here below, a similar action would be regretted. If a person knew that before their self-portrait, another who was loved manifested great contempt, that person would be unhappy with the action. Well, how much greater reason there is always to respect any crucifix or portrait we see of our imperial Majesty! Although I have written of this elsewhere, I am glad to write of it here, for I saw that a person went about in distress when ordered to use this remedy.[14]

I don't know who invented a thing that could so torment a person who wasn't able to do anything else than obey when her confessor gave her this counsel. This is because she thought she would go astray if she didn't obey him. My counsel is that even though a confessor gives you such advice, you should humbly tell him the reason for not accepting his counsel. The good reasons given me by the learned man I mention I have found very acceptable.

14. A wonderful benefit that the soul draws from this favor of the Lord is that when the soul thinks of him, or his life, or his passion, it remembers his most meek and beautiful countenance. This remembrance is the greatest consolation. It is just like our experience here below when it is far more consoling to see a person who has done a great deal of good for us than someone we had never met. I tell you that so delightful a remembrance brings much consolation and benefit.

Visions bring many other blessings. But since so much has been said about such effects, and more will be said, I don't want to tire myself or tire you. I advise you strongly that when you hear that God grants these favors to souls that you never beg nor even desire His Majesty to lead you by this path.

15. Although the path may seem very good to you, one to be highly esteemed and reverenced, desiring it is inappropriate for certain reasons. First, the desire to be given what you have never deserved shows a lack of humility. I believe that whoever desires this path will not have much humility. Just as the thoughts of a lowly workman are far from any desire to be king, since such a thing seems impossible to him, and he thinks he doesn't deserve it, so too with the humble person in similar matters. I believe that these favors will never be given to those who desire them, because before granting them God gives the person a deep self-knowledge. How will the ones who have such desires understand in truth that they are being given a great favor by not being in hell? Second, such a person will surely be deceived or in great danger because the devil needs nothing more than to see a little door open before playing a thousand tricks on us.

Third, the imagination itself, when there is a great desire, makes people think that they hear and see what is strongly desired. It is like those who desire something during the day, and who are thinking about it a great deal, dream of it at night. Fourth, it would be extremely bold to want to choose a path while not knowing what suits me more. Such a matter should be left to the Lord, who knows me. The Lord leads me along a path that is fitting—so that in all things I might do what His Majesty desires. Fifth, do you think that the trials suffered by those to whom the Lord grants these favors are few? No, they are extraordinary and of many kinds. How do you know you would be able to bear them? Sixth, by the very way you think you will gain, you will lose, as Saul did by being king.[15]

16. In sum, sisters, besides these reasons, there are others. Believe me, the safest way is to want only what God wants. He knows more than we ourselves do and loves us. Let us place ourselves in his hands so that his will may be done in us. We cannot err if we will always maintain this attitude with a determined will. You must note that greater glory is not merited by receiving a large number of these favors. It is rather to the contrary. The recipients of these favors are obliged to serve more because they have received more. The Lord doesn't take away from us that which, because it lies within our power, is more meritorious. So there are many holy persons who have never received one of these favors, and others who receive them but are not holy. Do not think the favors are given continuously. Rather, for each time the Lord grants them, there are many trials. Thus, the soul doesn't think about receiving more, but about how to serve what has been received.

17. It is true that this vision must be a powerful help to possessing the virtues with higher perfection. But the person who has gained them at the cost of her own labors will merit much more. I know a person, actually two people—one was a man—to whom the Lord had granted some of these favors. They were so desirous of serving His Majesty at their own cost, without these great delights, and so anxious to suffer, that they complained to the Lord because of the favors that were bestowed upon them! If they could have declined receiving these gifts, they would have.[16] I am speaking not of the delights coming from these visions—for in the end, these persons see that the visions are very beneficial and to be highly esteemed—but of those the Lord gives in contemplation.

18. It is true that these desires also, in my opinion, are supernatural and characteristic of souls very much inflamed with love. Such souls would want the Lord to see that they do not serve His Majesty for pay. Thus, as I have said, they never think about receiving glory as a motive for making the effort to serve more. Their desire is to satisfy love. It is love's nature to serve with deeds in a thousand ways. If it could, love would want to discover ways of consuming the soul within itself. If it were necessary to be always annihilated for the greater glory of God, love would do so very eagerly. May God be praised forever, Amen. In lowering himself to commune with such miserable creatures, His Majesty wants to show his greatness!

Chapter Ten

Tells about other favors God grants the soul, in a way different from those just mentioned, and of the great profit that comes from them.

1. The Lord communicates himself to the soul in many ways with these apparitions. He grants some of them when the soul is afflicted. Others are granted them when a great trial is about to come. Others are granted so that His Majesty might take delight in the soul and give delight to it. There's no reason to go into further detail about each, since my intention is only to explain the different favors there are on this road, insofar as I understand them. Thus, you will know, sisters, of their nature and their effects, lest we fancy that everything imagined is a vision.

When what you see is an authentic vision, you won't go about disturbed or afflicted if you understand that such a thing is possible. The devil gains much and is extremely pleased to see a soul afflicted and disquieted, for he knows that disturbance impedes it from being totally occupied in loving and praising God. His Majesty communicates himself in other ways that are more sublime and less dangerous because the devil, I believe, will be unable to counterfeit them. Thus, since these latter are something very secret, it is difficult to explain them, whereas the imaginative visions are easier to explain.

2. It will happen, when the Lord is pleased, that while the soul is in prayer and very much in its senses, a superstition will suddenly be experienced in which the Lord will reveal deep secrets. It seems the soul sees these secrets in God, for they are not visions of the most sacred humanity. Although I say the soul sees, it doesn't see anything, for the favor is not an imaginative vision but very much an intellectual one. In this vision it is revealed how all things are seen in God and how God has all things in His Majesty. This favor is most beneficial. Even though it passes in a moment, it remains deeply engraved in the soul and causes greatest confusion. The evil of offending God is seen more clearly, because while being in God (I mean being within God), we commit great evils. I want to draw a comparison—if I succeed—so as to explain this to you. For although what I said is true, and we hear it often, either we do not pay attention to this truth or we do not want to understand it. If the matter were understood, it doesn't seem it would be possible to be so bold.

3. Let's suppose that God is like an immense and beautiful dwelling or palace and that this palace, as I say, is God. Could the sinner, perhaps, so as to engage in evil deeds, leave this palace? No, certainly not! Rather, within the palace itself, that is, within God, the abominations, indecent actions, and evil deeds committed by us sinners take place. O frightful thought, worthy of deep reflection, and very beneficial for those of us who know little. We don't completely understand these truths, for otherwise it wouldn't be possible to be so foolishly

audacious! Let us consider, sisters, the great mercy and compassion of God in not immediately destroying us there, and be extremely thankful! Let us be ashamed to feel resentment about anything that is said or done against us. The greatest evil of the world is that God, our creator, suffers so many evil things from creatures within his very self, and that we resent a word said in our absence and perhaps with no evil intention.

4. O human misery! When will we imitate this great God, O my daughters? Let us not think we are doing anything by suffering injuries. We should very eagerly endure everything. Let us love the one who offends us, since this great God has not ceased to love us even though we have offended His Majesty very much. Thus, the Lord is right in wanting all to pardon the wrongs done to them.

I tell you, daughters, that even though this vision passes quickly, it is a great favor from our Lord if one desires to benefit from it by keeping it habitually present.

5. It also happens very quickly and ineffably that God will show within himself a truth that seems to leave in obscurity all those truths that there are in creatures like us. One understands very clearly that God alone is Truth, unable to lie. What David says in a psalm about every person being a liar is clearly understood.[17] However frequently the verse may be heard, it is never understood as it is in this vision. God is everlasting Truth! I am reminded of Pilate, how he was often questioning our Lord when, during the Passion, Pilate asked our Lord, "What is truth?"[18] How little we understand here below about this supreme truth!

6. I would like to be able to explain more about this, but it is unexplainable. Let us conclude, sisters, that in order to live in conformity with our God and Spouse in something, it will be well if we always study diligently how to walk in this truth. I'm not merely saying that we should not tell lies, for in that regard, glory to God, I already notice that you take great care in these houses not to tell a lie for anything. I'm saying that we should walk in truth before God and people in as many ways as possible. Especially, there should be no desire that others consider us better than we are. In our works we should attribute to God what is God's, and to ourselves what is ours. Then we should strive to draw out the truth in everything. Thus, we shall have little esteem for this world, which is a complete lie and falsehood, and as such will not endure.

7. Once I was pondering why our Lord was so fond of this virtue of humility. This thought came to me quite suddenly. It is my opinion, and not a result of any reflection. It came because God is supreme Truth. To be humble is to walk in truth, for it is a very deep truth that of ourselves, we have nothing good, but only misery and nothingness. Whoever does not understand this walks in misery and in falsehood. The more anyone understands this, the more that person pleases

the supreme Truth because that one walks in the truth. Please God, sisters, we will be granted the favor never to leave this path of self-knowledge. Amen.

8. Our Lord grants these favors to the soul because, as to one to whom he is truly betrothed, one who is already determined to do his will in everything, he desires to give it some knowledge of how to do his will and of his grandeur. There's no reason to deal with more than these two things I mentioned, since they seem to me very beneficial. In similar things there is nothing to fear. Rather, the Lord should be praised because he gives these gifts. The devil, in my opinion, and even one's own imagination have little capacity at this level, and so the soul is left with profound satisfaction.

Chapter Eleven

Treats of some desires God gives to the soul that are so powerful and vehement they place it in danger of death. Treats also of the benefits caused by this favor the Lord grants.

1. Do you think that all these favors the Spouse has bestowed upon the soul will be sufficient to satisfy the little dove or butterfly, so that it may come to rest in the place where it shall die? Do not think that I have forgotten it! Certainly not. Rather this little butterfly is much worse! Even though it has been receiving these favors for many years, it always moans and goes about sorrowful because they leave it with greater pain. The reason is that since it is getting to know ever more the grandeurs of its God and sees itself so distant and far from enjoying this God, the desire for the Lord increases much more! Love increases in the measure that the soul discovers how much this great God and Lord deserves to be loved. This desire continues! Gradually, it grows in these years to reach a point of suffering so great as that of which I shall now speak. I have said "years" so as to be in line with that person I have mentioned here. I well understand that one must not put limits on God! In a moment God can raise any of us to the lofty experience mentioned here. His Majesty has the power to do whatever is desired and God is eager to do many things for us.

2. Well, here is what sometimes happens to a soul that experiences these anxious longings, tears, sighs, and great impulses that were imagined. All of these seem to proceed from our love with deep feeling. They are all nothing in comparison with this other experience that I'm going to explain, for they resemble a smoking fire that—though painful—can be endured. While this soul is going about in this manner, burning up within itself, a blow is felt from elsewhere (the soul doesn't understand from where or how). The blow comes often through a sudden thought or word about death's delay. Or the soul will feel pierced by a fiery arrow. I don't say that there is an arrow. But whatever the experience, the

soul realizes clearly that the feeling couldn't come about naturally. Neither is the experience that of a blow, although I did say "blow"! It causes a sharp wound.

In my opinion, it isn't felt where earthly sufferings are felt, but in the very deep and intimate part of soul, where this sudden flash of lightning reduces to dust everything it finds in this earthly nature of ours. While this experience lasts, nothing can be remembered about our being. In an instant, the experience so binds the faculties that they have no freedom for anything except those things that will make this pain increase.

3. I wouldn't want what I say to appear to be an exaggeration. Indeed, I see that my words fall short because the experience is unexplainable. It is an enrapturing of the faculties and senses away from everything that is not a help, as I said, in feeling this affliction. For the intellect is very alive to understanding the reason why the soul feels far from God! His Majesty helps at that time with a vivid knowledge of himself in such a way that the pain increases to a point that makes the one who experiences it to cry aloud.

Though she is a person who has suffered and is used to suffering severe pains, she cannot then do otherwise. This feeling is not in the body. It is in the interior part if the soul as was said before. As a result, this person understood how much more severe the feelings of the soul are than those of the body. She reflected that such must be the nature of the sufferings of souls in purgatory. The fact that these souls have no body doesn't keep them from suffering much more than they do through all the bodily sufferings they endure here in earth.

4. I saw a person in this condition![19] Truly she thought she was dying. This was not so surprising because certainly there is great danger of death. Thus, even though the experience lasts but a short while, it leaves the body very disappointed. During that time, the heartbeat is as slow as it would be if a person were about to render the soul to God. This is no exaggeration! The natural heat fails, and the fire so burns the soul that—with a little more intensity—God would have fulfilled the soul's desires.

This is true not because a person feels little or much pain in the body, although it is disjointed as I said. For three or four days afterward, one feels great sufferings and doesn't even have the strength to write. It even seems to me that the body is always left weaker. The reason one does not feel the pain must be that the interior feeling of the soul is so much greater that one does not pay any attention to the body. When one experiences a very sharp bodily pain, other bodily pains are hardly felt even though they may be many. I have indeed experienced this! With the presence of this spiritual pain, I don't believe that physical pain would be felt, little or much, even if the body were cut in pieces!

5. You will tell me that this is an imperfection and ask why the soul doesn't conform to the will of God, since it is surrendered to His Majesty. Until now it could do this and has spent its life doing so. As for now, the reasoning faculty is

in such a condition that the soul is not the master of it, nor can the soul think of anything else than of why it is grieving, of how it is absent from its God, and of why it should want to live. It feels a strange solitude because no creature in all the earth provides company, nor would any heavenly creature. Neither of these is the One whom the soul loves.

Instead, everything torments it. The soul sees that it is like a person hanging, who cannot support itself with anything on earth nor can it ascend to heaven. It is on fire with this thirst but cannot get to the water. The thirst is not one that is endurable, for it is already at such a point that nothing will take it away. The soul does not desire that it be taken away except by that water of which our Lord spoke to the Samaritan woman.[20] Yet no one gives such water to the soul.

6. O God, help me! Lord, how you afflict your lovers! But everything is small in comparison with what you give them afterward. It is natural that what is worth much costs much. Moreover, if this suffering is to purify this soul so that it might enter the seventh dwelling place—just as those who will enter heaven must be cleansed in purgatory—it is as small as a drop of water in the sea. Furthermore, in spite of all this torment and affliction, the soul feels the pain is precious. This is true even though the suffering cannot be surpassed by any earthly affliction.

(This person had suffered many bodily as well as spiritual pains, but they all seemed nothing by comparison with this suffering.) The soul understands very well that the pain is so precious that one could not deserve it. However, this awareness is not of a kind that alleviates the suffering in any way. But with this knowledge, the soul suffers the pain very willingly and would suffer it for all of its life, if God were to be served by it. The soul would not then die once but be always dying, for truly the suffering is no less than death.

7. Well, let us consider, sisters, those who are in hell who do not have this conformity or this consolation and spiritual delight that is placed in the soul by God. They do not see that their suffering is beneficial, but they always suffer more and more. The torments of the soul are so much more severe than those of the body. The moment that souls in hell suffer is incomparably greater than the suffering we have here mentioned, and must, it is seen, last forever and ever. What then will the suffering of these unfortunate souls be? And what can we do or suffer in so short a life that would amount to anything if we were thereby to free ourselves of those terrible and eternal torments?

I tell you it would be impossible to explain how keenly the soul feels suffering and how different that is from the suffering of the body if one had not experienced this. The Lord himself desires that we understand this so that we may know the extraordinary debt we owe him. He has brought us to a state in which—through his mercy—we hope he will free us and pardon our sins.

8. Well, let us return to the soul who has been left with much pain. The in-

tensity of the pain lasts only a short while. In my opinion, it will last three or four hours at most. If it were to last a long time, natural weakness would not be able to endure it other than by a miracle. It has happened that the experience that left the soul in pieces lasted no more than a quarter of an hour. Truly, during that time the person lost her senses completely. The pain came in intensity merely from her hearing that life would not end. This happened while she was engaged in conversation during Easter week, the last day of the octave. This was after she had spent all of Easter in so much dryness she almost did not know it was Easter.

In no way can the soul resist this dryness. It cannot do this any more than it can stop flames from having heat and burning it if it is thrown in a fire. This feeling is not one that can be concealed from others. Those who are present are aware of the great danger in which the person abides, although they cannot be witnesses to what is taking place interiorly. True, they provide some company, as though they were shadows. All earthly things appear like shadows to this person.

9. In case you might sometime have this experience, you must realize what happens because of your weakness. The soul dies with the desire to die, as you have seen. The fire afflicts so deeply that it seems nothing can keep the soul from leaving the body. The soul truly fears that it might end up dying from wanting the pain to cease. The soul is aware that this is a weakness that is natural, for its desire to die is not taken away. A remedy cannot be found to remove this pain unless the Lord himself takes it away. Usually this is done through a great rapture, or with some vision, where the true Comforter consoles and strengthens the soul that it might desire to live as long as God wills.

10. This experience is a painful one, but the soul is left with the most beneficial effects. The fear of the trials that can come its way is lost. When the trials are compared to the painful feeling experienced in the soul, the trials don't seem to amount to anything. The benefits are such that one would be pleased to suffer the pain often. But there is no way that one can do this, nor is there any means for suffering the experience again. The soul must wait until the Lord desires to give this favor, just as there is no way to resist or remove it when it comes. The soul is left with greater contempt for the world than before because it sees that nothing in the world was any help to it in that torment. It is now much more detached from creatures because it now sees that only the Creator can console and satisfy it. It now has greater fear of offending God, for the soul sees that God can torment as well as console.

11. It seems to me that two experiences that lie on this spiritual path can put a person in danger of death. The first is the pain, for it is truly a danger and no small one. The second is overwhelming joy and delight. This reaches such an extraordinary height that I think the soul swoons to the point that it is

hardly kept from leaving the body. Indeed, its happiness could not be considered a small happiness.

Here you will see, sisters, whether I was right in saying that courage is necessary, and whether the Lord is right in answering your petitions for these favors as he did the sons of Zebedee. "Are you able to drink the chalice?"[21]

12. I believe all of us will answer "yes," sisters. This is rightly so, for His Majesty gives strength to the one who has need of it. He defends these souls in all things. When they are persecuted and criticized, he answers for them as he did for the Magdalene.[22] If this is not in words, it is in deeds. In the very end, before they die, he will pay for everything at once, as you will now see. May he be blessed forever, and may all creatures praise him, Amen!

The Seventh Dwelling Place[23]

This contains four chapters. The first deals with the favors God grants to those who have entered the seventh dwelling place. The following are some descriptions of the effects of the marriage of the soul with God.

7. . . . Each day the soul becomes more amazed, for the three Persons never seem to leave it any more. The soul clearly beholds that they are within it in the way that was mentioned. They are present in the extreme interior. This is a place very deep within oneself. The soul perceives this divine company, but it does not know how to explain this any further because of a lack of learning.

8. You may think that as a result the soul will be outside itself and so absorbed that it will be unable to be occupied with anything else. It is just the opposite! The soul is much more occupied than before with everything pertaining to the service of God. Once its duties are over, it remains with that enjoyable company. In my opinion, if the soul does not fail God, God will never fail to make his presence clearly known to the soul. The soul has strong confidence that since God has granted this favor, the soul will not be allowed to lose it. Though the soul knows this, it still goes about with greater care than ever not to displease God in anything.

9. It should be understood that this presence is not felt so fully, I mean so clearly, as when revealed the first time or at other times when God grants the soul this gift. For if the presence were felt so clearly, the soul would find it impossible to be engaged in anything else, or even to live among people. But even though the presence is not perceived in very clear light, the soul finds itself in this company every time it takes notice.

The experience resembles that of a person who is in a bright room with others. Once the shutters are closed, the person is in darkness. The light that enabled the person to see the others has now been taken away. Until the light returns, the others cannot be seen. However, that does not prevent the person from knowing that others are present. It might be asked whether the soul can see these others when it desires and the light returns. To see them does not lie in its power, but depends on when our Lord desires that the window of the intellect be opened. Great is the mercy the Lord shows in never departing from the soul and in desiring that the soul perceive him so manifestly. . . .

Chapter Two discusses the spiritual marriage and how it differs from spiritual union. A number of examples and comparisons—some of which follow—are used to illustrate the difference.

1. . . . The first time the favor is granted, His Majesty desires to show himself to the soul through an imaginative vision of his most sacred humanity so that the soul will understand and not be ignorant of receiving the gift. With others, the favor may be received in another form. With regard to this person, the Lord represented himself to her just after she had received communion. He was in the form of shining splendor, beauty, and majesty, as he was after his resurrection. He told her it was now time that she consider as her own what belonged to him. He would take care of what was hers.

2. It may seem that the experience was nothing new since at other times the Lord had represented himself to the soul in such a way. The experience was so different that it left her stupefied and frightened. Why? First, the vision came with great force. Second, because of the words the Lord spoke to her and because of the interior of the soul in which he represented himself were not like previous visions. You must understand that there is the greatest difference between the previous visions and those of this dwelling place. The difference between the spiritual betrothal and the spiritual marriage are as great as that which exists between two who are engaged and two who can no longer be separated.

3. . . . It should be understood that in this state there is no more thought of the body than if the soul were not in it. One's thought is only of the spirit. In the spiritual marriage there is still much less remembrance of the body because this secret union takes place in the very interior center of the soul, which must be where God is. In my opinion, there is no need for any door for God to enter in here. I say there is no need of any door because everything that has been said up until now seems to take place by means of the senses and faculties, and this appearance of the humanity of the Lord must also.

But that which comes to pass in the union of the spiritual marriage is very different. The Lord appears in this center of the soul not in an imaginative vision but in an intellectual one, although more delicate than those mentioned. It is as he appeared to the apostles without entering through the door when he said to them "Peace be to you."[24] What God communicates here to the soul in an instant is so great and a favor so sublime—and the delight the soul experiences is so extreme—that I do not know what I can compare it to. I can only say that the Lord wishes to reveal for that moment, in a more sublime manner than through any spiritual vision or taste, the glory of heaven.

One can say no more—insofar as can be understood—than that the soul, I mean the spirit, is one with God. Since God is also Spirit, His Majesty has desired to show his love for us by giving some persons understanding of the point to which this love reaches so that we might praise God's grandeur. His Majesty has desired to be so joined with the creature that, just as those who are married cannot be separated, God does not want to be separated from the soul.

4. The spiritual betrothal is different, for the two are separate. The union is also different because, even though it is the joining of two things into one, in the end the two can be separated and each remains by itself. We observe this ordinarily, for the favor of union with the Lord passes quickly, and afterward the soul remains without that company. I mean the soul remains without the awareness of that company. In the other favor, the soul always remains with God in its center. Let us say that the union is like the joining of two wax candles to such an extent that the flame coming from them is one, or that the wick, the wax, and the flame are all one. Afterward, one candle can be easily separated from the other and there are two candles....

I am laughing to myself over these comparisons, for they do not satisfy me. Yet I do not know any others. You may think what you want, but what I have said is true.

Chapter Three describes the effects of the prayer of union upon the soul. There is a difference in the quality of these effects as they are described. The benefits include a self-forgetfulness so that God's glory is the main concern. The soul is content to follow God's lead so that it no longer initiates any suffering or detachment. There is an interior joy and peace in allowing God to be God. There are almost no experiences of dryness in prayer.

Chapter Four concludes the reflections, trying to answer why the Lord grants the spiritual favors to some and not to others. Teresa insists that the reason favors are granted is to fortify human weakness. This enables the soul to endure whatever sufferings may come as did the apostles and other followers of Christ. The purpose of the spiritual marriage is the birth of good works.

7. This is the true sign of a thing or favor being from God, as I have already told you. It benefits me little to be alone making acts of devotion to our Lord,

proposing and promising to do wonders in his service if I then go away, and when opportunity presents itself, do just the opposite....

9. I repeat, it is necessary that your foundation consist of more than prayer and contemplation. If you do not strive for the virtues and practice them, you will always be dwarfs. And, please God, it will be only a matter of not growing. You already know that whoever does not increase decreases. I hold that love, where present, cannot possibly be content with remaining always the same....

12. This is what I want us to strive for, my sisters. Let us desire and be occupied in prayer, not for the sake of our enjoyment, but so as to have this strength to serve. Let's refuse to take an unfamiliar path, for we shall get lost at the most inopportune time. It would indeed be novel to think of having these favors from God through a path other than the one he took and the one followed by all the saints. May the thought never enter our minds....

14. ...Apart from the fact that by prayer you will be helping greatly, you need not be desiring to benefit the whole world, but must concentrate on those who are in your company....

15. ...In conclusion, my sisters, let me summarize by saying that we should not build castles in the air. The Lord doesn't look so much at the greatness of our works as at the love with which they are done. And if we do what we can, His Majesty will enable us each day to do more and more, provided that we do not quickly tire. But during the little while this life lasts—and perhaps it will last a shorter time than each of us thinks—let us offer the Lord interiorly and exteriorly the sacrifice we can. His Majesty will join it with that which he offered on the cross to the Father for us. Thus, even though our works are small, they will have the value our love for him would have merited had they been great.

16. May it please His Majesty, my sisters and daughters, that we all reach that place where we may ever praise him. Through the merits of his Son who lives and reigns forever and ever, may God give me the grace to carry out something of what I tell you. Amen.

For I tell you that my confusion is great. Thus I ask you, through the same Lord, that in your prayers you do not forget this poor wretch.

NOTES

1. Michael Cox, *Handbook of Christian Spirituality* (San Francisco: Harper and Row, 1985) 153–64. For a readable explanation of the *Spiritual Exercises* of Saint Ignatius, see James Skehan, *Place Me with Your Son* (Washington, D.C.: Georgetown University Press, 1991).

2. Richard Woods, *Christian Spirituality* (Chicago: Thomas More Press, 1989) 267–69.

3. *The Study of Spirituality*, ed. Cheslyn Jones, Geoffrey Wainwright, and Edward Yarnold (New York: Oxford University Press, 1986) 365–75.

4. A specific example among many can be found in Teresa of Ávila's *The Interior Castle*, trans. Kieran Kavanaugh and Otilio Rodriguez (New York: Paulist Press, 1979) 156–70.

5. John of the Cross, *Ascent of Mt. Carmel*, trans. David Lewis (London: Baker, 1906), vi.5; 2, xxvii.2–3; *The Complete Works of St. Teresa of Jesus*, ed. and trans. Edgar Allison Peers (New York: Sheed and Ward, 1946). *The Way of Perfection*, xxi.2; *The Book of Her Life*, xiii.15 are from *The Complete Works*.

6. Teresa of Ávila, *The Interior Castle*, 1–31, provides a brief introduction to these works.

7. Carolyn Humphreys, *From Ash to Fire* (New York: New City Press, 1992) 9–23.

8. The translation is that of Kavanaugh and Rodriguez. All page numbers refer to this edition of *The Interior Castle*.

9. Chapters nine, ten, and eleven are the last three chapters of the Sixth Dwelling Place. Chapter nine is found in full between 156 and 171.

10. This refers to the intellectual visions of chapter eight.

11. It was a popular belief in sixteenth-century Spain that certain stones—such as the bezoar—had curative powers.

12. This person is Teresa.

13. Acts 9:3–4.

14. The person is Teresa.

15. 1 Sam 15:10–11.

16. This probably refers to Teresa and to John of the Cross.

17. Ps 116:11.

18. John 18:36–38.

19. This is Teresa.

20. John 4:7–14.

21. Matt 20:22.

22. Luke 7:40–48.

23. The full text is found between 172 and 194.

24. John 20:19–21.

BIBLIOGRAPHY

Auclair, M. *Teresa of Avila*. Translated by Kathleen Pond. New York: Pantheon Books, 1953.

Humphreys, Carolyn. *From Ash to Fire*. New York: New City Press, 1992.

Jones, Cheslyn, Geoffrey Wainwright, and Edward Yarnold, eds. *The Study of Spirituality*. New York: Oxford University Press, 1986.

Peers, Edgar Allison. *Handbook to the Life and Times of St. Teresa and St. John of the Cross*. Westminster, Md.: Newman Press, 1954.

Peers, Edgar Allison. *Studies of the Spanish Mystics*. 2 vols. New York: Macmillan, 1927–30.

Rodriguez, Otilio. *The Teresian Gospel: An Introduction to a Fruitful Reading of the Way of Perfection*. Darlington: Carmel, 1974.

Teresa of Ávila. *The Collected Works of Teresa of Ávila*. Translated by Kieran Kavanaugh and Otilio Rodriguez. Vol. 1. *The Book of Her Life, Spiritual Testimonies, Soliloquies*. Washington, D.C.: ICS, 1976.

Teresa of Ávila. *The Interior Castle*. Translated by Kieran Kavanaugh and Otilio Rodriguez. New York: Paulist Press, 1979.

Trueman Dicken, E. W. *The Crucible of Love*. New York: Sheed and Ward, 1963.

Woods, Richard. *Christian Spirituality*. Chicago: Thomas More Press, 1989.

– 15 –

JANE FRANCES DE CHANTAL

(1572–1641)

Strike Back with the Heart

Jane Frances de Chantal mirrors a French spirituality rooted in a history of changing times, influences, and spiritual schools. Fourteenth-century France witnessed the struggles for power between an Avignon papacy and a Roman papacy. Fourteenth- and fifteenth-century France witnessed a renewed interest in mysticism accompanied by fears of heresy and witchcraft. The burning at the stake of French mystics Marguerite Porete (1310) and Joan of Arc (1431) affirmed how dangerous it could be for women to make claims about the voices and visions they experienced.[1]

The Inquisition was as actively vigilant in France as it was in Spain. This was one reason for the Roman pontiff Paul III setting up a general Holy Office of the Inquisition in 1542. This papal court would oversee the trials of the national church tribunals of the Inquisition. In sixteenth-century France there was a strong sympathy with the German Peasants' Revolt advocated by Luther's treatise of 1520. The common people were becoming increasingly anticlerical as the aristocratic clergy became enmeshed in political power struggles.

In the first half of the seventeenth century, French spirituality had great influence in Europe. French writers like Pierre de Bérulle, Francis de Sales, Jane Frances de Chantal, and a host of other religious foundresses and founders affected the next three hundred years of Christian spirituality. The seventeenth-century French schools of spirituality were marked by authentic fervor and countercultural emphases that some admired and others despised.

A favorite Christ image of the period was of the Servant who was annihilated in his love for humans. Jesus Christ was surely the Lord of all creation and the center of the world's meaning and longing. But Jesus Christ was also the Servant who did not vie for political and religious status among the people. He died to himself in the process of living unto God. Seventeenth-century French spirituality emphasized this perspective to counter the paradigm of power and wealth so popular with many civil and church leaders. The mystery of the Incarnation was perceived as an annihilation, for Jesus Christ left the glory of God for the servant status of humans. The presence of Jesus Christ through the eucharistic bread and wine was also perceived as annihilation, for Jesus continues to be of service to humanity even while he is the Christ of glory.

This theology of annihilation stressed that those who wish to imitate this servant Jesus must die to themselves in order to live unto God. Dying to self was sharing in the crucifixion of Jesus Christ. The emphasis on annihilation led to a piety that reverenced the symbols of the Sacred Heart, the crucified Christ, the infant Christ, and Christ present in the eucharistic bread and wine as paradigms of love at the service of others. This stress on the servant Christ was the theological grounding for leaders of the French school, like Pierre de Bérulle (1575–1629) stressing the importance of Christians taking a vow of servitude.[2]

The emphasis on self-sacrifice in order to be united with Jesus Christ was a constant in this school of spirituality. The body was looked on as posing a threat to the soul or spirit. Heroic bodily mortification was a means for attaining the liberty of spirit necessary for the annihilation into God:

> We must first of all labor for the mortification of self. Then, being dead to the flesh, we must endeavor to live by the Spirit. Without this, we shall never do anything, and all other exercises will only serve to our loss. All the rest is like a salve that encloses our evil without removing it, which hides it and in no way heals it.[3]

Although the word *annihilation* could well have negative connotations for twentieth-century readers, French spiritual writers felt this was another way of stating the emptying that is the fullness of Philippians 2:6–11. Those who are united or in communion with Christ live as Christ lived and love as Christ loved. The virgin Mary was a prime example of one who emptied herself to receive the fullness of the Word, Jesus Christ. As Jesus and Mary were one heart, one soul, and one life, Mary's ministry of giving Jesus to the world became a model for Christians desiring holiness.[4] The vow of servitude to Jesus and to Mary came out of this context of self-emptying being a simultaneous filling. Lourdes, La Salette, and other centers of devotion to Mary were testimonies to this spirituality of service and abnegation.

In the seventeenth century there were two major distortions of the French spirituality of annihilation, Jansenism and Quietism. Jansenism was named after the Dutch Jesuit Cornelius Jansen (1585–1638), a theologian at Louvain who was made bishop of Ypres in 1636. Jansen taught that St. Augustine questioned the corruption of human will and that possibly even grace could not change the basic corruption. Jansen's written work, published after his death, was immediately attacked by some of his fellow Jesuits; others, however, defended the theological precision of his reflections on Augustine.

The perspectives of Jansen were spread by his friend, Abbé St. Cyran, who instructed the celibate men and women at Port Royal, a community of spirituality that influenced many fervent people of seventeenth-century France. Jansen's teachings that this community passed on to others included the perspective that humans were the victims of determinism. Grace, once given, is irresistible. This compromised the teachings about free will. There were also strict standards for the sacramental disciplines. Penitents should not be given the benefit of the doubt. Respect for Holy Communion required occasional abstention as a disciplinary measure. Any pleasurable experience was questionable and ought to be avoided by those desiring a fervent spiritual life. Attending the theater, dancing, and enjoying pleasing sights and sounds were suspect.

The self-righteousness of the Jansenists caused their eventual undoing. The community of Port Royal was condemned by the church, but not before it had strongly influenced the religious community of the Oratorians. The Jansenist influence affected the worship of the church by encouraging repetitions of gestures and prayers like triple crosses over the chalice, triple recitation of invocations, and the necessity of sacramental confession before receiving holy communion.

Quietism was the other expression of spirituality that came under negative scrutiny in seventeenth-century France. This movement is traced to Miguel de Molinos (1628–96), a Spanish priest who studied in Rome and then returned to France. He encouraged the nuns he directed to destroy all paintings and images of Jesus Christ because these visual images stimulate the lower, sensual, visual, or bodily imagination. Molinos allowed nuns to receive communion every day because the sign of bread was in no way connected to the sensual or visual presentation of Christ that their imaginations might suggest.

Molinos said evil thoughts should be simply allowed or passively endured until they ran their course. He felt that the sacramental reception of confession or communion could activate demonic powers, so one should be hesitant and careful in approaching these sacraments. Molinos was condemned by the Inquisition for these teachings and imprisoned for life. His quiet endurance of this and his kindness to the oppressors made him a heroic figure for many people. One of his most influential disciples was the wealthy and pious Madame de Guyon (1648–1717).[5]

Into this time of fervor and excesses, Jane Frémyot was born in 1572. The Protestant Reformation had already influenced the position of married women. Educational opportunities for women increased, in spite of lessening the viable options for women's adult choices. The Reformers' insistence on the importance of individual interpretation of the word of God gave women and men access to instructions.[6]

In seventeenth-century France the new humanism had already provided a foundation for interpretation of the self-giving that was involved in human loving. Jesus Christ died and experienced annihilation as a testimony to the cost of loving God and neighbor. The dynamics of this friendship with God and humans served as a model for the relationship between dedicated men and women of the period. Francis de Sales (1567–1622), the gentle bishop of Geneva, and Jane Frémyot de Chantal, his intimate friend, portrayed the best of Christian humanism that countered both Jansenism and quietism.

The two would eventually cofound the Sisters of the Visitation some years after their meeting in 1604. The mutually influential friendship of these two diverse personalities can be better appreciated by a brief tracing of each life prior to that providential meeting.

Francis de Sales was born in the war-torn period of the Protestant Reformation and the Counter-Reformation. Francis was a brilliant, sensitive child. He was well trained in the humanities at Clermont College and studied theology on his own. When he went to Paris for further schooling, he admits that he engaged in the typical pursuits of Parisian men who fancied women.

At Paris Francis experienced a faith crisis through his limits in controlling himself. His earlier strong convictions of care and sensitivity to others were demolished by his new experiences of the loss of self-discipline. He left the University of Paris for Padua, where he continued graduate studies under a Jesuit tutor, Possevin. His desire for a life of contemplative beauty and love was nourished in Paris. At age twenty-five, in 1592, he left for a seminary and was apprenticed to a bishop near Geneva. Strongly influenced by the works of Teresa of Ávila, he eventually became the bishop of Geneva in 1602. Jane Frémyot, the baroness de Chantal, would enter his life two years later.

Jane Frémyot was born in Dijon. Her mother died when Jane was eighteen months old. Jane and two other children were then raised by an aunt and her father, who was a lawyer. All three children learned the financial, legal, and practical matters of life from their father, as well as the strictness of Catholic faith. In 1592, at age twenty, Jane married Baron Christophe de Rabutin-Chantal, a wealthy, good-hearted man whose spending practices quickly encouraged her to take charge of his estate.

A devoted wife, Jane took over the financial rehabilitation of her husband's estate while remaining the lively hostess at his extravagant parties. Jane and Christophe loved each other deeply. Two of their six children died at birth. After the baron survived military service, Jane nursed him through a debilitating disease. Shortly afterward, he was killed in a careless hunting accident. She fell into a process of grief for several years.

Her father-in-law threatened to take her four children away from her if she would not sell Christophe's estate and come to take care of him. Although her own father also needed care, Jane went to the estates of Chantal in the country. Her youngest child was still under eight years of age when they left for Chantal. During this period in the country, Jane sought spiritual direction from Francis de Sales. She asked him to help her discover how she could live out the great desire she felt for a more total dedication to God.

Over a six-year period Jane and Francis shared their common quest for greater love of God. In the process both came into contact with other women who desired a greater dedication to God, although they—like Jane—had young children. Francis and Jane envisioned a community of women who might dedicate themselves in a formal way to God. They devised a community in which women and their dependent children could live a form of community life, pray a shortened form of morning, noon, and evening prayer, visit the sick and the poor during the day, and continue the dual vocation of mother and sister. This community would be known as the Visitation Sisters.

Jane continued to run the estate of her husband, to care for her father-in-law, to raise her children and arrange for their education, and eventually to arrange marriages for one daughter and her son. In a period of fifteen years, there were established more than eighty convents of the Visitation Sisters. Widowed and single women joined the group. The prayer and service were fitting for their own life circumstances. During the period of the foundation of the Visitation community, Marie, Jane's oldest daughter, married Bernard, the brother of Francis de Sales. Charlotte, her middle daughter, died. Her youngest daughter, Françoise, and her youngest child, her son, Celse Bénigne, lived with Jane. Meanwhile, she was superior of the Visitation community and the one to whom the other superiors of the houses had recourse.

In 1602, Francis became bishop of Geneva. His reputation as a preacher, teacher, and reformer grew rapidly, and he was often away from Geneva on preaching tours. The friendship between Jane and Francis grew. Both answered many letters from a variety of correspondents who sought their advice on the spiritual life. In 1618 both Jane and Francis opposed the bishop of Lyons, who insisted that women ought to be cloistered.

The work of Francis de Sales, *Introduction to the Devout Life*, became a classic for laity of the period. It was no longer expected that only the clergy ought to follow a set guide for growth in the spiritual life. The handbook of Francis de Sales remained a popular and practical guide for centuries. The letters of Jane as well as those of Francis illustrate the letter as a popular form of spiritual direction in the seventeenth century. Their letters reflect that each person has a different way to follow in the growth of their affective life, their sense of discipline, and their unique call to follow the gentle Christ.

Although letters of spiritual direction did not become a fixed form of spiritual literature for approximately another century, the letters of Jane and Francis can be considered to represent spiritual direction. The letters show basic wisdom about the unfolding of the spiritual life for different persons in different circumstances. Although many of Jane's letters were not preserved, those that were show the balance that prevents her from being characterized as either a quietist or a Jansenist.

The letter of Francis de Sales to Jane that is included in this chapter indicates moderation and balance. He encourages Jane to trust her heart and his, and not to fear affection. He loves her without embarrassment and assures Jane that such good movements can be of God. He advises her not to engage in intellectual debate with the devil, but to let her feelings strike against the devil. If necessary, she can invoke the use of the discipline for liberation's sake, but not too rigorously. Her spirit of liberty should be used for good. A sign that it is used for good is the lack of anxiety or scruples that ought to accompany true liberation.

Both Jane and Francis believed sincere Christians could take a discerning look at their life and assess what was happening affectively and intellectually. Jane's counsels to her daughter Françoise, to superiors, and to a priest show a commonsense spirituality. Jane's letter to her priest brother upon the death of Francis reveals the depth of her feeling about him. She acknowledges that her loss has already given way to the hope of eternal reunion. The friendship of the saints had been a means for transforming both of them into Christ.[7] As Jane was dying in Moulins, Vincent de Paul recounts that he was praying for her. Then he experienced a vision that he interpreted as a final union of the two friends, Jane and Francis:

> There appeared to him a small globe of fire which rose from the earth to the upper regions of the air to be united with another globe which was larger and more luminous. Then these two became one, mounting even higher, entering and being incorporated into yet another globe which was infinitely greater and more resplendent than the others.[8]

Letters of Loving Advice

Letter from Francis de Sales to Jane, October 14, 1604[9]

Madam,

I have a very great desire to make myself clearly understood in this letter. Please God I will find the means to match my desire! I am sure that you will be encouraged by my response to part of what you asked me about. This is about the part of the two doubts which the enemy is suggesting to you concerning your choice of me as your spiritual director. So I am going to tell you what I can, in order to put into a few words what I think you need to consider in this matter.

First of all, the choice you have made gives every indication of being a good and legitimate one; so please have no further doubts about this. My reasons are the following: the strong impulse of your heart which carried you to this decision almost by force, yet with joy and contentment; the time I took to deliberate before agreeing to your wish; the fact that neither you nor I relied on ourselves but sought the opinion of your confessor, who is a good, learned, and prudent man; the fact that we allowed time for your first enthusiasm to subside in case it had been misplaced, and we prayed about this. We prayed not only for one or two days, but for several months. Without a doubt, all these are infallible signs that we acted according to God's will.

Impulses that come from the evil spirit or from the human mind are very different. They are frightening, vehement, and vacillating. The first thing they whisper to the agitated soul is not to listen to any advice. Or, if the soul does listen, it listens only to the advice of persons of little or no experience. These impulses urge us to hurry up and close a deal before having discussed the terms. They are satisfied with a short prayer which serves as a pretext in deciding most important questions.

Our case was not at all like this. Neither you nor I made the final decision in this matter. It was made by a third person who had no reason to consider anything but God's will. The fact that I hesitated at first—and this was because of the deliberation I was bound to make—ought to put your mind completely at rest. You may be sure it was not from any disinclination to serve you spiritually, for my inclination to do so is great beyond words. But in a decision of such moment, I didn't want to follow either your desire or my inclination, but only God and God's providence. So please stop right there and don't go on arguing with the enemy about it. Tell him boldly that it was God who wanted it and who has done it![10]

It was God who placed you under that first direction, profitable for you at the time. It is God who has brought you under my direction, and the Lord will make it fruitful and useful to you, even though I, the instrument, am unworthy.

As to your second point, my very dear sister, be assured of this. As I said from the very beginning when you consulted with me about your interior, God gave me a tremendous love for your soul. As you became more and more open with me, a marvelous obligation arose for my soul to love yours more and more. That's why I was prompted to write you that God had given me to you. I didn't believe that anything could be added to the affection I felt for you, especially when I was praying for you. But now, my dear sister, a new quality has been added—I don't know what to call it. All I can say is that its effect is a great inner delight which I feel whenever I wish you the perfect love of God and other spiritual blessings. I am adding nothing to the truth. I speak in the presence of the "God of my heart" and yours.[11]

Every affection differs in some particular way from every other affection. That which I have for you has a certain something about it which brings me great consolation. When all is said, it is extremely good for me. Hold that for the modest truth and have no more doubt about it. I didn't intend to say so much, but one word leads to another, and I think you know what I mean.

To me, it's an amazing fact, my daughter, that holy church, in imitation of her Spouse, teaches us to pray, not for ourselves only, but always for ourselves and our fellow Christians. "Give us . . . " she says, and "grant us . . . " and similar all-inclusive terms. It had never occurred to me when praying in this general way to think about any persons in particular. But since leaving Dijon, whenever I say "we" I think of particular individuals who have recommended themselves to my prayers. Ordinarily, you are the one who first comes to mind, and when not first—which is barely the case—then last so that I have more time to think of you. What more can I say than that?

But for the honor of God, do not speak about this to anyone. I may be saying a little too much, though I say it in total honesty and purity. This should be enough to help you answer all those temptations in the future, or at least to laugh at the enemy and spit in his face! I'll tell you the rest someday, either in this life or the next.

In your third point, you ask me what remedies there are for the suffering caused you by the temptations the devil suggests to you against the faith and the church. At least, that's what I understand to be the difficulty. I shall tell you what God inspires me to say. In this kind of temptation, we must take the same stance that we take against temptations of the flesh. That is, we do not argue at all, but do as the Israelite children did with the bones of the paschal lamb. We do not try to break them but simply throw them into the fire.[12] In no way must we answer or even pretend to hear what the enemy is saying, no matter how hard he pounds on the door.

We must not even say, "Who is it?" "That's true," you tell me. "But he is so annoying and is making such a loud racket that those inside can't even hear each other speak." It's all the same. Be patient. Speak by means of signs. We must prostrate ourselves before God and stay there at God's feet. The Lord understands very well from this humble gesture that you are his, and that you want his help, even though you are unable to speak. Especially, stay inside and don't so much as open the door either to see who is there or to chase the pest away. Finally he will grow tired of shouting and will leave you in peace. "It's about time!" you will tell me.

. . . So, courage then! Things will improve soon. So long as the enemy doesn't get in, the rest doesn't matter. Still, it's a very good sign that he is raging and beating at the door. It's a sign that he doesn't yet have what he is after. If he had it, he would no longer carry on this way. He would come in and stay. Remember this, so that you never get caught up in scruples.

Here is another remedy for you. The temptations against faith go directly to the understanding to draw it to argue, and to get caught up in these things. Do you know what you should do while the enemy wastes his time trying to scale the walls of your intellect? Slip out the gate of your will and take the offensive against him. That is... let your affective side attack him with full force, and even let your thoughts be reinforced by your voice, crying out, "You traitor! You wretch! You left the church of the angels, and you are trying to get me to leave the church of the saints! Disloyal, unfaithful, perfidious one! You gave the apple of perdition to the first woman and now you want me to bite it, too!"[13]

"Get behind me, Satan! It is written: you shall not tempt the Lord your God."[14] No, I will not argue with you. When Eve tried to dispute with you, she lost. She argued and was seduced. "Live, Jesus, in whom I believe! Long live the church to which I cling!" Say these and similar impassioned words. You must speak also to Jesus Christ and to the Holy Spirit in whatever way God inspires you. Even pray as well to the church. "O Mother of the children of God, may I never be separated from you. I want to live and die in you."

I don't know if I am making myself clear to you. What I'm trying to say is that we have to strike back with the heart and not with our reason. We strike back with intense feelings and not with arguments. It's true that at such times of temptation, our poor will is without feeling. So much the better! Its blows will strike the enemy that much harder. When the enemy discovers that—instead of delaying your progress—he is giving you every opportunity of expressing countless virtuous affections, particularly that of affirming your faith, he will finally leave you alone.

As a third remedy, it would be good once in a while to take fifty or sixty strokes of the discipline—or only thirty—depending on what you can take.[15] It's surprising how effective this measure has been for someone I know. Undoubtedly that's because the physical sensation distracts from interior suffering and calls forth the mercy of God. Moreover, when the devil sees his partner the flesh is being subdued, he gets afraid and runs away. But this third remedy must be taken in moderation, depending on the good it achieves. This you will know after trying it out for a few days....

If you really like the prayers you are used to saying, please don't drop them. If you happen to leave out some of what I am telling you to do, have no scruples about it. Here is the general rule of our obedience written in capital letters:

DO ALL THROUGH LOVE, NOTHING THROUGH CONSTRAINT;
LOVE OBEDIENCE MORE THAN YOU FEAR DISOBEDIENCE.

I want you to have the spirit of liberty, not the kind that excludes obedience (this is freedom from the flesh), but the liberty that excludes constraint, scruples, and anxiety. If you really love obedience and docility, I'd like to think this. When some legitimate or charitable cause takes you away from religious exercises, this would be for you another form of obedience, and that your love would make up for whatever you have to omit in your religious practice....

It looks to me as if I will never finish this letter which I've written only with the intention of answering you. Still, I really must finish it now, asking for your prayers, which are a great help. How I need them! I never pray without including you in my petitions. I never greet my own angels without greeting yours. Do the same for me, and get Celse Bénigne[16] to pray for me also. I always pray for him and all your little family. You may be sure that I never forget them in my Mass, nor their deceased father, your husband.

May God be your very heart, mind, and soul, my dearest sister. I am in the Lord's merciful love, your very devoted servant....

Letter of Jane to Her Daughter, Paris, 1620[17]

Darling,

Since M. de Toulonjon is free for eight or ten days, he is hurrying off to see you to find out firsthand whether you think he is suitable for you or not. He hopes his personality will not displease you. As for me, frankly, I see nothing to find fault with in him. In fact, I couldn't wish for more. Our Lord has given me so much satisfaction about this match that I can't remember ever having had such a good feeling about a temporal matter. I am not so much attracted by his good background and refinement as by his intelligence, pleasant disposition, sincerity, sound judgment, integrity, and good reputation. In a word, dear Françon, let us thank God for such a match.

Out of gratitude, dear, try to love and serve God better than you ever have. Don't let anything stop you from continuing to go frequently to the sacraments or from trying to be humble and gentle. Take the *Devout Life* for your guide. It will lead you safely. Don't waste time fussing about jewelry and fashions. You will be living in plenty. But, my darling, remember always that we are meant to use the good things God gives us without being attached to them. Such is the attitude that we should have toward all that the world values. From now on, try to live honorably, modestly, and sensibly in the new way of life that is before you.

I'm certainly very happy that your relatives and I arranged this marriage without you. This is how things should be, and, my dearest, I want you always to follow my advice. Moreover, your brother, who has good judgment, is delighted about your engagement. True, M. de Toulonjon is about fifteen years older than you. But, darling, you will be much happier with him than with some rash, dissolute young fool like the young men of today. You are marrying a man who is not at all like this. He is not a gambler, has lived honorably on the battlefield and has received high appointments from the king. You would be lacking the good sense I believe you to have if you did not accept him cordially and sincerely. I beg you, dear, to accept him graciously. Be assured that God, who has been mindful of you, will not forget you if you abandon yourself to that tender love. The Lord guides all those who place their trust in him.

Letter of Jane to Her Daughter, Paris, April 13, 1620[18]

My dearest daughter,

Praise God, who so far has guided you so well in these preliminary steps toward your coming marriage! I hope this divine goodness will give you complete peace. I must say, darling, that I myself am more and more pleased about the match. In my opinion, M. de Toulonjon is as fine a man as one could find anywhere. He has returned as happy as can be, and we have every reason to feel the same. Truly, dear Françon, you have pleased me very much by placing such total confidence in me. If you only knew how much I have prayed and longed to see you happily settled and how much more keenly I feel your concerns than my own. Of course, I shall always prefer your happiness to my own. There's no doubt about that. You may be sure that on this occasion I acted with great affection because I saw it was for your happiness.

We owe everything to the goodness of our Lord, who has watched over you and me and heard our prayers. You can see by the enclosed letter how much the archbishop of Bourges wants this marriage also. So, stand fast if you are disturbed by fears and imaginings. Shut the door upon them and do not let such feelings enter, under any pretext whatever. In everything, use common sense and follow my bit of advice. It is for your good, and if you continue to follow it, you will not regret it.

Write me, as you have promised, all the feelings in your heart. And if, as I hope, God has bound you to M. de Toulonjon—for that is what I desire above all else—then I trust that God will have blest your first meeting. For my part, darling, I tell you frankly, I find him altogether to my liking, as I have already said. Really, I like him very much. All our relatives and friends who know him couldn't ask for more.

As to your rings, M. de Toulonjon is very busy about them and wants to have lots of precious stones sent to me from Paris so that I may buy as many as I like for you. I would prefer that you not buy any at all, for, frankly dear, ladies of rank here no longer wear them. Only the townswomen do. However, you can make your own choice when you get here. I don't know how to make M. de Toulonjon understand this, for he begs me—at least for now—to let him send you pearls, earrings, and a locket covered with diamonds, which is what all the ladies are wearing on the front of their gowns.

Dearest, we mustn't let M. de Toulonjon be extravagant about buying so many things for you. He has such an intense desire to please you in every possible way, but we must not allow that. If ever there was a perfectly happy woman, it is you. But don't you see, dearest, you must be very discreet and hold him back in this. It will be better to put aside a little of your money and spend it more usefully than to squander it on trinkets and vanities. For my part, I hope that my Françon will not be swept off her feet by all this. My reputation would be at stake, for, since you are my daughter, you are expected to be circumspect and to conduct your affairs wisely and prudently.

I can just picture you as a lady, mistress of the heart and home of our dear M. de Toulonjon! That's why it will be up to you to manage your affairs carefully. Since he wants you to send me a design of the dress you like, do so, but I am going to allow only one gown to be sent to you. More than one, considering all the other things he is getting for you, would be unreasonable. You yourself, if M. Coulon wants to help you,[19] may also have one made. However, I would prefer that he simply send you the money for it. We could have it made in today's style and out of fashionable fabric so that it could be worn anywhere.

See to it that Foretz is sold.[20] Moreover, you shouldn't have a wedding dress made. Today that appears ridiculous among both the ladies at court and the gentry. Besides, I want you to have a quiet wedding, and I want you to trust me in this. M. de Toulonjon tells me that you do not want to be married in May. Good heavens! Don't be scrupulous about this, for it's only a superstition. However, I don't think a May wedding is possible anyway, even though he would like it very much. That's because he wants to please you at any cost. I'd be in favor of a May wedding too if it meant your getting rid of your scruple about it.

He wrote you about how he was prevented from coming here as soon as he had hoped. He didn't tell you how he did get here. It happened that while he was waiting at the relay station, a friend of his who is a state councilor was going by in his carriage. M. de Toulonjon jumped right in without his sword. He hadn't had time to eat, but came just as he was. He was sorry not to have been able to send you anything today, but he will on Thursday. Really, the more I see him, the more I like this man, and the more I realize how much you and I should praise God for this fortunate match. Write him a courteous, warm answer and speak honestly and openly with him, returning his affection. The time to stand on ceremony is over. His man is waiting downstairs for my letter.

Dearest Françon, I want you to love your fiancé perfectly. May you be as happy as you have reason to be happy. As for me, I am completely happy, and with good reason. Good-bye, dearest love. Write to me quite openly.

P.S. A thousand greetings to our dear relatives. Good-bye again, darling. Let us love wholeheartedly him whom God has given us.

Letters of Spiritual Direction

Letter to a Visitandine[21]

I return your greeting and also wish you a "forever," not of this perishable life, but of a blessed eternity. This will be yours to claim after you have lived a long, holy life of service to God through a faithful observance of your Rule. Our blessed Father used to say that the best means of grasping the spirit of our vocation was to put into practice the instructions found in our Rules. You know that the principal virtues are humility, self-effacement, and a holy simplicity that does away with all kinds of vanity, self-seeking, and self-satisfaction. If you put these virtues into practice, it will become apparent in all that you say, do, and write. Now it is this very simplicity that I especially want for you because it is the distinctive quality of the daughters of the Visitation.

Your indulgent heart, which I love most sincerely, gives me confidence to mention something in passing that I think you won't mind hearing. I find your letter very well written, but, it seems to me, it contains too many expressions that lack simplicity. That's why I hope that the virtues that I have just spoken of will be seen in your thoughts, words, and deeds, and that there will be nothing in your manner of speaking or writing that smacks of affectation. In truth, I would rather have us appear unskilled in letter writing than be considered affected....

I beg you, dearest daughter, to pray to God for me. I wish you the attainment of a most holy perfection.

Letter to a Superior[22]

My dearest daughter,

...If it appears that a sister has done something to lessen the mutual love and confidence that should exist among us, I prefer that—before taking the rumor seriously and talking—you write to her quite candidly. Write not as if you believe the story being spread, but to learn the truth from her directly and to believe her.

I beg you, my dear sister, govern your community with great expansiveness of heart. Give the sisters a holy liberty of spirit, and banish from your mind and theirs a servile spirit of constraint. If a sister seems to lack confidence in you, do not for that reason show her the least coldness. Rather, gain her trust through love and kindness. Don't entertain thoughts against any one of the sisters, but treat them all equally.

Lead them not with a bustling, anxious kind of concern, but with a care that is genuine, loving, and gentle. I know there is no better way to succeed in leading souls. The more solicitous, open, and supportive you are with them, the more you will win their hearts. So be present at the community prayers and other functions as often as you can, and let the sisters know how much you enjoy being with them.

You tell me that you can no longer stand the burden of being superior. Dear sister, don't ever let me hear you say that again! Do you want to bury your talents and render useless all the gifts God has lavished upon you? God has given you these many graces so that the glory of the Lord may be increased in whatever houses are given to your governance. So, look beyond your timid, fearful hesitations. Trample them underfoot, my dearest daughter. Keep your eye on God's good pleasure and the eternal plan for you. Surrender all the remaining days of your life to God, and let the Lord use these for such activities and services as will be pleasing to God and not to yourself. Finally, I place in the Lord's hands all of your consolations. Believe that I am always yours....

Letter to André, 1622[23]

[*Francis de Sales, bishop of Geneva, died in 1622. Jane's response to the death of this friend was partially conveyed in her letter to her brother, André.*]

Dear André,

You say you want to know what my heart felt on that occasion. Ah, it seems to me that it adored God in the profound silence of its terrible anguish. Truly, I have never felt such an intense grief nor has my spirit ever received so heavy a blow. My sorrow is greater than I could ever express. It seems as though everything serves to increase my weariness and cause me to regret. The only thing that is left to console me is to know that it is my God that has done this, or at least, has permitted this blow to fall. Alas! My heart is too weak to support this heavy burden. How it needs strength! Yes, my God, you put this beautiful soul into the world; now you have taken him back. May your holy name be blessed. I don't know any other song except, "May the name of the Lord be blessed!"

My very dear brother and dear Father, my soul is filled with grief, but also full of the peace of God's will which I would never oppose with the least resistance. No, my dear Father, I affirm what it pleased God to do—to take away that great flame which lit up this miserable world and let it shine in the kingdom, as we truly believe. May the name of the Lord be blessed! God has chastised me as I deserved because I am certainly too insignificant to merit such a great blessing as well as the contentment that I had in seeing my soul held in the hands of such a great man of God.

I believe that God, in that supreme goodness, does not want me to take any more pleasure in this world. I don't want to take any more either except to hope to have the joy of seeing my dearest Father in the bosom of God's everlasting goodness. Yet I still will to remain in exile. Yes, my dear brother, I truly do. It's a terribly difficult exile for me, this miserable life. But I want to stay here, as I said, as long as it is God's plan for me. I will let the Lord do with me as he wishes.

Remember me as well as this little family of the Visitation in your holy sacrifices. They are so sorrowful and suffer with such grace and resignation that I am consoled. We will leave here soon to go back to poor little Annecy. My pain will be redoubled by seeing our sisters there. God be blessed in and for everything. Long live the will and the pleasure of the Lord!

Letter to a Superior, Annecy, after 1623[24]

Take care, dearest daughter, not to dismiss the novice with the pulmonary disorder. What would our blessed Father say? "But she will die," you will reply. Well, wouldn't she die in the world? And wouldn't she be happy to die as a spouse of Jesus Christ? There is a postulant here at Annecy with the same illness, but she is certainly not being sent away because of it. "It's flesh and blood that gives such advice," our blessed Father used to say. He never wanted candidates to be sent away because of any physical infirmity unless they had a contagious disease. So let us be unyielding in this matter, holding on to what we have received from our holy founder. I know this is what you really want to do.

I promise you, I do not choose the most capable or most virtuous sisters to be superiors. Rather, I choose those that I see have the God-given talent of governing well. I have put to the test those who are intelligent, attractive in the eyes of the world, and devout, as well as those who are genuinely holy. I found that neither kind was successful unless they learned how to govern and had the true humility, prudence, and sincerity that the institute calls for. But if they had these virtues, even if they had other imperfections which I saw they were trying to overcome, I didn't hesitate to put them in charge. This is what our holy Father did, with the hope God would bless them. Still, he did look at the external talents of those whom we thought of making superiors so that, as he put it, they might satisfy and attract secular persons.

Your answer to the archbishop is fine, except for this. Instead of submitting to an infringement of this point in the constitution if he ordered it, you should have asked him very humbly to let you continue the practice which obliges you to show your accounts to the ecclesiastical superior every year when he asks to receive them, or to the one making the visitation, but not to anyone else. This is an obligation of the Rule.

My dearest sister, we must—in all humility—resolve to maintain our observances. Otherwise, if we break down on one point, then all the rest will be dissipated. Let us be obedient toward our ecclesiastical superiors in everything that they ask as long as it is not contrary to our institute. Let us always be faithful to our founder's recommendations. Our ecclesiastical superiors are there only to see that we observe our Rule, not to destroy it. What would happen if each one of these superiors wanted to make changes? It would soon look very different. Dearest, let us be constant in our fidelity. Once small irregularities creep in, the big ones follow. Our holy founder so often advised us not to fail in any detail or soon we would lose everything.

...As for people making fun of us, that won't last. I am not worthy of such suffering. But we should be careful not to bring any ridicule on ourselves.

I greet all your dear daughters, but especially the older sisters. May God keep each of us according to his heart.

Letter to Mother Marie-Adrienne Ficher, Superior at Rumilly, Annecy, 1627[25]

...As for your temptations, pay no attention to them, and do whatever is necessary to keep your mind off them. These efforts, though forceful, must reflect moderation. You see, dear, the way by which you are being led is at once mild yet strong and solid. God hides the prize of eternal glory in our mortifications and in the victory over ourselves, which we always strive for with great gentleness. Otherwise, your impulsiveness would cause you—and others—to suffer. In the end, gentleness plays a large part in the way we govern. Every day I notice that kindness, gentleness, and support, as well as generosity, can do much for souls. You know that God has given me a very special love for your house. It seems to me that it is like a dormitory annex of Annecy.

So people are talking, are they, saying that your house is unlucky because you have had so much misfortune.[26] That's the language of the world! God speaks quite a different one. It is a great mark of God's blessing when a house is stricken with some tribulation or other which does not offend our Lord. Death of the sisters is an example of this. It is not bad luck, but the contrary, for God is glorified by this sorrow because these dear souls have gone to heaven to praise God forever.

Furthermore, be more and more careful that your corrections are not too harsh, for that would be neither beneficial nor useful. Those who are responsible for others cannot always say with St. Paul (sic): "I am innocent of your blood," that is, of the faults his people were committing. We, on the other hand, are usually guilty, as much for the faults of others as for our own, either because we overcorrected or tolerated too much. Or else we corrected too harshly or neglected to correct; or we failed to include in our correction the sweetness of holy charity.

Dearest, here is the money for the new habit which you sent me, and please, send me back the one which the sisters kept. There is nothing that bothers me more than their attachment to these external signs of imaginary holiness in me. These are traps which the devil puts in my way to make me stumble into the bottomless pit of pride. I am already weak enough, and enough of a stumbling block to myself, without anyone adding another. So I beg all of you not to be an occasion of such temptation for me. If anyone has anything belonging to me, do me the kindness of burning it. If only our sisters would treat me as I deserve to be treated before God, then I would have some hope of becoming, through these humiliations, what they imagine me to be. But to be presenting me with continual temptations to vanity is intolerable. This brings sadness to my heart and tears to my eyes as I tell it to you.

Dear ______ and ______ seem to be happy to have to bear so many external humiliations. For this, I love them even more, and believe them to be even greater in the sight of God whose judgment is so different from ours.

Letter to Mother Marie-Aimée de Rabutin, Superior at Thonon, Annecy, 1639[27]

My dearest daughter,

...Concerning the lack of gentleness that you show your sisters when they bother you for trifles, you know that you must not behave in this way. The superior has a duty to listen to and answer all who wish to speak to her. After you have listened to the sisters, you may point out to them that what they say is either trivial or useless. But you must not guard your privacy so jealously that the sisters don't dare approach you except for very important matters.

About those souls who are somewhat difficult, I can't tell you anything more on the subject. You'll have to handle them according to whatever light God gives you, and not torment yourself so much by wondering if you're the cause of their failures. Please, don't tell me about this all over again, and don't think about it so much. Must you continue to be your own cross? I can see that no matter which way God leads you, you change everything into bitterness and trouble for yourself by constantly examining yourself and brooding over everything.

For the love of God, stop behaving like this. You gave your whole being to God and surrendered yourself to the care of the Lord. Stay that way and replace all this self-scrutiny with a pure and single glance at God's goodness. In that glance, let all your fears and introspections die. I can't help repeating this and telling you that, really, if you don't stop being so hard on yourself and despairing over all your problems, I won't answer you again. I see you wallowing in your misery and choosing to make yourself a martyr!

Letter to a Priest, August 14, 1634[28]

My very honored and most dear Father,

Well, my dear Father, I see you have fallen into the condition where I've always feared your great fervor would bring you. Even so, you tell me that you're afraid of flattering yourself, yet do not fear enough your own fears....

All God wants is our heart. God is more pleased when we value our uselessness and weakness out of love and reverence for the Lord's will than when we do violence to ourselves and perform great works of penance. Now, you know that the peak of perfection lies in our wanting to be what God wishes us to be. So, having given you a delicate constitution, the Lord expects you to take care of it and not demand of it what he—in his gentleness—does not ask for. Accept this fact. What God, in his goodness, asks of you is not this excessive zeal which has reduced you to your present condition. God asks a calm, peaceful uselessness, a resting near with no special attention or action of the understanding or will, except a few words of love or of faithful, simple surrender, spoken softly, effortlessly, without the least desire to find consolation or satisfaction in them. If you put that into practice, my dear Father, in peace and tranquillity of mind, I promise you, it will please God more than anything else you might do.

Just one more word. Do believe me when I say that instead of spending four or five hours on your knees, you should try just one hour—a quarter of an hour after rising; another in preparation for holy Mass; the same in thanksgiving; and a short quarter of an hour for the evening examination of conscience. That's enough! Try, for the love of God, to restore your former strength by getting enough rest, physically and mentally, and by taking plenty of good nourishing food. This I beg of you, my dear beloved Father, by all that you hold most dear in heaven and on earth. If it weren't that I felt impelled to request this, I wouldn't be writing to you so soon. I hope that in the great kindness and fatherly affection that you have for us—for our consolation—you will not neglect to do whatever you can to regain your health.

NOTES

1. In 1456 Pope Callistus III reversed the decision of the Court of Inquisition and declared Joan of Arc "blessed." Benedict XV declared her a saint in 1920 with a feast on May 30.

2. Bérulle, *Grandeurs de Jesus*, discourse 2. *Oeuvres complètes*, ed. Migne (Paris: Migne, 1856) 181ff., 1161ff.

3. *Introduction à la vie chrétienne*, ch. 8, in *Oeuvres complètes de M. Olier* (Paris: Migne, 1856).

4. Olier, *Journée chrétienne*, part 2, end, in *Oeuvres complètes de M. Olier* (Paris: Migne, 1856).

5. Michael de la Bedoyere, *The Archbishop and the Lady: The Story of Fénelon and Madame Guyon* (New York: Pantheon, 1956).

6. Natalie Davis, "City Women and Religious Change," in *Society and Culture in Early Modern France* (Stanford: Stanford University Press, 1975) 65–95.

7. A well-written source for this is Wendy Wright, *Bond of Perfection* (New York: Paulist Press, 1985).

8. This is quoted in ibid. 208; see her citation, 239 n. 6.

9. Francis de Sales, Jane de Chantal, *Letters of Spiritual Direction*, trans. Péronne Marie Thibert, V.H.M. (New York: Paulist Press, 1988). Letters of St. Francis de Sales, *Oeuvres*, 12, 352–70. Letter 234. 130 n. 65. The full text of the letter can be found on 130–43. Subsequent letters will be from Thibert's translation and citation, indicated as *LSD* and page number.

10. The citation is from Ps 115:3; Ps 135:6.

11. Psalm 73:26 (or Ps 72:26 in the Vulgate translation).

12. Exod 12:10.

13. Gen 3:1–6.

14. Matt 4:10, 7.

15. The discipline was a form of self-inflicted wounds from a knotted metallic instrument that resembled the scourging whip, although on a much smaller scale.

16. Celse Bénigne was Jane's young son whose piety was admired by Francis de Sales.

17. *Sa Vie et ses oeuvres*, 4, 390–91. Letter 236, *LSD* 210.

18. *Sa Vie et ses oeuvres*, 4, 401–4. Letter 243, *LSD* 211–13.

19. M. Coulon oversaw Françoise's estate.

20. Foretz was Françoise's property.

21. *Sa Vie et ses oeuvres*, 8, 542. Letter 1,764, *LSD* 264.

22. *Sa Vie et ses oeuvres*, 8, 556–57. Letter 1,872, *LSD* 264–65.

23. *Sa Vie et ses oeuvres*, 5, *Lettres* 2, 90–92, *LSD* 76.

24. *Sa Vie et ses oeuvres*, 6, 47–49. Letter 784, *LSD* 252–53.

25. *Sa Vie et ses oeuvres*, 7, 49–51. Letter 1185 *LSD* 253.

26. At this time in 1623 many sisters in the young, struggling community of Rumilly drowned on September 29, 1625, and many were stricken with a long and dangerous illness.

27. *Sa Vie et ses oeuvres*, 8, 154–56. Letter 1,212, *LSD* 255–56.

28. *Sa Vie et ses oeuvres*, 8, 192–95. Letter 1341 *LSD* 194.

BIBLIOGRAPHY

de Chantal, Jeanne-Françoise. *St. Francis de Sales: A Testimony by St. Chantal*. Translated by Elisabeth Stopp. London: Faber and Faber, 1967.

de Chantal, Jeanne-Françoise. *The Spirit of Sister Jane Frances de Chantal as Seen in Her Letters*. Translated by the Sisters of the Visitation, Harrow on the Hill. New York: Longmans, Green, 1922.

de Chantal, Jeanne-Françoise. *The Spiritual Life: A Summary of the Instructions on the Virtues and on Prayer, Compiled from the Writings of St. Jane Frances de Chantal.* Sisters of the Visitation, Harrow on the Hill. London: Sands, 1928.

de la Bedoyere, Michael. *The Archbishop and the Lady: The Story of Fénelon and Madame Guyon.* New York: Pantheon, 1956.

de Sales, Francis. *Introduction to the Devout Life.* Translated by John K. Ryan. New York: Doubleday, 1982.

de Sales, Francis, and Jeanne-Françoise de Chantal. *Letters of Spiritual Direction.* Translated by Péronne Marie Thibert, V.H.M. New York: Paulist Press, 1988.

Stopp, Elisabeth. *Madame de Chantal: Portrait of a Saint.* Westminster, Md.: Newman, 1963.

Wright, Wendy. *Bond of Perfection.* New York: Paulist Press, 1985.

– 16 –

SOJOURNER TRUTH

(c. 1797–1883)

They All Know Jesus! I Am So Happy!

Sojourner Truth was born in Hurley, New York, approximately twenty-one years after the beginning of the American Revolution. She was born to James and Betsey, slaves who worked on the estate of Colonel Hardenbergh of Hurley. James and Betsey named this ninth child of theirs Isabella. James, a tall and stately man, was given the name of Bonnetree because of his height and straight posture. Betsey was affectionately called Mama Betts by the children of the Hardenbergh estate. Isabella was called Belle by those who knew her. Because slaves were given the name of their current master, Isabella was called Belle Hardenbergh at this point in her life.

By the time Belle was born, her older brothers and sisters had either died or been sold to other slave owners, with the exception of her three-year-old brother, Peter. Belle's first memories as a child were of her mother making the children solemnly promise that they would never steal or lie, because "God" was there to help when they felt desperate. Betsey taught her children African songs and the Lord's Prayer in Low Dutch, the language spoken in the Hardenbergh household. Belle learned a little about her brothers and sisters from her parents' stories that recounted the great sadness of the day each child was auctioned away.

Master Hardenbergh died when Belle was a very small child. She remembered only very little about his death, except that the other slaves were talking about their next master. She did recall that Charles Hardenbergh, son of Master Hardenbergh, was respected for his kindness to the slaves. James, Betsey, and their children Peter and Belle stayed to work for Master Charles. James had two former wives who had been sold by other masters; he was relieved that Betsey, Belle, and Peter could stay together a while longer.

Charles Hardenbergh, the new master, allowed the slaves to stay in the basement quarters underneath the large house he had built for himself. This unheard of kindness to slaves was very appreciated by them. Twentieth-century readers may not consider this such a good deed when they read the description of the place:

> The space beneath the loose boards of the floor and the uneven earth below was often filled with mud and water. The uncomfortable splashings of this were as annoying as the noxious vapors were chilling and fatal to health... both sexes and all ages slept on those damp boards, like the horse, with a little straw and a blanket.[1]

In time, Charles Hardenbergh decided to sell Belle's brother, Peter. Peter was only four years old at the time. A sister who was the tenth child and who was younger than Belle would be sold at the same time. Belle was young but old enough to remember the cold, New York winter day on which her brother and sister were sold:

> A large, old-fashioned sleigh was seen to drive up to the door.... This event was noticed with childish pleasure by the unsuspecting boy. But when he was taken and put into the sleigh, and saw his little sister actually shut and locked up in the sleigh box, his eyes were at once opened... like a frightened deer, he sprang from the sleigh and, running into the house, concealed himself under a bed. But this availed him little. He was reconveyed to the sleigh and separated forever from those whom God had constituted his natural guardians and protectors.[2]

Master Charles Hardenbergh died after a debilitating illness in 1808. His heirs decided to sell the estate and its holdings. They decided at the same time to free James for his years of faithful service. They also freed Betsey so that she could take care of James, who was much older, as well as arthritic and sickly. The strangers who purchased the estate allowed James and Betsey to stay in the basement if they wished. Meanwhile, the plot of land that the old master, Colonel Hardenbergh, had left to them, provided a small amount of money and food for their survival in old age.

Belle was now eleven years old, mature for her age, a good worker, and very healthy. It was clear that she would bring a good price on the auction block. As Belle related her story to her autobiographer, she remembered her fear at the reality of being sold. After the auction, she was dragged away by a new master with only a brief moment allowed to embrace her mother and utter a brief goodbye to her father. As she walked past her father, he whispered that she wasn't going too far and he would come to see her. James was getting used to saying good-byes to his children, painful as it was.

Belle's new owner, John Neeley, was unaware that Belle knew only Low Dutch. He and his wife spoke English and assumed that any slave would know the language spoken in their household. Belle recalled that she was most confused by this strange mixture of words and received constant beatings for "laziness" and "disobedience." After one exceptionally severe night beating by John Neeley, Belle decided that she would escape at the first opportunity she could find. She asked the God of her early childhood, the "God in the sky," to make her father come to see her so she could get his advice on her plan.

It was almost a year after she was sold before her father ever came. By this time James could hardly walk. He had to find someone who would be kind enough to come with a sleigh—at a price—to get him to Belle. Mrs. Neeley, the woman of the house, did not let the two visit alone. Belle couldn't say what she wanted to say until she and her father took the short walk to the sleigh that enabled their conversation to be unheard. It was during these brief minutes that she burst into tears and pleaded with her father to find another master to buy her. James promised he would do his best for her. Simple as this promise was, it did bring Belle a glimmer of hope in a hopeless situation.

For weeks after her daily work was over, she walked to the precise place where her father had made the promise. Since the winter snows were still holding fast, she could walk in the remains of the large footprints of James that were left in the snows. Then the snows melted, the spring came, and she could no longer walk in the hopeful footprints that were tied to the promise.

It was still spring in New York State when Belle heard a kind voice ask, "Would you like to come with me?" The kind voice belonged to Martin Schryver who had just paid $105 for her. Martin had known Belle's father. He informed Belle that, at her father's urging, he had purchased her to work on his farm and occasionally in his tavern. Belle was treated so well by Martin and his wife that she thought even the "freedom" being discussed by some of the slaves could not be much better than this experience.

She was only thirteen at this time but was already six feet tall, resembling her father's side of the family. Unfortunately for Belle and for Martin, times became tough for him. One day while Belle was working in the tavern, she overheard Martin's wife talking with a customer about Belle's industriousness. It was only a few minutes later into the conversation when Belle heard Mr. Dumont, the customer, send for Martin. Dumont was prepared to give Martin a profit for Belle. He would offer $310 for this hardworking slave. Mrs. Schryver urged Martin to consider the profit. He gave in to her demands and sold Belle, much to Belle's dismay.[3]

Mr. Dumont, the new master, was kind to Belle. He was very happy with her hard work and eventually assigned her to work in the house rather than in the fields. His wife disliked Belle, however. Although Mrs. Dumont did allow her to receive messages from her parents, she refused to let her visit them on her days off. Finally, Belle was given permission to see her parents when it was clear that her mother was dying. She finally found a way to get to her father's house. He met her on the way to tell her that her mother had died. James was almost blind and penniless by this time. Once Betsey died, he had no one to care for him.

Years later, Sojourner Truth described parting from her father that day. "Oh, how he cried! Aloud like a child. Poor old man. I remember his cry as if it were yesterday."[4]

In 1817, seven years after Belle had begun working for the Dumonts, New York State declared that any slave who was forty years old or older could be freed. New York also decreed that all slaves must be given their freedom in 1827. This caused great excitement among the slave population. For Belle, who was only twenty, ten years seemed like a long time to wait for freedom.

At the same time, her life at the Dumont estate became much happier because of a strong young man named Bob. Bob was a slave from the adjoining estate who befriended her, shared her hope for freedom, and came to see her often. The two grew to love each other. Bob's English owner, Mr. Catlin, was afraid that Bob might marry Belle and then try to escape to freedom with her. Like most other slave owners, Catlin made his slaves marry each other so that their offspring would enlarge his work force, since the master owned the children of slaves as well as the slaves.

Catlin forbade Bob to continue seeing Belle, but older slaves protected Bob and Belle's secret meetings in a number of ways. Bob continued to come to the Dumont estate in the late hours of the night and into the early morning. Belle and Bob grew in their love for each other.

Mr. Catlin suspected that Bob was still seeing Belle. While in town one day, Mr. Dumont, Belle's owner, overheard a conversation between Catlin's men. The men said that they were going to "stalk" Bob to catch him in the act of seeing Belle. This would give them better status with their master. It was already late at night, so Dumont decided to get back to his estate to warn Belle and Bob of the danger that the night's meeting held.

Before Dumont could get home, Catlin's men had caught Bob on Dumont's property. Dumont arrived only after Bob had been severely beaten in the head and back with hard canes. Catlin's men had forced Belle, along with other awakened slaves, to watch the bloody beating that almost cost Bob his life. By the time Dumont arrived and demanded that the beating stop, it was too late. Although Dumont did not allow any beating of slaves on his property, Bob was not "his property." Bob was carried away, close to dead, and Belle never saw him again.

In the shock of being forced to witness the beating of someone she loved, all that Belle could remember was that Bob uttered only one word during the beating. It was the name "Jesus." Belle did not remember ever hearing that name. She could only remember her mother teaching her children the words of an "Our Father" and believing in some God "in heaven" above the stars.

Belle wondered who this "Jesus" could be that meant so much to Bob. She never again saw Bob to ask him. On the Dumont estate Belle was told to marry Tom, an older slave who wanted a wife. There was little choice in the matter when a master wanted a marriage. Belle and Tom soon had three children in three years. The children were named Diana, Peter, and Hannah. Elizabeth and baby Sophia came within the next three years.

Peter was especially bright and charming. Mr. Dumont told Belle he would sell Peter to a gentleman who would see to it that Peter was educated and brought up like a son in the family. Since Peter was Belle's only son, she was heartbroken. Dumont tried to make the action less offensive. He promised Belle that she could have her freedom one year before New York law would officially allow her to go free. He also promised that she and Tom would be given a small house on the estate in which to raise their remaining four daughters.

Belle worked hard all year in anticipation of the freedom that was to be hers in 1826. Like other masters before him, however, Mr. Dumont did not consider it unjust to break his promise to a slave and did not free her in 1826. Belle decided that God in the heavens would help her to escape, for she had kept her promise to work hard for the master. Belle decided to take only baby Sophia with her as she tried her escape from the Dumont estate. She knew the other slaves would care for her remaining children and so would Tom. She also knew that if she told Tom of her plans, he would tell the master.

In the darkness of night, Belle and Sophia fled through woods to the house of a lawyer named Levy Rowe. Belle had heard that this lawyer was a strong abolitionist. From the description of other slaves, she knew his house was on the escape path in the woods. When she arrived there, she was told to come in. Levy Rowe was ill and bedridden, but he told his servants to direct Belle and Sophia to the Von Wageners, a Quaker couple who purchased slaves and then set them free.

This couple arose from bed early in the morning and welcomed Belle and Sophia warmly. The Von Wageners fed them and then put them to bed. The next morning Dumont appeared, demanding the return of Belle and Sophia. Because Belle had worked for him for sixteen years, she was worth a great price. Mr. Von Wagener settled the issue by buying Belle:

> I'm not in the habit of buying and selling slaves. Slavery is wrong and I'll have no part of it. But rather than have thee take the mother and child back, let me buy her services from thee for the rest of the year. She'll be lost to thee in any case come next July.[5]

Belle was sold for twenty dollars and Sophia for five dollars. Within a year Belle would be legally free. Thus, Dumont was satisfied and left. When Belle turned to address Mr. Von Wagener to thank him and to call him "master," the new owner told her to never to call him "master." There was only one master in the house, and that was Jesus Christ. Belle and Sophia were told to join the family at the table and not to wait on them, for they were all one family in Jesus. Belle learned some things about this Jesus whom Bob had named while he was being beaten. At the same time, she was afraid to ask too many questions since she was still technically a slave.

Belle had only been in the Von Wagener household for a few months when she became homesick for her children, her husband, and the other slaves. It was close to Pentecost. On the Christian estates, Pentecost was an event that the slaves were used to celebrating for a week. This celebration meant that the slaves were free from duties for that time.[6]

As if he could sense Belle's desire, Dumont arrived at the Von Wagener's to see if Belle wanted to come back to his estate for the weeklong celebration. She decided that she would like to do so. All was arranged between the Von Wageners and the Dumonts. Mr. Dumont himself drove the wagon to pick her up and take her back to his estate for the festivities.

The day came for the return, and Belle made her way to the waiting wagon. It was at this moment that she received her first revelation of the light. The God she hardly knew but prayed to when things were not going well "saw" her with "a look" she could never forget.

It was "with the suddenness of a flash of lightning, showing her in the twinkling of an eye... that there was no place that God was not."[7] She wished she could hide from the gaze of God, but where could she flee? She was now aware of her sins and afraid that God might give her another such "look" and she would be extinguished. She could no longer talk to God as she had before, for she had imagined God to be another person like herself. A great chasm opened up between herself and God. She wished that God would let someone stand between her sinful self and God and speak for her. When she returned to herself, she saw that Dumont had gone, for some time had passed. She returned to the house.

She tried to go back to work, but the moving experience drew her back inside herself. Soon it seemed that a friend appeared and stood between herself and the deity. This "friend" was not really recognizable to the sight, however. Belle asked herself if it was her friend Deencia? Upon a closer look, Belle decided it was not. Then the vision brightened into a distinct form that beamed with the beauty of holiness and radiant love. Belle felt that she should know the form but she could not put a name on it:

> I know you and I don't know you.... You seem perfectly familiar; I feel that you not only love me, but that you always have loved me—yet I know you not—I cannot call you by name.[8]

When she said, "I know you," the vision remained calm. When she said, "I don't know you," the subject of the vision became agitated and restless. Belle remembered that she was afraid to have the vision cease, for it was so invigorating. So she kept saying, "I know you." Finally, she felt the cry of her whole heart, her whole person, begging to know who this was. An answer came distinctly to her saying, "Jesus." "Yes," she responded. "It is Jesus!"[9]

Belle recalled that after this encounter the world seemed a different place. This "Jesus" was so lovely and powerful. How she wished she could see him again. But she was not sure where to look. She watched for his bodily appearance among her friends. Maybe she could go to live with him. At the time she did not wish to speak of this "Jesus" to any other. She was afraid that others with greater status might take him from her. After all, she was only a slave woman and an uneducated one at that. She did not at that time believe Jesus to be God, for then "how could he stand between me and God? I saw him as a friend, standing between me and God, through whom love flowed like a fountain."[10]

Years later Belle described her conversion to many groups of people. She recalled that when things were going well, she'd give up praying. When things were going badly, she'd remember to ask God for help. But she did not meet God until the night when she was going toward the wagon, and after that meeting she received insight into the meaning of love:

> Then, all of a sudden, it (the vision) stopped, and I said, "There's the white folks that have abused you, and beat you, and abused your people—think of them!" But then there came another rush of love through my soul and I cried out loud—"Lord, Lord, I can love even the white folks!" Honey, I just walked around and around in a dream. Jesus loved me; I knew it! I felt it! Jesus was my Jesus. Jesus would love me always. I didn't dare tell nobody. It was my great secret. Everything had been taken from me that I ever had. I thought that if I let the white folks know about this, maybe they'd take him away too.[11]

In her later life as Belle told the story of her conversion experience, her Christian listeners found it hard to believe that she had never heard about Jesus Christ. Belle's response was always logical enough. She had never heard any Christian preacher in her days as a slave. She had never been allowed to go to the "campground meetings" like some of the other slaves. So when she heard the name of Jesus from Bob's lips or the lips of others, she thought he was like another Lafayette.

It was after her vision that she finally attended a campground meeting. Here at this Methodist gathering she was surprised to find out that her secret "Jesus" was known by others:

> There was a Methodist meeting somewhere in our parts, and I went. They got up and began to tell their experiences. The first one began to speak. I was startled, because the man had told about Jesus. "Why," I said to myself, "that man's found him too!" And another got up and spoke. I said, "He's found him too!" And finally I said, "Why, they all know him!" I was so happy![12]

Belle's happiness was aided by the emancipation of slaves in New York State on July 4, 1827. New York emancipated all male slaves who were twenty-eight or over and all female slaves who were twenty-five or over. The Von Wageners conducted a small religious ceremony for Belle and Sophia in their home. Belle wished to stay on with them because she had no other place to go. The Von Wageners were also willing to help her find her son, Peter, who had been taken from her when he was still a very young child.

With the help of friends and the Quaker community, Peter was finally found in Alabama. He had been illegally sold out of New York State. The hearing of the case was placed in an Alabama court. Belle went south after giving her daughter to the slaves at the Dumont place to care for in her absence. She worked in Alabama to make money to partially pay a lawyer. Her Quaker friends assisted her in this.

When she finally located Peter, she discovered that he had been treated as a son by the man who raised him. The court gave Peter back to Belle, but Peter had to be forcibly taken away from the master he loved. The man was gracious to Belle in spite of his great sadness at losing Peter.

Belle returned to the Von Wagener estate with Peter. On the first night that she saw the scars and welts on Peter's body from neck to thighs, she was angrier than she had ever been. When she could ask Peter about the beatings, she heard the tales simply told. "Sometimes I crawled under a stool to hide, my blood running all over me and my back stickin' to the boards. And sometimes Miss Liza would come and grease my sores when everyone was asleep."[13] As Belle tried to remember how she accidentally met the lawyer Romeyne, who was so essential to her getting her son back, she recalled that a stranger on the road had told her exactly where to go and what to say. The more she tried to remember the face, the surer she became that the stranger on the road had been Jesus.

Like other young men helped by the Von Wageners, Peter got a job not far from their estate. Meanwhile, Belle had met a woman at the Methodist church she now attended. This woman, Miss Geer, was a schoolteacher from New York City, who was returning there in the fall. Miss Geer invited Belle and Peter to come with her, their passage paid, so that Peter could attend school in New York. At the time, there were no schools for black people in Hurley. Miss Geer promised to pay Peter's tuition and to have one of her friends hire Belle for good wages. In late summer 1829, Belle, Peter, and Miss Geer went to New York City.

In New York, Belle joined a Methodist church for a time. Then she joined the African Zion Church. Eventually she joined the Zion Hill community, a Christian communal group that did missionary work with prostitutes in New York. The Zion Hill group were charged with "financial scams" that resulted in the group's members being arrested. When other members were brought to trial with Belle, they implicated her as the instigator of all the criminal activity, although she never knew anything about it.

Meanwhile, Peter found companions in New York who were not for his good. He was constantly in trouble, skipping school, spending any money he had, and unable to keep a job. A man named Mr. Williams took Peter and other disadvantaged boys under his care. Peter borrowed money from Mr. Williams that he never intended to pay back. Belle was mortified when she heard what Peter had done. Although Peter was always "repentant," he kept drifting from job to job and was constantly in and out of jail.

It seemed to Belle that Peter's only hope for maturity was to sign up on a merchant ship. This would at least enable him to stay out of prison. Belle went to the pier to see Peter off on his first voyage in 1839. She heard from him a year later. Since she could neither read nor write, her employer, Mr. Whiting, read the letter to her:

> My dear and beloved mother,
>
> I take this opportunity to write to you and to inform you that I am well and in hopes to find you the same. I am got on board the same unlucky ship, Zone of Nantucket. I am sorry for to say that I have been punished once severely, for shoving my head in the fire for other folks. I would like to know how my sisters are. I wish you could write me an answer as soon as possible. I am your son that is so far from your home in the wide, briny ocean. Mother, I hope you do not forget me, your dear and only son. I hope you all will forgive me for what I have done.
>
> Your son, Peter Von Wagener[14]

Belle had Mr. Whiting write Peter immediately. Nonetheless, Peter wrote more than five letters in three years, each time claiming he had received no reply from Belle. Mr. Whiting wrote back immediately after each letter came, but for some reason they never were given to Peter. After 1841, Belle received no more letters from Peter, nor did any of the family ever see him again.

In 1843, Belle was washing the floors for Mrs. Whiting when she felt a clear call come to her. She had been getting strong feelings for some time that God wished her to do something else with her life. But it was not until June 1, 1843, that the message became clear, telling her that she was to stop working as a servant for others and become a servant of the Lord. Belle did not know exactly what kind of work God was calling her to do, but she did know it would involve speaking the truth to people. God had shown her the truth, so she must share it with others. She asked where she should go, and the answer was simply, "East."[15]

With twenty-five cents, a loaf of bread, and some cheese carried in a pillowcase, Belle told the Whitings good-bye and headed east toward Brooklyn. Belle, now forty-six, was not sure where she was going. She took the ferry to Brooklyn and kept walking east down sandy roads through cornfields and never looked back. She knew the Lord would give her direction in this pilgrimage:

> In my wretchedness I said, "Oh, God, give me a name with a handle to it. Oh, that I had a name with a handle!" And it came to me at that same moment, like a voice as true as God is true: "Sojourner Truth." And my heart leaped for joy—Sojourner Truth. "Why," I said, "thank you, God. That is a good name. Thou art my last Master and thy name is Truth. So shall Truth be my last name until I die."[16]

Sojourner walked east as she had been told. She came to Long Island, staying in sheds for the night. She eventually came upon a camp meeting that had thousands of families in attendance. They shared their food with her as they listened to anyone who would care to speak. Sojourner stood to tell them about her conversion to Jesus. Then she concluded with a song, and many stopped to talk with her. Although she had never learned to read, she could quote the Bible at length from having heard it read. She decided to memorize all the Bible said about Jesus so that she could be of more help to others looking for him. She traveled and preached widely on the East Coast, working if people needed help, and taking only food and lodging for her preaching. Her reputation grew quickly and so did her audiences, white and black.

The abolitionist movement was gaining supporters across the country, so it became a favorite topic of many camp meetings as well. At one such meeting in Northampton, Massachusetts, a number of young white men threatened to attack any black preacher, and especially any black woman, who dared to address the audience. Sojourner was frightened by the threats and felt like running away, as some advised her to do to avoid violence. She decided that God would protect her, for she was a servant trying to please her God. She came forth from the common hiding place and walked toward the open fields of the campground:

> Sojourner walked some thirty rods to the top of a small rise of ground, commenced to sing in her most fervid manner, with all the strength of her most powerful voice, the hymn of the resurrection of Christ.... All who have ever heard her sing this hymn will probably remember it as long as

they remember her. The hymn, the tune, the style, are too closely associated with her to be easily separated from herself; when sung in one of her most animated moods, in the open air, with the utmost strength of her powerful voice, it must have been truly thrilling.

As she commenced to sing, the young men made a rush toward her, and she was immediately circled by a body of rioters, many of them armed with sticks or clubs as their weapons of defense, if not of attack. As the circle narrowed around her, she ceased singing, and after a short pause, inquired in a gentle but firm tone, "Why do you come about me with clubs and sticks? I am not doing harm to anyone." "We ain't going to hurt you, old woman; we came to hear you sing," cried many voices simultaneously. "Sing to us, old woman," cries one. "Talk to us, old woman," cries another. "Pray, old woman," says another. "Tell us your experience," says a fourth.

"You stand and smoke so near me, I cannot sing or talk," she answered. "Stand back," ordered several authoritative voices . . . the speakers declaring with an oath that they would knock down any person who would offer her the least indignity.

She looked about her, and with her usual discrimination, said inwardly, "Here must be many young men in all this assemblage, bearing within them hearts susceptible to good impressions. I will speak to them." She did speak and they silently heard and civilly asked many questions. It seemed to her that she was gifted at the time with truth and wisdom beyond herself. Her speech had operated on the roused passions of the mob like oil on agitated waters. They were, as a whole, entirely subdued, and only clamored when she ceased to speak or sing. . . . They kindly assisted her to mount a wagon from which she spoke and sang to them about an hour. Of all she said to them on this occasion, she remembers only the following.

Well, there are two congregations on this ground tonight. It is written there shall be a separation of the sheep and the goats. The other preachers have the sheep. I have the goats. And I have a few sheep among the goats, but they are very ragged! This produced great laughter. . . .

Children, I have talked and sung to you as you asked me. . . . If I sung one more hymn for you, will you then go away and leave this night in peace? . . . I want you all to answer! She reiterated the words once again. "Yes, yes, yes!" came from the mouths of the entire mob. "Amen! It is sealed," repeated Sojourner in the deepest and most solemn tones of her powerful and sonorous voice. Its effect ran through the multitude like an electric shock. . . . Before she concluded her song, she saw them turn from her and in the course of a few minutes, they were running as fast as they could in a solid body.[17]

In June 1843, Belle heard a strong inner voice urging her to change her name to "Sojourner" and to start her journey. She began walking through Long Island and Connecticut without knowing anything more than her inner voice dictated. She preached about love wherever she went, attended varieties of church gatherings and religious meetings, and depended on the goodness of people for daily necessities.

It did not take long for her reputation to precede her coming. In Massachusetts William Lloyd Garrison and Frederick Douglass made it a point to meet her. They invited her to join with them as they traveled to promote the abolitionist cause. On one of her travels Sojourner met Olive Gilbert, who convinced Sojourner that a narrative of Sojourner's life would be of interest to many people. It would be among the first narratives about a freed woman slave. Sojourner agreed when Olive told her that she could use the money made from her book to support herself. Olive wrote what Sojourner narrated and saw to it that *The Narrative of Sojourner Truth* was published in 1850.[18]

The year 1850 was also the year in which the Fugitive Slave Law was passed. This law now allowed marshals to hunt down any runaway slaves and return them to their masters. The slave was not allowed to give any self-testimony. Even freed slaves could be arrested without warrant or trial and sent back to masters who felt they had more work coming from them. The abolitionists considered this a step backward in the fight for human rights.

In summer of that same year the first women's rights meeting was held in Worcester, Massachusetts. Sojourner was one of the delegates chosen to represent the state of Massachusetts. The meeting was the subject of much ridicule, both by the public press and by the mainline churches. It was referred to as a meeting of hens who were mistakenly "trying to crow." The topic for the meeting was not only women's rights but the broader issue of human rights for all. Although the meeting drew more ridicule than positive public attention, those who attended were inspired to commit themselves to spreading the theories of freedom that so many were denied.

In August 1850, Frances Gage and her husband encouraged Sojourner Truth to attend a women's rights meeting in Akron, Ohio. They were aware of the long trip that would be required for Sojourner, but friendship won out. Sojourner agreed to go and stay with her friends, attending the convention with Frances Gage, the convener. The Gages fought for years for the abolition of slavery and for women's rights. Their strong support of the gathering for women's rights drew much public publicity.

On the second day of the convention, ministers came from all over the Ohio Valley. Their presence was intimidating to many of the less well educated women, as was their assurance about what God intended for women. "Of course the Lord intended man to have the superior rights and privileges. Did not the

Lord make a man's intellect superior to that of a woman?" "Was not the Christ a man? Would not God—at that time—have given some token of his wish to have women equal if he had wished such a thing?" "According to the Bible, it was not man but woman who sinned by accepting the apple from the serpent. Was not that a proof of God's wish to make her inferior?"[19]

Whereas most were intimidated into silence by such assured and loud statements by the ministers, Sojourner slowly got to her feet and approached the altar, getting the acknowledgment to speak from the chairwoman, Frances Gage. Sojourner's resonant voice was easily heard by all in the church:

> Where there is so much racket, there must be something out of kilter. I think between the Negroes of the South and the women of the North—all talking about rights—the white men will be in a fix pretty soon. . . .
>
> That man over there . . . he says women need to be helped into carriages and lifted over ditches and to have the best everywhere. Nobody ever helps me into carriages, over mud puddles, or gets me any best place . . . and ain't I a woman?
>
> Look at me! (showing her strong arm) Look at my arm. I have ploughed, and I have planted, and I have gathered into barns. No man could beat me. And ain't I a woman?
>
> I could work as much and eat as much as any man—when I could get it—and bear the lash as well. And ain't I a woman? I have borne children and seen them sold into slavery, and when I cried out with a mother's grief, none but Jesus heard me. And ain't I a woman?
>
> He talks about intellect (pointing to a former speaker). What's intellect got to do with women's rights or black folks' rights? If my cup won't hold but a pint, and yours holds a quart, wouldn't you be mean not to let me have my little half-measure full?
>
> That little man in black there (pointing to another). He says women can't have as much rights as man because Christ wasn't a woman. . . . Where did your Christ come from? Where did he come from? From God and a woman.
>
> If the first woman God ever made was strong enough to turn the world upside down all alone, we women together ought to be able to turn it back and get it right side up again. And now that we are asking to do it, the men better let us. (She stooped to pick up the sunbonnet she had dropped at her feet, then turned to conclude in sweetness.) Obliged to you for hearing me.[20]

Sojourner joined Frederick Douglass in Salem, Ohio, in late summer at an anniversary convention of the Antislavery Society. The Fugitive Slave Law had caused immeasurable suffering to thousands of black people trying to flee to Canada and other havens. Douglass stunned the audience by his strong assertion that there was no hope for justice now unless they staged a bloody rebellion. This was a dramatic change from his former strategy for freedom. Sojourner could not accept this new aggressive and fiery abolitionist creed. She asked Frederick if he thought that God was dead, to which he did not reply. Sojourner's God was a God of peace, so she and Douglass would no longer travel together.[21]

Sojourner began a wide range of further addresses about the evils of slavery, of oppression of both white and black women, and of prejudice against darker-skinned blacks. She remembers that when she came to the Ohio Valley or to any crossroads, she would simply drop the reins and tell God to drive. She did not know how else she could get to whatever place God wished her to go next.[22]

Sojourner met Harriet Beecher Stowe in 1853. Harriet read parts of her book that was to be published soon as *Uncle Tom's Cabin*. Sojourner objected to the part of the book that seemed to indicate only those blacks with light skin were intelligent. The section was altered.

In 1857, Sojourner had enough money to buy a simple cabin in Battle Creek, Michigan. The cabin was near a spiritualist seminary. Many of Sojourner's Quaker friends were involved with spiritualism, a popular movement in North America at the time. The movement taught that it was the Spirit of God who gave gifts to individuals, men and women, slave and free. Consequently, whoever had gifts was encouraged to use them for the good of the community. Understandably the movement attracted a number of devout Christians from mainline churches. The spiritualists taught direct access to the divine, a teaching denounced by the more hierarchical churches. The spiritualist doctrine of the living communicating with the dead had many interpretations and became a source for various break-off groups whose practices were condemned by mainline churches.

Whether Sojourner ever became a member of this group or whether she simply accepted their generous hospitality on her travels is difficult to know. What is known is that her travels took her to groups of whites as well as to groups of blacks, to church conventions as well as to civil rights and abolitionist meetings, to former slave groups, and to Washington, D.C., where she met President Abraham Lincoln, who invited her to stay in that city. During her stay she helped former slaves living in camps around Washington to learn how to live as free people. She brought the attention of the courts to the practice of Maryland slaveholders kidnapping the children of freed slaves in the Washington, D.C., camps. She also assisted in the structuring of the Freedman's Hospital.[23]

In Washington, Sojourner consistently tested laws in her journey to freedom. During the Civil War, blacks could ride only in special "Jim Crow" streetcars. Whites often rode these cars if they were in a hurry. This meant that whites sat and blacks stood. It also meant that some conductors drove past waiting black people or tried to shut the door after the white people got on. Sojourner learned to push her way on, to sit without rising, and to cause a great stir when forced to do otherwise. She complained to the president and to a senator from Massachusetts about the abuses she experienced on the street railway. It did not take long for Congress to ban all segregated public transportation in Washington, D.C.

In 1865 Elizabeth Cady Stanton strongly encouraged Sojourner Truth to attend the Equal Rights Convention whose topic was black rights. Sojourner spoke eloquently at this convention and began to lobby for the idea of a black state. She petitioned President Grant for public land where the many blacks who lived in refugee camps could come without fear of retribution. That particular idea never materialized as it was conceived, but many blacks did move westward to Kansas and Missouri in the 1870s.

At the Equal Rights Convention of 1867 Sojourner was one of the official speakers. There was much dissension at the time because some wished to have a clear distinction made between the various rights issues. In spite of the Emancipation Proclamation of 1863, there was still disagreement among and within churches about membership of blacks in formerly white faith communities. Women's common roles in churches were still in providing support services and not leadership services, although there were a few exceptions. The call for voting rights was another part of the broad agenda, as well as the rights of black women in particular. It was about this latter topic that Sojourner was to speak to the group. Her address was typically straightforward:

> I want women to have their rights. In the courts, women have no right, no voice. No one speaks for the women. I wish women to have her own voice there among the pettifoggers. If that place is somehow not fit for a woman, then it must be unfit for men as well.
>
> I am above eighty years old. It is about time for me to be going now. I have been forty years a slave and forty years free. I wish I would be here for forty more years if it meant equal rights would come for all. I suppose I am kept here because there is something more that I should do. I suppose I am yet to help break the chain.
>
> I have done a great deal of work. I did as much as a man but did not get so much pay. I used to work in a field and bind grain, keeping up with the cradler. Men did no more than I did. Yet they got twice as much pay. . . . We women do as much. We eat as much. We want as much. I suppose I am about the only colored woman who goes about to speak for the colored women. I want to keep the water stirring now that there is a crack in the ice. What we women want is a little more money. You men know that you get twice as much as women, when you write or for whatever you do.

> When we get our rights, we shall not have to come to you for money, for then we shall have money in our own pockets, and maybe then you will even ask us for money. But you must help us until we get it. It is a good consolation to know that when we have got this battle once fought, we shall not be coming to you any more....
>
> I am glad to see that men are getting their rights. But I also want women to get their rights. While the water is stirring, I will step into the pool. Now there is a great stir about colored men getting their rights. It is time for women to step in the water and have theirs. I am sometimes told that, "Women ain't fit to vote. Why, don't you know that a woman had seven devils in her? And do you suppose that a woman is fit to run this nation?" Seven devils ain't of no account. A man had a legion in him! When the devils didn't know where to go, they asked that they might go into the swine. They thought that was as good a place as they came from. They didn't ask to go into the sheep—no, into the pig. The pig is the selfish beast fit for devils. Men are so selfish that they've gotten women's rights and their own. Yet, they refuse to give women their rights. They keep them all to themselves![24]

Sojourner's agenda from that point on would include women's suffrage in addition to the other human rights issues that she had fought for all her life. The majority of abolitionists at the convention, however, would not saddle their cause with women's rights. The black suffrage cause was unpopular enough without adding to it the even more unpopular cause of women's suffrage. Even Frederick Douglass, who was a staunch supporter of women's rights, refused to allow the joining of the two causes as one cause of "human rights."

Sojourner Truth was one of the few speakers at the convention who had experienced the double bias of being black and a woman. She refused to separate the issues of abolition of slavery, black suffrage, women's suffrage, and basic rights issues. Whenever and wherever she appeared, crowds of people would gather to hear her. She did not agree with her dear friend Frederick Douglass as he began to advocate rebellion among the blacks, even if it cost the lives of many. Sojourner understood Frederick's frustration, for the people had been patient for too long, but she insisted that God would move the hearts of good people to join blacks in the cause of dignity and justice. Although neither convinced the other, they stayed friends in spite of their differences on the way to go about furthering human rights.

In her travels around the country, Sojourner addressed more white audiences than black audiences in her attempts to get people to work together. Leaders of churches sent moving testimonial letters to other leaders of churches to welcome Sojourner Truth when she came their way. At one meeting at a Methodist

Episcopal church in New Lisbon, Ohio, she sang an original song to conclude the evening.

I am pleading for my people, a poor downtrodden race,
Who dwell in freedom's boasted land with no abiding place.

I am pleading that my people may have their rights restored,
For they have long been toiling, and yet had no reward.

They are forced the crops to culture, but not for them the yield.
Although both late and early, they labor in the field.

While I bear upon my body, the sores of many a gash,
I am pleading for my people who groan beneath the lash.

I am pleading for the mothers who gaze in wild despair
Upon the hated auction block, and see their children there.

I feel for those in bondage—well may I feel for them.
I know how fiendish hearts can be that sell their fellow men.

Yet those oppressors steeped in guilt—I still would have them live;
For I have learned of Jesus, to suffer and forgive!

I want no carnal weapons, no machinery of death.
For I love to not hear the sound of war's tempestuous breath.

I do not ask you to engage in death and bloody strife.
I do not dare insult my God by asking for their life.

But while your kindest sympathies to foreign lands do roam,
I ask you to remember your own oppressed at home.

I plead with you to sympathize with sighs and groans and scars,
And note how base the tyranny beneath the stripes and stars.[25]

Sojourner Truth actively traveled for the cause of human rights until 1880. Her friendships included some of the most prominent public figures of the century, many of whom had written in her Book of Life, a small book she always carried. As she sensed that people shared her vision of human dignity, she would ask them to sign her book of life. This book was a strong symbol of hope, especially in times when equality and dignity were denied to so many people.[26] In 1880, Sojourner returned to her small cabin in Battle Creek, Michigan, where she continued to enjoy the visits and letters of friends from around the world. She had hoped to live until she saw women obtaining the right to vote, but this was not to be.

In 1883, she became ill and was in great pain for many months. Sojourner thought she was too young to die, since she thought she was only in her eighties "somewhere." Friends claimed that she was 105 that year. Regardless of her real age, it became clear that she was in her last stages of life. One of her friends who came to visit during this period recalls asking her about her faith as death neared. "Sojourner, suppose there is no heaven. What will you say if you never get there?" "What will I say if I never get there? Why, I'll say, 'Bless the Lord! I had a good time thinking I'd get there!' "[27]

Sojourner Truth died quietly on November 26, 1883. She was buried in Oak Hill Cemetery in Battle Creek, accompanied to this final resting place by a long line of carriages. In time a white stone shaft, six feet high, would mark the grave. On the back a cross is formed by the letters, IN MEMORIAM, SOJOURNER TRUTH. On the front, the inscription reads:

Born a slave in Ulster County,
State of New York, in 18th Century.
Died in Battle Creek, Michigan,
November 26, 1883. Aged about 105 years.
"Is GOD DEAD?"[28]

NOTES

1. Sojourner Truth, *The Narrative of Sojourner Truth: A Bondswoman of Olden Times*, told to Olive Gilbert (Boston, 1850); published in Battle Creek, Mich., 1878. This was first published for the author. It was printed by Arno Press and the *New York Times* in 1968. The direct quotations included here are from the 1968 edition. The early memory cited here is on p. 14.

2. *Narrative* 16.

3. Jacqueline Bernard, *Journey toward Freedom: The Story of Sojourner Truth* (New York: Norton, 1967) 24–34.

4. Ibid. 39.

5. Ibid. 61.

6. Slaves in North America were free to celebrate major and minor festivals of the Catholic Church and the Church of England. Slaves were paid extra if they decided to work. Religionists generally agreed with Frederick Douglass that such times were essential safety valves for owners as well as slaves; see *Narrative* 63–64.

7. Ibid. 65.

8. Ibid. 67.

9. Ibid.

10. Ibid. 69.

11. Ibid. 159.

12. Ibid.

13. Bernard, *Journey* 82.

14. Ibid. 112.

15. *Narrative* 117.

16. Bernard, *Journey* 122.

17. *Narrative* 116–20.

18. This is a summary of Bertha Pauli, *Her Name Was Sojourner Truth* (New York: Avon, 1971) 150–62.

19. Bernard, *Journey* 164–65.

20. Ibid. 166–67.

21. Ibid. 167–68.

22. Ibid. 168–76.

23. Pauli, *Her Name Was Sojourner Truth* 195–217.

24. Address to the American Equal Rights Convention, New York City, 1867. The text and introductory material used here are from Gerda Lerner, ed., *The Female Experience: An American Documentary* (New York: Oxford University Press, 1992) 488–89. The context for the speech can be found in Elizabeth C. Stanton, Susan B. Anthony, and Mathilda J. Gage, *History of Woman Suffrage*, vol. 2 (New York: Fowler and Wells, 1881–1922) 193–94.

25. *Narrative* 303–4.

26. Many of these people, their notes, and letters are included in part 2, Book of Life, in *Narrative* 129–320.

27. Bernard, *Journey* 251–52.

28. Ibid. 253.

BIBLIOGRAPHY

Bernard, Jacqueline. *Journey toward Freedom: The Story of Sojourner Truth*. New York: Norton, 1967. (The bibliography has a number of additional resources.)

Fauset, Arthur Huf. *Sojourner Truth, God's Faithful Pilgrim*. Chapel Hill: University of North Carolina Press, 1938.

Ferris, Jeri. *Walking the Road to Freedom*. Minneapolis: Carolrhoda, 1988.

Gayraud, Wilmore. *Black Religion and Black Radicalism: An Interpretation of the Religious History of Afro-American People*. Maryknoll, N.Y.: Orbis, 1983.

Krass, Peter. *Sojourner Truth*. New York: Chelsea House, 1988.

Mathews, Donald G. *Religion in the Old South*. Chicago: University of Chicago Press, 1977.

McKissack, Pat. *Sojourner Truth: Ain't I a Woman?* New York: Scholastic, 1992.

Pauli, Bertha. *Her Name Was Sojourner Truth*. New York: Avon, 1971. (This work has an extensive bibliography.)

Raboteau, Albert. *Slave Religion: The "Invisible Institution" in the Antebellum South*. New York: Oxford University Press, 1978.

Sojourner Truth. *The Narrative of Sojourner Truth: A Bondswoman of Olden Times*. Told to Olive Gilbert. Boston, 1850. First published in Battle Creek, Mich., 1878; republished by Arno Press and the *New York Times* in 1968.

Stanton, Elizabeth C., Susan B. Anthony, and Mathilda J. Gage. *History of Woman Suffrage*. New York: Fowler and Wells, 1881–1922.

Stegnan, H. M. *Battle Creek: Its Yesterdays*. Battle Creek, Mich., 1931.

– 17 –

MARIA W. STEWART

(1803–LATE NINETEENTH CENTURY)

You Are Made in God's Image

Some historians of North American religion call the early nineteenth century the time of the "Second Great Awakening," a religious awakening that occurred between 1795 and 1830. The years that precede such events are times of social turmoil, including religious turmoil. The causes of the turmoil are all related to the fact that an old world is passing, although many cling to it in the hope that it can be revived. The new world that is simultaneously arriving cannot be seen clearly and consequently is difficult to control or direct. Things seem out of control.

The early nineteenth century was characterized by the same realities that accompany any period of social turmoil preceding a great awakening. There was a general loss of faith in institutions and the authority of their representatives. Formerly held popular values and dreams no longer inspired the people. There was a growing uneasy awareness that the people together—not the official leaders—were the common source of wisdom. Out of this wisdom would come the eventual defining of new dreams and visions that could order the new world in process. Till this eventual time arrived, there was pain and ambiguity.[1]

Maria W. Stewart lived in the early nineteenth century, as North America was painfully passing from an older world to a new one. The "old ways" of racism were slowly beginning to die. The "old ways" of sexism were also beginning to die. Some of the familiar old ways of working were being made obsolete by machines. Old ways of churches and government that unintentionally oppressed minorities and women were being reshaped to fit the meaning of American liberty and justice for all.

Within the Christian churches there was a lack of agreement about the practical meaning of equality in Christ. There were contradicting claims about what Jesus Christ meant to happen in the churches that bore his name. Some popular preachers of the nineteenth century, like Charles Finney, strongly advocated the rights of women to pray, to preach, and to lead congregations of Christian believers. The revivals and campground meetings of the nineteenth century experienced black women preachers who ranked among the best of the evangelical preachers.

Women like Maria Stewart and Sojourner Truth enriched the lives of thousands of people by their testimonies to Jesus Christ. The campground and revival meetings were a sign of the religious awakening that came on the heels of social change. The numbers of people who attended the various forms of revivals varied from a few hundred to a few thousand. The renewed sensitivity to God and to religion was alive and well as the nation experienced the shift from the old to the new order.[2]

Evangelical revivalism furthered the agenda of reexamining the meaning of universal liberty and justice. This included the movement that would eventually be placed under the umbrella label of "feminism." If feminism is described as "a belief in—and commitment to—the moral and social autonomy of individuals, male and female," the second awakening in North America furthered feminism. Evangelical revivalism also provided an arena for reexamining the oppression of the African people through the institution of slavery.

Both Maria Stewart and Sojourner Truth identified the universality of Christianity in their many preaching engagements. Some religious leaders used Christianity to limit or to openly oppose liberty for African Americans and women. Others joined their voices with those of their people to demand liberty and justice as God intended, that is, for all.[3]

For African American women writers in the nineteenth century, the autobiography was a popular way to set forth convictions that had religious implications. The two religious autobiographies discussed in this book illustrate the teaching intent of the genre. The writings of Maria Stewart and the work of Sojourner Truth are not private reflections intended to help people remember them. The writing is part of their ministry to proclaim the liberty that Jesus Christ died to reveal.

These autobiographical writings in the mid-nineteenth century had a purpose similar to that of the earlier women mystics like Margery Kempe, Julian of Norwich, and Teresa of Ávila. The purpose was to awaken readers to a conversion of heart. These religious autobiographies would address two clear areas that required conversion.

The first area of conversion needed by many was the acceptance of the fact that people of color had a spiritual life (soul). The second area was the admission that people of color were redeemed by Christ just as anyone else was redeemed. The religious autobiography provided direct and indirect responses to prejudices. How? If Jesus Christ could converse with the writer and empower her to be filled with the Spirit, obviously that person was spiritual (had a soul) and was also redeemed in the Spirit.

The religious autobiographies of African American women were somewhat different, however, from those of their African American brothers. The women's writings had to address gender bias as well as prejudices against their race. These prejudices included perceptions of African Americans that doubted their capacity for intellectual learning, for ethical and reasonable behavior, for hard work, and for the adult use of liberty.

Women had to address all of these assumptions through the second biased perception of both white and black patriarchal attitudes. These attitudes persisted among women as well as men. Social and religious limits were set on women. Educational expectations differed. Expectations about religious ministries differed. Leadership of church communities in prayer and worship differed. Religious equality in Christ that all agreed occurred in baptism was not externally visible in use of gifts for ministry to the community. The same selective interpretations of Jewish and Christian Scriptures limiting ministries were used across Christian traditions.

The religious autobiography of Maria Stewart, like those before and after her, rejects any selective interpretation of the message and meaning of Jesus Christ. Her conversion experience reflects a clear consciousness of her call to a deeper life. Like that of other male and female mystics, her conversion to Christ comes in stages, unfolds through events of daily life, awakens her to a sorrow for any evil in her life, and calls her to proclaim the love of Christ for all as she grows into deeper commitment and communion with him. She has no doubt that she can be an apostle for Christ and that her gender does not limit her proclamation, her leadership of communities or her call to lead those communities in prayer and worship.

Maria Stewart and Sojourner Truth had no doubt about the mission to which Jesus Christ called them. They were not fearful of their call. They responded with the conviction that their experience of Jesus Christ and their conversion stories were as authentic as the experience and conversion of male preachers of their day. The ability of women preachers to inspire others to conversion or to Christ testified to their reception of the Spirit that could touch the Spirit in the hearts of others. As black women, they were living proof that people of color were spiritual and as loved by Jesus Christ as any other person.[4]

Both Maria Stewart and Sojourner Truth were part of the Second Great Awakening in North America. This was a time when it was necessary for serious Christian evangelists to travel throughout the country, since most people lived in rural areas. The travels of the evangelical men and women during the nineteenth century testified to the universality of their love for all in need of the Gospel. Maria Stewart and Sojourner Truth endured the same hardships of travel as the men of their time. They went wherever they were invited to go or wherever the spirit of Jesus Christ led them.

Maria Stewart was born in Hartford, Connecticut, in 1803. Both of her parents died when Maria was five years old. The family of a clergyman took her in but made no effort to educate her through the school system. She left that family at fifteen and attended various Sabbath schools until she was twenty. In 1826, she married James Stewart, but he died three years later. While mourning his death, Maria slowly came to a new sense of her true mission in life. In 1831, she made a public profession of faith.

This profession was her response to the mission to which she felt called, namely, to preach the word of God to her people. Like other black women preachers, she faced some opposition from male clergy who believed only men could preach and teach. The response of the people affirmed, however, that she could preach and teach, so she continued to follow her call. In spite of her fiery challenges to the men and women of her day, she was well liked, exerting a positive influence on the self-esteem of African Americans. By popular demand some of her meditations and lectures were published in 1835.

In the selections of Maria Stewart's writings that follow can be seen a spirit of commitment, honesty, and boldness in Christ. Her addresses and meditations point to a practical Christianity that claims her hearers simply need to accept the courage given them in the Spirit. The story of her own conversion reflects the stages of conversion that could serve as an encouragement to others who have gone forward and backward in their life journey.

The Productions of Mrs. Maria Stewart [5] show that she has overcome the feeling of powerlessness that both her society and her church had placed on her. Clearly acknowledging that God's gifts have enabled her to do what she has been called to do, she encourages her audiences to claim their own gifts from God and to remember their dignity. She boldly tells both men and women to accept responsibility for their own futures and that of their children. It is their proud heritage to claim their lives and decide on a future they will bring into being.

For Maria Stewart, the world was already getting smaller and freedom was becoming a universal cry. The mighty work of a new reformation was already beginning and it would not be stopped. All her hearers needed was to decide to courageously move it forward as best they could. She often reminded her hearers that they were "made a little less than the angels," but they would have to prove it by their lives.

She has seized authority in her own life and wants that Spirit to continue empowering her hearers to do the same. Her meditations show that she has little patience with those who refuse to take some small action to better their situation. At the same time, she offers practical advice on how to make improvements.

Productions of Mrs. Maria W. Stewart[6]

"Religion and the Pure Principles of Morality"[7]

All the nations of the earth are crying out for Liberty and Equality. Away, away with tyranny and oppression! Shall Africa's sons be silent any longer? Far be it from me to recommend to you either to kill, burn, or destroy. But I would strongly recommend to you to improve your talents. Let not one talent lie buried in the earth. Show forth your powers of mind. Prove to the world that:

> Though black your skins as shades of night,
> Your hearts are pure, your souls are white.

This is the land of freedom. The press is at liberty. Every one has a right to express an opinion. Many think, because your skins are touched with a sable hue, that you are an inferior race of beings. But God does not consider you as such. God has formed and fashioned you in the divine image, and has bestowed on you reason and strong powers of intellect. The Lord has made you to have dominion over the beasts of the field, the fowls of the air, the fish of the sea. You have been crowned with glory and honor. You have been made a little less than the angels.

According to the Constitution of these United States, God has made all people free and equal. Then why should one say to the other, "Keep down there while I sit up yonder. I am better than you!"? It is not the color of skin that makes one human, but the principles that have formed the spirit.

Many will suffer for pleading the cause of oppressed Africa, and I shall glory in being one of her martyrs. I am firmly persuaded that God in whom I trust is able to protect me from the rage and malice of my enemies and from them that rise against me.

Boston, 1831

My Respected Friends,

I feel almost unable to address you, almost incompetent to perform the task. At times I have felt ready to exclaim, "Oh that my head were waters and my eyes a fountain of tears, that I might weep day and night, for the transgressions of the daughters of my people." Truly my heart's desire and prayer is that Ethiopia might stretch forth her hands unto God. But we have a great work to do.

Never, no never, will the chains of slavery and ignorance burst until we become united as one, and then cultivate among ourselves the pure principles of piety, morality, and virtue. I am aware of my ignorance, but the knowledge that God has given to me I also can impart to you. I am aware of former prejudices, but it is high time for prejudices and animosities to cease from among us.

I am aware I expose myself to calumny and reproach, but shall I remain silent because I fear the weak who shall someday die? Shall I—for fear of scoffs and frowns—hold my tongue?

No, I speak as one who must give an account at the awful judgment seat of God. I speak as a dying mortal to other dying mortals. O you daughters of Africa, awake! Awake and arise! Sleep and slumber no longer! Distinguish yourselves! Show forth to the world that you are endowed with noble and exalted faculties! O you daughters of Africa! What have you done to immortalize your names beyond the grave? What examples have you set for this coming generation? What foundations have you laid for the unborn generations yet to come? Where is our union and where is our love? Where is our compassion that weeps at another's suffering and hides the faults that we see?

And our daughters, where are they? Are they blushing in innocence and virtue? And do our sons strive to become crowns of glory for our heads? Where is the parent who is conscious of having faithfully discharged the duty of parent, and at the last awful day of account can say to the Lord, "Here I am, Lord, your poor unworthy servant and the children you have given me?" And where are the children who will rise up to call the parents blessed?

O God, forgive me if I speak out of turn or wrongly. The minds of our tender babes are tainted the moment they are born. They go astray, it seems, from the womb. Where is the maiden who will blush at vulgarity? Where is the youth who has written upon his manly brow a thirst for knowledge, whose ambitious mind soars above trifles and longs for the time to come when he shall redress the wrongs of the fathers and plead the cause of their people? Did the daughters of our land possess a delicacy of manners combined with gentleness and dignity? Did their pure minds hold vice in abhorrence and contempt? Did they frown when their ears were polluted with vile language?

If so, would not their influence become powerful and would not our people fall in love with their virtues? Their spirits would become fired with a holy zeal for freedom's cause! They would become ambitious to distinguish themselves! They would become proud to display their talents! Able advocates would arise in our defense. Knowledge would begin to flow and the chains of slavery and ignorance would melt like wax before the flames.

I am but a feeble instrument, as one particle of the dust of the earth. You may frown or smile. After I am dead, perhaps before then, God will surely raise up those who will more powerfully and eloquently plead the cause of virtue and the pure principles of morality better than I do. O virtue, how sacred is your name....

When I consider how little improvement has been made in the past eight years, the apparent cold and indifferent state of the people of God; how few have been hopefully brought to the knowledge of the truth as it is in Jesus; that our young men and women are fainting and drooping by the wayside for want of knowledge; when I see how few care to distinguish themselves either in religious or moral improvement; and when I see the greater part of our community following the vanity of life with so much eagerness.... I think we are in as wretched a state as the house of Israel was in the days of Jeremiah.

I suppose many of my friends will say, "Religion is always your theme." I hope my conduct will prove me to be what I profess, a true follower of Christ. It is the religion of Jesus alone that will constitute your happiness here and support you in your dying hour. Oh, then, do not trifle with God and your own souls any longer. Do not presume to offer God the dregs of your lives. Now, while you are still blooming in health and vigor, consecrate the remainder of your days to the Lord.

Do you wish to become useful in your day and in your generation? Do you wish to promote the welfare and happiness of your friends, as far as your circle extends? Have you one desire to become truly great? Oh, then become truly pious! God will endow you with wisdom from on high....

O Lord God, the watchers and protectors of Zion have cried, "Peace, peace!" But there is no peace. They have been—as it were—blind leaders of the blind. Why have you withheld your Spirit from us for so long? Why have you hardened our hearts and blinded our eyes? It is because we have honored you with our lips when our hearts were far from you....

Cause your face to shine upon us and we shall be saved. Visit us with your salvation. Raise up sons and daughters of Abraham and Sarah, and grant that there might be a mighty shaking of dry bones among us, and a great gathering in of souls. Enliven your confessing children!

Grant that the young may be encouraged to believe that there is a reality in religion, and a beauty in the fear of the Lord. Have mercy on the afflicted sons and daughters of Africa. Grant that we may soon become so distinguished for our moral and religious improvements that the nations of the earth may take notice of us! Grant that our cries may ascend to your holy throne like incense.

Grant that every daughter of Africa may consecrate her sons to you from birth. Do you, Lord, bestow upon them wise and understanding hearts. Clothe us with humility of soul, give us a dignity of manner that we may imitate the character of the meek and lowly Jesus. Grant that Ethiopia may soon stretch forth her hands to you!

Now Lord, be pleased to grant that Satan's kingdom may be destroyed and that the kingdom of the Lord Jesus Christ may be built up. May all nations and kindreds and tongues and peoples be brought to the knowledge of the truth, as it is in Jesus. Then may we at last meet around your throne and join in celebrating your praises.

Boston, 1831[8]

Friends,

I am of the strong opinion that the day on which we unite, heart and soul, and turn our attention to knowledge and improvement, that day the hissing and reproach among the nations of the earth against us will cease. And even those who now point at us with the finger of scorn will aid and befriend us. It is of no use for us to sit with our hands folded, hanging our heads like bulrushes, lamenting our wretched condition. Let us make a mighty effort and arise! If no one will promote or respect us, then let us promote and respect ourselves....

Why cannot we do something to distinguish ourselves, and contribute some of our hard earnings that would reflect honor on our memories and cause our children to arise and call us blessed? Shall it any longer be said of the daughters of Africa they have no ambition and they have no force? By no means!

Let every female heart become united, and let us raise a fund ourselves! At the end of one year and a half, we might be able to lay the cornerstone for the building of a High School, that the higher branches of knowledge might be enjoyed by us. God would raise us up and aid us in our laudable designs. Let each one strive to excel in good housewifery, knowing that prudence and economy are the road to wealth. Let us not say we know this, or we know that, and practice nothing. Let us practice what we know!

How long shall the fair daughters of Africa be compelled to bury their minds and talents beneath a load of iron pots and kettles? Until union, knowledge, and love begin to flow among us. How long shall a mean set of men flatter us with their smiles, and enrich themselves with our hard earnings, their wives' fingers sparkling with rings and they themselves laughing at our folly? That will last until we begin to promote and patronize each other. Shall we be a by-word among the nations any longer? Shall they laugh us to scorn forever? Do you ask what can we do?

Unite and build a store of your own.... Fill one side with dry goods and the other with groceries. Do you ask, "Where is the money?" We have spent enough money on nonsense to do whatever building we choose. We have never had an opportunity for displaying our talents. Therefore, the world thinks we know nothing. We have been possessed by a far too belittling and cowardly disposition.... Do you ask what disposition I would have you possess?

Possess the spirit of independence! The Americans do and why shouldn't you? Possess the disposition of bold, enterprising Americans, fearless and undaunted. Sue for your rights and privileges! Know the reason that you cannot attain them. Weary them with your importunities! You can but die if you make the attempt, and we shall certainly die if you do not!

The Americans have practiced nothing but head work these past two hundred years, and we have done their drudgery. Is it not high time for us to imitate their example, practice headwork too, keep what we've got, and get what we can? We need never think that anybody is going to feel interested in us if we do not feel interested in ourselves. On that day, we as a people will have listened to the voice of the Lord our God, walking in the word and ways of the Lord, becoming distinguished in our manner, elegance, grace, and virtues. On that day the Lord will raise us up, aid and befriend us, and we shall begin to flourish.

If every gentleman in America realized as one that they had become bondmen, and their wives, sons, and daughters were forever servants to Great Britain . . . their countenance would be filled with horror. Every nerve and muscle would be forced into action. Their souls would recoil at the thought. Their hearts would die within them, and death would be more preferable. Then why do Africa's sons and daughters not have a right to feel the same? Are not their wives, their sons, and their daughters as dear to them as these are to the white parent? Certainly God has not deprived them of the divine influences of the Holy Spirit, the greatest of all blessings if they would but ask the Spirit.

Why should any person deprive other human beings of their rights and privileges? O, America, America, foul and indelible is thy stain! Dark and dismal is the cloud that hangs over you for the cruel wrongs and injuries to the fallen sons and daughters of Africa. The blood of her murdered ones cries to heaven for vengeance against you! You have become almost drunk with the blood of the slain. You have enriched yourselves through their toils and labors. Now you refuse to make even a small return. You have caused the daughters of Africa to commit whoredoms and fornications, but it is upon you that their curse shall descend.

O great and mighty men and women of America! You who are rich and powerful, many of you will call for the rocks to fall upon you and hide you from the wrath of the Lamb, from the wrath of the One who sits upon the throne! Many of the sable skinned Africans you now despise will shine forever in the kingdom of God like the stars! Charity begins at home. Those who do not provide for their own are worse than infidels.

We know that you are raising contributions to aid the gallant Poles. We know that you have befriended Greece and Ireland. You have rejoiced with France for her heroic deeds of valor. You have acknowledged all the nations of the earth, except Haiti. You may publish as far as the East is from the West that you have over two million Negroes who aspire no higher than to bow at your feet, and to court your smiles. You may kill, tyrannize, and oppress as much as you choose, until our cry shall come up before the throne of God.

I am convinced that God will not allow you to quell the proud, fearless, and undaunted spirits of the Africans forever. In God's own time, our Lord will plead our cause against you and pour out upon you the ten plagues of Egypt. We will not come out against you with swords and sticks as against a thief; but we will tell you that our spirits are fired with the same love of liberty and independence with which your spirits are fired. We will tell you that too much of your blood runs in our veins, and too much of your color in our skins, for us not to possess your spirits. We will tell you that it is our gold that clothes you in your fine linen and purple, and causes you to eat sumptuously every day.

It is the blood of our ancestors and the tears of our people that have enriched your soils. WE CLAIM OUR RIGHTS! We will tell you that we are not afraid of those who can kill the body but after that can do no more. We will tell you whom we do fear. We fear our God, who is able—after killing the body—to destroy soul and body in hell forever. Then, my people, sheathe your swords and calm your angry passions. Stand still, and know that the Lord is God! Vengeance belongs to the Lord alone, who will repay evil!

This is a long future.... When you begin to thrive, America will begin to fall. God has raised up a Walker and a Garrison for you. Though Walker sleeps, yet his spirit lives! His name shall be held in everlasting remembrance. I, even I who am but a child and inexperienced when compared to many of you, am still a living witness that can testify to you this day that I have seen the wicked grow powerful and then pass away....

It is God alone that has inspired my heart to feel for Africa's woes. Do not worry because of the evildoers. They shall be cut down as the grass and wither away like the green herb. Trust in the Lord and do good, and then you shall dwell in the land and you shall be fed. Encourage the noble hearted Garrison. Prove to the world that you are not orangutans, nor a species of animal, but that you possess the same powers of intellect as those of the proud, boastful Americans.

I am aware, my friends, that many of you have been deprived of advantages and kept in ignorance, and that your minds are darkened. If any of you have tried to aspire after high and noble enterprises, you have met with bitter opposition and become discouraged. For this very reason, a few of us have ventured forth to expose our lives in your behalf and to plead your cause against the great. But this will be of little use unless you feel for yourselves and your little ones and exhibit the courage of the strong. Turn your eyes to knowledge and improvement, for knowledge is power! God is able to fill you with wisdom and understanding and to allay your fears. Arm yourselves with the weapons of prayer and put your trust in the living God!

Though all the powers of earth and hell were to arm against me... still would I trust in the Lord and take joy in the God of my salvation. For I am persuaded that God will bring me victory, and yes, even more than that, through Jesus who has loved me and given himself for me!

Farewell Address to Her Friends in the City of Boston, September 21, 1832[9]

My *Respected Friends,*

You have heard me observe that the shortness of time, the certainty of death, and the instability of all things here, induce me to turn my thoughts from earth to heaven. Borne down with a heavy load of sin and shame, my conscience filled with remorse; considering the throne of God forever guiltless, and my own eternal condemnation as just, I was at last brought to accept salvation as a free gift, in and through the merits of a crucified Redeemer. I was brought to see . . . we are saved by grace alone abounding through the Son. . . .

I found that religion was full of benevolence. I found there was joy and peace in believing. I felt as though I had been commanded to come out from the world, be separate, go forward and be baptized. I thought I heard a spiritual interrogation that asked, "Are you able to drink of the cup that I drank? Can you be baptized with the baptism I underwent?"

My heart made the reply, "Yes, Lord, I am able!" Yet, amid these bright hopes, I was filled with fears, lest my hopes were false. I found that sin still lurked within me. It was hard for me to renounce all for Christ when I saw my earthly prospects blasted. It was a bitter cup but I drank it. It was hard for me to say, "Thy will be done," yet I bent my knee and accepted all for my Redeemer's sake. Like so many, I was anxious to retain the world in one hand and religion in the other. "You cannot serve God and evil," sounded in my right ear. With great strength, I plucked out my right hand and eye—as it were—thinking it better to enter the kingdom of God without them rather than have everything cast into hell. Conflicts ended and I received the heart cheering promise, "Neither death, nor life, nor principalities, nor powers, nor things present, nor things to come, shall be able to separate us from the love of Christ Jesus, our Lord."

Truly I could say with St. Paul that at my conversion, I came to the people in the fullness of the gospel of grace. In one city where I visited previously, I saw the flourishing condition of the churches and the progress made in the Sunday schools. I visited Bible Classes and heard of the union that existed in the Female Associations. When I returned later, I could find very few individuals still interested in these things, except Mr. Garrison, and his friend, Mr. Knapp. Hearing that those gentlemen had observed that female influence was powerful, my soul became fired with a holy zeal for your cause. Every nerve and muscle in me was engaged in your behalf. I felt that I had a great work to perform. I was in haste to make a profession of my faith in Christ that I might be about my Father's business. Soon after I made this profession, the Spirit of God was upon me and I stood to speak before many!

When I went home, reflecting upon what I had said, I felt ashamed and did not know where I could hide myself. Something said within me, "Press on and I will be with you." My heart replied, "Lord, if you will be with me, then I will speak for you as long as I live." So far, I have every reason to believe that it is the Holy Spirit operating within my heart that has led me to have any success in the feeble and unworthy efforts I have made.

But let me begin my subject. You have heard that it was said, "Whoever is angry with brothers or sisters without cause shall be in danger at the judgment. But whoever calls another 'fool' is in danger of hell fire." I believe that the Almighty saw the affliction with which I was suffering, the false representations of me, and there was no one to help. I cried unto the Lord in these troubles. For wise and holy purposes known best to God, I was delivered from the hands of my enemies and God vindicated the wrongs in the sight of the people....

I believe that God has put divine testimony within me, and sealed my forehead. With these weapons I have been able to conquer the evil ones of the earth and hell. What if I am a woman? Is not the God of the ancient times still the God of these days of ours? Did God not raise up Deborah to be a mother and a judge in Israel? Did not Queen Esther save the lives of many Jews? Was not Mary Magdalene the first to declare the resurrection of the Lord Jesus? "Come," said the woman of Samaria, "see a man who has told me all things. Is he not the Christ?"

St. Paul declared that it was shameful for a woman to speak in public. Yet our great High Priest Jesus did not condemn any woman for this. Neither will he condemn me, for God will not break the bruised reed, nor quench the smoking flax until judgment is sent forth on all the earth. If St. Paul could know today of our deprivations and our sufferings, I presume he would make no objection to us pleading in public for our rights.

Holy women ministered to Christ and to the apostles. Women of refinement in all ages, more or less, have had some voice in moral, religious, and political subjects. Why the Almighty God has given me the power to speak like this I do not know. Jesus lifted up his head to the Father and said, "I thank you for hiding things from the wise and the prudent that you have revealed to the little ones. It has seemed to be good in your sight."

To convince you of the high opinion that was formed of the capacity and ability of women by the ancients, I refer you to "Sketches of the Fair Sex." Read page 51 and you will find that several of the Northern nations imagined that women could look into futurity, and that they had something inconceivable about them that approached divinity. Perhaps that idea was simply the effect of the wisdom common to the sex, and the advantages that their natural reflections gave them over rough warriors. Perhaps the barbarians, surprised at the influence that beauty can have over force, were led to ascribe a supernatural charm to that which they could not comprehend.

The belief that the Deity more readily communicates divine mystery to women has, at one time or another, prevailed in every quarter of the earth. This is not only among the Germans and the Britons, but among the Scandinavian peoples as well. Among the Greeks, women delivered the oracles. The respect the Romans paid to the Sybils is well known. The Jews had their prophetesses. The predictions of the Egyptian women got a good hearing in Rome, even under the Emperors. In the most barbarous nations, all things that have the appearance of being supernatural, the mysteries of religion and the rites of magic, were in the possession of the women.

If such women have once existed, let us then no longer be astonished, my friends. God at this eventful period can raise up your own women to strive, by their example in both private and public spheres, to assist those who are trying to stop the strong current of prejudice that flows against us at present. Do not ridicule the efforts of these women, for that shall be counted as sin. God makes use of feeble means, sometimes, to bring about the most exalted purposes!

The fifteenth-century period of this spirit is worth observation. If we lived then, we might have seen women preaching and mixing themselves in controversies, women occupying the chairs of Justice and Philosophy, women haranguing in Latin before the Pope, women writing in Greek, and studying in Hebrew. We would see Nuns who were Poetesses and students of Divinity. There were young women who had studied Eloquence and would—with the sweetest countenances and most plaintive voices—encourage the Pope and Christian princes to declare war against the Turks. Women in those days used their leisure hours for contemplation and study. The religious spirit that has animated women of all ages showed itself in these times. It made them martyrs, apostles, warriors, theologians, and scholars.

Why can't such a religious spirit animate us now? Why can't we become the theologians and scholars? Although formal learning is somewhat required, remember that those great apostles Peter and James were ignorant and unlearned. They were taken from their fishing boats to be the fishers of all people.

In the thirteenth century, a young lady of Bologna devoted herself to the study of the Latin language and of the Laws. At the age of 23, she pronounced the funeral oration in Latin in the great church of Bologna. To be admitted as an orator, she did not need some special indulgence because of her youth or of her sex. At 26, she attained the degree of Doctor of Laws, and began publicly to espouse the Institutions of Justinian. At the age of 30, her great reputation raised her to a Chair, where she taught the law to the most prestigious scholars from all nations. She joined the charms and accomplishments of a woman to the knowledge of a man. Such was the power of her eloquence, that her beauty was only admired when her tongue was silent.

What if such women so admired would arise from our sable race? It is not impossible! It is not the color of the skin of a woman or man, but the principles formed in the soul. Brilliance will shine and come from where it will. Genius and talent will not be hidden by skin.

To return to my theme, I say again that the mighty work of reformation has already begun among our people. The dark clouds of ignorance are being dispersed. The light of science is bursting forth. Knowledge is beginning to flow, and its moral influence will not be extinguished until its refulgent rays have spread over us from East to West, from North to South. This mighty work has begun but it has not yet finished. Christians must awake from their slumbers. True Christianity must flourish before the church will be built up in unity and immorality be suppressed.

Yet, knowing your own prospects are bright, I am about to leave you and perhaps never to return. For I find it is of no use for me as an individual to try to make myself useful among my own in this city. It was contempt for my moral and religious opinions in private that drove me to speak publicly. Had experience shown me more plainly that it was the nature of human beings to crush each other, I would not have thought it so hard.

But my respected friends, let us no longer talk about prejudice of others until prejudice becomes extinct at home. Let us no longer talk of opposition of others until we cease to oppose our own. For as long as these evils exist, to talk about them only is to do no more than to give breath to the air. Though wealth is more highly prized than humble goodness, none of these things move me. With God as my friend and my portion, what do I have to fear? Promotion comes neither from the East nor from the West; I rejoice that I am as I am as long as this is the will of God. Humans in their most important feelings can be but vanity.

Some people have risen from obscurity to eminence. I, although a female of darker hue, far more obscure than the men of whom I speak, will prove virtuous in spite of the fact that I hang my harp upon the willows and bend my head. If it is the will of my heavenly Father to reduce me to a state of poverty and want, I am still ready to say "Amen, so be it." "The foxes have holes and the birds of the air have nests, but the Son of Man has nowhere to lay his head."

During the short period of my Christian warfare, I have indeed had to contend with the fiery darts of the devil. If it were not for the truth that the righteous are kept by the mighty power of God for faith unto salvation, I should have been like the seed on the wayside long ago. There were times when it actually seemed like the powers of earth and hell have combined to overthrow me. Yet, in the midst of these powers, I found the Almighty God to be a friend that is closer to me than anyone. God does not forsake those who lean upon that Love. The Lord may chasten and correct, but that is for our best interest. "As a father has mercy upon his children, so the Lord has mercy on those who fear our God."

Some of you have said, "Do not talk so much about religion. People do not wish to hear you, for we all know these things. Tell us something we do not know." If you knew these things, my friends, you would be much happier and far more prosperous than you are now.... Religion is the most glorious of the themes about which mortals speak. The older it grows, the more new beauty it shows. Earth, with its brilliant attractions, appears as nothing by comparison with religion. Religion is a fountain that never dries up. Those who drink of it shall never thirst. It is a well of water springing up in the spirit for everlasting life.

Those ideas of greatness that are held up to us are no more than delusions, airy visions that we shall never realize. All that we say or do can never elevate us, for the important things are those that we and God do together. How?

Let us stop all political discussion in our behalf, for these, in my opinion, sow only discord and strengthen the seeds of prejudice. A spirit of animosity has already arisen, and unless it is quenched, it will burst forth as a fire and devour us. Our young will be slain by the sword. It is God's will that our condition should be in such a way.... Shall the clay say to the creator, "Why have you created me thus?" It is time to stop the political discussions and when our day comes for deliverance, God will provide a way for us to escape and fight our own battles.

Finally, my people, let us follow in God's ways and in the way of peace. Cultivate your own minds and morals. Real merit will elevate you! Pure religion will burst your fetters. Turn your attention to industry, and try to please your employers. Save what you earn; remember that in the grave all distinction withers. High and low are equal.

I draw to my conclusion now. I will long remember the sympathy and kindness of my friends, especially those who have stood by me in the midst of difficulties. May many blessings rest upon them. Gratitude is the only gift I have to offer, but a rich reward awaits them.

To my friends who remain unconverted, I say that my frame will shortly be laid to rest in the ground and lie in ruins. O solemn thought! But why should I revolt, for it is the glorious hope of blessed immortality beyond the grave that has supported me through this vale of tears. Who among you will strive to meet me at the right hand of Christ? The great day of retribution is fast approaching and who shall abide that coming? You are forming characters for eternity. As you live, so shall you die. As death leaves you, so judgment will find you.

Then shall we receive the glorious welcome, "Come you blessed of my Father, inherit the kingdom prepared for you from before the foundation of the world." Or hear the heart rendering curse, "Depart from me you wicked into the everlasting fire prepared for the devil and his angels." When thrice ten thousand years have rolled away, eternity will be but just begun. Your ideas will just have begun to expand. O eternity, who can fathom thine end or comprehend thy beginning?

Dearly beloved, I have made myself contemptible in some eyes that I may win over some others. It has been like labor in vain. "Paul may plant, and Apollos water, but God alone giveth the increase." To my brothers and sisters in the church, I say, Be clothed with the breastplate of righteousness and have yourself wrapped with the garment of truth, prepared to meet your Bridegroom at his coming. Blessed are those servants who are found watching.

Farewell! In a few short years from now, we shall meet in those upper regions where parting will be no more. There we will sing and shout and shout and sing, and make heaven's high arches ring. There we shall range in rich pastures, and partake of those living streams that shall never dry. O, blissful thought! Hatred and contention shall cease, and we shall join with the redeemed millions of people in giving glory to the Lamb that was slain and to the One who sits upon the throne! Eye has not seen, ear has not heard, nor has it yet entered into the heart of anyone to conceive of the joys that are prepared for those who love God.

Thus far, my life has been almost a life of total disappointment. God has tried me as if by fire. Well was I aware that if I contended boldly for the cause of God, I would suffer. Yet I chose to suffer affliction with my people rather than to enjoy the pleasures of sin for such a short time. I believe that the glorious declaration is about to be made for me that was made to God's ancient covenant people by the prophet, "Comfort, take comfort my people. Say unto her that her warfare is accomplished and her iniquities are pardoned." I believe that a rich reward awaits me, if not in this world, then in the world to come.

Oh, blessed hope. The bitterness of my soul has departed from those who endeavored to discourage and prevent me from Christian progress. I can now forgive my enemies and bless those who hated me. Cheerfully can I pray for those who have despitefully used and persecuted me.

May you fare well! (Written in New York for publication in 1834)

The Negro's Complaint

Forced from home and all its pleasures,
   Africa's coast I left, forlorn,
To increase a stranger's treasures,
   O'er the raging billows borne.
Men from England bought and sold me,
   Paid my price in paltry gold;
But—though slave they have enrolled me—
Minds are never to be sold.

Still in thought as free as ever,
What are England's rights, I ask;
Me from my delights to sever?
Me to torture, me to task?
Fleecy locks and black complexion,
Cannot forfeit nature's claim.
Skins may differ, but affection
Dwells in white and black the same.

Why did all creating Nature,
Make the plant for which we toil?
Sighs must fan it, tears must water,
Sweat of ours must dress the soil.
Think, you masters iron hearted,
Lolling at your jovial boards,
Think how many blacks have smarted
For the sweets your cane affords.

Is there—as you sometime tell us—
Is there one who reigns on high?
Has God bid you buy and sell us,
Speaking from that throne, the sky?
Ask God if your knotted scourges,
Fetters, blood extorting screws,
Are the means which duty urges,
Are agents of God's will to use!

Hark! God answers—wild tornadoes,
Strewing yonder sea with wrecks,
Wasting towns, plantations, meadows,
Are the voice with which God speaks.
God, foreseeing what vexation
Africa's children undergo,
Fixed the tyrant's habitation
Where the whirlwind answers, "NO!"

By our blood in Africa wasted,
before our necks received the chain;
By the miseries which we tasted,
Crossing in your barks the main.
By our sufferings, since you brought us,
To the humanly degrading mart;

All sustained with patience, you taught us
  Only by a broken heart.

Deem us as just brutes, no longer,
  For some reason you will find
Worthier to regard and stronger
  Than the color of our kind.
Slaves of gold! Your sordid dealings
  Tarnish all your boasted powers;
Prove that you have human feelings,
  Before you proudly question ours!

(England had 800,000 slaves and she has made them FREE. America has 2,225,000 slaves, and she holds them fast! For sale at the Office of the Massachusetts Anti-Slave Society, No. 46, Washington St., Boston, by B. C. Bacon, Agent and Secretary; and by David Ruggles, No. 67, Lespenard St., New York City.)

NOTES

1. William G. McLoughlin, *Revivals, Awakening and Reform* (Chicago: University of Chicago Press, 1978) 1–22; Anthony C. Wallace, "Revitalization Movements," *American Anthropology* 58 (1956) 264–81.
2. Roger Finke and Rodney Stark, *The Churching of America: 1776–1990* (New Brunswick, N.J.: Rutgers University Press, 1992) 90–101.
3. Nancy A. Hardesty, *Women Called to Witness: Evangelical Feminism in the 19th Century* (Nashville: Abingdon, 1984) 9–12.
4. Susan E. Houchins, ed., *Spiritual Narratives* (New York: Oxford University Press, 1988) xxix–xli.
5. *The Productions of* Mrs. *Maria Stewart* was first published by Friends of Freedom and Virtue in Boston, 1835.
6. The following excerpts are all taken from the reproduction of the original in Houchins, *Spiritual Narratives.* Page numbers refer to this source.
7. Ibid. 4–11.
8. Ibid. 15–22.
9. Ibid. 72–84.

BIBLIOGRAPHY

Dodson, Jualyne, and Cheryl Townsend Gilkes, "Something Within: Social Change and Collective Endurance in the Sacred World of Black Christian Women." In *Women and Religion in America.* Vol. 3. Edited by Rosemary Radford Ruether and Rosemary Skinner Keller. San Francisco: Harper, 1991.

Hardesty, Nancy A. *Women Called to Witness: Evangelical Feminism in the 19th Century.* Nashville: Abingdon, 1984.

Houchins, Susan, ed. *Spiritual Narratives*. New York: Oxford University Press, 1988.

Jones, Charles Edwin. *Black Holiness*. Metuchen, N.J.: American Theological Library Association, 1987.

Mathews, Donald G. *Religion in the Old South*. Chicago: University of Chicago Press, 1977.

McLoughlin, William G. *Revivals, Awakening and Reform*. Chicago: University of Chicago Press, 1978.

Sernett, Milton C. *Black Religion and American Evangelicalism: White Protestants, Plantation Missions, and the Flowering of Negro Christianity*. Metuchen, N.J.: Scarecrow, 1975.

Smith, H. Shelton, Robert T. Handy, and Lefferts A. Loetscher, eds. *American Christianity*. Vol. 2. New York: Scribner's, 1963. 167–214.

– 18 –

GABRIELLE BOSSIS

(1874–1950)

Each Soul Is My Favorite

Gabrielle Bossis was born in Nantes, France, in 1874. The youngest of four children in a wealthy middle-class family, Gabrielle was a sensitive, shy, and fearful child who often preferred to be alone rather than to play with other children. This shyness soon passed. She slowly grew into a graceful, joyous young woman with an adventurous spirit. The aloneness that was part of her childhood and remained throughout her life was not observable to her friends. She was extremely sociable and outgoing in the eyes of others. At the same time, she was gifted with a deep sense of God's presence and a contemplative spirit that grew as she aged.

Gabrielle was always loved and appreciated in her family. She spent her earlier life between the family home in Nantes and the summer home on the Loire River in Fresnes. Her early years passed in joy and peace, for she had no worries about making a living or choosing some career. Her family's closeness and wealth gave her a secure existence. At the same time, she had always had a desire to help others, so she was constantly engaged in some project for those who were not as well off as she was. She obtained a degree in nursing to care for the poor and assisted in various of parish mission projects for the less fortunate.

Gabrielle was an energetic person of many interests and talents. She enjoyed her training in the fine arts, and learned painting, music, and sculpture. She took time from her busy life to engage in horseback riding, one of her favorite sports. Given the family's status, she was invited to many parties and other social gatherings. She especially loved to dance and was very popular as a dance partner at gatherings of young adults her age.

The inner life she experienced since she was a child had always been characterized by a sense of God's presence, which made it easy for her to engage in "simple talks" with Jesus Christ. These conversations occurred throughout the days and nights, even when she was busy about many things. Eventually she told her Franciscan spiritual director about the lifelong communication with Jesus

Christ. The director urged her to become a nun. Gabrielle was quite sure that Jesus Christ did not want her to be a nun. She felt her director was wrong in his judgment, for her conversations with Christ made her sure she should live as a single woman.

As a popular and charming woman, Gabrielle received a number of proposals for marriage at various times in her life. Although she appreciated the depth of her friendships with men and women alike, she did not feel that marriage was her life's vocation. After some discernment she decided that she would decline each proposal as it came along. After each of these decisions she would renew her dedication to God as a single woman living her life for God's glory.

It was not until Gabrielle was sixty-two years old and had lived a full life that she discovered she had a real talent for writing. She was particularly skilled in writing in the genre of moral comedy. Moral comedies were very popular in France in the early part of the twentieth century. Gabrielle not only wrote moral comedies, she also decided to play the major part in her first attempt. Both the play and her acting were so successful that she was well known as both playwright and actress in a short time.

Her reputation spread quickly. Many French playhouses requested that she perform her works. Soon directors outside France invited her to their countries to do her plays and to act in them. In the midst of her busyness and exciting life she continued her dialogues with Jesus Christ. These dialogues went on any time and in any place. Sometimes the voice of Jesus Christ was so strong that she was filled with awe and surprised that no one around her heard anything. From the outside, people viewed Gabrielle as a fun-loving and attractive woman. Few ever knew about her contemplative center.

As Gabrielle began one of the busiest periods of her life, after age sixty-two, she experienced the presence of Jesus Christ in a sure and permanent way. She did all she could to provide some spaces for a more traditionally contemplative life, but for the most part her contemplation had to be energized by—and flow through—her action. She wondered briefly if she ought to slow down her life, but then came to a new realization that her mission was to spread the love of Christ through doing whatever she was doing.

From that point on, her interior voice became a sure and constant guide for the rest of her life. It was during this latter part of her life that Gabrielle began to write and keep her journals. She continued to do so till a few weeks before her death in 1950.

These journals combine travelogues and revelations of Jesus Christ. Like other mystics before her, Gabrielle was quite sure that her writings were not intended to be just for her own good. She intended to have them published after her death. Then the voice of Christ told her the journals would do others good if they could read them. She decided to have the first published without using her name. The first volume, published anonymously, sold out quickly, and people clamored for more of this kind of writing.[1]

No more volumes were published until after Gabrielle's death. In the interim, she continued to write her journals and was in excellent health. She loved to travel and was told by Christ that her travels and associations with many people were giving him glory. Always her manner of meeting people and affirming their goodness made her a desirable companion and friend, even to those who met her only briefly after a performance.

In May 1950 she became ill for one of the first times in her life. She was surprised to learn that her heart was becoming weaker and nothing could be done about her advancing death. Although she was surprised by the diagnosis, she faced death in the same lighthearted way she had embraced life. When she no longer had the strength to eat, she knew death was very near. The final entry in her journal was made on May 25, 1950:

> Have I come to the end of my life? Is this the moment when I celebrate my first and last Mass? Where are you, Loving Presence?... And afterward, what will it be?
>
> It will be I. It will be I. Forevermore![2]

Gabrielle Bossis died on June 9, 1950. Like the death of any well-known actress or playwright, hers' was noted by the usual headlines and then forgotten.

It was not until Daniel Rops wrote his preface to a second volume of her journal that Gabrielle's many friends discovered she had written the first one. They had not known their friend had a contemplative side. Her life had been so socially active and public. Enthusiastic readers of the second volume requested others as well. Eventually, seven volumes were published, with volume six being her autobiography.[3]

True to Gabrielle's adventurous and fun-loving personality, her dialogues with Jesus Christ reveal a loving and gentle Christ. There is a basic joyfulness about the dialogues that show that Jesus Christ respects the freedom of humans to accept or reject his offers of love.

Like others before her, Gabrielle acknowledged a faith that made God present to her throughout her life. She did not have any dramatic conversion from sinfulness to grace. She did not give all away to follow the vocation to which she was called. Rather, she lived with the social status and privileges that were hers, assured by Christ that she could give glory to him through her use of these gifts. Gabrielle was remembered as one who always dressed well, lived comfortably, traveled the world, and died with more wealth than many people made during their whole lifetime.

Gabrielle's vocation to a contemplative life illustrates one of the many forms that Christian holiness can take. She renounced both marriage and motherhood out of a sense that God wanted her to embrace the single life. She became more grounded in the freedom to affirm that choice many times. In spite of the relative unpopularity of a woman choosing the single life as a call to holiness, she never doubted that this was her vocation.

She remains an example of a professional woman whose busy life does not rule out mystical experience. Gabrielle's journals reflect an integrity of temporal and spiritual, material wealth and holiness, friendship with Jesus Christ and friendship with others. Her journal reveals the reality that all one's life is graced if there are eyes to see. The Christ of her life was one who respected her freedom, her need for action, her lifestyle of comfort, her theatrical career, and her ability to love.

The Christ in Gabrielle's writings is one whose love is sensitively attuned to the unique way in which each human enters into human and divine relationships. The mystery of the humanness of Christ has not disappeared in the eternal humanity of the risen Christ. Gabrielle's revelations point to the need for Christ to join us in our efforts to be renewed and to be renewers of the earth. In her journal she daily provides the mirror and means to touch the divine. The few selections that follow from Gabrielle's journal illustrate how one person's life that was "ordinary" became a window to the "extraordinary."

He and I[4]

Dec. 28, 1936[5]

I transform your prayers into my prayers. But if you don't pray.... Can I make a plant that you haven't sown bear blossoms?

Feb. 14, 1937[6]

You saw that kindness in the face of that young girl? Be like that always. If my followers were good to others, the face of the world would be transformed.... In your soul there is a door that leads to the contemplation of God. But, you must open it.

April 9, 1937

Don't get the idea that a saint is a saint at every moment. But there is always my grace. You must aim at perfection, but the perfection of your own nature. This is the way you will please me. (And he made me understand that the work of perfection of one soul is not the same as that of another.)

May 8, 1937

If you must pass judgment, judge according to the good rather than the evil. Do not go to so much trouble to make plans. I am the one who does your planning for you.

May 25, 1937

Why should you create solitude for yourself if I want you before the public? My beloved little child, take me to others. Be Christlike.

June 26, 1937

Is it because I am God that you believe I have no need of tenderness? Do you think I remain silent with those who want to talk with me? Talk with me....

June 30, 1937

Sometimes you feel me more, sometimes less, but I never change. Don't let praying tire you. Why do you give yourself so much trouble? Let it be utterly simple and heartwarming, like a family chat.

Jan. 1, 1938[7]

This year you will love me in my people. Do for them what you would do for me. If I give you favors of tenderness, it is to encourage you to make sacrifices for your sisters and brothers. Give as you have received. I want to go down to the very heart of your heart and make my home there. It will be simple and habitual.

Jan. 4, 1938

Consolations? Give them to others.

April 1, 1938

Be happy, my friend. Speak to me, as it were, with smiles. So many people look upon me as an executioner or an inexorable judge. My heart wants to be your gentle friend. What would I not do for those who really want to give themselves to me in confident and childlike surrender?

April 7, 1938

From now on, spend your life delighting me. You will feel transformed. Please me and live for me. This is the true meaning of your divinity.

June 12, 1938

Say "Good Morning" to me every time you awaken just as though you were arriving in heaven. Do you remember your first communion? You didn't dare to move, you were so sure that I was in your body. Well, I am there.

June 21, 1938 After communion

Certainly I am there to receive your praises, but above all I am with you to serve you. So take what you want. All of you, come and eat. When you say, "Sacred Heart of Jesus, have mercy on us" with love, I grant you more grace than for a long-drawn-out prayer that you repeat mechanically.

You thank me today for the sun and you do well. But be just as grateful for the dark weather. Everything comes from my providence.

Dec. 3, 1938

When you talk to my mother, be one with me. I poured out my heart to her while I was on the earth. Use your feet, your hands, your breath as if these were mine. What I want most is to be one with you.

When you pray to the Father, pray with my lips. If you are humiliated, remember that your humiliations complete mine. One does not feel sorry to be sacrificed to love.

March 1939[8]

Don't say your prayers just to get them finished, but saturate your soul with love. Otherwise, it would be better to say less.

When I give you power, if you keep it for yourself, it remains with you. If you share it with others, it multiplies a hundredfold. So have the courage to pass it on.

April 24, 1939

What other prayer could equal the one I composed myself?

Love your prayers, the Our Father, the Hail Mary. You who love works of art, love your prayers. When you pray, I guide the words on your lips as one guides the steps of a little child.

April 28, 1939

Enjoy me. Give yourself a rest from saying prayers, so that you may enjoy my love!

June 1, 1939

Write! I don't want people to be afraid of me any more, but to see my heart full of love and to speak with me as with a dearly beloved brother.

For some, I am unknown. For others, a stranger, a severe master, an accuser. Few people come to me as to one of a loving family. And yet my love is there waiting for them.

So tell them to come, to enter in, to give themselves up to love just as they are. Just as they are, I'll restore and transform them. They will know a joy they have never known before. I alone can give that joy, if only they would come. Tell them to come!

June 3, 1939

When you ask, believe that I am good enough to answer you. Otherwise, you will deprive me of giving.

Be crucified with me. To be crucified is to be stretched against your desires, against the love of self, in poverty, obscurity, and obedience to the Father.

Remember that the crucifixion is the prelude to the resurrection, that is, to all joys!

June 22, 1939

Be very simple with me. You know how people act in the family. They kiss each other affectionately morning and evening, and this is perfectly natural. And sometimes during the day, a word or a gift makes them exchange a loving look. There are outpourings of tenderness. If only I were allowed to be one of the family!

Oct. 10, 1939

Don't drag your past along with you constantly if it burdens you and hinders you from coming close to me. Just as you are, throw yourself into my arms for your joy. Can I give you anything else?

Jan. 17, 1940[9]

You don't always feel me in the same way, but don't let the darkness hinder you from going forward. Humble yourself, and go on your way faithfully. Keep going. You don't see me or feel me, but I'm there—Love itself, holding my arms out to you. Nothing ever makes me lose sight of my children on earth. Their ideas and their thoughts are short lived, and so they imagine that I am like them in this. But I am perfect Poise, the same, yesterday, today, and forever, for I am perfect constancy. I am the presence, the loving look. The entire cosmos is cradled in me. I am this second of time and I am eternity. I am the lavishness of Love, the one who calls, so that you may come without fear and throw yourself upon my heart.

I call you, at least you, my child, to be my response.

Jan. 26, 1940

Don't you understand that the bonds of my union with a soul must be tightened as it draws near to eternity? Try to be no longer in yourself, but in me. You were touched when you read that I was in the Gospels, hidden in the sacrament of the Word. But how much more I am present in the sacrament of human life! O my children who live in grace, let us never leave one another!

April 9, 1940

Don't think that a saint must look saintly in the eyes of humans. Saints have an outer nature, but it is the inner nature that counts. There is a fruit whose rough—even thorny—skin gives no inkling of its sweet and juicy taste. That's how it is for my saints. Their value is in their hearts.

May 4, 1940

Today I ask you to keep your mind in a state of pure simplicity, your thoughts rising pure like candle flames toward my power and majesty. . . .

Even if you don't see the result of your prayers or efforts, do not let this hold you back. Just keep in mind that I know everything, and place yourself once more in the hands of your redeemer.

Remember this: I will be for you what you want me to be. If you treat me as a stranger, I'll be only a judge. If you trust me, I'll be your Savior. If you live in my love, I'll be your loving bridegroom, the being of your being.

June 28, 1940

Tell me that it doesn't bother you to walk beside me. What you do cheerfully for me pleases me all the more.

I am in the position of one who fears to impose upon a friend, and so is overjoyed when that friend expresses ever new happiness to be together. I am not an exacting master. I am the fullness of love, so give yourself with open arms. You know how little children leap to be caught and lifted up into the arms of their father.

July 26, 1940

Be just as gracious toward the little ones as toward the great ones. Make an effort particularly when you are with people who seem vulgar to you. Go to everyone with the same gentleness. You are all sisters and brothers in me. Wasn't I everyone's brother? Don't take your eyes off your model!

Aug. 9, 1940

Don't be discouraged. There are many ways of advancing, even by your stumblings. Call out to me! Don't be afraid to cry if you fall. But let your cry go straight to your matchless friend. Believe in my power. Didn't I catch hold of Peter when he was sinking beneath the waves? And don't you think I'm more ready to help you than to lose you?

The smaller and weaker a child is, the more closely one holds it to one's heart!

Aug. 22, 1940

Take power from the power of the saints, from the power of the holy one. Be one with them. Give me the joy of helping and transforming you. Surrender everything; let yourself go! Tell me often about your great longing. Do you think that I would resist? That would be to misunderstand me!

If you are generous, how much more am I! You know the violent wind and the bird of prey? I too carry off. I am a Ravisher. Do not struggle. Because you let yourself be taken captive, I will bring you into my secret garden among the flowers and the fruit. You will wear the wedding ring on your finger. Your step will be in time with mine, and I will stoop down to your likeness so that we may talk together easily....

As you gaze on me, you will understand that the suffering that passes leads to life eternal. You will say, "How simple it is." Because we love, everything is simple. You will say, "You were nothing but goodness and mercy and I didn't know it."

Then the veil will be torn and you will have the face-to-face vision of all that I suffered for you. Now you are working and fighting in the dark, in the night.... But even now you must say, "Lord, I believe. I adore you in the mystery of it all. To whom should I go but you?"

Then surrender yourself to my peace.

Aug. 29, 1940

Even if you did nothing but repeat the wish, "Glory be to the Father and to the Son and to the Holy Spirit," for the whole hour, you would not have wasted your time. Not one of your prayers goes unheard. If people only knew how attentive the Father is to the actions and words of his little children! For in fact, many of them remind the Father of his only son toiling on the earth.

The Holy Trinity is in each one of you, more or less according to the space that you allow. For as you know, God never forces anyone. God only asks and waits. When you remain faithful, you are sure of the joy—I was going to say of the celestial joy—that it gives heaven. Keep this thought always before you. It is while you are living on earth that I enjoy you, my beloved faithful ones. But in heaven, it will be you who will enjoy me.

My little children, consider my simplicity and how easy it is for you to please me. It means only doing everything as well as you can for my love's sake in order to grow, to advance and to go higher. Hold out your two weak arms to me, and I will help you! We will do the work together in unequal shares. It is for the

Father to shoulder the heavier end of things. If the little child fixes eyes lovingly on the Father's eyes, the painful task will seem so little.

A look of love . . . what power for you and what joy for me! Anyone who loves me has the right to see me. Even if you loved me each day with a heroic love, it would be little compared to the love you will have throughout eternity! Then love me continually. Tell me about your love and live it continually. I'll receive it day by day, new in your heart and ever new in me. For I never grow weary of you!

Sept. 12, 1940

Never drain your cup of pleasure to the last drop. Keep a little for me as a sacrifice, my part. . . . Since we are together in everything, if you took it all, what would be left for me? You would be alone with yourself. "May God be with you. . . ."

I begin my life on earth again with each one of you—my life wedded to yours—if only you want to invite me. Do you remember how I walked with the disciples at Emmaus? . . . I do this for you as well. I walk along the same path with you, the path I chose for you from all eternity—in this family, in this country where you live. It is I who placed you there with a special love. So live there, full of faith, remembering that there is where you will win heaven, where you will win eternal love in exchange for this brief moment in time.

So pass through this life with the great desire to respond to my tenderness, and with constant eagerness to know me at last—to know me, your loving Savior. You have always been a thought in my eternal mind. It would be only fair for yours to be filled with me, my poor little children so often ungrateful!

Sometimes I stand at the door, waiting even before you call me. Do you remember this or that danger you escaped? And you believed it all happened by itself. Nothing happens by itself. So never lose sight of my watchful, kindly providence. Thank me for my invisible care. My love loves to plan for you and does everything for your good.

Sept. 14, 1940

Live in my heart. You have discovered the warm nest of the golden-crested wren hidden in your acacia tree? It is in the reach of any hand—but invisible.

Invite the angels to help you in your upward climb. So great is my longing to have you come nearer. I have so much to say to you, so much to give you! . . . Come nearer, always nearer.

Sept. 19, 1940

It's a strange thing, isn't it, that a creature can comfort its God. Yet, this is a fact. My love reverses the roles, inventing new ways for people to reach me—by allowing them to give me a protective tenderness. So great is my need of all your ways of loving! Great is my need for all your ways of being tender!

Oct. 11, 1940

Do not simply ask that I be loved, but offer every one of your deeds for this purpose. Nothing could bring me more balm. For although it may seem strange to you, there is grace that I cannot give unless you ask me for it.

This grace is the work of two—your Christ and you. You know how much I love to be one with you. We each have our share, and since I never impose upon you, you must invite me. You must make me act with you. In this way, I live my life again on earth.

This is why I sometimes say to you, "My dear daughter, continue my life." Your life is a gift from me, so I ask you to give it to me through all your actions. Don't you feel the greatness of it—to make God live? And it's so simple. If you only knew how very simple it is!

Just imagine what it would be like if at this moment all the people on the earth let me live in them through grace! What a spectacle for heaven! Because you are all performing before the angels and saints, you see, you are still on the stage....

My poor little ones. Don't neglect anything that could increase your tenderness....Call to me often. Isn't an earthly father delighted to hear his little one's appeals? Sometimes he does not answer immediately. But this is only in the hope that the child will call again. Do you remember when I seemed to rebuke the Canaanite woman? I wanted to lead her to me; so beautiful and humble was her answer....And so, if I seem not to hear you, call again and you will give me joy.

I am always eagerly awaiting you—particularly my very poor and little ones. The weakest and the poorest are already in my heart. How happy are the underprivileged!

Nov. 4, 1940

Do you at last believe with all your heart that I created you in order to make you eternally happy? It was out of pure love that I made you—not for my own interest, but for yours to give you infinite bliss.

Thank me for your creation. Turn your life toward me. Never cease to look at my love enfolding you. Then feeling loved, love me. You know how much more intensely one loves when one feels loved. It's like an animated conversation. Only in this one, there is no need for words. We love, that's all. And I am so much yours that you don't even feel that I come down or that you rise up. But it seems quite simple to you that we talk to each other on the same level, share as equals, even exchange our two hearts...although you give yourself utterly, you keep your personality and only enhance it the more!

Nov. 9, 1940

You may be sure that human nature cannot love suffering for itself. My human nature didn't love it either. But transformed human nature uses suffering as an instrument to serve God, either for its own purposes—and this is most perfect—or for the grace that we want to if it is God's will to give it.

Always my daughter, be at one with me in my sufferings. To quicken your will to love, you may choose some of my particular sufferings from childhood, adolescence, public life, those caused by other people's words and acts, and the ingratitude of those I loved. And my suffering for the anguish I caused my mother and friends during the ordeal of my passion. Do not waste a single one of your precious sufferings. Steep them in supernatural joy.

Jan. 9, 1941[10]

Come and watch me suffer in the garden, just as though it were that very night. It is always that very night, for God sees all time at a glance. Do not leave me! I am like a terrified child begging not to be left alone! Stay here and let me know you are with me. A human presence is comforting. Hold my hand, for I am now a poor man full of distress—even though I am God! No one will ever understand the depth of my desolation. I feel the need of being surrounded by my dear ones, for I see all the powers of evil let loose and I am alone in defending myself. Pray with me!

Do you have a firmer faith in my love now that you see me suffer so? Give me this kindness, this offering of faith! How much it means to me to see faith, hope, and love in my people....

Learn to desire. And since you have heard the words, "Be perfect as your heavenly father is perfect," dare to the utmost. Alone, you can't do anything. But trusting in me, leaning on me, submerged in me, you can do everything! That's why I keep on saying, "Lose yourself in me and humbly ask me to act for you, and I'll act."

Feb. 26, 1941 (Gabrielle's Birthday)

Remember this. As one lives, so one dies. If, during these moments that divide you from death, your heart is full of me; if zeal for my kingdom consumes it; if you thirst for my glory, death will find you like that and you will pass on with a thought of love.

To pass on... it's not long. It is just to leave the life on earth to enter into that other life. This is your true birthday, for this is being born to life everlasting. And I am Life, I, your Christ.

May 1, 1941

You thank me for the springtime with its flowers and the birds that sing in your linden trees, for the first butterflies and all my beautiful creatures. And you are right, for I am beauty itself. But the springtime that I bring to souls by my grace—this is what you should thank me for most of all. These springtimes full of the elixir of eternity are paid for with the shedding of my blood and create splendors you cannot see. But the angels and the saints gaze on them.

Oh, my dear children—when my Love is unloved, how deep is the wound I bear.... Lean upon my heart and the burden of you will be my joy. I will flow into you as the sap from the root of the vine flows into the branch. Your life will be my life. You are nothing at all by yourself.

Aug. 28, 1941

Even when your faith is no bigger than a mustard seed, you must strive to make it grow. Look upon these special blessings of today as my love, attentive to every detail of your life. At every step of the way, you will find me watching, going ahead of you. Have you ever gone anywhere that I have not been waiting for you? You often ask me to take care of your precious belongings. But for me, aren't you more precious than all?

Entrust yourself to me constantly. And always give me each moment as it passes. Isn't it better in my hands? Doesn't it say in the gospel, "He laid his hands on them and healed them." I'll take out of the present moment whatever clings too much to the earth—the selfishness that sullies your intention.

Always trust. Trust more and more—even to the point of expecting a miracle. Don't stop halfway or you will set limits to my love. When you have enfolded your confidence, you will unfold it still more without ever being able to exceed what I expect of you.

Always count on me and never on yourself. You will advance and soar with wings like an eagle.

April 11, 1942[11]

Don't you understand that I prefer someone who has fallen many times but who is humbled at my feet to the self-righteous person who thinks there is no fault within? My dear daughter, tell me every day how sorry you are for any way you have pained me. Take a steady look at your failures and stains and offer them to me so I can wash them away....

Say, "My friend, help me. You know only too well how helpless I am but with you I can do anything." And then go on your way again, trusting in me day by day. Do you understand? Even if you see no progress at all, be more patient than ever. Be ready to persevere to the very end. Didn't I need that kind of courage as I climbed up the hill to Calvary?

April 23, 1942

Even though you don't always feel me beside you, I never leave. Sometimes I come nearer, as I did yesterday in the garden when you said, "Good morning, my darling God!" It seemed to you almost as though I had answered you. I hide behind a veil so that you will learn to walk by faith and merit through learning. My love still surprises you. There is only one explanation—God's extravagance. The only thing you need to do is to believe with utter simplicity in this love of an all-powerful Being, a Being totally different from you. Give yourself up to the infinitely delicate and tender omnipotence. Become a captive of my love....

Think only of heaven, where I am waiting for you to celebrate our wedding day. Tell me of your impatience and submission, your eagerness under my will.... And you will come.

May 21, 1942

Don't ever grow weary of me, my friend. Fall in love with me over and over again. Let your way of loving me always be new. Don't worry if you don't hear my voice. Don't begin to think I am far from you. I'm in the very center of your being with the Father and the Spirit. Give yourself to us. Surrender by getting rid of your self-love and even your self-awareness. Never mind if you don't understand very well....

Come closer, always closer. Give up everything that separates us—the lack of confidence and hope. It is a great thing to hope. Hope for holiness. Would I ask every person to be holy if it were impossible? Very well, then. Believe in my help. Call me often. Don't be afraid of being too insistent.

Sept. 10, 1942

Why should you begrudge the help you give your neighbors? Don't forget that in serving them, you are serving me. That should give you courage. You'll need great courage to become holy. Never lose sight of the goal—holiness; that means to be always in readiness for me. It's so very simple. Would I ever ask anything from you that was impossible?

Adore and give thanks. And when I ask you to be simple, I mean above all in your relations with me. Don't get the idea that I need any special words or gestures. Just be yourself. Who is closer to you than God?

Oct. 8, 1942

How can you make progress all by yourself? Let yourself be carried in stronger arms, just as you did when you were little. Don't be ashamed of being weak and imperfect. I'll only love you the more. Don't lose sight of the path of spiritual childhood.

Cultivate your confidence. Let it blossom as a flower. You can trust me, can't you?...Come to me little by little, your heart on fire at the moment of death. Find a sweeter name for death. Call it the Meeting. And even now, even though you can scarcely see me in the twilight of time, you will stretch out your arms to me. Oh, the charm of an impatient heart longing to be entwined in mine!

Nov. 12, 1942

My daughter! You can be sure of this. Even though I am no longer on earth, your neighbor is there. Your desire to love me, to receive me, to serve me, and to give me rest, as in the home of Martha and Mary, may be realized in what you do for others. How ready you would be to smile at everyone if you could only see your Jesus in them. So remember this and don't economize on kindness. It is I myself who will receive it all. I have a thousand ways of responding to those who try to please me.

Jan. 30, 1943[12]

Why should my people offer me only their trials? Don't you think your joys would please me just as much? They do if you give them with as much love, your smallest joys with your greatest love.

July 15, 1943

Picture me as a living being loving you more than you could ever imagine, even in your deepest longing. Keep before you the thought that this living being who gave his life for you is waiting with infinite yearning for the moment of our Meeting....

Picture me often this way, as a real person, not just someone near you but actually in you. One whose presence never leaves you.

Feb. 3, 1944[13]

I lived my last hour as you will. Get ready now to unite your death with mine. Close together, you and I, above all at the final moment. In times of danger, you know how the members of a family throw themselves in each other's arms. You will keep yourself still closer to me when the last hour is drawing near....

Oct. 3, 1944

You may be sure that to do your duty is one way of loving me. In this way you can love me all day long. You don't notice this, but I do. Your offering in the morning has told me. Are you ever so busy that you haven't even a moment to glance at me?...

Be my voice for others. It is not enough to be good. You must be my goodness. Do you understand the difference?

Nov. 23, 1944

Don't forget to look at me through your days and nights. Don't grow weary. How could you grow weary of so tender a friend? When tempted against the faith, say a little word to him and the temptation will go away....

I am like a master who gives his instructions behind a curtain in order to hide his great love for his pupils. I am like a player who slips quickly away in order to excite and prolong the chase. Don't be afraid of me. Be afraid to be afraid.

March 1, 1945[14]

It's not enough to know about this love; above all, you must have faith in it. How much comfort people would find and what happiness even in the midst of trials if they only believed that everything that happens to them comes from my desire to do them good. All is fitted to the measure of each one.

Instead of that, some think I am spiteful toward them, and they plot vengeance against their God. It would be so simple and so heartwarming for them to contemplate my immense love.... Ponder these words, He and I. Live them. I and you. I in you.

April 20, 1945

Remember the value of a free gift, the gift of self, when offered out of tenderness. What inexpressible joy shall belong to the one who receives this gift! I will multiply the blessings of the recipient, who will be lost in wonder and gratitude, saying, "What have I done to deserve the kindness of my God?" I shall simply reply, "You loved me with all your might, and you let me love you."

Nov. 28, 1945

Why do you doubt, you of little faith? Am I less great than yesterday? Could my love ever fail? Do I love you for what you are worth? Close the eyes of this fear that paralyzes you and throw yourself into my arms. I am the very gentle shepherd. You know that I'll give you rest on my heart. What matters most of all is the fusion of our wills.

Jan. 3, 1946[15]

Why do you have such difficulty in believing in my love? This scenery that you find so enchanting is my love. That sunset that calls to your mind a bleeding host is my love.... Isn't it perfectly clear to you now that my love arranges all things? You always think that such things just happen. Nothing just happens. I am in everything and I am all love.

April 4, 1946

Don't be afraid of anything. Death? Of course not! You will receive the grace to clothe yourself in death. You will enter into death as you enter into a task received from me. I shall help you as always.

April 11, 1946

The proof of your love for God is the affectionate care you take of your neighbor. Be sure that you see me in your neighbor.... Begin today to do your best to speak to me when you speak to your neighbor. I expect this of you when you get together this afternoon with your friends.

Hunt for me everywhere! I'll let myself be captured with such joy! How could you expect to find me if you didn't search? And when you have found me, give me to others. There are people I am waiting to reach only through you. This is the mission foreseen for you from all eternity. Do not be unfaithful to it.

March 6, 1947[16]

As you look back over your life, do you see that my will was always for your good? This is because I love you, and it is the same for everyone, since I love each of you individually. I see you each differently. I see every detail about you. Do you understand? My love is not a general one.

I need every one of you as though you were the only person in the world, as though the cosmos had been created for you alone! My love is greater than the cosmos. So let this thought be a strength for you and a smiling calm.

Nov. 27, 1947

My dear daughter, do you know when you are speaking like me? It is when you put kindness and charm in your words, when you touch hearts, when you counter an acidic remark with a gracious answer, when you make excuses for someone, when you serve, when you give, when you calm someone who is angry, when you comfort, when you keep an even temper under all circumstances, when you remain humble without seeking to shine, when you are grateful for the kindness of others, and when you are generous in other ways.

Jan. 22, 1948[17]

I am like a shy human. I prefer you to discover my love on your own. I am afraid of speaking it, because I fear that would be interpreted as forcing it upon you. But then, you are free. But how great is my joy when—of your own free will—you seek ways of multiplying our meetings and deepening our intimacy! I let you be the one to come and to call. I hide myself to increase your desire for me.

Sept. 30, 1948

Each day is a first creation, for no day is like another. I never stop creating. It is all for you. . . . Pray for those who receive my gifts without wanting to know me, to love me and to serve me. They too would cease to exist were I not holding them up. So I wait for them. Pray that they may seize every opportunity of returning to me.

June 16, 1949[18] *(Feast of Corpus Christi)*

You know there need not be any interruption between Corpus Christi on earth and Corpus Christi in heaven. The procession never stops. The last altar of repose is heaven. Do you know what an altar of repose is? It is a life of love and joy, an outburst of enthusiasm. So put altars of repose in your life, into each one of your days.

May 18, 1950[19]

What are you going to say to me on arriving? What am I going to say to you? Oh, this moment of Meeting! Put your whole soul into it. Believe in the infinite tenderness.

May 23, 1950 (During Communion of the Sick)

You've waited until the very last minute of your life to really believe in my boundless compassion, in final forgiveness! Have no more fear of anything. It would wound me if you were afraid. Surrender your whole being to Love, my dearly beloved!

May 25, 1950

Have I come to the end of my life? . . .

It will be I, forevermore!

NOTES

1. Only the first volume of *Lui et moi* (*He and I*), a seven-volume work by Gabrielle Bossis, was printed by Beauchesne. The first volume of *Lui et moi* was published in Paris, 1948.

2. Gabrielle Bossis, *He and I*, ed. and trans. Evelyn M. Brown (Sherbrooke, Canada: Éditions Paulines, 1969) 385.

3. Evelyn Brown has condensed the essentials of volume 6 in her introduction to the one-volume edition of *He and I*, ibid. 7–21.

4. All page citations will be from the one-volume source edited by Evelyn M. Brown.

5. The 1936 excerpt is from 27.

6. The 1937 excerpts are taken from 28, 32, 33, 34, 37, 38.

7. The 1938 excerpts are found on 49, 51, 52, 55, 56, 60.

8. The 1939 excerpts are found on 64, 65, 68, 69, 72.
9. The 1940 excerpts are found on 76, 77, 82, 84, 89, 91–96, 100, 103–4, 106.
10. The 1941 excerpts are found on 112, 118, 121, 126.
11. The 1942 excerpts are found on 131, 133–34, 142, 144, 146.
12. The 1943 excerpts are found on 150, 153–54.
13. The 1944 excerpts are found on 169, 179–80.
14. The 1945 excerpts are found on 195–96, 215.
15. The 1946 excerpts are found on 219, 224–25.
16. The 1947 excerpts are found on 249–50, 269–70.
17. The 1948 excerpts are found on 277–78, 304.
18. The 1949 excerpt is found on 338.
19. The 1950 excerpts are found on 384–85.

BIBLIOGRAPHY

Bossis, Gabrielle. *He and I*. Edited and translated by Evelyn M. Brown. Sherbrooke, Canada: Éditions Paulines, 1969.

Dansette, Adrien. *Religious History of Modern France*. Vol. 5.2, bk. 3. New York: Herder, 1961.

Jones, C., G. Wainwright, and E. Yarnold, eds. *The Study of Spirituality*. New York: Oxford University Press, 1986.

Woods, Richard. *Christian Spirituality: God's Presence through the Ages*. Chicago: Thomas More Press, 1989.

– 19 –

DOROTHY DAY

(1897–1980)

The Only Solution Is Love

Dorothy Day was born on November 8, 1897 at Bath Beach in Brooklyn, New York, to Grace and John Day. Grace was a strong and stable influence both on John and on Dorothy. John Day was an avid fan of horse racing and a good journalist. Both parents were sensitive to the needs of many people, and yet neither practiced any particular religion. As different job possibilities beckoned John, the family moved from Brooklyn to Oakland, California, when Dorothy was six. She had a baby sister named Della and two older brothers, Sam and Donald.

Dorothy and her siblings were brought up to love God and to deal justly and lovingly with all people. As a child in California, Dorothy discovered she loved being alone and reading the Bible. One Sunday she attended a Methodist church with one of her girlfriends and recalls how moving it was. "No one went to church but me," she recalls. "I was alternately lonely and smug."[1]

John Day enjoyed his job writing about horses and horse racing for a local paper in Oakland. However, the earthquake of 1906 destroyed the building that housed the paper. The paper stopped publication, and John Day was out of a job. At the same time, Dorothy recalls the happiness she felt as her family shared what they had with others who were devastated by the earthquake. John Day decided to move the family to Chicago, where he felt he could get a job as a reporter.

The years in Chicago were happy ones. Dorothy doted on a new baby brother, John. While her mother worked, Dorothy cared for John and had time to read as avidly as she chose. Her father's gifts for writing seemed to have been passed down to her. In spite of their battles of will, Dorothy knew that in many ways she was very much like her father.

At fifteen, during her senior year of high school, she won a Hearst newspaper scholarship that enabled her to attend the University of Illinois. The family was not able to help her out financially, so Dorothy set tables in the dining hall of the YWCA. Her lack of financial resources made it impossible for her to socialize with other teenagers.

Due to her many hours of work, she could not take an active role in the social groups of the campus. She decided to behave as if she didn't care. She took up smoking, learned how to speak crudely, and became critical of campus religious organizations. When she joined a campus socialist club, she lost her YWCA job.

After two years at the University of Illinois Dorothy was quite happy to leave when her father announced the family would move to New York, where he had obtained a job as sports editor for the *New York Morning Telegraph*. When John found out that Dorothy intended pursuing a career in journalism, he forbade her to work. Dorothy could not accept his strict views about women remaining at home and not working, so she left the family home.

John Day encouraged all his newspaper friends to refuse to give Dorothy a job. He was secretly hoping this would force her to return home. Dorothy, however, finally found a job with *Call*, a socialist newspaper. She was paid five dollars a week for her work.

She worked at *Call* for eight months and lived on the Lower East Side of New York City. After covering some of the protests against the entrance of the United States into World War I, Dorothy became the editor of a paper called the *Masses*. The paper was listed on the government's "communist leanings" list for investigation because it lampooned political policies. It was shut down in 1917.

Dorothy then went to Washington, D.C. to be part of the suffragists' march. When the police tried to break up the demonstration and pushed the marchers aside, Dorothy bit and kicked so hard that she was thrown into solitary confinement in a Washington jail. By pardon of President Wilson she and others were allowed to go home on Thanksgiving. Dorothy did not go to her family home, but she did return to New York and found part-time jobs. She stayed with friends at night, since these jobs did not pay enough for her to afford a place of her own.

While Dorothy and a friend, Mike Gold, were attending a play, Mike introduced her to Eugene O'Neill. He and Dorothy talked a long time. She told him of the restlessness she had always felt in her search for God. O'Neill suggested that she read St. Augustine's *Confessions*. On another occasion O'Neill recited Francis Thompson's "Hound of Heaven" in its entirety by heart. Although he had had too much to drink, he did not miss a cadence. Dorothy recalls trying to hide how deeply moved she was as she heard of God's pursuit of the human heart. Dorothy remembers that during the time she spent with O'Neill she stopped in at a Roman Catholic Mass on her way home, even though she was not sure what the ritual meant.[2]

In 1918, Dorothy decided that she should become a nurse. In this way she could help alleviate the suffering caused by war. While she trained at King's County Hospital in Brooklyn, she met Lionel Moise, a known womanizer, with whom she became infatuated. It was her first romance. She became pregnant six months after their relationship started, and she had an abortion several months later—by this time Moise had already left her. A German family took Dorothy in as she dealt with the emotional and physical toll that the events took on her. She attempted suicide twice during this period of recuperation.

Soon after her period of recuperation she married Barkeley Tobey, an acquaintance from work, who had been married a number of times before. They were together for a very short time on a European honeymoon. Barkeley returned home to work and Dorothy went to Capri, where she spent six months writing her book *The Eleventh Virgin.* It became clear to her that, for all practical purposes, this marriage was over. She returned to Chicago in 1922.

In 1923, Dorothy went to New Orleans to work as a reporter, a job that lasted for several months. During that time she received word that the Liveright publishing house was selling her manuscript of *The Eleventh Virgin* to a movie producer. She received $2,500 as part of the transaction. This was an incentive to Dorothy to buy a ticket back to New York, which she had always felt was her true home. By April 1924 Dorothy found a house she could afford—it overlooked the bay. Another love of hers, Forster Batterham, moved in with her. While Forster fished and collected specimens from the sea, Dorothy wrote stories and articles to make enough money for food and taxes. Their child, Tamar, was born in March 1926. Dorothy was never happier.

The birth of Tamar moved Dorothy to reflect on making some formal commitment to God in some religion. She decided she would like to be a Catholic and have Tamar baptized a Catholic. She knew that this meant she would have to encourage Forster to marry her. Forster did not want to undertake such a commitment, with its responsibilities. For years Dorothy and Forster tried to come to some understanding, but the distance between them only grew greater. Finally it became clear to Dorothy that she would have to be willing to have Forster leave her if she was ever to be baptized. She decided to be baptized and live without Forster.

After a period of instruction Dorothy and Tamar were baptized. Forster left them and Dorothy decided to take Tamar to Mexico. Here she could live more simply, write, and enjoy her growing daughter. Her commitment to the Roman Catholic Church was a consolation to her during this period. At the same time, Dorothy never closed her eyes to the inadequacies of the church. She would write often of her love for it because it was Christ made visible. She would also write that she did not love the church for itself, because it was often a scandal to her.

The Great Depression settled over the United States in 1932, a development that caused Dorothy to return to New York. In December she received an assignment from *America* to cover a hunger march that was to take place in

Washington, D.C. The experience awakened her restless desire to do more for the poor.[3]

The police kept the marchers in their cars for days. This prevented them from marching on the Capitol. Because the demonstration was communist sponsored, Dorothy felt she could not actively participate, even though she thoroughly approved of the cause. No leading Catholic figures were joining in the event, a fact that Dorothy understood and yet detested. She was aware that Catholics or any other religious denominations attempting to help the poor were accused of being communists. Yet she wondered if the communist movement was really a more powerful torch for renewing the world than the church.[4]

After Dorothy returned to New York, she encountered a French peasant and former philosophy teacher named Peter Maurin who came to her door. He convinced her that the two foundation stones of Christianity were concern for the poor and commitment to the community. He believed that the church provided a path to God. Those who found this path and walked on it would find freedom, creativity, and renewing humanism. He talked with Dorothy about the material-spiritual unity of persons, and the need for each to share what they had.

Peter and Dorothy developed a deep friendship from which the Catholic Worker movement started. Peter's ready wit and philosophical insights complemented Dorothy's own idealism and pragmatism. The friendship grew and developed over their lifetimes.

The effects of the Great Depression called for movements like the Catholic Worker. The poverty ushered in by the depression demanded that Christians and other religious people share their wealth with the less fortunate. The Catholic Worker movement recruited workers who were dedicated to nonviolence. They also had to be dedicated to hospitality and to the sharing of their resources. The workers could reside at the Catholic Worker House or in houses of hospitality where the workers were indistinguishable from the guests who came for short stays. All ate the same food and shared in the same chores so that there was no class society.

Many disturbed people came as guests off the street to the Catholic Worker House. This made life in the house quite tense. Dorothy was constantly trying to assess her own feelings, her idealism, and the realism or pragmatism of the daily situations. She attempted to make sense of the adjustments required for the Catholic Worker to succeed. One decision was to accept the mentally unstable into the living space:

> When we accepted anyone into the group and gave them a bed, we were accepting them as one of a family.... On the one hand, we have to change the social order in order that people might lead decent Christian lives; on the other hand, we must remake people to remake the social order.[5]

Dorothy and Peter began publishing the *The Catholic Worker* in 1933. In this paper Dorothy often wrote of the relationships between Jesus Christ's gospel of love and the pacifist position she and Peter so strongly advocated for Christians. She was roundly criticized for her editorials, but she never backed down from her staunch stand against violence.[6]

There were occasions when the Roman Catholic hierarchy tried to close down Catholic Worker houses. The bishops feared the movement had a "communist foundation," for it stressed community and the sharing of all things. The Catholic leaders of New York were afraid that the church, which had only recently been freed from anti-Catholic bias in America, would once again be viewed as an unpatriotic religion. The pacifist actions of the Catholic Worker people made church leaders nervous about their image.

How did pacifism play itself out in a time of war, when patriotism was associated with war efforts? When Catholic Worker houses refused to participate in air raid drills, its workers and inhabitants were jailed.[7] Dorothy and Peter felt that their nonparticipation in these drills could stand as a sign of their opposition to war. In spite of the various criticisms hurled at the Catholic Worker houses, Dorothy stood her ground. Continuing to participate in antiwar movements, she always felt her antiwar actions were simply what any good Christian ought to do. Her protests were built on the conviction that humans are meant to live in love and not by destruction.

In the 1950s, Dorothy participated in many marches on behalf of civil rights. While taking part in one such march in Georgia, she was shot at while staying at a farm. This incident opened her eyes again to human fear and to the hatred that can come from fear. In the 1970s, she was jailed with migrant workers in California because she joined them in protesting their unjust treatment.[8]

Peter Maurin, her longtime friend, did not take part in such overt demands for equal rights for all, but he was a constant supporter of Dorothy's activism. His role on behalf of justice was that of organizer and theorist. With humor and great affection for Dorothy, Peter would constantly say that he proposed but Dorothy disposed.

Peter had a severe stroke and eventually lost his ability to communicate. He needed care that was an embarrassment to him. The slow and painful process of Peter's death took a great toll on Dorothy, as her autobiography records. After Peter died, it became even clearer that he had made a unique contribution to the Catholic Worker movement:

> He taught us what it meant to be children of God, and restored to us a sense of responsibility in a chaotic world. He was holier than anyone we ever knew.... The undertaker had tried to sell us artificial grass to cover up the soil, the unsightly grave as he called it. But we loved the sight of

> that earth that was to cover Peter. He had come from the earth as we all had. To the earth he was returning.[9]

Dorothy died in 1980, and people of all classes and from all walks of life attended her funeral. Typically, she wished her funeral to be celebrated in the midst of the people for whom her life had been given. She requested that there be no distinctions made in seating for those of title or rank. For her there should be no more spatial distinctions among the community gathered around Christ's table than there were among the people gathered around the Catholic Worker House table. In the end as in the beginning, "The final word is love."[10]

In the varieties of reflections and meditations that follow, the contemplative side of Dorothy Day will be evident. The prayerful grounding of her activity was never an embarrassment to her, nor did she ever feel the need to hide it from her coworkers. She made it quite clear to those who served others in the Catholic Worker houses or on the farm that they needed times of renewal as much as she did. What others thought of her or of her actions was never much of a concern as long as there was an authentic Christian community that shared concerns for others. The selections that follow provide but a small glance at the mystic and prophetic gifts that marked Dorothy Day's life and her legacy to the next generations.

Loaves and Fishes[11]

About the Time in the Women's Detention Center

For years, we at the Catholic Worker performed all the works of mercy except visiting the prisoner. We had tried to accomplish the equivalent of this through working for the release of political prisoners and speaking in their behalf. We had a chance to practice this act of love in another way in recent years. We visited prisoners by becoming prisoners ourselves for five years running.

We wanted to act against war and against getting ready for war. We made our gesture by disobeying the Civil Defense Act, one provision of which stated that everyone must take shelter during the sham air raid. We women were held in the Women's Detention Center. We were two in a cell on the most airless corridor with one 25 watt bulb in the cell.

From the time one is arrested until the time one leaves a prison, every event seems calculated to intimidate and to render uncomfortable and ugly the life of the prisoner. While in prison, I received a letter inviting me to speak on television. It had already been opened by the censor. The girls begged me to plead their case to the world.

"You must tell how we are put here for long terms, and about the cold turkey cure too, how we are thrown into the tank and left to lie there in our own filth too sick to move." I can only tell what I have seen with my own eyes. How many times I heard it said as a girl was released, "You'll be back here." It was like setting a stamp of hopelessness on any effort the prisoner might make to try to reform. I wondered if the attempt to keep prison unattractive really required so many small indignities to be heaped upon the prisoner.

One of the greatest evils of the day among those outside of prison is their sense of futility. Young people say, "What good can one person do?" They cannot see that we must lay one brick at a time; we can be responsible only for the one action of the present moment. But we can beg for an increase of love in our heart that will vitalize and transform all our individual actions, and know God will take them and multiply them as Jesus multiplied the loaves and fishes.

Next year again, God willing, we will go again to jail. Conditions will perhaps again be just the same. Shut in by walls, bars, concrete, noise, heavy iron screenings that impede the vision of the sky even from the roof, mind and body suffer from the strain.

If those who read this will pray for the prisoners—if New York readers, when they pass by the Women's House for Detention would look up and perhaps wave a greeting or say a prayer—there will be the beginning of change. Most prisoners look out through the bars and perhaps they will see the wave. It could also be that they will feel the caress of the prayer, and a sad heart lightened.

Christ is with us today not only in sacrament and where two or more are gathered in his name, but also in the poor. Who could be poorer or more destitute in body and soul than these companions of ours from the twenty-five days in prison?

I spoke earlier of how often I have failed in love. When we were locked up that first night in a narrow cell, we passed through an experience that was as ugly and horrifying as any I had ever been through. We had been processed, were dressed in the wrappers given to prisoners, floppy slippers, and the women prisoners surrounded us with sordid language, comments, quarreling, and grabbings. The officers were laughing at this, but finally separated us from the others and put us in cells.

The five hundred women were not quiet when the lights went out at nine thirty. Noise, singing, vile story telling, shouting, vile language continued through the night. The other prisoners certainly did not harbor any special hostility toward us. I judged myself for my interior fears and judgment.

Yes, we fail in love. We make judgments and fail to see that we are all one people, seeking love, seeking God, and seeking the beatific vision. All sin is a perversion, a turning from God. If only our love had been stronger, casting out fear, I would not have taken the stand I did in the jail.

Thank God for retroactive prayer! St. Paul said he did not judge himself and we must not judge ourselves either. We must trust Jesus to make up for our falls, our neglects, and our failures to love.

Collected Meditations[12]

All are called to be saints, but all are not called to the extraordinary. If sanctity depended on doing the extraordinary, there would be few saints. The need for saints is greater now than ever before. Never has the world been so organized—press, radio, education and also recreation—to turn minds away from Christ. St. Paul was converted when he had murder in his mind. We are all called to be saints. God expects something from each one of us that no one else can do. If we don't do it, it will not be done.[13]

The world is too much with me in the Catholic Worker. The world is suffering and dying. I am not suffering and dying in the Catholic Worker. I am writing and talking about it. I will not be saved alone. Wherever we are, we are with people. We drag them down or pull them up. Or we get dragged down and pulled up. In recognition of this latter fact, I recognize the need for helps and counsels in the journey to God.

That is why—as soon as possible—primarily for myself, I will try to organize days of recollection. I will not be able to stand the impact of the world otherwise. We can do nothing without saints, big ones and little ones. The only weapons we will develop will be prayer and penance. The world will leave us alone saying, "After all, they are not doing anything. They are just a bunch of smug fools praying."

We will not be as tormented by the scorn of the world as we are by the praise of the world for works of mercy, houses of hospitality and farming communes. It is only by the grace of God that these things have sprung up and prospered.[14]

California, Feb. 13. The Sixties

I stayed in feeling exhausted. Sorrow and grief exhaust me. Tonight, the prayer, the rosaries I have been saying, were answered. The feeling that prayers are indeed answered when we cry out is a comforting one. I had the assurance my prayers were answered even though it might not be now. Perhaps I would not see the results. But "praised be God who comforts us in our afflictions that we may comfort those who are in trouble with the same consolation we have had from Christ." (1 Cor. 1:3–7)

We are praying constantly for the world. We must pray as regularly as we eat in order to grow. We must pray with humility and confidence, for we are nothing without God. We can do nothing, not even lead a natural life. We depend every moment on God. Pray with confidence. Ask and you shall receive. That is a condition laid down by God, and God does not lie. Ask for love. Ask for grace. Do it even at moments of sin. God answers always.[15]

We all want someone to lean on and we all feel alone and we rebel against freedom and responsibility. We always will. But we have to endure this. The only remedy is prayer. Usually we will put that off and look for someone to lean on and give us comfort. We might as well make up our minds that we are not going to find it. We may think we find it but such support crumbles under us.

You can depend on nobody except God and yourself. It is a hard enough fight to control yourself without trying to control others. I always feel that we should expect everything from people—they are a little less than the angels. Then on the other hand, we must not be surprised or disappointed about anything, remembering they are but dust.

July 12, 1957. From Jail for Not Heeding an Air Raid Warning

Today I felt such an immense sense of love of God for all creatures. I was wondering if I would have had this strong sense alone. Being with others, sharing with others, makes the cross so much easier. God has provided a natural way to heaven, generally speaking. Walking with others, the pains of fatigue are lessened. Suffering cold with others—a blanket seems to wrap one and all.[16]

We pray to bring the life of Christ into our own life, into our own time. When we do this, we are asking for the cross, for suffering. Suffering is to surrender our own will. Pray always that our whole life be used to further God's glory and to loving Christ in others. If you keep on praying in that way, you will be a saint. If we do not become holy, it is our own fault.

Prayer is an effect of love. If you love, you pray. Prayer is raising our hearts and minds. It is not directed to ourselves as an outlet for our feelings. It must be an effort to touch God. Prayer has to be doctrinal, not sentimental or overly subjective. Good will is not enough. Prayer has to have good sense.

If your prayer is an ordeal, giving you no sensible consolation, but seeming to be a waste of time and even a subtle hypocrisy—this is all the better. Then you are praying by faith and not by sense. Prayer is always a weariness to the natural person.

Every day sees us making a new start. It seems the old person never dies, and the new one is never born.

My nights are always in sadness and desolation. It seems as soon as I lie down, I am on a rack of bitterness and pain. Then in the day I am again strong enough to make an act of faith and love and go on in peace and joy.

When any person says they have done enough, they have already perished.

Some movement is always necessary—forward or backward. There is no vacation in the spiritual life.

I think to myself, with a touch of bitterness, that the ordinary person does not hear the word of God. I have never heard it as I hear it now, each year in retreat and with the sureness that it is the gospel I am hearing. The average Catholic is baptized, instructed for first Holy Communion, then confirmation, then—Sunday after Sunday—short masses repeat themselves with inadequate sermons, all the announcements, appeals for money. The shepherds are not feeding the sheep. But the shepherds themselves have not been fed.

The sad part is, the people are poor and do not know they are so poor. Poor, undernourished, and even starving as far as spiritual nourishment goes.

The poor often are poor all around. They can be poor in gratitude. But they are not put in our way to be judged, only that we may purchase heaven from them.

Being judged is perhaps the greatest burden the destitute have to bear, the contempt, the judgment of others. "If they would only do this, they would get along better." "If they would think this way, the way I think, if they would do as I do, they would not have had this mental breakdown." There is always that assumption of superiority in us, of having in some way managed better, knowing better than anyone else.

This is even in the attitude of those who help the poor. It is everywhere. It is in us who go to live with the poor and try to serve them. We intrude on them with our advice. Oh yes, we have many plans to help the poor. If we could only feed them, shelter them, clothe them without question, without assuming we have all the answers.[17]

It gives glory to God to choose poor instruments. We feel and have always felt that when we accepted a person in our group and gave that person a bed, we accepted another member of a family. It is hard to remake anyone. This is not a matter of a few months or even a few years. On the one hand, we have to change the social order in order that people can live decent Christian lives. On the other hand, we must renew people to remake the social order. Order cannot be imposed from above. It is going to be a long, slow, suffering process.

But the more we suffer with it, the more we are going to learn. Infinite patience, suffering is needed. It is never ending. As for getting rid of those who are offensive, and then taking in others, one may as well understand that the new batch will be exactly as the last.

What we need is an interior change, the life of Christ in us. But we are always thinking about external organization and the life of the world outside us.

Sept., 1953[18]

To see Christ in others, especially those in authority as David saw Saul, even when Saul was trying to kill him, is difficult. To see Christ and only Christ when one is following one's conscience in what looks like defiance and disobedience is also difficult. To guard the spirit in which one resists—the spirit of a child combined with the judgment of an adult—is always a challenge. We obey when we go to jail.

I am afraid I have not kept the spirit of respect toward Senator McCarthy.[19] Still, there is no room for contempt of others in the Christian life. I speak and write so much better than I perform. But we cannot lower the ideal because we fail in living up to it.

During WW II

Nationalism has been superseded by the doctrine of the Mystical Body, which is as old as Christianity. It is the mystery of Christ in us. Because Jesus lives in you and me, we are one. This truth comes down from heaven. We must try to grasp the reality that lies behind these words. In the conversion of St. Paul, one sentence contains the truth. "I am Christ whom you persecute." There is a real, vital, and energizing union between the person and Jesus Christ. We are one with Christ as Christ is one with the Father. How this can be is a mystery.

When you think of Christ, think of the whole Christ, the fullness of Christ in space and time, a real existence. That the Mystical Body includes only the Roman Catholic Church is heresy. The Mystical Body is the inseparable oneness of the human race from Adam to the last person. Can I have any animosity toward any Japanese, German, Italian—black or white?[20]

If we have animosity, we are liars in Christ. There is no nationality. The only foreigner is the one who does not have Jesus Christ within. But in all human creation, there is no one that does not have Christ within. If only men and women could recognize this, there could never be war.

Practical Meditations[21]

I know that what I write will be tinged with all the daily doings, with myself, my child, my work, my study, as well as with God. God enters into them all and is inseparable from them. I think of the Lord as I wake and as I think of Teresa's daily doings.

Perhaps it is because I have a wandering mind. But I do not care. It is a woman's mind, and if my daily written meditations are about the people about me, of what is going on, then it must be so. It is a part of every meditation to apply the virtue, the mystery, to the daily life we lead.

Because I am a woman involved in practical cares, I cannot give the first half of the day to these things. I must meditate when I can, early in the morning and on the fly during the day. This is not in the privacy of a study—but here, there, and everywhere—at the kitchen table, on the train, on the ferry, on my way to and from appointments, and even while making supper or putting Teresa to bed.[22]

June, 1941[23]

I often think that our Lord must have been terribly bored with the disciples very often, humanly speaking. Certainly, he wasn't picking out brilliant, accomplished, pleasing personalities with whom to live. Isn't it in today's epistle where the mother of James and John wanted the best place for her two sons?

So even the relatives were hanging on to see what they could get out of the situation! He certainly had to get away from them every now and then and do a lot of praying.

They say a mystic is someone who is in love with God, again using that comparison as the kind of love we should feel. This is one of the most absorbing problems of all the work we do, this relationship we have to all those around us. It is a tie that holds us all together around the country.

Sept., 1942[24]

No one asked us to do this work. The mayor of the city did not come along and ask us to run a bread line or a hospice to supplement the municipal lodging house. Nor did the Bishop or Cardinal ask that we help out the Catholic Charities in their endeavor to help the poor.

No one asked us to start an agency or institution of any kind. Because of personal responsibility, because we are each the keepers of each other, we began to try to see Christ in each one that came to us.

If someone came in hungry, there was always something in the icebox. If someone needed a bed and we were crowded, there was always a quarter around to buy a bed on the Bowery. If someone needed clothes, there were always friends to be appealed to, after we had taken the extra coat out of the closet first of course. It might be someone else's coat, but that was all right too.

Feb., 1943[25]

People come to join us in our "wonderful work." It all sounds very wonderful, but life itself is a haphazard, untidy, messy affair. Unless we can live simply, unquestioningly, and solitary, one might say, in the midst of a mob, then we cease to be a personalist. The more we live with people in a community, the more we must look to ourselves and regard the beam in our own eyes. The more we live with a babbling crowd, the more we must practice silence. "For every idle word we speak, we will be judged."

True Love[26]

True love is delicate and kind, full of gentle perception and understanding, full of beauty and grace, full of joy unutterable. Eye has not seen, nor ear heard what God has prepared for those who love the Lord.

There should be some flavor of this in all our love for others. We are all one. We are one flesh in the Mystical Body, as man and woman are said to be one flesh in marriage. With such a love, one would see all things new. We would begin to see people as they really are, as God sees them.

We may be living in a desert when it comes to such perceptions now, and that desert may stretch out before us for many years. But a thousand years are as one day in the sight of God, and soon we will know as we are known. Until then, we will have glimpses of true community. In play, in suffering, in serving, we will begin to train for that ultimate communion.

July 1964[27]

The works of mercy are the works of love. The works of war are the works of the devil. "You do not know of what spirit you are," Jesus said to his disciples when they would call down fire from heaven on the inhospitable Samaritans. This is to look at things in the large context of modern war.

But as for the hostilities in our midst, the note of violence and conflict in all our dealings with others—everyone seems to contribute to it. There is no room for righteous wrath today. In the entire struggle over civil rights, the war which is going on in which one side is nonviolent, suffering martyrdoms, every movement of wrath in the heart over petty hostilities must be struggled with in order to hold up the strength of the participants.

Jan., 1967[28]

There is plenty to do for each one of us, working on our own hearts, changing our own attitudes, in our own neighborhoods. If the just person falls seven times daily, we each fall more than that in thought, word, and deed. Prayer and fasting, taking up our cross daily and following Christ, doing penance are the hard words of the gospel.

As to the Church, where else shall we go, except to the Bride of Christ, one flesh with Christ? Though she is a harlot at times, she is our Mother. We should read the Book of Hosea, which is a picture of God's steadfast love not only for the Jews, the chosen people, but also for the Church, of which each one of us is a potential member.

Since there is no time with God, we are all one, all one body. Whether Chinese, Russian, Vietnamese, the Lord has commanded us to love one another. "A new commandment I give, that you love others as I have loved you," is not to the defending of your life, but to the laying down of your life.

This is a hard saying. "Love is indeed a harsh and dreadful thing," to ask of us, of each one of us. But this is the only answer.

All the Way to Heaven[29]

We are not expecting utopia here on this earth. But God meant things to be much easier than we have made them. Any person has a natural right to food, clothing, and shelter. A certain amount of goods is necessary to lead a good life. A family needs work as well as bread. Property is proper to people. We must keep repeating these things.

Eternal life begins now. "All the way to heaven is heaven, because he said, 'I am the Way.'" The Cross is there of course, but "in the Cross is joy of spirit." Love makes all things easy. If we are putting off the old and putting on Christ, then we are walking in love and love is all we want. But it is hard to love, from the human standpoint, and from the divine standpoint, in a two-room apartment. We are eminently practical, realistic.

Dec., 1969[30]

We have heard this same word, "a band-aid for a cancer," from Boston and Milwaukee and even from the Australian bush within the last year. Perhaps it is only those words of the gospel about the corporal works of mercy, which in a way include the spiritual works of mercy, that has kept us going all these years.

We are commanded over and over again by Jesus Christ to do these things. What we do for the least of the people, we do for him. We are judged by this. It is the picture of the Last Judgment in Matthew 25.

Actually, we at the Catholic Worker did not start these soup lines ourselves. Years ago, John Griffin, one of the men from the Bowery who moved in with us, was giving out clothes. When they ran out, he began sitting down the petitioners to a hot cup of coffee, or a bowl of soup—whatever we had. By word of mouth, the news spread. One after another they came, forming lines (during the Depression) which stretched around the block.

The loaves and fishes had to be multiplied to take care of it, and everyone contributed food, money, and space. All volunteers who come, priests and people, nuns and college students, have worked on that line and felt the satisfaction of manual labor. They begin to do without things themselves to share with others, and a more intense desire to change the social order that left people hungry and homeless.

The work is as basic as bread. To sit down several times a day together is community. It is also a means of growth in the knowledge of Christ. "They knew him in the breaking of bread."

Postscript to the Long Loneliness[31]

We were just sitting there talking when Peter Maurin came in.

We were just sitting there talking when long lines of people began to form saying, "We need bread." We could not say, "Go and be filled." If there were six loaves and a few small fishes, we had to divide them. There was always bread.

We were just talking when people moved in on us. Let those who can take it, take it. Some moved out and made room for more. And somehow, the walls expanded.

We were all just talking when someone said, "Let's all go live on a farm." It was just as casual as that, I often think. It just came about. It happened.

I found myself a barren woman, the joyful mother of children. It is not always easy to keep in mind the duty of delight.

The most significant thing about the Catholic Worker is poverty, some say. The most significant thing is community, others say. We are not alone any more.

But the final word is love. At times it has been, in the words of Father Zossima, a harsh and dreadful thing. Our very faith in love has been tried through fire.

We cannot love God unless we love each other. To love we must know each other. We know the Lord in the breaking of the bread and we know each other in the breaking of the bread.

We are not alone anymore. Heaven is a banquet and earthly life is a banquet too. This is true even with a crust of bread where there is companionship.

We have all known the long loneliness and we have learned that the only solution is love. Love comes with community.

It all happened while we sat there talking. And it is still going on!

NOTES

1. Dorothy Day, *The Long Loneliness* (New York: Harper and Row, 1981) 20.
2. William D. Miller, *All Is Grace: The Spirituality of Dorothy Day* (New York: Doubleday, 1987) 1–15.
3. Ibid. 15–20.
4. Day, *Long Loneliness* 158–66.
5. Miller, *All Is Grace* 20–27.
6. Ibid. 136.

7. Day, *Loaves and Fishes* 160–78.

8. June E. O'Connor, *The Moral Vision of Dorothy Day* (New York: Crossroad, 1991) 63–86.

9. Day, *Long Loneliness* 281.

10. Ibid., Postscript.

11. Dorothy Day, *Loaves and Fishes* (New York: Harper and Row, 1963) 161–78.

12. The following meditations and the page numbers cited are from Miller's collection, *All Is Grace.*

13. 102.

14. 103.

15. 107–11.

16. 115–16.

17. 134–37.

18. Senator Joseph McCarthy, from Wisconsin, was one of the senators whose fear of communism led his committee to accuse many individuals and groups of subversive communist activity in the 1950s.

19. 145–47.

20. These particular ethnic groups are singled out because their countries were at war with the United States and its allies.

21. *Meditations*, ed. Stanley Vishnewski (New York: Newman, 1970), is the source to which page numbers in this section refer.

22. 6.

23. 79.

24. 54.

25. 60.

26. 61.

27. 54–55.

28. 74.

29. 79–80.

30. 80.

31. Day, *Long Loneliness*, Postscript. There is no page number.

BIBLIOGRAPHY

Callahan, Annice Marie. "Dorothy Day: Peacemaker in Our Nuclear Age." In *Spiritual Guides for Today*. New York: Crossroad, 1992.

Day, Dorothy. *The Eleventh Virgin*. New York: A. and C. Boni, 1924.

Day, Dorothy. *From Union Square to Rome*. New York: Arno Press, 1978.

Day, Dorothy. *House of Hospitality*. New York: Sheed and Ward, 1939.

Day, Dorothy. *Loaves and Fishes*. New York: Harper and Row, 1963.

Day, Dorothy. *The Long Loneliness*. New York: Harper and Row, 1963.

Day, Dorothy. *On Pilgrimage*. New York: Catholic Worker Books, 1948.

Day, Dorothy. *On Pilgrimage: The Sixties*. New York: Curtis Books, 1972.

Day, Dorothy. *Therese*. Notre Dame: Fides, 1960.

Ellsberg, Robert, ed. *By Little and by Little: The Selected Writings of Dorothy Day*. New York: Alfred Knopf, 1983.

Miller, William D. *All Is Grace*. New York: Doubleday, 1987.
O'Connor, June E. *The Moral Vision of Dorothy Day*. New York: Crossroad, 1991. (The bibliography cites numerous primary and secondary sources.)
Vishnewski, Stanley, ed. *Meditations*. New York: Newman, 1970.

– 20 –

CARYLL HOUSELANDER

(1901–1949)

A Christian Has No Enemies

Caryll Houselander was an English woman whose life in the twentieth century carried on the active humanness of Margery Kempe and the reflective warmth of Julian of Norwich. Although there has always been diversity in English spirituality due to the numbers of peoples who voyaged to and who pillaged parts of Britain, there have also been general characteristics that describe English spirituality since the Middle Ages.

These characteristics include an appreciation for and meditative reading of the Scriptures, a loving devotion to the humanity of Jesus Christ, a harmony between the more intellectual approach to Christian spirituality and the more affective approach, and a preference for the practical—as opposed to theoretical—approach to living a Christian life. These characteristics have parallels in the spiritual traditions of other countries, but the way in which they are lived out by the English is its own unique combination of the characteristics.[1]

The history of English spirituality since the Reformation included a variety of movements for renewal and reform. Henry VIII and Thomas Cranmer, two pillars of early Anglicanism, set forth a liturgical tradition that initially remained quite close to the Roman Catholic tradition.[2] Doctrinal differences in the relationship to Rome as well as in interpretation of sacraments remained through the centuries. Anglican clergy were well educated through the university system and imbibed some humanistic ideals. Roman clergy were less educated and generally narrow in their more medieval interpretations of Scripture and tradition. There was a certain vindictiveness of the Roman Curia toward Elizabethan England, which led to the middle and upper classes having difficulty remaining Catholic.

The wedding of church and state in England continued through the centuries, with the king or queen retaining the power to appoint bishops. Roman clergy were not linked to the authority of the monarch, but were under the papal authority of the Roman Church.[3] In general, the composition of the Roman

Catholic Church included more of the immigrant and socially lower classes than the Anglican communion.[4]

The Roman Church at the turn of the nineteenth century was still suffering from tensions between popes and national rulers as nationalism dominated the world environment. The uneasy fears of reformation liberty and progressive theological renewal affected the papacy of Leo XIII (1878–1903). Even though he was statesman enough not to use the infallibility claim to seize papal power in a world that threatened it, the Curia urged him to be firm in dealing with national leaders. His positive attribute was his strong sense of social justice and the challenge to national leaders to act with compassion for the victims of poverty.

Pius X (1903–14) fostered a renewed sacramental life. He encouraged an approach to the Lord's Supper or Holy Communion that invited people to a frequent reception of the Eucharist. Communion was not to be looked on as a reward for goodness, but as an aid to people still on the journey to God. Pius X inherited the power struggles that caused strong anticlerical tensions in France and Germany at the time. His fearful Curia became a dominating force at the end of his life. In 1910, he required that all seminary professors take an "antimodernist oath," which prevented professors from teaching certain "modern" views of theology and biblical studies. This set Roman Catholic theological and biblical research back by fifty years and widened the credibility gap between Catholic theologians and other scholars.

Benedict XVI (1914–22) spent most of his life trying to prevent World War I and to end the antimodernist heretic hunts inside the Roman Church. He refused to take sides during the war and was a strong advocate for the care of war orphans and other victims. His efforts for the release of prisoners of war were quietly effective. He was the first pope to identify and to discourage the colonialism that affected the Roman Catholic Church in Asia and Africa. He did what he could to encourage native clergy. His successor, Pius XI (1922–39), was a man of contrasts. On the one hand, he desired strong uniformity in Catholic teaching, but on the other hand, he fostered the Catholic Action movement of the laity. The movement was controlled by clerics, but it also acknowledged that the laity had a more active role to play in transformation of the world than was formerly accepted.[5]

Caryll Houselander's life reflected the vitality of the Catholic Action movement, although she was not directly involved in that particular movement. She and her friends would eventually shape their own movement for the powerless. But first, she would grow through the uncertain period of World War I and its aftermath.

Caryll was baptized into the Roman Catholic Church when she was six, along with her mother, who had undergone a sudden and strong religious conversion to Catholicism. The religious fervor of her mother influenced Caryll's own commitment to Christ. As her mother became more fervent, her father could no longer accept the relationship with his wife. Caryll's parents divorced when she was eight. The emotional trauma of the father leaving them took years for Caryll to integrate into her life.

Caryll's mother ran a boardinghouse in order to make a living for both of them. She did well enough to be able to send Caryll to a French convent boarding school when Caryll was eleven. During this time Caryll became close to the only Bavarian lay sister in the community. The sister seemed to understand Caryll's sensitivity and loneliness. Occasionally Caryll helped the sister shine shoes or aided her in other ways in the menial tasks she did for the children.

One day as this Bavarian sister was shining the children's shoes, Caryll noticed that she was weeping. This was in the early days of World War I, when the French and Bavarian peoples were set against each other. It became clear to Caryll that the only Bavarian lay sister in a French community must feel somewhat estranged and lonely. She went over to the sister and asked if she could help. As the sister looked up, Carol's first visionary experience occurred. She saw a crown of thorns encircling the head of the sister.[6]

She did not understand the significance of this initial vision until years later when two further visions would clarify its meaning. Caryll eventually got more involved in the social and educational life of the school and finished with a fine education. If she expected to get into the social middle class, however, she would need more schooling.

At sixteen she decided to attend St. John's Wood Art School. Her artistic talent was significant, although making a living as an artist was not a practical hope. Her mother had continued to help her pay for the education and suggested that Caryll set up a sort of art studio in the garden by the mother's house. In the meantime, Caryll had a negative experience with a particular Catholic church that affected her for eight years.

She had decided to attend a Sunday service, and as she tried to enter the church, she was asked to pay "pew rent." She had no money with her at the time and tried to explain this. The usher would not allow her to enter. She walked away indignant and promised herself she would not go to a Catholic church again. She spent eight years keeping that promise.

In these years of early adulthood Caryll was not sure what she wanted to do with her life. She had accepted an engagement ring only to finally admit to herself that she did not want to be engaged. She was simply too sensitive about hurting the young man's feelings if she said no. She returned the ring and the engagement ended.

Caryll was a promising artist and writer, but could not make a living without total dedication to one field or the other. As she reflected on her real concerns, however, she identified a vocation that grew out of a long-term care and concern for the poor and powerless, especially prostitutes and helpless children. As long as she could remember, she had returned home from walking the streets of London with a deeper compassion for the many poor and underprivileged people who merely existed on the streets.

Caryll had her second vision while walking these streets. One evening she was hurrying down a crowded street to buy potatoes. She looked up to see a massive Russian icon, the crucified Christ the King, stretched out over the London sky. Shortly after this vision, she passed a newspaper stand and saw headlines about the assassination of the czar of Russia. When she looked more closely at the picture of the czar, she saw his face was identical to the face of Christ in her vision.[7]

Reflecting on the meaning of her visions led her to seek a job working with Russian immigrants in London. During the postwar period, Caryll became increasingly sensitive to the plight of displaced citizens, especially children. As she and a coworker did all they could for the immigrants, she fell in love with him. His name was Sidney Riley, and he worked for the British Intelligence Agency. A strong friendship slowly bonded them and changed them both in the process. As they learned more about each other, their mutual commitment to the poor and the hope they had for the powerless drew them closer. In time, Sidney met and then married another woman, but the insight each had given to the other remained a powerful force in both their lives.

It was not long after Sidney's marriage that Caryll experienced a third vision. This vision lasted intermittently for days. Caryll was on her way home in the London underground and in the midst of the usual crowd of people getting into the train when the vision occurred. She began to notice that wherever she looked, each person seemed to be another Christ. If the person looked sad or upset, it was the suffering Christ that she saw. If the person was joyous and vigorous, she saw a different Christ. When she left the subway for the crowded streets, the same phenomenon occurred. The vision lasted for several days, a much longer period than her prior visions.

Caryll reflected on all three visions. The last was the one that enlightened her about the inner meaning of all three. If every person was "another Christ," then the destruction and hatred manifest through wars between nations was a crime against Jesus Christ. If anyone was in need, Christians were obliged to do something to remedy the situation, for that was service to Christ. The asceticism of Christian life was not some externally imposed penance but the asceticism that flows from the attempts to love as universally as Christ loves.[8]

In a country in which there was a history of some antipathy between major denominations of Christians, and in a church where a pope had refused to choose sides in a war, Caryll worked out the meanings of loving as Christ loved. For her, the mystical body of Christ meant that everyone was loved and called to be a member of the Christian community. There was no special privilege that separated Christian from Christian, cleric from lay. All were called to holiness as Christ intended. There was not a ranking of vocations according to which ones brought the highest expectation of holiness, at least not in her mind. All of the baptized had the obligation to live the corporal and spiritual works of mercy.

Although Caryll was always skeptical about the hierarchical definitions and restrictions that characterized the church of her day, she did return to the Catholic Church in her mid-twenties. The sense that Caryll had of the mystical body of Christ posed a lifelong tension for her. She was thoroughly convinced that the church ought to be serving everyone in need, regardless of their religious background. At the same time, she was aware that the Roman Catholic hierarchy equated itself with the fullest expression of the Christian tradition, and others should simply accept that. She never felt it was that simple.

As a younger adult, Caryll was constantly pulled between her artistic work, her writing, and her conviction that she ought to be meeting the demands of countless poor people. Like many of the poor she served, Caryll often struggled to make ends meet. She eventually confided to her close friends that her artistic gifts could never fully develop because she had made a choice about the direction of her life that would never place her in the upper class of English society. She had chosen to remain a single woman so that she could serve others.

In the England of the 1940s, the vocation of the single life was not understood or affirmed. As a Roman Catholic in England, Caryll knew that motherhood or vowed religious life constituted the two "vocations" that many people in the church believed women could follow. She refused to live in such restrictive lines. She considered her expression of "spiritual motherhood" to be a vocation that affirmed life, nurtured the needy, and brought some fullness to the body of Christ. This "spiritual motherhood" was as valid a form of motherhood for her as the motherhood that accompanied married life.

As Caryll's sense of the embodiment of Christ in everyone grew, her work at the British Censorship Office was directly affected. She became painfully aware of the propaganda directed against the "enemy" nations, especially Germany. She was sure that hating an enemy is a form of self-destruction, since the only thing hatred accomplishes is further division and hatred. For reasons of conscience, she had to leave the job.

The aftermath of World War I had left many people, including children, homeless, maimed, and deprived of family members. The poverty, suffering, and fear that plagued postwar nations led Caryll to envision the people as helpless children. Her book, *The Passion of the Infant Christ* identifies this tragedy of war and begs Christians to respond to the suffering.[9]

Caryll and her friends were always distrustful about any organized spirituality that resembled a ledger approach to charity. If Christians had to measure their good or kind deeds against their sinfulness, life became an un-Christian drudgery. For Caryll, love that imitated Christ's love was simple. Everyone is sister and brother to Christ because Christ is brother to everyone. This strong insight led Caryll and her friends to do something pragmatic about the poor children and adults who went hungry each day. They decided to open a small place where meals would be free. The effort was simply named Loaves and Fishes.

Loaves and Fishes was—and is—an effort that encourages ordinary people to share what they have with those who are less fortunate. This is accomplished with volunteers who come to share and distribute food to the hungry. Caryll and her friends loosely organized this effort in England while they retained anonymity.

The Loaves and Fishes pattern was eventually picked up by many groups who were convinced that lay action is necessary to save the church. The movement spread rapidly during the economic depression of the 1930s. For Caryll and her friends, these personal efforts to help others were not really an option but a commandment to love as Christ loves us.

Perhaps because her life was lived in the aftermath of World War I, Caryll's writings often deal with suffering and forgiveness. Suffering of any kind is intended to enlighten human hearts and call forth deeper love. Anyone who suffers is enabled to understand and be sensitive to the sufferings of all. Only love can span the distance that divides people and nations.

Caryll could laugh at her eccentricities.[10] Although committed to the health and care of the poor, she continued to be a chain-smoker. Although living a social spirituality that preceded official church writings, she considered herself a conventional Roman Catholic. Although she maintained a very active life, she also spent time away to renew the inner space that nourished her life. And whereas her desire to be unnoticed was sincere, she admits her delight in becoming the first woman to be named president of the Royal Society of Medicine. The honor enabled her to collaborate with Dr. Eric Strauss in using art therapy in a school for "disturbed boys." This was one of many forms of care that would mark Caryll's relatively short but full life.

Caryll's vocation was deeply rooted in her conviction that each person must follow the call to love in a manner that both respects and challenges the status quo. In her eyes, to be just as God is just did not mean one could inflict destructive punishment. God's justice meant to forgive so that love could be a real possibility again. Caryll's spirituality of loving as Christ loves meant doing something about the little ones, the powerless ones who are often forgotten in a fast-paced society. To be poor in spirit as Christ was poor in spirit meant to accept that God can—and in time will—do all things through those who try to act as God would act.

Elements of the spirituality of Caryll Houselander that flows through the excerpts that follow may seem strange to modern ears. Caryll will speak about the "passion of the infant Christ." The phrase is used symbolically to emphasize the suffering of the powerless, namely, children and others who are powerless to change their oppressive situations. Caryll will speak about the need for individual action in situations that seem so overwhelming that many feel an individual gesture is useless. She often wrote about alleviating the suffering of Christ in the children and poor of the world, pointing out that a slow resurrection is existing side by side with oppression.

Caryll Houselander's perceptions are more than fifty years old. Yet some of them remain meaningful in these last years of the twentieth century. The passion of Christ is still inflicted on the poor and the little ones by those who have greater power. There is still disregard for the suffering of Christ that is manifest in lives dehumanized by the oppressive use of power. At the same time, Caryll's hope that some would work for justice in pragmatic ways is also being realized.

Loaves and Fishes is a movement that has gone beyond English shores. The sharing of food with the less fortunate occurs in many cities through a variety of agencies. There are still those who—like Caryll—reach out in little ways to pragmatically address great problems. These people continue to act as the body of Christ, receiving hope as Caryll herself did. To others and to herself she said often, "Lift up your eyes and see the star!" The excerpts of her works that follow indicate some of the light that she saw in her life of service and following the star.

Redemptive Childhood and Justice[11]

Meditation on the unity of Christ's life, of how the passion is in the infancy and how the infancy is in the passion, proves to us that our own lives need not be lived on an heroic scale to be redeeming. This is of huge significance to us today, faced by the appalling suffering in the world.

It seems that human anguish is a gathering tide, a storm rising higher and higher, sweeping its dark waves wider and wider and closer and closer. We feel futile and utterly helpless to do anything about it. It is a feeling of helplessness that is like being face-to-face with an ocean sweeping toward us in a flood of towering waves and we were told to stop it with our naked hands.

The magnitude of suffering makes our lives seem even more futile than we have realized. We ask ourselves, what have we done to help even one persecuted child in the misery of Europe? Of what use to the multitudes of suffering people is our life? Of what use is our little circumscribed life to anyone when it consists of doing the same meaningless things every day for the same monotonous number of hours, winding up with the same frustrating weariness and drowsiness each night?

We seem useless even to those in our immediate circle, our family and friends. When one of them meets with real grief, we are helpless before it. We can do nothing. More often than not, we cannot even find words to express our sympathy, or we are too self-conscious to express them and we let the moment of meaningful spoken compassion go by. If we look superficially, it could seem that every life must be lived in spiritual isolation, as if we create our own prison.

The longing to help humanity, to be in communion with other people, is genuine enough in most of us. But we remain frustrated, or imagine ourselves to be, by the insignificance of our circumstances, our limits, and our lack of skill or opportunity. Even in something about which we agree in our hearts, namely, the necessity of avoiding a new war, we can feel helpless. Evidently fear, that is strong enough to destroy and separate us, is not strong enough to unite us.

This problem is of a spiritual order. Our life is sacramental, that is, integral in body and soul. This is why we can never escape the obligation to help each other materially even if the attempt looks like Don Quixote tilting at a windmill. This is why the inward meaning of life must ground our efforts. The inward meaning of life is Christ, who says, "Without me, you can do nothing." The power to do anything in this world is the power of Christ's love in us.

If we only had our own puny hands with which to hold back the flood of the world's suffering, it is without question that we should drown in it. The only hands that can hold back the world's suffering are the crucified hands of Christ. In the world, in the human race as a whole, just as in each human life, love and death are face-to-face. Love is Christ on the cross facing the world with his arms wide open. This is translatable into any language: it is the Word telling of the Father's love to all. Whatever suffering any individual anywhere in the world offers up for humankind in the crucified Christ becomes this Word uttered in love.

All those who offer any suffering for the world are one. They live together as one body in Christ. Christ on the cross is the oneness of our world. In him, our individual suffering is integrated in one redeeming act of love. In the crucified Christ, the Christs of every nation meet as one. This oneness in the Passion of Christ is the love that is redeeming the world.

A Christian has no enemies. Those who formerly wounded one another bleed together from the same wounds, the wounds of the crucified Christ. Poured again from his wounds, the blood sows the seed of love into the world. Those who have killed one another in war may still rise in him overcoming death. In Christ, those who rise will come together and greet each other with his greeting, "Peace be to you."

Suffering does not redeem simply because it is suffering. It does not help those in need more or less because it is more or less suffering. Suffering does not necessarily help at all. Suffering does not necessarily unite us to God. In fact, suffering can separate us from God, for it can make us bitter, cynical, cruel, and even drive us to despair.

God's presence or absence can be known by the effect of suffering on us, especially the small suffering of every day. In those in whom Christ abides, it is Christ who suffers. It is not what we suffer that redeems and heals; it is with whom we suffer, Christ in us. Our lives are lived by Christ in us. Therefore the way to the world's healing, to cessation of the world's suffering, is simply to foster the life of Christ in us. If the Christ in us is the infant Christ, then in our own littleness we can be stretched to the size of the cross.

The massacre of the innocents that started in Bethlehem has spread all over the world today. It is always the children who are the first victims of tyranny. Herod ordered the children to be killed because he was afraid any one of them might be the Christ. Any child might be the Christ! The fear of Herod, of modern Herods, is the hope of every Christian. What processions of little children have followed across the world in our own times! Thirty years ago, Russian children were driven before the Red Army to be tossed alive into open graves in the Steppes.

From Czechoslovakia, France, Belgium, Holland, Java, Korea, Greece, Poland, Estonia, Latvia, Lithuania, Rumania, Bulgaria, Albania, Yugoslavia, Finland, Hungary, Austria, Serbia, Çroatia, Slovenia, Bosnia, Montenegro, and Macedonia, children have been driven out or killed by tyrants. Whether these tyrants bear the name of one ideology or another, they can equally be identified with Herod. On earth, the answer to these Herods is still the same. It is the birth of Christ into the world through the least and the littlest that can change its course. It is spiritual childhood that must return, Christ in each for the good of all.

Abroad, the infant Christ is hunted and persecuted. In England, he has become a foundling. He who has said to us with such tenderness, "I will not leave you orphans," has been left an orphan. He is orphan in countless souls where he lives, but is forgotten, neglected, and even unknown.

There are many of whom this tragic indictment is true and yet who are not culpable for it. The vast number of English people received baptism, but it was regarded by their parents as a social occasion, not a sacrament. Godparents were chosen not for their faith but for the material advantages that might result from the compliment that was paid to them. These people have been brought up "free to choose their own religion," which means, without any definite teaching about any religion at all, in an atmosphere of shifting prejudice, doubt, and materialism and with no Christian practice in their homes. Instead of it, there was a general understanding that any outward adherence to God is in bad taste, and the whole subject of faith is sufficiently embarrassing to be taboo in polite conversation.

Divorce, arrogance, and thoughtlessness have given us a nation of spiritually starved children. Over one thousand of them between six and twelve years of age, evacuated from London during the war, were questioned concerning their knowledge of God by a group of people temporarily responsible for them. Out of them all, one only was familiar with Christ's holy name—as a swear word. Not one knew that Christ was God, or even who God is.

The Christ-Child in the soul of the average English person is a forgotten, unwanted child, waiting for adoption in a children's home that is not a home, for it is without beauty and without love.

To be a foster parent of the orphaned Christ is a sublime vocation. It exacts a profound humility from those who are called to it, and confers a unique majesty upon them. Very often, the worldly pass such people by with a vague uncomfortable contempt. They regard celibacy itself as either a disease or a disgrace, and, in either case, a disaster. I am talking about the lives that are neither those of married people nor of vowed religious, which are not breathless with social success or obsessed with making money. I am speaking of lives so empty that there is time to "go about doing good" as Christ did on earth. These lives are in fact spent largely with the lowly and the outcasts. Such lives spent with the "insignificant" seem to the vast masses of mediocre people to be deserts of arid waste, stony, uncultivated wilderness. But in the eyes of God, they are the wilderness that flowers.

These foster parents of Jesus are not those terrible reformers of individual lives who, urged and driven by an unrecognized sense of power or vanity, interfere with people's lives. These are not the ones who fumble at the locked doors of the souls of others with clumsy fingers, bruising when they touch to heal. They are—to the contrary—sensitive people. They approach others with sympathy, not with exhortations. They approach not with self-satisfaction but with humility. They give and they listen. They see the spark of life wherever it is and fan it by the warm breath of their humanity. They reverence the solitude of other people's souls. They bear other people's burdens and rejoice in their joy, without imposing upon them. Not only do they tread delicately not to crush the broken reed, but they go down on their knees to bind it up.

They are those people who will be amazed when Christ calls them on the day of judgment and greets them by telling them that they gave him food and shelter and clothed him and came to him in prison. It is not those who make a double entry account of their kindness, and have a balance sheet of merit who will receive this lovely recognition and be astonished by it!

When we say, "I must have justice!" we usually mean, "I must have the relief of hurting as I have been hurt, of despoiling as I have been despoiled." Christ has commanded us to forgive as often as we are injured. Christ has made the forgiveness we give the very condition of our own forgiveness in his day of judgment. If we knew the human heart as God knows it, and the network of interdependence which spreads the responsibility for every sin not only among countless people but over many generations, we should not attempt to untwist the skeins of right and wrong. For us, justice is to forgive and to make reparation ourselves for all sin. We must be just not because we are judges, for that we are not. We must be just because we are trustees of God's love to the world. Justice is a supreme expression of God's love.

Today, justice must restore the kingdom of heaven to the little nations. These are those sorrowful countries in the power of tyranny, outwardly depersonalized by the pattern of ideology imposed upon them by force. Their own characteristics and racial beauty are effaced for the time being as they are stripped of their national dress, just as Christ was stripped of his garments. These are the countries that are poor as children, subject as children, and helpless as children.

Lift up your eyes and see the star! The star burns over the martyr countries of the world. Justice constrains us to insist openly on the rights of the little nations, to make penance for the sins against them, in our own lives, to give all that we can for their relief. We must be ready if it is expedient to do so, to give our lives for the restoring of the freedom of the Divine Child in their midst. In them, Christ will be born again. In any humble, frustrated life, Christ may be born. It may be that in the heart of an old peasant, who has lost all sons and daughters, the Divine Child shall be born and the old will be made new. The life of this Christ shall renew the earth.

When Christ, born secretly in the little nations, in the martyr countries of the world, is recognized and worshiped openly, those countries will be clothed in their own particular heritage of beauty once more. They shall receive back their own individual character. Then the bereaved will see the Child King again. This child will have the face of their own children. In Germany, it will be the fair child with wide, blue eyes. In Poland, the child will be grave, but it is childhood's gravity. In France, the scepter will be the crook of the shepherd. In Japan, the Christ Child shall walk among the reeds on naked delicate feet. To every parent, the Child of Ivory shall come. In Russia, the Child shall come among the peasants, his holy face caressed by the flickering of the icon lamps. When the Christ Child is crowned again in the little nations, then, and only then, shall there be peace on earth!

The Comforting of Christ[12]

If we are not interested in the minds, the feelings, the hopes, fears, sorrows and joys of everyone with whom we come in contact, we are not interested in Christ.

Whatever we do to anyone, we do to him. If we are impatient with the mental suffering, the doubting, the questioning and the wrestling with the angel of the more sensitive minds, then we are impatient with the mind of Christ bleeding under the crown of thorns. If we shrink from the broken lives of sinners, then we draw away from Christ fallen and crushed under his cross. If we will not go to the sick and the poor to help them, we will not help Christ.

How shall we educate ourselves to face other people's sufferings? First, we can start with the physical. We can now go into the hospitals and work for the sick. Those who do this will come to life if they see the wounds of Christ in each one. They must cease thinking of people in the wards as casualties, decrepits, cases, or operations. They must think of them as Christ's.

Outside of hospitals, outside of national service, there is the great harvest of the forgotten poor. In our zeal for our country, we have forgotten that if we do not work to keep the little homes and lives of our people, our victory will mean nothing. We are not fighting for might. We are trying to keep the conditions that can still enable the love of Christ to flower, that can lift an innocent face to God from the earth. If we forget our poor now, we might as well have surrendered to those who trampled the Christian faith into the mud.

There is another more general way of teaching oneself to face the world's suffering. Instead of simply forgetting, remember. Remember that everywhere there are people in need. You must face this need. Learn to do without so that others can have more. When I was a child I used to rage when I was told to eat my disgusting rice pudding because lots of starving little girls would like it. That struck me as a very good reason to give it to them!

I have not changed this view. Now I add to it the practice of leaving the table a little bit hungry, give up something that I do like, and share it with those who are hungry. If we train ourselves to do without some of our small amusements, clothes, cigarettes, we can give to Christ in his need. We might even get into a habit of sharing and giving. None of us is so poor that we cannot find another in greater need than ourself. It takes far greater skill to attend to a broken heart than it does to attend to a broken limb.

The Risen Christ[13]

It requires no courage to accept the fact that the joy of Christ's love is given to us in the mystery of his risen life, which is now our life. The very meaning of Christianity is that we are to increase the life of the world by giving this love to one another. But if we consider how Christ loves us and therefore how we are to love, courage is asked of us.

We think of the risen life in us as a summer of Christhood in the world, a splendor of flower and fruit, a harvesting of love. So it is, but not unconditionally. Christ has told us himself what the condition is. The seed must be buried deep down in the darkness under the weight of the earth. Then the seed must be subject to the winter, the season of frost, of long darkness and short light. The slow pace, the long pause in periods of growth is the condition for bearing fruit.

Christ has clearly told us that our love must be as his. His commandment is that we love as he has loved us (John 15:12–13). This is a love that dies to self so that it can be given to everyone. Obedience to God is acceptance of the plan of our lives. In loving at all, we know an element of suffering. We realize the frailty of those we love. We fear the loss and the parting of those we love. By a strange paradox, falling in love brings us a deep realization of our own nothingness or helplessness to do and to be all that we would wish to be for the beloved.

The dying to self which makes our love like Christ's is not selfless. Selfless love would not be love at all. Rather it is the surrender of ourself in love that is true love. Many who imagine that they love are really concerned with nothing except that they be loved. Their parents, husbands, wives, friends, children, become their victims. Their love is plaintive, possessing, and suffocating. They depend upon others for constant reassurance that they are loved. This love cannot go out from itself and give life even to those in the household. It cannot certainly give life to the ends of the earth.

Yet we are to love everyone and to exclude no one. The rich must love the poor and the poor must love the rich. The white race must love the races of color and the races of color must love the white race. The wise must be hospitable to the foolish and the foolish must also be hospitable to the wise. We are to love those who hate us and who are indifferent to us, which is often harder. Most baffling of all, we are to love those we don't even know!

When we think of what this means, the mystery deepens. When we consider the martyrs, how mediocre our ability to love. Martyrs give the world everything that they suffer, even their deaths. What they do belongs to us because we are in communion with them. What we do belongs to them because we are in communion with them. We are all one Body in Christ.

Equally, we are one with the sinners of the world. Just as we realize that the martyrs give us much and we give back so little, so we realize that sinners may need much. We give sinners so little because we are sinners too. How can any one person, limited in knowledge, imagination, circumstances, as most of us are, reach out in love to such widely different people?

Only through a yet closer and real identification with Christ. So far we have thought of how we can be one with him in our love of one another. If we are to reach the world, we must be one with him in his love of the Father.

In our communion with Christ on earth, we do reach each other through the span of the cross. We can love all people, known and unknown, through literally loving with Christ's love. It would not be fantastic in our days to ask if love, to be literally like his, might not demand of us that we should actually die for one another. So many have done this and are doing it. But how we are to die is God's secret for each of us. The sacrifice of self at the heart of each life, offered to the world, to God, is a complete expression of the sacrifice of the cross.

Christ expressed his sacrificial love in everything he did in his life. His very birth was a surrender of himself to death. Every act was an act of the same love that was consummated on Calvary. There are many people today in forced labor camps hidden away from the world. There, unknown, nameless martyrs will die. The few who have escaped tell us that of all their sufferings, the worst was a sense of having been forgotten. But they are not forgotten. Those who willingly share in Christ's suffering every day are always with them. When there seems no comfort left, suddenly small miracles happen. A gleam of sunlight, a bird's song, a whispered word of encouragement, an unexpected hand clasp, can be means of hoping again. Some older woman somewhere, a little child in a distant place, is giving them the gentle solace of Christ's love.

Some people learn to love the whole world through the love of God. For them, the way of sacrifice is direct and informed with joy. Others learn to love God through loving one another. There are not two kinds of love in Christ, one his suffering love and one his risen love. There is only one love. This love is part of the glory of the Risen Lord. This love, even here, is the beginning of the answer to his prayer that all may be one.

Because Christ comes to us in human hands as he once came to us first in a woman's arms, no one need ever be quite alone and without human help. He comes to the loneliest, to outcasts, degenerates, strangers, to prisoners, and to men and women in the condemned cell. He comes through the hands of other creatures who are led by the spirit of love.

Christ lives in each of us and in each of us he waits to receive human kindness from another. It is for us to allow that to happen to Christ in us. Even the greatest sinner, though he waits until the hour of death, not only receives comfort from a priest but also gives comfort to Christ.

Christ knew the interdependence of human creatures and felt it himself in little things and in great things. As a human being, he accepted the limitations of human beings. He discarded false heroics. When he needed rest, he sought it without complaining if he was disturbed or frustrated. He was not one of those disheartening people who, when they have exhausted their whole household by the endless fever of their activities, say, "If you want a thing done properly, do it yourself!" Christ often delegated his work. He still delegates it to us today.

There are many "commonsense Christians," afraid to spend themselves on anyone from whom they do not get favorable results. They are ready for hard work for reform. They pour out good advice. They are proud to be realists, who repudiate anything impractical, including the poetry of Christ. They have no use for those baffling creatures who won't play the game by their rules. Such realists refuse to see that there are problems which cannot be solved, griefs which cannot be healed, conditions which cannot be cured. These are impatient with the suffering they cannot end. They refuse to accept such realities because they cannot—they think—do much about it.

We cannot make an end of Christ's suffering. For as long as the world goes on, the Passion of Christ will go on in his members. He will ask, not for his suffering to be mitigated, but for sympathy. In Gethsemane, Christ tried to awaken his apostles, not because they could take away his pain, but because they could give him compassion.

Compassion is giving oneself to suffer in sympathy with the thing that cannot be changed in another's life. Sympathy with Christ in those who suffer his Passion is a rare thing.

Christ rose bearing his wounds. There are other Christs today who are not always recognized as such because they carry wounds, stigmata—his stigmata. People who bear a burden of hereditary disease, temperament or temptations, and neurotics or borderline cases may be shunned by society. Mentally ill people who are often abandoned by their families, elderly people who have outlived their friends and feel unwanted, people broken in mind or spirit are people in whom Christ asks for compassion. In these, Christ asks that we be awake to his presence and to his suffering in them and visit them with the redeeming sympathy of love.

Our bodies play an enormously important role in our life in the Risen Christ. The Incarnation has given a sacramental quality to our flesh and blood, so that we can offer an unceasing prayer of the body that can begin here and never end. This prayer sanctifies not only the suffering of the body but its joys as well. The prayer of the body is preparation for the eternity when our bodies will be glorified as the risen body of Christ is glorified now.

When Christ rose from the tomb, he rose with the same body that had grown in his mother's womb. It was the same body that had labored in Nazareth and fasted in the wilderness. This was the body that had hungered and thirsted, slept, been wounded, suffered, and died. It was the body that was given in the breaking of the bread at the Last Supper.

Long before Christ gave us his body in his own hands, these hands were hardened by toil, beautiful with the line and muscle and sinew of the hands of an artisan. But in the consummation of his self-giving, these hands that had given in so many ways were helpless, fastened immovably to a plank.

Sooner or later, our prayer of the body becomes the helpless hands, the falling away of the self, the breaking of the bread. Sickness, old age, death must come.

When these come, it can seem as if our service is over. There is an exhaustion which makes it at first difficult and eventually impossible to even lift up the hand to make a sign of the cross. There will be no more liturgical acts in daily life, no gestures that worship God and bring Christ's love to others.

Everything falls away from us, even memories and the weariness of the self. This is the breaking of the bread, the supreme moment in the prayer of the body, the end of the liturgy of our daily lives. Then we are broken in communion of Christ's love for the world.

But this is not the end of the prayer of the body. There is no end to the prayer of the body of Christ, of our own body. The morning of resurrection wakens up this body, glorified and living forever.

Most of us want to feel the presence of Christ all the time. We want to experience the continual sweetness of devotion and sense that our prayers are like flowers opening. We can become distressed when our prayers bring no sweetness at all, no consolation. We forget that if we go on praying without any consolation from God, we might be consoling God by giving God what is due.

We are impatient because we do not immediately feel the healing of our wounds, or do not at once recover from the effects of our sins. We may still be tempted and be unwilling to recognize that it takes time to unform a bad habit.

The beginning of peace and rest that allows the Spirit to flood our hearts consists in accepting God's plan. In God's plan for us, there is winter as well as spring, spring as well as summer, and autumn with its harvest. This means we must deliberately refuse to be anxious.

There are times when we shall not feel the indwelling of Christ. There are times when we shall not feel we have faith. In these times, the blessed winters of the spirit, Christ is growing within us. There are times of dryness in prayer. If we are honest, we know we have not entered into some "dark night of the soul" but simply become bored with prayer. Being human, our emotions move around in great cycles.

After a period of intense consolation or sweetness, of going out of ourselves for others, we can anticipate a succeeding period of emptiness and flatness. That time of emptiness is the preparation for the new influx of life, the new sweetness, which we cannot force. It will come when there is an empty heart and a receptive mind awaiting the inrush of Heaven's life.

To be at rest means to accept God's plan of our nature and our limits with tranquillity. This is in order that Christ may grow in us and that we may be made new in his way. We must accept this new spring when it comes. Gloomy Christians who repudiate joy and dwell exclusively on suffering cannot open their hearts in readiness for new life. They refuse to be tranquil in the winter of the heart because they are avid in their desire to feel suffering. They mistrust the spring.

At the present time, such tranquillity is not easy for anyone. It is particularly difficult for those who feel the kingdom of Christ is solely in their hands or in their keeping. It can be difficult for Christians to withdraw from time to time and simply rest, trust, and accept. Too many anxious Christians feel they must preach and teach and enter into unending activities in saving the world. They feel this does more to save the world than their quiet surrender into God to become deeply Christ-bearers.

Christ himself prepared for resurrection by resting in the tomb, as he prepared for birth by resting in the womb. After the resurrection, he told the apostles to wait for the Spirit. They should not run away, make plans of their own, be troubled over their failures, or fear the dangers all around them. They must simply wait for the Comforter to come, to make them strong, to heal their wounds.

The preparation for the coming of the Spirit is the same today. This is true whether we think of today as one needing the rebirth of Christ in the hearts of many, or the return from the grave of a Christ whose blood is shed again by the martyrs of our time. The preparation is the same, waiting with open heart and mind while the life of the world to come already grows within, pointing to the flowering of everlasting joy that no one can take from us.

NOTES

1. Joan M. Nuth, "English Mystical Tradition," in *The New Dictionary of Catholic Spirituality*, ed. Michael Downey (Collegeville, Minn.: Glazier/Liturgical Press, 1993) 337–47.

2. This was true of Cranmer's first Book of Prayer. His second Book of Prayer shows the effects of Zwingli and is not reflective of Catholic sacramental piety.

3. *Orthodox Spirituality and Protestant and Anglican Spirituality*, ed. Louis Bouyer (London: Burns and Oates, 1969) 99–168.

4. John C. Dwyer, *Church History* (Mahwah, N.J.: Paulist Press, 1985) 350–65.

5. Ibid., 364–73; see also Richard P. McBrien, *Report on the Church* (New York: HarperCollins, 1992) 89–110, for expansion of "Catholic Action" perspectives today.

6. Caryll Houselander, *Rocking Horse Catholic* (New York: Sheed and Ward, 1955) 72–74.

7. Ibid. 110–17.

8. Ibid. 137–39.

9. Caryll Houselander, *The Passion of the Infant Christ* (New York: Sheed and Ward, 1949).

10. Maisie Ward, *Caryll Houselander: That Divine Eccentric* (New York: Sheed and Ward, 1962), introduction.

11. Houselander, *Passion* 89–98, 101–3, 105–12.

12. Caryll Houselander, *The Comforting of Christ* (New York: Sheed and Ward, 1947) 124–25, 205–7.

13. Caryll Houselander, *The Risen Christ* (New York: Sheed and Ward, 1958) 13–15, 17–19, 22–23, 54–55, 57–58, 64, 73–74.

BIBLIOGRAPHY

Houselander, Caryll. *The Comforting of Christ.* New York: Sheed and Ward, 1947.
Houselander, Caryll. *The Dry Wood.* New York: Sheed and Ward, 1947.
Houselander, Caryll. *The Flowering Tree.* New York: Sheed and Ward, 1945.
Houselander, Caryll. *Guilt.* New York: Sheed and Ward, 1951.
Houselander, Caryll. *The Mother of Christ.* London: Sheed and Ward, 1978.
Houselander, Caryll. *The Passion of the Infant Christ.* New York: Sheed and Ward, 1949.
Houselander, Caryll. *The Reed of God.* London: Sheed and Ward, 1944.
Houselander, Caryll. *The Risen Christ.* London: Sheed and Ward, 1958.
Houselander, Caryll. *Rocking Horse Catholic.* New York: Sheed and Ward, 1955.
Ward, Maisie. *Caryll Houselander: That Divine Eccentric.* New York: Sheed and Ward, 1962.
Ward, Maisie, ed. *The Letters of Caryll Houselander.* New York: Sheed and Ward, 1965.

– 21 –

PAULI MURRAY

(1910–1985)

Hope Is a Song in a Weary Throat

Pauli Murray was born on November 20, 1910, in her parents' home in Baltimore, Maryland. Throughout her life she exhibited the qualities of a "Sunday child" with her laughter, determination, gentleness, and boldness. Pauli's mother, Agnes Fitzgerald Murray, was a nurse. William H. Murray, Pauli's father, was a schoolteacher. Years later she still remembered the many hours he spent both preparing lessons and counseling his students. His strong dedication to teaching inspired many of his Negro[1] students to fight for admission to college in spite of the racism that denied it.

Pauli's mother died giving birth to her seventh child. Agnes Murray had been a healthy woman, but complications set in that could not be reversed. William Murray had become mentally impaired through a long bout with typhoid fever. He was not able to care for seven children after Agnes died, for he was subject to periods of depression and extreme forgetfulness. The three older children fought to stay with William and they succeeded. Four-year-old Pauli and the younger children, however, were taken by relatives and raised in different places.

One of William's sisters, Aunt Pauline, took Pauli to live with her in Durham, North Carolina. Aunt Pauline was the godmother after whom Pauli was named. She took care of her parents, Pauli's grandparents, who lived in the same house. An active four-year-old like Pauli was too much for the aging grandparents to deal with throughout the day, so Aunt Pauline decided that Pauli would have to come with her to her primary classroom each day so that the grandparents could have some peace and quiet.

Aunt Pauline instructed Pauli that she was to be quiet, and to do her "special lessons" while the other children were being taught. A few nights a week Pauli attended Aunt Pauline's adult reading class. Near the end of their first year together, five-year-old Pauli surprised her aunt one evening as she quietly told an adult some words he did not know. She had apparently been listening and learning along with Aunt Pauline's primary students as she did her own special lessons.

Although many of her memories of childhood faded, Pauli always remembered her home in North Carolina. "A wooden cross stood in the center of the mantelpiece as a reminder of our faith and a tall red candle graced either end. On the wall above the cross hung Miss Mary Ruffin Smith's painting."[2] Grandmother Cornelia Smith loved this painting of her blood relative, her owner, and her loving friend who cared little for what anyone thought of her.

As Pauli grew up in North Carolina, she was not conscious of racism in their small town. "The two races lived close together, and within the limits of the strict racial code considerable familiarity existed in their dealings with one another."[3] She was told she could greet the "coloreds" but not the "whites" on her way home from school. This was difficult for a spontaneous and extroverted child, but she accepted it as she did other rules that children were supposed to obey.

Two incidents that occurred when Pauli was eleven and thirteen were the first direct experiences she had of racism. The first happened when Aunt Pauline and she were visiting relatives in Baltimore. The second took place some years later when her father died.

Aunt Pauline and Pauli had received word in Baltimore that Pauli's grandfather was dying. The relatives arranged for Aunt Pauline and Pauli to get to the railroad station to travel home to Durham. The two arrived at the station just in time to see their train pulling into the depot. As Pauli and Aunt Pauline ran to catch the train, Aunt Pauline slipped and fell full force to the ground. Her glasses broke and her cheeks were deeply cut as she struck the ground. Pauli was frightened at the sight of so much blood and tried to get the only two men she could find to come and help. The men were white and refused to move.

Eventually Aunt Pauline got herself up. She took Pauli into the waiting room as she quickly tried to clean herself up, although she could not see without her glasses. Two white men got up and stood menacingly close without saying a word. They followed Aunt Pauline and Pauli as the two ran to the Jim Crow car of the train. They stayed close without saying anything. When the train started up, they got off. Only later did Pauli realize that they had crossed the "color line" in the station, an action for which others had been lynched. "The incident awakened my dread of lynchings, and I was learning the dangers of straying, however innocently, across a treacherous line into a hostile world."[4]

The second incident occurred in 1923, the year Pauli's father died. After the death of her mother, Pauli's father had had increasingly severe bouts with depression. The aftermath of the damage done by typhoid fever grew progressively worse. Finally, William Murray had to be committed to a state home. When Pauli was twelve Aunt Pauline took her to see her father in the home. The effect was both confusing and frightening. William could hardly remember his daughter, whom he had last seen when she was four.

Pauli's vague memories of a strong man with dancing eyes and infectious laughter were shattered by what she saw. The skeletal figure that appeared in the state home was frightening to her, though their embrace at the end of the visit was a comfort. That was the last time that Pauli saw her father alive.

Within the year the family was informed that William Murray had died and that the body would be shipped back to Durham after an autopsy. The family waited for weeks. Finally the burial box came and was hauled to the parlor of the home in which Pauli and Aunt Pauline and William's parents lived. The family gathered for the opening of the casket. No one was prepared for the sight. Pauli never forgot her shock:

> His face was purple and swollen, his head was shaven, and his skull had been split open like a melon and sewed together loosely with jagged stitches crisscrossing the blood-clotted line of severance.... I kept returning to stare at the puffed eyelids, the battered face and lips, the butchered skull.... I remember reaching down under the coffin lid, touching the hands, holding them and trying to convince myself that the wretched thing I saw in the ill-fitting suit was in fact my father.[5]

The investigation into the cause of death revealed what the family had suspected. The official record was clear:

> He (Mr. Murray) was taken to a basement and there beaten with a blunt instrument resembling a baseball bat over the buttocks and over the head. This was done in the presence of some other patients and was also witnessed by another attendant.[6]

William Murray was buried in Laurel Cemetery next to his wife. In time the cemetery went bankrupt, the overgrown markers became invisible, and a shopping mall was constructed on the site. There was no regard for the relatives of those who were buried in the cemetery. The people buried there were simply treated as if they had never existed.

From that point on, Pauli Murray became very aware of both the racism and the sexism that limited her in accomplishing what she hoped to do with her life. Like others of her race, she was forced to attend a segregated high school. Well-trained and dedicated teachers urged their students to show people the errors of racism that claimed Negroes had "smaller brains" and "less intelligence."[7] Most young men dropped out of Pauli's class of 1926. The graduating seniors included only three men and thirty-seven women.

Pauli decided she would not attend a segregated college, which was her only choice if she remained in the South. Aunt Pauline encouraged her to go to New

York and seek admission to Hunter College. Pauli was informed that she would have to return to a New York high school for at least eighteen months to meet the admission standards. She went back to high school, passed both her state exams and admission exam with honors, and entered Hunter College in the fall. One thing she learned early on at Hunter was to stop using the word *colored* and to use the correct term, *Negro*. She used the word consistently in her own publications, in spite of the changing designations for the race.

Pauli and other Hunter students worked as waitresses to make some money. The first evening she discovered that a color line existed among the employees with regard to the meal that was provided for them. Pauli had to eat alone in a different room from her white friends. Although all the students protested by skipping the provided meal, the boycott had no effect on the policy.

Pauli graduated in 1933, and like many others in the country, she joined President Roosevelt's Works Progress Administration to aid the depressed economy. She taught for five years before applying to the University of North Carolina for admission. She had decided to study law, a field that could make a contribution to changing unjust social structures. Pauli was denied admission because no Negroes could attend the University of North Carolina at this time.[8]

Because President Franklin Roosevelt had received an honorary degree from the University of North Carolina in 1938, Pauli decided to write him. The president had praised the university for its liberal American tradition of furthering the democratic principles of "equality and justice." Pauli's letter asked:

> Have you raised your voice loud enough against the burning of our people? Why has our government refused to pass anti-lynching legislation?... What does equality and justice mean for Negro Americans? Does it mean that... the University of North Carolina is ready to open its doors to Negro students seeking enlightenment or that again we are to be set aside and passed over for more important problems?[9]

Eleanor Roosevelt answered Pauli personally. Mrs. Roosevelt had already made headlines in Negro papers for her boldly symbolic stands at various national conferences. Consistently she would place her chair midway between the segregated seating at such national conferences. The meaning of this act was clear to all who witnessed it. These actions did not escape Pauli Murray, whose correspondence with Mrs. Roosevelt eventually gave way to personal meetings and a long friendship. However, in spite of the backing of Mrs. Roosevelt and pressure from President Roosevelt, Pauli was not admitted. She decided to seek admission to Howard University School of Law in Washington, D.C.

Pauli was admitted without difficulty. Howard University provided invaluable experience as well as a first-rate education in law. In the 1940s Howard University professors and students became very active in the NAACP, and a variety of Negro rights movements in Washington. Led by Howard Law School faculty, the students unearthed the 1872 civil rights, law which had never been observed in the nation's capital. This particular law was a foundation for the 1953 Supreme Court decision banning discrimination and segregation in public places in Washington.

While Pauli attended Howard, she was able to have closer contact with Mrs. Roosevelt, a powerful ally in the cause for civil rights. Her personal warmth and graciousness to Pauli and other Howard students was treasured. Mrs. Roosevelt, a strong advocate in the equal rights movements of the 1940s, was a source of constant encouragement to agitators like Pauli, who spent time in jail for public actions of peaceful protest.

Eleanor Roosevelt invited Pauli and some other Howard Law School students to contribute their expertise to a document on international human rights. Mrs. Roosevelt's leadership in forging the Universal Declaration of 1948 incorporated many contributions from the students who had experienced racism and sexism. The document would become the standard for human rights across the world, but it would be another sixteen years before equal rights would gather enough momentum to effect needed changes in the United States.

Pauli graduated cum laude from Howard in 1944. In 1945 she received a master's degree from the University of California School of Law at Berkeley. She tried unsuccessfully to enter Harvard Law School in 1944 and in 1946, but this school did not admit women until 1949. Pauli decided to learn on the job and wait for doctoral education.

Although Pauli had graduated with honors, the double bias of race and sex made it extremely difficult for her to find work as a lawyer. Finally, she secured a job as a law clerk for twenty-five dollars a week in New York City. From 1948 until 1960 she served in private law practice, associated with the New York firm of Paul, Weiss, Rifkind, Wharton, and Garrison. She was encouraged to seek election to the state assembly as a third-party candidate, but the time was not right for a Negro professional woman to make her way into this body.

Pauli engaged in varieties of equal rights movements. She also wrote poetry that captured her deep concern that violence not be repaid with violence. Martin Luther King's influence on her was evident. She was strongly affected by the blood shed in the name of justice. Her poetic "Collect for Poplarville" was written during this time, based in part on the evening prayer of the Book of Common Prayer:

> "Lighten our darkness, we beseech you, O Lord."
> Teach us no longer to dread
> hounds yelping in the distance,
> the footfall at the door,
> the rifle butt on the window pane....

Teach us that most difficult of tasks—
to pray for them,
to follow, not burn, thy cross![10]

The universality of the dream for deeper freedom was brought home to Pauli during a sixteen-month stay in Ghana, where she was senior lecturer of constitutional and administrative law at the national School of Law. During this time she wrote a historical study of the first constitution of the new Republic of Ghana.

Pauli entered Yale Law School and was appointed to the President's Commission on the Status of Women in 1963. Having earned her doctorate in 1965, in 1969 she was appointed to a working committee of the World Council of Churches that was planning an international conference on racism. The meeting in Uppsala, Sweden, had a lasting effect on her:

> Uppsala fired me with a renewed determination to return to the United States and proclaim through my own life and work the universal sisterhood and brotherhood I experienced during those eighteen days.[11]

Brandeis University offered her a visiting professorship in American civilization, which included developing a program in Afro-American studies. She taught law at Brandeis for years until another moving event changed her life direction. Her reflections on that event and its results follow. The reader may discover hints of the heroic faith of Pauli Murray in spite of the brevity of the selection. That faith included a willingness to go wherever she was led with a vitality that one of her friends describes well:

> Pauli was always insatiable and restless for more life and more challenges. She was like a mountain climber whose stamina increases with each new climb.... She had always been in search of life's meaning. Over and over again, right until the end, she found it.[12]

Song in a Weary Throat[13]

The early 1970s found me responding alternately to the competing demands of the black movement and the women's movement, often taking the lonely and unpopular position of calling for a broad, inclusive expression of feminism at a time when many prominent Negro women felt impelled to subordinate their claims as women to what they believed to be the overriding factor of "restoration of the black male to his lost manhood." As a self-supporting woman, I saw this as a shortsighted view and said, in an article I wrote for Mary Thompson's book *Voices of the New Feminism*, published by Beacon Press in 1970:

> Reading through much of the current literature on the Black Revolution, one is left with the impression that for all the rhetoric about self-determination, the main thrust of black militancy is a bid of black males to share power with white males in a continuing patriarchal society in which both black and white females are relegated to a secondary status.

Pointing to the triple handicap under which black women labored—race, sex, and economic exploitation—I argued: "black women can neither postpone nor subordinate the fight against discrimination to the Black Revolution.... As a matter of sheer survival black women have no alternative but to insist upon equal opportunities without regard to sex in training, education and employment. Given their heavy family responsibilities, the outlook for their children will be bleak indeed unless they are encouraged in every way to develop their potential skills and earning power." I saw the liberation of black women in terms of feminine solidarity across racial lines.

> Because black women have an equal stake in women's liberation and black liberation, they are key figures at the juncture of these two movements.... By asserting a leadership role in the growing feminist movement, the black woman can help keep it allied to the objectives of black liberation while simultaneously advancing the interests of all women.

I also envisioned feminist solidarity achieving a broader objective than would be possible if black women confined themselves solely to the demands of black militancy.

> Beyond all the present conflict lies the important task of reconciliation of the races in America on the basis of genuine equality and human dignity. A powerful force in bringing about this result can be generated through the process of black and white women working together to achieve their common humanity.

As I struggled with the racial and sexual conflicts of the period, I clung to the twofold legacy left to the world in the 1960s—the life and work, respectively, of Eleanor Roosevelt and Martin Luther King, Jr. Each in different ways had emphasized the moral and spiritual imperatives of the ongoing struggle for human dignity and had demonstrated the power of love to transcend divisions of race, sex, or class. Pondering the source of the great influence on their times led me to reflect more deeply upon the meaning of the Christian faith.

Yet had anyone suggested in 1972 that within less than a year I would resign my now tenured faculty position to enter seminary as a candidate for holy orders in the Episcopal Church, I would have questioned that person's sanity. I had been named Louis Stulberg Professor of Law and Politics in the American

Studies Department at Brandeis, and that spring was also a lecturer at the Boston University School of Law, teaching my favorite subject, the enforcement of constitutional rights and liberties. My articles were being published in law reviews and journals of opinion, and I had even found time to begin my memoirs, work postponed since 1968. The burgeoning women's movement absorbed much of my energies, for I was serving on a faculty committee to improve the status of women at Brandeis, on the national board of the ACLU to win support for the Equal Rights Amendment, and on the Commission on Women organized by Church Women United and chaired by my good friend Thelma Stevens.

Although I was active in ad hoc groups seeking wider recognition of women's ministries in the Episcopal Church, and strongly supported women's ordination to the priesthood, I had no conscious desire to enter the ordained ministry itself. At the same time, I was being drawn into the ferment growing among women I met at what was then the Episcopal Theological Seminary and is now the Episcopal Divinity School in Cambridge. Their passionate commitment to their calling left a deep impression.

The church's slow response to women's appeals spurred me to greater activism. In the summer of 1969 a special convention of the Episcopal Church meeting at South Bend, Indiana, refused to seat a woman as a delegate to the House of Deputies, although she had been duly elected from her diocese in California. The fact that the church excluded women from its national deliberative body while it accepted millions of dollars collected by women through the United Thanks Offering so incensed me that I joined in a telegram of protest signed by six active Episcopal lay women and addressed to the presiding bishop, John E. Hines, and the president of the House of Deputies, Dr. John B. Coburn. In a follow-up memorandum sent to these officials, I analyzed the system of discrimination against women within the Episcopal Church and pointed to the dire consequences if women became so alienated that they withdrew their support from the church. The memorandum created a little flurry in church circles when Church Women United got permission to reproduce it and distributed it to five hundred key women in other denominations.

Several months later, in early 1970, I was surprised to receive notice that I had been appointed to a special commission on Ordained and Licensed Ministries to study the issue of women's ministries and make a report. Along with the letter of appointment, however, the secretary of the convention sent a communication advising commission members that since no money had been allocated to finance the commission's work, we should file a report of "No Progress" and request the 1970 General Convention to provide the necessary funds.

By this time, the movement for women's ordination was beginning to escalate. That spring I attended a weekend conference of forty-five episcopal women at Graymoor Monastery in New York State, at which we attempted to formulate a position on the aspirations of women in our denomination. At least eight or ten of the women were seminary graduates or were attending seminary and actively seeking ordination, among them the redoubtable Jeannette Picard, a former balloonist who had ascended higher in space than any other woman of her time, had earned a doctorate, and was a consultant to NASA. Then in her seventies, Jeannette told me she had been waiting almost fifty years to fulfill her call to the ordained ministry. The body adopted a strong resolution calling for equality of women in every aspect of the life of the church, including admission to all levels of the clergy. The Graymoor Conference was a precursor of the Episcopal Women's Caucus, which would later mobilize wide support for women's ordination.

My involvement with the issue deepened later that spring when I met the Reverend Henry H. Rightor, a lawyer-priest, then professor of pastoral theology at Virginia Theological Seminary and an ardent supporter of women's ordination. The Reverend Rightor, who had also been appointed to the Commission on Ordained and Licensed Ministries, was a veteran of general convention politics and knew that such an issue could drag on for years unless the convention was forced to deal with it promptly. He proposed that our commission not postpone deliberations but that we meet at our own expense and produce a report in time for the General Convention meeting in Houston in October.

We held a one-day meeting on September 19 in Baltimore, during which Henry Rightor and I examined the Constitution and Canons of the Episcopal Church and reported that there was no language in that official document which specifically prohibited the ordination of women as priests. (Obviously, the drafters of the original Constitution had taken for granted that women would never be considered for ordination and so had felt no need to make explicit their exclusion.) This finding led us to assert that there would be no need to invoke the cumbersome procedure of amending the Constitution, a process that would require approval by two consecutive conventions and usually took at least six years to become effective. We argued that a simple resolution concurred in the House of Bishops and the House of Deputies at a single convention was all that was necessary to remove any doubt about the eligibility of women for ordination. Moreover, the Commission concluded, there was no need to undertake still another review of the issue. The time had come for decision. Our report was brief and to the point; it recommended immediate approval of the admission of women to all levels of the ordained clergy. Henry Rightor volunteered to have copies of the Commission's report reproduced and to attend the Houston convention in the hope of having our recommendations accepted.

It was naive to hope that any effort to overturn such deeply entrenched tradition would be that simple. The General Convention of 1970 bypassed our report, but it did move one step forward by removing language that limited the lowest level of the ordained ministry, the diaconate, to males, thereby opening the way for women to enter the ordained clergy. I was so disappointed over a half-measure intended to keep women in a subordinate category that I stopped going to church. Like many other women on the periphery of organized religion, I began to question the authority of a traditional faith which continued to treat half of its membership as less than fully human. My rejection of the church left me floundering in a wilderness of doubt. At the time, I was living in Boston, next to the Massachusetts Avenue Bridge to Cambridge, in an apartment on Beacon Street. On Sundays I used to walk my black Labrador, Roy, along the banks of the Charles River, at war with myself because I was not in my accustomed place singing in the choir at Saint James Church over in Cambridge.

I was still in a morass of indecision about the church when calamity struck one of my dearest friends, Renee Barlow, and I was put to a stern test of faith. Over the years, Renee and her mother, Mary Jane Barlow, had remained part of my extended family. Mrs. Barlow was now ninety-three, housebound, and very frail, and Renee herself was showing increasing signs of illness.

Because of my experience with my own aging aunts, I felt great sympathy for mother and daughter in their struggle against the encroaching debilities of age. As the years passed I had watched Renee juggle the demands of her busy life to meet her mother's growing infirmity with countermoves designed to make her comfortable: relocation from their walk-up apartment on Second Avenue to a sunny, spacious apartment in Peter Cooper Village overlooking the East River; the employment of a series of paid companions so that Jenny Wren—as we called Mrs. Barlow—would not be alone. Numerous projects kept her busy—mending friends' clothing, shortening skirts, knitting caps, and making dolls and toys for children in the church who had little for Christmas.

During the summer of 1972, Renee celebrated the fifth anniversary of her surgery for cancer. It was an important milestone, and she thought hopefully that she might be out of the woods. I noticed whenever she visited me in Boston on a weekend she spent most of her time sleeping. She called my apartment the Murray Rest Home and thought of it as a place where she could get away from constant pressures and be quiet for a few hours. That fall we kept in close touch by telephone, Renee explaining she was calling because there was something wrong with her hand. "I can't type," she said once. On several occasions she reported she had been trying to reach me, "But I keep getting wrong numbers."

I knew something was terribly amiss, but Renee's casual references gave me no clues. When I stopped over in New York during the Thanksgiving weekend, I was shocked at the way she looked. She told me she had to get away for a little rest and was planning a two-week trip to Montego Bay, Jamaica, where we had spent several winter vacations. Renee had always come back from those trips refreshed and renewed. Elizabeth Lehmann, a mutual friend, had agreed to go with her. They were to meet in Miami.

The trip was disastrous. On the plane to Florida, Renee became ill with severe vertigo and was unable to go on. She and Elizabeth returned by train. Renee tried to go back to work, but within a few days one leg was dragging and she could hardly walk. Elizabeth, who lived in Philadelphia, came over to give her a hand and called me in desperation. Renee, normally practical in emergencies, was suddenly refusing to call her physician. I had one more week of classes at Brandeis before the semester ended and I would be free to come to New York. Meanwhile, Elizabeth and I consulted daily by telephone. We knew someone had to take charge, given Mrs. Barlow's eggshell frailty.

Finally, Renee gave in and on January 10, 1973, she was admitted to Harkness Pavilion at Columbia-Presbyterian Medical Center for observation and tests. I arrived and was aghast. Her right side was partially paralyzed and her right arm and hand were useless. She could not focus her vision, her speech was slurred, and she could not complete her sentences.

Renee was suffering from a brain tumor. Brain surgery was not possible because the tumor was so close to vital centers of speech and sight. The alternative was to administer heavy doses of steroids to reduce the swelling in the brain, followed by a series of cobalt treatments. Renee had not been informed of the extent of the illness. I held her power of attorney, so I was expected to be available to the hospital authorities at all times to give the necessary consents for radical procedures.

This fateful knowledge was a staggering blow. I was stunned not only by the magnitude of Renee's illness but by the awesome responsibility of having to make life-and-death decisions on her behalf. I had no experience in dealing with a severely ill patient, but over the sixteen years of our friendship, Renee and I had been honest and respectful with one another. Painful as it might be, I knew I would have to insist that Renee's physicians be candid about her situation, respecting her right to make her own decisions about her future as long as she was able to communicate her wishes.

Renee was probably more aware of the true nature of her illness than any of us realized. Before she went into the hospital, she talked with Elizabeth about her youth and spoke of her fiancé, a young medical student who had died of a brain tumor. Renee had chosen to go on alone, picking up the fragments of her life shattered by an inconsolable loss. Unable to marry the man she loved and have children of her own, she had gone about mothering everyone else. Now, when faced with the same catastrophic illness, she accepted the medical diagnosis with characteristic calm. Her quiet courage throughout her ordeal enabled me to carry on with some semblance of strength.

Over the next ten days Renee made what seemed to be a miraculous comeback, thanks to the steroids. Her speech and vision improved, she was able to sign her own checks and insurance forms and walk with the aid of a metal walker and a nurse's assistance. Her inimitable humor returned and she laughingly referred to the hospital staff and the many friends telephoning from places around the country as her "cast of thousands."

My most immediate problem was trying to persuade Renee's mother to go to Connecticut to stay with her other daughter, Doris Maycock. Mrs. Barlow could not be left without constant care, but she had a will of iron. Her fierce determination to stay in her New York apartment, where she was able to do as she pleased, defeated every effort I could make short of risking the shock of telling her the truth about Renee's illness. Mrs. Barlow clung tenaciously to life, once telling her nurse companion, "I'm not afraid to die; I just don't want to leave Renee." She yielded only when Renee made the effort to telephone her and, putting the problem as gently as she could, told her mother there was "pressure on the brain" and she would have to be in the hospital a long time.

Before signing her consent for cobalt treatments, Renee discussed her situation with her physicians and was fully aware of the risks she was taking. As she weighed the matter, she told me, "I've had a good life, and I don't know whether I've got what it takes to fight this thing." It was as close as we came to speaking of death, but I could no more accept the thought of Renee dying than, at the time, I could accept the thought of my own death. I replied, "If we have to go down, we'll go down fighting." I told her I didn't think God intended human beings to be resigned to their fates until they had made every effort, but that when they had done their best, they could leave the outcome to God.

Renee did not tell me she might be paralyzed and lose her sight, although she knew of those risks. I think she wanted to spare me the terrible anxiety of anticipation. In any case, I do not believe I could have accepted the risk, for it had fallen to me as her legal representative to decide upon cobalt. The treatments began on January 22, her fifty-ninth birthday, a day memorable because it was the day President Richard Nixon announced a cease-fire in the Vietnam War, and later the news was flashed that former President Lyndon B. Johnson had died of a heart attack. That night a blizzard hit New York, and in the midst of the heavy snowfall an electrical storm lighted up the skies like a spectacular display of northern lights.

I rode home from the hospital with one of Renee's medical team, who said it was hoped the treatments would give her a little time—six months, a year, perhaps two years—and that it was also hoped she would "be herself" during whatever time she had left. I clung to this shred of hope, pushing back the reality of a death sentence and helping Renee to plan her convalescence. Anticipating the loss of her hair, she ordered a wig from Lord and Taylor and amused friends who visited her with her "new look." She also talked of how she would spend the next few months when she left the hospital. The treatment had gone so well that her physicians planned to discharge her after the first series, having her return for outpatient treatment. I was sufficiently encouraged by this to go back to Boston for a few days to take care of my personal affairs, so I could be with her when she left the hospital.

While I was gone Renee had a sudden setback. I rushed to New York on February 5 and found that the tumor had spread to the right side of the brain, partially disabling the left side of her body. Tests also showed a shadow on her lung. Her eyes remained tightly closed and her nurse believed she had lost all sight. She was conscious when awake, was able to call my name and answer "yes" or "no" to questions, and even smiled when I said something humorous. But she kept slipping into a deep sleep. Her doctors had done all medical science could do and she seemed to be resting comfortably without noticeable pain.

The situation was so critical that I telephoned her sister immediately and Doris came down to New York. We stayed at the Harkness Pavilion, apartments rented to relatives of gravely ill patients. We could be close by and also handle the many telephone calls that flooded the hospital switchboard. We were both so shattered by Renee's stillness that we could not look at her without weeping. I would stand by her bed, speak to her, and she would squeeze my hand, then I would have to rush out of the room to a linen closet down the hall, where she could not hear my uncontrollable sobs. Doris had to return to Connecticut after ten days because Mrs. Barlow's health was failing fast, and I was virtually alone with my grief.

Renee had once described our friendship as that of two independent spirits who "meshed" in crises and "disengaged" when it was no longer necessary to act as a unit. Now I had to stand by helplessly, our teamwork torn apart by forces neither of us could control. Through all of this I had to deal with the many sorrowing people who hung on to the telephone each day, seeking a word of hope or comfort, each one relating to me how Renee had helped them through some crisis in their own lives. Each one, like myself, refused to believe that their sturdy, reliable friend was dying. I was overwhelmed by the great outpouring of love and gratitude in letters, telegrams, and telephone calls, all the more poignant because Renee was unaware of the enormous response to her lifetime of ministering to the needs of countless others.

For several days I lived in a state of split consciousness. Part of me functioned as a lawyer, organizing Renee's business files and papers in preparation for the administration of her estate by the law firm for which she then worked. The other part of me carried on a dialogue with God alternately praying, "Thy will be done," and arguing angrily, "It isn't fair, Lord." When I went to the hospital I would sit by Renee's bed, sometimes talking to her as if she had all her faculties, although I had heard those dreaded words "brain death." I found myself speaking to God about the choices she was making: that if she went on she would be with all those loved ones who had gone on before her; that if she decided to stay with us we would be with her all the way....

I had always been terrified of death and had avoided funerals as much as possible. Now I had to watch death approaching my closest friend and I could no longer avoid pondering the ultimate mystery of life.... Why should one fear what is as natural as birth, or what is, perhaps, merely crossing a threshold? I recalled that a friend who was an undertaker's assistant once said there was always peace on the faces of dead people, even those who had died violent deaths. I began to think of the experience of death as a transition in which a person may swing back and forth between two states of being, not quite out of this world and not quite into the next. And, I thought, perhaps those who love the person most can be a hindrance to the process. They may hold on when the one who is dying is ready to die....

That night, when Renee's special nurse had been called elsewhere, Renee grew restless. Her head tossed; her breath came in gasps; her moans made me cry out silently, "Take her, God. I can't bear to see her suffer this way." No priest was available, so I stood by her bed reading the Twenty-third Psalm. When I finished, I kissed her good-bye and said, "Rest." When I left the hospital that night, I knew I could not come back....

Renee died the next morning around ten o'clock. Time hung like an eternity in the hours before her death. Everything in my private world was waiting. When the hospital called, and I knew that her heart had stopped beating, time began to move again. I felt a flood of relief and joy that she was at last released from pain. Although it was bitterly cold outside, I opened all the windows of her apartment to let fresh air blow through, and put on her favorite record—Schumann's Piano Concerto in A Minor—in celebration of the passing of a beautiful spirit....

I had been called upon to minister to my friend in her final hours and my ministry to her family and friends continued through her funeral and the memorial service held three days later. When it was all over, Tom Pike commended me on a beautiful service. I was astonished when he added, "You may not have realized it, but you have been acting as an enabler, a function of a deacon in our church. Have you ever thought of ordination?" Late that afternoon as I drove back to Boston thinking of Tom Pike's words, an exquisite sunset of gold, blue, pink, and aqua filled the western sky. It was as if Renee's spirit was smiling in approval as she bade me farewell.

Renee's death changed my life. It was more than the loss of a close friend. In Renee's dying hours, I had come face to face with my own mortality. I felt an urgency to complete my mission on earth in the days left to me. From its beginnings, our friendship had centered around the church, and it was in the church that I had found the comforting belief that the living and the dead are bound together in the "communion of saints." For the second time in my life I had been called upon to be with a devout Christian to minister in ways I associated only with the ordained clergy. As I reflected upon these experiences, the thought of ordination became unavoidable. Yet the notion of a "call" so astounded me that I was unable to eat or sleep as I struggled against it.

In spite of my vigorous advocacy of women's ordination in the Episcopal Church, my age and my sense of unworthiness had insulated me against such a possibility for myself. Once I admitted my call, it seemed that I had been pointed in this direction all my life. In spite of the opposition to women's ordination, which was widespread in the Episcopal Church at the time, I took the fateful step of applying for admission to Holy Orders.

The bishop of the Diocese of Massachusetts, Right Reverend John M. Burgess, and the Suffragan Bishop Morris F. Arnold were both supportive. I was accepted as a candidate in June 1973. This was the same year the General Convention of the Episcopal Church voted down the ordination of women. The Convention left women seminarians as well as women who were already ordained deacons with an uncertain future in the church. This continuing barrier had serious implications for me as I approached my sixty-third birthday. Having given up my academic career and the financial security it provided, I would be severely handicapped by my age in seeking professional employment. No official action would be taken by the church for another three years. I petitioned the faculty to change my status to that of a regular three-year student and a candidate for the Master of Divinity Degree.

Those three years of seminary subjected me to the most rigorous discipline I had ever encountered, surpassing by far the rigors of any law school training. One's personality is under the continuous scrutiny of instructors and schoolmates as well as under constant self-examination. In addition to daily devotions and corporate worship, seminarians have to absorb an immense body of learning. Throughout the process they have to satisfy various layers of the church hierarchy not only that they are academically competent but also that the spiritual formation essential to a priestly calling is plainly evident.

Women seminarians were in a peculiarly ambiguous position in the mid-1970s. Although we were formally accepted as candidates for degree and for ordination to the diaconate, we were the center of bitter controversy, the targets of veiled and sometimes overt hostility. Our numbers were few and our presence in a community designed for men only was more tolerated than encouraged. Not only was I the only Negro woman enrolled, but I felt set apart because of my age and professional experience, which was greater than most of my professors. Most of my classmates were white males in their twenties. My legal training was a mixed blessing. It contributed to clarity of expression but my "probe and debate" training also disturbed some of my professors who gave me a reputation of being "abrasive."

The convention of 1973 had angered many women seminarians. I felt compelled to say that the church was losing its authority as a Christian body and it was no longer speaking with an authentic voice if women were treated as outcasts when they sought to answer God's call to the priesthood. Supportive male clergy had joined the women in strategizing what needed to be done before the 1976 Convention when the issue of women's ordination would come up again. Several dramatic confrontations happened in the three years.

In mid-December 1973 five male deacons were ordained to the priesthood at the Cathedral of Saint John the Divine in New York City. At the ceremony, five women deacons—whose qualifications were identical to the males except for sex—also presented themselves in vestments to Bishop Paul Moore, Jr., for ordination. It was the first dramatic confrontation over an issue that threatened to rock the unity of the Episcopal Church. Right before the Consecration, when the five deacons knelt before Bishop Moore in silent appeal for the ordination, he told them with sadness, "Go in peace, my sisters." Clearly rejected, they simply turned and walked with bowed heads down the middle aisle out of the church. No funeral procession could have been more sorrowful. More than half the congregation joined them as they too left the church and went to a nearby building to finish the agape as a church in exile.

The incident had immediate repercussions at General Seminary where the community divided into warring camps. Heated exchanges took place in the corridors and in the dining room. Some male seminarians condemned the women's actions as a scandal. Some who had shown lukewarm support for women's ordination now railed against using a "civil rights" tactic which they felt had no place in the solemn liturgy of the church. Others contented themselves with hostile stares at those of us who supported the women deacons by our attendance at the ordination service. I learned that disputes among the faithful, although usually fought with polite words, can be as acrimonious in their language as a street brawl.

At times when theological arguments were invoked against the ordination of women, I shuttled between faith and inner doubt. These arguments carried the force of a two-thousand-year tribal taboo. They were so deeply imbedded in the psyche that on the morning of July 29, 1974, when I took the train to Philadelphia to attend the ceremony in which eleven women deacons were ordained priests without the official approval of their own bishops, I experienced sudden terror. My panic was so great that I might have left the train at Newark if I had not met two clergy women of the United Church of Christ, whose obvious enthusiasm for the event calmed some of my fears.

In Philadelphia, we joined a throng of two thousand people from many parts of the country, who crowded into the Church of the Advocate to witness a dramatic turning point in the struggle for women's ordination. None of us knew what to expect. When the point in the service was reached where the Bishop invites anyone "who knows of an impediment or crime because of which we should not proceed" to make it known, a few male priests screamed their objections. Their hysterical outburst was received calmly and they eventually left the church and the ceremony proceeded with customary dignity and solemnity. By the end of the service, the joyous spirit that enveloped the congregation swept away all of my doubts as to the rightness of the action that occurred that day. My most cherished memory of the occasion was kneeling before the newly ordained Jeannette Picard to receive her blessing.

This ordination took place in a church at the heart of the Philadelphia ghetto, and a Negro congregation provided hospitality. Symbolically, the rejected opened their arms to others who were rejected. They understood each other.

The Episcopal Church could never be the same. The House of Bishops called an emergency meeting and a majority of those present condemned the ordinations as "invalid." Although lively debates among church scholars followed as to whether the ordinations were "invalid" or merely "irregular," the sacramental act could not be rescinded, and the new priests could not be ignored. For many women like me, their existence revolutionized our feelings about the church and about its sacraments. In the days following Philadelphia, some of us met in a small group for a house communion celebrated by one of the Eleven.

Public celebrations would eventually follow. Reverend Alison Creek was the first woman to publicly celebrate the Holy Eucharist in an Episcopal church in the United States. She celebrated at the churches of Saint Stephen and the Incarnation in Washington, D.C. As such things happened, the male rectors of these churches had canonical trials and were charged with violating their ordination vows. The flames of dissension grew.

During my senior year in seminary I did my field work at Saint Philip's Chapel in Aquasco, Maryland. My Aunt Pauline, Aunt Sallie, and Grandmother Cornelia had all worshiped in this church, so it linked me with the spiritual pilgrimage of my family. I remained there through graduation and diaconate, enjoying the community there and my various ministries.

In September 1976, the General Convention met in Minneapolis. After much debate, the ordination of women to the priesthood was finally approved. The Convention's approval would become effective on January 1, 1977. The Right Reverend William F. Creighton, bishop of the Diocese of Washington, D.C., and a firm supporter of the ordination of women, scheduled the ordination ceremony for January 8, 1977. In November 1976, a fire destroyed the little church where I was serving and I mourned the loss much as one mourns the loss of a friend.

In early December, Adina Stewart Carrington, my friend Maida's mother, who was like a second mother to me, suffered a stroke. I rushed to Brooklyn to be with her and Maida in the crisis. I felt overwhelming sorrow seeing this once vibrant woman, whose home had been filled with laughter, stricken and unable to speak to me when I entered her bedroom. She could only smile in recognition as if to say all would be well. For three days, Maida, Mrs. Fleming, a nurse, and I kept vigil as the pulse rate got slower and slower. When the end came, Maida was reading the Ninety-first psalm aloud as her mother gave a slight gasp and slipped into eternity.

Maida had been determined that her mother would die with dignity at home as she wished. Mrs. Fleming now sent Maida from the room and asked me to help with the usual ministrations upon death. All pain had vanished from Mrs. Carrington's face and she looked like a young woman who had simply fallen asleep. I took part in her funeral as a member of the clergy, reading the Ninety-first psalm without letting my voice falter.

On January 8, I was one of three women and three men to be ordained at the same service in which the ordination of two "irregular" women priests was affirmed. All of this occurred at the Washington Cathedral. The circumstances gave the ceremony unusual prominence. Several days before this ordination, I was suddenly seized by an agony of indecision, as though I had been assaulted by an army of demons. The thought that the opponents of women's ordination might be right and that I might be participating in a monstrous wrong terrified me. As a sister priest put it later, "I felt that God might strike me dead before it happened." I have since been told by other priests, male and female, that they faced a similar ordeal before ordination.

January 8 was a bitter-cold, gray morning in Washington, with ice and snow covering the ground. Three thousand or more people packed the Washington National Cathedral, a number of them my relatives and friends. The usual long procession of vested clergy walked down the aisle followed by lay presentors (or sponsors) of the ordinands, and then ourselves who were to be ordained. The liturgy moved forward majestically through the solemn ritual. I was the last of the six to be consecrated. As Bishop Creighton placed his hands on my forehead, the sun broke through the clouds outside and sent shafts of rainbow-colored light down the stained glass windows. The shimmering beams of light were so striking that members of the congregation gasped. After we were thus consecrated and vested, and the words "The Peace of the Lord be always with you," were spoken, the cathedral throng exploded into a joyous outburst such as one seldom sees at the usual staid Episcopal services. It was a resounding affirmation of our community's call to serve as priests.

On Sunday, February 13, in a little chapel where my Grandmother Cornelia had been baptized more than a century earlier as one of "Five Servant Children

Belonging to Miss Mary Ruffin Smith," I read the gospel from an ornate lectern engraved with the name of that slave-owning woman who had left part of her wealth to the Episcopal Diocese of North Carolina. A thoroughly interracial congregation crowded the chapel and many more stood outside until they could enter to kneel at the altar rail and receive communion. There was great irony in the fact that the first woman priest to preside at the altar of the church to which Mary Ruffin Smith had given her deepest devotion should be the granddaughter of the little girl Mary sent to the balcony reserved for slaves. But more than irony marked that moment. Whatever future ministry I might have as a priest, it was given to me that day to be a symbol of healing.

All the strands of my life had come together. Descendant of slave and slave owner, I had already been called poet, lawyer, teacher, and friend. Now I was empowered to minister the sacrament of One in whom there is no north or south, no black or white, no male or female—only the spirit of love and reconciliation drawing us all toward the goal of human wholeness.

Pauli Murray held posts in a number of Episcopal churches in the Baltimore and Washington, D.C., area. She was in constant demand as a pastor and a preacher. She continued to write many articles in theological publications, challenging many on a wide range of justice issues. Differences of culture, appearance, nationality, religion or any other difference were a source of enrichment and not a barrier to human relationships. . . . She died on July 1, 1985, while still working with her editor on this book. —ED.

NOTES

1. The word *Negro* will be used throughout this chapter out of respect for Pauli's preference.

2. Mary Ruffin Smith was a wealthy white woman who encouraged the marriage of her brother, Sidney, to a Negro-Cherokee slave, Harriet. Their daughter was Pauli's paternal grandmother, Cornelia Smith, who helped raise Pauli. Pauli Murray, *Song in a Weary Throat* (New York: Harper and Row, 1987) 1–15.

3. Ibid. 34.

4. Ibid. 39.

5. Ibid. 56.

6. Ibid.

7. In addition to these stereotypes, Christian churches had also debated the full humanness of Negroes; for background, see *American Christianity*, vol. 2, ed. H. Shelton Smith, Robert T. Handy, and Lefferts A. Loetscher (New York: Scribner's, 1963) 167–214.

8. The University of North Carolina did not admit its first Negro student until 1951.

9. Murray, *Song* 112.

10. Pauli Murray, "Collect for Poplarville," in *Dark Testament and Other Poems* (Wharton, Conn.: Silvermine, 1970) 38.

11. Murray, *Song* 385.
12. Ibid., Eleanor Holmes, introduction, xii.
13. Ibid. 415–37.

BIBLIOGRAPHY

Lake, Verge and Pauli Murray, eds. *States' Laws on Race and Color,* 1955 Supplement. Edited by Verge Lake and Pauli Murray. Cincinnati: Board of Missions of the Methodist Church, 1951.

Murray, Pauli. *Dark Testament and Other Poems.* Wharton, Conn.: Silvermine, 1970.

Murray, Pauli. *Proud Shoes.* New York: Harper and Row, 1978.

Murray, Pauli. *Song in a Weary Throat.* New York: Harper and Row, 1987.

Rubin, Lesli, and Pauli Murray. *The Constitution and Government of Ghana.* London: Sweet and Maxwell, 1964.

Smith, H. S., R. T. Handy, and L. A. Loetscher, eds. *American Christianity.* Vol. 2. New York: Scribner's, 1963.

Zickmund, Barbara Brown. "Winning Ordination for Women in Main-stream Protestant Churches." In *Women and Religion in America.* Vol. 3. Edited by Rosemary Radford Ruether and Rosemary Skinner Keller. San Francisco: Harper and Row, 1991. 339–84.

– 22 –

LAURA LÓPEZ AND SILVIA MARIBEL ARRIOLA

(TWENTIETH CENTURY)

If We Love, We Must Show It

The women in this chapter dared to act boldly against the forces of death in El Salvador. Like thousands of Salvadoran victims, their hopes for their people were not accomplished in their lifetimes. Their stories are part of a long history of dehumanization of the indigenous people of Latin America.

In 1492, one hundred million people lived in the Caribbean and in Latin America. By 1570, the number had plummeted to approximately ten to twelve million. In less than a century, eighty million people had been wiped out. This was the greatest genocide in recorded human history.

The Spanish conquistadors began the genocide under the guise of colonial Christendom, and legitimated the massive destruction in the name of conquest for Christ. Five hundred years later, the contemporary Christian church is slowly casting away the colonial attitude and becoming a church of, with, and for the oppressed indigenous people.[1]

The historical victimization of indigenous women has been brutal. Past and present patriarchal authoritarian war practices treat the wives of conquered men as property. In the fifteenth century the additional practices of giving women to invaders as signs of hospitality, as barter for favors, as seals of alliance, or as tokens of possible shared power were common.

The colonizing Catholic Spaniards of the fifteenth century baptized native women so that they could be "concubines" according to church law. This meant the conquerors would not offend canon law if they used the women sexually. Many of the conquerors used women in this way for as long as they wished and then gave them to lesser officers or common soldiers as "gifts" for their use.[2]

Victimization of the indigenous people by the wealthy ruling classes and by the military regimes continued until a massive uprising of peasants occurred in El Salvador. Thousands of peasants were slaughtered and power remained with the conquerors. From then on there was such a deep-seated fear for self and for family that no further mass uprising occurred, in spite of the oppressive conditions.

In 1968, all Roman Catholic bishops of the hemisphere were called to meet in Medellín, Colombia. The purpose of the meeting was to assess what the church could do to alleviate the oppression of the native peoples. Prior to that meeting Pope Paul VI challenged the prominent citizens of Bogotá to mend their ways:

> What can I say to you, men of the ruling class? What is required of you is generosity. This means the ability to detach yourselves from the stability of your position, which is a position of privilege, in order to serve those who need your worth, your culture, your authority.... Your ears and your hearts must be sensitive to the voices crying out for bread, concern, justice, and a more active participation in the direction of society.[3]

The assembled theologians and bishops at Medellín realized in a new way that—through the centuries—many men who represented the church had unwittingly contributed to the oppression. It was time for the official church to become a more active and visible force for liberation. In spite of disagreements, a socially active church of the poor began to take conscious shape at Medellín.

By 1970, Rutilio Grande, a Salvadoran Jesuit, had gone to live and work among the peasants whom he organized into small communities of reflective faith. The groups met weekly to reflect on the Scriptures and to talk about their responsibility to act for transformation of the unjust structures that oppressed them. The number of these groups, the base communities, spread widely throughout the countryside. Grande was assassinated on March 12, 1977, because his work was threatening to those in power. His murder did not stop the movement, however. It had the opposite effect of adding strength to the resolve of the peasants and their church workers. The base community movement continued to threaten those who held political and military power.

Between 1970 and 1976, more than fifteen thousand pastoral workers and catechists (teachers of faith) were trained in pastoral centers opened by the Catholic Church. By the late 1970s, the countryside of El Salvador was dotted with these communities of hope and resistance. Peasants began to feel the power of communities bonded in Christ as they continued meeting around the Scriptures.

The catechists brought a threefold message to the small peasant communities. First, the peasants were as important in God's eyes as the privileged groups. Second, any suffering the people were enduring was not God's will, but an abuse of God's will by the oppressors. Third, God was with the people in their struggle for liberation, dignity, and equality. Nonviolent resistance was encouraged.

Many clergy, women and men religious, lay leaders, and peasant communities were bonded together as those who shared varieties of gifts. Like the earliest

Christian communities, they endured the possibility of death because they insisted on equality and dignity. Some bishops, like Archbishop Oscar Romero, were particularly bold in openly condemning oppression. In 1979, Romero publicly denounced the victimization in his weekly sermons over the radio. In the midst of mounting violence he urged the Salvadorans to reflect on their deeds and stop killing their brothers and sisters. His pastoral letter affirmed the right of the people to defend themselves through "insurrectional violence" if necessary. He quoted from Paul VI's *Populorum progressio:*

> When a dictatorship violates human rights and attacks the common good of the nation, when it becomes unbearable and closes all channels of dialogue, of understanding, of rationality . . . the church speaks of the legitimate right of insurrectional violence.[4]

Romero also encouraged the thousands of trained pastoral workers to accompany the poor, that is, to disperse throughout the land and be with the oppressed. Thousands of dedicated Christians did just that. Salvadorans and those who had come to Salvador from other countries as pastoral workers continued to take their lives in their own hands as they gathered peasants together. The small communities of faith increasingly became a threat to the powerful.

The formation of people's councils in the villages was a way to experience a small form of democracy. A military coup backed by the United States in 1979 led to a repression of such efforts. By January 1980, land reform movements that were supposed to be for the good of the people were actually a means of eliminating the leaders among the peasant communities. The decade of the 1980s became a decade of increasing bloodshed. Archbishop Romero continued his outspoken criticism of the government. He also realized in new ways that it was not that a single person could be called "prophet," but rather that the whole community was prophetic. This was a shift in emphasis for the church:

> I've never felt I was a prophet in the sense of being the only prophet of the people. I know that you and I, the people of God together, compose the prophetic people.[5]

A prophetic people share the vision and hope of God for the world. They attempt to act as God acts, with compassion and hope for the present and future. When prophecy is alive in a community, the death of one person does not dissolve the prophetic spirit. Others will come forth with similar gifts to be leaders, so that the liberation movement continues. This was the case with the base community movement in Latin America. As the list of those who were tortured and martyred grew, new leaders among the people stepped forward. There was mounting opposition to victimization, in spite of the increased number of killings. But the people did not cease their opposition despite death squad activity. The people accepted that if they were to follow Christ's call to liberation, there would be some form of the cross before they would have the experience of resurrection.[6] A prophetic people realize that their gift is for the future of the people.

> Perhaps the gift we have given to the world is that it is possible to make something new . . . Jesus came for a specific purpose: to announce the good news to the poor and to live among them. So this is the church that does not exist at the present time. It's being built with the efforts of thousands of people. . . . The church of the poor is a church that is always creating. It's not satisfied to remain stuck in the past.[7]

The need for new models of the church is slowly being realized as communities reflect on the meanings of being a "new people of God." These reflections have led to a deeper realization that men and women are equals and are equally the image of God. The new people of God must live as an inclusive community of graciousness open to ongoing revelation. This means there will be an eventual development of political and church structures that will be better vehicles of God's hope. After five hundred years of a colonial version of Roman Catholicism and after one hundred and fifty years of Protestant presence, the Christian churches are still in need of interior liberation if they are to be credible. The churches that continue to keep women voiceless and invisible in official leadership cannot simply criticize political injustices if they remain unchanged. A credible liberation must occur in the church if it is to be a powerful voice for change.[8]

The Christ who is the model for the liberation movement in Latin America shows passionate concern for the community. A privatized Jesus Christ cannot empower communal liberation. Jesus Christ is met in the midst of the pain, struggle, and strength of the community. Scriptural reflections are set in this vision in which Jesus Christ continues to send forth his spirit. There is no feeling that revelation has stopped with the written word of the Scriptures. The Spirit continues to reveal what is of God, and a prophetic people knows its vision is partial. "We are aware of the provisional nature of certain affirmations. In the midst of historical conflict, things will change and will change us."[9]

The lives of the two women whose stories are told in this chapter testified to the liberating love of Christ for the prophetic community. Each experienced Jesus Christ with and among his people. Those who knew Laura and Silvia sensed their commitment to the church of the future that the people were shaping in the present. It was with and for the church of the poor that each woman was called to live. In the midst of rising repression these women lived with the hope that their people would continue to allow love to conquer fear.

They are escalating the war, the repression. I hope that fear will not weigh heavier than our love for our people. Our convictions and our faith must overcome them.[10]

Silvia Maribel Arriola and Laura López are but two of the countless martyrs of Salvador. Silvia and Laura were native Salvadorans who felt the call to work among the poor of that country. One life began in a context of poverty, whereas the other was cast in privilege. Each woman underwent a conversion that led her to a deep sense of mission. Each life ended violently, but the violence of the death did not stop the liberating movement of their communities.

At the time that this is being written, the death squads in Salvador continue to murder those among the people who are influencing their communities to demand equality and dignity. In spite of this unchecked cruelty, the many martyrs like Sylvia and Laura seem to remain more subversive in death than in life. Their memory is dangerous, as the accounts will show. For the communities that meet to "remember" these women and their other martyrs, remembering provides a source of inspiration. Others are inspired to take the place of the martyrs. The blood of Silvia and Laura has now mingled with the blood of countless others who tried to make Salvador a sacred ground befitting its name.

For the Salvadoran people, Silvia and Laura are not silent victims. They stand among the people as potent reminders that there is always a choice of resignation or resurrection for Christian believers. The death of a martyr is not in vain. Those who will not let the dead die are saying that they shall continue the revolution, the way of the cross for a resurrection, a better tomorrow.[11] The prophetic promise contained in the lives that are remembered in this chapter provide insight into the true meaning of the body of Christ. Silvia and Laura could truthfully say with Jesus Christ, "This is my body given for you."

Laura López (d. 1985) Go Forward![12]

The people called Laura López their bishop because she was all they had. No priest had baptized a baby, blessed a wedding, or said the words of Eucharist for years on the Guazapa volcano. No priest would dare. The Salvadoran military considered Guazapa a haven for guerrillas. Thus the people who fed them were targets. Laura went to Guazapa in 1979 to live as a pastoral worker.

Laura had been part of the pastoral team of Sister Ana, a pastoral worker who had rooted herself among the people in the war zones. Laura emerged as a leader through election by her community to be a "delegate of the word." Such delegates performed the sacramental functions of a priest with the exceptions of presiding at a wedding and officially celebrating a Catholic Mass. Laura pledged that she would go into the war zones to accompany the people.

Sister Ana blessed Laura's mission. Laura went with her small children, three daughters and two sons, to Guazapa. The troupe slowly lugged their possessions up the side of the mountain. Laura left her house, animals, and basic grains. The family took only what they could carry up the terrain of eighteen miles. Laura carried her infant in her arms. Upon arrival in Guazapa, Laura went from village to village, meeting with the various Christian base communities. She encouraged them, as she imagined Paul encouraged his early church communities. She reminded them that if they were persecuted for the sake of the people, they should count themselves highly for such love and courage. Laura was truly the bishop of Guazapa. The only symbol of her authority was a knapsack she carried on her back. In the knapsack, she had alcohol for wounds, communion bread, and money for the breadless.

Laura's husband had preceded her to Guazapa. In 1981, three years after his arrival, he stepped on one of the hidden land mines and was killed. Laura's loneliness after her husband's death was the loneliness of one who lost the person who best understood her commitment. She was well loved in the midst of her own loneliness. Critics could not help but ask why she was doing what she was doing. What did she offer the people since she was not a priest? Her own brothers said that if they ever saw her they would kill her. They were members of the death squads.

Her children never questioned her, even when she walked them into a war, saying only, "If we love, we must show it." After the death of the father, the oldest boy told Laura that even if she would return to their home, he would now stay with the poor people. But it was the people whose lives called to Laura to stay on, even though her original plan was to stay only for a three-year period.

The air war began in 1985. Laura met the bombardment with innocent fury, documenting the bombings of the civilians. As planes droned overhead, she grabbed camera and tape recorder and captured the invasion. She sent communiqués to the International Red Cross, letters to Christian churches, and to international press agencies. She noted the destruction of lives, fields, and the numbers of the common people who were captured or who disappeared. On March 8, 1985, she wrote from an underground shelter as two A-37 bombers flew over Mirandia and El Zopote dropping ten bombs.

> All of us are hidden in a bomb shelter because we are well aware that their bullets are waiting for us.... At this moment, one A-37 is in our vicinity. We are on the shore of the lake.... Meanwhile another plane is bombing

> Cinquera. We are trying to defend our lives, although we can no longer defend our huts or belongings.

She closed the communiqué with characteristic simplicity, followed by the fierce confidence the peasants of Guazapa depended upon. "God doesn't want it to be that way. They want to terrorize us but we will not be swayed."

Laura was never swayed. God alone knows what her people felt as they scampered from village to village without homes or safe houses. They were a community living under the trees, this pueblo of poor farmers. Children hid from the military who were determined to "sanitize" Guazapa. The community hid underground, holed up for days, thirsty, terrified to surface as they watched their children's wounds fill with worms because they had no antiseptic. Laura's ability to calm her people even in the midst of crises is still well remembered.

Between December and March the bombings took place daily. Laura's desperation drove her to risk travel to the archdiocesan office in San Salvador. Her delegation walked all day and all night. She told a journalist in San Salvador, "We were barely able to cover the bus fare to the archdiocesan office." The total bus fare was the equivalent of a dollar and a half. She feared that people would die of hunger because General Blakon had said the offensive would last three months. "We can hardly bear two weeks," she said. "How shall we bear three months?"

The suffering of the people was tearing at her. Her own children were so sick that she had to leave them in San Salvador. The community of Guazapa was being pulverized. The army could starve them out. Their homes, crops, and animals had been devastated during the search and destroy missions. Yet her reflections that were taped during the liturgies she led called for a realm of the spirit to transform the impossible grief.

> The martyr's cross has been placed on our shoulders. Our people have decided to end this way of the cross, but the final triumph is still far down the line. We are Christians and we know what we have to do. But first, we must sacrifice and make a serious decision to do so.

Whatever Laura felt about her own life, she was clear on who would be the first casualties. "The first to die are always those with faith."

On Palm Sunday, in the midst of hell, the peasants of Las Delicias spoke of hope, reflecting on Jesus' triumphal entrance into Jerusalem. The peasants of Guazapa believe they will be resurrected. Their fire cannot be put out by counterinsurgency. Laura's reflections pointed the way.

> We have gotten used to hating, to being afraid. We have to put an end to that. We have to confront ourselves, to kill the false pride within our soul,

> so that a new person may arise, so that a new civilization may come into being—one composed of love.

In the same Palm Sunday reflection Laura spoke about violence and nonviolence. "We should not place our faith strictly in weapons, thinking that the gun is God and that the gun will give us liberty and justice." Then, echoing Archbishop Romero's words, she added, "If it weren't for the compañeros in arms, we would all be killed even though we have faith.... We can't remain passive in the face of this situation."

On April 6, 1985, Laura met with all the pastoral workers in Guazapa. Her communiqué says, "Despite the fatigue, after making an escape from an invading army, we give thanks to God for protecting us. The work of the base communities must continue, because if it were otherwise, what would become of us?" The army invaded again on April 22, and Laura was worried. "We can't take off and leave the people here. We have already offered our lives for them." It was characteristic of Laura to talk like that in the face of rising panic, to remind everyone—including herself—of the reason for their commitment.

The shelling continued relentlessly. When bombardment was close, Laura and her family fled for a shelter. When a family with children couldn't enter the overcrowded hideout, she and her thirteen-year-old daughter ran into the canefields of Valle Verde, trying to outrun the ground patrols. They were surrounded. Her daughter recalls the event.

> I was running along, just about at my mother's side, when she was hit by a bullet in the back. I said, "Mama, they've hit you!" Perhaps she hadn't felt it just yet because she kept on running. Then another bullet hit her.... She couldn't run anymore.... She gave me the knapsack and told me to go forward!

This final moment symbolizes the church of the poor in which the only promise is that—if you fall—someone else will take your place. The knapsack is handed over. It is a symbol of that church which is bloodstained and passes on a pastor's contraband, passes on the spirit of the one who died.

Laura's daughter ran into tall grass to hide, carrying the knapsack. Crouched in the grass, she could see the soldiers shoot Carlos, a six-year-old boy from her village. He was hit in the testicles and left for dead. Laura's daughter took off her socks, made a bandage to stop the bleeding, then carried him through the cover of the canefields under the protection of nightfall. She carried the boy for three days until they could break through the military encirclement and find villagers to care for the child. On Saturday, April 27, the daughter and others searched for Laura's body.

> They found my mother with her skull caved in, and it was barely connected to her body. She had been tied up like an animal for the slaughter. They found two other bodies near her, people who couldn't run fast enough to escape and they shot them down. I remember how the soldiers shouted, "Don't run! We won't hurt you!" Then they shot them down.... We buried my mother along with the two other people.

Among the peasants Laura still lives. "Laura López and Padre Caceres (a young martyred priest) were ours," says a villager named Teresita. "They are martyrs of this people. They gave us their lives."

We (the author and others) attended a liturgy that evening amid candle flames, wildflowers, and the murmur of cicadas. A large picture of Laura López was tacked on the wall of the open shed "chapel." Sitting beneath Laura's smile, the pastoral team gathered to speak with me. All of them seemed under the age of 25. An older member who was on Laura's pastoral team ended by explaining Laura's title of bishop.

> Laura was the bishop of Guazapa because she refused to abandon the people even when the bombing had driven many away. She once told us that the Good Shepherd never deserted the sheep, and she would stay on in Guazapa preaching the gospel if only one person remained.

Then the small company repeated Laura's legendary last charge. "Adelante!" Forward!

Silvia Maribel Arriola (1951–1981) Don't Seek Me in the Tomb![13]

Silvia Maribel Arriola was born to privileged parents in Santa Ana, El Salvador, in 1951. She was sent to an exclusive Catholic girls' school in San Salvador. When the violence in San Salvador grew worse, only Silvia and her father remained behind in the country. Silvia joined a traditional San Salvador religious order of teachers and nurses. As she and another sister attended the meetings of the base communities, she became convinced that her vocation was to work within these communities. The decision meant that she would have to leave the more traditional order.

She decided to renew her vows as a woman religious, but did so in the midst of the people who were her base community. She recited her vows, which were received both by Archbishop Romero and the people.

> In a society whose ideals are power, possession, and pleasure, I pray that I may be a sign of what it really means to love. I will do my best to be a sign that Christ Jesus alone is Lord of history, that he is present here in our midst, and that he is capable of inspiring a love mightier than our own instincts, mightier than all the economic and political forces, mightier than death itself.... I promise our Lord that I will be faithful—in sickness and in health, in youth and old age, in tranquility and persecution, in joy and sorrow. I promise to do my best to share in his incarnation among the poorest of the poor, and to imitate his poverty and solidarity with them in their liberation struggle... concentrating all my will and affections on him and on all my sisters and brothers.[14]

Silvia and the sisters of her community were a surprise, a gift that the poor did not expect. Each step Silvia took dismantled her identity as a middle-class professional. As she acted to construct a new church, she constructed a new self that she discovered in the common longing and jeopardy of the poor. Silvia learned to become empty in order to enter into the heart of life. A difficult loss was silence for prayer.

Living in a slum with four other sisters, working half-time to help pay living expenses, ministering to the homeless refugees pouring into the city for the other half of the day, and attending base community meetings at night left Silvia with little time for contemplative silent prayer. When Silvia let go of that longing, the people became her prayer and she became theirs. Magdalena, a co-madre, recalls Silvia's surrendering to the people.

> I remember her gentleness and patience with the people. What really touched me was that she learned to be poor even though she had never been poor like us. She was rich. I'll never forget this, never.... Her deep commitment brought her to martyrdom.

At the same time that Silvia was working with base Christian teams, mass popular organizations were also emerging. This provoked some tensions in the church. Previously, the community had been shaped by the witness of Martin Luther King and Gandhi. But at the time the popular movements grew, there was need to deal with the more militant revolutionary organization of the FMLN (Frente Farabundo Martí para la Liberación Nacional) as well. People's suffering helped the sisters to understand the commitment of others who were also trying to change things.

During this period Silvia met Emma and her youth group in the poor Mejicanos neighborhood in San Salvador. It was Holy Week when the sixteen-year-old Emma attended the traditional Way of the Cross. She had heard it was being led—incredible as it seemed—by a woman named Silvia.

> We had always had a traditional Way of the Cross, but Silvia's reflections were very different and beautiful. It made an impression on me that a woman who was so young was leading the Way of the Cross. Also I had never seen a religious who was on the streets with the people and not cloistered in a convent. At that moment I spoke to Silvia and said, "Who are you? Why have you come?"

That first encounter with Silvia was powerful for a young woman like Emma, who had deep spiritual ideals and lived in a country at war. Meeting the demands of committed youth in El Salvador requires in an adult not ordinary maturity but heroism. Silvia did not disappoint. She was more than Emma's youth group could keep up with. In life and in death Silvia was just a step ahead. According to Emma, what compelled the youth group of Mejicanos was not the charism of Silvia but her love and friendship.

> Silvia truly identified with us. Besides being a friend, she was a sister with whom we could share. We could go to confession to her better than with a priest. For me she was someone who fulfilled herself, who was happy in her work.

Emma described Silvia's patience and dedication to the youth group, taking them more seriously than they had taken themselves. Once a week under the trees at Planes de Rendero, Silvia and the youth group had lunch meetings as the group spoke of their hopes and dreams. "We were searching for a life in which our spiritual longings could be fulfilled. Silvia was the occasion of awakening my vocation." In time Emma's journey would take her directly into the war. Meanwhile, as the repression expanded, the pastoral team divided into groups and went into different regions.

Silvia went to El Amate for a year. Then a death threat from one of the right-wing para-military groups caused Silvia to be a pilgrim. She lived from village to village, only staying briefly with a family so that her presence would not endanger them. Silvia, like so many others, had become *quemada* (wanted).

On January 3, 1981, Silvia went to Santa Ana in order to accompany the people. Her little community of sisters affirmed her decision. People had asked Silvia to be with them in the war zones, and the community discerned that it was right to do this. While working in Santa Ana, Silvia continued to return to her base community in San Salvador. As the human needs of people under siege grew desperate, Silvia returned to one family in the community of San Salvador. This was just weeks before the FMLN offensive would sweep Santa Ana.

In 1981, just before the rebel offensive, the Salvadoran soldiers in the Santa Ana garrison mutinied and joined the FMLN. Then the FMLN took over the town of Santa Ana. During this period Silvia gave a talk in the town plaza on the theme of Christian commitment. The crowd was struck that a woman religious, Silvia, was in a place like this. Addressing the assembled people, the mutineers, and the guerrillas was like a twelve-year-old Jesus addressing the Jewish elders in the temple. "They were amazed at the strength of a faith that prompted her to such a commitment."

Following the mutiny, everyone understood the army would return bent upon reprisals. The town prepared to depart or join the guerrillas. Silvia chose to go with the FMLN contingent with the intention of offering her nursing skills in care for the wounded. A Maryknoll sister who worked in Santa Ana describes the FMLN takeover of the town in January and the events that followed.

> The guerrillas went house to house advising us to stay in and not be fearful. By 9:00 p.m. the barracks were taken. During the night the Green Cross center was used for the wounded brought in from the outskirts of the city. That night was quiet and so was the first part of the next day. People went about daily life. The young boys were instructed in the use of guns. There was a fearless, cozy attitude. But later in the morning when I was at the Green Cross Center, a helicopter came in and began firing. The houses were frail. We heard bombs in the city but we did not feel them in Lamatapec. But then canons fired on us. Helicopters came in and people fled into the chapel and convent where we set up mattresses against the bullets. We played a game to calm our fears.
>
> At 3:00 p.m., the army came with tanks and the guerrillas fled. An office and a clinic were destroyed. The baby scale, which was difficult to come by, was taken. We saw this from the chapel. At 4:00 p.m., the Salvadoran military set up a transmitter and guided the movement of the helicopters, directing them to follow those who had fled over the hills. We were appalled at this, knowing it was U.S. technology that would track that group that would otherwise have been free. It was an American voice that I heard across the street. Someone said, "That's all. Let's go."
>
> Days later, the group of guerrillas, doctors, and nurses who served with Silvia were caught on the road to Metapan.

Silvia and ninety-one others ran for three days. Their legs pumped with the fury of animals outrunning the hunters, hunters with precise, high-powered rifles. Traced by radar, pursued by helicopters and planes, the bands of FMLN militants, the wounded, doctors and nurses like Silvia, were surrounded and virtually incinerated. It was January 17, 1981. After the slaughter they were thrown into an open grave.

When Silvia's base community heard of her death, they were stunned with grief. But it was people in the poor barrio of Mejicanos where Silvia had worked who had the deepest response. Two members of her youth group responded to her death as an invitation to a more committed life. When Silvia fell, two others took her place. Maria and Emma, now Sister Maria and Sister Emma, decided to enter Silvia's small community, publicly vowing themselves to obedience, charity, poverty, and to the God of the poor. Emma recalls the response of the youth group to Silvia's death.

> At the moment we learned Silvia had been killed, the youth group came together to reflect upon her life. Sister Maria and I asked to be accepted into the community. Two boys from the youth group who wished to enter the seminary went to the war front and are still there. Three more stayed in the city and joined in the base Christian community ministry. The other four became frightened, left the work, stayed behind, and even now they do nothing.

There is no marker on Silvia's grave. "The zone is still controlled by armed forces so we cannot find it," said Emma.

> But when the revolution triumphs, we shall make a pilgrimage to that spot. For me, Silvia is not dead. She lives on in my ideals. She lives on in the commitment of the Christian community. Silvia could die if we let go of our faith.

Where does the meaning of Silvia's life lie? For her community, the meaning of Silvia's life is discovered in the effect of her life on those for whom and with whom she struggled. On the fifth anniversary of Silvia's death, her community celebrated a Mass in remembrance of her. The people offer gifts: flaming ocote, a knotty wood cross, doves that flutter upward following the light of the high windows of the church. Her community sings the song written to commemorate her, "Silvia, where are you going?" It is in this song that Silvia speaks to the community once more. She points beyond herself.

> Don't seek me in my tomb.
> I am among the people.
> I go opening pathways
> of a new history.

NOTES

1. Pablo Richard, "1492: The Violence of God and the Future of Christianity," in *1492–1992: The Voice of the Victims*, ed. Leonardo Boff and Virgil Elizondo (London: SCM Press, 1990) 59–67.
2. Julia Esquivel, "Conquered and Violated Women," in ibid. 68–77.
3. Quoted by Ana Carrigan in *Salvador Witness: The Life and Calling of Jean Donovan* (New York: Simon and Schuster, 1986) 82–83.

4. Quoted by Jenny Pearce, *Promised Land* (London: Latin American Bureau, 1986) 184.

5. Jon Sobrino, *Archbishop Romero: Memoirs and Reflections* (Maryknoll, N.Y.: Orbis, 1990) 239.

6. Renny Golden, *The Hour of the Poor, the Hour of Women* (New York: Crossroad, 1991) 25–39.

7. These are some reflections of a twenty-three-year old catechist named Reina in her interview with Renny Golden, ibid. 64.

8. Aracely de Rocchietti, "Women and the People of God," *Through Her Eyes: Women's Theology from Latin America* (Maryknoll, N.Y.: Orbis, 1989) 96–117.

9. Nelly Ritchie, "Women and Christology," in ibid. 82.

10. Interview with Reina, in Golden, *The Hour of the Poor* 66.

11. Ibid. 134–35.

12. This edited version of Laura's story is from the full text by Golden in *The Hour of the Poor* 135–45.

13. Silvia's story is told in full by Golden, ibid. 155–63.

14. Pablo Galdámez, *Faith of a People* (Maryknoll, N.Y.: Orbis, 1986) 48–49, cited in Golden, *Hour of the Poor* 201 n. 58

BIBLIOGRAPHY

Boff, Leonardo, and Virgil Elizondo, eds. *1492–1992: The Voice of the Victims*. London: SCM Press, 1990.

Carrigan, Ana. *Salvador Witness: The Life and Calling of Jean Donovan*. New York: Simon and Schuster, 1984.

Golden, Renny. *The Hour of the Poor, the Hour of Women: Salvadoran Women Speak*. New York: Crossroad, 1991.

Gutiérrez, Gustavo. *The Power of the Poor in History*. Maryknoll, N.Y.: SCM Press/Orbis, 1983.

Lernoux, Penny. *The Cry of the People*. New York: Penguin, 1980.

Ortiz, Noemi. "Martyrdom Does Not Come from Death, but Life." *Central American Report* 11:3 (June 1991).

Sobrino, Jon. *Archbishop Romero: Memoirs and Reflections*. Maryknoll, N.Y.: Orbis, 1990.

Tamez, Elsa, ed. *Through Her Eyes: Women's Theology from Latin America*. Maryknoll, N.Y.: Orbis, 1989.

Thompson, Marilyn. *Women of El Salvador*. London: Zed Press, 1986.

FILMS RELATED TO THE MARTYRS OF SALVADOR

Choices of the Heart
Romero
Roses in December

– 23 –

MOTHER TERESA

(1910–1997)

We Need the Poor to Touch Christ

Mother Teresa spent most of her life working in the rich cultural and religious heritage of India. Diverse Christian and non-Christian spiritualities can be found in India, where they exist side by side within a long history of oppression. Similar to other colonized lands, it is the indigenous Indian people who have been placed at the bottom of the Hindu caste system.

In the 1990s approximately 225 million out of 700 million people are the tribal peoples and the *dalits* or poorest caste of the "untouchables." All are indigenous peoples who lost their land and were enslaved as the Brahman civilization arose centuries ago. The Brahman priests and ruling classes institutionalized inequality in the political-religious caste system within which they have special religious and political status.

India was under British colonial rule for more than two hundred years. Traditional arts, crafts, and economic systems were essentially wiped out by the colonizers, who considered their ways superior. The Westminster model of parliamentary democracy was imposed by British rulers. This form of government did not take ethnic and cultural diversities into account. Consequently, the most oppressed people continued to be powerless in the political arena. An economic model that enmeshed India in a global economic network has had disastrous results for the nonwealthy. The educational system continues to perpetuate the interests and rule of an elite caste, as unemployment rises for the poorer people.

Indian independence was won from Britain in 1947. The impoverishment of the people has not changed, however. Socially, politically, and spiritually, there is still a caste system in place that keeps the poor impoverished. The intricate web of oppressive political and religious socialization was pushed into a more global consciousness through the women's movement in the early 1970s.

Like some earlier movements, the women's movement in India began to address the injustices inherent in the caste system. Women and others of the untouchable caste still have low legal and minimal economic status. The women's movement protested the political marginalization of women and of the rest of the poor. The degree of change in oppressive laws is not great, but some change has occurred in laws about rape and in former laws that protected men who abused women in the name of religious and political order. Fundamentalist religious and political forces still target women for acceptable patriarchal violence and control. However, women have begun to band together with the *dalits* and the tribal peoples to insist on the necessity of dignity for all, regardless of caste.

The clash between those who presently hold privileged positions and those who are becoming communities of resistance and change will only be resolved through a new paradigm for a new India. In the present, as in the past, whenever the poorest people try to claim dignity and human equality, they are opposed by a form of fascism that masquerades as "Indian nationalism." The ideology of Hindu nationhood and Brahman culture has been a dangerous weapon in the hands of the state. The privileged classes that claim the divine will wants only a few to be privileged and hold power is a perversion of the spiritualities that are foundational to Indian culture.

Centuries before the birth of Jesus Christ, Buddhism was a formative religion in India. This religion was named after its religious founder, Gautama, a Buddha or enlightened one. Gautama Buddha rejected caste and gender discrimination, attacked greed, stressed the need for his followers to better the lot of people in this world, and insisted on respect for all life. Buddhism was one path for transforming an emerging culture of violence in India toward one of liberating peace. Although there are many different expressions of Buddhism, there is similarity in the religious philosophy that guides the expressions.

Buddhism teaches a threefold way of spirituality (*dharma*). Insight, enlightenment, and wisdom are the three gifts that reveal the illusions of the world (*maya*). The three ways of living spiritually include action, devotion, and love. Right action (*karma*) confronts injustice directly. The ways of universal love and devotion (*bhakti*) are open to all. The particular expression of Buddhism that is Sikh spirituality teaches that holiness can only be experienced through service, community, hospitality, refusal of gender distinctions, refusal of priestly hierarchies, and the tradition of acting and governing in a democratic and respectful manner.

Muhammad was another religious leader whose teachings strongly influenced Indian spirituality. In his time Muhammad was directly engaged in trying to liberate the poor and victimized of his day. The spirituality of Muhammad is a spirituality of the Qur'an (Koran), which emphasizes a God of mercy and compassion. The God of the Qur'an hates injustice and calls believers to fight against injustices of all kinds. The true wisdom of the Qur'an respects equality of persons, sexes, nations, tribes, and all other religions.

Christianity has its clear Way, Truth, and Life in Christ Jesus. In Christ there can be no separational inequality of women or men, slave or free, classes, races, or ethnic groups. There must be action and passion for justice and love. Love of all is at the heart of Christian spirituality. It calls for liberating action to bring about the equal dignity that Christianity asserts. The Christian Gospel shows Jesus Christ mingling with the outcasts and religiously or socially victimized people. The little ones heard what he was saying and saw what he was doing. They heard the true message about the reign of God and the kingdom that was for all. Those who were trying to keep dying institutions alive could not hear of the newness.

The spiritualities of bhakti, Sufi, and Christian tradition are similar in their paths to liberation. None of these spiritualities links political systems to institutionalized religion. The countercultural vision of these traditions calls for the people to break down the walls of divisiveness, privilege, and oppressive caste systems. The spirituality that is shared by the diverse religions of India calls for liberation from unjust practices and institutionalized privilege and oppression. The stress on the need for both action and discerning love provides a wisdom that can guide the long-term process of transformation.

Protest, conflict, suffering, and ultimately a communion with others who share the same dreams of authentic selfhood will carry the process forward. There will not be an easy peace or a simple immediacy about the transformation from caste system to a new system of dignity and equality for all people. There will be further social upheaval because of protest movements. In the long run, the upheavals will bear fruit if there is the will to sustain the effort with nonviolent wisdom.[1]

If Christianity is to be an equal partner in the movement for transforming the present institutionalized inequity, the Christ who must appear through Christian witness is a Christ who cares about the present physical suffering of the people. The humanity of a compassionate Christ that can encourage women as well as men to follow his way of love is especially important. In the midst of a history of oppression of women, the maleness of Christ can be an obstacle to the thousands of women who have associated maleness with privilege and oppressive power:

> If we ascribe maleness to Jesus Christ, we are also committing the mistake of ascribing the pagan/Hindu notions of sexuality to our God who transcends this. The church in India needs to recognize the personhood of Jesus Christ and the fact that Christ is the representative human being for all people, including Indian women.[2]

Christianity will be credible to the extent that Christians do what Jesus did for the poor and the outcast. This is the agenda of Mother Teresa and her sisters, brothers, and coworkers throughout the world. The loving concern of Christ for the outcast has become not only their concern but their reason for existing.

Mother Teresa insisted that this spirituality is not a special gift, but one that can be followed by everyone who is Christian. Whereas this may be true in theory, the life of Mother Teresa does suggest that, in fact, her living spirituality was a gift that was developed in her in a special and unique way.

Before reflecting on her vision of the Christian life, it may be helpful to learn something about the woman. Not much is known about her childhood, primarily because she chose not to discuss the past as much as the present. Biographers who interviewed Mother Teresa about her life were usually surprised by this attitude.

Over the years Mother Teresa seldom spoke of herself. Her response to questions about herself was quite predictable. "Write about the work and my people." "Personalities are not important." "That's not necessary." Then she would shift the topic to something that removed the focus from herself. One of her admirers said in response to questions about Mother Teresa, "There are no legends. The remarkable thing about Mother Teresa was that she was ordinary."[3]

What is known about Mother Teresa is that she was born of Albanian parents in Skopje, Yugoslavia, on August 27, 1910. Her parents named her Agnes Gonxha Bojaxhiu. Her father was a grocer and her mother took care of the home and family. Agnes had one brother and one sister. She attended the government school and became a member of a sodality as a teenager.[4] The Jesuits who ran the sodality were Yugoslavians. Some of the Yugoslav Jesuits were in Calcutta in 1925 doing work for the poor, and one of them sent back enthusiastic letters from the Bengal mission that were read to the members of the sodality. Agnes, who had decided to be a missionary when she was twelve years old, was so moved by the letters that she volunteered for the Bengal missions. She was put in touch with a community of sisters who were working in Bengal, the Loretto community in Ireland.

In November 1928 she went to the Loretto Abbey in Dublin to learn English, the major language of India. After schooling in Dublin, Agnes was sent to begin her novitiate in Darjeeling, India. She had expected to see poverty, but the novitiate was in the foothills of the Himalayas. Although this disappointed her at the time, she knew she would someday be working with the poor. She took her first vows as a Loretto sister in 1931 and made final vows in 1937. She was disappointed when she was sent to teach high school at Entally, Calcutta. This school was for daughters of wealthy Europeans and Indians, not for the poor. Eventually she became principal of this school.

She was successful at her work but maintained the desire to work with the poor. On September 10, 1946, while on a train going to Darjeeling, she received her "inspiration." The voice of God seemed to directly address her. The voice told her to leave her convent to live among the poor and to work with them directly. To do this she had to secure permission from her own community to live outside the cloister. In that same year, she applied to Rome for permission to set aside the traditional habit of the Loretto sisters for a more typically Indian dress, a white sari. She added a cross to the shoulder. This would be the habit or dress she would wear while living among the poor. She recalls the suffering that leaving the community brought upon her. "To leave Loretto was my most difficult sacrifice, the most difficult thing I have ever done."[5]

She went to Patna for three months to study nursing with American Medical Missionary Sisters. Here she met Mother Dengal, a woman who had fought with Rome to get permission for her sisters to practice surgery and midwifery. Mother Dengal gave the young Sister Teresa much advice, help, encouragement, and valuable training in a short time. While at Patma, Sister Teresa decided that she would start her own congregation of sisters. The members would have to live like India's poorest people. She and her followers would eat and dress like the poorest of the poor of India. When she decided that the diet would be only rice and salt, Mother Dengal pointed out that this would not be adequate if the sisters were working all day. Sister Teresa took the wise advice.

In December 1948 Sister Teresa arrived back in Calcutta, confronted by an impoverished city. It was only a year earlier that India had gained independence from the British. However, independence came only after Pakistan had been partitioned as a Muslim state. Hostile religious groups killed so many Muslim and Hindu people that there was a flight of eight million fearful Muslims and Hindus to Bengal. The number of people in Bengal was a contributing factor to Bengal being divided into a western and eastern section. Calcutta became the capital of West Bengal.

The British colonial city of Calcutta in Bengal had been known as a city of palaces when the British were ruling it. However, it turned into a living nightmare after the division of Bengal that independence brought. The number of lepers, diseased, and homeless of Bengal was incalculable. Sister Teresa lived with the Little Sisters of the Poor as she worked in Bengal. At this time she decided to formally renounce her Yugoslav citizenship and become a citizen of India.

After she became an Indian citizen, she began her work by opening a small school, which was no more than a space among the crowded huts in Moti Jheel. The children of this slum were taught reading and also hygiene. Some former students of Sister Teresa and some friends of hers from the Loretto community came to help her. The school grew and she eventually found a place to live that was closer to the people. Others desired to join her in her work, and the number of concerned workers grew.

With the growth in numbers and the shared vision for the poor, Sister Teresa decided to regularize the community as an official group. She set forth a rule of life (constitution) and asked for approval from Rome. On October 7, 1950, Pope

Paul VI approved the Constitution and the Congregation of the Missionaries of Charity, whose founder was Mother Teresa. The center house would be located in Calcutta. Its members would take vows to free them to love Christ above all and to serve him in the poor. In 1963, the Missionary Brothers of Charity were founded and blessed by the archbishop of Calcutta.

At the conclusion of a 1964 Eucharistic Congress in Bombay, India, Pope Paul VI gave Mother Teresa a new limousine that had been donated by the American people for his use at the congress. The pope presented it to Mother Teresa to aid her work. Since no one could imagine Mother Teresa or any of her community riding in such a car, they felt she would simply sell it to get money for the missions. She decided she would get more money by running a raffle. The government allowed her to do this, in spite of some questions about the laws governing such a form of gambling. She would have gotten approximately $15,000 from selling the car in 1964. However, the raffle netted over $64,000. The money was used to open a home for lepers, a project she had long hoped to undertake.

The Missionary Sisters and the Missionary Brothers of Charity spread rapidly to various parts of the world. In 1969 a branch of Co-Workers was added to the group. Paul VI received their constitution and blessed the new project. In 1970 a novitiate was opened in England to train people from Europe and the Americas to become members. Increasing numbers of people throughout the world continued to offer their lives and their service.

The work of Mother Teresa and her community has become well known in the past twenty years. Leaders of states and nations as well as leaders of religious organizations have publicly honored Mother Teresa. Some of the public honors she received include the John XXIII Peace Medal; the John F. Kennedy International Award in 1971; the Jawaharlal Nehru Award in 1972; the Templeton Award for Progress in Religion presented by Prince Philip in 1973; and the Nobel Peace Prize in 1979. Mother Teresa consistently accepted the honors so that the human needs of the poor and the work that must be done for people in need could receive attention and elicit support.

Although Mother Teresa would have preferred working with the poor to traveling around the world, she looked on traveling as part of her ministry to the poor. She jokingly admitted that she would probably go to heaven quickly because she endured so much unnecessary publicity.[6] She consistently stressed that the poorest of the poor are not only those whose material needs were not met. The poorest of the poor can also be the abandoned and lonely ones who may be materially affluent. These include the addicted in any form, the disenfranchised, the criminal, the ignorant, the special people, and all people who are looked on as burdens rather than blessings. One of her typical acknowledgments was that the one way that Jesus Christ appears today is through these poor. It saddened her when she saw that "today when Jesus comes among us, his own, we often don't recognize him."[7]

For Mother Teresa, as for many women mystics before her, the contemplation of the Lord and action with and for his body, were one reality. For her, the body of Christ was present twenty-four hours a day through as many expressions as there were people in her life. Her spirituality proclaimed in action that love transforms the world wherever humans live it. Something as simple as a smile can affirm this love. Mother Teresa believed that every Christian is called to do Christ's missionary work in some form. She made no claim to a "special holiness" because of the work that she and her sisters did. But her quiet heroism and love have led others to claim that hers was a special holiness.

The former prime minister of India, Indira Gandhi, summarized Mother Teresa's life as she paid tribute to her. Using the prayer of St. Francis of Assisi as a basis for her reflection, Gandhi had this to say:

> Who else in this wide world reaches out to the friendless and the needy so naturally, so simply, so effectively? She lives the truth that prayer is devotion, prayer is service. Service is her concern, her religion, her redemption. To meet her is to feel utterly humble, to sense the power of tenderness, and to know the strength of love.[8]

The selections that follow will reveal some of the tenderness and strength of Mother Teresa. The Christian universality of love that grounds her life points to a way that one woman embraced the particular conditions of culture and responded to the needs that were evident in that culture. For Mother Teresa heaven was manifest through whatever shape the passion and resurrection of the Lord assume in daily life. Although biographers had to gather pieces of reflections in between busy segments of her day, there was still a consistent grounding of all the reflections in the hopeful assurance that Christ is met twenty-four hours a day in the loving response to those we meet.

Reflections of Mother Teresa[9]

On Love of God

"You shall love the Lord your God with your whole heart, your whole soul, and with your whole mind." This is the commandment of the great God who cannot command the impossible. Love is a fruit that is in season at all times. It is within the reach of every hand. Anyone may gather it and no limit is set. Everyone can reach this love through meditation, spirit of prayer, sacrifice, and an intense inner life.

On Prayer

It is not possible to engage in the direct apostolate without being a person of prayer. We must be aware of our oneness with Christ, as Christ was aware of oneness with the Father. Our activity is truly apostolic only insofar as we permit Christ to work in us and through us, with his power, with his desire, and with his love. We must become holy, not because we want to feel holy, but because Christ must be able to live his life fully in us. We are to be all love, all faith, all purity, for the sake of the poor we serve. Once we have learned to seek God and the will of God, our contact with the poor will become the means of great sanctity to ourselves and to others.

Love to pray. Feel often during the day the need for prayer and take trouble to pray. Prayer enlarges the heart until it is capable of containing God's self-gift. Ask and seek, and your heart will grow big enough to receive the Lord and keep the mystery as your own.

On Silence

We need to find God. God cannot be found in noise and restlessness. God is the friend of silence. See how nature—trees, flowers, grass—grows in silence. See the stars, the moon, the sun, and notice how they move in silence. Is not our mission to give God to the poor in the slums? This is not a dead God, but a living and loving God. The more we receive in silent prayer, the more we can give in active life. We need silence to be able to touch the human spirit. The essential thing is not what we say but what God says to us and through us. All our words will be useless unless they come from within—words which do not give the light of Christ increase the darkness.

On Holiness

Our progress in holiness depends on God and on ourselves, on God's grace and on our wills to be holy. We must have a real living determination to reach holiness. "I will be a saint" means I will free myself of all that is not God. I will strip my heart of all created things. I will live in poverty and detachment. I will renounce my will, my inclinations, my whims and fancies, and make myself a willing servant to the will of God.

On Humility

Let there be no pride or vanity in the work. The work is God's work. The poor are God's poor. Put yourself completely under the influence of Jesus, so that he may think his thoughts in your mind. Do his work through your hands, for you will be all powerful with him who strengthens you.

On Submission

Make sure that you let God's grace work in your souls by accepting whatever the Lord gives you, and giving to God whatever is taken from you. True holiness consists in doing God's will with a smile.

On Suffering

Without our suffering, our work would be just social work, very good and very helpful. But this would not be the work of Jesus Christ, not part of the Redemption. Jesus wanted to help by sharing our life, our loneliness, our agony, our death. Only by being one with us has he redeemed us. We are allowed to do the same. All the desolation of the poor people, not only their material poverty, but their spiritual destitution, must be redeemed. We must share it, for only by being one with them can we liberate them, that is, by bringing God into their lives and bringing their lives into God.

On Joy

Joy is prayer, joy is strength. Joy is love, joy is a net of love by which you can catch human spirits. God loves a cheerful giver. She gives most who gives with joy. The best way to show gratitude to God and the people is to accept everything with joy. A joyful heart is the normal result of a heart burning with love. Never let anything so fill you with sorrow as to make you forget the joy of the Risen Christ.

We all long for heaven where God is. But we have it in our power to be in heaven with God right now, to be happy in God at this very moment. Being happy with God at this time means:

loving as God loves
helping as God helps
giving as God gives
serving as God serves
rescuing as God rescues
being with God twenty-four hours a day
touching God in the Lord's distressing guise.

On Kindness

Be kind and merciful. Let no one ever come to you without going away better and happier. Be the living expression of God's kindness: kindness in your face, kindness in your eyes, kindness in your smile, kindness in your warm greeting. In the slums, we are the light of God's kindness to the poor. To children, to the poor, to all who suffer and are lonely, give always a happy smile. Give them not only your care, but also your heart.

On Our Lady

Let us ask our Lady to make our hearts meek and humble as was her Son's. It is so very easy to be proud and harsh and selfish, so easy. But we have been created for greater things. How much we can learn from our Lady! She was so humble because she was all for God. She was full of grace. Tell our Lady to tell Jesus, "They have no wine," the wine of humility and meekness, of kindness and sweetness. She is sure to tell us, "Do whatever he tells you." Accept cheerfully all the chances he sends you. We learn humility through accepting humiliations cheerfully.

On Thoughtfulness

Thoughtfulness is the beginning of great sanctity. If you learn this art of being thoughtful, you will become more and more Christ-like. The heart of Christ was meek. He always thought of others. Our vocation, to be beautiful, must be full of thoughts for others. Jesus went about doing good. Our Lady did nothing else in Cana but thought of the needs of others and made their needs known to Jesus.

On Leaving Loretto (Her Former Community)

Our Lord wants me to be a free nun, covered with the poverty of the Cross. Today I learned a great lesson. The poverty of the poor must be so difficult for them. When looking for a center (to be a home for the poor), I walked and walked until my legs and arms ached. Then I thought how much the poor ache in soul and body as they look for a home, food, health. The former comfort of Loretto came to tempt me. But out of my own free choice, my God, and out of love for you, I desire to remain and to do whatever your will is in my regard. Give me courage now at this moment.

Peace

We shall make this year a year of peace in a particular way. To be able to do this, we shall try to talk more to God and with God, and less with people or to people. Let us preach the peace of Christ like he did. He went about doing good. He did not stop his works of charity because the Pharisees and others hated him or tried to spoil his Father's work. He just went about doing good. Cardinal Newman wrote: "Help me to spread thy fragrance everywhere I go—let me preach to you without preaching, not by words but by example—the catching force; the sympathetic influence of what I do; the evident fullness of the love my heart bears to you."

Our works of love are nothing but works of peace. Let us do them with greater love and efficiency—each in her own or his own work in daily life; in your home, in your neighborhood. It is always the same Christ who says:

I was hungry—not only for food, but for peace that comes from a pure heart.

I was thirsty—not for water, but for peace that satiates the passionate thirst of desire for war.

I was naked—not for clothes, but for that beautiful dignity of men and women shown forth in their bodies.

I was homeless—not for a shelter made of bricks, but for a heart that understands, that protects, that loves.

This year let us be this to Christ in our neighbor wherever the Missionaries of Charity and their Co-Workers are. Let us radiate the peace of God and so light this light of the Lord. Let us extinguish in the world and in the hearts of all people any hatred or love for power. Let the Missionaries of Charity and the Co-Workers, in every country where they are, meet God with a smile—everywhere they go, in everyone they meet.

Apostle of the Unwanted

The biggest disease today is not leprosy or tuberculosis, but rather the feeling of being unwanted, uncared for and deserted by everybody. The greatest evil is the lack of love and charity, the terrible indifference toward one's neighbor who lives at the roadside assaulted by exploitation, corruption, poverty and disease.

As each one of this Society is to become a Co-Worker of Christ in the slums, each ought to understand what God and the Society expect from her. Let Christ live and radiate his life in her, and through her in the slums. Let the poor seeing her be drawn to Christ, and invite him to enter their lives and their homes. Let the sick and the suffering find in her a real angel of comfort and consolation. Let the little ones of the streets cling to her because she reminds them of him, the friend of the little ones.

Our life of poverty is as necessary as the work itself. Only in heaven will we see how much we owe to the poor for helping us to love God the better because of them.

Holy Communion

In Holy Communion we have Christ under the appearance of bread. In our work we find him under the appearance of flesh and blood. It is the same Christ. "I was hungry, I was naked, I was sick, I was homeless."

Daily Prayer for the Children's Home

Dearest Lord, may I see you today and every day in the person of your sick ones. While nursing them, may I minister unto you. Though you hide yourself behind the unattractive disguise of the irritable, the exacting, the unreasonable, may I still recognize you. Enable me to say, "Jesus, my patient, how sweet it is to serve you."

Lord, give me this seeing faith. Then my work will never be monotonous. I will ever find joy in humoring the fancies and gratifying the wishes of all the poor sufferers.

O beloved sick, how doubly dear you are to me, when you personify Christ. What a privilege is mine to be allowed to tend you.

Sweetest Lord, make me appreciative of the dignity of my vocation and its many responsibilities. Never permit me to disgrace it by giving way to coldness, unkindness, or impatience.

O God, while you are Jesus, my patient, please be to me a patient Jesus, bearing with my faults. Look only to my intention, which is to love and serve you in the person of each of your sick.

Lord, increase my faith, bless my efforts and work, now and forevermore. Amen.

On Conversion[10]

Oh, I hope I am in the process of conversion. I don't mean what you think. I mean I hope we have converting hearts. Not even the almighty God can convert a person's heart unless the person wants it. What we are all trying to do by our work of serving the people is to come closer to God. If in coming face to face with God, we accept the Lord in our daily lives, then we are converting.

We become a better Hindu, a better Muslim, a better Catholic, a better whatever we are. Then by being better, we come closer and closer to God. If we accept the Lord fully in our lives, then that is conversion. What approach would

I use? For me, naturally, it would be a Catholic one. For you it may be Hindu and for another, it may be Buddhist, according to one's conscience. What God is in your mind, you must accept. But I cannot prevent myself from trying to give you what I have.

I am not afraid to say that I am in love with Jesus Christ. He is everything to me. But you may have a different picture in your life. This is the way that conversion has to be understood. Some people think that conversion happens overnight. It is not like that. Nobody, not even your father or your mother, can make you do that. Not even almighty God can force a person. Even Jesus Christ, though he was God, could not convert the hearts of people unless they allowed him to do it.

I very much want people to come to know God, to love and serve the One who brings true happiness. What I have, I want everyone in the world to have. But it is their choice. If they have seen the light, they can follow it. I cannot give them the light. I can only give the means to the light. If I breathe into Kalighat, and do some work there and really serve the people with great love and sacrifice, naturally they will come to know. And once they know, they will want to love. If they love, they will want to serve.

There are many Hindu ladies who want our way of life, the life of poverty, prayer, sacrifice, and service. They want the life of a missionary. But they wish to retain their faith, their own belief in God. Now I don't know how this works. You see, they want to take vows. They want prayer. They want complete dedication. I am trying to think of a way. We are not social workers, though we do social work.

On Belief

What we allow God to use us for is important. What God is doing through us is important. Because we are women religious, our vocation is not to work for the lepers or the dying. Our vocation is to belong to Jesus Christ. Because I belong to Jesus Christ, the work is a means for me to put my love for him into action. So it is not an end but a means. Because my vocation is to belong to God completely, and to love the Lord with an undivided heart, I take religious vows.

I see Christ in everyone I touch because Christ said, "I was hungry. I was thirsty. I was naked. I was sick. I was suffering. I was homeless. And you took me. . . ." It is as simple as that. Every time I give a piece of bread, I give it to him. That is why we must find a hungry one, and a naked one. That is why we are totally bound to the poor.

The vows we take are essential to religious life. The vow of chastity is nothing but an undivided love for Christ. Poverty is nothing but freedom. The total surrender to God is obedience. If I belong to God, then I belong to Christ. Christ must be able to use me. That is obedience. Christ may use me to give whole-hearted service to the poor, and that is service or ministry. Prayer and service complete each other. That is our life.

If you really belong to the work that has been entrusted to you, then you must do it with your whole heart. You can bring salvation only by being honest and by really working with God. It is not how much we are doing but how much love, how much honesty, how much faith, is put into doing it. It makes no difference what we are doing. What you are doing, I cannot do. What I am doing, you cannot do. Sometimes we forget that and spend more time looking at somebody else and wishing we were doing something else. We waste our time then. We waste time thinking of tomorrow, then let today pass, and meanwhile yesterday has already gone.

On Love

The poor must know that we love them and that they are wanted. They themselves have nothing to give but love. We are concerned with how to get this message of love and compassion across. We are trying to bring peace to the world through our work. But the work is really the gift of God.

People today are hungry for love, for understanding love, which is greater. This is the only answer to loneliness and great poverty. That is why we are able to go to countries like England and America and Australia where there is not much hunger for bread. But there are people suffering from terrible loneliness, terrible despair, terrible hatred, feeling unwanted, feeling helpless, feeling hopeless. They have forgotten how to smile. The have forgotten the beauty of the human touch. They are forgetting the meaning of human love. They need someone who will understand and respect them.

The poor are not respected. People do not think that the poor can be treated as people who are lovable, as people who are like you and me. But the young are beginning to understand. They want to serve with their hands and love with their hearts. They want to love to the full, not in a superficial way.

Love can be misused for selfish things. This can happen if I love you but at the same time want to take from you as much as I can, even the things that are not mine to take. Then there is no true love, for true love hurts. Love always has to hurt. It is painful to love someone. It is painful to leave them and you may have to die for them. When people marry, they have to give up everything to love each other. The mother who gives birth to her child suffers much. It is similar for us in religious life. To belong fully to God, we have to give up everything. Only then can we truly love. The word "love" is so misunderstood and misused.

A young American couple told me once, "You know a lot about love. You must be married." I said, "Yes, but sometimes I find it difficult to smile at my husband."

On Death

We help the poor die with God. We help them to say they're sorry to God. That is between God and them alone. No one has the right to intrude on that alone time. We just help them to make their peace with God because that is the greatest need—to die in peace. We live that they may die in peace. We live that they may go home according to what is written in their book, be it written according to Hindu or Muslim or Buddhist or Catholic or Protestant or any other belief. There are some societies that collect their own dead. We have never had any trouble.

Nobody in Nirmad Hriday (a house in Calcutta) has died depressed, in despair, unwanted, unfed, or unloved. That is why I think this is the treasure house of Calcutta. We give them whatever they ask according to their faith. Some ask for Ganges water. Some ask for holy water. Some ask for a prayer or for a word. We try to give them whatever they need. Some just ask for an apple or bread or a cigarette. Others just want somebody to sit with them.

In the beginning we weren't accepted at all. We had quite a lot of trouble. At one time, some young people were going around threatening and destroying and our people were getting more and more frightened. One day, I said, "If this is the way you want it, kill me. I will go straight to heaven. But you must stop this nonsense. You cannot go on like this." After that, it finished and everything was all right.

We had one of the priests here from the temple who died very beautifully. The others could not understand because he was so bitter when he came here. He was very bitter and very young, only about twenty-four or twenty-five. He was the head priest of the temple, I think. No hospital would take him. He was thrown out, which is why he was so bitter. He did not want to die when he came, but he changed.

He became quiet and peaceful. He was with us only two weeks. People from the temple used to come and visit with him every day. They could not believe the change in him. I suppose, surrounded by people who were suffering in the same way, he learned to accept. The people themselves are of tremendous help to each other. I often wonder what would happen to the world if innocent people did not suffer so much? The innocent sufferers are the ones interceding the whole time. They are so pleasing to God. By accepting suffering, they intercede for us.

On Faith

Why these people and not me? That person that was picked up from the drain—why is that person here and not me? That is the mystery. No one can give the answer. But it is not for us to decide. Only God can decide life and death. The healthy person may be close to dying, or even more dead than the one who is dying. The healthy might be spiritually dead, but it doesn't show. Who are we to know or to decide?

Where there is mystery, there must be faith. Faith cannot be changed no matter how you look at it. Either you have it or you don't. For us it is very simple because our feet are on the ground. We have more of the living reality. There was a time when the church had to show majesty and greatness. But today people have found that it does not pay. They have found the emptiness of all that pomp, so they are coming down to the ground. But in coming down, some have not yet found their real place.

God has created all things. All the butterflies, the animals, the natural world has been created for us. To other things, God has not given the will power to choose. They have only instinct. Animals can be very loving and very lovable. But this is instinct. Only the human being can choose. Will power or choosing is one thing God does not take from us. I want to go to heaven and I will it, with the grace of God. If I choose to commit sin and go to hell, that is my choice too. God cannot force me to do otherwise.

Our expanding knowledge does not dim our faith. It only shows the size and grandeur of God's creation. Often we do not understand. I don't know if you have read St. Augustine's life. It is a beautiful example. St. Augustine was trying to understand God, to understand the Trinity, to understand the magnitude of God's creation. His human mind could not grasp it. He was searching here and there when he came upon a small boy who was trying to fill a hole in the ground with water. St. Augustine asked him what he was trying to do. The child said, "I am trying to fill this hole with the ocean." St. Augustine said it was impossible. Then the child, who in truth was an angel, said, "It is still easier to put the ocean into this hole than for you to understand the mystery of God." And that is still true.

On Her Work

Since we began our work, something wonderful is happening. More and more poor people are coming from the villages into Calcutta, but there is a difference. Ordinary people are beginning to get concerned. Before, they used to pass by a person dying on the streets. Now, when they see something like that, they immediately do something. If they can't get an ambulance, they bring the person to us by rickshaw, or taxi, or take them to Kalighat, or phone us. The big thing is that they do something. That is wonderful, is it not?

At least our work has broadened people's minds. They are no longer frightened. They used to be frightened of getting involved with the police, but they know now that there is a place to go and that there are sisters who will stand by them.

We do not help the dying only. We also help the living. There's Shishu Bhavan, our dispensaries, and our schools... I did not know that our work would grow so fast or go so far. I never doubted that it would live, but I did not think it would be like this. I never had doubts because I had this conviction that if God blesses our work, it would grow. Humanly speaking, it is impossible and out of the question, because none of us has the experience. None of us has the things the world looks for to be successful. This is the miracle of all the little sisters around the world. God is using them as instruments. They have their own convictions. As long as any of us has this conviction, we will be fine, and the work will prosper. But the moment we begin to say, "This is my work," it has become selfish. Nothing will be necessary, and the Congregation and the work will die.

That is why we begin with this conviction. That is why we need the Eucharist. We need Jesus to deepen our faith. If we can see Jesus in the appearance of bread, we can surely see him in the broken bodies of the poor. That is why we need oneness with Christ and deep faith in Christ. When we are deeply united with Christ, we can touch the broken bodies. We need the poor to touch Christ. We feed ourselves in the Eucharist. After we are fed, we want to use that energy and to give it. That is why you see the sisters run and not walk. They call us the running Congregation!

On Sin

God dwells in us. That's what gives God a beautiful power. It doesn't matter where you are as long as you are clean of heart. God is there with you and within you twenty-four hours a day. That's why Christ says, "Love one another as I have loved you." To be clean of heart means to be open, to be free, to have the detachment that allows you to love God without obstacles. When sin comes into our life, that is a personal obstacle between me and God. Sin means God cannot act through me or give me strength where there is sin between us. Sin is nothing but a slavery.

When I choose evil, I sin. That's where my will comes in. When I seek something for myself at the cost of everything else, I deliberately choose sin. I say, for example, that I am tempted to tell a lie. Then I choose to tell the lie. Well, that means my mind is clouded. I have just burdened myself by putting an obstacle between God and myself. The lie has won and I have preferred the lie to God.

This is why poverty is such a gift to all of us—there are fewer obstacles. Very often, in our desire to get something, we are greedy. We can also be jealous. We can be distracted. Then we cannot see God, so these are obstacles.

More than any other congregation, our congregation needs poverty. Only this real poverty gives us the detachment and the real freedom we need to understand the poor people with whom we work.

On Prayer

You should spend at least half an hour in the morning and an hour in the evening in prayer. You can pray while you work. Work doesn't stop prayer, and prayer doesn't stop work. It requires only that you raise your mind and heart to God. Do small prayers like, "I love you, God; I trust in you; I believe in you; I need you now." Such small things are wonderful prayers.

Excerpts from the Nobel Lecture, December 10, 1979[11]

We believe what Jesus has said. "I was hungry; I was naked; I was homeless; I was unwanted, unloved, uncared for—and you did this for me."

I believe that we are not really social workers. We may be doing social work in the eyes of the people. But we are really contemplatives in the eyes of the world. We touch the body of Christ twenty-four hours a day. We have twenty-four hours a day in the presence of Christ. So do you. You too must try to bring that presence of God into your family. The family that prays together stays together. I think that we in our human family do not need bombs and guns to destroy or to bring peace. We can just get together and love one another.

That will bring peace, strength, and joy in the home. If we all did that, we would be able to overcome all the evil in the world. There is so much suffering, so much hatred, so much misery. We with our prayer and sacrifice are beginning at home. Love begins at home. It is not how much we do, but how much love we put into the doing.

I want you to find the poor here, right in your own home first. Begin your loving there. Be good news to your own people. Find out about your next-door neighbor. Do you even know who they are?

With this prize that I have received as a prize of peace, I am going to try to make the world home for many people that have no home. Because I believe that love begins at home, if we can create a home for more and more of the world's poor, love will spread. We will be able to bring peace and good news to the poor through this understanding of love. Let us do this to the poor in our own family first, then in our neighborhood, and then in the world.

To be able to do this, our lives have to be woven with prayer. They have to be woven with Christ to be able to understand and to share. Today there is so much suffering that it is clear the passion of Christ is being lived all over again. Are we there to share that passion, to share that suffering of the people around the world? I have found the poverty of the West so much more difficult to remove than that of economically poor countries.

When I pick up a hungry person from the street, I can give the person a bowl of rice, a piece of bread, and see satisfaction. I have removed the hunger. But a person that is shut out feels unloved, unwanted, terrified. The person closed out from society or community has a poverty so hurtful that I find it difficult. That poverty is the kind our sisters face in the West.

A smile is the beginning of love. So let us always meet each other with a smile. Once we begin to love each other, naturally we will want to do something for each other. Pray for all of us, our sisters and brothers and Co-Workers that we remain faithful to the gift of God.

Pray that we—and you—may love and serve the poor. Whatever our sisters and brothers have done would not be done without prayers, gifts, and continual giving by people like yourselves. I don't want you to give from abundance, but give until it hurts.

I think we all must live life beautifully. We have Jesus with us who loves us. If we could only remember that God loves us and we have the opportunity to love others as we are loved! If small things were done with great love, this Norway would be a home of love! How beautiful Norway would be as a center for love and peace from war, a gift that can be given here. As you become a burning light of peace in the world, then really the Nobel Peace Prize becomes a gift of the entire Norwegian people to the world!

God bless you!

NOTES

1. "An Indian Search for a Spirituality of Liberation," a shared reflection by Indian theologians Stella Balthasar, Stella Faria, Arutu Gnanadason, Cresey John, A. P. Nirmal, Mirmal Minz, and Samuel Rayan, in *Asian Christian Spirituality: Reclaiming Tradition*, ed. Virginia Fabella, Peter K. H. Lee, and David Kwang-sun Suh (Maryknoll, N.Y.: Orbis, 1992) 64–84.

2. Monica Melancthon, "Christology and Women," in an address given in Singapore, November 1987. This paper has been edited and included in *We Dare to Dream: Doing Theology as Asian Women*, ed. Virginia Fabella and Sun Ai Lee Park (Maryknoll, N.Y.: Orbis, 1990) 15–23. The edited quotation can be found on p. 20 of this text.

3. Desmond Doig, *Mother Teresa: Her People and Her Work* (San Francisco: Harper and Row, 1976) 46.

4. A sodality is a group of Christians who promise to follow a mode of Christian life that includes particular daily prayers and meditation, reaching out to aid the needy, and meeting regularly with the group and its moderator. Sodalities were especially popular in the 1930s to 1960s in North America.

5. Kathryn Spink, *Miracle of Love* (San Francisco: Harper and Row, 1981) 23.
6. Ibid. 239.
7. Ibid. 142.
8. Doig, *Mother Teresa,* foreword. The reflections are dated September 26, 1975.
9. Malcolm Muggeridge, *Something Beautiful for God* (San Francisco: Harper and Row, 1971) 65–74.
10. Doig, *Mother Teresa* 156–66.
11. The full text can be found in Spink, *Miracle of Love* 229–39.

BIBLIOGRAPHY

Doig, Desmond. *Mother Teresa: Her People and Her Work.* San Francisco: Harper and Row, 1976.

Fabella, Virginia, and Mercy Amba Oduyoye, eds. *With Passion and Compassion.* Maryknoll, N.Y.: Orbis, 1988.

Fabella, Virginia, Peter K. H. Lee, and David Kwang-sun Suh, eds. *Asian Christian Spirituality: Reclaiming Tradition.* Maryknoll, N.Y., 1992.

Muggeridge, Malcolm. *Something Beautiful for God.* San Francisco: Harper and Row, 1971.

Spink, Kathryn. *The Miracle of Love.* San Francisco: Harper and Row, 1981.

– 24 –

CHO WHA SOON

(born 1934)

The Church Is for All People

Cho Wha Soon was born in Inchon, Korea. Like other rural women, Cho's mother had little formal education. Her father was well educated and an active participant in the Korean independence movement, which reached its height in March 1919. After the movement failed, Cho's father was thrown into prison. He escaped to Inchon, where he met and married Cho's mother.

As a child Cho was encouraged to be whatever she wished to be. She remembers the joyful and freeing atmosphere of her preteen years. As a teenager, she joined others in a Methodist youth group that studied discrimination against rural workers in Korea. The close-knit group of friends decided they would dedicate their lives to bettering the conditions of poor rural workers and women. The Korean War of 1950–53 changed their hopes.

This war was a result of the heightened animosity between the northern and southern sectors of Korea, a division made after World War II. Russian troops occupied North Korea and U.S. troops occupied South Korea. In 1948, the United Nations recognized South Korea as the Independent Republic of Korea. The North Korean army invaded South Korea in 1950. The Chinese joined forces with the North Korean army in 1951, when Cho was sixteen.

It became clear to those who had lived long enough that Korea was again entering into the process of an ancient, repetitive cycle of war, suffering, and poverty. The cycle always resulted in the powerful becoming more powerful and the poor being victimized by struggles that did not involve them. In the familiar cycle, villages of the poor would be destroyed. Eventually they would rebel. The rebellion would fail, and the result was loss of life, reprisals, new sufferings, and ongoing poverty.

Ancient feudalism, patriarchalism, militarism, capitalism, and neocolonialism continued to keep the common people (the *minjung*) poor. Throughout the centuries rural women in particular were victimized by their limited access to education, by cultural-religious discrimination, and by customs that rewarded oppressive situations for women.

In 1961, Park Chung Hee seized power in South Korea through a military coup. His regime used traditional and patriarchal norms to strengthen its position and power over the people. Korean Confucian culture reinforced the practices of the Park regime, which fostered a strong sexual discrimination and authoritarianism. A slight change in the Constitution of the Republic of Korea gave nominal rights to women without changing the system of discrimination and without bettering the working conditions of women and poor people.

President Park's educational and cultural policies emphasized traditional loyalty and filial piety. Official awards were given to self-sacrificing women who proved they were virtuous wives and faithful daughters-in-law. This meant that the women were rewarded by President Park for providing hard labor for meager wages. Compared to men in the same labor force, women worked in poorer conditions for longer hours and for less pay. The virtuous wives were also full-time parents, providers for their husbands and children, primary caretakers of husbands' parents as well as their own, and caretakers of brothers who were in need.

President Park had planned to build a self-sufficient economy by focusing on labor-intensive light industries through the 1960s and the 1970s. In the later 1970s, he planned to implement heavy industries. Foreign capital was needed for such a long-range economic policy. As the foreign capital was provided, the economy became better but the national debt increased. One way of lessening the debt was to enforce a lower wage policy. This policy was implemented for women and for the poorer workers, but did not touch the wealthy. This policy prevented the poorest people from sharing in any benefit of the "economic growth."

By 1984, more than 88 percent of the workers received wages that were below the minimum cost of living. The wages were the worst for women who were single, young, and from the rural areas. These women were often sent to work in the factories to help out their families and to aid in the education of their brothers. The women were not given access to education as their brothers were. Long hours and poor conditions in textile companies were a health hazard for many women, but there were always others to take their place.

The Korean Christian Church became actively involved in bettering working conditions and wages for women workers. Women worked for less than minimum wage as a result of the pressures on them to help their families. To respond to such injustices, the Korean Christian Church inaugurated the Urban Industrial Mission.[1] The mission was carried out by pastors working in the same conditions as underpaid workers and trying to organize the workers to demand more humane conditions and salaries.

The ancient religious roots of Korea militated against the Urban Industrial Mission project, however. Shamanism and Confucianism strongly affected Korean cultural ideology. Both systems legitimized the dehumanizing treatment in the guise of a religious system.

Confucian ethics required that a woman obey her father, her husband, and her son. This notion of obedience also extended to employers, shamans, authorities, and male workers in the same positions as the women. This subjugation of women was so extreme that the whole of women's existence was governed by men.

Korean shamanism is called a "religion of the people" because it is the religion of the majority of poor and oppressed people. Shamanism is a family-centered religion that "protects" the welfare of the family by exorcising (ritually casting out) evil spirits that dwell in and around the house. It reconciles the family with good household spirits and enables the family to be in harmony with the spirits of its dead members. The family is shown to be "religious" when it is blessed with wealth, success, male children, and health. Any anger caused by being oppressed (*han*) must also be released by a shamanistic ritual if the victimized are to be free spirits.

Korean Christianity has been influenced by shamanism in its more familial, individualistic, and materialistic concerns. This has led to a lack of social concern among Christians for the injustices suffered by others. As concerns for the impoverished conditions of the people entered Christian consciousness, projects like the Urban Industrial Mission succeeded. Such projects, however, were—and still are—suspect, for they seem to be contrary to deeply ingrained cultural sensitivities. Some Christian churches are beginning to see that shamanistic rituals can have meaning for Christian people. Resistance and subversion can be strengthened as victimized rural people use the Christian shamanistic rituals to transform destructive angers into a power for liberation.[2]

If Christianity is to be a transforming religion for the Korean people, a liberating image of Christ must be presented as a central image. A Christ who liberates, who works with and for the poor, who feeds the hungry, and who has power to reintegrate outcasts into the society will be credible to the people. Christian pastors will need to share in the lot of the poor as they also simultaneously organize the people to effect their own liberation. "Disciples must become victims of the present order or else they have no right to denounce it. The struggle for the poor is a mission entrusted only to those who are or have become poor."[3]

This is the reality that Cho Wha Soon accepted in her call to be a Methodist minister in Korea. Although Christianity remains a minority religion, Cho's life proclaims its strength in bringing hope and transformation to society. In the reflections that follow, Cho tells her life story to reveal the power that Christ has shown in and through her. Like the actions of other women before her,

Cho's action to change unjust systems is nourished by her intimacy with Christ. A life that began in comfort in Inchon was forever changed by events in her teenage years, events that led her to become a quiet but forceful presence of Christ among the people. In these selections Cho tells her story of ministering in a war-torn Korea and the war's aftermath.[4]

Let the Weak Be Strong[5]

[*In 1950 the choir in which Cho sang was ordered to perform for the soldiers stationed in Pusan. When the group arrived, the Korean army officer in charge had received no word about the performance. The war had become so widespread that the group could not return to Inchon. That afternoon the choir members became war refugees who had no money and no place to stay. The girls were taken to an army "hospital" to tend wounded soldiers. The boys were taken to places near a U.S. army camp and given jobs. Cho was sixteen at the time. The experience left a lasting impression.*]

> Through my life as a nurse at that time, I became aware of God's calling for me. It was a very valuable period of my life.[6]

We were separated into three different rooms for our work, intensive care, regular patients' ward, and "light" patients' ward. My sixteen friends were sent to care for patients in the regular and light wards. I was the only one sent to intensive care. There I experienced a sensation of life and death mingled together. Some patients had already stopped breathing. Some were still alive but just like dead bodies. Others looked on in despair as they themselves waited to die. When I opened the door I could hardly breathe for the smell of decaying bodies. The air was filled with groans of pain and suffering. Foamy spit ran from mouths. There were screams, blood and sweat, the laughter of mental breakdown. How can I describe it all? There was one doctor, one nurse aide, and one nurse-hygienist. They were unable to meet patients' needs.

I worked all day running and serving the patients. Mostly, I dressed wounds, washed the men, and fed those who could not feed themselves. It was difficult and tiring work. By supper time, I was exhausted. When I finally reached my bed, I was irritated because the others still had energy to talk about the things that had happened that day. They were able to still enjoy themselves, laughing and playing. I complained to God for being so unfair to me. Why should I have to endure the hardship when I had been no more sinful than any of the others?

The more I thought about it, the angrier I became. One of my friends understood and wisely said to me, "Do not blame God like that. You ought to thank God. Among the seventeen of us, who else of us could have endured that kind of work? Who else?" She went through the sixteen names and I finally realized that none of the others would do such drudgery without complaining. "See? You are the only one who could do it. God has especially commissioned the work to you. It seems that you are getting a special favor from God." That really struck me and I began to have a different attitude. God had appointed me for the special work because I could do it!

My relationship with the patients changed wonderfully. They began to call me "respected" nurse. None of the others were called that. Since we were not registered nurses and were all very young, they just called, "Come here!" and treated our group roughly. They acted as if we were servants to them. But I was treated quite differently. Perhaps it was because they felt love from my hands, for I did whatever I could to help them. I sang songs; I listened to stories; I encouraged them to have hope and remember family and good things from their past.

The patients forgot that I was younger than they were. They liked me more like a mother or a sister. One day I looked at the patients lying there with bare feet. It was a cold winter and the heating was not enough to keep them warm. Looking at the bare feet made me sad. I decided to make socks for their feet. I found some old bloodstained blankets in a storage room. After my work, I took the blankets to a frozen stream. I broke the ice and washed the blankets in the freezing water. I blew on my hands to keep them from freezing. I watched over my patients carefully during the day, but as night came, I started sewing their socks. I could sew about ten pair of socks a night. Finally, I finished and took the socks to the room. I put each one on my patients' feet with care. It is impossible to describe the joy that each of them felt when I personally put the socks on their feet. When I saw the degree of their happiness, I felt a wonderful joy myself.

When Inchon was reclaimed after four months, my nursing came to an end. I received a small piece of rice cake made by my patients as a thank-you. We all cried at the sadness of this separation. This had been one of the most worthwhile pieces of my life! It was a time of special spiritual experience as well. I realized God's love through being chosen for such a difficult work. I was born again, for I now realized that no matter how miserable one's situation is, it can become a beautiful experience if one is awakened to the deeper meaning of life.[7]

[Cho returned to Inchon and found that her parents had lost so much in the war that they were too poor to send her to high school. Together they decided to sell a last valuable item, a piano. Cho finished high school, passed the teacher's examination, and became a primary teacher. She and some friends who were dedicated to the role of education as a liberating tool taught primary children by day and adults from the rural areas at night. Reading was taught to the adults while remedial classes were held for their children who had missed school due to home chores. Cho was assigned to teach at

Namsa Primary School when she was twenty years old. Here she met another teacher who became her first love.]

When we first met, he was a teacher at Namsa school. He was five years older than I and already married. Even though I was always bright and active, I was as strict as a Puritan. Having no experience of love, I did not even know our relationship was love. He always listened to me attentively even when I said things in fun. Sometimes I noticed him gazing at me like a mindless person while I was teaching the children. When we called on students' homes, two teachers always formed a team. He always arranged to make me his partner so that we could go together. In the evening we would walk along the tree-lined path and share refreshing, friendly talk.

One day on the way home after visiting students' homes, he asked me, "Cho Sun-saeng (Teacher Cho), you won't stay here forever, will you? If you find better circumstances for the rural movement, you surely will leave. Then you will naturally forget me, won't you? Even if we are apart, how about your being my adopted sister and I being your brother, to continue the relationship between us?" I did not take it seriously and responded with a joke. I was so excited and interested in my schoolwork that other things could not matter much to me.

Finally, on a study tour, he acknowledged that he was in love with me. "Coming to know you, I found that I was a new person. My married life is dead and without love, but you are vivid and make me alive." We did not have any special dates, but just met as we went back and forth in our work. Later I realized deep in my heart that I was in love with him. Being with him made me excited about my work. He was not a Christian, but sometimes said that through me he saw God. When I entered the Methodist seminary, I could no longer meet him. If I had agreed to our "adopted" relationship as he had proposed, I could have met him with that excuse. Now I had no acceptable reason.

Being unable to meet him made me long for him so much that it was unbearable. At last I realized that I was deeply in love with him too. Then a letter came from him. He wrote me love letters three times a day. Each letter was written beautifully and consisted of five full pages. His letters were so emotional that they often made me cry. But in any case, I had to cut off ties with him since he had a family and I knew our relationship was not right. So I did not reply to his letters. I was alone and sick with a broken heart. Of course he must have suffered just as much.

Three years later I went to the wedding of a friend who had been a teacher with me. There I met him again and we greeted each other with our eyes only, as I was busy helping her with the wedding. After the wedding, I was feeling lonely. When I got home, he was there, and was greeting my father. He carried on a very lively and kind conversation with my family. After a long visit, he left. My family liked him very much and asked about my relationship with him. "Don't miss the chance to get such a good man for your husband," they told me. I walked with him that night and he asked me to meet him again the next day. I could not meet him the next day because I could not trust myself that I could reject his offer. If he was not a married man, I would marry him immediately. I think that loving such a person was the will of the Lord for me.

He always watched me with much love. I sensed that the loving gaze was a mixture of passion and the agony of controlling himself. He seemed to be near wherever I went. When I was sent to Dokjokdo as the missioner for a pioneer church, I became terribly ill. I was alone and there was no chance to notify my family about the illness. I don't know how he found out, but he sent me a long letter with money for medicine. I didn't know anything about him and yet he seemed to know everything about me.

Ten years later, when I first started industrial mission work, I met him on the street in Inchon quite by accident. He asked me for a date. Because so many years had passed, I felt that I could now agree to meet him and say a formal good-bye. The next day we walked in the park and I felt myself losing my certainty. We stayed together until five minutes before the curfew. As we parted, his face seemed very lonely. I will never forget his loving eyes! Once, as he walked away, he turned his face to me. When I saw his eyes, my eyes overflowed with tears. I dreamt of him with great longing. I could not keep myself from loving him.

Five or six years passed before we met again. In 1972, I was on the way to the Christian Academy in Suwon for an education program. A friend told me that he was in Suwon and held a high position in the education field. We met over the lunch hour and he asked me to go to his home. I did and it was here that he said, "I truly love you. From the first time we met until now, I have not forgotten you even for a minute. The agony I have suffered for twenty years is whether I should throw away everything for love: my wife, my children, and all my property. But I find that I do not have the courage to abandon them. Yet it is so painful that I am not able to come to you."

I sat touching the flowers in front of me with my heart pounding. His wife returned and set the table for lunch. I knew who she was, without knowing the relationship. After lunch, I said good-bye. His wife walked me outside and caught a cab for me. Once inside the taxi, I realized that our love of twenty years was like a rose-colored dream. But reality is not a rose-colored dream. He became a middle-aged man with everything, who was willing to throw away nothing. He had a wife, a son, a daughter, a well-furnished home, and a firm place in society. I knew now that I had no room to squeeze in there. I also finally knew that I was at last seeing the truth about him and myself. My emotions calmed down and seemed cleansed. Facing the reality, the lingering feeling of attachment left and the beautiful dream slowly ended.

From then on I felt comfortable even when we accidentally met. The feeling of love dissolved as I saw that there was a large gap in our feelings about social issues. I was already in the midst of the industrial mission work and was standing against the regime of Park. He supported the regime and worked for it as a sincere servant, an educator. Once he came to try to persuade me not to work for the Urban Industrial Mission. I was under heavy guard by the secret police (KCIA). It was then that I suspected he may have been an agent of the secret police, though he probably was only concerned for my safety. He advised me to let up on my involvements against the regime, as I had been on television, radio, and in the newspapers. I explained my stand reasonably and I think he understood it.

Now, because of my age, as I look back on the agony I went through, I feel it is a precious and beautiful memory. Everything is kept very quietly in my heart. Can a memory always be so beautiful?[8]

[*The twenty years of this relationship saw much change in Cho's maturity of faith. After graduating from Methodist seminary, she was sent to the island of Dokjokdo, her first experience of being a pastor. This island was inhabited by an influx of refugee boat people from the aftermath of the Korean War. Since the island had no running water, human excrement was all over the road, in empty buildings, and in the abandoned church that Cho was to pastor. The church had no members, for the refugee boat people were afraid that if anyone believed in Jesus, the whole village would be destroyed.*]

The people avoided talking to me, saying that if they got close to a Christian they would have bad luck. I decided that I would develop this church. For several days, Kyung Hyun, a friend, and I removed all trash and excrement, washing the floor of the church many times! After thoroughly cleaning the church, I held the first Sunday service. The only attendee was a mentally disturbed man from a neighboring village. I wondered what to do when I remembered, "Jesus said he would leave ninety-nine sheep to go and find the one that was lost." For one month, this was the only one who came to the church to hear my sermon!

As I walked through my village, and as Christmas was soon coming, I invited any of the children—who had little to do—to come to the church to play, to act, to have fun. With songs, dances, and plays, we decided to do a Christmas pageant. We got a pine tree from the hill and decorated it for Christmas. Most of the people came to the village church to see the play since it was winter and there was nothing else to do. The people were fishermen so I gave a short sermon on the love of Jesus for fishermen. I also told them, "The church is a joyful place for all people. Please come when you are sad or suffering, or in agony, or any other time. You are welcome here!" Most only came when they wanted to kill time, but they came. However, on Sundays, there was only the poor man and once in a while, his mother.

Two neighboring churches heard my story about the needs of my church and helped me with money. I became convinced that my church should exist for the development of the community. I started to visit the people. Since they were workers in the fields, I would dig and weed with them and share stories. I tried to encourage the youth to have some concern for their village. "Let's think hard and make efforts together for this village."

In the early 1960s, when the military revolution had taken place, the government carried out a booming reconstruction project all over the country. It was a coincidence that helped make my dream come true. I held many public lectures. The content was not "believe in Jesus," but rather the daily living problems faced by village people. I opened a night school; I became a counselor. People who once just stared at me because I was a Christian became my friends.

A problem in this village was a gang of twenty-one and twenty-two-year-old youths who went around and made trouble. They would break into people's homes for no other reason than to steal rice, harass, tease young women, and make gambling money. One Christmas they took all the rice cake that had been prepared for the church celebration. One day as I was walking along the road, they stood in front of me to block my way. I did not know what to do, so I said, "Do you know how to dance the twist?" They relaxed and smiled. "What's the twist?" "You really don't know when the city people have been dancing it as the popular dance of the day? If you want to learn, come and follow me." I walked on around them, but they did not follow.

After some days, several of the group appeared in my house and said, "We want to learn the twist." I pretended that I was a good dancer and showed them what I knew. We all had a very good time and even laughed a lot together. From then on, they came to my room fairly often to just dance and eventually talk. If they came when I was preparing a service for the church, I would simply say, "Gentlemen, I am really sorry, but today I am preparing a worship service, but if you could come back tomorrow, I would help you." They would in turn help me get ready for the service.

Once they actually came to a worship service for a first time. That was after a year. I introduced the eight former troublemakers to the congregation during the fellowship hour as men who had committed their lives to Jesus. Hands clapped like thunder since our congregation were overjoyed about the change of heart! The youths themselves were stunned by their "reception." They had just come to the service without any motive and were suddenly treated like sincere Christians! I admit it was a one-sided push.

After the service, I did organize them as a core group for youth fellowship and what it could do for the village. The war had been over for ten years, but the people here were still called refugees. The youth opened a shop where they sold basic daily necessities, including wood they chopped from the mountains. I taught the villagers some basic nursing skills I had learned during the war so that they could treat minor wounds and diseases. I still meet these young people from time to time. The three years here were hard years and yet I was able to realize my childhood dream of being involved in rural development.[9]

One day a man about fifty came to the church. "I have no right to bother you, but have come to ask a favor. I have a daughter who is engaged and should marry. But she has suddenly gone out of her mind and I do not know the reason. If the groom's family hear of this, they will break the engagement. I am not a Jesus believer, but I've heard people say that if one believes in Jesus, mental disease can be cured. Won't you come to our home and pray for us?"

I agreed to come, but I spent the night worried, pacing the floor, and restlessly mumbling prayers. "God, what shall I do? In spite of my inability, I said I would heal her. I am in big trouble! In your name, I am dishonoring you. Please punish this sinner, myself, your servant. Tell me what to do."

Around nine in the morning, a young man came to see me. He came just to visit the pastor, for his father was an elder in my church. While conversing, he mentioned that he had experience in healing the sick and the mentally disturbed. I told him what I was doing that day and he slapped his knee in surprise. "I had a dream last night! Now I know why I am here! Let's go to that home tonight and you watch what I do. I believe I can cure her. You have the worship service and I will take charge after that!"

So we went to the home and I held the worship service there. During the service, someone fell on the floor with a loud "Oh!" I was shocked and my own body felt numb. When everyone calmed down, we found that the one who had fallen to the floor was the brother, not the young woman! He was shouting and twisting his whole body and acting like he was insane. The parents looked shocked and pale. Not only the daughter but also the son was ill. The young man who visited me had said that sometimes the devil goes into the weakest one of a family. I had not believed any of this, but it was happening!

Meanwhile the young man said to the brother's devil, "What kind of devil are you?" "Tosan." "Who is the most fearsome person with the strongest faith among us?" I was so afraid that I would be identified by the devil as the one with least faith before he identified the one with the most faith. Actually, I felt it was nasty of the young man to ask a question that might be answered with an opposite as well, again naming me as the worst sinner among them. Then the young man possessed by the devil spoke. "This woman who is holding me from behind is the most fear-inspiring one who is also the most faithful!" I was astonished! I repented my faithlessness and thanked God at the same time for choosing me, a person so lacking in faith, to be here. I silently confessed to God that in the future, I would try to do whatever was asked of me.

Suddenly, I became convinced that with God's help, I could be a servant in healing this man's illness. My fears disappeared and I could talk with the possessed man. There was a prediction by the devil that the family's business of importing preserves would suffer a setback. Shipments of shrimp preserves did arrive spoiled in the days ahead, in spite of the usual precautions! I prayed five days and five nights for the young man. It was the coldest winter in thirty years and I was one who suffered from cold. Yet as I prayed, sweat poured all over my body. I then prayed, "If my life needs to be taken for this healing, take it." Only a miracle would remove the superstition of the island people about devils and possessions and the power of Jesus.

On the fifth day, the young man wept unrestrainedly and said, "Since this household treats me so badly, there is no way out except to get out of here." I replied, "Then you must go back to hell." The devil responded, "It's not time to go to hell yet." The young man recovered his normal self completely.

Long after the experience, I found myself wondering whether this might have been just an accidental happening with no relationship between my prayers and the young man's healing. I was again convinced that God had been with me. From that experience, I developed faith that—together with God—I could overcome whatever hardship might confront me. That strength gave me the strength to endure later on, when I was suffering from government oppression. Even now, I believe that God is with me and I live on in the strength of that faith.[10]

[*In November 1966 Reverend Cho Wha Soon was sent to Hwasudong, Inchon, to work in the Dong Il Textile Company. This was her first experience in a factory, working in the conditions that oppressed Korean women. Here she was treated as miserably as all other women workers. The cursing, crudeness, and verbal abuse were at first shocking to her. As the days went on, she understood the deep frustration of the young girls who in turn vented their anger and abuse on each other. The young women were dutifully sending some money home to their parents and to their brothers for their education. They used a minimal and inadequate sum for their food. There was seldom anything left to help them eventually attain their own dreams, if they had any.*]

> My new understanding turned into compassion, and this compassion developed into love. I sincerely repented my life so far. I decided that from now on, I would live for the workers.[11]

[*Cho tried hard to organize the women to secure better futures. She was an avid advocate for the democratic unionizing that some places in Korea were attempting by the 1970s. Although the Park regime wanted no democratizing of unions, the woman workers were strongly convinced that this was the best way to secure more human conditions and be paid equally. Two different kinds of unions resulted from the tensions. One kind was allied with the Park regime and had mainly male members. The other kind included the democratic unions and consisted primarily of women; they were often headed by women chairpersons.*

Initially the textile company for which Cho worked and the Methodist Church's Urban Industrial Mission worked well together. But by 1975 the Park regime was already sending secret police to threaten the workers who protested their conditions. A group of women workers continued to ask for elections to decide which kind of union the workers preferred. The police pressured company officials to disregard these pleas, and the officials decided there would be no ballot boxes for any form of democratic election.

On July 27, 1976 the women demonstrated against these repressive measures. The riot police appeared in buses and broke up the demonstration and threatened the women workers. The women responded by taking off their clothes, hoping this would shame the police into leaving the building. Instead, the police started beating the women with clubs. Three hundred workers managed to escape, but seventy-two were arrested. Within days some had died, others went into shock, and two became insane. The workers who had escaped managed to put enough pressure on the company and media to obtain some basic betterment of conditions. By April 1977 a third woman chairperson was elected to be the voice of the union.

On February 21, 1978, some of the male workers were mobilized by members of the Park regime to intimidate male workers who were siding with the women for a democratic union election. The women workers who heard of it staged a sit-in at the factory. The women were shocked when male fellow workers appeared with clubs, destroyed their ballot boxes, and then took pails of liquid dung to throw over them or to force down their throats. Policemen were present to "guard the elections" and simply looked on as the women appealed to them for help.

On March 10, Korean Labor Day, the women saw a way to make their cause known to the nation. The large stadium rally provided a television audience. The official male union leader for the government party was speaking when eighty women workers staged their placard protest for the television audience. It was enough to draw attention to their plight and disrupt the ceremonies. The women were arrested, as was expected.

That night the Reverend Cho Wha Soon preached at the Cathedral Church Service celebrating Labor Day. She graphically told of the events surrounding the day's protests and the injustices that were heaped upon the women. The majority of laborers who made up the congregation agreed to join the labor cause, to fast, and to sit in. Cho Wha Soon was placed under surveillance, and the Catholic Church was blacklisted as well.]

> Persons like Reverend Cho are imprisoned for working for justice while powerful perpetrators of injustice continue the blatant destructive dehumanizing policies in view of everyone. Reverend Cho has been kept under surveillance while the demonic forces outside are free to brutalize whoever they choose.[12]

[*Cho's imprisonment in 1978 followed an address to a youth group at a local YMCA. A pastor friend had begged her to come and tell of the incident with the dung as a means of informing the younger people about injustices in the land. The address concluded with an observation that was not fiery or inflammatory but a statement of her experience. "Our country is world-famous for two things: one is dictatorship, and the other is torture."*[13] *The YMCA lecture was reported and Cho Wha Soon was detained in jail for seven days. During this period she was given a handful of barley and a few pieces of salted radish for each meal. Then she was moved to a prison.*]

In contrast to my first imprisonment, this time there were fewer disturbances. Pusan Prison had been built fairly recently, so it was very clean—quite different from the dirty and smelly Seodaemoon Prison. I even had a clean flowered quilt, just like in a hotel. It seemed to me that the change to such a clean and bright atmosphere had been the result of the efforts of persons such as political prisoners and prisoners of conscience who had fought for better prison conditions. I was deep in thought for some time, remembering their tears and suffering. The guard told me that the Dong Il textile workers had been in this room before their transfer to Taegu. I felt a surge of emotion.

One day I got a written notice of arraignment. I was charged with "Violation of Presidential Emergency Decree No. 9" and "Violation of the Law on Meetings and Demonstrations." I read the prosecution note, which was immature and awkward. For just a few antigovernment words I was being treated as if I had committed high treason. Receipt of the written arraignment meant I had to go to court for a trial. I had been released from my first prison without a court trial. This time was different. Many thoughts kept me awake. "When I stand in court, will I be able to speak well? The students who have stood trial for their student movement were very eloquent. What can I say in my summary statement?"

The day before the trial, a woman guard opened the door and told me to come out. I was surprised, but I followed her. This was unusual because as a rule the door was opened once in the morning and once in the evening. Now it was after the evening check, and very late. I followed the guard into a room, where I saw the prosecutor assigned to my case. He immediately got up. "Ah, Reverend, it has been a long time. You have been through much hardship." I sat there for four hours listening to his monologue, as he turned the topic from this to that. The main point, however, was that I should speak carefully at the trial tomorrow. Then I could be freed. He told me that the arrest had been his doing, but the release was up to me.

I spent that night in agony. Should I get out or should I stay in? . . . Actually, without having done anything worth mentioning, it was regrettable to be imprisoned for several years. It would be more effective to get out sooner and to work harder. Tossing and turning, agonizing over what to do, I suddenly thought, "If this were Jesus, what would he do?" The answer was very clear. Jesus would say, "Satan, go away!" Then my action as a confessed servant of this Lord was also very clear. I was ready to face my conviction.

The next morning I went to the court. The others on trial were tied with a white rope. I was handcuffed and my arms were tied behind my back with several coils of green rope. There was a red sticker placed on my chest, as if I were a death row prisoner or a spy. The other prisoners looked at me strangely. As I entered the courtroom I saw many familiar faces, ministers and priests from Pusan and workers from Inchon. At the sight of them, my eyes filled with tears. I greeted them quickly with a glance. As I sat in the front row of prisoners, my heart was pounding. I prayed quietly to God and I felt better.

At last my turn came and the questioning started. Among other things, the prosecutor asked me, "Was not your action for the sake of class struggle?" I answered, "I do not know. I am ignorant of such things. What is meant by class struggle? I have only tried to follow the words of the Bible, acting as a shepherd."

The prosecutor presented the demand for sentencing. "As the prosecutor in charge of this event, I request that the defendant, Cho Wha Soon, be penalized by seven years' imprisonment." The moment I heard this, I remembered that in Rev. Park Hyung Kyu's similar case not long before, the prosecution demanded ten years of imprisonment. So I shouted loudly, "Is this sexism? You demanded ten years for Rev. Park. Why do you demand only seven years for me? Give me ten years!" The judge, prosecutor, and prison guard looked startled.

The judge told me to make my summary statement. "I grew up in a rich home. When I was a child, my home was the richest one in the village. I did not know the suffering of the poor and I had never had any special difficulty in my life. When I entered prison, I talked with people there and found out that most of them had experienced severe hardships in their lives, far different from me. I was surprised to hear from people my own age how hard a life they've had. When I went to the factory to work and live with the laborers, I could not help weeping in repentance. At first, I met them simply to evangelize and teach the gospel, but it was no use. It was like pouring water into a bottomless jug. After a long time, I realized that there is a systemic evil. To solve this problem, it is necessary not only to worship but also to demolish that systemic evil."

I turned to the courtroom audience and shouted, "As a disciple of Jesus, I am doing this work as a disciple of Jesus. We will fight the devils of this land, not fearing death. The righteous anger (*han*) of the oppressed, poor, and marginalized will turn into the sword of God's judgment! Our chief, Jesus, is leading us. We will surely have victory. Hurrah for the workers of this land! Hurrah for God!" The judge tried to stop me, but the people in the audience stood up and clapped loudly as they wept.

Several prison guards came running toward me and took me away. I was thrown into a black sedan as workers gathered to shout their approval. My tears fell. I was sentenced to five years and taken to Taegu prison. The prison was dirty. The toilet was full of maggots, and rats came into the room through the toilet. I had a hard time with the rats.

President Park Chung Hee was assassinated by one of his own men on October 29, 1979. When I heard the news, I was glad and yet not sure. I was reminded of the words of patriot Kim Ku, who fought for Korea's independence from Japan. When Korea was emancipated, he said, "If it had happened just a little bit later, we could have accomplished our own emancipation. This has happened by foreign power, so it has no meaning." Park's death should have happened through the strength of our own people, so this had little meaning.

A few days after political prisoners were released, I was in court again. A few persons held an informal trial and I was sentenced to a year of imprisonment with a two-year suspension of the execution of sentence. So I was released in a few days with my sack of clothing. What would be my destiny? I could not rid myself of an uncomfortable premonition.[14]

During my involvements with the labor and political movements, I felt there were times when our spirit or soul was too dry. We cannot let that happen if we are to be the seedbed for the society or new order that Jesus Christ proclaimed. What this means is that the formation of the true human being occurs in self-repentance before God, the creation of a new being through the inner revolution of the self. For the new age, there must be a new being. This is because the new world must be realized through a change not just of the forms but of the very core of humanity.

The new human will be the bridgehead supporting the quality of the new society. The whole ongoing process of the revolutionary movement must be accompanied by such an inner revolution! There was a time when I knew nothing about social movements and thought narrow-minded personal salvation was all that mattered. But from the time that I became involved in the industrial mission, the social salvation aspect was emphasized and for a while I decided the social movement was all. Now I have turned round again, and realize the necessity of uniting the two things, personal integrity and renewal with social concerns. Outer social-structural change and change of the inner human being must proceed together.

In this sense, I have never seen another teacher as great as Jesus. In his time, there were many lines of movement for the liberation and independence of Israel. The Zealots advocated revolution through political struggle. They felt an urgency to finish everything in a short time. On the other hand, there were groups like the Essenes, who expected to achieve salvation through their ascetic life in separation from others. Yet others were like the Pharisees. It is highly unlikely that Jesus never thought of revolution. But how can we distinguish Jesus from all the other revolutionaries?

He proclaimed, "Repent, the Reign of God is at hand." Repent is the answer. Be born again as a new person, new wine in new wineskins. The Reign of God is fundamentally different from the present world. The new society is a breaking of the whole present evil circle. This was the unique liberation theory of Jesus. Some say Jesus was not a revolutionary, basing their rationale on his use of the word, "Repent." But this is not true.

Jesus' liberation is a movement for the simultaneous achievement of social revolution and the inner revolution of the person. It is indeed a revolution to create the new future. In this sense, prayer is very important. Jesus prayed before he began anything. He prayed at times of hardship, agony, and temptation. In the case of the non-Christian movement worker, prayer may be expressed as self-reflection.

The continuous effort to objectify oneself before God and to be faithful before God and history is what creates real love and achieves real revolution. The social revolution, democratization, and human rights movements we are advocating must be actions coming from such inner sincerity. In this sense, I want our movement to be a praying movement or a praying revolution.

I think the road we are walking is wide and its destination is far. It is a process not only of rejecting the established system, but of creating the new order. We who are involved in the movement should lead the way in becoming persons of the new future.

A thing that has caused me pain for twenty years was the unequal treatment of women. I also experienced the agony of discrimination and alienation caused by sexism. Women are oppressed wherever we go—at home, at work, in society, and even before the law. The have-not class gets continually poorer and oppressed. Among these, the people suffering the most oppression and alienation are the women.

Mothers in the slum areas suffer greater injustices than their husbands or sons. Women laborers in the factories are working under worse conditions and getting less pay than their male counterparts. The women laborers' suffering does not stop at the physical level; they also endure severe mental stress. The cultural climate with its long accumulated habits of discrimination against women attempts to rationalize sexism. Especially in Korea, this discrimination has deeper roots because of the Confucian thinking that man dominates woman and woman must follow "three ways," i.e., as a child she obeys her father; as a wife, her husband; and as a mother, her own son.

I think the women's movement has a character that is inclusive, that is sociocultural and at the same time cannot help being political. Women are the most oppressed class in this society historically, as they are under the capitalist economic structure. Working women are probably the class that has borne the greatest burden of historical oppression created by human society up to now. That is why I think their struggle is most important for the real freedom and liberation of our society. Because of its inclusiveness, the women's movement should of course be developed wherever sexism exists. But the women laborers' movement is especially important. Other women's movements should be in solidarity with it.

True human liberation can be accomplished only when the women's liberation movement is realized at the same time. The working class is generally said to be the most important class in solving the contradictions of capitalistic society. It is thought that liberation will be achieved through the laborers' struggle. However, we must think not only in terms of laborers. We must also think in terms of women and their liberation. Women's oppression does not exist only in theory. The women's liberation movement is not a by-product of some other movement. However, men usually think it is. Amazingly, even many movement workers think like that. Women bear a historical task that is twice as hard and important as men's labor movements because women have the additional task of the women's issue besides the low wage issue. Women need to have more autonomy, more ability, more skill to do the jobs men do, and more persistent fighting power as well. Women must stand for their freedom even until the end.

Recently, I have been thinking that our movement should proceed more systematically. Without organized power, there will be no victory. Women must organize themselves carefully because they face many problems in relation to the overall political and labor movements. In the political movement group or in the labor movement group, a women's opinion is often ignored or marginalized by the men. No matter how hard she tries to be heard, she will be pushed away from the center against her will and eventually be left out completely. This kind of thing happens quite often. I myself have had such experiences. The wounds from these experiences are deep ones.

I am now gathering such wounded women together. Other women movement leaders have had the same kind of experience. There is increasing concern about this situation, not only among the members of the women's movement in general, but also among the labor movement. I believe we should have an inclusive, organized women's movement that includes the grassroots women's laborer movement. Such a movement will not only open up a new future to ourselves as women, but will lead the way to the true liberation of all. It is almost impossible for an individual woman to have any power for changing systems. This is true whether it is a church or secular framework. The only way to break through the established male world is to have organized collective power.

Among the Urban Industrial Missions (UIMs), no other woman was involved when I was, so I was needed by the majority of male colleagues like seasoning to food. When I was ending my work in the Urban Industrial Mission, I felt alone. I discovered that the male solidarity that works as group caucuses, protecting and taking care of each other, did not apply to me. I felt the necessity of forming a women's group. I discovered that as women we did not have such a pressure group of a political nature.

The males established in the status quo looked for me when they needed assistance. But when they became self-sufficient, they could do without my help. They no longer wanted me. Women working with the National Council of Churches in Korea go through the same experience. That is the reason we formed "The Women with Democracy, People, and Nation." Now the National Council of Churches asks two representatives of women in the democratic movement to participate in their decision-making process on a regular basis.

At the end of 1984, I finished my work at Inchon Urban Industrial Mission after eighteen years. There were several complex reasons for my resignation. The most important was that—from my standpoint—my role in the labor movement was no longer that important. Even if it was, I must not continue in the same way. I was needed in the beginning. I cried with the laborers and rejoiced with them as we found out the problems together. I was needed when the unconscientized laborers began their first struggle. Now those laborers have developed and grown and what is needed are competent new professional leaders.

If one person stays too long and tries to handle everything, it limits the development of the movement. But the sad thing is that there is no one right now with my experience who can continue development in the next stage. I am already inadequate for that next stage. Whoever is involved in the labor movement as an intellectual should have pretraining through sharing the real life of the laborers. There are many cases of persons from the student movement being involved in the labor movement. Their desire is good, but the problem is that they try to lead the labor movement in student movement styles.

There were many problems with my moving back to Dalwol Church, but I chose pastoral work again due to my concern for grassroots expansion of the people's movement. I know institutional work is important, but institutions have many limitations. It fits my personality better to work with people "at the bottom." However, for a person like myself who became well known through the Urban Industrial Mission work, it is difficult to find a church that wants me.

Our still conservative churches in Korea do not call radical ministers like myself. It is true that some danger exists, which is one reason why few Industrial Mission pastors have succeeded in local church ministry. But in my case, God made this possible and I am at Dalwol Church.

During Passion Sunday, we have the footwashing ceremony. The first year, I as pastor did the footwashing of the twelve elders. As I washed each one's feet, I did pray fervently for each of them, mentioning the life situations each was in. As I prayed for them, I wept with love and the congregation did as well as they prayed with me. I think that was the initial event that overcame the basic suspicion and prejudice against me. One year I washed the feet of the elders; the elders did the deacons and deaconesses; the deacons and deaconesses washed the laypeople. In that way, everybody got into the act.

When I administer communion, I do it on the basis of the family unit. I listen to the stories of each family, including the children, and I pray for them. I do all that I can to have everyone involved in the sacraments and worship. Once the unified support of the congregation is gathered, the programs of our church to help society can progress without much controversy. We now have three major programs. These are the Farmer's Credit Union, a Community Newsletter, and the Nursery and Kindergarten. Dalwol Church initiated the Farmer's Credit Union in the village, a worldwide movement originally founded by Catholics. It is a self-reliant monetary organization where one can borrow necessary money for the cheap interest rate of 2 percent. The trust is a mortgage, and the community makes all the decisions.

In the village where the church is located, people have nothing to read. In order to give some meaningful reading material to the people and educate them on national problems, the church publishes a weekly newspaper. We print 400 copies and distribute them to every one of the 249 family units. We send the rest to outer rural areas. The men read it for the most part, for the majority of women are still illiterate.

I have a new desire in these years. The parts of the pastoral work that concerns me most are the church renewal movement, the lay movement, and the youth movement. I am still very cheerful and childish. I feel joyful and excited as I consider new things. I believe I will be able to do whatever work the Lord gives me to do. The Lord uses me always as a servant and I am thankful for his liberation. I wish to live the life to which the Lord calls me and I thank him for the wonderful life he has called me to live![15]

NOTES

1. Lee Hyo Jae, "Industrialization and Women: The Social Background of Cho Wha

Soon's Ministry," in Cho Wha Soon, *Let the Weak Be Strong: A Woman's Struggle for Justice* (New York: Crossroad, 1990) 146–50.

2. David Kwang-sun Suh and Lee Chuing Hee, "Liberating Spirituality in the Korean Minjung Tradition," in *Asian Christian Spirituality: Reclaiming Traditions*, ed. Virginia Fabella, Peter K. H. Lee, and David Kwang-sun Suh (Maryknoll, N.Y.: Orbis, 1992) 31–43.

3. Aloysius Pieris, *An Asian Theology of Liberation* (Edinburgh: T. and T. Clark, 1988) 23.

4. Text in brackets is intended to put Cho's excerpts in context.

5. Subsequent page references are from Cho Wha Soon, *Let the Weak Be Strong.*

6. 17.

7. 17–19.

8. 24–27.

9. 32–37.

10. 38–43.

11. 53.

12. "Korean Women's Reflections" by Kim Soon Myung in *Let the Weak Be Strong* 158.

13. 96.

14. 97–101.

15. 139–44.

BIBLIOGRAPHY

Cho, Wha Soon. *Let the Weak Be Strong: A Woman's Struggle for Justice.* New York: Crossroad, 1990.

Chung, Hyun Kyung. *Struggle to Be the Sun Again: Introducing Asian Women's Theology.* Maryknoll, N.Y.: Orbis, 1990.

Fabella, Virginia, ed. *Asia's Struggle for Full Humanity: Towards a Relevant Theology.* Maryknoll, N.Y.: Orbis, 1980.

Fabella, Virginia, and Sergio Torres, eds. *Irruption of the Third World: Challenge to Theology.* Maryknoll, N.Y.: Orbis, 1983.

Fabella, Virginia, and Sun Ai Lee Park, eds. *We Dare to Dream: Doing Theology as Asian Women.* Maryknoll, N.Y.: Orbis, 1990.

Fabella, Virginia, Peter K. H. Lee, and David Kwang-sun Suh, eds. *Asian Christian Spirituality: Reclaiming Traditions.* Maryknoll, N.Y.: Orbis, 1992.

Pieris, Aloysius. *An Asian Theology of Liberation.* Edinburgh: T. and T. Clark, 1988.

Thistlethwaite, Susan Brooks, and Mary Potter Engel, eds. *Lift Every Voice: Constructing Christian Theologies from the Underside.* San Francisco: Harper, 1990.

Torres, Sergio, and Virginia Fabella, eds. *Doing Theology in a Divided World.* Maryknoll, N.Y.: Orbis, 1985.

– 25 –

MERCY AMBA ODUYOYE

(born 1934)

God Alone Gives and Distributes Gifts

Mercy Amba Oduyoye was born on October 21, 1934, in Asamankese, Ghana, to the Reverend Charles Kwaw and Mercy Dakwaa Yamoah. Charles Kwaw was a theological educator and Methodist pastor. As part of his ministry, he was pastor for three parishes in Akan semi-urban communities. Mercy received an early appreciation of Akan culture through her life with the Akan communities. The presecondary Methodist school in Mmofraturo, Kumasi, that Mercy attended successfully incorporated the best of the Ashanti culture into its curriculum. Mercy learned much about variants of the Akan culture through families of her friends and through her visits to northern Ghana. The secondary school she attended at Achimota, Accra, provided the possibility of learning the native Ga language. A broad perspective of Ghanaian culture grounded the curriculum. The coed institution stressed excellence in education. There were no gender limitations in the curriculum, so each student could study whatever subjects each chose to study.

In 1954 Mercy received a postsecondary certificate of education from Kumasi College of Technology (now the University of Kumasi). Her teaching certificate from the Ministry of Education was also received that year. She taught for several years at a Methodist girl's middle school in Kumasi before continuing undergraduate education at the University of Ghana in Legon, Accra. She received a B.A. in the study of religion in 1963, and then attended Cambridge University in England, receiving a B.A. in theology in 1965 and an M.A. in theology in 1969. The Academy of Ecumenical Indian Theology bestowed an honorary doctorate on her in September 1990, as did the University of Amsterdam in January 1991.

Mercy recalls that the missionaries with whom she grew up did not mix with the people but stayed mainly with Europeans. This was much more noticeable to her than the separateness of other British administrators. Although her education had been a liberating experience, she eventually felt discrimination both from her own Akan culture and from the Christian church. "With

African culture, Islamic norms, Western civilization, and the church's traditional antifeminism piled on African woman, the world has been led to see African women as not more than the quintessence of the status called 'the oppressed.'"[1]

Mercy is proud of her Akan heritage. It has enabled her to be brought up with a sense of the centrality of women in the community. "It is as an African that I am a Christian. I have no conflicts with that, only periodic depression with regard to how little the Church in Africa concerns itself with social issues."[2]

Mercy has served as youth education secretary for the World Council of Christian Education, the World Council of Churches, from 1967 to 1973. During 1970–73 she was also the youth secretary for the All-Africa Conference of Churches. She taught in the Religious Studies Department at the University of Ibadan, Nigeria, from 1974 to 1986, a time when she also was assistant editor and then editor of *ORITA*, the Ibadan Journal of Religious Studies. She has served as the vice president of the Ecumenical Association of African Theologians from 1980 to 1984, and as a research assistant at Harvard Divinity School in 1985 and 1986. As the Henry Luce Visiting Professor at Union Theological Seminary from 1986 to 1987 she became better known to North American students. Since that time she has held various visiting lectureships in the United States and England.

In 1987, she became deputy general secretary of the World Council of Churches, a position she continues to hold at the time this is being written. Mercy is the first woman and the first African to serve as president of the World Student Christian Federation. She is the first African woman to become a member of the World Council of Churches' Commission on Faith and Order. This position has widened her participation in global conferences and in ecumenical assemblies.

Her research interests and publications reflect her concern for the liberation of women who are being oppressed through social, religious, or cultural ideologies. She has consistently pointed out to the Western Christian world that Africans have a great potential for contributing to Christian theological development. Mercy has often written that the Christian liberation of African women is necessary if Jesus Christ is to be credible, a conviction she has spent much of her life sharing. She is an articulate spokeswoman for the unique contribution of African women to the development of Christian theologies.

Her writings and lectures consistently stress that theological plurality must remain grounded in basic unity. She has a sensitivity to the culturally specific influences that condition the hearing of the Christian Gospel. In the context of her own culture, she is well aware of the rich grounding African oral tradition provides for Christian theology. Mercy has a deep appreciation for the oral and written traditions of her people, but she also views these traditions with critical theological eyes. She insists that theologians must keep their eyes, ears, and hearts open to the living community that surrounds them. To her, this means that basic Christian doctrines and sacraments need ongoing reinterpretation in culturally specific contexts. At the same time, the cultural traditions need critique by Christian theology.

Mercy Oduyoye has not hesitated both to affirm and to criticize the so-called liberation theologians of the Third World peoples. In spite of the central theme of justice for all, some of these theologians will not address the injustices against women:

> There have been several international meetings at which Third World representatives have said that antisexism is not their priority. At times they have even said it is not an issue in their world, where men and women know their place and play their role ungrudgingly. . . . The fact is that sexism is part of the intricate web of oppression in which most of us live, and that having attuned ourselves to it does not make it any less a factor of oppression.[3]

In the 1990s Mercy has been particularly active in the World Council of Churches' project "The Churches in Solidarity with Women." This project was one priority of the World Council of Churches for the decade 1988–98. It is hoped that the project will further the equality and dignity of women throughout the world. Christian churches are participating as they are able.

Mercy has spent her life in a variety of causes for the liberation of people, men as well as women. She has many concerns for the Christian churches today and is especially convinced that the churches must hear and respond to the cries of the poor in the world:

> I have arrived at a point where I no longer wish to be patient with sexism, racism, and injustices against the dignity that rightly belongs to beings made in the image of God. . . . As long as I am a woman and black and refuse to accept any attitude toward me that makes me feel less than accepted and included, I stand with all who are trampled upon and with all who want to struggle to see the end of inhumanity in the human community.[4]

Mercy is married to Adedoyin Modupe Oduyoye, who is the literature secretary of the Christian Council of Nigeria and the manager of Daystar Press in Ibadan. He is a member of the Anglican Church of Nigeria. Mercy and Adedoyin have five foster children. The family belongs to the congregation of All Saints Jericho, an ecumenical congregation which has some ties with the Methodist Church.

The ecumenical perspectives of Mercy Amba Oduyoye flow from a life of Christian commitment to furthering the dignity of all people in Christ. For

Mercy, Christian liberation is affirmed to the degree that Christians work for justice for everyone who is oppressed. Her strong commitment to the universality of the love of Jesus Christ and the meaning of that love in today's world is part of the reflections that follow.

Christianity in Africa[5]

A Liberating Perspective

In order to begin the experience of fully human living, whatever gender we are, we are called to refuse to be what others require us to be, instruments against our own convictions, people who acquiesce to their own marginalization. Positively put, we are called to struggle for the transformation of relationships. We have to live the life of the future even as we seek to bring it into existence by our insistence on personal accountability, participation, and on the importance of becoming authentic reflectors of the image of God. In this way we hope to build a human community whose obligations arise from within ourselves rather than from outside ourselves. This view challenges the traditional view of authority. It is a part of the liberation process that will surely encompass all persons.

Women and men are depicted by Scripture as being equally the objects of God's love. They experience God's love to the extent that their personal inclinations allow. The variety of gifts described in Acts had no gender limitations; neither does the list described by Paul. The will of God is the matter of who does what for me declared clearly by the fact that women—freed from cultural taboos, though constrained by circumstances or tradition—have been able to contribute to human community. Being "a little lower than the gods" applies equally to both men and women, just as sin knows no gender boundaries. The myths that seek to blame the woman do not exonerate the man. Both are endowed with the ability to respond to God, and baptismal grace knows no sexist boundaries.

Baptism into Christ compels Christians to see themselves at the beginning of a new humanity modeled after Christ. Just as Galatians 3:27–28 has been evoked on behalf of the abolition of slavery and racism . . . it shows that sexism is also incompatible with our being in Christ. We are baptized into Christ as persons, irrespective of our social status, so that—just as the male is taken into the Christ—so is the humanity of the female. . . . A Christian contribution to the -isms that seek to shape the meaning of life needs the experience of the women. This experience calls for a return to God-intended relationships that we have lost through our dichotomizing sexuality and making its biological manifestations and implications the foundation of our human relations.

We cannot be happy and unashamed in each other's company if we are hiding behind our gender to shirk responsibility. As baptized people, our suffering is salvific when taken on voluntarily. Our sharing of the gifts of others gives us the ability to thank God who made us male and female. When we are all willing to see the humanity of the other, then we can begin the task of understanding a Christian anthropology.

Our baptism into the name of the Trinity means that we should stand not for monarchies and hierarchies but rather for participation. In God's economy, we find a sharing of power and of responsibility. Our baptism into the name of the Trinity also means that we share Jesus' acceptance of solidarity with sinners that led him on the path of self-giving, not just on behalf of the baptized, but on behalf of the whole world.

Africa belongs to the world of the powerless and the dispossessed. As a woman who feels the weight of sexism I cannot but go again and again to the stories of the exodus, the exile and other biblical motifs in which the "least" are recognized and affirmed, are saved or held up as beloved of God or at least are empowered to grow at the fundaments of the structures of injustice until these fundaments cave in on themselves. These narratives have been for me the bearers of good news.

Therefore, in spite of the entrenched patriarchal and ethnocentric presuppositions of the Bible, it is a book I cannot dispense with and indeed may not since I remain in the Christian community. That community means more to me than my personal hurts. For the same reason, I cannot be anything else but African. So, bringing my whole being and life experience to bear upon what I hear of God through Christ, I do not see truth as a given that I have to accept or reject. Rather, I see myself in community with others and in the enabling power of the Holy Spirit. I am called to participate in fuller understanding of what God is about. Neither the Bible, nor the African corpus of sociocultural history can be treated as fossilized touchstones. Critical apparatus exists for their use, and the theologians are making others aware of this factor.

In my reflections, I have not ruled out the possibility of coming to know Christ more fully, of comprehending God's future better, and of listening for what the Spirit is saying to the churches and to the African world. For this reason in these reflections, I seek understanding not only from the Bible and the Christian tradition but also from what some may consider unlikely sources. When I read theological theory my pragmatic approach to life is at its keenest where prescriptions are decreed. I never cease to ask myself who is benefiting from a particular stance? Theology bears the mark of ideology.

In the Akan worldview that operates in the dark mysterious center of my being, there sits a sense of being mystically incorporated into an ever-expanding principle of human be-ing. This is why I am attracted to the themes of community and selfhood. Liberation/freedom/salvation cannot be conceived as being at the expense of "the other."

As we Africans reread the Bible and books on Western missionary theology, we unmask their ideological components but we draw toward the ecumenical truths they embody. We are thereby freed to move to re-interpretation and re-statement and to uncover aspects of the truth that may have remained concealed to the Western mind.

We heard about sin and evil in humanity and in African culture. Now we know and can name the structures of injustice. The embodiments of evil and sin take on broader and deeper meaning. We do not simply "name" injustices. We seek empowerment from the Gospel to dismantle what is demonic in society and to exorcise the demons that turn persons into oppressors. We heard the mission theology of salvation of individual souls; now we know that salvation cannot but be in a familial context and encompass the whole person as an integrated being.

We heard about being created in God's image and as such being moral agents, a little lower than the gods, knowing good and evil and able freely to respond to God. Now we know that to be fully human we have to have the freedom to respond, to initiate, and to participate. We have to have the freedom to be able to obey God rather than human beings. We heard "you shall have no other gods." Now we know that any response made because of the principalities and powers of this world rather than because of a faith-in-God stance is idolatry.

We heard of the dangers of attempting to find out whether God indeed has witnesses in all human cultures, and we felt the dismissal of African culture. Now we know we are not alone in our search. We attempt to respond to the Christ who confronts us in the Bible, who comes to us as African women and men, black and poor people of the South who are prone to manipulation of the rich North. Knowing ourselves, having a sense of history, believing in the future and the transformation brought about by the cooperation of the divine and the human in Jesus the Christ, we are (I am) freed to take part in the building up of theologies that will contribute to the transformation needed in the church and in society.

The Christ of Scriptures and Tradition[6]

Most Christians refer to Scripture as meaning the Hebrew Bible and its Christian supplement, the New Testament. But we would like to start with a reference to the "unwritten Scriptures" of the Fante of Ghana. When the Fante were journeying to their present home in southern Ghana, they crossed vast tracts of waterless plains and they thirsted. Such was the agony of a people on the move.

But their leader, Eku the matriarch, did not despair. She spurred them on. They were to press forward until they came to a place where they could settle in peace and prosperity. Following her encouragement, they dragged their weakened legs along. They then came to a pool of water. Having suffered much treachery on their journey, none dared to salve the parched throat with the water now presented invitingly before them. It could have been poisoned by their enemies.

Matriarch Eku took her life into her hands, drank from the pool, and gave to her dog to drink. The people waited. They peered at the woman and her dog with glazed eyes. Neither human nor animal had suffered from drinking water of the pool. All fell to and drank their fill, shouting "Eku aso" (Eku has tasted). Thus, the place where this happened is to this day called Ekuaso. Eku has tasted on our behalf. We can now drink without fear of death![7]

All human communities have their stories of persons whose individual acts have had lasting effects on the destiny and ethos of the whole group. Such are the people remembered in stories. Not all are Christ figures. Only those whose presence has led to more life and wholesome relations are commemorated as having been "God-sent." In the Hebrew story, the idea of the "God-sent" figure crystallized into that of the Messiah, the anointed of God. The Messiah was expected to be a male figure of power, as a ruler of God's people, and a prophet called by God to guide the people. Much else accrued to the figure of the Messiah as the people passed through political changes.

One such metamorphosis taken over by Christians is the Messiah as the Suffering Servant of God. But even cast in this lowly mold, the figure of the Messiah remains powerful and victorious and male. Messiah is a servant who suffers, but one whose presence always tells the people how God's future for humanity stands inviolate in spite of all appearances. As Jesus of Nazareth and almost all who fell into his way of teaching were Jews, they had been brought up on the various images of the messianic figure and had prayed for the timely arrival of the anointed one of God, who was being expected by the whole nation.

The predominant myth of Christianity in Africa remains the paradise to come: the messianic hope of a golden age has even begun to surface in political terms as "African unity." In the church, it is stated in terms of a single unified church. As these ideals retreat, or tarry too long, people either buy deeper into the apocalypticism of the "Coming One," and therefore of Christ the King who sits in judgment upon his subjects to reward faithful Christians with bliss and unbelievers with torment, or they simply give up.[8] This Christ is not up to the task of empowering Christians with life in Africa today, with all its material and spiritual demands. It masks the relevance of Christ in the business of living today and in the immediate future.

Africans require a holistic view of life. This demands a Christ who affects the whole of life and demonstrates that there is nothing that is not the business of God. There is need to rewrap Christology in African leaves.

The devil is a reality in Africa. Witches actually operate to release life-denying forces into the world. Individual people may be possessed and used by negative forces to prevent life-affirming and life-giving environments and activities. Evil is real, and evil is embodied in persons as well as unleashed on persons by spiritual forces. This spirit world is a powerful reality in Africa.

God created not only the palpable world but living spirits whom we do not see but whose presence we certainly feel and who, we believe, impinge upon our lives to do good. Such a cosmology calls for a Christ in relationship to God, to the spirit world, and to the African experience of being related to God. Is the Christ the "chief executive," giving us confidence that—however precarious our circumstances—all is in fact under control?

The theology of the people sees Christ in this role.... The Christ of the theology of the people is the Christ who breaks the power of evil and empowers us in our life's journey. In Africa, one's forebears retain an ongoing interest in one's affairs. The ancestors continue to be involved in earthly life long after they have departed to join their forebears. This ancestor precedence has a strong hold on the regulation of ethical life. Is Jesus our ancestor the quintessence of a life of faith? If so, then one begins to formulate Christology in terms of mediation and of participation in the divine human axis that links humanity to divinity.

In Jesus of Nazareth we see the return to earth of the Divine Spirit of God, the source of life, as an individual—just as in African tradition the ancestors return in the birth of new babies. This could, of course, imply that there can be many Christs as the spirit of a grandmother returns to grandchildren in perpetuity as long as such children are named after her, that is, called by her name.

Does Christianity have room for the concept of many Christs, persons in whom the Spirit of God dwells in its fullness? Has history seen many Christs and will such Christ-figures continue in perpetuity? These would be legitimate questions for a Christology that focuses upon Jesus of Nazareth as our ancestor in religious obedience.

In Africa, where physical suffering seems endemic, where hunger and thirst are the continuous experience of millions, a suffering Christ becomes an attractive figure. However, Jesus of Nazareth is seen as a comrade who did not accept deprivation as the destiny of humanity. Rather, he demonstrated in his dealings with people that such suffering is not in the plan of God. You cannot be sad when Jesus is around. You cannot fast. Healing and eating and drinking were the experiences of those who were with him. When they told the story, they did not neglect to say so. In fact, they assigned large portions of their stories to the telling of these experiences. They were as impressed by these as by his death and resurrection. They did not report only what Jesus said, for they saw what he taught as made up of what he did and what he said. His presence saved situations.

This is another one of the reasons for the growth of African charismatic churches, whose prophets and healers are seen as mirroring the Christ. Jesus Christ in his life enhanced life where it had been overshadowed by death, even bringing life where physical death had arrived prematurely. Christ, the great Healer, is seen as the center of the Christology of these charismatic churches.[9]

The Christ who is on the side of life is seen as being on the side of God. He not only taught that laws which frustrate and stifle life are to be scrapped. He himself did that, healing on the Sabbath and defending his disciples against the scruples of religious legalism. Even his acceptance of death can be read as the outcome of love for life, since the will of God can only foster life, even if the path has to be through death. Africa's business has to be that of turning death into life.

What an African Woman Says about Christ

Although most of the published studies on Christ in Africa are by male theologians, nonetheless there exist reflections by women, which are virtually unknown. Among these are the reflections, stories, and prayers of praise of Afua Kuma of Ghana.

Afua Kuma lives and works in the tropical forest of Ghana, a farmer and midwife from the Kwawu area. She belongs to the Church of the Pentecost. When in church, she is called Christiana Afua Gyane. She has had published prayers and praises to Jesus that capture vividly the language, culture, proverbs, folk tales, and court poetry of the Akan. Afua's theology and precisely her Christology—as most of her words refer to Jesus—is one that comes from the interplay of faith and life.

From Afua's words one gets some insight into what Christ means for the many in African churches to whom the word of God comes as a story, and who then make their own connections with Christ as they go about their daily routine....

Afua uses much contemporary imagery as the rural and urban are linked together when relations move to and fro. Her imagery of Jesus can be that of the ordinary folk, like teachers who influence the society for good. Jesus is the enabler of a variety of people. He is the spokesperson for lawyers, the helper of the police, the one who gives victory to soldiers, and food to prisoners. Because Jesus is all this, women praise him. Afua Kuma blesses people in the holy name of Jesus, promising them his gifts. "The one who gives to thousands, Jesus, has come. He has brought gifts for his people. This morning, what you are looking for, your hands will touch."[10]

The needs of the people include food and shelter. Afua refers to Jesus as having a great hall that will accommodate all who come. Children, who are the subjects of a large proportion of African prayers, appear only once, when Afua refers to Jesus as the one who makes the sterile give birth to twins. But she is preoccupied with the difficulties of clearing the forest and of meeting wicked people in the forest. In all this, one thing is clear. With Jesus, difficulties are bound to melt away.

The Christ for African Women

The Christ images of most Christian women in Africa will have a familiar ring. This causes no small wonder, as the men and women of Africa share the same reality and tradition and learned their Christianity from the same Western, male-centered, clerically minded missionaries.

African women, however, have a different experience of this common reality and of lived Christianity. For example, when Pobee (an African male theologian) suggests that Christ is the okyeame of God the ruler, to him the okyeame can be nothing else but a male. Whereas in the Akan system of rule, the oykeame can be either a man or a woman. In the Christological statements of the male African theologians, the cross, which looms so large in the theologies of Western-trained academics and preachers, gets very scanty treatment in Afua's theological reflections.

The cross, she says, has become the fishing net of Jesus. It is the bridge from which Christians can jump into the pool of saving blood that leads to everlasting life. Here is a perception of the cross that demands not only that we admire what Jesus has done, but that we too stand ready to jump into the pool of blood through which we shall reach the life that is life indeed.

Although, in general, the women affirm the Christological position of the African men, at times they go beyond it or contradict it altogether. This can be gleaned not so much from the writings of African women as from the way they live and from their Christianity. In other words, their spirituality witnesses to what Christ means for their lives.

The Christ whom African women worship, honor, and depend upon is the victorious Christ. They know that evil is a reality. Death and life-denying forces are the experience of women. So, the Christ who countered these forces and who gave back the child to the widow of Naim is the African women's Christ.

This Christ is the liberator from the burden of disease and the ostracism of a society riddled with blood taboos and theories of inauspiciousness arising out of women's blood. Christ liberated women by being born of Mary and by demanding that the women bent double with gynecological disorders should stand up straight. The practice of making women become silent "beasts" of societies' burdens, bent double under racism, poverty, and lack of appreciation of what fullness of womanhood should be, has been annulled and countered by Christ. Christ transcends and transforms culture and has liberated us to do the same.

Jesus of Nazareth, by countercultural relations he established with women, has become for us the Christ, the anointed one who liberates, the companion, the friend, teacher, and true "child of woman." In Christ, the fullness of all that we know of perfection is revealed. He is the caring, compassionate nurturer of all. Jesus nurtures not just by parables but by miracles of feeding. With his own hands, he cooked that others might eat; he is known in the breaking of the bread. Jesus is Christ—truly woman (human) yet truly divine, for only God is the truly compassionate One.

Christ for us is the Jesus of Nazareth, the Servant who washed the disciples' feet, the Good Shepherd who leads us only to green pastures, to the heavenly reign of God, who in fact comes after us to draw us back to God. Christ seeks to save. Jesus Christ is "Lord" because Jesus of Nazareth was a servant, meeting the needs of humanity in obedience to the will of God, even to the point of dying so that we might be freed from fear of death.

Christ for us is the Jesus of Nazareth who agreed to be God's "Sacrificial Lamb," thus teaching that true and living sacrifice is that which is freely and consciously made. Jesus pointed to the example of the widow who gave all she had in response to God's love. Christ is the Jesus of Nazareth who approved of the costly sacrifice of the woman with the expensive oil, who anointed him as king, priest, prophet in preparation for his burial. Thus, Jesus approved of all that is noble, lovely, loving, and motivated by love and gratitude.

Jesus of Nazareth, designated "the Christ," is the one who has broken down the barriers we have erected between God and ourselves as well as among ourselves. The Christ is the reconciler, calling us back to our true selves, to one another, and God, thereby saving us from isolation and alienation, which is the lack of community that is the real experience of death.

In Christ, all things hold together. The integrity of the woman as a person, born into a particular culture, and yet belonging to the community of Christ is ensured. The integrity of woman as a person is recognized and promoted by the way Jesus Christ lived and interacted with women, with handicapped persons, with persons oppressed by death-dealing cultural demands and by physical and material needs. The Christ has held body and soul together by denouncing oppressive religious practices that ignored well-being.

It is this Christ that has become for us, for African women and for Africa, the savior and liberator of the world. This Christ dominates the spiritual churches of Africa, such as the one to which Afua Kuma belongs. The women give expression to a spirituality that enables them to face human struggles and problems. In fact, women have founded some of these churches and within them exercise their spiritual gifts of healing, solving marital problems, and so forth. God wears a human face in Christ. God in Christ suffers with the women of Africa.

In conclusion, an African woman perceives and accepts Christ as a woman and as an African. The commitment that flows from this faith is commitment to full womanhood (humanity), to the survival of human communities, to the birthing, nurturing, maintenance of life, to loving relationships, and to a life that is motivated by love.

Having accepted Christ who is refugee and guest of Africa, the woman seeks to make Christ at home, and to order life in such a way as to enable the whole household to feel at home with Christ. The woman sees the whole space of Africa as a realm to be ordered, as a space where Christ has truly "tabernacled." Fears are not swept under the beds and mats, but are brought out to be dealt with by the presence of Christ. Christ becomes truly friend and companion. Christ liberates women from assumptions of patriarchal societies, honoring, accepting, and sanctifying the single life as well as the married life, parenthood as well as the absence of progeny. The Christ of the women of Africa upholds not only motherhood, but all who, like Jesus of Nazareth, perform "mothering" roles of bringing out the best in all around them. That is the Christ, high priest, advocate, and just judge in whose reign we pray to be.

This has serious consequences, for Jesus of Nazareth has pointed out the Christ figures among us. Whatever we do or do not do to the least of these figures, we are assured that we are relating to the Christ through our interaction with—or avoidance of—such people by the contribution we make to the oppression they live. The only way we can convince Africa that Jesus of Nazareth is uniquely the Christ of God is to live the life we are expected to live as Christ believers. Do not call "Lord, Lord" while ignoring the demands of God.

Christology down the ages, though derived from the experiences of the early companions of Jesus of Nazareth and those of their immediate associates, has been formulated in response to the actual historical realities of each age and place. Persons have contributed by the way each perceives and experiences Christ. "Christ" has been explained through imagery, cosmology, and historical events understood by both "speakers" and "listeners." This process continues in Africa. One thing is certain: whatever the age or place, the most articulate Christology is that silently performed in the drama of everyday living!

Who Will Roll the Stone Away?[11]

One of the most difficult words to get a handle on is the word church. In the World Council of Churches, the shortened way of identifying a church is to look at what the community calling itself a church believes. Of course there are a variety of institutional forms of ministry, liturgy, discipline, and so on. Churches vary in their understanding of what it means to incorporate women into the body of Christ by baptism. In some churches, even the baptismal rite differentiates between baby girls and baby boys. Gender seems to be a deeply theological issue. It is a factor in the extent, form, and meaning of the participation of the individual in the body of Christ.

A most sensitive theological issue for and of the decade is that of ordination, an issue which the World Council of Churches has faced for over forty years. It continues to engage the churches. Ordination is a divisive factor and, for that reason, one we cannot gloss over.

There is, however, an unease in some quarters that the issue, if it continues to be canvassed, will hamper the progress of the many other facets of such a call for solidarity with women. It is even feared that it will jeopardize the quest for visible Christian unity. Can the churches afford to maintain a posture of sacrificing women on the altar of visible unity?

The forty years of the World Council of Churches' advocacy on behalf of women, and the many fine statements the council has issued, are meant to change the actual lifestyles and attitudes of churches and people toward women's potential for promoting the vision of a new age in Jesus Christ. The issue of women in the churches is a deeper issue than one of status. It is a question of the very nature of human beings. It is also a question of the nature of the church. If the church anticipates the reign of God, then we who are the church are called upon to face the harsh realities of the anti-reign of God in history. This includes the history of our churches, and the present history of our churches in regard to women.

Affirming the Humanity of Women

The ecumenical Decade (1988–98) calls attention to women's development. It is a question of justice. Women are anxious to see the churches own the Decade and demonstrate solidarity with women and their search for a fuller expression of their humanity and their obedience to baptismal vows.

Women know there are churches that cannot accept the ordination of women into the eucharistic ministry, but will only provide for the participation of women in the life of the churches, especially in the area of diakonia. The Orthodox churches have made it clear that their support of the Decade excludes the ordination issue. It is an important caveat, but its import pales in the context in which the churches do not accept one another.

The whole of the Christian understanding of mission and ministry is what is at stake. The power, primacy, and honor that go with being in the eucharistic ministry should be seen in the context of the responsibility to serve. "I am among you as one who serves" is a Jesus statement that applies most aptly to what Christian women are in the church.

In recent years the call to a clarity of our understanding of what or who the church is has become more and more pressing. Theologians, especially those who oppose so vehemently the eucharistic ministry of women, should be encouraged to articulate their ecclesiology. Some ecclesiastical authorities are saying that they have heard the argument from our common baptism far too often.

It should be their responsibility, then, to make clear by what theology, sacramental or ecclesiological, they insist upon excluding women from eucharistic ministry. That will be a crucial contribution in the deliberations during this ecumenical Decade. The Decade is about the church; it is for the churches to state clearly where they are with women.

In this Decade women are called to unveil their true womanhood, to reinvent themselves, to piece themselves together from the bits of humanity that various cultures and religions have left for them. They are called to reproduce women's own images of true humanity. In this Decade, women must become self-defined human beings.

Out of the leftovers of the fabric of history, women will make a cloth of many colors. This cloth will force both church and society to notice the variety of ways there are to be women. Women will demonstrate that the wonderful diversity of human character, accepted in the case of men, also exists among women. All women are not from one mold. Women do not have a common eye or voice or language. Out of the poverty of women's presence in history, many creative portraits of women's history are coming alive.

Women's struggle for presence has gone on for centuries. Now the churches are being called to participate in the endeavor. Women can no longer be projected as "the other." Nor can they be assimilated any longer into the dominant ways of doing things in the church. It can no longer be assumed that human authority can only be exercised by men.

Partnership and power are to be seen together. The churches will show their solidarity with women when they demonstrate a new understanding of power and their willingness to share its exercise with the whole community of people. Biblical injunctions against women teaching men must be put in their original context for understanding. These texts must be seen in the light of faith that realizes God alone gives and distributes gifts to all persons.

Churches today are beginning to hear and be open to the leading of the Spirit. Sharing responsibility, sharing the possibility for action, removing the obstacles to women's full sharing in the church's being and doing are all beginning to happen.

Partnership

Power sharing is a prerequisite for the realization of co-responsibility. Created equally human, God made women and men stewards of creation and gave us authority to jointly fill the earth and manage it. The present state of the partnership of men and women in all cultures, on all continents, and in all churches, is a state of sin. The one-sided development of the source of human authority has reduced stewardship to domination, husbanding to control, and complementarity to the paternal determining the scope of being for the maternal. Patriarchy has distorted partnership.

This is what women are raising as an issue of grave implication, not only for the relation between women and men within the human community but also for the relationship of human beings to the rest of creation. Miners, farmers, industrialists, and all people must consider their relationship to the earth with its mountains, plains, rivers, plants, animals, and atmosphere on which life depends.

The community study that preceded the Decade underlined the efforts needed to bring about just relations between men and women. Under the rubric of partnership, we examined how the church community may seek ways of working for the restoration of its wholeness. We became conscious of the various ways and levels of exclusion of women, and we began to engage in advocacy for the participation of women in our collective consciousness as the church. What the decade calls for now are acts to bring about the significant changes that will move women and men into fuller partnership based on the diversity of gifts given to each as an individual.

One line of action is to move toward equity in representation of women and men in decision-making bodies. Questions still unresolved in this connection are who represents the church and speaks for the churches. Questions are being raised that pitch numerical and qualitative participation against each other. This suggests that the participation of women lowers the authority and prestige of a body and therefore that of its decisions.

In this Decade, we have to face our inability to link women with authority. This is a manifestation of our disbelief in scripture that the Spirit of God is poured out on men and women and that the Spirit of Wisdom and understanding operates in women as in men for the common good of the community (1 Cor 12; Eph 14).

The partnership issue goes beyond numbers, but at least presence is an index of recognition of one's responsibility to be in active partnership. We note sadly, however, that the visible, physical presence of women in the church at worship has not ensured the presence of women's experience in the determination of policies and priorities.

We suggest that some of this is due to the fact that often the very language that is in vogue at worship ignores their presence. This makes women act as spectators to the goings-on in the altar area and the boardroom. This Decade calls for listening to women state their perceptions and taking them into account when decisions are made.

Participation means empowering women to become active partners in determining the quality of the life of he church as a community and of its presence in the world. Visible involvement of women in this manner is an essential element of the unity we seek in order that the world may believe.

For me one of the saddest effects of the intransigence of churches on this issue of partnership is the creation of "women churches." The women church is a challenge to assess why we are so divided. The Decade is for the churches to face the question of unity, asking and seeking answers to the questions on the role of the gender factor in our search for the unity of the church and the renewal of the human community.

Unity and Gender

The church from its beginnings bore within its body the seeds of diversity. That this diversity has led to divisiveness is the result of human sin. We now have women churches as the visible expression of the deep hurt of women arising out of their marginalization. The presence of women in the church is taken for granted; so is their lack of voice. Their active service in creating an environment for physical and mental health is taken for granted. They are in the church as facilitators for the men who are the makers and actors of the church. Women's silence complements men's speech. There is no unity. There is only a community in which one sector conforms to the forms of participation imposed upon it by the other.

The language of deliberations on unity in recent times has taken a most unfortunate turn. Women are being portrayed as obstacles to the unity of the churches as if women were not of the church. The churches will demonstrate solidarity with women when bilateral and multicultural deliberations claiming to seek the visible unity of the church admit women's presence and listen with seriousness to the points women raise. Women, both in church and in society, are challenging their marginalization because it visibly disrupts the unity of the community.

Churches such as the Lutheran Church in Tanzania are responding by taking steps toward the ordination of women into the eucharistic ministry while the Orthodox Church is reviving the ancient diaconate order as a ministry in itself and not necessarily a step toward priesthood. In Africa, the media are beginning to pick up the issue of the ordination of women.

The experimental project of young women doing theology and the various associations of women theologians, especially in the Third World, have highlighted the inescapable link between doing theology and living daily life. They have unearthed sociocultural biases against women doing theology. Christian theology is not univocal. It cannot be whole or complete if it is carried out by male voices only. The same can be said for all areas of human life. In theology, as in any other issue, gender has been a negative factor in the search for visible unity.

In society women ask for reciprocity as a sign of unity. They ask why a wife should need a husband's signature to buy land when the husband does not need the wife's signature to do the same. The unity of the church, like the unity of the human community, becomes a reality when women are recognized as legal and economic and sacramental agents.

The low percentage of women holding political offices is comparable to that of women in ecclesiastical offices. Apart from cultural factors, both have roots in the lack of education appropriate to the office. Women in many parts of the world have internalized their state of "subordination." They live with a low self-esteem and in silence, apathy, and with servile attitudes to men and to the structures of church and society. The Decade calls upon men to stand by the women who have chosen to obey God.

On the agenda of many church groups are the issues of racism, militarism, health hazards of nuclear testing, and the dumping of nuclear waste. The exploitation of creation and the need for ecological wisdom, justice, peace, survival of creation are all related.

In many countries, it is religion as a whole that is the context of solidarity that women require. Where there is religious fundamentalism, women's traditional place and roles are curtailed in ways that seriously limit possibilities of personal development. Women are accused of violating traditional norms of the community when they seek to assert their individual wish to grow in nontraditional roles. All religions tend to do this with women.

Women's spiritual heritage is circumscribed by what fundamentalism allows. The entrenched sexism in religion is hard to tackle. Women need the solidarity of men to review the whole area of human sexuality and its links with religion, rituals, and taboos. Many churches have it on their agenda to challenge institutionalized sexism in the structures, ethics, and theology of the churches.

Sayings and Doings

The emerging trends are encouraging. On several of the issues, one observes efforts to speak out and to act for change. The most visible area is the empowering of women to move the church into action. Women are saying clearly that this is the agenda of the church. In many places women have taken advantage of this to take up research and write women's histories and women's contribution to the mission of the church, which remains unrecognized.

Church women are consciously linking up with women of other faiths and secular women's groups on issues that affect society as a whole. The Church of Christ cannot afford to do other than seek justice and act in compassion.

My expectation is that the churches will come to demonstrate to the world community that religion is an integral part of human life. Churches must show that they are an inescapable element in our understanding of society, and therefore in the struggles for peace and justice. I hope the Decade will raise the awareness that a society's attitude toward women is directly related to its understanding of what it means to be authentically human and truly religious.

For the church this is crucial. Human dignity is none other than the respect due to the image of God in us. The Decade calls the churches to be clear on what they really believe is the nature and purpose of human existence. Should some human beings be treated differently from others—and differently from what God wants them to be?

Let me end with a well-known story.

A young woman preparing herself for marriage is confronted with a most unwelcome message. She is to become pregnant before she begins her married life. It is totally unexpected and deeply embarrassing. The shame of it will be enough to kill her. She is being asked to do what is wholly against her religion and social upbringing. She is to sacrifice her social standing and expose herself to society's disapproval. She is being asked to put the plan of God above her social and religious expectations. Who will believe that what she is carrying is of the Holy Spirit and that her act of obedience will profoundly affect the history of all humanity? Against all conventional wisdom she says "yes" to this plan of God for her.

That young woman, Mary of Nazareth, has gone down in history as the mother of God.

What about the man who is to marry her? He stood by her because he too has heard the voice of God and he too believes Mary's submission to God's purposes will bring new life to the whole human community.

Joseph too is going against custom and tradition when he takes a pregnant woman for his wife. We never stop to think how embarrassing his own position is. What will his parents say? What will his friends say?

Here is a man who stood in solidarity with a woman he loved and trusted. This man had an ear tuned to what God was saying to him and to the world.

Does the story have a message for us?

NOTES

1. Mercy Amba Oduyoye, "Christian Feminism and African Culture: The 'Hearth' of the Matter," unpublished presentation given to Union Theological Seminary in February 1987.

2. Mercy Amba Oduyoye, "The Empowering Spirit of Religion," in *Lift Every Voice: Theologies from the Underside*, ed. Susan Thistlethwaite and Mary Potter Engel (New York: Harper and Row, 1990) 245.

3. Mercy Amba Oduyoye, "Reflections from a Third World Woman's Perspective:

Women's Experience and Liberation Theologies," in *Irruption of the Third World: Challenge to Theology*, ed. Virginia Fabella and Sergio Torres (Maryknoll, N.Y.: Orbis, 1983) 249.

4. Oduyoye, "The Empowering Spirit" 246.

5. Mercy Amba Oduyoye, *Hearing and Knowing: Theological Refections on Christianity in Africa* (Maryknoll, N.Y.: Orbis, 1986). The reflections in this section are from 135–49.

6. Elizabeth Amoah and Mercy Amba Oduyoye, "The Christ for African Women," in *With Passion and Compassion* (Maryknoll, N.Y.: Orbis, 1988); the selections are from 35–46.

7. Graecia Adwoa Asokomfo Tewiah, a specialist in children's education and a collector of Fante legends, has narrated this tale.

8. J. S. Mbiti, *New Testament Eschatology* (London: Heinemann, SPCK, 1971) 57–61.

9. Worship in the African charismatic churches incorporates many prayers that are a call for life; see A. Omoyajowo, "Prayer in African Indigenous Churches," in *The State of Christian Theology in Nigeria, 1980–1981*, ed. Mercy Amba Oduyoye (Ibadan: Daystar Press, 1986).

10. The prayer is quoted in Amoah and Oduyoye, "The Christ for African Women" 42.

11. Mercy Amba Oduyoye, *Who Will Roll the Stone Away?* (Geneva: World Council of Churches, 1990) 49–56, 64–69.

BIBLIOGRAPHY

Oduyoye, Mercy Amba. *And Women, Where Do They Come In?* Lagos: Methodist Literature Department, 1980.

Oduyoye, Mercy Amba. *Hearing and Knowing: Theological Reflections on Christianity in Africa*. Maryknoll, N.Y.: Orbis, 1986.

Oduyoye, Mercy Amba, ed. *The State of Christian Theology in Nigeria, 1980–1981*. Ibadan: Daystar Press, 1986.

Oduyoye, Mercy Amba. *The Will to Arise*. With Musimbi R. A. Kanyoro, coeditor. Maryknoll, N.Y.: Orbis, 1992.

Oduyoye, Mercy Amba. *Who Will Roll the Stone Away?* RISK Series. Geneva: World Council of Churches, 1990.

Oduyoye, Mercy Amba, and Virginia Fabella, eds. *With Passion and Compassion*. Maryknoll, N.Y.: Orbis, 1988.

– 26 –

EDWINA GATELEY

(born 1943)

Being Missionary Means Being on the Edges

Edwina Gateley was born in 1943 in Lancaster, England. Her older brother, Colin, and her younger sister, Maureen, "were both better looking than I and, I felt, more intelligent."[1] At an early age, Edwina was encouraged to cultivate a competitive spirit so that she could continue her schooling rather than work in a local factory.

Even while she was still a child, Edwina recalls that God broke into her life and called her to some form of service in the Roman Catholic Church. When she was fifteen, Edwina decided she was being called to be a missionary. After completing college in 1964, she went to be a volunteer in one of the schools in Uganda, East Africa. The school was run by the Sisters of Our Lady of Africa. After a year at this school, Edwina went to the local Ugandan bishop, Adrian Ddungu, to see if she might meet other needs in his diocese.

She ended up in a small village, Kyamaganda, and built up a school for the eleven- to eighteen-year-old Ugandans. The people taught Edwina how to live life in the present as she taught them their school subjects. She returned to England in 1967, knowing she would continue to be a missionary in some form.

In 1968 the way became clear. After a retreat, Edwina knew she would found a volunteer lay missionary movement. However, after spending much time in selling her ideas to those she hoped would support the establishment of such a group, it seemed like the idea would not assume reality. She returned to Uganda in 1968. The following year there was an offer of funding for her movement, and she returned to England to organize the venture. By 1979 the Volunteer Missionary Movement had already sent over five hundred lay missionaries to twenty-six countries. After leading the movement for ten years, Edwina decided it was time for new leadership.

In 1979 the leadership was given to Maria Gabriel, and in 1981 Su Hood became the first director of the U.S. branch of the Volunteer Missionary Movement. Edwina went to the Sahara desert for a three-month retreat of thanksgiving and solitude. In September she went to the Catholic Theology Union in Chicago and received a master's degree in theology in June 1981. At this time she sensed that the Spirit of God was calling her to a mission, but she was unable to identify just what this mission might be. She spent nine months in a forest hermitage in Yorkville, Illinois, a place near one of the missionary houses.

During this time she prayed and fasted in the solitude of the woods while discerning which direction would open to her. After the first five months there was still no clear sign of direction:

> I am anxious and looking around for signs. I must stop looking or I will miss them. I am accustomed to action and clear direction, and my first instinct, if there isn't any clear direction, is to create one! How hard it is to BE! I must believe that this time . . . is part of a process of becoming available and learning to wait on God. God is not gone—it is only that I cannot find God's face for a while. I did not know that it was so hard to listen in a very deep silence.[2]

A variety of responses to the rhythmic felt absence and presence of God occurred. When some days hung heavily, Edwina remembered that life takes time. On days like this, she could recall the wisdom of others:

> A friend of mine, Maria, once said to me, "The rocks and the earth . . . we call dead matter because we cannot think slowly enough to see them live." There is a lot of wisdom here.[3]

In time, the wisdom of waiting opened new doors to what was happening. The journey in solitude enabled Edwina to discover that action for others and discovery of some future event was not the primary purpose of her time in the woods. For this time in life, "God left me to experience aloneness, because I was the event. . . . My ministry at this point is me. It is not my business to worry about where I shall go or what I shall do."[4]

A thirty-day retreat experience closed the period of solitude and discernment. As the retreat progressed, Edwina experienced an ambivalence about a sacramental church that she had always loved and called home. An outer face of that church misused power and authority and ignored the sacramental gifts of women:

> I went to the Eucharist this morning and suffered through it. The language was sexist, the theology unsound. . . . This church has smiled upon me, applauded me as a good, obedient girl. But now I have become a woman and can acknowledge my pain at experiencing prejudice in this church. . . . The church needs my brothers and sisters who have grown to be men and women, and continue to give birth to love and hope in our world, but she is too blind to see. I am sad and grieving.[5]

As the retreat was drawing to a close, Edwina had a vision of an old and gentle woman who did not speak, but only spoke with her compassionate eyes. The woman had a strong, tender being. She and Edwina had tea and simply gazed at each other for a long time:

> She called me woman. I called her Mary. She leaned over to me, embraced me and then held my hand. I felt hers—rough. She was crying. There were tears running down her face. She was suddenly sad. "Be compassionate. Don't condemn. Love."[6]

Slowly the future became clearer. It was time to extend the compassion of Christ to those who knew little compassion. The call to minister to the suffering women of the streets, the prostitutes of Chicago, took shape. The mission was an ordination to a new ministry on the streets. It was clear that this is what God wished Edwina to do at this time in her life.

> There were no crowds at my ordination.
> The church was cold and bare.
> There was no bishop to bless and consecrate,
> No organ music filled the air.
> No solemn procession went before me,
> No cross or incense smell.
> There were no songs, nor incantation,
> And no pealing triumphant bell.
>
> But I heard the children laughing
> In the stench of the city slums.
> And I heard the people sobbing
> At the roaring of the guns,
> And the stones cried out before me
> As the sirens wailed and roared
> And the blood of women and children
> In the arid earth was poured.
>
> There were no crowds at my ordination.
> The church was cold and bare.
> But the cries of the people gathered
> And songs of birds filled the air.
> The wind grew cold before me.
> The mountains rose and split.
> As the earth shuttered and trembled
> And a flame eternal was lit.[7]

In January 1983 Edwina moved to one of the poorest areas of Chicago and began to walk the streets. God was now giving Edwina a new group of guides and teachers on her journey. Her deep faith and humor enabled her to simply flow where she was being led without planning everything. In January 1984 she established Genesis House of Hospitality for the care of the people of the streets. As the house of hospitality grew, Edwina continued to know the many faces of Christ through the cries of the poor.

Her own life continues to be one that remains committed to serving the poor. She remains an active volunteer missionary with other brothers and sisters who share her vision:

> Christ was available to all, and reached out to the poor, the sick, and the rejected. He was one of them. His mission is now ours. Our mission is to be wherever there is injustice of any kind. We see the Spirit at work in those to whom we go as well as within ourselves.... We praise and bless the Lord who calls us to live and to be in the world and to share his mission of love and peace with all men and women of every color and belief.[8]

In the reflections that follow, Edwina shares her insights about the challenges that Christian mission holds for individuals and for the community called church. Her humor and compassion do not blind her to the shortsightedness of institutional Christianity and individual believers who can get too settled in older ways.

Prophetic Mission: Sniffing Out the Kingdom[9]

Prophetic mission is about challenging and stretching ourselves, the church, and the world to be just and to be holy. Mission by its very nature is prophetic. It follows that missionaries are the church's avant-garde, the ones who walk ahead, the ones who break new ground and plow new furrows. Because our essential task is to go out beyond the normal boundaries we therefore experience the strange, the new, the different and it is this very journey which gives the missionary the unique task of being an agent of transformation, constantly calling ourselves and our communities to check on whether we are growing and moving toward the reality of God's rule, or whether we are stagnating, or indeed going backward.

Do you know that little animal called the mole? The mole lives below the earth and she is a furry little thing. Do you know that the mole is blind? She cannot see a thing. She lives under the earth and although she is blind, she has developed over the centuries an instinct for the rain, an instinct for the sunshine. She has been endowed with an incredible sniffing ability and so she sniffs her way below the earth in the darkness, even though she is blind.

We missionaries must be like the mole. We must sniff in the darkness for God's reign. We don't know where we are going and that's all right. In our heart we have been endowed with the gift of faith that tells us that God is with us as long as we continue to sniff for God's justice, to sniff for God's light in the darkness.

Charting New Territory

The missionary, therefore, has the ongoing task of being particularly committed to charting new territory and inviting God's people to experience and live out the Good News in ever new and life-giving ways. This is no easy task. If faithfully pursued, it means for the most part that missionaries will be a bit of a nuisance because we must rock the boat that lies still. We must question constantly whether the kingdom of God is indeed among us, and if so, where and how... and it may well be that the kingdom of God is not exactly where we thought it was. In actual fact it may look quite different from what we once thought.

There was a time when we thought the kingdom was all about gathering, getting people all together—with the same language (Latin)—in the same building (the Roman Catholic Church)—professing the same faith and creed (ours)—all under the same hierarchical leadership (the Pope and his bishops)—all centered in the one place (Rome)—and worshiping the one white male God. But it is not like that. In fact, it is very different. It looks like the nicely packaged Good News—that we have spent so long parceling, labeling, and marketing—spilled out and burst its packaging.

What we have been gradually discovering these past few years since Vatican II is that God, and God's rule, is a great deal bigger and a great deal more difficult to get a handle on than we could ever have thought in our early evangelizing days. It is the missionary in particular who is becoming more and more conscious of this and is seeking new ways of understanding mission and its praxis.

Reaching Out

As you may know, I work on the streets of Chicago. I remember meeting one of my first, if you like, clients. She was one of the women to whom I was sent, to evangelize, to reach out to. She was flat, horizontal on the pavement, drunk, a street woman, a prostitute. Everything in me said, "Save her, reach out to her!" You know that wonderful feeling of helping that we get when we do something for the poor. So I reached out and scooped up this prostitute off the streets and I took her home to help her so that she might be like me—middle class, white, and educated.

I gave her a shower and I gave her clothes and I said to her, "You don't have to be a prostitute. You don't have to be on the streets. You can get your life together." As a missionary, I thought this is what I was supposed to do. I took care of her and I did everything I could for her. After a few weeks—off she went, back to the streets and the drink. I went after her and I brought her back—back to the center, back to possibilities, back to health. We began again. And off she went again! Being a good Catholic missionary, I went after her again. I went in pursuit of the one that got away!

Over a period of three years that woman shot off a dozen times, two dozen times fleeing from the Good News. Can you believe that! Fleeing from the kingdom! One day I said to myself, "I'm finished. I won't pursue her any more." After three years of desperately trying to call her forth, I gave up. Late one night, three o'clock in the morning, I received a phone call from the prostitute saying, "Please come." I said, "No—I will not be co-dependent." (We're all trying not to be co-dependent now!) Then I got another phone call from the Chicago police asking, "Do you know this woman who has killed herself? She's in this dirty apartment building in Chicago. She's dead."

Finding God Present

I said to my God, "I have been faithful and you weren't. I have pursued what I believed to be evangelization and you didn't do anything."

I could not understand what this God was doing. How far do you go in pursuit of the Good News? I was numb with grief. We had the funeral in a small funeral parlor in the area where I work because there are many poor people there and they can't afford big funerals. The coffin was by a little altar. I was to do the service. We only had a dozen chairs so I stood by the coffin and I didn't understand why she had to die.

Then the door opened and in came the shopping bag ladies with their trolleys which they wheeled up to the altar and parked beside the coffin. And they looked at the dead woman and said, "She looks better now than she did when she was alive!" The shopping bag ladies sat down and in came some priests from the local parish. Then came some prostitutes, drug addicts, pushers, and pimps from the streets of Chicago, followed by some nuns from the suburbs.

The prostitutes and the pimps sat down among the priests. The bag ladies and the drug addicts shoved up against the nuns. There we were all scrunched up together—priests and prostitutes, nuns and bag ladies, drug addicts and sophisticated white Christians from the suburbs. We took the hymn book and began to sing of God's presence in our world.

As I saw the dead body of the one I worked with for so long, and saw all the people gathered—black and white, pimps and prostitutes, nuns and priests, I suddenly realized that God was indeed present in a different way. God was here in the breaking down of barriers between people who would never normally have come together. God revealed God's self and reign to me. It was not in the way I chose and it was not in the way I wanted. I wanted to see one woman live and God chose to show me that if you are faithful even to death God will bring together priest and prostitute, black and white, lay and religious and that this was mission. I didn't understand it at all. It was a different agenda from my own.

And in the Northern Hemisphere

Mission, once narrowly perceived as "going out" with the Good News to the outsider in foreign lands, and building monuments and cathedrals as symbols of the triumph of Christianity, is now being recognized as an activity that might well be based at home, directed at the insiders, including ourselves! It may have a lot more to do with inner healing and nurturing rather than with preaching and building.

We are beginning to recognize that many of the problems facing the Southern Hemisphere—the poverty, injustice, and hunger prevalent there—are linked directly to the economic and political power as well as lifestyle of our own Northern Hemisphere. We in the Northern Hemisphere are a people obsessed by progress and success, moving at a devastatingly fast pace and, in the process, suffering from all sorts of addictions and diseases which, in turn, affect the whole globe.

If we are to understand mission not simply as limited to furthering the Roman Catholic Church, but as the much wider call to bring about God's rule in the world, then we missionaries have to start again—at home! Most of us have a deep fear of mission at home—how many of us prefer to stay in the Southern Hemisphere? Why do you think that is? Are the problems, the lifestyle, the pressures, harder for us at home than in the bush? Are we nervous about proclaiming God's kingdom where no one, perhaps, really wants to hear about it? Are we afraid?

Being Carried by God

Once when I was in the forest, I found a little chipmunk. It had been caught by two cats and they were playing with her, throwing her from one paw to the other. The little thing was flying through the air terrified. I ran in and rescued the chipmunk. She was shaking and nervous. I lifted her up and told her, "You'll be all right. I'll put you in a safe place." I carried her and as I walked with her, she bit me hard! I again tried to reassure her that she would be all right. She bit me again and this time drew blood. Everything in me wanted to say, "You stupid chipmunk!" I felt like hitting her but I took her to a safe place feeling extremely frustrated that I could not communicate with her that I was taking care of her and everything would be fine.

Afterward I asked myself how I felt and I realized I was so frustrated because I was unable to get my message across. Then I thought about God. Is it like this for God? Is God carrying us in the palm of her/his hand and are we biting all the way because we are not sure? Is God covered in bites? Who is inflicting them? Surely we missionaries know that God carries us in the palm of the hand with the message of evangelical wholeness, "Tell my people not to be afraid. It's all right."

Surely, we are the ones that must understand that God will never leave the people if we are faithful. But we shiver and shake at the thought of how mission is going to be today. How can we face the kinds of problems we see prevalent in the First World? Our God says, "Don't be afraid!... Remember, I carry you in the palm of my hand."

Walking the Prophetic Edge

God longs for our transformation. In all our research we must not forget that. What happens to us often, in the North, is that we become so overwhelmed by the problems and sense of helplessness that we allow ourselves to be somewhat anesthetized.

We missionaries are called to walk on the prophetic edge. It's very tight and it's very fine. We have to balance ourselves between the world and God's reign. We know the world and its problems but we have another dream—of world peace, justice, and transformation. We walk the prophetic edge but what happens is that often we look so much at the world and its problems that we let go of the prophetic edge and its sharpness. We go "blob" like jelly. We say, "I cannot do anything about it." It's safer just to settle down and say, "It's not my problem."

The missionary who is sharp and alert, walking on the tight edge says, "I must not allow myself to become like a jelly. I must not settle. I must keep moving along right on the precipice." It's a balancing act at which the missionary must become adept. The temptation for our church and especially for its missionaries is to be pulled back into the jelly mold. But if we are pulled back, there will be no evangelization, no kingdom. We must maintain the prophetic edge of evangelization. We must not buy into the system that would settle down. We must continue to sniff for the light even in our own darkness.

In the United States and Britain, the church often vacillates between finding the prophetic edge, feeling its sharpness, and then moving rather rapidly back into the jelly mold. The American bishops (and I suspect the European ones too) occasionally come out with prophetic statements—for example, the pastoral letters on peace and the economy. But on other issues, for example, mission, and women—two major issues, they fell well short of reality, let alone prophecy! Gospel people cannot be choosy and selective about justice. They must be a just people on all issues, and on a global level. The Vatican Council puts it like this:

> Wherever there are people in need of food and drink, clothing, medicine, housing, employment, education . . . wherever people lack the facilities necessary for living a truly human life or are afflicted with serious distress or illness or suffer exile or imprisonment, there Christian love should seek them out and find them. (Apostolate of the Laity 8:4)

Call to Conversion—Beginning with Ourselves

Seeking out such injustice and poverty is a lot easier when the search is focused out there and far away. As we know from our past missionary history it is a rather comfortable feeling to dip into our excess and help out the poor folks in another land. It is much more difficult to challenge our own selves, our churches and governments to change lifestyles and attitudes in the name of the gospel.

Mission is, indeed, a call to conversion and, without any doubt, it begins with ourselves. As missionaries, we are to be tuned in to God's Spirit permeating the world, ever calling us to individual and institutional conversion. If we are open, if we let go of our penchant for power and control, we will hear this Spirit and we will understand the call. If we recognize the mess and are repentant about it, we will experience new possibilities. But this will not be without cost! Not without the cost involved in letting go and listening and suddenly finding that we are rather small and helpless before this great God of ours.

Letting Go

I have yet to get involved in a new experience of mission that was not proceeded with a whole letting go of the familiar and the traditional. It took me eighteen months to start the Volunteer Missionary Movement in England in 1969. It was eighteen months of struggling, believing in a mission for laity in mission, believing that mission for me was to stretch the church to be open to laity. Eventually it happened and the Volunteer Missionary Movement began—a new and different thing in the history of the church in England. There was growth, numbers, consolidation. I was nominated Catholic woman of the year. All in ten years! I was proud of my mission. It was good to be popular. But mission is not about popularity or establishment. It is about sniffing for the kingdom and even moving in pursuit of it.

Maybe we need to be in the wilderness to get back in touch with the promise. When I felt the call of God whom I call "The God of the Belly Button," to let go of my position, of the responsibility, the power and the status, I didn't want to hear. I felt so much a part of the establishment, and let me tell you it is comfortable to be there. As God was telling me to let go, to move on, I was protesting. "I know the bishops well, and lots of people here; and my name is in the *Catholic Universe* and the *Catholic Trumpet;* and my mother is proud of me." God kept saying, "Move on" and I kept answering, "Go away and leave me in peace. I can proclaim your message here where I feel comfortable."

Praying and Listening

I went to the Sahara desert to try and make sense of the call I was experiencing, to let go of the Volunteer Missionary Movement and all it meant to me. It was in the wilderness that I felt this God saying, "I will never leave you but you must be faithful to the sniff! You must keep moving on." It was for me a painful experience.

Maybe it's appropriate for us now to consider a new mission today. It's called "Letting go." I can smell that it's time to let go, to consider a new mission today. I can smell it, breathe it, touch it, and something in me trembles. I will not cry. But it is time to go; time to step out of the world I shaped and watched become. Time to let go of the status of administration. Time to turn my back on a life that throbbed with my vigor and a spirit that soared through my tears. Time to go from all I am to all I have not yet become. I will not cry but tremble at the death within me—the lonely, brave departure while my being shudders in utter nakedness.

I lost a great deal of ground, it seems, in letting go of my mission and all its accoutrements. But I was trying to be faithful to the sniff!

If we pray and listen, we will know what we must do even if it may not make a great deal of sense. Most of the time, Jesus did not make a great deal of sense to his hearers. He disappointed his followers and friends; he was elusive; he refused to be fixed; he refused to let the kingdom be concretized or pigeonholed. The kingdom was leaven-salt-mustard seed—among you and within you. The kingdom is about the children-the poor-the dispossessed.... No wonder he was not popular!

We missionaries who are about the same business of sniffing out the kingdom, must take the inevitable risk involved in being faithful to mission. We are not to be at the center of things, but at the fringes, the periphery, ever stretching God's people to greater faithfulness. The sniffing that we do requires reflection and prayer as a prerequisite to action.

Call to Mission—U.S.A.

The missionary sniff led me to the United States eleven years ago. I went to study theology at the Chicago Theology Union. As a Catholic laywoman, missionary, minister, I had never studied theology. I didn't know the language of the professional missionary and I wanted to know what it is that they do, what it is they learn in those big buildings called seminaries where all the young men go in one door and five years later they come out the other door wearing their collars—a sign of mission as a priest. I wanted to know what I as a Catholic laywoman had been missing all these years. And I got it—a degree in theology!

I said, "Look, God, I got it! I'm a Catholic laywoman missionary minister with a degree in theology!"

And God said, "Put it away. You don't need that right now. Why don't you listen?"

"I don't want to listen, God. I've learned it all."

"Why don't you do nothing?"

"What do you mean, do nothing? God, don't you know the world is hungry, the world is suffering and oppressed?"

"Edwina, I have something to tell you which is a secret. The world has already been saved. Just listen and let me get to know you."

That was a very difficult thing for me to do as a missionary—to feel the call, to let go of my activity, and to listen. I got myself a little hermitage and put it in a forest in Illinois. I did not understand why I was there or where I was to go next. I hoped that in my uselessness and lack of activity and being faithful to doing nothing I would have a vision or two, or a dream, or be filled with a great sense of God's presence.

I sat alone in that stupid forest asking God to tell me what to do. Nothing came to me. No dreams, no revelations, just the day-after-day longing for God to be present. I found myself walking through the forest talking to the squirrels. I do not know what it was that kept me in the forest but maybe it was that tiny little grain of faith. I believed that God would not leave me in my darkness, in all the mess, and I knew I had to hold on even though I knew it looked crazy.

In the ninth month, suddenly God was alive. God was a person! I thought of a woman in childbirth. The seed of new life requires the darkness, the silence and the warmth but the not knowing of the womb. The God seed in you also requires darkness and silence as God's word matures in the heart of the people. We must allow for the gestation. Yet how close we are to an abortion! We constantly hear of physical abortions. But what about spiritual abortions because we cannot wait to hear God's words or cannot wait to understand what we must do?

Instead we have our five-year plan or our three-year plan. We must know what the process is. But God operates in darkness and the people must be familiar with God's ways. Listen deeply. We cannot enter anyone's darkness until we have entered our own.

To Work the Streets

Called to work on the streets was not my idea of mission, U.S.A. Apparently one of the wealthiest countries in the world, having more Christian churches, huge cathedrals and well-established rich dioceses than I had seen anywhere else in the world, it seemed to me incongruous to do mission in U.S.A.

I asked God to send me back to Africa. "I'm good in Africa, you know, God. Or send me back to England and let me work with the church in England—I'm okay with the British, or let me teach. I can teach, you know."

Then God said, "I want you to go to the prostitutes."

"Stop right there, God. That's not my agenda. I don't know anything about prostitution. When I was in the seminary there was no department of brothels and prostitution. I read no books on how to evangelize prostitutes or how to minister to street people or drug addicts or pimps. And there was nothing about the church pimping."

And God said again, "I want you to work with the women in prostitution."

"But God, I've no plan. I don't know anything about it. Who is going to pay? Do you think anyone is going to believe me? Does anybody believe you, God? Do you think I can go to the cardinal and say 'Eminence, I feel called by God to work with women in prostitution, and would you please pay my medical insurance, or would you please support me?' No way!"

As a church, we do not embrace the edges. We have things nicely set up and organized for the center. I told God that I wished I'd never gone to that silly forest because I listened so deeply that I had heard God's whisper. When we stop and listen deeply in the darkness, it's dangerous business to pray because then God gets very excited and says, "A fool! I can send her or him out to places where only an idiot would go. I can send them out to tasks which may be a little frightening for them."

God is always looking for opportunity, always tempting and daring the missionary church to go to the edges—to take the Good News to the women in prostitution.

Walking on the Water

This call reminded me of Jesus going to the hills to pray while the disciples were in a boat rowing away in the midst of a storm. While they were rowing against the elements Jesus was off in the hills to communicate with his God. He comes back the following morning. The disciples are still in the boat and Jesus walks on the water. The disciples think it's a ghost. Jesus calls the disciples—dares them—and Peter jumps into the water and goes toward the vision, the dream, toward that which calls him. Peter isn't thinking. He's following. As he goes on the water toward the vision of the kingdom, he begins to think about what he is doing and he begins to sink.

The moment we begin to rationalize the kingdom, to ask, is it possible? can it be done? will we be all right?—we drown. Missionaries on the prophetic edge have to stop thinking, stop planning, stop trying to work it all out and follow the belly button. That is the only way God gets a chance to show us miracles. When we try to work the miracles with our brains and computers, the kingdom never fits into it. We need to loosen up and allow our hearts to lead us.

I was more at home with mission in an African village than I was with hanging about the dirty streets of Chicago with no handle on my mission at all! But then perhaps, I was the mission event. When we are too secure, when we are too strong, we are part of the problem. Perhaps I had to pursue the kingdom blindly in Chicago in order to enter a process of mission conversion myself, one in which all my notions of mission would be turned upside down and transformed once again.

Saying "Yes" to God

My first encounter with women on the streets confirmed for me that in spite of my tears and insecurity, God was very real and present in my new call to mission. I will share with you my first encounter with the women on the streets of Chicago late one night thinking, "What am I doing here?!" I saw them smoking their reefers and standing around on the street corner wearing long boots and short miniskirts. They were flagging down the cars of those poor innocent middle-aged men who just happened to be driving along the road at midnight!

I went up to the women and said, "Hi." And they looked me up and down and then said, "f— off!" And I did. I got out of there as fast as I could because you see in my mission in Africa, nobody ever told me to "f— off!" When I was in church with the people in Africa, they said, "Welcome. How nice to see you. How are you?" And here I was in Chicago trying to be faithful to the sniff and they didn't want either it or me. I went home and told God what to do with the prostitutes, and God said, "Go back." God never gives up calling the people to mission. Mission is God's problem. All we need to be is fools and say to God, "Yes! We will go and do it but you work it out!"

I went back the next day and there they were doing the same thing and I went up to them and I said, "Hello."

"Hey, baby, we told you to f— off! What the f— are you doing here?"

"I can stand here. I have a right to stand here on this street corner."

"We told you to f— off. Get your a— out of here!"

"No, I can stand on this street corner."

"Hey, are you a cop?"

"No, I'm not a cop."

"Are you a journalist? Are you going to write a report on us?"

"No, I'm not a journalist."

"Are you a nun?"

"No, I'm a laywoman."

"Well, why are you on our turf? We don't have no Christians in our place."

"I'm an alien." (I have this card from the U.S. Immigration Office and in big blue letters it has the word ALIEN, and I showed it to them. My thumbprint is on one side of the card and on the other side is a picture of my ear. The U.S. government believes that the ear is unique. There is no ear in the universe like mine! Can you imagine God making all those millions and billions of ears! What fun she must have had!)

The women in prostitution looked at my card and said, "She's not nobody. She ain't nobody." And I heard God laugh. When they take away the pulpit, and take off the vestments and take away the Bible and all the credibility—you ain't got nothing. And then the poor don't feel threatened. The poor and the marginated who know what it is like to be on the edges, to be on the periphery don't need to be scared of us. Because we are nobody.

Taking Risks

God's ways are different. God throws away all the strength and all the power and all the symbols and all the glory and triumph and finds those who will walk with nothing and go to places where only fools will go so that God will manifest power in the world. We missionaries have to be right there on the sharp edge of discipleship. It is God who will transform the world—not with jelly but with the prophetic edge of authentic discipleship which dares to take risks in order to see God's miracles.

We gospel people should know that God will provide if we are about the business of the kingdom. Having learned from my African experience that listening is vital to mission I knew that my task was simply to hang around the streets and do just that. It became one of the most painful learning experiences of my life.

America the Beautiful

I found myself in the midst of an overwhelming poverty. It was exacerbated by the cosmetic wealth, power, and freedom of which the United States boasts. Here is a country which flies its flag proudly and dares to proclaim itself the defender of world freedom and democracy. Yet here is a country of approximately 57 million Catholics in which:

- one out of every four women are raped
- $31 million per hour are spent on arms
- 80 percent of all households are headed by women
- more people are in prison relative to its population than any other country in the world
- one in seven people live in poverty (as judged by U.S. standards)
- planning is occurring to build more Trident missiles than the seven already built (one is capable of destroying all the cities in the Northern Hemisphere!)
- economic fairness in distribution of income ranks last among all the industrialized nations
- 7,000 tons of toxic waste are produced daily
- over 90 percent of women involved in prostitution are victims of incest or abuse as children
- 10,000 children a year die in poverty
- 350,000 children bring guns to school every day

The list could go on and on.

Where Is the Kingdom?

Mission-evangelization-the kingdom. Where is it? What must we do about it? We must cry aloud where the kingdom of God is not present. But the church is not good at crying. The church is good at organizing and planning. Maybe we need to learn to weep again, old-fashioned weeping. Where must we be to sniff out and call forth the kingdom? A poem in my recent book attempts an answer.

> America the beautiful—salute the flag
> while down the dirty alley
> old ladies scavenge for cans and garbage scraps.

And Mick, bent and broken,
shuffles down the streets picking up the fag ends,
center of his life.

America the beautiful—salute the flag
while the lines at the soup kitchen
all ragged and shamed get longer and longer
in winter's cold dusk.

America the beautiful—salute the flag
and in the darkened hallways
the old folks huddle under yesterday's papers
claiming a stronger, rising dollar.

America the beautiful—salute the flag,
and raise it in the shelters
where the weak and hungry in their dirty, smelly clothes
are too sick, too old, too poor,
to raise the flag themselves.

America the beautiful—
Ah, bury, bury your flag,
until the smallest of your children
can raise it themselves.

The Church of the Northern Hemisphere Called to Conversion

As I became more and more aware of the terrible problems and the injustice prevalent in the United States, I knew that God's Spirit was indeed alive and well and calling for new mission awareness and activity right in the heart of the Northern Hemisphere. In Washington, millions of dollars are being spent to continue the building of a basilica to honor the mother of Jesus. Yet, women and children are the most oppressed and poverty-stricken population in the U.S.A.

An authentic church cannot afford to be ambiguous. It seems to me that conversion—yes!-repentance-old-fashioned repentance!—a change of heart, for those who hold the power and the resources, is indeed the new challenge of mission. One way or another, it is meant for all of us, but in particular for the church. We have preached enough. We need to sit with the pain in order to be open to transformation.

I work in the brothel system in Chicago. The brothel is a house of prostitution. It is a strange experience sitting in a brothel instead of a church and not knowing what to say. If I am preaching—when I am allowed to preach—I know what to say and I know my audience. When you are in a brothel, what do you say to women in prostitution? "Why don't you stop that? I'll get you a job in McDonald's?" What do you say? I sit there with the women and I have nothing to say. We are so used to having our role set out that we need that security. When God calls us and moves us to the edges, to the periphery, we are not secure and we don't know what to say. What we need to say to each other is, "That's fine—just fine!"

Mutuality of Evangelization

I remember once being invited to preach some homilies in a western suburban church in Chicago. I went to the brothel and just for conversation said to the madam that I would be preaching in church next week. Madam said, "Girls, Edwina is preaching. We're going."

I said, "Oh, no. That's not necessary." The last thing I wanted was to have the women in prostitution hear me preaching. At the church the following week I went up to the lectern. There they were—a whole row of prostitutes right in the middle of the church. I couldn't believe it! I got through my homily.

Afterward I went to the back of the church and there was the madam and there were the girls at the edge by the wall, trying to disappear into the wall. I said, "Thank you for coming! Thank you for your support." The madam said, "Well, we missed a morning of business, but it was worth it." Again I thanked them. Then one of the women said, "Edwina, you come and sit with us in our place. You come and you sit in our house with our problems. We know you ain't doing so well in your church, you being a woman and all, so we come and support you when they let you preach." And again I heard God laughing!

Solidarity

The women in prostitution wanted to support me, to be in solidarity with me because of the oppression found in our very own church institutions. It's as though the women were saying, "We go and we hear you, a woman, preach. You come and you sit and you see us in our poverty. You see us in our abuse, and you support us by loving us, even though we are in that darkness." This is the mutuality of evangelization! In spite of this darkness and the struggles, the missionary church must be faithful.

Bearing Fruit

When I was in the Sahara desert one day, I was feeling very lonely and very alienated. I'd been there for months and I hadn't heard God's voice. I sat on the sand and leaned against the remains of a little old mud hut. I let my head fall back and began to think, "Is God really with us?" Curling down from the remains of this hut was a grapevine and at the top a whole bunch of grapes was growing in the desert. And I heard God saying, "Even in the desert, especially in the desert, I bear fruit."

We are in the desert, and it is all right because God is with us and it is God that bears the fruit. All over Europe and America prophetic individuals and communities are trying to be faithful, to bear fruit and make a difference.

Last Sunday I was in a place called Rock Island in the state of Illinois. I had been invited to preach and to give a talk in a church that dared to invite a woman because it was committed to justice and peace. They told me that although they had invited me, they were unable to announce in public that I was speaking because I might then have been banned. Why would I be banned? Because I am a woman and because I am preaching! I am a gospel woman and for twenty-five years I have tried to understand and preach the Good News. Yet, in our church, gospel women like me are not allowed to preach the Good News.

That particular parish is on the verge of being closed because of its commitment to justice and peace, and because the pastor's activities are not in conjunction with the institutional church nor with his bishop. This pastor and his community, many of whom spend time in jail for protesting against nuclear arms, and who invite a woman to preach, are on the prophetic edge. The reality is that the parish may be closed. The reality is that a church, a small community, stays on the edge which is where they believe they must be.

Prophetic Challenge

Our Volunteer Missionary Movement in the U.S. received no support from the U.S. Catholic bishops because we dared to use the word "ecumenical" in our public statements. Although we are 90 percent Catholic, we opened out our movement to our Protestant brothers and sisters. So we are an ecumenical movement with Catholic roots. We are disqualified from Catholic support in the U.S. because of this ecumenical stance. We cannot afford to be ambiguous in the church. The prostitutes say, "Tell it like it is!" Preach the truth, not ambiguously, not changing it, but straightforwardly.

The truth is we are ecumenical. That is what we are called to be. We come from traditional Catholic roots but we will not sell ourselves for the money or for the power.

The Volunteer Missionary Movement in Europe is also on the line now in Scotland. The bishops want to know what we think of the Eucharist. They heard that we were allowing people who are not Catholic to receive the Eucharist. What do we do when we are in a community of missionaries and we are gathered to break the bread? Do we say to one, "You can have some" and to another, "You can't have some, because—although you serve and walk with us—you aren't Catholic?" The Scottish bishops say, "Tell us exactly what you are doing. If we do not agree with it, you lose your funding."

The God who called us to mission and evangelization says, "Tell it like it is! Do not play games with the gospel and do not play games with the Good News." If that means we lose ground financially or materially or powerwise, then so be it. But we will try to be faithful to the gospel of Jesus Christ.

Genesis House

Genesis House, the only house of hospitality in Chicago for women leaving prostitution, served 4,500 prostitutes over the last few years and helped them to get their lives together and to live more wholesome and dignified lives. It lost its support from the institutional church because it taught "safe sex." You cannot go to a prostitute and say, "My dear, why don't you be celibate?"

You cannot preach chastity and celibacy to women who have known only violence and who do not give a damn about themselves, and who are selling their bodies on the streets because they don't know anything else. You have to say, "At least I'll try to save your life." Safe sex! The church as an institution, coming from an entirely different position says, "No."

These people are hungry for the Good News, hungry for resurrection, hungry for nurturing, and not hungry for rules and ethics. You cannot say to an incest victim, a rape victim, or a deviant who has been in and out of jail, "Be celibate." You must say, "I will try to make your life a little bit better." In doing this, we do lose support from the institutional church, which looks like a power broker in this case. We have to "say it like it is" both to the prostitutes and to the institutional church. We know what's going on. It is a difficult place to walk, but maybe we missionaries, the avant-garde, have to be in dangerous places and constantly question much of what we do and how we do it.

Women Questioning the Institution

Because of entrenchment attitudes in the U.S. and British churches, the whole institution is being questioned. This is particularly true of women who are coming up with alternatives. One alternative is Mary's Pence for women (as opposed to Peter's Pence for the support of the Vatican). Mary's Pence says that if the institutional church does not understand women, the poor, and the prostitutes, the women will gather together and come up with alternative ways of reaching out to the widow and the orphan, the abandoned mother and wife. They will find resources elsewhere.

If the resources which we have in the church cannot be shared with those who challenge the system, then maybe we should find our resources elsewhere. I spent the last three summers in England, Scotland, and Ireland at the request of scores of Catholic women throughout these countries. In Britain, the U.S., and Australia, the mothers, the wives, and the daughters are creeping out and saying, "Edwina, let me tell you something. There's little left for us in the Catholic church!" Or others say, "What am I going to say to my three daughters? They won't even let them be altar servers!" And others, "Edwina, what are we going to do?"

These women are hungry and they are not being nurtured. They are coming out along the edges and asking, "Can we gather and nurture our children in different ways? Do we have a message of good news for them?"

The women are rebuilding the church. They are sniffing the call to mission and to a meaningful spirituality. We, the missionaries, must not lose that connection. We must be part of the underground movement that is moving forward from the poor and the dispossessed, especially the women. We must know about it and be in tune with it if indeed we are to be the evangelizing arm of the Catholic Church.

The Radical Jesus

If it is to survive, the church, like the radical Jesus, must speak aloud on behalf of the poor and oppressed, both at home and elsewhere. The church, like the radical Jesus, must have no truck with the power dealers and their tables. The church, like the radical Jesus, must listen to the Spirit who cries aloud for justice at the city gates and in the market place. The church, like the radical Jesus, must be missionary, and being missionary means being a pilgrim. It means being on the edges.

The Escape of the Spirit

I will end with a story. Once upon a time we captured God and we put God in a box and we put a beautiful velvet curtain around the box. We placed candles and flowers around the box and we said to the poor and the dispossessed, "Come! Come and see what we have! Come and see God!" And they knelt before the God in the box.

One day, very long ago, the Spirit in the box turned the key from inside and she pushed it open. She looked around in the church and saw that there was nobody there! They had all gone. Not a soul was in the place. She said to herself, "I'm getting out!" The Spirit shot out of the box. She escaped and she has been sighted a few times since then. She was last seen with a bag lady in McDonald's.

The missionary task is to be alert; to look for where the Spirit escaped to; to ask, "Where did she go?" Then we say to the community, "Look, we think, maybe here; it could be there." At least we are on the journey; at least we are moving!

NOTES

1. Edwina Gateley, *Psalms of a Lay Woman* (Trabuco Canyon, Calif.: Source Books, 1992) 83.
2. Edwina Gateley, *I Hear a Seed Growing* (Trabuco Canyon, Calif.: Source Books, 1992) 11–12.
3. Ibid. 30.
4. Ibid.
5. Ibid. 39–40.
6. Ibid. 53–54.
7. Ibid. 79–80.
8. Ibid. 109, 112.
9. *SEDOS Bulletin* 28:6, 7 (June 15–July 15, 1991) 193–205.

BIBLIOGRAPHY

Gateley, Edwina. *A Warm, Moist, Salty God: Women Journeying toward Wisdom*. Audio Tape. Trabuco Canyon, Calif.: Source Books, 1993.

Gateley, Edwina. *Giving Birth to God in the Contemporary World*. Audio Tape. Trabuco Canyon, Calif.: Source Books, 1992

Gateley, Edwina. *I Hear a Seed Growing*. Trabuco Canyon, Calif.: Source Books, 1992.

Gateley, Edwina. *I Hear God Laughing*. Audio Tape. Trabuco Canyon, Calif.: Source Books, 1992.

Gateley, Edwina. *Psalms of a Lay Woman*. Trabuco Canyon, Calif.: Source Books, 1992.

Gateley, Edwina. *Rediscovering and Claiming the Feminine Soul: Turning the World Upside Down*. Audio Tape. Trabuco Canyon, Calif.: Source Books, 1992.

ACKNOWLEDGMENTS

Grateful acknowledgment is made to the following publishers, groups, and individuals for permission to reprint the following materials, to which minor editorial revisions have been made:

All Is Grace: The Spirituality of Dorothy Day by William Miller; copyright 1985 by William H. Miller; used by permission of Doubleday, a division of Bantam Doubleday Dell Publishing Group, Inc. U.S.A.

Book of Margery Kempe by Margery Kempe; copyright by Devin-Adair Publishers, Inc., Old Greenwich, CT 06870; permission granted to reprint *The Book of Margery Kempe* by Margery Kempe, ed. W. Butler-Bowdon, 1944; all rights reserved.

Catherine of Siena: The Dialogue, trans. Suzanne Noffke; copyright 1980 by The Missionary Society of St. Paul the Apostle in the State of New York; used by permission of Paulist Press, Mahwah, N.J.

Francis de Sales, Jane de Chantal: Letters of Spiritual Direction, trans. Péronne Marie Thibert; copyright 1988 by The Missionary Society of St. Paul the Apostle in the State of New York; used by permission of Paulist Press, Mahwah, N.J.

Hadewijch: The Complete Works, trans. Mother Columba Hart; copyright 1980 by The Missionary Society of St. Paul the Apostle in the State of New York; used by permission of Paulist Press, Mahwah, N.J.

He and I by Gabrielle Bossis, trans. Evelyn M. Brown; copyright 1969 by Éditions Paulines; used by permission of Éditions Paulines, Sherbrooke, Quebec, Canada.

Hearing and Knowing by Mercy Amba Oduyoye; copyright 1986 by Orbis Books; used by permission of Orbis Books, Maryknoll, N.Y.

The Hour of the Poor, the Hour of Women by Renny Golden; copyright 1991 by The Crossroad Publishing Company; used by permission of The Crossroad Publishing Co., New York, N.Y.

I Hear a Seed Growing by Edwina Gateley; copyright 1990 by Edwina Gateley; used by permission of Source Books, Trabuco Canyon, Calif.

Julian of Norwich: Showings, trans. Edmund Colledge and James Walsh, S.J.; copyright 1978 by The Missionary Society of St. Paul the Apostle in the State of New York; used by permission of Paulist Press, Mahwah, N.J.

Let the Weak Be Strong by Cho Wha Soon; copyright 1990 by The Crossroad Publishing Company; used by permission of The Crossroad Publishing Co., New York, N.Y.

Meditations with Dorothy Day by Stanley Vishnewski; copyright 1970 by Newman Press; used by permission of Paulist-Newman, Mahwah, N.J.

The Narrative of Sojourner Truth: A Bondswoman of Olden Times by Sojourner Truth, 1850, as told to Olive Gilbert; republished by Arno Press/*New York Times*, 1968; copyright 1968 by Arno Press; used by permission of Arno Press, Manchester, N.H.

The Passion of the Infant Christ by Caryll Houselander; copyright 1949 by Sheed and Ward; used by permission of Sheed and Ward, Kansas City, Mo.

"Pelagia: Beauty Riding By," in *Harlots of the Desert* by Benedicta Ward, S.L.G., copyright by Benedicta Ward; used by permission of Benedicta Ward, S.L.G. and Geoffrey Chapman Co., London, England.

"Productions of Mrs. Maria Stewart" by Mrs. Maria Stewart; excerpted from *Spiritual Narratives*, ed. Susan Houchins; copyright 1988 by Oxford University Press, Inc.; reprinted by permission.

The Revelation of Mechthilde of Magdeburg (1210–1297); or, *The Flowing Light of the Godhead* by Lucy Menzies; used by permission; copyright 1953 by Iona Community/Wild Goose Publications, Glasgow, Scotland.

The Risen Christ by Caryll Houselander; copyright 1958 by Sheed and Ward; used by permission of Sheed and Ward, Kansas City, Mo.

A Rocking Horse Catholic by Caryll Houselander; copyright 1955 by Sheed and Ward; used by permission of Sheed and Ward, Kansas City, Mo.

Sainted Women of the Dark Ages by Jo Ann McNamara, John E. Holberg, and E. Gordon Whatley, 1992; copyright by Duke University Press; used by permission of Duke University Press, Durham, N.C.

Scivias of Hildegard of Bingen by Bruce W. Hozeski; copyright 1986 by Bruce W. Hozeski; used by permission of Bruce W. Hozeski and Bear and Co., Santa Fe, N.M.

Selected excerpts from pages 488–89, "Address to the American Equal Rights Convention," of *The Female Experience: An American Documentary*, ed. Gerda

Lerner; copyright 1992 by Gerda Lerner; originally published: Indianapolis: Bobbs-Merrill, 1977; reprint: New York: Oxford University Press, 1992; used by permission of Gerda Lerner and Oxford University Press, New York, N.Y.

Selected excerpts from pages 161–78 of *Loaves and Fishes* by Dorothy Day, copyright 1963 by Dorothy Day; copyright renewed; reprinted by permission of HarperCollins Publishers, Inc.

Selected excerpts from *The Long Loneliness* by Dorothy Day; copyright 1952 by Harper and Row, Publishers, Inc.; copyright renewed 1980 by Tamar Teresa Hennessy; reprinted by permission of HarperCollins Publishers, Inc.

Selected excerpts from pages 229–39 of *The Miracle of Love* by Kathryn Spink; copyright 1981 by Colour Library International, Ltd.; reprinted by permission of HarperCollins Publishers, Inc.

Selected excerpts from pages 156–66 of *Mother Teresa: Her People and Her Work* by Desmond Doig; copyright 1976 by Nachiketa Publications; reprinted by permission of HarperCollins Publishers, Inc.

Selected excerpts from pages 193–205 of *SEDOS* Bulletin, Vol. 28:6–7 (June 15–July 15, 1991); copyright by *SEDOS*; used by permission of P. Walter von Holzen, Director of SEDOS, Rome, Italy.

Selected excerpts from pages 65–74 of *Something Beautiful for God: Mother Teresa of Calcutta* by Malcolm Muggeridge; copyright 1971 by The Mother Teresa Committee; reprinted by permission of HarperCollins Publishers, Inc.

Selected excerpts from pages 415–37 of *Song in a Weary Throat: An American Pilgrimage* by Pauli Murray; copyright 1987 by the Estate of Pauli Murray; reprinted by permission of HarperCollins Publishers, Inc.

Teresa of Avila: The Interior Castle, trans. Kieran Kavanaugh and Otilio Rodriguez; copyright 1979 by The Missionary Society of St. Paul the Apostle in the State of New York; used by permission of Paulist Press, Mahwah, N.J.

Who Will Roll the Stone Away? by Mercy Amba Oduyoye; copyright 1990 by World Council of Churches Publications; used by permission of the World Council of Churches, Geneva, Switzerland.

With Passion and Compassion, ed. Virginia Fabella and Mercy Amba Oduyoye; copyright 1988 by Orbis Books; used by permission of Orbis Books, Maryknoll, N.Y.

INDEX